CW00705532

Living by the
WORD

BECOMING DISCIPLES
OF CHRIST

OTHER BOOKS
BY ED J. PINEGAR AND RICHARD J. ALLEN:

Latter-day Commentary on the Old Testament

Teachings and Commentaries on the Book of Mormon

Teachings and Commentaries on the Doctrine and Covenants
(with Karl R. Anderson)

Living by the WORD

BECOMING DISCIPLES OF CHRIST

Ed J. Pinegar and Richard J. Allen

Covenant Communications, Inc.

Covenant

Cover painting *I Am the Way* © 2005 Simon Dewey. Courtesy of Altus Fine Art.
www.altusfineart.com

Cover and book design © 2005 by Covenant Communications, Inc.

Published by Covenant Communications, Inc.
American Fork, Utah

Copyright © 2005 by Ed J. Pinegar and Richard J. Allen

All rights reserved. No part of this work may be reproduced by any means without the express written permission of Covenant Communications, Inc., P.O. Box 416, American Fork, UT 84003. This work is not an official publication of The Church of Jesus Christ of Latter-day Saints. The views expressed within this work are the sole responsibility of the author and do not necessarily reflect the position of The Church of Jesus Christ of Latter-day Saints, Covenant Communications, Inc., or any other entity.

Printed in Canada
First Printing: September 2005

11 10 09 08 07 06 05   10 9 8 7 6 5 4 3 2 1

ISBN 1-59156-707-6

ACKNOWLEDGMENTS

We express our sincere thanks to the editors and design staff of Covenant Communications for their outstanding professional service in bringing forth this publication. In particular we recognize the committed service of Shauna Humphreys, Peter Jasinski, Annalisa Wiggins, and Linda Prince. In addition, may we express our appreciation to our wives, Patricia P. Pinegar and Carol Lynn Allen, and other family members for their devoted support and encouragement in the completion of this work over a period of many years.

CONTENTS

INTRODUCTION

Upon the loom of the Lord is woven the fabric of our lives—formed of myriad shining threads, each representing a different principle of the gospel of hope. From faith to forgiveness, from reverence to revelation, from motherhood and fatherhood to peace and patience—all of these themes and dozens of others are the pervasive spiritual themes of our daily lives. To understand such principles and apply them consistently and valiantly for the blessing of mankind is the substance of our mortal experience and the undergirding of our quest for perfection. By striving to live the gospel of Jesus Christ in all of its dimensions, we prepare ourselves for the transition to a higher mode of discipleship in which we become more and more like the Savior and Redeemer, taking on His nature and attributes, grace for grace—as the scriptures declare, "line upon line, precept upon precept; here a little, and there a little; giving us consolation by holding forth that which is to come, confirming our hope!" (D&C 128:21; see also Isa. 28:10, 13; 2 Ne. 28:30).

This volume is designed as a practical roadmap for traversing the landscape of our mortal experience in consistent daily alignment with gospel values. Each of the over one hundred articles (presented alphabetically) is constructed so as to illuminate one of the key principles and themes of the gospel in a proactive, accessible way. Following a concise defining statement, each article provides an array of pertinent scriptural references and applications, quotations from modern prophets, ideas for daily living (organized in succinct bullet format), one or more vignettes illustrating the theme, and a brief concluding summary. The format lends itself to ready-reference application for personal or group study, family home evening presentations, talks or lessons, and doctrinal research.

This organizing structure makes it easy for you, as reader, to identify one or more categories that you may want to work on. By striving for daily improvement, we can all harvest great blessings. The benefits of living the gospel of Jesus Christ include peace, joy, wisdom, hope, enduring relationships of harmony with loved ones, and an inner confidence with the potential to "wax strong in the presence of God" (D&C 121:45). Living the gospel grants a clarity of vision that opens up the vista of hope for ultimate redemption, as the audience of King Benjamin learned: "And we, ourselves, also, through the infinite goodness of God, and the manifestations of his Spirit, have great views of that which is to come; and were it expedient, we could prophesy of all things. And it is the faith which we have had on the things which our king has spoken unto us that has brought us to this great knowledge, whereby we do rejoice with such exceedingly great joy" (Mosiah 5:3–4). Above all, living the gospel brings into the present moment—*immediately*—the efficacy of the Atonement on behalf of the faithful and devout: "Yea, I would that ye would come forth and harden not your hearts any longer; for behold, now is the time and the day of your salvation; and therefore, if ye will repent and harden not your hearts, immediately shall the great plan of redemption be brought about unto you" (Alma 34:31).

The authors express the hope that this volume will serve as a useful adjunct learning system to assist the reader in the practical application of the principles of the restored gospel. We say "practical application" since it is our conviction that the essence of learning and education extends beyond the mere internalization of concepts—as important as that is—to embrace the active expression of principles and doctrines in an exemplary way. Alfred North Whitehead confirmed this perspective when he stated, "Education is the acquisition of the art of the *utilization* of knowledge" (*The Aims of Education and Other Essays* [New York and London: Free Press, 1969], 4; emphasis added). President Harold B. Lee taught: "Your place in the celestial kingdom will be measured by what you do. The Lord's judgment will be according to the deeds of men and women done in the flesh—not by what they profess. It isn't enough just to *be* good in this church. The all-important thing is that we *do* good" (*The Teachings of Harold B. Lee,* ed. Clyde J. Williams [Salt Lake City: Bookcraft, 1996], 143). And King Benjamin solemnly proclaimed: "And again, believe that ye must repent of your sins and forsake them, and humble yourselves before God; and ask in sincerity of heart that he would forgive you; and now, if you believe all these things see that ye do them" (Mosiah 4:10).

Let us all, therefore, make a stronger commitment to incorporate into our behavior the principles in which the gospel of Jesus Christ is anchored. Let us believe and then do. Let us strive on a daily basis to fulfill the commandment of the Savior: "Therefore I would that ye should be perfect even as I, or your Father who is in heaven is perfect" (3 Ne. 12:48).

This process of perfection will not happen all at once, but one day at a time, as we strive earnestly to live "by every word that proceedeth out of the mouth of the Lord" (Deut. 8:3; see also Matt. 4:4). What we see now in but luminous outline form, by the vision of faith ("through a glass, darkly"—1 Cor. 13:12), will, through obedience and action, become ever more clear and familiar to our awakening eyes: "Beloved, now are we the sons of God, and it doth not yet appear what we shall be: but we know that, when he shall appear, we shall be like him; for we shall see him as he is. And every man that hath this hope in him purifieth himself, even as he is pure" (1 Jn. 3:2–3).

ACCOUNTABILITY

We are accountable for the knowledge and blessings we receive from our Heavenly Father. In other words, we will have to account to Him for what we have done with what we have been given. We will be held accountable for our thoughts, words, and deeds, as well as for the worthy things we neglect to do that we should do (sins of omission). The gift of moral agency requires that all people be accountable for their choices; this accountability begins at age eight. A central part of the plan of salvation is that we receive rewards or punishments according to our works. Therefore, specific blessings or consequences are predicated on what we do, think, and say.

THE SCRIPTURES TEACH US

Articles of Faith 1:2. *We believe that men will be punished for their own sins, and not for Adam's transgression.*

Alma 12:14. *For our words will condemn us, yea, all our works will condemn us; we shall not be found spotless; and our thoughts will also condemn us; and in this awful state we shall not dare to look up to our God; and we would fain be glad if we could command the rocks and the mountains to fall upon us to hide us from his presence.*

Mosiah 4:30. *But this much I can tell you, that if ye do not watch yourselves, and your thoughts, and your words, and your deeds, and observe the commandments of God, and continue in the faith of what ye have heard concerning the coming of our Lord, even unto the end of your lives, ye must perish. And now, O man, remember, and perish not.*

It is abundantly clear from these scriptures that we are accountable for our own sins. We cannot transfer our wrongdoings to anyone else. We have the power to choose, and we have been given grand resources to help us—the light of Christ, the Holy Ghost, the word of God, the counsel of living prophets, and the assistance of many loving associates. However, it is up to us to act in valiant and responsible ways.

Doctrine and Covenants 101:78. *That every man may act in doctrine and principle pertaining to futurity, according to the moral agency which I have given unto him, that every man may be accountable for his own sins in the day of judgment.*

There will one day be a time of ultimate reckoning for each of us concerning our performance in this mortal life. At the Day of Judgment we will be restored—good for good and evil according to that which is evil (see Alma 41:3–4).

MODERN PROPHETS SPEAK

Joseph Smith:
> Men not unfrequently forget that they are dependent upon heaven for every blessing which they are permitted to enjoy, and that for every opportunity granted them they are to give an account. (*History of the Church,* 2:23–24)

Joseph F. Smith:

> If there is one principle of the gospel of Jesus Christ that goes directly to the very foundation of justice and righteousness, it is that great and glorious and God-like principle that every man will have to render an account for that which he does, and every man will be rewarded for his works, whether they be good or evil. (*Gospel Doctrine: Selections from the Sermons and Writings of Joseph F. Smith,* comp. John A. Widtsoe [Salt Lake City: Deseret Book, 1939], 69)

Neal A. Maxwell:

> Nor should we rationalize our responsibilities simply because we are often in short-term relationships with other people. The hungry or thirsty stranger, Jesus said, represents more than himself or herself (see Matthew 25:31–46). We are accountable for doing our part in all relationships and for providing what leadership, service, and influence we can. Those within our circles of influence constitute our present sample of humanity; they are neither mere functionaries nor strangers in a transit lounge. (*A Wonderful Flood of Light* [Salt Lake City: Bookcraft, 1990], 112)

IDEAS FOR DAILY LIVING

Here are some ideas to help us remember that we are accountable for our thoughts and actions.

1. **Learn to manage your personal life according to the principle of being accountable.**
   - *Mental preparation*—Pray. Prepare your mind. Realize that every action or decision results from our thoughts and intents. Prayer keeps our minds and hearts turned to God and His will.
   - *Pondering*—Each time you make a decision, ponder the consequences. Will the decision bring you and your loved ones closer to your Father in Heaven? Decide not on the basis of pleasure or gratification, but according to a higher order of living. Don't deceive yourself with lust; pleasure is short-lived.
   - *Values*—Choose your governing values in life so that when the time comes to make a decision, you are already disposed to choose the right and act responsibly.
   - *Keep a journal*—Take a daily personal accounting of your motivations and actions.
   - *Study the word of God*—Read the scriptures and the words of the prophets daily to learn what the Lord expects of us and to enjoy the inspiration and motivation that come from God's word.
   - *Remember who you are*—Think of yourself as bearing the name of the Savior. Christ will one day require an account of how we have borne His name.
   - *Listen to the Spirit within*—By listening to the Holy Ghost, you will know what is right.

2. **Establish an environment for proper decision making.**
   - *Choose that which edifies*—Fill your life with wholesome pastimes and worthy causes. We are free to do much good. Our environmental choices influence in large measure our decisions in life.
   - *Surround yourself with positive reminders*—Adorn your environment with appropriate symbols of the gospel (such as pictures of the temple, the prophet, the Savior, your family) as reminders to be more holy and valiant.
   - *Fill leisure hours with uplifting influences*—Fill your mind with good music, stimulating literature, wholesome conversation, and uplifting thoughts. Purge your hours of superficial television programming, riotous music, and other forms of idle or degrading entertainment.

3. **Use Church experiences to sharpen your sense of being accountable.**
   - *Sacrament*—Use the sacrament time each week to refresh your commitment to obedience.

- *Testimony bearing*—Bear your testimony regularly. This is a form of accounting to the Lord and to others for the guidance of His Spirit and the blessings He grants to you through the gospel.
- *Interviews*—Make your temple recommend interview and other important interviews a rehearsal for your ultimate account to the Savior for your life's actions and all your inner dispositions.
- *Temple attendance*—Go to the temple often to experience the process of accounting to our Father in Heaven for all we do.

4. Work with others effectively.
- *Responsible leadership*—In whatever roles we fill (spouse, parent, home/visiting teacher, ward/stake callings), we have a stewardship. Fulfill these callings to the best of your ability, and account to your leaders.
- *Lessons*—Make yourself accountable for what you've been taught by setting goals and applying gospel lessons to your life. Do this in your families to teach accountability.
- *Praise*—Praise others for their good work. Sincere and appropriate praise reinforces good behavior.
- *Help others to understand accountability*—A natural consequence often teaches accountability. Except in situations of an immediate, life-threatening nature, be cautious about interceding in the affairs of others (especially children) to take away the consequence of their actions. Often, great lessons can be learned from natural consequences.

ILLUSTRATIONS FOR OUR TIMES

Elder Robert Wood of the Seventy relates this story and teaching concerning accountability:

There is a fairy tale about a king who offered the hand of his daughter in marriage to the young man who would do or create the most extraordinary, unbelievable thing. Young men from all over the kingdom brought to the royal city marvelous works of mind and hand and tremendous demonstrations of physical agility. Finally, one young man created a tremendous clock that not only told the minutes, hours, days, months, and years, but also had carved within it the figures of the great poets, philosophers, and prophets of history, who on the appointed hours expounded the wisdom of the ages. The people exclaimed, "What an unbelievable thing!" But then another young man appeared on the scene who, sledgehammer in hand, began to destroy the masterpiece. Again the people exclaimed—this time in horror—"Why, *this* is the most unbelievable thing we've seen!" And so it appeared that the king was to be compelled to hand his daughter over to the ruffian. But, this being a fairy tale, suddenly all the stone figures reassembled, became flesh, and drove the young man from the town.

When I first read this tale to one of my daughters, she asked, "What was everyone doing while the young man was wrecking the clock?" A very sensible question! For too many, responsibility seems to end with hand-wringing and exclamations of dismay. Yet talk without action accomplishes little. We need to be vigorously engaged in the world. If our schools are inadequate or destructive of moral values, we must work with fellow members of the community to bring about change. If our neighborhoods are unsafe or unhealthy, we must join with the civic-minded to devise solutions. If our cities and towns are polluted, not only with noxious gases but soul-destroying addictions and smut, we must labor to find legitimate ways to eliminate such filth while respecting freedom of conscience.

But what can one man or woman or a handful of Latter-day Saints accomplish? Much. The dynamics of history are driven, on the one hand, by the few who are engaged, and on the other hand, by the many who are apathetic. If we are not among the few engaged, we are, despite our concerns and voices of alarm, among the apathetic. May it never be said of us, "Because thou art lukewarm, and neither cold nor hot, I will spue thee out of my mouth" (Rev. 3:16).

We are among the most blessed people in all of history. There is no place for complaining, no excuse for inaction, no "escape from freedom." Being so richly blessed, we have the responsibility to be a blessing to others, to our nation, to the world. When we stand at the great judgment bar of Jehovah, He may ask: Did we honor our personal responsibility? Did we bear the burdens of our neighbors? Did we heal? Did we comfort? Did we bring peace? Did we instill virtue? Did we spend ourselves in the service and uplift of mankind? May we at that day be able to answer in the affirmative and then hear the words pronounced, "Well done, thou good and faithful servant. Enter into my rest." ("On the Responsible Self," *Ensign,* March 2002, 27)

SUMMARY

Accountability is a basic tenet of the gospel of Jesus Christ, "for it is required of the Lord, at the hand of every steward, to render an account of his stewardship, both in time and in eternity" (D&C 72:3). Our every deed and action, our use of time, even our very thoughts belong to our personal history and will ultimately have to be accounted for. Yet it is a process of becoming, and it takes time to become a responsible and accountable person. Every blessing with which the Lord blesses our lives is part of His eternal investment in our well-being and must inevitably show up in the balance sheet of our life. Our agency is a God-given gift, without which salvation would not be possible. Because of that gift, we can look forward to a harvest of rich and empowering blessings based on valiant and righteous choices, or a recompense of punishment and woe based on unrepentant disobedience. It is up to us.

ADVERSITY

Adversity is a reality of life. It can come from disease, accidents, physical or emotional injuries, natural disasters, wars, ignorance, willful disobedience, and even chastisement from the Lord or a special trial He gives us for our particular tutoring and growth. Often it comes as afflictions upon an innocent victim (see Hel. 3:34). It is always present, and we must come to terms with it in order to learn to navigate the mortal pathways leading to a higher quality of life. Frequently, adversity is not manifest in just the situation itself, but in our attitude toward the situation and the events and relationships around us. How we view the situation is the key to dealing with adversity. Perceiving things from a higher perspective invariably leads to greater understanding and, frequently, to the discovery of ultimate solutions in overcoming adversity. Remember that opposition in all things is essential for our growth. Without opposition, we could not understand or appreciate joy in contrast to sorrow, or righteousness in contrast to wickedness. Without opposition, everything would be "a compound in one" (see 2 Ne. 2:11)—devoid of vitality and bereft of the opportunity for eternal progression.

THE SCRIPTURES TEACH US

2 Nephi 2:11. *For it must needs be, that there is an opposition in all things. If not so, . . . righteousness could not be brought to pass, neither wickedness, neither holiness nor misery, neither good nor bad.*

Opposition is necessary in order for us to grow. When we realize that adversity, trials, tribulations, and opposition are for our growth, our attitude and behavior will change. Adversity will become an opportunity rather than a stumbling block. We need to look at life as the time to prove ourselves worthy, not to be free from adversity.

Doctrine and Covenants 122:7. *And if thou shouldst be cast into the pit, or into the hands of murderers, and the sentence of death passed upon thee; if thou be cast into the deep; if the billowing surge conspire against thee; if fierce winds become thine enemy; if the heavens gather blackness, and all the elements combine to hedge up the way; and above all, if the very jaws of hell shall gape open the mouth wide after thee, know thou, my son, that all these things shall give thee experience, and shall be for thy good.*

In all the difficulties of life, let us never lose sight of our purpose: We are here to become like our Heavenly Father and our Savior Jesus Christ. We agreed to the test of mortality in the premortal life. We need this experience in order to grow. In our trials, we learn how to help others by applying the lessons we learn, even as Christ did in suffering the ultimate sacrifice (see Alma 7:11–12).

Doctrine and Covenants 136:31. *My people must be tried in all things, that they may be prepared to receive the glory that I have for them, even the glory of Zion; and he that will not bear chastisement is not worthy of my kingdom.*

Heavenly Father knows what is best for us (see Prov. 3:5–6). We become perfected through the processes of sacrificing, enduring to the end, and learning to submit to all things that the Father should inflict upon us (see Mosiah 3:19). Let us cultivate an attitude full of hope and faith to overcome adversity and go forward knowing of the goodness of God.

MODERN PROPHETS SPEAK

David O. McKay:
> There are those who have met disaster, which almost seems defeat, who have become somewhat soured in their natures, but if they stop to think, even the adversity which has come to them may prove a means of spiritual uplift. Adversity itself may lead toward and not away from God and spiritual enlightenment; and privation may prove a source of strength if we can but keep a sweetness of mind and spirit. (*Gospel Ideals: Selections from the Discourses of David O. McKay* [Salt Lake City: Improvement Era, 1953], 390)

Ezra Taft Benson:
> Our great purpose in life is to overcome adversity and worldly consideration as we strive for things of the Spirit. (*The Teachings of Ezra Taft Benson* [Salt Lake City: Bookcraft, 1988], 449–50)

Gordon B. Hinckley:
> If as a people we will build and sustain one another, the Lord will bless us with the strength to weather every storm and continue to move forward through every adversity. (*Teachings of Gordon B. Hinckley* [Salt Lake City: Deseret Book, 1997], 7)

James E. Faust:
> Many in today's generation have not fully known nor appreciated the refining blessings of adversity. Many have never been hungry because of want. Yet I am persuaded that there can be a necessary refining process in adversity that increases our understanding, enhances our sensitivity, makes us more

Christlike. Lord Byron said, "Adversity is the first path to truth" (*Don Juan,* canto 12, stanza 50). The life of the Savior and the lives of His prophets clearly and simply teach how necessary adversity is to achieve a measure of greatness. ("The Blessings of Adversity," *Liahona,* May 1998, 3)

IDEAS FOR DAILY LIVING

The question in dealing with trials is, How can we gain a better perspective on adversity and learn to appreciate its role in our lives so that we can grow from our experiences? The following ideas may help you view and respond to adversity in a positive manner:

1. Adversity is a universal experience.
- *We all face adversity*—Without adversity we may forget God (see Hel. 12:2–3). No one person has a monopoly on adversity—we are all in this together.
- *Adversity can lead to good*—Learning to overcome adversity is part of life. It will be for our good (see D&C 98:1–3).
- *Face adversity with courage*—To wish away adversity will only make one weak. The result will be little or no growth.
- *Rise above adversity*—Great souls are those who handle adversity positively, maintain a good attitude, and have a proper perspective on life.
- *Trust in God*—Adversity teaches us to trust in the Lord (see Prov. 3:5–6).
- *The Lord chastens those He loves*—We are chastened in adversity (see 2 Ne. 5:25; Mosiah 23:21) and then blessed as we grow from it (see Mosiah 24:8–15).

2. You already have access to effective tools for overcoming adversity.
- *Faith in Jesus Christ*—Heavenly Father has given each of us abilities that we can utilize. As we exercise our faith in Jesus Christ, we will receive the strength to overcome our adversity (see 1 Ne. 7:17).
- *The word of God*—There is power in the word (see Alma 31:5). It will tell us all things that we should do (see 2 Ne. 32:3).
- *The Spirit*—The Holy Ghost will guide us in all things (see 2 Ne. 32:5) and comfort us as well (see John 14:16).
- *Prayer*—The scriptures teach us clearly that if we but ask, the Lord will help us (see James 1:5–6; Mosiah 27:14; Alma 13:28).
- *Hope*—When you are full of hope, knowing that in the end all things shall work together for your good, you can endure and transcend adversity (see D&C 122:7).
- *Patience*—As we exercise patience, time will become our ally. Patience is a righteous response to adversity (see Alma 26:27). The process of overcoming was never meant to be easy or quick; it is a process of becoming (see D&C 24:8).
- *People*—Family, friends, associates, and even caring strangers are there to lend support (see D&C 108:7).
- *Positive response*—We have moral agency. We can choose to face adversity positively in the strength of the Lord or allow it to destroy us.

3. There are great benefits that come through adversity.
- *Humility*—Adversity cultivates humility—knowing our relationship to and dependence upon God—which is the beginning virtue of exaltation.
- *Self-worth*—Overcoming adversity brings great personal satisfaction and a sense of self-worth and self-confidence.

- *Strength*—Overcoming adversity brings us an enduring kind of spiritual strength.
- *Gratitude*—Adversity is the teacher that helps us remember the good times and the blessings of God.
- *Spirituality*—From adversity we can become closer to God, knowing that He not only gives us the strength to overcome, but provides blessings in the process.
- *Blessings from the Lord*—The Savior continually nurtures us and strengthens us in our adversity and afflictions (see Alma 7:11–12).

ILLUSTRATIONS FOR OUR TIMES

The following well-known quote provides many examples of those who overcame great adversity to become some of the most accomplished human beings in modern history.

Portraits in Overcoming Adversity

Cripple him, and you have a Sir Walter Scott. Lock him in a prison cell, and you have a John Bunyan. Bury him in the snows of Valley Forge, and you have a George Washington. Land him in poverty, and you have an Abraham Lincoln. Subject him to bitter religious strife, and you have a Disraeli. Strike him with infantile paralysis, and you have a Franklin D. Roosevelt, the only president of the United States to be elected to four terms of office. Burn him so severely in a schoolhouse fire that the doctors say he will never walk, and you have a Glenn Cunningham, who set a world record in 1934 for running the mile in 4 minutes, 6.7 seconds.

Deafen a genius composer who continues to compose some of the world's most beautiful music, and you have a Beethoven. Drag him more dead than alive out of a rice paddy in Vietnam, and you have a Rocky Blaier, that beautiful running back for the Pittsburgh Steelers. Have him or her born black in a society filled with racial discrimination, and you have a Booker T. Washington, Harriet Tubman, or Martin Luther King Jr. Have him born of parents who survived a Nazi concentration camp, paralyze him from the waist down at the age of four, and you have an Itzhak Perlman, the incomparable violinist. Call him "retarded" and write him off as "uneducable," and you have an Albert Einstein.

After losing both his legs in an airplane crash, let an RAF fighter pilot fly, and you have World War II ace, Douglas Bader, who was captured by the Germans three times and escaped three times on two artificial limbs. Label him too stupid to learn, and you have a Thomas Edison. Label him a hopeless alcoholic, and you have a Bill Wilson, the founder of Alcoholics Anonymous. Tell her she is too old to start painting at 80, and you have a Grandma Moses. Blind him at age 44, and you have a John Milton, who 10 years later, wrote Paradise Lost. Call him dull and hopeless and flunk him in the 6th grade, and you have a Winston Churchill.

Tell a young boy who loved to draw and sketch that he had no talent, and you have a Walt Disney. Rate him mediocre in chemistry, and you have a Louis Pasteur. Take a crippled child whose only home was an orphanage, and you have a Louis E. West, the first chief executive of the Boy Scouts of America. Spit on him, humiliate him, betray his trust, say one thing and do another. Mistrust those whom he loves. Mock him. Make him carry a heavy wooden cross, and then crucify him— and he forgives you and calls you a friend.

—Anonymous

SUMMARY

We came to this earth to be tested, to see if we would obey (see Abr. 3:25). In this test, opposition is the environment in which we can grow. Let us have the wisdom to understand and appreciate, even as the Prophet Joseph, that all of this opposition will be for our good, for our growth in becoming like our Savior Jesus Christ. When we recognize this, we can cope with adversity and opposition and say, like our close colleague and friend, John Covey, himself no stranger to hardship: "Just think how much I will grow when I overcome this." Remember that the Lord will not give us anything that we cannot eventually overcome—for He strengthens us and will provide a way (see Alma 26:11–12; Ether 12:27; 1 Ne. 3:7).

AGENCY

Agency is a gift. The right to choose is necessary for our growth. We are a result of the use of our agency. Our choices and decisions determine our blessings, or the consequences of our actions. Agency can operate because there is (1) opposition in all things, (2) knowledge of good and evil, (3) laws and commandments given by God, and (4) the freedom to choose. This gift is better referred to as moral agency, which connotes responsibility and accountability in regard to our choices.

THE SCRIPTURES TEACH US

2 Nephi 2:16. *Wherefore, the Lord God gave unto man that he should act for himself. Wherefore, man could not act for himself save it should be that he was enticed by the one or the other.*

We must realize that without opposition, trials, and temptation, we would be unable to exercise our agency and progress toward eternal life. We should recognize and be grateful for our opportunities for growth through challenges in life.

2 Nephi 2:27. *Wherefore, men are free according to the flesh; and all things are given them which are expedient unto man. And they are free to choose liberty and eternal life, through the great Mediator of all men, or to choose captivity and death, according to the captivity and power of the devil; for he seeketh that all men might be miserable like unto himself.*

We are free to choose and follow Christ to eternal life, or the devil to captivity. We should make our choices with this motto in mind: "What would Jesus have me do?"

Doctrine and Covenants 101:78. *That every man may act in doctrine and principle pertaining to futurity, according to the moral agency which I have given unto him, that every man may be accountable for his own sins in the day of judgment.*

Moral agency connotes that we are accountable for our actions. We will be judged by our actions; Christ is our judge and is the keeper of the gate (see 2 Ne. 9:41). We should have a great desire to keep His commandments, knowing that we must look into His face, knowing that He paid the price for our sins. We want to be able to do so with a clear conscience, not with a soul full of sorrow and regret for misdeeds (see Alma 36:15).

Moses 4:3–4. *Wherefore, because that Satan rebelled against me, and sought to destroy the agency of man, which I, the Lord God, had given him, and also, that I should give unto him mine own power; by the power of mine Only Begotten, I caused that he should be cast down; And he became Satan, yea, even the devil, the father of all lies, to deceive and to blind men, and to lead them captive at his will, even as many as would not hearken unto my voice.*

Satan seeks to take away our agency by making us think that our decisions have no consequences. He does his insidious work through subtlety, lies, and half truths (see 2 Ne. 28:7–9; Alma 12:4; 3 Ne. 2:2).

MODERN PROPHETS SPEAK

Brigham Young:

> The volition of the creature is free; this is a law of their existence and the Lord cannot violate his own law; were he to do that, he would cease to be God. . . . When the Lord made man, he made him an agent accountable to his God, with liberty to act and to do as he pleases to a certain extent in order to prove himself. (*Discourses of Brigham Young,* sel. John A. Widtsoe [Salt Lake City: Deseret Book, 1954], 62)

Ezra Taft Benson:

> The gospel can prosper only in an atmosphere of freedom. This fact is confirmed by history, as well as by sacred scriptures. The right of choice—free agency—runs like a golden thread throughout the gospel plan of the Lord for the blessing of His children. (*The Teachings of Ezra Taft Benson* [Salt Lake City: Bookcraft, 1988], 81)

Lorenzo Snow:

> There is the principle of God in every individual. It is designed that man should act as God, and not be constrained and controlled in everything, but have an independency, an agency and the power to spread abroad and act according to the principle of godliness that is in him, act according to the power and intelligence and enlightenment of God, that he possesses, and not that he should be watched continually, and be controlled, and act as a slave in these matters. (*The Teachings of Lorenzo Snow,* ed. Clyde J. Williams [Salt Lake City: Bookcraft, 1984], 4)

Gordon B. Hinckley:

> I should like to suggest three standards by which to judge each of the decisions that determine the behavior patterns of your lives. These standards are so simple as to appear elementary, but I believe their faithful observance will provide a set of moral imperatives by which to govern without argument or equivocation each of our actions and which will bring unmatched rewards. They are: 1. Does it enrich the mind? 2. Does it discipline and strengthen the body? 3. Does it nourish the spirit? ("Caesar, Circus, or Christ?" *BYU Speeches of the Year,* October 26, 1965, 4)

IDEAS FOR DAILY LIVING

There is wisdom in striving to understand and apply the principles and doctrines that are necessary for agency to operate:

1. Enlarge your perspective to view opposition and temptation (i.e., the need to overcome temptation) as eternal verities.

- *See opposition as the key to growth*—Opposition is not a hindrance to our growth, but a necessary ingredient in life that makes it possible for us to learn how to make correct choices and lift ourselves to a higher plane of wisdom.

- *Cultivate an attitude of hope and persistence in the face of opposition*—Our attitude towards opposition and temptation often determines our decisions. A positive attitude grounded in faith leads to an upward course in life. A negative attitude based on resignation and surrender leads to a downward course in life. We should try to be courageous and resilient in coping with difficult situations.

- *Seek the noble and the spiritual dimension of life*—The devil seeks to tempt us with pride, greed, lust, and all the vain things of the world. Take control when the choice is placed before you—choose the right.

- *Control your environment*—Remember that we often put ourselves in situations that are tempting and conducive to sin. We actually get on the "road to sin" and sooner or later the result *is* sin. Let us avoid compromising situations and remove ourselves out of temptation.

- *Follow the Spirit*—In all the temptation and opposition we face, let us never doubt our capacity to make correct choices. As we act by the Spirit, with faith, we can make good decisions.

- *Sin and bad decisions limit our power to use moral agency properly*—Sin separates us from God, and we lose the Spirit and the power to make good decisions. Bad habits can lead to addiction. The hopelessness caused by sin creates the feeling that our decisions don't matter or that we can't change. Unrighteous traditions (personal, family, or cultural) can negatively influence our choices (see Mosiah 10:11–12; Alma 37:9). An attitude that we can sin a little, receive a little punishment, and then go on with life (see 2 Ne. 28:8) is also a poor use of agency.

2. Knowledge of good and evil is necessary to exercise agency.

- *Cultivate a clear understanding of the outcomes of actions*—Knowledge of good and evil will teach us of the blessings and consequences of our actions.

- *Study the word of God*—The scriptures are the authoritative guide on agency. Make a plan to search and feast upon the word of God, thus arming yourself with the knowledge of God.

- *Seek to become grounded in the doctrines of Christ*—Knowledge and understanding of the doctrines, principles, and covenants of the Church will help us make correct choices.

- *Remember that the devil seeks to destroy you*—Wrong choices—or thinking that your choices really don't count—often cause one to misuse one's agency. Though he may make disobedience seem easier or more appealing, the devil wants us to be miserable (see 2 Ne. 2:27). Remember, "wickedness never was happiness" (Alma 41:10).

3. Laws and commandments are required for the test of our agency.

- *View the commandments as instruments of liberty*—Heavenly Father has given us laws and commandments to help us return to His presence. They do not infringe our liberties or constrict our progress; rather, they are the means to obtain higher liberty, even eternal life.

- *Understand the connection between the commandments and happiness*—The laws of God are designed to bring us happiness. Obedience to the commandments in an environment of opposition and moral choice leads to joy: "Then shall thy confidence wax strong in the presence of God" (D&C 121:45).

- *View love as the bridge to obedience*—Build in your heart and mind an understanding that obedience ultimately comes from love, not fear or merely a sense of outward compliance to duty. When we love God, we will keep the commandments (see John 14:21).

- *Seek the strength of the Spirit*—The blessing of always keeping the commandments is to always have His Spirit to be with us. This is what we covenant and are promised each week as we partake of the sacrament.

4. When we exercise our agency, we learn over time the godly manner of making choices.

- *Enthrone accountability as the anchor of your life*—Moral agency carries with it a responsibility and accountability for our actions. To accept this as a principle of life is to establish an inviolate inner compass to guide our lives.
- *Listen to the Spirit*—Choices and decisions should always be made by the Spirit (see 2 Ne. 32:5). The Spirit knows all things and can tell us all things we need to know (Moro. 10:5).
- *Remember to do as Jesus would do*—Whenever we have doubts or questions as to how we should act, remember that we have a perfect example to follow (see 3 Ne. 27:27).
- *Set the standards high ahead of time*—We should choose our values and standards to live by. We can know what is right and wrong through the Light of Christ (see Moro. 7:15–17), and so can make decisions based on the Spirit in advance of the situation or temptation.
- *Pray and Fast*—We will be strengthened (see Hel. 3:35; 3 Ne. 18:18) and directed in our decisions (see D&C 9:7–9) as we commune with Heavenly Father in this way.
- *Ordinances empower us*—The power of godliness is manifested in us as we keep the ordinances of the gospel (see D&C 84:20).
- *Ask for priesthood blessings*—Priesthood blessings, fathers' blessings, and patriarchal blessings can help us in our use of agency.
- *Remember we are the result of our choices*—The law of the harvest is part of every choice. "But behold, they are in the hands of the Lord of the Harvest, and they are his; and he will raise them up at the last day" (Alma 26:7).

ILLUSTRATIONS FOR OUR TIMES

Because we have the blessing of agency, we are not "compelled in all things" (see D&C 58:26). We must learn to stay close to the Spirit and make good decisions based on inspiration and our own judgment and promptings, as the following illustrates:

Your Decisions Will Make You

Now sometimes there are problems that you face that really aren't significant enough for the Lord to bother with. You think, "Well, I don't understand that. The Lord is supposed to answer all my prayers."

There is some good evidence in Section 61 of the Doctrine and Covenants that illustrates what I am talking about. This is where the Prophet and his party were traveling between Independence and St. Louis, Missouri, on the Missouri River. They had been given direction that a number of the party should go quickly on a mission. And as they were riding down the Missouri River one of the brethren saw, in open vision, the devil riding on the face of the water. That so startled them all that they stopped. They pulled over to shore in their boat and decided they had better talk this over. They talked about it among themselves, and they were in disagreement. One said, "Oh, the water is cursed, so let's don't go on the water, let's go on land."

Others said, "No, we are doing the work of the Lord, therefore he is going to protect us. It will be just as safe on the water as it will be on the land."

They couldn't agree and so they didn't do anything. They just sat there. They sat there all night. The next morning the Prophet prayed to the Lord and received an answer. It is a very interesting answer, part of which reads as follows:

"I, the Lord, was angry with you yesterday, but today mine anger is turned away.

"Wherefore, let those concerning whom I have spoken, that should take their journey in haste— again I say unto you, let them take their journey in haste.

"And it mattereth not unto me, after a little, if it so be that they fill their mission, whether they go by water or by land; . . ." (D&C 61:20–22.)

In other words, "It doesn't make any difference to me how you go, but get going. Move out." And so it is important that you make a decision on your own sometimes. . . .

Sometimes we belabor the Lord on little insignificant things like this on which we are perfectly capable of making the decision. It really won't make any difference to him. He told them here he didn't care whether they went by water or by land—just go. Be sure and get the job done—but go.

If you live for it, you deserve and can have the guidance of the Spirit in making decisions. And that, of course, is the thing that is most important, because the Lord knows the end from the beginning; things that sometimes appear insignificant to you on the surface may not be. If you are in tune, the Spirit will tell you, for instance, whether or not you should accept a call to fill a stake mission when you had planned on going to night school—it may seem insignificant. A lot of such calls are turned down, yet this may be a very significant decision in your life because it could put you on a course that will lead you to exaltation.

The Lord knows why you are here. Many times you don't know. Consider the course we have talked about today, think about it, weigh, seek advice of people who have been through the experience, pray unto the Lord, be clear on your principles and don't depart from them, and then all those decisions that deal with honesty and virtue and other things of eternal import will be made for you in advance. Take advantage of your advance preparation. That is the easy way to do it. Keep yourself in condition so you can get the spirit of the Lord, the guidance of the Spirit in all that you do. Then your decisions will be good decisions. Your decisions will *make you.* (Hartman Rector Jr., *Speeches of the Year,* July 15, 1969, 12–14)

SUMMARY

We can use our agency wisely by using the Light of Christ (Moro. 7:15–17) and living by the Spirit (2 Ne. 32:5). Let us remember that when we fail to act on the promptings and knowledge we receive, we are still using our agency by our decision to be passive or indecisive. Passivity in the face of choice is agency by omission (failure to choose). Of all of our blessings, the freedom to choose and act should be most cherished by mankind. Heavenly Father ordained it so because He loves us and seeks only our eternal life and happiness. Our choices can bring us happiness through the Atonement of the Lord Jesus Christ. It behooves us to use our agency wisely.

ANGER

Anger has always brought innumerable problems to all of society, perhaps more so than any of the other weaknesses of man. Anger is the inner response to a problem or event, and it is usually followed by an outward verbal or physical outburst. It is the cause of so many sins and social ills—abuse, hurtful rage, physical trauma, emotional scars, and even murder. To all of us, it can present serious problems at home, at school, at play, and at the workplace. Its damaging effects can cause physical and emotional trauma and destroy relationships. Uncontrolled anger truly is one of mankind's greatest weaknesses and is rooted in selfishness and lack of self-control. Anger is a choice. It is a major character flaw. Whether manifest in attitude or action, anger reflects a poor internal reaction to our circumstances.

THE SCRIPTURES TEACH US

Psalms 37:8. *Cease from anger, and forsake wrath: fret not thyself in any wise to do evil.*

Harboring and expressing anger is not only inherently a sin, but it can result in many other unrighteous acts. This is why the Lord is so adamant about freeing ourselves from anger.

Proverbs 15:18. *A wrathful man stirreth up strife: but he that is slow to anger appeaseth strife.*

When we control our anger, we prevent discord and contention. Contention is of the devil and must be avoided at all costs (see 3 Ne. 11:29).

Proverbs 16:32. *He that is slow to anger is better than the mighty; and he that ruleth his spirit than he that taketh a city.*

In this proverb the Lord teaches us that He cares deeply about our well-being and personal development. He wants us to overcome the flesh and perfect ourselves spiritually. This is the purpose of earth life. It takes greater strength and power to overcome our anger than to be ruled by it.

JST, Matthew 5:22. *But I say unto you that whosoever is angry with his brother, shall be in danger of his judgment; and whosoever shall say to his brother, Raca, or Rabcha, shall be in danger of the council; and whosoever shall say to his brother, Thou fool, shall be in danger of hell fire.*

In the King James Version the words "without a cause" are present. In both the JST and the Book of Mormon they are not present. This teaches us a great lesson. There is no place for anger, just like there is no place for pride. The Lord has made it clear that anger is not acceptable to God. We can be disappointed, but we must resolve things in love and harmony rather than in anger (see Eph. 4:31–32). This is easy to say but hard to do. The point then is simply to be better each day in controlling any expression of anger. With effort—and the blessings of heaven—we will then eventually root out all anger from our dispositions, replacing it with a genuine concern for others and self-control within ourselves.

3 Nephi 11:29–30. *For verily, verily I say unto you, he that hath the spirit of contention is not of me, but is of the devil, who is the father of contention, and he stirreth up the hearts of men to contend with anger, one with another.*

When we are upset and respond in an angry manner, we are under the influence of the devil. He seeks to stir us up to anger so that we will behave in an un-Christlike manner. The Lord expects us to cease from contention and do away with anger.

MODERN PROPHETS SPEAK

Gordon B. Hinckley:

> There is too much trouble in our homes. There is too much anger, that corrosive, terrible thing called anger. I make a plea with you, you men of the priesthood: Control your tongues. Walk out the door instead of shouting. Get control of yourselves. Love your children. Respect them. No good will come of beating them. It will only make them resentful. Treat them with love, kindness, and respect, and I do not hesitate to promise you that the day will come that you will get on your knees and thank the Lord for his blessings upon you and your family. (*Teachings of Gordon B. Hinckley* [Salt Lake City: Deseret Book, 1997], 25)

Brigham Young:

> Now I charge you again, and I charge myself not to get angry. Never let anger arise in your hearts. No, Brigham, never let anger arise in your heart, never, never! Although you may be called upon to chastise and to speak to the people sharply, do not let anger arise in you, no, never! (*Discourses of Brigham Young,* sel. John A. Widtsoe [Salt Lake City: Deseret Book, 1954], 265)

> All the power that is gained by contending with people is usurped power. (*Journal of Discourses,* 1:273)

Neal A. Maxwell:

> In the same way that aggressive, evil thoughts should not be offered a chair and invited to sit down, so anger should never be an overnight guest! (*If Thou Endure It Well* [Salt Lake City: Bookcraft, 1996], 115)

IDEAS FOR DAILY LIVING

Here are five things to help you understand anger and take steps to overcome it.

1. Understanding and communication often dispel anger.
- *Get the facts*—Take time to get the facts before acting. Strength of character is the ability to hold off until all the facts are in.
- *Seek perspective*—Look at things first from a higher perspective, as the Savior Jesus Christ would do. Such behavior is an admirable display of leadership.
- *Talk understanding*—If you feel you are on the verge of anger, use language such as, "Let me see if I understand what you are saying (doing)." "Can you help me to understand your position on this?" "Do I understand correctly? Are you saying . . . ?" Often, such an approach will dispel misperception and save you from acting foolishly.
- *Seek empathy*—True communication involves empathy—the ability to feel what others are feeling. Empathy brings understanding, which then can dispel anger.
- *Be quick to forgive*—When you feel tempted to take offense, consider the other person's perspective. Maybe he or she wasn't at peak performance, or didn't know or understand the situation.
- *Realize that anger is your own problem*—Don't seek to blame others for your response to a situation.

- *Admit when you are wrong*—It is exhausting, damaging, and deceptive to persist in arguing after you realize you may not be entirely right. "Agree with thine adversary quickly" (Matt. 5:25) ought to be even easier if deep down we see the wrongness of our actions.

2. Control your environment and control your anger.

- *Find a better moment*—Anger often occurs when we are tired, frustrated, or have had negative experiences. Wait for a better moment to raise issues with loved ones and associates.
- *Take time*—The old adage of counting to ten before you react can often diffuse the situation.
- *Pray*—Pray for strength to overcome your expressions of contention and anger in the environments that often affect you, such as athletic contests, competitive situations, or driving your car. Pray for understanding and patience with others.
- *Reminders*—Use little signs or special things that remind you to be slow to anger, or even better, to not be angry at all.
- *Cultivate humor*—We all admire those who can diffuse a tense situation through the skillful use of humor, which often brings disagreeing parties together long enough to gain needed perspective. "Humor is laughing in spite of it all" (Wilhelm Busch).

3. Anger may have survival roots, but it is the wrong form of expression.

- *Survival reflex*—It is good to respond when we discover that our survival is at risk, that the innocent are being abused, or that wholesome principles are being violated. However, there is a correct way to respond, devoid of anger and violence.
- *The choice is ours*—If we sense anger within ourselves, we know that we face a choice of how to express our concerns—whether through physical violence or moral leadership, retribution or peacemaking, instant retaliation or the search for long-term solutions. Anger is the tripwire for taking charge in purposeful ways.
- *Maximum good*—Anger is observed more often in selfish people than in selfless people. Therefore, seek solutions that lead to the maximum good for the most people.

4. Rewards exist for controlling anger.

- *Balance*—Anger is an expression of imbalance. Learning to control anger will promote greater well-being and balance, physically, emotionally, and spiritually. Understanding that anger is a cause of physical malaise, that it has an adverse effect on your physical health, is motivation enough to find a better way.
- *Unity*—To control your anger will promote togetherness, unity, teamwork, and family solidarity.
- *Appeal*—To control your anger will make you more inviting to others and promote friendship and unity.

5. If you recognize you have a lingering problem dealing with anger, there are certain things you can do to overcome it.

- *Recognition*—Once you recognize the problem and acknowledge it to your Heavenly Father, ways will present themselves to overcome your feelings or expressions of anger. Noting the moment of anger enables us to seek alternatives, and over time effectively put them in place.
- *Put in a "good" word*—In expressing anger, you could use the statement: "I feel (upset, frustrated, angry, offended, etc.) concerning the situation." This brings anger to a "feeling" level to be resolved, rather than being left as an explosive verbal or physical reaction.
- *Get informed*—Additional useful information about anger management can be obtained from books, tapes, and CDs, colleagues, and the Internet.
- *Seek counseling*—If the anger persists, seek professional guidance.

ILLUSTRATIONS FOR OUR TIMES

The following story demonstrates how we can control our anger by looking at a situation from another's perspective.

Dealing with Anger and Contention

The key to overcoming a spirit of anger and contention, then, is to overcome selfishness—to try to infuse empathy and compassion into our relationships. Consider an example: Ann had just finished straightening the living room in preparation for guests who would arrive in an hour. As she walked back into the room, she couldn't believe what she saw. Right in the middle of her perfectly cleaned room, four-year-old Elizabeth had dumped the contents of the vacuum, spreading a filthy dust pile nearly three feet wide in front of the fireplace. She was looking up at her mother with a helpless expression.

"What are you doing?" were the first, almost automatic words that escaped from Ann's lips.

"I don't know!" cried the frustrated child, knowing that her mother had reason to be angry.

Her words suddenly made Ann see the situation from her daughter's perspective. Her anger vanished as she realized that Elizabeth had watched her preparing the room for guests and had known that vacuuming the room was a usual part of her mother's preparations. So she had attempted to help. Somehow, though, as she dragged the vacuum into the room, the bag had come loose on the floor.

When Ann saw the situation from her daughter's point of view, her initial feelings of anger melted into understanding. Without pretense, Ann was able to scoop Elizabeth up in her arms and say, "Thank you for helping me with this big job. I appreciate you very, very much. Can you help me put that dirt back in the vacuum so we can finish this job together?"

Recalling the incident, Ann says, "As upset as I was, I was able to see through my false desire to control Elizabeth and recognize that she had been trying to help me. That recognition softened my heart, and I responded the way I would like to always."

No amount of anger would have cleaned the mess up any sooner, nor would the child have learned through a demonstration of anger any worthwhile lesson that would prevent future accidents. But if the parent had responded in anger, what the child *would* have learned was that anger is the appropriate response in this situation. (*Ensign,* September 1988, 62)

* * *

This story illustrates how following the Lord's counsel to love our enemies, though difficult to do, can bless both their lives and our own. It also shows us how holding back when we are justifiably upset is living the higher law and is a more excellent way.

A More Excellent Way

As a young man, Brother Vern Crowley said he learned something of the crucial lesson . . . to "love others, even our enemies as well as friends." This is a good lesson for each of us.

After his father became ill, Vern Crowley took responsibility for running the family wrecking yard although he was only fifteen years of age. Some customers occasionally took unfair advantage of the young man, and parts were disappearing from the lot overnight. Vern was angry and vowed to catch someone and make an example of him. Vengeance would be his.

Just after his father had started to recover from his illness, Vern was making his rounds of the yard one night at closing time. It was nearly dark. In a distant corner of the property, he caught sight of someone carrying a large piece of machinery toward the back fence. He ran like a champion athlete and caught the young thief. His first thought was to take out his frustrations with his fists and then drag the boy to the front office and call the police. His heart was full of anger and vengeance. He had caught his thief, and he intended to get his just dues.

Out of nowhere, Vern's father came along, put his weak and infirm hand on his son's shoulder, and said, "I see you're a bit upset, Vern. Can I handle this?" He then walked over to the young would-be thief and put his arm around his shoulder, looked him in the eye for a moment, and said, "Son, tell me, why are you doing this? Why were you trying to steal that transmission?" Then Mr. Crowley started walking toward the office with his arm around the boy, asking questions about the young man's car problems as they walked. By the time they had arrived at the office, the father said, "Well, I think your clutch is gone and that's causing your problem."

In the meantime, Vern was fuming. "Who cares about his clutch?" he thought. "Let's call the police and get this over with." But his father just kept talking. "Vern, get him a clutch. Get him a throwout bearing, too. And get him a pressure plate. That should take care of it." The father handed all of the parts to the young man who had attempted robbery and said, "Take these. And here's the transmission, too. You don't have to steal, young man. Just ask for it. There's a way out of every problem. People are willing to help."

Brother Vern Crowley said he learned an everlasting lesson in love that day. The young man came back to the lot often. Voluntarily, month by month, he paid for all of the parts Vic Crowley had given him, including the transmission. During those visits he asked Vern why his dad was the way he was and why he did what he did. Vern told him something of their Latter-day Saint beliefs and how much his father loved the Lord and loved people. Eventually the would-be thief was baptized. Vern later said, "It's hard now to describe the feelings I had and what I went through in that experience. I, too, was young. I had caught my crook. I was going to extract the utmost penalty. But my father taught me a different way."

A different way? A better way? A higher way? A more excellent way? Oh, how the world could benefit from such a magnificent lesson. (*Ensign*, May 1992, 61)

SUMMARY

The stories about the consequences of anger are legion. They are found in every country, city, and home. Uncontrolled anger is a character flaw that needs to be addressed at every level—personal, family, school, workplace, and society at large. May we as individuals do all we can to assure that anger does not destroy; rather, let us replace it with empathy, love, and peace. Let us remember to structure our lives according to the principles of persuasion, long-suffering, gentleness, meekness, love unfeigned, kindness, pure knowledge, charity, and virtue (see D&C 121:41–45).

ATONEMENT

Understanding the Atonement of Christ and its relationship to our eternal existence is the greatest knowledge we can have in our quest to return to God, our Eternal Father. The Atonement is the center of the gospel of Jesus Christ. When we diligently apply its principles to our lives through the covenant process—through faith unto repentance, baptism, and receiving the gift of the Holy Ghost—we become liberated from our fallen state. We become free through Christ by obedience (see Gal. 5:1). Yet it is by the grace of God that we are saved, after all we can do (2 Ne. 25:23). We apply the Atonement to our lives through the gospel and through priesthood authority in The Church of Jesus Christ of Latter-day Saints.

It is this knowledge of the Atonement and Christ's role in our lives that will motivate and cause us to change. This is why the Book of Mormon was given to us as another witness and testament that Jesus is the Christ, the Anointed One. The Lord said, "Behold I have given unto you my gospel, and this is the gospel which I have given unto you—that I came into the world to do the will of my Father, because my Father sent me. And my Father sent me that I might be lifted up upon the cross; and after that I had been lifted up upon the cross, that I might draw all men unto me" (3 Ne. 27:13–14).

It is by such means that the Atonement will draw us to the Lord. The reality of the Atonement demonstrates the tender mercy and the goodness of God.

THE SCRIPTURES TEACH US

2 Nephi 9:7. *Wherefore, it must needs be an infinite atonement—save it should be an infinite atonement this corruption could not put on incorruption. Wherefore, the first judgment which came upon man must needs have remained to an endless duration. And if so, this flesh must have laid down to rot and to crumble to its mother earth, to rise no more.*

The Atonement is the center of the gospel plan in saving mankind. God loved us so much that He gave His Only Begotten Son (see John 3:16). This is the grace of God which enables and empowers us to be saved, resurrected, and exalted after all we can do (see 2 Ne. 25:23). We would have been subject to the devil, to rise no more, were it not for the Atonement of the Lord Jesus Christ (see 2 Ne. 9:8–10). This is why we should be moved to gratitude for our Savior, full of love and eager to keep the commandments.

2 Nephi 9:21–22. *And he cometh into the world that he may save all men if they will hearken unto his voice; for behold, he suffereth the pains of all men, yea, the pains of every living creature, both men, women, and children, who belong to the family of Adam. And he suffereth this that the resurrection might pass upon all men, that all might stand before him at the great and judgment day.*

The Atonement can save us if we hearken to the will of the Lord, that is, if we listen and do His will. He has suffered these things that we might come before Him, repentant and worthy of the Father's presence. If we don't repent we must suffer even as He suffered (see D&C 19:15–19). Remember that the Lord employs no servant at the gate—we must come before Him and account for how we have used His Atonement in our lives (see 2 Ne. 9:41).

Alma 7:11–12. *And he shall go forth, suffering pains and afflictions and temptations of every kind; and this that the word might be fulfilled which saith he will take upon him the pains and the sicknesses of his people. And he will take upon him death, that he may loose the bands of death which bind his people; and he will take upon him their infirmities, that his bowels may be filled with mercy, according to the flesh, that he may know according to the flesh how to succor his people according to their infirmities.*

The suffering of our Savior through the Atonement makes possible the Lord's understanding of our needs. He will succor us. He will understand and help us in our trials, tribulations, and even our infirmities. One comes to realize, as did father Lehi, that the Lord will encircle us in the arms of His love (see 2 Ne. 1:15).

Alma 42:23. *But God ceaseth not to be God, and mercy claimeth the penitent, and mercy cometh because of the atonement; and the atonement bringeth to pass the resurrection of the dead; and the resurrection of the dead bringeth back men into the presence of God; and thus they are restored into his presence, to be judged according to their works, according to the law and justice.*

The Atonement has the power to bring us back to the presence of God. There is no other way (see Hel. 5:9). The question is, Did we repent that we might make claim upon the mercy of God? Were our works the works of righteousness? Eternal life comes only to those who believe on His name (see Alma 11:40); then are just men made perfect (those who live by faith and keep the commandments; see D&C 76:69).

MODERN PROPHETS SPEAK

Bruce R. McConkie:

> To us, the central thing in the plan of salvation is the atoning sacrifice of Christ. The blessings of the creation and the fall have passed upon all mankind. Those who kept their first estate earned the right to a mortal probation. But only those who believe and obey will gain the full blessings of the atonement. (*A New Witness for the Articles of Faith* [Salt Lake City: Deseret Book, 1985], 132)

Howard W. Hunter:

> What does the Atonement have to do with missionary work? Any time we experience the blessings of the Atonement in our lives, we cannot help but have a concern for the welfare of our brethren. (*The Teachings of Howard W. Hunter,* ed. Clyde J. Williams [Salt Lake City: Bookcraft, 1997], 248)

Henry B. Eyring:

> Now, for me, at the right moment, I can begin to feel the pain the Savior felt for sins, yours and mine. His groan within himself came after he had paid the price for us, after the Atonement. His being troubled was not some abstract grief for our sins and those of the house of Israel. His was real pain, recently felt, as he took upon him the sins of the world. I can't experience that, but I can sense it enough to have sorrow for what I have added to it. I can resolve to add no more. And I can feel determination that I will help offer the full blessings of the Atonement to as many as I can, because that passage helps me feel, in a small way, what taking upon him the sins of all mankind cost the Savior. (*To Draw Closer to God: A Collection of Discourses* [Salt Lake City: Deseret Book, 1997], 69–70)

Boyd K. Packer:

> Nowhere is the generosity and kindness and mercy of God more manifest than in repentance. Do you understand the consummate cleansing power of the atonement made by the Son of God, our

Savior, our Redeemer, who said, "I, God, have suffered these things for all, that they might not suffer if they would repent"? (D&C 19:16.) I know of no sin connected with transgression of the moral law which cannot be forgiven, assuming, of course, full and complete repentance. (*Things of the Soul,* [Salt Lake City: Bookcraft, 1996], 115)

Gordon B. Hinckley:

No member of this Church must ever forget the terrible price paid by our Redeemer who gave his life that all men might live—the agony of Gethsemane, the bitter mockery of his trial, the vicious crown of thorns tearing at his flesh, the blood cry of the mob before Pilate, the lonely burden of his heavy walk along the way to Calvary, the terrifying pain as great nails pierced his hands and feet, the fevered torture of his body as he hung that tragic day, the Son of God crying out, "Father, forgive them; for they know not what they do." (Luke 23:34.) . . . We cannot forget that. We must never forget it, for here our Savior, our Redeemer, the Son of God, gave himself a vicarious sacrifice for each of us . . .

Everything depended on Him—His atoning sacrifice. That was the key. That was the keystone in the arch of the great plan which the Father had brought forth for the eternal life of His sons and daughters. Terrible as it was to face it, and burdensome as it was to realize it, He faced it, He accomplished it, and it was a marvelous and wonderful thing. It is beyond our comprehension, I believe. Nevertheless, we glimpse it in small part and must learn to appreciate it more and more and more. (*Teachings of Gordon B. Hinckley* [Salt Lake City: Deseret Book, 1997], 26–27, 30)

IDEAS FOR DAILY LIVING

Some things to remember and do to make the Atonement effective in our lives include:

1. Understand the necessity of the Atonement within the plan of happiness.

- *The Atonement is the foundation upon which the gospel stands*—Without the Atonement, the plan of salvation would fail. Man would never be redeemed from the Fall or be resurrected. Without the redeeming power of the Atonement, we would never fill the design of our creation.
- *Cultivate gratitude through understanding*—The more we understand and appreciate the Atonement, the greater our gratitude will be. Gratitude draws us to Christ (see 3 Ne. 27:14–15). The Atonement is the greatest motivating force in our lives, and it is worthy of the highest priority among our lifelong themes of study.
- *Consider the power of the Atonement*—The Atonement overcomes sin and death, lifts us above our fallen state, and resolves our separation from our Heavenly Father. It makes possible repentance and resurrection. It makes possible the return to the presence of our Heavenly Father—the "at-one-ment." In the fullest sense the Atonement makes all things possible, including exaltation. Through the Atonement, Christ is the great Mediator, Reconciler, and Advocate. In Him is the fulness of the Father manifest (see JST, John 3:34–35).
- *Consider the fate of mankind without the Atonement*—Mankind is otherwise subject to the devil and becomes even angels to the devil (see 2 Ne. 9:8–10). Without the Atonement, there is no resurrection (see 2 Ne. 9:7). There would be no eternal life or eternal families.

2. Recognize and remember the goodness of God and the suffering of our Savior.

- *The love of God and Christ is supreme*—Heavenly Father loved us so much that He gave us His Son (see John 3:16). Christ gave His life because He loved us (see 2 Ne. 26:24).

- *Remember that the Lord's work centers on His children*—Everything our Heavenly Father and our Savior do is for our immortality and eternal life (see Moses 1:39). This is their work and glory. Our work and our glory should similarly be for the welfare of all mankind.
- *Ponder that Christ suffered beyond our comprehension*—Our Savior sweat great drops of blood in anguish for our sins (see D&C 19:18; Luke 22:44). Much has been written to help us attempt to comprehend this transcending event. Our finite minds try, yet only by the Spirit can we gain an insight into this magnificent, infinite, and eternal sacrifice. We should seek through prayer understanding and appreciation for our Savior.

3. Remember with gratitude the personal blessings that come from the Atonement.

- *Repentance and forgiveness*—We can repent and be forgiven because of what Christ suffered, but only by coming unto Him and taking His name upon us. This means we accept Him as our Savior and recognize and honor His atoning sacrifice through obedience. To be forgiven, we must go through the process of repentance (see *Repentance*). Because of His sacrifice, He has promised us that if we truly repent He will remember our sins no more (see D&C 58:42–43).
- *Freedom from guilt*—The Atonement does not provide amnesia, else we could too easily forget and not learn from our experiences; rather, we receive peace. Our guilt can be swept away (see Enos 1:6). We have joy in having a peace of conscience, knowing that we have been forgiven. Can anything be sweeter than knowing we are forgiven and that our Savior's joy is full (see D&C 18:13)?
- *The Savior succors us*—Because of what He suffered, He knows how we feel, what we're going through, and what we need. By this He helps us and strengthens us at all times (see Alma 7:11–12). He blesses us as we seek to serve and strengthen others (see D&C 84:85–88).

4. Apply gospel principles regularly.

The blessings of the Atonement can come to us as we apply the principles of the gospel in our lives. We exercise faith unto repentance (see Alma 34:15–17), make covenants through baptism (see D&C 20:37), and then receive the gift—and gifts—of the Holy Ghost (see D&C 33:6). The blessings of exaltation can be ours as we live worthy of and receive our temple covenants and ordinances. All good things come to us because of our Elder Brother's ultimate sacrifice, which wrought the eternal and infinite Atonement.

5. Renew and remember our covenants.

- *Partake of the sacrament*—Our baptismal covenants are renewed when we partake of the sacrament. We promise to keep the commandments. As the sacrament prayers indicate, this process of recommitment should help us to always remember the Savior and the infinite grace that He has extended to us.
- *Attend the temple*—Even though we do not renew our covenants in the temple, we certainly refresh in our minds the things that we have agreed to do as we perform vicarious service.
- *Pray*—On bended knee we come to our Heavenly Father through our Savior Jesus Christ. We can come to Him *because* of His Son. Our Savior has reminded us to always call upon the Father in His name (see 3 Ne. 18:20–23). Through prayer we receive the blessings of God and deepen our understanding of our covenants, thus enabling and empowering us to make a recommitment to our Savior and Heavenly Father.

ILLUSTRATIONS FOR OUR TIMES

The following is an account given by Orson F. Whitney in regard to a very personal application of the Atonement:

Then came a marvelous manifestation, an admonition from a higher source, one impossible to ignore. It was a dream, or a vision in a dream, as I lay upon my bed in the little town of Columbia, Lancaster County, Pennsylvania. I seemed to be in the Garden of Gethsemane, a witness of the Savior's agony. I saw Him as plainly as ever I have seen anyone. Standing behind a tree in the foreground, I beheld Jesus, with Peter, James and John, as they came through a little wicket gate at my right, leaving the three Apostles there, after telling them to kneel and pray, the Son of God passed over to the other side, where He also knelt and prayed. It was the same prayer with which all Bible readers are familiar: "Oh my Father, if it be possible, let this cup pass from me; nevertheless not as I will, but as thou wilt."

As He prayed the tears streamed down his face, which was toward me. I was so moved at the sight that I also wept, out of pure sympathy. My whole heart went out to him; I loved him with all my soul, and longed to be with him as I longed for nothing else.

Presently He arose and walked to where those Apostles were kneeling—fast asleep! He shook them gently, awoke them, and in a tone of tender reproach, untinctured by the least show of anger or impatience, asked them plaintively if they could not watch with him one hour. There He was, with the awful weight of the world's sin upon his shoulders, with the pangs of every man, woman and child shooting through his sensitive soul—and they could not watch with him one poor hour! . . .

All at once the circumstances seemed to change, the scene remaining just the same. Instead of before, it was after the crucifixion, and the Savior, with the three Apostles, now stood together in a group at my left. They were about to depart and ascend into Heaven. I could endure it no longer. I ran from behind the tree, fell at his feet, clasped Him around the knees, and begged Him to take me with Him.

I shall never forget the kind and gentle manner in which He stopped, raised me up, and embraced me. It was so vivid, so real. I felt the very warmth of his body, as He held me in His arms and said in tenderest tones: "No, my son; those have finished their work; they can go with me; but you must stay and finish yours." Still I clung to Him. Gazing up into His face—for He was taller than I—I besought him fervently: "Well, promise me that I will come to you at the last." Smiling sweetly, He said: "That will depend entirely upon yourself." I awoke with a sob in my throat, and it was morning.

. . . I had never thought of being an Apostle, nor of holding any other office in the Church, and it did not occur to me even then. Yet I know that those sleeping Apostles meant me. I was asleep at my post—as any man is who, having been divinely appointed to do one thing, does another.

But from that hour, all was changed. I was never the same man again. (As quoted by Spencer W. Kimball, *Faith Precedes the Miracle* [Salt Lake City: Deseret Book, 1972], 26)

SUMMARY

We must more fully understand the Atonement. While we cannot completely understand it, we need to strive to appreciate it and bring it into our hearts. We apply the Atonement of Jesus Christ to our lives by partaking of the principles and ordinances of the gospel. We do this through faith unto repentance, by covenanting through baptism and taking the name of Christ upon us, and by receiving from the Father the gift, power, and blessing of the Holy Ghost. We receive the ordinances and covenants of the temple that we might gain eternal life. Then we endure to the end and, through hope and charity, return to the presence of our Father and our Savior Jesus Christ. Then is the Atonement fully effective in our lives.

ATTITUDE

Our feelings and thoughts about a situation often determine our actions and the ensuing results. Literature is replete with guidance on attitude and power: "Your attitude determines your altitude," "You are what you think you are," "When the going gets tough, the tough get going." And the list goes on and on. A positive attitude is an important building block in one's life. The big question is: What can you do in daily doses to maintain a positive attitude about life?

THE SCRIPTURES TEACH US

Proverbs 23:7. *For as he thinketh in his heart, so is he.*

The heart is the center of the soul, the mirror of the mind, and the emotional center of our very beings. Our lives eventually become the results of the feelings and yearnings of our hearts. Often, we act on our thoughts and our feelings.

1 John 3:3. *And every man that hath this hope in him purifieth himself, even as he is pure.*

When our attitude is one of hope, looking forward and being positive with faith, we tap into the power of our Savior Jesus Christ, with astounding results. Hope has power because it is interrelated to faith and charity.

Moroni 7:6–8. *For behold, God hath said a man being evil cannot do that which is good; for if he offereth a gift, or prayeth unto God, except he shall do it with real intent it profiteth him nothing. For behold, it is not counted unto him for righteousness. For behold, if a man being evil giveth a gift, he doeth it grudgingly; wherefore it is counted unto him the same as if he had retained the gift; wherefore he is counted evil before God.*

The attitude and motivation for our actions can make all the difference. If our attitude is good and motivated by love, our deeds are acceptable before God. As we act with hope in Christ, our capacity for righteousness increases.

MODERN PROPHETS SPEAK

Gordon B. Hinckley:

I hope that we will cultivate an attitude of looking for positive elements that lead to growth and enthusiasm. (*Faith: The Essence of True Religion* [Salt Lake City: Deseret Book, 1989], 77)

The Lord has said: "Wherefore, lift up thy heart and rejoice, and cleave unto the covenants which thou hast made" (D&C 25:13).

I believe He is saying to each of us, be happy. The gospel is a thing of joy. It provides us with a reason for gladness. Of course there are times of sorrow. Of course there are hours of concern and anxiety. We all worry. But the Lord has told us to lift our hearts and rejoice. I see so many people . . . who seem never to see the sunshine, but who constantly walk with storms under cloudy skies. Cultivate an attitude of happiness. Cultivate a spirit of optimism. Walk in faith, rejoicing in the beauties of nature, in the goodness of those you love, in the testimony which you carry in your heart concerning things divine. ("Words of the Prophet: The Spirit of Optimism," *New Era,* July 2001, 4)

Howard W. Hunter:

I want to tell you that despair, doom, and discouragement are not an acceptable view of life for a Latter-day Saint, however high they are on the charts of contemporary news. We must not walk on our lower lip every time a few difficult moments confront us.

I have seen a bit more of life than you. I want you to know that there have always been difficulties in mortal life and there always will be. But knowing what we know, and living as we are supposed to live, there really is no place, no excuse, for pessimism and despair. ("Why Try?" *New Era,* January 1994, 4)

Neal A. Maxwell:

At the center of our agency is our freedom to form a healthy attitude toward whatever circumstances we are placed in! Those, for instance, who stretch themselves in service—though laced with limiting diseases—are often the healthiest among us. The Spirit can drive the flesh beyond where the body first agrees to go! (*The Neal A. Maxwell Quote Book,* ed. Cory H. Maxwell [Salt Lake City: Bookcraft, 1997], 24)

James E. Faust:

The Savior reminds us, "All things are possible to him that believeth" (Mark 9:23), and "All things shall work together for your good" (D&C 90:24). The attitude with which we submit to "all things" is important. Maintaining a positive attitude and being cheerful are helpful. A belief that "all these things shall give thee experience, and shall be for thy good" is like a spiritual stabilizer. (D&C 122:7.) (*Reach Up for the Light* [Salt Lake City: Deseret Book, 1990], 83)

IDEAS FOR DAILY LIVING

Here are four strategies you might try for improving your attitude:

1. Orient your being toward Christ and His gospel.

- *Remember your heritage and your destiny*—Knowing we are children of God Himself can help us have a better perspective of ourselves and others. We have been promised eternal life if we keep the commandments.
- *Faith in Christ is the source of a positive attitude*—Because of the Savior's Atonement, there is hope for a better life now and in the eternities. The more we exercise faith and hope, the more positive we will feel and the better we will do.
- *Living the gospel requires thinking in gospel terms*—Since mental outlook has such a dynamic power in our lives, it would seem that to live the gospel requires a positive attitude. Doing much good is both the result and the perpetuation of good thoughts.
- *Your deeds reflect your attitude*—Our attitude towards our eternal roles and our Church callings will be reflected in our performance.

2. Focus on the benefits.

- *Self-esteem*—A good attitude encourages good works and thoughts, which in turn encourages self-esteem, self-worth, and self-confidence.

- *Peace*—A good attitude brings peace, and peace, in turn, helps sustain a good attitude. When you are at peace with your life as it relates to your values and behavior, your attitude toward life and others is good. To feel well and be well, we must think and do well.
- *Health*—Research has repeatedly shown a positive relationship between attitude and physical and emotional health.
- *Contagious benefits*—Your attitude affects everyone you come in contact with. All will see and feel your "upbeat spirit."
- *Gratitude*—An attitude of gratitude is a catalyst for righteousness.
- *Overcome problems*—When you have a positive attitude, your problems often become stepping stones rather than stumbling blocks, and your capacity to do good increases.

3. Give yourself the choice.

- *Teach yourself*—Remember that attitudes can be learned—the earlier the better. Just as you can teach a child to have a positive outlook on life, you can do the same for yourself. Set goals to create habits that cultivate a more positive attitude.
- *Keep learning*—The saying "What you are not up on, you are down on" confirms that knowledge and understanding not only give you power, but a change in attitude.
- *Adjust your perspective*—You can choose to look at things in a positive way (for example, the glass is always "half full" rather than "half empty").

4. Serve others.

- *Lift yourself by lifting others*—Thinking of others always helps your own attitude and well-being; selfishness only hurts your attitude.
- *Be patient*—Withholding judgment and practicing patience will usually keep your attitude on a positive note.
- *Give praise*—Receiving praise always makes one's attitude better. Praising others sincerely is one way you can help them develop a better attitude, and help improve your own attitude at the same time.

ILLUSTRATIONS FOR OUR TIMES

This story about a child's difficult day at school demonstrates the fact that a positive attitude can make all the difference in our lives.

The Little Quarters of Life

A story told to me many years ago by a friend proved the point that a good attitude can make the difference in everybody's life. It was picture day at school, and the little girl talking with her mother said, "Oh, Mom, what dress can I wear?" Her mother said, "Oh, sweetheart, let's have you wear that beautiful new white dress."

Well, she was so excited. March fifteenth—what a glorious day! Picture day. As you all know, she got to the bus stop first. She drew a little line in the dirt off the side of the road and stood there straight and true, first in line to get on the bus. She thought, *Picture day at school, and I'm first in line for the bus.* Along came a car she didn't notice. Turning slightly, the car hit a chuckhole; mud splattered all over and just showered her, and she was a mess. She began to cry and ran home to her little house just a block away. "Mommy, Mommy, look, look. I'm ruined. My dress is ruined."

Her mother said, "Oh, sweetheart, you left so early. Quick, let's put on another dress. We'll put on your second best dress. It's so nice."

They put on her second best dress, and she ran back to the bus stop. Just as she got there, the bus was almost ready to pull away. She reached for the door, and the bus driver not seeing her slammed the door right on her nose. Blood was everywhere. The bus driver said, "Oh dear, I'm sorry, little sweetheart." She helped her in, gave her a hankie and there she was having a nosebleed right on the bus. The children all said, "What happened to you?" Well, tears streaming down her cheeks, she rode to school.

When she got to school her nose had stopped bleeding, and things seemed to be okay. Well, when it was time for first recess she went out on the north side of the building. To her surprise there was still a little snow. Some of the boys were just having their typical snowball fights, and one snowball went the wrong direction and hit her right in the eye. Oh, it was icy, and it did hurt. She ran in to the teacher, "Teacher, teacher!" Her eye began to swell up. The teacher said, "Oh, sweetheart, you've got to go on the south side of the building where it's warm today." Well, tears streaming out of her one good eye, she said, "Okay."

Lunchtime came and with a little extended recess she went out to play. Gleaming in the distance were the "trick-bars." She climbed to the top and waved to a friend. She lost her balance and fell to the bottom. She landed on her arm and something snapped. She yelled out in pain, but as she did so she noticed something shiny on the ground, and she clutched it in her one good hand. She ran as best she could into the teacher. The teacher took her quickly to the school nurse. The nurse said, "I'm afraid we have to go the doctor. Your arm may be broken." They put the arm in a sling and called her mother to come and take her to the doctor.

She went outside to wait. There she stood . . . scabby nose, eye swollen shut, arm in a sling, and wearing her second best dress. A smile came on her face. Her mother pulled up and while helping her into the car she said, "How can you smile at a time like this?" She replied, "Oh Mommy, Mommy my lucky day, my lucky day. I found a quarter." Let's make all our little quarters of life into a positive attitude.

—Ed J. Pinegar

SUMMARY

Remember: Time is your ally. Positive attitudes bring blessings to one's life in every respect. With patience, you can cultivate a positive attitude that will be enduring. From the little train that "could," to the athlete who picked himself up from sure defeat to go on to victory, experience proves time and again the power of your mental attitude. To cope with life it is well not just to *understand* the value of a positive attitude, but to *practice* it as well.

BOOK OF MORMON

The Book of Mormon is the word of God. The Prophet Joseph said, "I told the brethren that the Book of Mormon was the most correct of any book on earth, and the keystone of our religion, and a man would get nearer to God by abiding by its precepts, than by any other book" (Joseph Smith, *History of the Church,*

4:461). It contains the fulness of the gospel of Jesus Christ and stands as another witness that Jesus is the Christ. Throughout the Book of Mormon we are privileged to view panoramically the great blessings and tender mercies the Lord has shown to His children here upon the earth, and especially on the American continent. When one comes to know the truthfulness of the Book of Mormon, one will know that Jesus is the Christ, that Joseph Smith was indeed a prophet of God, and that this is the "only true and living church upon the face of the whole earth" (D&C 1:30), once again established here in the latter days (see the title page of the Book of Mormon).

THE SCRIPTURES TEACH US

Isaiah 29:4. *And thou shalt be brought down, and shalt speak out of the ground, and thy speech shall be low out of the dust, and thy voice shall be, as of one that hath a familiar spirit, out of the ground, and thy speech shall whisper out of the dust.*

Isaiah saw our day. The Book of Mormon would come forth and would bring again the gospel of Jesus Christ (see D&C 20:9). It would spring forth out of the earth bringing us truth (see Ps. 85:11). We should cleave to this record because it not only contains the gospel message, but the plain and precious things that are still there in their purity (see 1 Ne. 13:29).

Ezekiel 37:19. *Say unto them, Thus saith the Lord GOD; Behold, I will take the stick of Joseph, which is in the hand of Ephraim, and the tribes of Israel his fellows, and will put them with him, even with the stick of Judah, and make them one stick, and they shall be one in mine hand.*

The Bible is the stick of Judah and the Book of Mormon is the stick of Joseph. Ezekiel saw our day and knew of the coming forth of the Book of Mormon. The rendering of this scripture is even clearer in 2 Nephi 3:12.

John 10:16. *And other sheep I have, which are not of this fold: them also I must bring, and they shall hear my voice; and there shall be one fold, and one shepherd.*

The Lord referred to the Nephite colony as His other sheep (see 3 Ne. 15:21). The Bible makes reference to this other people or their record (see John 10:14–16). The angel Moroni is referred to as bringing the gospel to preach to every nation, kindred, tongue, and people (see Rev. 14:6).

Doctrine and Covenants 20:8–9. *And gave him power from on high, by the means which were before prepared, to translate the Book of Mormon; Which contains a record of a fallen people, and the fulness of the gospel of Jesus Christ to the Gentiles and to the Jews also.*

The Book of Mormon contains the fulness of the gospel. The Prophet Joseph was given power from on high to translate it. The gospel is the foundation of the Church. The beginning of the Restoration began with the Prophet Joseph as he saw God the Father and the Savior Jesus Christ. It then continued with the bringing forth of the word of God that truth might again be established here upon the earth, and with the bestowal of keys and powers needed to administer the ordinances of the gospel.

Doctrine and Covenants 84:57. *And they shall remain under this condemnation until they repent and remember the new covenant, even the Book of Mormon and the former commandments which I have given them, not only to say, but to do according to that which I have written.*

As members of the Church, we are blessed with the gift of the Book of Mormon. The Lord has warned us not to take this sacred book lightly. It is up to each Latter-day Saint to individually take this gift into his or her own life, lifting the Lord's condemnation for taking it lightly.

MODERN PROPHETS SPEAK

Gordon B. Hinckley:

> Without reservation I promise you that if you will prayerfully read the Book of Mormon, regardless of how many times you previously have read it, there will come into your hearts an added measure of the Spirit of the Lord. There will come a strengthened resolution to walk in obedience to his commandments, and there will come a stronger testimony of the living reality of the Son of God. (*Teachings of Gordon B. Hinckley* [Salt Lake City: Deseret Book, 1997], 41)

Ezra Taft Benson:

> The honest seeker after truth can gain the testimony that Jesus is the Christ as he prayerfully ponders the inspired words of the Book of Mormon. Over one-half of all the verses in the Book of Mormon refer to our Lord. Some form of Christ's name is mentioned more frequently per verse in the Book of Mormon than even in the New Testament. He is given over one hundred different names in the Book of Mormon. Those names have a particular significance in describing His divine nature. . . .

> The Book of Mormon must be re-enthroned in the minds and hearts of our people. We must honor it by reading it, by studying it, by taking its precepts into our lives and transforming them into lives required of the true followers of Christ. President Joseph Fielding Smith said: "It seems to me that any member of this Church would never be satisfied until he or she had read the Book of Mormon time and time again, and thoroughly considered it so that he or she could bear witness that it is in very deed a record with the inspiration of the Almighty upon it, and that its history is true. . . . No member of this Church can stand approved in the presence of God who has not seriously and carefully read the Book of Mormon." . . .

> I have a conviction: The more we teach and preach from the Book of Mormon, the more we shall please the Lord and the greater will be our power of speaking. By so doing, we shall greatly increase our converts, both within the Church and among those we proselyte. The Lord expects us to use this book, and we remain under His condemnation if we do not (see D&C 84:57). (*The Teachings of Ezra Taft Benson* [Salt Lake City: Bookcraft, 1988], 56, 57, 58)

IDEAS FOR DAILY LIVING

Some ideas for making the Book of Mormon a powerful influence in your life include:

1. Follow the compass points given by the Book of Mormon itself—Moroni's title page to the Book of Mormon makes clear the four-fold purpose of the volume: "Which is to show unto the remnant of the House of Israel what great things the Lord hath done for their fathers; and that they may know the covenants of the Lord, that they are not cast off forever—And also to the convincing of the Jew and Gentile that Jesus is the Christ, the Eternal God, manifesting himself unto all nations." As Moroni consigned the plates to the earth until the time of the Restoration and looked back over the centuries covered by this sacred volume, he encapsulated the essence of the work in terms of (1) great stories of God's blessings from the past, (2) great covenants for the present, (3) great hope for the future (through the Atonement we are not "cast off forever")—all built upon the (4) foundation of Jesus Christ. This pattern is a prism for viewing the Book of Mormon.

- *Stories of God's blessings*—The Book of Mormon is a storybook of unsurpassed grandeur and inspiration. Watch for the greatness of God and His mercy and kindness toward His children. Throughout the Book of Mormon there are many examples of how the Lord provided for His children—from deliverance from the Egyptians, to obtaining the plates of Laban, to building the ship and protecting the emigrants at sea, to delivering them from their enemies in times of war and captivity. In all things they received strength and blessings from the Lord. This is one of the main purposes in the Book of Mormon (see Title Page).
- *See your own covenants in the mirror of holy writ*—By studying the pages of the Book of Mormon, which chronicle the history of a remnant of God's covenant people, you can see reflected with clarity your own opportunities and destiny as you strive to fulfill the promises you have made to your Father in Heaven and His Son Jesus Christ.
- *Cultivate hope*—The Book of Mormon is a handbook of hope. Become aware of the benefits of reading it regularly. Focus on what you feel when you study it thoughtfully, prayerfully, and gratefully—new energy, harmony, peace, faith, hope.
- *Recognize and appreciate the central doctrine taught that will bless your life: Jesus is the Christ*—Knowing that Jesus is the living Christ is absolutely essential for our salvation and exaltation. In the Book of Mormon there are hundreds of references to the Savior (over 1300, an average of one every 1.7 verses). In 1982 the words, "Another Testament of Jesus Christ" were placed just below the title. Through this book that continually testifies of Christ, we come to know Him and His role as our Savior.

2. Likening the scriptures to our lives. A standard feature in every topic of this book is to see what the Lord has said in His scriptures and then use that truth by applying it to our lives. This is how Nephi taught (see 1 Ne. 19:23). See also *Scriptures* in the present volume, which discusses how to apply the standard works to our lives. Here are just a few examples of what you can do to make the Book of Mormon a familiar and helpful influence.

- *Consistent daily study*—You can read the Book of Mormon every nine months by reading three pages a day, or every four-and-a-half months by reading six pages a day, and so on. The key is to search daily from the pages of the Book of Mormon. As vitamins taken daily are for the body, so likewise is the word of God for the spirit: You need a daily dose. Reading it just to get through it is like eating a feast without savoring the food—it just shouldn't be done in that hasty way. Ponder the word carefully, seeking to understand, applying it to your life, and sharing it with your family and associates.
- *Adopt a hero*—Think of the principal figures from the Book of Mormon, the paragons of spiritual strength who traverse the pages of this book from God, as your heroes. Adopt their examples for your life. Nephi's courage and obedience, Alma's resiliency and penitence, Abinadi's singular commitment, General Moroni's leadership, the faith of the Brother of Jared—any or all of the figures such as these can become an internalized friend and companion whose sterling qualities you can strive to emulate.
- *Make it part of your environment*—Frame your favorite scripture from the Book of Mormon and put it out on display as a memory device. Decorate your home or workplace with reminders of the message and witness of the Book of Mormon. Posters, quotes, personalized memorabilia—all of these can help remind you of the blessings of God.

3. Share your witness of the Book of Mormon with others.

- *Bear testimony*—Bear witness of the truth of the Book of Mormon often, and your testimony of it will continue to grow.
- *Spread the word*—Send copies of the Book of Mormon to colleagues and friends who are open to the message of the Restoration. Often a personalized, inscribed testimony is an effective way to introduce the book to others.
- *Personalize your witness*—If you feel inspired to do so, seek ways to express your love for, and testimony of, the Book of Mormon through creative means: entries in your personal journal, writing stories from your own life reflecting truths from the Book of Mormon, or creative expression through art, music, sculpture, dance, and so on.

4. Remember that to study the Book of Mormon is both a commandment and a blessing.

- *We cannot take lightly the Book of Mormon*—The Prophet Joseph and later President Ezra Taft Benson reminded us that Zion stands under condemnation because we have treated lightly the things that we have received, especially the Book of Mormon. "The Lord expects us to use this book, and we remain under His condemnation if we do not (see D&C 84:57)" (Ezra Taft Benson, *The Teachings of Ezra Taft Benson* [Salt Lake City: Bookcraft, 1988], 58).
- *We live by every word that proceedeth from the mouth of God*—This is clearly taught in Doctrine and Covenants 84:43–48. The word of God in the Book of Mormon is plain to our understanding (see 1 Ne. 13:40; 2 Ne. 31:2–3). The word will help us change more than any other thing (see Alma 31:5). The word, when we hold to it with all of our being, will lead us through temptation (see 1 Ne. 15:24; Hel. 3:29). The word will be our compass (see Alma 37:37–47). If we nurture the word with faith, diligence, and patience, we can enjoy the love of God and the blessings of eternal life (see Alma 32:40–43).

ILLUSTRATIONS FOR OUR TIMES

The following testimony of the Book of Mormon's influence was given by Abigail Leonard, one of the early converts to the gospel in this dispensation, at the age of eighty-two:

In 1829 Eleazer Miller came to my house, for the purpose of holding up to us the light of the gospel, and to teach us the necessity of a change of heart. He did not teach creedism, for he did not believe therein. That night was a sleepless one to me, for all night long I saw before me our Saviour nailed to the cross. I had not yet received remission of my sins, and, in consequence thereof, was much distressed. These feelings continued for several days, till one day, while walking alone in the street, I received the light of the spirit.

Not long after this, several associated Methodists stopped at our house, and in the morning, while I was preparing breakfast, they were conversing upon the subject of church matters, and the best places for church organization. From the jottings of their conversation, which I caught from time to time, I saw that they cared more for the fleece than the flock. The Bible lay on the table near by, and as I passed I occasionally read a few words until I was impressed with the question: "What is it that separates two Christians?"

For two or three weeks this question was constantly on my mind, and I read the Bible and prayed that this question might be answered to me.

One morning I took my Bible and went to the woods, when I fell upon my knees, and exclaimed: "Now, Lord, I pray for the answer of this question, and I shall never rise till you reveal to me what it is that separates two Christians." Immediately a vision passed before my eyes, and the different sects passed one after another by me, and a voice called to me, saying: "These are built up for gain." Then, beyond, I could see a great light, and a voice from above called out: "I shall raise up a people, whom I shall delight to own and bless." I was then fully satisfied, and returned to the house.

Not long after this a meeting was held at our house, during which every one was invited to speak; and when opportunity presented, I arose and said: "Today I come out from all names, sects and parties, and take upon myself the name of Christ, resolved to wear it to the end of my days."

For several days afterward, many people came from different denominations and endeavored to persuade me to join their respective churches. At length the associated Methodists sent their presiding elder to our house to preach, in the hope that I might be converted. While the elder was discoursing I beheld a vision in which I saw a great multitude of people in the distance, and over their heads hung a thick, dark cloud. Now and then one of the multitude would struggle, and rise up through the gloomy cloud; but the moment his head rose into the light above, the minister would strike him a blow, which would compel him to retire; and I said in my heart, "They will never serve me so."

Not long after this, I heard of the "Book of Mormon," and when a few of us were gathered at a neighbor's we asked that we might have manifestations in proof of the truth and divine origin of this book, although we had not yet seen it. Our neighbor, a lady, was quite sick and in much distress. It was asked that she be healed, and immediately her pain ceased, and health was restored. Brother Bowen defiantly asked that he might be slain, and in an instant he was prostrated upon the floor. I requested that I might know of the truth of this book, by the gift and power of the Holy Ghost, and I immediately felt its presence. Then, when the Book of Mormon came, we were ready to receive it and its truths. The brethren gathered at our house to read it, and such days of rejoicing and thanksgiving I never saw before nor since. We were now ready for baptism, and on or about the 20th of August, 1831, were baptized. (as quoted in Edward W. Tullidge, *The Women of Mormondom* [New York: Tullidge & Crandall, 1877],160–63)

SUMMARY

The Book of Mormon is the key to our understanding the gospel of Jesus Christ. It is the word of God. It is the keystone of our religion, and we should make it our lifetime study. It will bless our lives and the lives of our children. Let us learn of God and His Beloved Son through this precious scripture given for our day to bring us the knowledge of eternal life.

CHARACTER

"Sow an act, and you reap a habit; sow a habit and you reap a character; sow a character, and you reap a destiny." This profound statement by George D. Boardman truly puts into perspective the process of building character. It is a process that takes time and effort. It takes a value system based on the gospel of Jesus Christ. It takes self-discipline and integrity. Surely it takes all that one possesses to become a man or woman of Christ. The Savior stated with utter clarity the commission for our existence: "Therefore I would that ye should be perfect even as I, or your Father who is in heaven is perfect" (3 Ne. 12:48). He then later restated the commandment with similar unequivocal clarity: "What manner of men [and, by extension, women] ought ye to be? Verily I say unto you, even as I am" (3 Ne. 27:27). Such is the divine directive to build character and answer the call to honor and fulfill our destiny.

THE SCRIPTURES TEACH US

Articles of Faith 1:13. *We believe in being honest, true, chaste, benevolent, virtuous, and in doing good to all men; indeed, we may say that we follow the admonition of Paul—We believe all things, we hope all things, we have endured many things, and hope to be able to endure all things. If there is anything virtuous, lovely, or of good report or praiseworthy, we seek after these things.*

This is our "character" Article of Faith. The Lord expects us to strive for the stated qualities. These qualities, along with those necessary to obtain and practice charity, are the basis for having a Christlike character.

MODERN PROPHETS SPEAK

Ezra Taft Benson:
> Members of The Church of Jesus Christ of Latter-day Saints are to emulate the character of the Savior.
>
> And what is His character?
>
> He has identified the cardinal virtues of His divine character in a revelation to all priesthood holders who serve in His ministry. In this revelation, which was given a year before the Church was organized, He said, "Remember faith, virtue, knowledge, temperance, patience, brotherly kindness, godliness, charity, humility, diligence." (Doctrine and Covenants 4:6.) These are the virtues we are to emulate. This is the Christlike character. (*Come unto Christ* [Salt Lake City: Deseret Book, 1983], 48)

David O. McKay:
> And what is the crowning glory of man in this earth so far as his individual achievement is concerned? It is *character—character developed through obedience to the laws of life as revealed through the gospel of Jesus Christ, who came that we might have life and have it more abundantly.* Man's chief concern in life should not be the acquiring of gold nor fame nor material possessions. It should *not* be the development of physical prowess nor of intellectual strength, *but his aim, the highest in life, should be the development of a Christlike character.* (*Man May Know for Himself: Teachings of President David O. McKay,* comp. Clare Middlemiss [Salt Lake City: Deseret Book, 1967], 29)

IDEAS FOR DAILY LIVING

Here are four remedies to help you build character:

1. Anchor your life to the Lord Jesus Christ.
- *Commit to gospel standards*—Character is grounded in unchanging doctrines and principles, rather than in the shifting winds of fad and whim. Therefore, commit to living by enduring values and standards.

- *Stick with your principles*—Self-esteem and self-respect increase as you exercise self-control in accordance with your values and standards. This, in turn, will increase your desire to be a person of character. Be true to yourself and to God.
- *Learn from example*—Study the life of the Savior and other men and women of unquestioned character. Here are some of the qualities to look for: **C**—*courage* in the face of adversity; **H**—*honesty* in the midst of moral relativism; **A**—*alignment* with unchanging principles; **R**—*respect* for the rights of every person; **A**—*admitting* (and correcting) mistakes when you make them; **C**—*courtesy* in the presence of antagonism and arrogance; **T**—*trust* in a world of deceit; **E**—*empathy* for the disadvantaged; **R**—*resilience* in the wake of disappointment.
- *Christ's divine nature*—Increase in your faith, virtue, knowledge, temperance, patience, brotherly kindness, godliness, *charity,* humility, and diligence (see D&C 4:6; 2 Pet. 1:3–12). In charity we find the center of Christ's character; it is the trait and quality that makes us like Him. Make this your priority and goal, to become even as He is.

2. Make wise decisions every day.
- *Decide first to decide wisely*—"Good character is more to be praised than outstanding talent. Most talents are, to some extent, a gift. Good character, by contrast, is not given to us. We have to build it piece by piece—by thought, choice, courage and determination" (John Luther).
- *Make each moment count*—Character is a result of attitudes, desires, and choices. Remember: You are what you are because of your decisions. Have the courage to make wise decisions.
- *Stretch yourself*—Set high goals and make plans to keep them. Check your progress on a regular basis.
- *Build strong habits*—It takes up to 21 days to create a habit that forms your character, but only one day to break it. Build positive, character-building habits.

3. Put the well-being of others high on your agenda.
- *Build character through service*—"Character is established not on the sands of selfishness, but on the rock-hard commitment to leave behind good seeds for the present and coming generations" (East Asian Philosophy).

4. Welcome adversity and challenge as mentors.
- *Welcome challenge*—Character is more readily illuminated in times of trial and adversity than in moments of calm and bounty.
- *Welcome sacrifice*—Character is grown in the seedbed of sacrifice and trial. Sacrifice is often required to maintain your character.
- *Welcome difficulty*—Do something difficult as a proactive way to strengthen your character.

ILLUSTRATIONS FOR OUR TIMES

In the following account, notice how it is not so much the content of the evening this young man spent with President Benson's family, but the quality of the family and home life that drew him to them. It was the character of their lives.

We Need More of That Spirit in Our Home

I was seated in my office in Salt Lake City when I received a telephone call from a man in New York, a multimillionaire and one of our great industrialists. He had a son in a camp just outside

Salt Lake City who had been expecting to be shipped overseas, and then the war had ended and so the servicemen were crowded into that camp. This boy was discouraged and his father was worried about him, so he called and said, "Would you please call him on the telephone and see if you can cheer him up a bit." I said, "Of course, I would be happy to." And so I called him and said, "Wouldn't you like to come into the office for a little visit?" He said, "I surely would."

He was a bit delayed coming in and I was just ready to leave for home when he arrived. I said, "Wouldn't you like to go out to the house with me and take pot luck with the family? My wife doesn't know you are coming, but you will be welcome." He said, "I can't imagine anything I'd rather do tonight than that." So he went with me and we had our dinner and we had our prayer. Then we gathered around the piano afterward and enjoyed ourselves in some singing. After we visited for a while, I drove him down to the bus. In a few days, I got a letter from his father. And you know, you would have thought I had saved the boy's life! In the letter, the father quoted a letter from his son in which the son had said, "Father, I didn't know there were any people in this world who lived like that."

Yes, we take it all for granted. Here was a man worth millions of dollars, who could buy his son anything that dollars could buy and never miss the dollars, and yet this simple thing of prayer and devotion in the home had passed him by. We need to be more grateful. I think there is no true character without gratitude. It is one of the marks of a real strong character to have a feeling of thanksgiving and gratitude for blessings. We need more of that spirit in our homes, in our daily association, in the Church, every-where. It doesn't cost anything, and it is so easy to cultivate. It is so easy also to be dissatisfied and to be envious of other people. (Ezra Taft Benson, *God, Family, Country: Our Three Great Loyalties* [Salt Lake City: Deseret Book, 1974], 201–202)

SUMMARY

Your character truly does make your destiny. The words of Helen Keller show the price one must pay to develop character. She said, "Character cannot be developed in ease and quiet. Only through experience of trial and suffering can the soul be strengthened, ambition inspired, and success achieved." The Apostle John summarized the essence of our quest to acquire the divine character when he said, speaking of the lot of the valiant and obedient: "Beloved, now are we the sons of God, and it doth not yet appear what we shall be: but we know that, when he shall appear, we shall be like him; for we shall see him as he is" (1 Jn. 3:2). May we all strive with every fiber of our beings to transcend the tests of mortality and rise to the challenge of becoming, in our inmost character and patterns of living, even as He is.

CHARITY

Charity, the pure love of Christ, is the ultimate attribute of godliness. To have charity is to obtain the divine nature of Christ through faith, virtue, knowledge, temperance, patience, brotherly kindness, and godliness with all humility and diligence (see D&C 4:6). This pure love of Christ is total, complete, enduring, and characteristic of the divine Being. When one is possessed of this love, his or her desires are like unto our Savior's—to bless and serve mankind.

Charity never fails. Christ did not fail His Father, nor did He fail us; His pure love motivated His great sacrifice—the eternal, infinite, vicarious Atonement. Through the Atonement of Christ, we can gradually acquire this unconditional, godly love.

THE SCRIPTURES TEACH US

Moroni 7:44. *None is acceptable before God, save the meek and lowly in heart; and if a man be meek and lowly in heart, and confesses by the power of the Holy Ghost that Jesus is the Christ, he must needs have charity; for if he have not charity he is nothing; wherefore he must needs have charity.*

When we are meek and lowly, we are able to receive the Spirit more readily. With the Spirit, we come to know and testify of Christ. When we truly know Him, we strive to be like Him, thus obtaining a love like His, or charity. Charity should be the goal for each of us as we seek to become like Him.

Moroni 7:45. *And charity suffereth long, and is kind, and envieth not, and is not puffed up, seeketh not her own, is not easily provoked, thinketh no evil, and rejoiceth not in iniquity but rejoiceth in the truth, beareth all things, believeth all things, hopeth all things, endureth all things.*

When we truly have charity, this verse describes us. One can sense the joy that comes with the acquisition and application of a charitable disposition.

Moroni 7:46. *Wherefore, my beloved brethren, if ye have not charity, ye are nothing, for charity never faileth. Wherefore, cleave unto charity, which is the greatest of all, for all things must fail.*

Charity never fails because it is the pure love of Christ, which is eternal. In the end, charity is the greatest of all the gifts of the Spirit. Ultimately, we will not need the gift of tongues; the need for the gift of healing will pass away with mortality. But all through the eternities, we will need the godlike attribute of charity.

Moroni 7:47–48. *But charity is the pure love of Christ, and it endureth forever; and whoso is found possessed of it at the last day, it shall be well with him. Wherefore, my beloved brethren, pray unto the Father with all the energy of heart, that ye may be filled with this love, which he hath bestowed upon all who are true followers of his Son, Jesus Christ; that ye may become the sons of God; that when he shall appear we shall be like him, for we shall see him as he is; that we may have this hope; that we may be purified even as he is pure. Amen.*

Why will it be well with us to have charity? Because by obtaining this love we become the sons and daughters of God (see 1 John 3:2). Peter taught us that when we have charity we take upon ourselves the Lord's divine nature, and that by pursuing this path of righteousness our calling and election will be made sure (see 2 Pet. 1:5–10). Through mighty prayer we seek this most precious gift if we are true followers of Christ.

1 Corinthians 13:2–3. *And though I have the gift of prophecy, and understand all mysteries, and all knowledge; and though I have all faith, so that I could remove mountains, and have not charity, I am nothing. And though I bestow all my goods to feed the poor, and though I give my body to be burned, and have not charity, it profiteth me nothing.*

Charity is not just what we say or do; it is not just how we treat others. It isn't giving service because we're *supposed* to; it's doing good because of our love for God and our fellowmen. Charity is part of who we are. Our good works profit us nothing if we are not truly seeking to become like Christ and do as He would.

MODERN PROPHETS SPEAK

Ezra Taft Benson:

> The final and crowning virtue of the divine character is charity, or the pure love of Christ (see Moroni 7:47). If we would truly seek to be more like our Savior and Master, learning to love as He loves should be our highest goal. Mormon called charity "the greatest of all" (Moroni 7:46). . . . Charity never seeks selfish gratification. The pure love of Christ seeks only the eternal growth and joy of others. . . . The Lord Jesus Christ liberated man from the world by the pure gospel of love. He demonstrated that man, through the love of God and through kindness and charity to His fellows, could achieve His highest potential. He lived the plain and sure doctrine of service, of doing good to all men—friends and enemies alike. (*The Teachings of Ezra Taft Benson* [Salt Lake City: Bookcraft, 1988], 275)

Joseph Smith:

> Until we have perfect love we are liable to fall; and when we have a testimony that our names are sealed in the Lamb's book of life, we have perfect love, and then it is impossible for false Christs to deceive us. (*Encyclopedia of Joseph Smith's Teachings,* ed. Larry E. Dahl and Donald Q. Cannon [Salt Lake City: Bookcraft, 1997], 105)

IDEAS FOR DAILY LIVING

Listed below are some ideas to help us be full of charity.

1. Start with ourselves.
- *Ask for a blessing of charity*—Let us pray with all the energy of our hearts to possess charity (see Moro. 7:48).
- *Make a personal commitment for improvement*—Make a plan to increase our faith, be more virtuous, etc., following the admonition in D&C 4:6 by continually incorporating in our lives the attributes of godliness.
- *Make the Savior the Exemplar for charity*—Remember the Savior in all things. Create a new motto for our attitude and behavior: "Do as Jesus would do."
- *See with the eyes of charity*—Charity is truly a way of looking at things. We can start by counting our blessings. Our hearts will be softened, the desire to do good will increase, and we will want to help others. To become full of charity requires a change of heart toward oneself, others, and God.
- *Be open to opportunities to help*—Remember: There are people less fortunate than you, people who are in need of help now! There is ample opportunity to be of service. Assist in the Lord's work with charity (see D&C 12:8).
- *Follow the Spirit*—Be sensitive to the Spirit and follow the promptings you receive in regard to your treatment of and attitude toward others.

2. Make your home the schoolhouse of charity.
- *Teach charity*—Teach children and loved ones by setting an example of the qualities of charity (see Moro. 7:45).
- *Recognize even small acts of charity*—Even the most humble contributions, when given in love, are acts of charity. Be aware of the small acts of kindness you can give others, as well as those you receive.

3. Do good for the right reasons.

- *Charity never judges*—We should help others unconditionally. Thinking that they have brought their unfortunate circumstances upon themselves is not our right or privilege. Why? Because we never have all the facts or the feelings and emotions of the situation. Thoughtful people know that circumstances could one day place them in a similar position to need charity; they do not judge.
- *Act from love alone*—By this we can know that our motivation is pure. We do good out of genuine concern for others, and we are readily willing to forgo recognition and credit for the good deed. Nothing is quite as noble as the anonymous charitable act. "Charity ever finds in the act reward, and needs no trumpet in the receiver" (Beaumont and Fletcher).

4. Have a plan for charitable giving.

- *Develop your own formula for sharing*—Look at your resources, your time, your talents, your goods, your money. Budget to give away a certain amount of all these for charitable purposes.
- *Give away knowledge*—Sometimes charity means helping others to learn how to help themselves, rather than giving them goods only. Goethe put it this way: "Treat a man as he is and he will remain as he is. Treat a man as he can and should be and he will become as he can and should be."
- *Give of yourself*—Sometimes the greatest gift is not just material offerings, but ourselves—our time, our counsel, our solace, our support, our acceptance, our encouragement, and our companionship.

ILLUSTRATIONS FOR OUR TIMES

In the following, Richard J. Allen tells of an elderly member of the Church who, while in the hospital with a serious illness, valiantly attempted to contact his home teaching families. Brother Allen then relates scriptures that reinforce the fact that our charity towards others is a sign of true conversion.

Charity—A Sure Sign of Conversion

He was in his senior years, having devoted all his days to service and building up the kingdom of God on earth. Now the toll of mortality was showing up more and more frequently in his life in the form of recurring infirmities and chronic discomforts. This time pneumonia had set in, together with a worrisome blood infection. As I greeted this venerable high priest that day in the hospital, my expectation was to hear of the vexations that come with advancing years. But he would have none of that. His number one worry—despite the manifest dangers of his condition—was not his own health, but rather his home teaching. Prior to his hospitalization, he and his companion had completed two of the three family visits assigned to them. One family remained. The good brother had made repeated calls from the hospital to try to arrange for backup assistance, but he had not been able to connect. When I asked about the remaining family, he mentioned an elderly widow who lived alone. "Oh," I said, "it turns out that, by coincidence, we of the high priests group leadership visited her just three days ago and left a spiritual message. Consider the visit done!" Coincidence indeed! Immediately his eyes brightened up and a look of peace came into his countenance. What a potent medicine is the divine elixir of charity in the heart of good people such as this older brother.

When Enos spent a day and a night in fervent prayer for a blessing of peace and forgiveness, the Lord favored him with the comforts of the Spirit. His conversion immediately invoked in him a feeling of selflessness in the form of an overwhelming desire for the welfare of his brethren. "And it came to pass that after I had prayed and labored with all diligence, the Lord said unto me: I will grant unto thee according to thy desires, because of thy faith" (Enos 1:12). It is that kind of faith that opens the doorway to charity. Mormon made this point very clearly in his famous sermon preserved by the hand of his son, Moroni:

"But charity is the pure love of Christ, and it endureth forever; and whoso is found possessed of it at the last day, it shall be well with him" (Moro. 7:47). It was this kind of charity that my good friend was displaying that day in the hospital. What better sign of conversion to the gospel of Jesus Christ could there ever be than a charitable and loving disposition transcending one's own needs?

—Richard J. Allen

SUMMARY

Christ's love for us endures forever. When we are possessed of it, it endures in our lives. Do we desire charity? Do we want to possess this love? Can we see the benefits and the blessings of love exercised in our lives? Let us with all the energy of our hearts, with all our souls, with all our minds, and in all of our decisions seek to be full of charity. Life will be beautiful and we will find peace as only the Lord can give. "And now abideth faith, hope, charity, these three; but the greatest of these is charity" (1 Cor. 13:13).

CHASTENING

The purpose of chastening is to help people reform, repent, and purify their lives. Righteous chastening is always based on love for the individual. The Lord chastens us because He loves us. He wants to help us stay on the straight and narrow path. He even helps us feel guilt to encourage us to repent. Sometimes He uses external means such as famine, pestilence, and many other hardships (see Hel. 11:4–18) to bring us to a state of humility so that we can be taught and persuaded to change our ways. Through chastening we can grow—provided we are easily entreated and don't consider the chastening as punishment, but rather as a "course correction" to keep us on the right course. Chastening from a priesthood leader or parent should always be motivated by a desire to help us repent from sin so that we can enjoy the blessings of the Spirit and ultimately return to the presence of our Heavenly Father.

When we need to chasten in performing our role or stewardship in life, we must follow the counsel given in Doctrine and Covenants 121:41–44: reproving (correcting) betimes (early on, without delay) with sharpness (with clarity) when inspired by the Holy Ghost. Let us then always remember to follow up with compassion and love, so that the individual will not take us for an enemy. When receiving chastening, we should be as contrite, humble, and easily entreated as possible.

THE SCRIPTURES TEACH US

Doctrine and Covenants 95:1–2. *Verily, thus saith the Lord unto you whom I love, and whom I love I also chasten that their sins may be forgiven, for with the chastisement I prepare a way for their deliverance in all things out of temptation, and I have loved you—Wherefore, ye must needs be chastened and stand rebuked before my face.*

The Lord loves us. We need to realize that in chastening us, He demonstrates that love and provides for us the opportunity to repent. We should learn to be grateful that those who love us care enough that they will practice the most difficult form of love—chastening.

Doctrine and Covenants 1:27. *And inasmuch as they sinned they might be chastened, that they might repent.*

Everyone who sins must come to realize the need to repent. Chastening can come in many forms to help us repent: godly guilt and sorrow, disciplinary councils, leaders exercising stewardship responsibilities concerning our behavior, external chastisement by physical means (earthly conditions) to bring us to a state in which we are willing to repent, visitations from heavenly beings (see Ether 2:14), and any other means the Lord sees fit to use in helping His children come back to Him.

Helaman 12:2–3. *Yea, and we may see at the very time when he doth prosper his people, yea, in the increase of their fields, their flocks and their herds, and in gold, and in silver, and in all manner of precious things of every kind and art; sparing their lives, and delivering them out of the hands of their enemies; softening the hearts of their enemies that they should not declare wars against them; yea, and in fine, doing all things for the welfare and happiness of his people; yea, then is the time that they do harden their hearts, and do forget the Lord their God, and do trample under their feet the Holy One—yea, and this because of their ease, and their exceedingly great prosperity. And thus we see that except the Lord doth chasten his people with many afflictions, yea, except he doth visit them with death and with terror, and with famine and with all manner of pestilence, they will not remember him.*

Let us always be careful to remember the goodness of God. When we forget God and His goodness, we set Him at naught and hearken not to His counsels (see 1 Ne. 19:7). At such times He will chastise us so that we will remember and repent.

Hebrews 12:5–11. *And ye have forgotten the exhortation which speaketh unto you as unto children, My son, despise not thou the chastening of the Lord, nor faint when thou art rebuked of him: For whom the Lord loveth he chasteneth, and scourgeth every son whom he receiveth. If ye endure chastening, God dealeth with you as with sons; for what son is he whom the father chasteneth not? . . . Furthermore we have had fathers of our flesh which corrected us, and we gave them reverence: shall we not much rather be in subjection unto the Father of spirits, and live? For they verily for a few days chastened us after their own pleasure; but he for our profit, that we might be partakers of his holiness. Now no chastening for the present seemeth to be joyous, but grievous: nevertheless afterward it yieldeth the peaceable fruit of righteousness unto them which are exercised thereby.*

As we learn from this scripture, chastening is difficult to receive. However, we know that we receive it only because Heavenly Father loves us, and any loving father would so care for and caution an errant child. Let us be patient and look forward to the fruit of righteousness as our reward for giving or receiving chastening.

MODERN PROPHETS SPEAK

Harold B. Lee:

> It's an interesting thing that sometimes it takes calamity to drive us together. It's a terrifying thing to think that that's necessary, but the Lord said through one of His prophets that sometimes we have to have the chastening hand of the Almighty before we will wake up and humble ourselves to do the thing that He has asked us to do (see Helaman 12:3–6). In talking about the conditions that would come, He warned the people that death and destruction and all sorts of difficulties would have to come before people would listen, before they would obey, and He removes His hand and lets these things occur, or our people would not repent and come unto the Lord. (*The Teachings of Harold B. Lee*, ed. Clyde J. Williams [Salt Lake City: Bookcraft, 1996], 191)

Brigham Young:

> We as a people, will be chastened until we can wholly submit ourselves to the Lord and be Saints indeed. (*Discourses of Brigham Young*, sel. John A. Widtsoe [Salt Lake City: Deseret Book, 1954], 226)

Neal A. Maxwell:

> Sometimes our chastening comes to us compressed in a difficult "little season" (D&C 103:4). Whatever the case, if we cannot endure chastening we do not yet qualify as true disciples: "My people must be tried in all things, that they may be prepared to receive the glory that I have for them, even the glory of Zion; and he that will not bear chastisement is not worthy of my kingdom" (D&C 136: 31). (*Not My Will, But Thine* [Salt Lake City: Bookcraft, 1988], 64)

IDEAS FOR DAILY LIVING

Here are some things to consider when we are called upon to either give or receive chastening:

1. Chastening others.

- *Follow the Spirit*—Chastening must always be directed by the Spirit and practiced with love.
- *Consider your stewardship*—You must first have the right as well as the responsibility, or the authority to chastise.
- *Listen*—First make sure you have the facts; ask questions and invite discussion.
- *Use the word of God*—Let the Lord speak to the situation through His scriptures and the pronouncements of His prophets.
- *Act only when the strategy is complete (ending with the spirit of healing)*—Never chastise if you don't have enough of the "balm of Gilead" to heal the wound with love.
- *Be discreet*—Chastening should always be in private.
- *Never in anger*—Use a soft voice with no wrath or anger

2. Receiving chastening.

- *Perceive the love behind the action*—Recognize that the one chastening loves you and is trying to help you.
- *Practice patience*—When you feel wrongfully accused, pray for the one doing the chastening. Be patient. Remember that time and more information can right the wrong.
- *Eschew vengeance*—Never seek retaliation. Leave justice to the Lord (see Rom. 12:19).
- *Be softhearted*—Be easily entreated.

ILLUSTRATIONS FOR OUR TIMES

From the example of the saints in the early days of the restoration, we learn that we must endure chastening with humility in order to receive the Lord's crowning blessings.

Chastened Even as Abraham

Amid relentless persecution and painful dislocation in Missouri, the Saints in Kirtland received on December 16, 1833, a remarkable revelation from the Lord through the Prophet Joseph Smith, telling them, "they must needs be chastened and tried, even as Abraham, who was commanded to offer up his only son. For all those who will not endure chastening, but deny me, cannot be sanctified" (D&C 101:4–5). The Lord gives them a grand promise that He will remember them, comfort them, gather them, and give them a crown. "Be still," He counsels them, "and know that I am God" (v. 16). Thus in an hour of great affliction, the Lord gives the Saints a loftier view of things, shows them that He is in charge of the flow of events, and reinforces the age-old pattern of righteousness: that all should repent, depend on Him, and humbly submit to divine chastening as a gateway to spiritual growth and ultimate victory. (See *History of the Church,* 1:458–64.) Against the background of this panorama of chastening and correcting so characteristic of the Restoration period, let us all learn to accept the chastening of the Lord in humility: "And seek the face of the Lord always, that in patience ye may possess your souls, and ye shall have eternal life" (D&C 101:38).

—Richard J. Allen

* * *

A personal story from the life of author Richard J. Allen shows us how our chastening of our children must be based on understanding and compassion.

The Wooden Splinter

In a special location at home I keep handy a small reminder of a big lesson I learned one time as a young father. It is a sharp wooden splinter about an inch-and-a-half in length that was retrieved from the tire of our family car many years ago at a time when one of our daughters was learning to drive. One day while she was driving that particular car, she rounded a corner and managed to bump up over the curb. Soon thereafter the tire went flat, which occasioned the need for a fatherly rescue. Making the not illogical assumption that the impact had caused the problem, I took the occasion to admonish her on being more careful. It was, I thought, the perfect teaching moment—and so it was, but for the father rather than the daughter. The repairman soon discovered the problem with the tire: it was not the bump but rather an imbedded wooden splinter that was at fault. I apologized to my daughter for the misplaced blame (she was always very forgiving) and resolved to be less judgmental in the future in carrying out my fatherly teaching duties. Recently I was counseling with my son on some family matters and retrieved the wooden splinter to relive for his benefit the lesson I had learned so many years ago. We enjoyed a good chuckle at my expense.

And so it is in life—as parents teach, they need to remember constantly that they, too, are imperfect and have need of continuing education and constant correction. When Alma exhorted his sons to live righteously, he did so in the context of his own grievous past. He taught repentance with authority, because he himself was an authority on repentance: "Yea, I say unto you, my son, that there could be nothing so exquisite and so bitter as were my pains. Yea, and again I say unto you, my son, that on the other hand, there can be nothing so exquisite and sweet as was my joy" (Alma 36:21). What a powerful testimony of the effects of repentance and the application of the principles of the Atonement. The Savior reminded us: "And why beholdest thou the mote that is in thy brother's eye, but considerest not the beam that is in thine own eye?" (Matt. 7:3; see also Luke 6:41–42). Parents as teachers would do well to clothe truth in humility, doctrine in compassion, principles in charity, and chastening in love.

—Richard J. Allen

SUMMARY

Chastening is a bold and firm method of correction that sometimes needs to be practiced in order to bless lives. As leaders, and especially as parents, we may need to practice "tough love" from time to time in order that we not be guilty of permissiveness. Permissiveness often condones the inappropriate action or sin. "Tough love" is upholding truth and righteousness. It must be practiced with sensitivity and compassion, thus communicating our love for the individual. Remember that the preaching of the word of God is always the first thing we should do (see Alma 31:5) to help strengthen the people we love and serve. Let us never forget that chastening should always be handled and received with caution, care, and love—and only as directed by the Spirit.

CHILDREN

Of all the tasks on earth, nothing is so difficult yet so rewarding as raising a child. Our joy truly is in our posterity. The trials seem almost overwhelming and the joys simply exhilarating. The question is, what can we do to help them grow without so many crises? What can we do to help prevent things that need not occur? What can we do to help them become truly converted to the gospel of Jesus Christ and have a desire to live it throughout their lives? What can we do to help them be prepared to share the gospel and keep the sacred covenants of the temple? What can we do to help them become mature young adults who are responsible and accountable? What can we do to help prepare them for marriage and their future family? As parents, raising children is the most important thing we will ever do. Our parental roles will go on through all eternity as we become worthy of exaltation.

THE SCRIPTURES TEACH US

Psalms 127:3. *Lo, children are an heritage of the Lord: and the fruit of the womb is his reward.*

Children are gifts from our Heavenly Father. We are responsible for the gifts and stewardship God has given us, for where much is given, much is required (see D&C 82:3).

Proverbs 22:6. *Train up a child in the way he should go: and when he is old, he will not depart from it.*

Early teaching and training is imperative in raising a child. This proverb has with it a promise of lasting value. Make a plan to teach your children in their early years, giving them the foundation they need to make good choices and live and serve in the Lord's kingdom.

Isaiah 54:13. *And all thy children shall be taught of the Lord; and great shall be the peace of thy children.*

The knowledge of the Lord brings peace to one's soul. Your children find peace in righteousness as they live the doctrines and principles you teach them.

Matthew 18:6. *But whoso shall offend one of these little ones which believe in me, it were better for him that a millstone were hanged about his neck, and that he were drowned in the depth of the sea.*

Never hurt, belittle, abuse, or in any way offend a child. Children are pure and seek love and learning from their parents and other adults. This love and learning requires discipline, but never cruelty. If we fail in this stewardship, or if we lapse into abuse, the consequences are severe. On the other hand, the joy of success is boundless.

Mosiah 4:14–15. *And ye will not suffer your children that they go hungry, or naked; neither will ye suffer that they transgress the laws of God, and fight and quarrel one with another, and serve the devil, who is the master of sin, or who is the evil spirit which hath been spoken of by our fathers, he being an enemy to all righteousness. But ye will teach them to walk in the ways of truth and soberness; ye will teach them to love one another, and to serve one another.*

While a crucial part of parenting, fulfilling the responsibility of providing food, clothing, and shelter to our children isn't enough. The major role of parents is to teach our children the principles of righteousness (see Moses 6:57–58). We have the responsibility to help keep our children on the straight and narrow path. We must also teach them to avoid contention, for contention is of the devil (see 3 Ne. 11:29). We will teach them to obey the commandments and to serve one another. Make a plan to teach by precept and example the gospel of Jesus Christ to your children.

Doctrine and Covenants 68:25–28. *And again, inasmuch as parents have children in Zion, or in any of her stakes which are organized, that teach them not to understand the doctrine of repentance, faith in Christ the Son of the living God, and of baptism and the gift of the Holy Ghost by the laying on of the hands, when eight years old, the sin be upon the heads of the parents. For this shall be a law unto the inhabitants of Zion, or in any of her stakes which are organized. And their children shall be baptized for the remission of their sins when eight years old, and receive the laying on of the hands. And they shall also teach their children to pray, and to walk uprightly before the Lord.*

Let us, as parents, take seriously our teaching responsibility even as Jacob did (see Jacob 1:19). We teach the gospel so that our children will walk uprightly before the Lord and be obedient.

Doctrine and Covenants 93:39–40. *And that wicked one cometh and taketh away light and truth, through disobedience, from the children of men, and because of the tradition of their fathers. But I have commanded you to bring up your children in light and truth.*

We should establish righteous traditions within our families: family prayer, family scripture time, family home evening, family council, family blessings and interviews, and family vacations that build family unity and combat the evil that would rule our families.

MODERN PROPHETS SPEAK

The First Presidency and the council of the Twelve Apostles:
> Husband and wife have a solemn responsibility to love and care for each other and for their children. "Children are an heritage of the Lord" (Psalms 127:3). Parents have a sacred duty to rear their children in love and righteousness, to provide for their physical and spiritual needs, to teach them to love and serve one another, to observe the commandments of God and to be law abiding citizens wherever they live. Husbands and wives—mothers and fathers—will be held accountable before God for the discharge of these obligations. ("The Family: A Proclamation to the World," *Ensign*, November 1995, 102)

Neal A. Maxwell:
> If . . . we truly want the best for our sons and daughters, we would want for them—not status—but more *meekness, mercy, love, patience,* and *submissiveness.* (*The Neal A. Maxwell Quote Book,* ed. Cory H. Maxwell [Salt Lake City: Bookcraft, 1997], 40)

Ezra Taft Benson:
> Teach your children the gospel in your own home, at your own fireside. This is the most effective teaching that your children will ever receive. This is the Lord's way of teaching. The Church cannot teach like you can. The school cannot. The day-care center cannot. But you can, and the Lord

will sustain you. Your children will remember your teachings forever, and when they are old, they will not depart from them. (See Prov. 22:6.) (*Come, Listen to a Prophet's Voice* [Salt Lake City: Deseret Book, 1990], 35–36)

IDEAS FOR DAILY LIVING

Listed below are four key ideas you might use to help your children grow in the gospel:

1. Make your children the center of your life.
- *They are your highest priority*—They are more important than fame, professional acclaim, or fortune. As David O. McKay was fond of saying, "No success can compensate for failure in the home."
- *They deserve your time*—Spend time with them, quality and quantity time. This will generate lasting memories and prove you truly care. "The best thing to spend on children is your time" (Arnold Glasow, in *Richard L. Evans' Quote Book* [Salt Lake City: Publishers Press, 1971], 18).
- *Always be there for them*—They need your presence more than your presents. They need to know that you are their refuge and their support, their mentor and their friend, their source of encouragement and comfort—no matter what.

2. Make the home the center of life for your children.
- *A place of safety*—Make your home a refuge for them, a place of peace and security. Make the home the center of their lives, not just a passing "pit-stop."
- *A gathering place*—Hold family home evening each week and schedule a time for special family activities.
- *Welcome their friends*—Allow their friends in; get to know the people your children like to be with. Make the home more inviting than any other place.

3. Make love the center of the home. Here are ten of the many faces of love:
- *Love is constant*—Show love often. Always show acceptance for your children.
- *Love listens*—Nothing will induce feelings of self-confidence and self-regard in a child more than a sense of really being listened to.
- *Love is flexible*—Each child is different. Parenting takes a customized approach for every child.
- *Love looks for the good*—Put the emphasis on catching them doing things right. Praise sincerely and frequently, always being specific about what is admirable.
- *Love is specific*—Take time to help them understand specifically what is expected of them regarding their attitudes and behaviors.
- *Love is balanced*—Balance children's need for strong discipline with their need to learn to make responsible choices. "You cannot teach a child to take care of himself unless you let him try to take care of himself. He will make mistakes; and out of these mistakes will come his wisdom" (Henry Ward Beecher).
- *Love accepts the individual*—Always separate behavior from the individual. You should accept your children, but not always everything they do. Avoid labeling them; instead, identify the behaviors they need to improve.
- *Love takes the long view*—Never chastise without enough of the "balm of love" to ensure your relationship will still be good (see D&C 121:41–44). There are dozens of ways to say "no" without causing ill feelings or lasting grudges.
- *Love measures carefully*—Give your children specific jobs to do and expect good performance. Help them to evaluate their progress. Have suitable rewards for reaching goals.

- *Love is patient*—Never forget that they are young and need time to become mature and responsible.

4. Teach your children.

- *Teach correct principles*—Teach your children the principles taught by the Lord. (Refer to all the scriptures at the beginning of this section.)
- *Help them build values*—Help your children establish a gospel value system to govern their behavior. Remember that agreed-upon values bring unity to the family.
- *Worship together*—Attend your church meetings together. Find regular ways for your family to show devotion and reverence for God and life. "If you can give your children a trust in God, they will have one sure way of meeting all the uncertainties of existence" (Eleanor Roosevelt).

ILLUSTRATIONS FOR OUR TIMES

President Joseph F. Smith is well known for his deep love for his children. The following is told by Charles W. Nibley:

Children: The Richest of All Earthly Joys

[President Joseph F. Smith's] love for little children was unbounded. During [a trip] through the southern settlements of St. George . . . , when the troops of little children were paraded before him, it was beautiful to see how he adored these little ones. It was my duty to try and get the company started, to make time to the next settlement where the crowds would be waiting for us, but it was a difficult task to pull him away from the little children. He wanted to shake hands with and talk to every one of them. . . .

I have visited at his home when one of his children was down sick. I have seen him come home from his work at night tired, as he naturally would be, and yet he could walk the floor for hours with that little one in his arms, . . . loving it, encouraging it in every way with such tenderness and such a soul of pity and love.

He showed great tenderness and love for his large and honorable family. In his last address to his children, November 10, 1918, his heart's dearest sentiments were expressed to them in these words: "When I look around me, and see my boys and my girls whom the Lord has given to me—and I have succeeded, with His help, to make them tolerably comfortable, and at least respectable in the world—I have reached the treasure of my life." (as cited in *Teachings of Presidents of the Church: Joseph F. Smith* [Melchizedek Priesthood and Relief Society course of study, 1998], 295–96)

SUMMARY

The list of ways to raise children in wisdom and love could go on infinitely. Suggestions such as the "Ideas for Daily Living" listed earlier not only work, but are truly necessary for the well-being of all children. Let us do all that we can to see that our children have the opportunity to grow up with love and high standards. The eternal rewards are measureless. As the Apostle John stated: "I have no greater joy than to hear that my children walk in truth" (3 Jn. 1:4).

CHOICES

The oft-quoted statement "You are the result of your decisions" is true. There is a seemingly limitless range of choices. Even when freedoms are curtailed, we are still free to choose our mental, emotional, and spiritual response to situations we face. We make decisions and choices every day, and they have an effect on every aspect of our lives. Even choices or decisions not made become decisions by omission. Recognizing that many facets of our lives are dependent on our choices, it would be well for each of us to consider how to make wise choices.

THE SCRIPTURES TEACH US

2 Nephi 2:27. *Wherefore, men are free according to the flesh; and all things are given them which are expedient unto man. And they are free to choose liberty and eternal life, through the great Mediator of all men, or to choose captivity and death, according to the captivity and power of the devil; for he seeketh that all men might be miserable like unto himself.*

While we recognize the great freedom we have to choose our path in life, we must never forget the responsibility we have with this freedom. Our choices will either lead us to eternal life or away from God forever.

Doctrine and Covenants 9:7–9. *Behold, you have not understood; you have supposed that I would give it unto you, when you took no thought save it was to ask me. But, behold, I say unto you, that you must study it out in your mind; then you must ask me if it be right, and if it is right I will cause that your bosom shall burn within you; therefore, you shall feel that it is right. But if it be not right you shall have no such feelings, but you shall have a stupor of thought that shall cause you to forget the thing which is wrong.*

In all our decisions we have the responsibility to exercise reason and wisdom, and then ask for confirmation by the Spirit to determine whether our decision is correct. That confirmation will come as both a *feeling* (in our hearts) and as an *insight* (in our minds) in understanding what we are to do. The Spirit will tell us the truth of all things (see Moro. 10:5).

MODERN PROPHETS SPEAK

Joseph B. Wirthlin:
> [The Holy Ghost] is a revelator and teacher who conveys information to our spirits with far more certainty than is possible by our natural senses. He can guide us in every choice and decision and will never deceive or mislead us. He is a comforter who brings peace to our souls in times of need. (*Finding Peace in Our Lives* [Salt Lake City: Deseret Book, 1995], 117)

M. Russell Ballard:
> We know that God has promised incredible blessings to those who learn in this life to walk by faith and exercise the moral agency He has given us to make good decisions and choices (including, it should be noted, the choice we all have to believe this eternal plan or not to believe it). That should

be enough. We don't have to know all of the details of those promised blessings. We just have to have confidence in them. And faith in Him. (*Our Search for Happiness: An Invitation to Understand The Church of Jesus Christ of the Latter-day Saints* [Salt Lake City: Deseret Book, 1993], 80)

Gordon B. Hinckley:

I should like to suggest three standards by which to judge each of the decisions that determine the behavior patterns of your lives. These standards are so simple as to appear elementary, but I believe their faithful observance will provide a set of moral imperatives by which to govern without argument or equivocation each of our actions and which will bring unmatched rewards. They are:

1. Does it enrich the mind?
2. Does it discipline and strengthen the body?
3. Does it nourish the spirit? . . .

This, my brethren and sisters, is our divine right—to choose. This is our divine obligation—to choose the right. God give us the strength, the courage, the faith in all our choices to choose that which will enrich the mind, strengthen and discipline the body, nourish the spirit, and thus give us growth and joy in this life and eternal life in the world to come. (*Teachings of Gordon B. Hinckley* [Salt Lake City: Deseret Book, 1997], 54)

IDEAS FOR DAILY LIVING

Here are four things to help you in your decision making.

1. Focus on that which is truly important.

- *Ultimate objectives*—What do you want to have happen in your life? What are your long-range goals? How will the decision that is before you advance these goals? The key to decision making is to understand first of all what you want the ultimate outcomes to be. Dwight D. Eisenhower declared: "The history of free man is never really written by chance but by choice—their choice."
- *Is it necessary?*—Is the choice you are facing something you *need* to have happen, or just *want* to have happen? Let us become students of how to determine the difference between wants and needs. Let us choose this day things that matter most and then make wise decisions accordingly. The deciding moment is where we act on priorities according to the governing question: "What will bring me closer to my goals than anything else?"
- *Does it complement the principles you stand for?*—Base your decisions on gospel principles. For example, if one of your guiding principles is honesty, then any decision you make has to be made in the spirit of honesty. If it's not honest, then you don't do it.

2. Timing is crucial.

- *Don't procrastinate key decisions*—Many times we need to choose our actions before we are confronted with a situation. Hasty decisions made "in the moment" can lead to regret. Choose now to be honest, to follow the Word of Wisdom, to stay morally clean, etc.
- *Act from strength*—Make key decisions when you are in an "up" mood. Negativity will cloud your perception and inhibit the inspiration of the Spirit. Be positive as you make choices.
- *Know that not deciding is deciding*—Recognize that every day is composed of time. Time is to be used wisely; therefore, anytime we do nothing, it becomes our decision to use our time unwisely.

3. Use reason.

- *Get the facts*—Collect all pertinent information first, and make sure of its accuracy. Make decisions calmly, not in haste or under duress, but in a reasoned, judicious manner.
- *Look at all the options*—Study the pros and cons of a certain decision. Maximize the benefits in your choice. Then seek confirmation. George Eliot observed: "The strongest principle of growth lies in human choice."

4. Consider all the people involved.

- *Weigh the consequences*—Factor in how your decisions will affect others. Understand the implications for the lives of all parties, now and in the future. Make sure the decisions are in the best interests of your children and loved ones.
- *Get input*—Confer with your circle of loved ones and associates before making a big choice. Always look ahead to the effects or the results of the decision. Will it bless people?
- *Avoid unilateral action*—Be careful in unilateral decision making or autocratic leadership—it often becomes difficult afterwards to rally support. Counseling together gives unity and strength to the decision, with greater chance for success.

ILLUSTRATIONS FOR OUR TIMES

Author Ed J. Pinegar shares four stories that emphasize the importance of good choices in shaping our character.

Four Illustrations

At every turn in the road of life we are faced with choices. It's not as simple as Yogi Berra quipped—"When you come to a fork in life, take it." Sometimes we *have* to make the difficult choice of going in one direction or the other. I have always loved to collect stories because they are the best teaching tools. In my collection of stories under the category of choices, here are just a few thoughts to get your mind working:

1. In Greek mythology there is a boy named Icarus. Imprisoned on the isle of Crete, he and his father created a pair of wings made of feathers and wax. With this marvelous invention, Icarus could raise himself up into the sky like a bird. At last, they thought, here was a means to escape their confinement. The father warned his son not to fly too close to the sun, lest the wax melt. But the free-spirited boy became obsessed with his newfound freedom and flew too high. The wax melted in the heat, and the boy fell to his death. Freedom and control must go hand in hand, or else freedom can become a curse to the individual.

2. I remember a "Peanuts" cartoon that showed Linus standing there with a snowball in his hand as Lucy enters the picture. She takes stock of the situation and says to Linus: "Life is full of choices. You may choose, if you wish, to throw that snowball at me. You also may choose, if you wish, not to throw that snowball at me. Now if you choose to throw that snowball at me, I will pound you right into the ground! If you choose not to throw that snowball at me, your head will be spared." Then Linus wisely throws away his snowball with the words, "Life is full of choices, but I never get any." Yes, Linus, you *do* get choices, but they always have consequences.

3. Isaac Stern, the world-famous musician-violinist, was once interviewed by a media personality and asked at what point in his life he had ultimately committed his energies toward a career as a concert violinist.

Mr. Stern contrasted the outcome of his first recital in San Francisco at a tender age with his first appearance in New York City. In the first instance the critics were effusively supportive of his promising career; in the second, the critics were unrestrained in their doubts. Greatly discouraged, the young artist boarded one of New York's double-decker buses and proceeded to ride aimlessly for a good deal of the day, pondering his fate. Should he quit or go forward? Were the New York critics right or wrong? Finally he returned to his apartment and said to his mother with full conviction: "I am going to *work,* mother—*work* at my music until it *works for me."* That choice resulted in Isaac Stern becoming one of the most acclaimed violinists in the world. Choice is a key part of character.

4. I remember reading about a sailor with standards. He chose to avoid the immoral antics of some of his shipmates whenever the ship was in port. One night, when he had chosen to retire alone in his bunk rather than party, he was awakened suddenly by the hand of one of his more belligerent shipmates. The huge man was drunk and was brandishing a hammer in a threatening manner. The sailor looked up from his bunk and realized that he could not escape, that his life was probably about to end. Then he discerned what the man was babbling at the top of his lungs: "Get your mask and fins. There is a man overboard, and you are the only one who can save him!" The sailor bounded out of bed and proceeded to accomplish the heroic deed that saved the life of one of the crew. He learned a powerful lesson in choice that night— for although his associates openly ridiculed him for his standards, they secretly admired his character and fortitude, and looked to him for leadership in a time of crisis.

From each of these lessons we learn the power of choice—not only to direct a course, but to mold a character.

—Ed J. Pinegar

SUMMARY

The Lord has given you the power to make good decisions. As He declared: "Verily I say, men should be anxiously engaged in a good cause, and do many things of their own free will, and bring to pass much righteousness; For the power is in them, wherein they are agents unto themselves. And inasmuch as men do good they shall in nowise lose their reward" (D&C 58:27–28). There are examples from the past of many great people who, regardless of the situations facing them, took decisive and prudent action of their own free will and thus made a difference in their own lives and often in the lives of many others. The consequences of wise decisions—useful inventions, important discoveries, ways to transform poverty into prosperity, despair into hope, and spiritual degeneracy into gospel joy and gratitude—enrich our lives every day. Enjoy life now and forever by making proper and wise choices.

CIVIC DUTY

As members of society we have a moral and civil responsibility to our neighborhood, community, county, state, nation, and the world at large. We are children of a loving Heavenly Father; therefore, all of us are brothers and sisters, and we should be our brothers' and sisters' keeper. We need to understand our unique role and capacity to help humanity. As Saints our overwhelming concern should be for our fellowmen; hence, we should serve them compassionately, both in and out of the Church (see Matt. 25:40; 1 Ne. 1:5;

Mosiah 2:17). We seek to make the world a better place to live that all might enjoy freedom and the pursuit of happiness.

THE SCRIPTURES TEACH US

Doctrine and Covenants 58:27–28. *Verily I say, men should be anxiously engaged in a good cause, and do many things of their own free will, and bring to pass much righteousness; For the power is in them, wherein they are agents unto themselves. And inasmuch as men do good they shall in nowise lose their reward.*

This oft-quoted scripture should resound in our hearts and minds, for the Lord outlines what true Saints should do. Never deny a loving or generous thought; make it efficacious by doing good.

Mosiah 2:17. *And behold, I tell you these things that ye may learn wisdom; that ye may learn that when ye are in the service of your fellow beings ye are only in the service of your God.*

When we truly understand the doctrine of the gospel of Jesus Christ, we will come to appreciate life-shaping principles, such as those reflected in the parable of the good Samaritan, the "Golden Rule," and the admonition of the Savior: "Inasmuch as ye have done it unto one of the least of these my brethren, ye have done it unto me" (Matt. 25:40). We will recognize that our service to God and our fellowmen is not restricted to "Church service," but is for blessing all mankind through volunteer service.

Doctrine and Covenants 98:10. *Wherefore, honest men and wise men should be sought for diligently, and good men and wise men ye should observe to uphold; otherwise whatsoever is less than these cometh of evil.*

It is incumbent upon all of us to seek righteous men and women to serve in leadership positions that affect our community and nation. When we choose unrighteous leaders, the people suffer.

Articles of Faith 1:12. *We believe in being subject to kings, presidents, rulers, and magistrates, in obeying, honoring, and sustaining the law.*

We are duty bound to sustain the laws of our land as long as they accord with this principle: "We believe that no government can exist in peace, except such laws are framed and held inviolate as will secure to each individual the free exercise of conscience, the right and control of property, and the protection of life. We believe that all governments necessarily require civil officers and magistrates to enforce the laws of the same; and that such as will administer the law in equity and justice should be sought for and upheld by the voice of the people if a republic, or the will of the sovereign" (D&C 134:2–3). The people should uphold the government where they reside, "while protected in their inherent and inalienable rights by the laws of such governments" (D&C 134:5). If there is something with respect to governance that needs changing, then the people should work within the law to establish something better.

MODERN PROPHETS SPEAK

Ezra Taft Benson:
> Edmund Burke once said, "All that is necessary for the triumph of evil is for good men to do nothing." It is not enough that we wring our hands and moan about conditions in America. We must become responsible citizens and carry out our civic duty. We should be "anxiously engaged" in good causes and leave the world a better place for having lived in it (D&C 58:27).

I think the Lord wants us to be good citizens of this country. I believe He wants us to keep our economic and social thinking straight and not be influenced by policies and programs that strike at the very foundation of all that we hold dear in this country.

We have a measuring rod that no other group has. We have the revelations of the Almighty to indicate to us whether a thing is right or wrong. The Lord has spoken. He has placed a responsibility upon us to see that our form of government is preserved and that good men and honest men are elected for public office. His counsel is found in the Doctrine and Covenants (see D&C 98; 101). We are not left to move in the dark. (*The Teachings of Ezra Taft Benson* [Salt Lake City: Bookcraft, 1988], 676–77)

We urge our members to do their civic duty and to assume their responsibilities as individual citizens in seeking solutions to the problems which beset our cities and communities.

With our wide-ranging mission, so far as mankind is concerned, Church members cannot ignore the many practical problems that require solution if our families are to live in an environment conducive to spirituality. Where solutions to these practical problems require cooperative action with those not of our faith, members should not be reticent in doing their part in joining and leading in those efforts where they can make an individual contribution to those causes which are consistent with the standards of the Church. Individual Church members cannot, of course, represent or commit the Church, but should, nevertheless, be "anxiously engaged" in good causes, using the principles of the gospel of Jesus Christ as their constant guide. (Ezra Taft Benson, *This Nation Shall Endure* [Salt Lake City: Deseret Book, 1977], 78–79)

Joseph Smith:
> "A man filled with the love of God, is not content with blessing his family alone, but ranges through the whole world, anxious to bless the whole human race." (*Teachings of the Prophet Joseph Smith,* sel. Joseph Fielding Smith [Salt Lake City: Deseret Book, 1976], 174)

IDEAS FOR DAILY LIVING

Here are six ideas to help us fulfill our civic duty and give volunteer service:

1. Be Informed.
- *Study the issues*—Be a student of civic and political affairs.
- *Seek information from reputable sources*—Read newspapers and position papers, watch television coverage, access applicable information on the Internet, listen to candidates, and discuss the issues with colleagues.

2. Support the election process for local, state, and national leaders.
- *Be proactive in mind and deed*—Get personally involved in the election process.
- *Always vote*—Exercise your franchise to express your choice.
- *Involve the family*—Make civic issues a matter of family discussion; teach these principles to your children.

3. Be active in volunteer service.
- *Use personal leadership*—Pick a cause or several projects that can use your service, expertise, energy, and leadership.

- *Cooperate with organized civic efforts*—Become familiar with government service agencies, medical associations (heart, kidney, lung cancer, etc.), hospitals, schools, foundations, county service, etc., and learn how you can get involved in good causes.

4. Attend community meetings.

- *Town meetings*—Make your presence known at meetings where important civic issues are being debated and discussed.
- *School-board meetings and PTAs*—Education is critically important; get informed and take a stand on the principles, values, and issues involved.
- *Informative lectures on current issues*—Watch for opportunities to learn from multiple points of view.

5. Stand for something—avoid apathetic feelings at all costs.

- *Cultivate the mindset of a civic leader*—Remember that one person can make the difference. If you don't take a stand on tough issues, who will do it for you?
- *Stand on values*—You and the truth are a majority. Seek to uphold principles of truth in the government arena.
- *Concentrate on things that matter*—Choose causes that make a difference in people's lives.

6. Remember and learn from the past.

- *Make civic duty a lifelong pursuit*—Learn from the past. Act in the present. Plan for the future.
- *Seek wisdom*—Learning comes from what we glean from experience. Let us grow from the past and not repeat negative actions.

ILLUSTRATIONS FOR OUR TIMES

Often we feel that we as individuals can't make a difference in the world around us. The following accounts from an *Ensign* article show how one can make a difference, and how by "small and simple things are great things brought to pass" (see Alma 37:6).

Getting Involved, Giving Service, Growing

> Members who reach out to serve others in their communities learn that their contributions multiply and that personal growth is inevitable. Latter-day Saints who contribute in their community simply to better it frequently find unexpected blessings of both greater capacity and increased opportunity to serve. Almost every ward or branch has members like the following who have tasted the joy that comes through service, acting alone or in cooperation with others. . . .

> *Helping Youth Make a Difference*

> Jeff Walker of the Green Valley Ward, Las Vegas Nevada Green Valley Stake, found that it only takes one concerned individual to make a difference but that continual motivating efforts are needed to help a program succeed.

> In spring 1997, 15-year-old Jeff Walker represented Green Valley High School in Henderson, Nevada, at a press conference featuring members of the class of 2000. The purpose was to discuss what it meant to be a member of this class and what students projected their world would be like in the next century.

Jeff, who had been elected Green Valley's sophomore class president for the 1997–98 year, realized that the class of 2000 might well receive more media and public attention than any previous group of graduates, saying, "I felt very uncomfortable with the idea of our class being takers of attention without having made a significant contribution to society."

Consequently, he developed a training program for community involvement to take to other sophomore class leaders in southern Nevada. The purpose of his program, "2000 Tomorrows," was to unite all participating classes in an effort to make positive changes in their communities.

The training program showed youth leaders step by step how to assess community needs, develop service projects, and involve as many classmates as possible. A banquet was scheduled for the end of the school year, when a panel of civic and business leaders presented a trophy to one of the schools.

Throughout the year, Jeff called participating class presidents monthly to encourage and assist them with their projects. "I've learned that it's really hard to motivate people," he says. Of the 15 schools that agreed to participate, 7 followed through, and 6,000 students took part. Cimarron High School in Las Vegas won the trophy for involvement. Students there volunteered at local junior high schools throughout the year, making presentations about teen pregnancy, peer pressure, and related issues, as well as helping younger students prepare for high school.

For 1998–99, the Nevada state student council became involved, and schools throughout the state were invited to participate. A primary requirement for a service project is that at least one member of the class of 2000 be involved in spearheading the project.

"Community service is a hard thing for many people to fit into their schedules, but they've got to ask themselves if they really are 'too busy,'" Jeff says.

"Service does affect people's lives, and I saw our project really help some people and change them for the better."

Mentoring Unmarried Mothers

Linda Petersen of the Unity First Ward, Burley Idaho Stake, was the originator for Brighter Beginnings, a mentor program that helps the community reach out to about 40 unmarried mothers each year.

"What alarmed us is that a third of the babies born in these two counties are born to young women who haven't even graduated from high school," says Sister Petersen, a member of the Mini-Cassia Child Protection Team, a volunteer organization operating in Minidoka and Cassia Counties, Idaho. She has often helped teach the importance of sexual abstinence, but unfortunately abstinence isn't always the choice young people make, nor is placing the baby for adoption, "so we felt we needed to help those young women who decided to keep and raise their children." It is important, she says, to give each young mother greater self-worth and the opportunity to learn good parenting skills in order to "make it the brightest future we can for her and that baby."

A few months after Sister Petersen shared her idea for the program with others on the child protection team, they had lined up a registered nurse and many volunteer mentor moms to help give Brighter Beginnings its start.

The group seeks to help young mothers graduate from high school and learn how to care for their children in a nurturing environment. Each mentor mom goes into a young woman's home once a month to teach parenting and safety skills and also makes herself available to answer the young woman's questions. It is hoped that the experienced mothers can be role models and "sounding boards" for the young women, Sister Petersen says. A registered nurse will visit and check on the baby's health at two and four months of age.

More than nurses and mentors are involved. Volunteers help in other ways. Laurel and Eagle Scout projects provide some quilts and wooden toys for the children. Once a month, senior citizens help babysit while young mothers get together at the local senior citizens' center to talk and receive instruction in such things as nutrition and safety. One of Sister Petersen's favorite memories is of an older gentleman tenderly cradling a little baby for an hour as the class went on.

Brighter Beginnings is funded by a government grant under the title "Building Stronger Families," but it is the mentor moms and other volunteers who give it life, Sister Petersen says. Without them, no amount of money could make the program work.

(The forgoing material is from "Getting Involved, Giving Service, Growing," *Ensign,* February 1999, 21ff)

SUMMARY

The exercise of our civic duty and carrying out volunteer service should be a natural expression of a Saint—a Latter-day Saint. These activities are the things true disciples of Jesus Christ do. Our vision of becoming like our Savior should include the vision of love of country, concern with how we can help those in need, a focus on whom we can serve today, and a motivation rooted in our desire to serve and bless. We need to be about our Father's business—blessing His children, our brothers and sisters.

COMMANDMENTS

Heavenly Father has given us the laws and commandments essential for gaining eternal life through His Beloved Son, Jesus Christ. If kept, these commandments will help us achieve happiness here and in the hereafter (see Mosiah 2:41). We are to "live by every word that proceedeth forth from the mouth of God" (D&C 84:44). The commandments have been established according to divine design, and when we fail to keep them, we don't break them, but rather break ourselves against them and suffer the consequences. When we truly love God, we will keep the commandments (see John 14:15; Moses 5:13). The test of mortality is about our willingness to keep the commandments (see Eccl. 12:13; D&C 93:1; Abr. 3:25).

THE SCRIPTURES TEACH US

Deuteronomy 6:17. *Ye shall diligently keep the commandments of the Lord your God, and his testimonies, and his statutes, which he hath commanded thee.*

Diligently keeping the commandments is not congruent with a casual attitude or passive behavior. Obedience requires a mindset of valor, and a lifestyle characterized by a careful and caring manner and by actions reflecting zeal and constancy. We need to make keeping the commandments the highest priority in our lives.

Ecclesiastes 12:13. *Let us hear the conclusion of the whole matter: Fear God, and keep his commandments: for this is the whole duty of man.*

Our moral obligation is to obey God. When we come to understand and appreciate the importance of this transcending doctrine, we will be submissive and choose to obey. After all Heavenly Father and our Savior have done for us, it is the least we can do.

Matthew 22:36–40. *Master, which is the great commandment in the law? Jesus said unto him, Thou shalt love the Lord thy God with all thy heart, and with all thy soul, and with all thy mind. This is the first and great commandment. And the second is like unto it, Thou shalt love thy neighbour as thyself. On these two commandments hang all the law and the prophets.*

Can there be any doubt that love is not only the great commandment, but the motivating force behind all that is good (see John 3:16; 2 Ne. 26:24)? When we truly love Heavenly Father and our Savior, our concern for our fellowmen will be without bounds. Because of this love, we will serve our fellowmen and seek righteousness.

Jarom 1:9. *And thus being prepared to meet the Lamanites, they did not prosper against us. But the word of the Lord was verified, which he spake unto our fathers, saying that: Inasmuch as ye will keep my commandments ye shall prosper in the land.*

The Lord is bound if we keep His commandments (see D&C 82:10). He wants to bless our lives, but He requires obedience to the commandments.

Doctrine and Covenants 29:35. *Behold, I gave unto him that he should be an agent unto himself; and I gave unto him commandment, but no temporal commandment gave I unto him, for my commandments are spiritual; they are not natural nor temporal, neither carnal nor sensual.*

Even though many temporal blessings come to us by keeping the Lord's commandments, we must never forget that all of His commandments are spiritual in nature. In keeping the commandments, we yield our hearts to the Lord and to His Holy Spirit, thus choosing to obey. This process is spiritual in nature and keeps us connected to our God.

MODERN PROPHETS SPEAK

Gordon B. Hinckley:

> We are a people who have taken upon us a solemn covenant and the name of the Lord Jesus Christ. Let us strive a little harder to keep the commandments, to live as the Lord has asked us to live. We are His children. He delights in our good behavior and I think He grieves when we misbehave. (*Teachings of Gordon B. Hinckley*, ed. Clyde J. Williams [Salt Lake City: Deseret Book, 1997], 146)

Howard W. Hunter:

> The Ten Commandments involve two major categories. The Decalogue or the ten laws were inscribed on two tablets of stone. Just how they were arranged is not known, but most students

divide them into two sets. The first division consists of those laws which are concerned with man's relation to God. These are: no other gods, no graven images, no blasphemy, and keep the Sabbath. Some have included honor thy parents, while others have put this in the category of the last five, which are the laws encompassing a system of moral duties to others—thou shalt not kill, commit adultery, steal, bear false witness, or covet.

Apparently the Savior had these two groups of laws in mind, the first defining man's duty to God and the second providing for a duty to neighbors [see Matt. 22:36–40]. (*The Teachings of Howard W. Hunter*, ed. Clyde J. Williams [Salt Lake City: Bookcraft, 1997], 23)

Ezra Taft Benson:
> Yes, it is "by grace that we are saved, after all we can do" (2 Nephi 25:23).
>
> What is meant by "after all we can do"? "After all we can do" includes extending our best effort. "After all we can do" includes living His commandments. "After all we can do" includes loving our fellowmen and praying for those who regard us as their adversary. "After all we can do" means clothing the naked, feeding the hungry, visiting the sick and giving "succor [to] those who stand in need of [our] succor" (Mosiah 4:15)—remembering that what we do unto one of the least of God's children, we do unto Him (see Matthew 25:34–40; D&C 42:38). "After all we can do" means leading chaste, clean, pure lives, being scrupulously honest in all our dealings and treating others the way we would want to be treated. (*The Teachings of Ezra Taft Benson* [Salt Lake City: Bookcraft, 1988], 354)

IDEAS FOR DAILY LIVING

Here are six ideas to help us keep the commandments:

1. Gain a knowledge and understanding of the commandments.
- *Study*—Search the scriptures (see 2 Ne. 32:3; Alma 31:5; D&C 84:43–44). Listen to the living prophets.
- *Ponder*—Ponder prayerfully to gain understanding and appreciation (see 1 Ne. 11:1; 3 Ne. 17:2–3; D&C 138:1–11).
- *Visit the temple*—Remember temple attendance for vicarious service and refreshing your mind concerning your covenants. In the temple you will be taught by the Lord (see D&C 97:13–14).
- *Seek counsel*—Seek counsel and instruction from your parents and leaders.
- *Follow the Spirit*—Remember the Holy Ghost can teach you all things, including how to enjoy and keep the commandments (Moro. 10:4–5; D&C 36:2; D&C 50:17–22).

2. Pray for strength.
- *We are nothing without the Lord*—In our finite and mortal state we need strength from the Lord (see 1 Ne. 4:31; Alma 26:11–12)
- *Follow the spiritual compass*—Remember, the Lord will provide a way for us to keep His commandments if we truly seek to obey (see 1 Ne. 3:7; 17:3).

3. Seek to be humble and submissive. Humility and contrition are a protective shield. Without these qualities we will eventually fall. They are imperative in order to keep the commandments (see Alma 7:23; Ether 12:27).

4. Live worthy of and pray to have the Spirit. We are promised the Holy Ghost as a constant companion. Living worthy of His companionship not only implies we are trying to live the commandments, but that we will have a higher capacity to do so (see 2 Ne. 32:5; 3 Ne. 19:9; Moro. 10:8–19; D&C 46:10–33).

5. Love God with all your heart, might, mind, and strength. In cultivating this love, we will only want to do good (see John 14:15).

6. Practice the principle of remembering to keep the commandments.
- *Signs*—Make signs and place them in prominent places to help you remember.
- *Systems*—Create mnemonic systems to help you remember to make right choices—a bell ringing, a penny in your shoe, a certain time each day, as you pray, and when you make your list of things to do.
- *Spiritual blessings*—Remember the promise that when we keep the commandments, we will always have His Spirit to be with us (see D&C 20:77, 79).

ILLUSTRATIONS FOR OUR TIMES

The following excerpt explains how keeping the commandments can be an anchor in our lives, keeping us secure and safe.

Keep the Commandments

> *Keep the commandments; keep the commandments!*
> *In this there is safety; in this there is peace.*
> *He will send blessings; He will send blessings.*
> *Words of a prophet: Keep the commandments.*
> *In this there is safety and peace.*
> *(Children's Songbook*, p. 146; *Hymns*, no. 303)

In July 1972 Harold B. Lee became the eleventh President of the Church. One hour after the announcement was made, he met with newspaper and television reporters. One of them asked him if he had a message for Church members.

President Lee said: "The safety of the Church lies in the members keeping the commandments. There is nothing more important that I could say. As they keep the commandments, blessings will come."

Barbara A. McConochie, a Church member, was so impressed with his words that she wrote the song "Keep the Commandments" (above) for Primary children. Its words tell us of two blessings that come from keeping the commandments: "In this there is safety and peace."

Sister McConochie says, "Keeping the commandments is the anchor for our safety amidst the storm. True peace will come to each individual, family, and nation only as we learn obedience to the laws of our Heavenly Father."

An anchor is a heavy object that sailors use aboard ships on the ocean. They lower the anchor on a chain to the ocean floor, and it keeps the ship from drifting. Even in storms, when the ship is being buffeted by waves and wind, the anchor keeps the ship where it should be.

We are like sailors lowering anchors when we use the commandments to keep ourselves safe. Commandments, like anchors, help keep us secure and in the right place. Even when we feel tossed about by temptations or by the unkind words or actions of others, the commandments can help us stay steady and safe. As we keep the commandments, we know in our hearts that we are doing what is right and that eventually good will come. In this there is safety and peace. (Judy Edwards, "Sharing Time: 'Keep the Commandments,'" *Tambulilit,* April 1994, 8)

SUMMARY

The greatest blessing that comes from being obedient and keeping the commandments is eternal life. Obedient children of our Father in Heaven are blessed both temporally and spiritually. The obedient are happier here on earth and will enjoy a state of never-ending happiness in the world to come (see Mosiah 2:41). Such exceeding joy can be experienced only as we keep the commandments by repenting of our sins and seeking eternal happiness as our life's quest—always displaying a broken heart and a contrite spirit before the Lord (see 3 Ne. 9:20; 12:19; Ether 4:15; D&C 20:37; 59:8). In keeping the commandments, you demonstrate your love of God and thus obey the greatest of all the commandments (see John 14:15).

CONSCIENCE

Conscience is the Light of Christ, a voice from within, that moral sense that helps us determine right from wrong, and then helps us try to do that which is morally right (see Moro. 7:15–19). We all have that voice within. Sometimes there's so much noise in our lives that we can't hear its counsel. Sometimes we're so stubborn, hard-hearted, greedy, or power hungry that we become deafened to this voice, or choose not to hear it at all. Then we are left to ourselves. In that case we allow our own selfishness, pride, and personal wants and appetites to dictate our behavior. The prescription for a moral life is lost. We must enhance our conscience, and then learn to obey it.

THE SCRIPTURES TEACH US

Titus 1:15. *Unto the pure all things are pure: but unto them that are defiled and unbelieving is nothing pure; but even their mind and conscience is defiled.*

When we seek righteousness and aspire to cultivate purity of heart and mind, our conscience protects us and leads us to do good. When we seek to do otherwise, we become contaminated and polluted to the point that our conscience cannot operate properly.

Moroni 7:15–17, 19. *For behold, my brethren, it is given unto you to judge, that ye may know good from evil; and the way to judge is as plain, that ye may know with a perfect knowledge, as the daylight is from the dark night. For behold, the Spirit of Christ is given to every man, that he may know good from evil; wherefore, I show unto you the way to judge; for every thing which inviteth to do good, and to persuade to believe in Christ, is sent forth by the power and gift of Christ; wherefore ye may know with a perfect knowledge it is of God. But what-*

soever thing persuadeth men to do evil, and believe not in Christ, and deny him, and serve not God, then ye may know with a perfect knowledge it is of the devil; . . . Wherefore, I beseech of you, brethren, that ye should search diligently in the light of Christ that ye may know good from evil; and if ye will lay hold upon every good thing, and condemn it not, ye certainly will be a child of Christ.

Everyone is born with a conscience because everyone has the Light of Christ. We know right from wrong; the only question is how we will use our agency. Mormon's words to his son Moroni are clear: your conscience will lead you to do good and persuade you to come unto Christ. Anything else is of the devil. Our duty is to search our conscience and then have the courage to obey it and overcome the temptations of the devil.

Doctrine and Covenants 84:45–47. *For the word of the Lord is truth, and whatsoever is truth is light, and whatsoever is light is Spirit, even the Spirit of Jesus Christ. And the Spirit giveth light to every man that cometh into the world; and the Spirit enlighteneth every man through the world, that hearkeneth to the voice of the Spirit. And every one that hearkeneth to the voice of the Spirit cometh unto God, even the Father.*

As we immerse ourselves in the gospel and the scriptures, the word of God will feed our spirit and the Word of God, even the Savior, will cause our pathways to be illuminated. We receive light and truth from the Spirit. The Holy Ghost enhances our conscience and we have greater power to choose righteousness (see Rom. 9:1).

MODERN PROPHETS SPEAK

David O. McKay:

> The first condition of happiness is a clear conscience. No man who does wrong or who is unvirtuous will be happy. No unvirtuous woman can ever be happy unless . . . she fully repents. Uprightness of character, honesty in dealing with your fellow men, honor bright, your word as good as your bond, then when your head touches your pillow at night, and you contemplate your actions during the day, you sleep with a good conscience. (*Gospel Ideals: Selections from the Discourses of David O. McKay* [Salt Lake City: Improvement Era, 1953], 498)

Spencer W. Kimball:

> Conscience stirs up a desire to repent. How wonderful that God should endow us with this sensitive yet strong guide we call a conscience! Someone has aptly remarked that "conscience is a celestial spark which God has put into every man for the purpose of saving his soul." Certainly it is the instrument which awakens the soul to consciousness of sin, spurs a person to make up his mind to adjust, to convict himself of the transgression without soft-pedaling or minimizing the error, to be willing to face facts, meet the issue, and pay necessary penalties—and until the person is in this frame of mind he has not begun to repent. To be sorry is an approach, to abandon the act of error is a beginning, but until one's conscience has been sufficiently stirred to cause him to move in the matter, so long as there are excuses and rationalizations, one has hardly begun his approach to forgiveness. (*The Teachings of Spencer W. Kimball*, edited by Edward L. Kimball [Salt Lake City: Bookcraft, 1982], 86)

IDEAS FOR DAILY LIVING

Here are three principles that can help us follow our conscience and strengthen its power in our lives:

1. Do things that amplify the voice within.

- *Meditate and ponder frequently*—Take time to meditate and evaluate your life as it relates to your values and behavior (see 1 Ne. 11:1; D&C 138:1–4, 11).
- *Pray always*—Pray for strength to overcome temptation (see 3 Ne. 18:18).
- *Search the scriptures*—Feast upon the word of God, which will strengthen your spirit and help you make correct choices (see 2 Ne. 32:3).
- *Purge mind and heart*—We enhance our conscience as we clean up our lives from sin and dead works (see Heb. 9:14).
- *Walk or exercise regularly*—Often physical activity away from the din of commercialism will enhance our sensitivity to the voice within.
- *Rise early*—Take occasion to retire to bed early and get up early. Often the sunrise will bring new insights (see D&C 88:124).
- *Tap your creative powers*—Do active, creative things—often the Light of Christ or the Spirit will give you insight during those moments (see 2 Ne. 32:5; Moro. 7:15–17).
- *Keep a journal*—Having a regular conversation with yourself about the important things in your life will often bring out and reinforce guiding principles (see 3 Ne. 5:14, 17–18).

2. Ask others.

- *Seek wisdom*—Solicit input and feedback from wise people around you. Often your own moral conscience will be confirmed and strengthened by the righteous counsel of others (see Prov. 27:9).
- *Follow the counsel of your church leaders and parents*—These are the people who have the stewardship to give you counsel, and they can help guide you in the light and understanding you receive from within.

3. Leverage the rewards through small, courageous acts.

- *Enhance your willingness*—Open up a willingness and a desire to listen to your conscience. Often a few moments of listening will pay enormous dividends (see D&C 19:23).
- *Remember the purpose of your conscience*—Your conscience will always lead you to do good and come closer to your Savior. It will enliven within you a sense of guilt that will encourage you to repent (see Alma 14:6).
- *Honor first impressions*—Consciously pick up on early promptings of inspiration that move you in wise directions. Follow through (see Job 32:8).
- *Take extra care in decision making*—Take time to weigh your decisions according to your moral values rather than just "doing what you want to." Look at the long-term rewards instead of the short-term pleasures (see D&C 9:7–9).
- *Exercise your conscience*—The more you obey your conscience the more it is enhanced, and the more sensitive you become to its guidance (see D&C 71:6).
- *Practice self-control and discipline*—Listening to your conscience can become a strengthening pattern for living, an empowering habit of moral courage (see 2 Ne. 32:8).
- *Be more loving*—Demonstrate compassion and love to all. A loving attitude reinforces the power of conscience (see Moro. 7:44–45).
- *Savor the peace of conscience*—Our conscience can bring us peace through repentance (see Mosiah 4:3).

ILLUSTRATIONS FOR OUR TIMES

Ed J. Pinegar tells a personal story wherein he followed his conscience in a tempting situation and found peace in his decision.

Don't Do It

My father died on Mother's Day, 1947. I was a twelve-year-old boy, the baby of the family. My mother, a living angel, became the true matriarch of the family. She taught me to live by high principles, including never taking anything into my body that would be harmful. I remember making a promise to her and to Heavenly Father that I would never do anything to hurt her or bring shame to her. It was sealed in my mind and my heart.

I went through the teen-age years without too many problems. Still, I recall the time when my values and standards that my mother had taught were put to the test. Our high school football team, on which I played tight end, had just won a game, and we were having a party at a friend's house. Everything was great. We were having a great time. No one was doing anything wrong. A friend asked the host for a drink of water. He was directed to the kitchen cupboard for a glass. As he was getting a drink, he noticed a big dark bottle of cherry cooking wine. It was almost full. He suggested we should all have a sip of alcohol to prove ourselves. They all came in for a little drink. Something in my heart and mind (my conscience) said, "Don't do it," and then I became bold and told them, "Don't do it." They said that one little drink wouldn't hurt. I told them no, and if they did that I would leave the party. They said, "Go ahead. We don't like babies anyway."

So I left. I was hurt because of their standards and their apparent lack of concern for me as their supposed friend. As I walked home, a good feeling came over me. I had obeyed the inner voice—my conscience. It had saved me from disappointing my mother. The memory lingers. Obeying your conscience brings peace to the soul.

—Ed J. Pinegar

SUMMARY

Always being obedient to one's conscience is—without a doubt—difficult. Our momentary desires and immediate gratification often win out. Self-control is sacrificed for the here and now. To be a person of conscience truly takes character and we have to *practice* disciplining ourselves. There is no doubt that trying to always listen to one's conscience is one of the great tests of life. Addressing this subject adequately is a challenge simply because listening to one's conscience is such a personal challenge, and so emotional in nature. But we can all be better at it if we focus our desire and intent on good outcomes such as spiritual tranquility and inner peace. The Savior said, "Learn of me, and listen to my words; walk in the meekness of my Spirit, and you shall have peace in me" (D&C 19:23). Living a life true to ourselves, true to the gospel, and true to our God gives us the peace so needed in today's turbulent world.

CONSECRATION

The Lord has asked His righteous people to consecrate their lives for the building up of the kingdom of God (see JST, Matt. 6:38). When we consecrate our lives, we dedicate and set apart our time, talents, and material goods. Consecration is uniquely related to the depth of our conversion to our Savior Jesus Christ. Through consecration we truly sacrifice all things for the Lord. We begin the process of purification of our own lives, and in turn we are better able to bless our brothers and sisters that they too might enjoy eternal life. This is truly building up the kingdom of God. Part of this law, as we now live it, requires us to provide for our family and be an instrument in the Lord's hands to bless our family and all those we associate with. Consecration is an attitude as well as an observable act of goodness.

THE SCRIPTURES TEACH US

Doctrine and Covenants 42:30–31. *And behold, thou wilt remember the poor, and consecrate of thy properties for their support that which thou hast to impart unto them, with a covenant and a deed which cannot be broken. And inasmuch as ye impart of your substance unto the poor, ye will do it unto me.*

All commandments are spiritual. The blessing of the poor and needy is a demonstration of pure religion, as if we had done it unto our Savior Himself (see Matt. 25:40; James 1:27).

Doctrine and Covenants 105:5. *And Zion cannot be built up unless it is by the principles of the law of the celestial kingdom; otherwise I cannot receive her unto myself.*

"Those who have the companionship of the Holy Ghost and are guided thereby in their lives are 'able to abide the law of a celestial kingdom,' including the law of consecration or anything else the Lord might ask of them. They are the ones who—'united according to the union required by the law of the celestial kingdom' (D. & C. 105:1–5)—will build up Zion in the last days." (Bruce R. McConkie, *Mormon Doctrine,* 2nd ed. [Salt Lake City: Bookcraft, 1966], 117)

Mosiah 4:21. *And now, if God, who has created you, on whom you are dependent for your lives and for all that ye have and are, doth grant unto you whatsoever ye ask that is right, in faith, believing that ye shall receive, O then, how ye ought to impart of the substance that ye have one to another.*

When we realize how much we've been given by the Lord, how can we begrudge others in need? Consecration requires the overcoming of the worldly desires of power and greed, as well as idleness. This is why it has always been difficult to live the law of consecration, unless the people were of one heart, and—as the Lord directs—equal in all things and sharing them in common. Having things in common brings forth the blessings of the Spirit (see Acts 2:43–44; 3 Ne. 26:19; 4 Ne. 1:3; D&C 70:14).

MODERN PROPHETS SPEAK

Lorenzo Snow:

> If we as elders fail to keep the covenants we have made, namely, to use our time, talents, and ability for the upbuilding of the kingdom of God upon the earth, how can we reasonably expect to come forth in the morning of the First Resurrection, identified with the great work of redemption? If we in our manner, habits and dealings, imitate the Gentile world, thereby identifying ourselves with the world, do you think, my brethren, that God will bestow upon us the blessings we desire to inherit? I tell you no, He will not! In all our business occupations we must prove ourselves better than any other people, or we forfeit all. We must build ourselves up in the righteousness of heaven and plant in our hearts the righteousness of God. Said the Lord, through the prophet Jeremiah, "I will put my law in their inward parts, and write it in their hearts; and will be their God, and they shall be my people." [Jer. 31:33.] This is what the Lord is endeavoring to do, and this He will accomplish in us if we conform to His will. (*The Teachings of Lorenzo Snow,* ed. Clyde J. Williams [Salt Lake City: Bookcraft, 1984], 44)

Ezra Taft Benson:

> Until one abides by the laws of obedience, sacrifice, the gospel, and chastity, he cannot abide the law of consecration, which is the law pertaining to the celestial kingdom. . . .
>
> The law of consecration is a law for an inheritance in the celestial kingdom. God, the Eternal Father, His Son Jesus Christ, and all holy beings abide by this law. It is an eternal law. It is a revelation by God to His Church in this dispensation. Though not in full operation today, it will be mandatory for all Saints to live the law in its fulness to receive celestial inheritance. You young people today abide a portion of this higher law as you tithe, pay a generous fast offering, go on missions, and make other contributions of money, service, and time. (*The Teachings of Ezra Taft Benson* [Salt Lake City: Bookcraft, 1988], 121–23)

Spencer W. Kimball:

> The Lord has blessed us as a people with a prosperity unequaled in times past. The resources that have been placed in our power are good, and necessary to our work here on the earth. But I am afraid that many of us have been surfeited with flocks and herds and acres and barns and wealth and have begun to worship them as false gods, and they have power over us. Do we have more of these good things than our faith can stand? Many people spend most of their time working in the service of a self-image that includes sufficient money, stocks, bonds, investment portfolios, property, credit cards, furnishings, automobiles, and the like to guarantee carnal security throughout, it is hoped, a long and happy life. Forgotten is the fact that our assignment is to use these many resources in our families and quorums to build up the kingdom of God—to further the missionary effort and the genealogical and temple work; to raise our children up as fruitful servants unto the Lord; to bless others in every way, that they may also be fruitful. Instead, we expend these blessings on our own desires, and as Moroni said, "Ye adorn yourselves with that which hath no life, and yet suffer the hungry, and the needy, and the naked, and the sick and the afflicted to pass by you, and notice them not." (Mormon 8:39.)
>
> As the Lord Himself said in our day, "They seek not the Lord to establish his righteousness, but every man walketh in his own way, and after the image of his own god, whose image is in the likeness of the world, and whose substance is that of an idol, which waxeth old and shall perish in Babylon, even Babylon the great, which shall fall." (D&C 1:16.) (*The Teachings of Spencer W. Kimball,* edited by Edward L. Kimball [Salt Lake City: Bookcraft, 1982], 357)

IDEAS FOR DAILY LIVING

Here are four ideas to help us understand and live the law of consecration:

1. Keep in mind the eternal purposes of Heavenly Father.
- *Our destiny*—He seeks our immortality and eternal life (see Moses 1:39).
- *Our happiness*—He wants us to be righteous and thus enjoy life here and in the hereafter (see Mosiah 2:41).
- *Our unity and love for others*—He desires that there should be no poor and needy among us (see Mosiah 18:27–29).
- *Our spiritual growth*—He wants us to grow and become like Him—and this requires sacrifice (see 3 Ne. 9:20).

2. Remember the goodness and mercy of God to His children.
- *Gratitude*—When we appreciate the blessings of God and feel the Spirit, we become grateful and have a greater desire to do good (see D&C 11:12). We are more willing to consecrate our lives.
- *Atonement*—Never forget the love of God (see John 3:16) and that of our Savior (see 2 Ne. 26:24). The Atonement was the ultimate sacrifice, making our very salvation possible. Christ died for us, and we ought to live for Him.

3. Set goals and make plans to live a consecrated life.
- *Plan for a full-time mission*—Such service provides a time when we have no other distractions and can concentrate on building up the kingdom of God (see D&C 138:56).
- *Remember daily opportunities for consecration*—Family togetherness time, providing for the needs of your family, and even taking the opportunity for wholesome recreation is part of living a consecrated life. Follow the Spirit in your efforts of consecration (see 2 Ne. 32:5, 9). The Holy Ghost can be your guide in knowing how to best give of yourself.
- *Use wisdom and prudence*—Don't run faster than you have strength (see Mosiah 4:27).
- *Use leadership*—Prioritize your life so you can organize every needful thing (see D&C 88:119).

4. Follow a pattern of consecration.
- *Go to the temple*—Attend the temple often and refresh your mind concerning your covenants (see D&C 138:53–54).
- *Fast with a purpose*—Don't simply go without food on fast Sunday (see Alma 17:3; Hel. 3:35). Use fasting as a means to bless others and strengthen yourself.
- *Study the word of God*—Regularly search the scriptures to receive instructions from the Lord concerning consecration (see 2 Ne. 32:3; D&C 84:43–45).
- *Foster a charitable attitude*—Remember to give willingly and not begrudgingly (see Moro. 7:6–11). Look for things to share, not simply to possess.
- *Live unselfishly and with gratitude*—Remember that everything we have is really the Lord's, for He is the Creator of all things (see 2 Ne. 2:14–15).
- *Practice modesty and humility*—Concentrate on your needs and not your wants (see Alma 32:14–15).

ILLUSTRATIONS FOR OUR TIMES

In a general conference address, Apostle Neal A. Maxwell explains how we often commit sins of omission and thus fail to fully consecrate ourselves to Heavenly Father.

Swallowed Up in the Will of the Father

> Whenever Church members speak of consecration, it should be done reverently while acknowledging that each of us "come[s] short of the glory of God," some of us far short (Rom. 3:23). Even the conscientious have not arrived, but they sense the shortfall and are genuinely striving. Consolingly, God's grace flows not only to those "who love [Him] and keep all [His] commandments," but likewise to those "that [seek] so to do" (D&C 46:9). . . .
>
> Consider three examples of how honorable people in the Church keep back a portion and thus prevent greater consecration (see Acts 5:1–4).

A sister gives commendable, visible civic service. Yet even with her good image in the community, she remains a comparative stranger to Jesus' holy temples and His holy scriptures, two vital dimensions of discipleship. But she could have Christ's image in her countenance (see Alma 5:14).

An honorable father, dutifully involved in the cares of his family, is less than kind and gentle with individual family members. Though a comparative stranger to Jesus' gentleness and kindness, which we are instructed to emulate, a little more effort by this father would make such a large difference.

Consider the returned missionary, skills polished while serving an honorable mission, striving earnestly for success in his career. Busy, he ends up in a posture of some accommodation with the world. Thus he forgoes building up the kingdom first and instead builds up himself. A small course correction now would make a large, even destinational, difference for him later on.

These deficiencies just illustrated are those of omission. Once the telestial sins are left behind and henceforth avoided, the focus falls ever more on the sins of omission. These omissions signify a lack of qualifying fully for the celestial kingdom. Only greater consecration can correct these omissions, which have consequences just as real as do the sins of commission. Many of us thus have sufficient faith to avoid the major sins of commission, but not enough faith to sacrifice our distracting obsessions or to focus on our omissions. (Neal A. Maxwell, "Swallowed Up in the Will of the Father," *Ensign,* November 1995, 22)

SUMMARY

In the temple, we covenant to live the law of consecration. This law is that we consecrate our time, talents, strength, property, and money for the upbuilding of the kingdom of God on this earth and the establishment of Zion. As we can see, consecration is not merely something we can measure in quantities. Consecration is a quality of attitude. It is not only how much time, money, and other possessions we give, but *how* we give them. If our hearts are truly set on building up the kingdom of God, even our widow's mites can be a great offering (see Mark 12:42).

CONVERSION

Conversion is the process of being born of God. "Born of God" or "born again" refers to the personal spiritual experience through which we receive a forgiveness of sins and a witness from God that if we continue to live the commandments and endure to the end, we will inherit eternal life. The scriptures teach that just as each of us is "born into the world by water, and blood, and the spirit," so must we be "born again" of water and the Spirit and be cleansed by the blood of Christ (see John 3:5; Moses 6:59). To be born of God implies a sanctifying process by which the old or natural man is supplanted by the new spiritual man who enjoys the companionship of the Holy Ghost and hence is no longer disposed to commit sin (see Col. 3:9–10; Mosiah 3:19; *Teachings of the Prophet Joseph Smith,* 51). When we are born again we are spiritually begotten sons and daughters of God and more specifically of Jesus Christ (Mosiah 5:7; 27:25). The Book of Mormon prophet Alma the Younger calls this inner transformation a "mighty change in your hearts" (Alma 5:14). (Adapted from the article by Ed J. Pinegar in *Encyclopedia of Mormonism,* 1–4 vols., ed. Daniel H. Ludlow [New York: Macmillan, 1992], 218)

THE SCRIPTURES TEACH US

Mosiah 5:7. *And now, because of the covenant which ye have made ye shall be called the children of Christ, his sons, and his daughters; for behold, this day he hath spiritually begotten you; for ye say that your hearts are changed through faith on his name; therefore, ye are born of him and have become his sons and his daughters.*

We become truly converted, or the sons and daughters of Jesus Christ, when we have made the mighty change in our hearts and, through baptism, have taken upon us His name. This carries with it a covenant and promise to remember Him and keep the commandments.

Mosiah 5:2. *And they all cried with one voice, saying: Yea, we believe all the words which thou hast spoken unto us; and also, we know of their surety and truth, because of the Spirit of the Lord Omnipotent, which has wrought a mighty change in us, or in our hearts, that we have no more disposition to do evil, but to do good continually.*

When we are truly converted by the Spirit, we will experience the "mighty change" and we will feel and act differently. We will have the desire to do good just like the subjects of King Benjamin. We will be united with Christ and His Church.

Alma 5:26. *And now behold, I say unto you, my brethren, if ye have experienced a change of heart, and if ye have felt to sing the song of redeeming love, I would ask, can ye feel so now?*

Conversion is not a momentary experience we have just when we are baptized. It is a state of being, a way of life that we must follow consistently to the end.

Alma 5:46. *Behold, I say unto you they are made known unto me by the Holy Spirit of God. Behold, I have fasted and prayed many days that I might know these things of myself. And now I do know of myself that they are true; for the Lord God hath made them manifest unto me by his Holy Spirit; and this is the spirit of revelation which is in me.*

Conversion comes through the Spirit. Even though Alma the Younger had seen an angel, he still had to fast and pray to receive the confirmation of the Spirit. Many others have seen wonders and angels without experiencing conversion (think of Laman and Lemuel). Conversion is found in the continual companionship of the Holy Ghost.

Moroni 8:25–26. *And the first fruits of repentance is baptism; and baptism cometh by faith unto the fulfilling the commandments; and the fulfilling the commandments bringeth remission of sins; And the remission of sins bringeth meekness, and lowliness of heart; and because of meekness and lowliness of heart cometh the visitation of the Holy Ghost, which Comforter filleth with hope and perfect love, which love endureth by diligence unto prayer, until the end shall come, when all the saints shall dwell with God.*

Through baptism and an active participation in the gospel, we will recognize a true change within our soul. We will start to feel the Spirit and enjoy the fruits of it in our lives. We will be more humble and loving in all things. We will sincerely be immersed in and converted to the gospel of Jesus Christ.

Moses 6:59. *That by reason of transgression cometh the fall, which fall bringeth death, and inasmuch as ye were born into the world by water, and blood, and the spirit, which I have made, and so became of dust a living soul,* *even so ye must be born again into the kingdom of heaven, of water, and of the Spirit, and be cleansed by blood, even the blood of mine Only Begotten; that ye might be sanctified from all sin, and enjoy the words of eternal life in this world, and eternal life in the world to come, even immortal glory.*

We must truly come unto Christ, or be born again through the grace of God in order to receive the blessings of eternal life (see John 3:5–7). This means that each of us must repent and bring forth fruit worthy of all acceptation of the Lord, thus proving ourselves worthy of returning to His presence.

MODERN PROPHETS SPEAK

Harold B. Lee:
> Conversion must mean more than just being a "card carrying" member of the Church with a tithing receipt, a membership card, a temple recommend, etc. It means to overcome the tendencies to criticize and to strive continually to improve inward weaknessess and not merely the outward appearances. (*Stand Ye in Holy Places* [Salt Lake City: Deseret Book, 1974], 355)

> It is very clear that the most important responsibility which we have in missionary work is to ourselves. There is no missionary work that takes precedence over the importance of the missionary work which we do for our own salvation. Someone has put it in this rather interesting way: "Our job is to look after the one behind the man in front of us." Now, have you discovered who that was? That is yourself. Now, the first convert you want to make in this church is yourself. When you are sure you have him converted, then you start on somebody else. (*The Teachings of Harold B. Lee,* ed. Clyde J. Williams [Salt Lake City: Bookcraft, 1996], 589)

Marion G. Romney:
> But all that has happened in the past has not, and all that occurs in the future will not change the truth that conversion to Jesus Christ and his gospel is the one and only way; for still it must be said that "there is none other way given under heaven by which men must be saved." (See Acts 4:12.) (Conference Report, October 1963, 26)

IDEAS FOR DAILY LIVING

Here are some things to remember and do in striving for true conversion:

1. Seek to align yourself with the qualities of a truly converted person.
- *Be mindful of your baptismal covenants*—Since you have been baptized, you have promised to be humble, have a broken heart and a contrite spirit, truly repent, take the name of Jesus Christ upon you, have a determination to serve Him to the end, and manifest by your works that you have received the Holy Ghost unto the remission of your sins (see Moro. 6:1–4; D&C 20:37). Remember, you have covenanted to bear one another's burdens, mourn with those that mourn, and comfort those that stand in need of comfort (see Mosiah 18:8–9).
- *Be blameless before the Lord*—Always be awakened to a sense of your duty and stand blameless before the Lord. Serve God with all your heart, might, mind, and strength (see D&C 4:2). This requires one to be humble, easily entreated, full of patience, temperate, diligent in keeping the commandments, prayerful in asking for all things both spiritual and temporal, and always giving thanks unto God (see Alma 7:23). If you exercise faith, are full of hope, and demonstrate charity, you will always abound in good works (see Alma 7:24).

- *Be spiritually born of God*—Conversion is anchored in a mighty change of heart, which is the process of becoming pure in heart. The heart is the center of your affections, the center of your soul, and your decision-making center. That is why the process of conversion is tantamount to yielding your heart to God (see Hel. 3:35) and to the enticings of the Holy Spirit (see Mosiah 3:19). Receiving the image of Christ in your countenance indicates that you have received a change of heart and have been born again. When you are born of the Spirit, you become like Him and take upon yourself His divine nature (see 2 Pet. 1:3–12).
- *Be obedient and endure to the end*—Cultivate a desire to follow Christ with steadfastness, hope, and the love of God, pressing forward to the end (see 2 Ne. 31:20).
- *Be charitable*—Make and follow a plan to do good and be good—a true disciple of Christ (see John 13:34–35). Demonstrate a true concern for the welfare of others as evidenced by good works (see Matt 25:40; Mosiah 28:3). Enos, Alma, and the sons of Mosiah are perfect examples of those who exhibited a Christlike behavior following their conversion.

2. Follow daily strategies to retain the spirit of conversion and remain strong in the Church.
- *Remember to pray*—Be prayerful and grateful. Express your love to your Father in Heaven and His Son often. Pray to overcome temptation (see Alma 13:28), for knowledge (see Alma 5:46), for humility and faith (see Hel. 3:35), and for all things (see James 1:5–6). Go with a prayer in your heart always (see 3 Ne. 20:1).
- *Search the scriptures*—Live by the word of God (see 2 Ne. 32:3). Feasting on the word daily draws the Spirit into our lives, takes us closer to the Savior, and brings our hearts closer to true conversion.
- *Gain understanding*—Seek to understand the doctrines and principles of the gospel of Jesus Christ, and live them (see Prov. 3:5; 7:27; Mosiah 1:2; Alma 17:2; 32:28).
- *Remain valiant*—Renew and keep your covenants made at baptism (see Mosiah 18:13).
- *Cultivate the spirit and practice of service*—Magnify your callings (see Jacob 2:2; Mosiah 2:17; D&C 107:99–100).
- *Build up the kingdom of God*—Spread the gospel and bless the lives of your brothers and sisters here on earth (see JST, Matt. 6:38; Alma 6:6; Morm. 9:22; D&C 88:81). The more we share the blessings of the gospel, the more committed and converted we are to it.

ILLUSTRATIONS FOR OUR TIMES

As you read the following story of Parley P. Pratt's conversion, notice that, as is any true conversion, his was characterized by hungering and thirsting after righteousness.

The Conversion of Parley P. Pratt

It was early in the morning, just at the dawn of day, I walked ten miles into the country, and stopped to breakfast with a Mr. Wells. I proposed to preach in the evening. Mr. Wells readily accompanied me through the neighborhood to visit the people, and circulate the appointment.

We visited an old Baptist deacon by the name of Hamlin. After hearing of our appointment for evening, he began to tell of a *book*, a strange book, a VERY STRANGE BOOK! in his possession, which had been just published. . . . He promised me the perusal of it, at his house the next day, if I would call. I felt a strange interest in the book. . . . Next morning I called at his house, where, for the first time, my eyes beheld the "BOOK OF MORMON"—that book of books—that record which reveals the antiquities of the *"New World"* back to the remotest ages, and which unfolds the destiny of its people and the world for all time to come; that Book which contains the fulness of the gospel of a crucified and risen Redeemer;—that Book which reveals a lost remnant of Joseph, and which was the principal means, in the hands of God, of directing the entire course of my future life.

I opened it with eagerness, and read its title page. I then read the testimony of several witnesses in relation to the manner of its being found and translated. After this I commenced its contents by course. I read all day; eating was a burden, I had no desire for food; sleep was a burden when the night came, for I preferred reading to sleep.

As I read, the spirit of the Lord was upon me, and I knew and comprehended that the book was true, as plainly and manifestly as a man comprehends and knows that he exists. My joy was now full, as it were, and I rejoiced sufficiently to more than pay me for all the sorrows, sacrifices and toils of my life. I soon determined to see the young man who had been the instrument of its discovery and translation.

I accordingly visited the village of Palmyra, and inquired for the residence of Mr. Joseph Smith. I found it some two or three miles from the village. As I approached the house at the close of the day I overtook a man who was driving some cows, and inquired of him for Mr. Joseph Smith, the translator of the "*Book of Mormon.*" He informed me that he now resided in Pennsylvania; some one hundred miles distant. I inquired for his father, or for any of the family. He told me that his father had gone [on] a journey; but that his residence was a small house just before me; and, said he, I am his brother. It was Mr. Hyrum Smith. I informed him of the interest I felt in the Book, and of my desire to learn more about it. He welcomed me to his house, and we spent the night together; for neither of us felt disposed to sleep. We conversed most of the night, during which I unfolded to him much of my experience in my search after truth, and my success so far; together with that which I felt was lacking, viz: a commissioned priesthood, or apostleship to minister in the ordinances of God.

He also unfolded to me the particulars of the discovery of the Book; its translation; the rise of the Church of Latter-day Saints, and the commission of his brother Joseph, and others, by revelation and the ministering of angels, by which the apostleship and authority had been again restored to the earth. After duly weighing the whole matter in my mind I saw clearly that these things were true. . . .

In the morning I was compelled to take leave of this worthy man and his family—as I had to hasten back a distance of thirty miles, on foot, to fulfil an appointment in the evening. As we parted he kindly presented me with a copy of the Book of Mormon. I had not yet completed its perusal, and was glad indeed to possess a copy of my own. I travelled on a few miles, and, stopping to rest, I commenced again to read the book. To my great joy I found that Jesus Christ, in his glorified resurrected body, had appeared to the remnant of Joseph on the continent of America, soon after his resurrection and ascension into heaven; and that he also administered, in person, to the ten lost tribes; and that through his personal ministry in these countries his gospel was revealed and written in countries and among nations entirely unknown to the Jewish apostles.

Thus revealed, written, handed down and preserved, till revealed in this age by the angels of God, it had, of course, escaped the corruptions of the great and abominable church; and been preserved in purity.

This discovery greatly enlarged my heart, and filled my soul with joy and gladness. I esteemed the Book, or the information contained in it, more than all the riches of the world. Yes; I verily believe that I would not at that time have exchanged the knowledge I then possessed, for a legal title to all the beautiful farms, houses, villages and property which passed in review before me, on my journey through one of the most flourishing settlements of western New York. (Parley P. Pratt, *Autobiography of Parley P. Pratt,* ed. Parley P. Pratt Jr. [Salt Lake City: Deseret Book, 1985], 20–22)

SUMMARY

True conversion is the beginning of a new life abounding in faith, hope, charity, and good works. When we are truly converted, we gladly give a life of service to our fellow beings. We share the gospel message, sacrifice our time, talents, energy, and resources for the benefit of others, and in general hold high the light of Christ. We become true disciples by inviting all to come unto Christ. Surely Enos, Alma, and the sons of Mosiah are examples of converted Saints: They immediately had the desire to share the gospel of Jesus Christ with all mankind. We should do likewise, committing our whole hearts to God and His work, and enduring to the end in our converted state of being, that we might return to live with Him.

COUNSEL

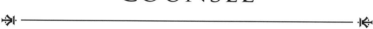

Counsel refers to advice, direction, information, caution, and even admonition or exhortation. We often need to give counsel within our stewardship as parents or leaders. As individuals we need to be easily entreated that we might be willing to receive counsel. Whether giving or receiving counsel, it is imperative that we always seek the Lord's direction (see Jacob 4:10; Alma 37:37).

THE SCRIPTURES TEACH US

Jacob 4:10. *Wherefore, brethren, seek not to counsel the Lord, but to take counsel from his hand. For behold, ye yourselves know that he counseleth in wisdom, and in justice, and in great mercy, over all his works.*

We can always depend upon the Lord, who giveth freely and upbraideth not (see James 1:5). His will and His ways are always the best. We must seek His will in prayer, and seek for confirmation in our minds and hearts to know His counsel (see D&C 9:7–8).

Alma 37:37. *Counsel with the Lord in all thy doings, and he will direct thee for good; yea, when thou liest down at night lie down unto the Lord, that he may watch over you in your sleep; and when thou risest in the morning let thy heart be full of thanks unto God; and if ye do these things, ye shall be lifted up at the last day.*

Our lives ought to be lived in continual communion with God and His will. When we act with faith to seek counsel from the Lord, we must have the courage to accept and follow His direction.

2 Nephi 9:28–29. *O that cunning plan of the evil one! O the vainness, and the frailties, and the foolishness of men! When they are learned they think they are wise, and they hearken not unto the counsel of God, for they set* *it aside, supposing they know of themselves, wherefore, their wisdom is foolishness and it profiteth them not. And they shall perish. But to be learned is good if they hearken unto the counsels of God.*

Our pride as it relates to our learning can be one of the most damning elements in our lives. The devil has full sway in our hearts when pride enters in. Remember that the learning and wisdom of man are so finite, even infinitesimal, compared to the Lord's (see Isa. 55:8–9; 2 Ne. 9:20). We must always seek counsel from the Lord and be submissive to His will.

MODERN PROPHETS SPEAK

Lorenzo Snow:

> Counsel that is given to us, when it comes from the proper authority, is given for a certain purpose; and that purpose is our happiness, so far as the present time is concerned; it is for the purpose of adding happiness unto us in the present state, and also for the purpose of communicating benefits unto us in a state hereafter. Upon this principle is counsel established, upon the principle of doing our fellowmen good; for the purpose of doing them good here and hereafter.

> It requires more energy and more strength of purpose in a man to follow out the counsel of one who is just above him than it does to follow a man that is a long way ahead of him.

> No man can give counsel to anyone, but what it has a tendency to benefit himself as well as others. We are so constituted and organized, that we cannot counsel that which will contribute to the benefit and exaltation of others without at the same time contributing to our own good. (*The Teachings of Lorenzo Snow*, ed. Clyde J. Williams [Salt Lake City: Bookcraft, 1984], 89)

Brigham Young:

> How my heart longs to see the brethren and sisters in a condition that when the words of truth and virtue—righteous words of counsel—are poured upon them, they will meet like drops of water meeting each other. How I long to see the brethren, when they hear the words of truth poured upon them, ready to receive those words because they are perfectly congenial to their feelings, and every soul exclaim, "Those words savor of the Spirit that is in me; they are my delight, my meat, and my drink; they are the streams of eternal life. How congenial they are, instead of their being contrary to my feelings."

> If we hearken to counsel, we shall be the best people in the world; we shall be as a bright light set upon a hill, that cannot be hid, or like a candle upon a candlestick. (*Discourses of Brigham Young*, sel. John A. Widtsoe [Salt Lake City: Deseret Book, 1954], 219)

IDEAS FOR DAILY LIVING

Here are some ideas that may help us in giving and receiving counsel:

1. **Follow the Spirit**—Be sure counsel is given and received by the Spirit (see D&C 36:2; 39:6).

2. **Remember that charity is the motivating force**—All counsel (or chastening, for that matter) should be designed to help and bless one another, to bring people closer to our Savior and Heavenly Father (see D&C 95:1).

3. Remember to love—All counsel and nurturing must be motivated by and given in love for our Savior, the Good Shepherd, and for all His sheep (see John 13:34–35; 21:15–17; D&C 12:8).

4. Look for the best teaching moments—Counsel is best received when a person asks for help. Help create a teaching or counseling moment. Being easily entreated is the key to receiving and acting upon the counsel given (see Alma 7:23; D&C 122:2).

5. Chasten when moved by the Spirit—Sometimes chastening is part of counseling. We must always use the standard for reproving as taught in D&C 121:41–44, doing so with sharpness when necessary, but in love.

6. Stay peaceful and controlled—Never give or receive counsel in anger (see Prov. 15:18).

7. Respect the individual—Always refer to the behavior and not to the individual. The sin is condemned; the sinner is given hope through repentance (see D&C 1:31–32).

8. Respect privacy—Never counsel an individual in public (see D&C 42:88).

9. Listen carefully—Seek to understand the individual's concerns and feelings (see Prov. 17:27).

10. Use the word of God—Counsel from the scriptures and in keeping with the spoken word of the prophets (see Jacob 4:10; D&C 105:37).

ILLUSTRATIONS FOR OUR TIMES

Richard J. Allen explains how a young couple's willingness to receive counsel led to repentance and prosperity in their lives.

The Light of the Gospel

Here was a delightful young couple preparing for marriage—bright, faithful in Church participation, eager to do the right thing. But now there was a problem, a compromising of values and propriety. They were embarrassed and heartbroken as they sat across from me, wondering what to do. We counseled. We sorrowed together. We pondered the consequences. But we also took comfort together in the process of repentance empowered by the Atonement. Yes, there needed to be change. There needed to be prayerful and godly sorrow and faithful commitment to a better lifestyle. But they had caught themselves at the edge of the precipice, and they had recoiled under the strength of conscience and now wanted to do right before the Lord. They were good young people with a desire for righteousness. The Lord loved them and wanted them to have the fulness of His blessings. There needed to be some regular appointments for a few weeks to give momentum to the new commitments. But things went very well, so we came up with a plan—a code just between the bishop and these two. When we crossed paths each week thereafter at the meetings, it took only a nod of the head and a twinkle in the eye as an indication that all was well. You can't disguise the light of the gospel in the eye. It is a sure sign that the Spirit is at work. And it was at work for them. They prospered. They rebounded. They rose to new heights, and once more the age-old story of the gospel transforming lives was repeated in a real-life setting. Thank heavens they were willing to receive by the Spirit counsel given through the Spirit. Thank heavens for the principles of the gospel. Thank heavens for the Atonement of Jesus Christ. "And how great is his joy in the soul that repenteth" (D&C 18:13).

—Richard J. Allen

SUMMARY

When we seek to receive or give counsel, let us always keep in mind the welfare of the individual. Counseling is a form of nurturing, instructing, inspiring, and, above all, giving one hope to carry on. We should never forget that we seek to be instruments in the hand of the Lord—saying and doing the things He would say and do if He were here. Occasions of counseling are pivotal moments in people's lives. Let us always follow the Spirit as we receive counsel, or are called on from time to time to assume the role of counselor.

COURAGE

Courage is the power to act in difficult situations. It can be an act of bravery in every sense of the word, whether in battle or in the personal trials of life. Courage is the attribute of character that often separates the winner from the defeated, success from failure, and happiness from misery. Courageous deeds are often acts of spontaneity on a grand scale, but there are millions of patient, quiet, and enduring acts of courage going on in our homes, schools, and workplaces every day. Courage in honoring one's covenants before the Lord, despite the world's views, is the highest form of this sterling quality.

THE SCRIPTURES TEACH US

Deuteronomy 31:6. *Be strong and of a good courage, fear not, nor be afraid: . . . for the Lord thy God, he it is that doth go with thee; he will not fail thee, nor forsake thee.*

In all our doings in building up the kingdom of God, let us remember that the Lord is with us always. He will be before our face, on our left and on our right, with His Spirit in our hearts, and His angels round about to bear us up (see D&C 84:88).

Psalms 31:24. *Be of good courage, and he shall strengthen your heart, all ye that hope in the Lord.*

Showing courage is an act of faith, for we put aside fear and doubt and move forward in the strength of the Lord. Each act of courage in dealing with a difficult situation will result in increased power to act and do good.

2 Timothy 1:7. *For God hath not given us the spirit of fear; but of power, and of love, and of a sound mind.*

Feelings of fear and discouragement don't come from God. We must be firm in our testimony (see 2 Tim. 1:8) and face whatever will come, with the strength of the Lord.

Alma 56:45. *And now I say unto you, my beloved brother Moroni, that never had I seen so great courage, nay, not amongst all the Nephites.*

The stripling warriors were courageous. Why? They knew that God was with them. They thought more about the liberty of others than themselves, because they were taught by their mothers that if they acted in faith, nothing doubting, God would deliver them (see Alma 56:46–48).

MODERN PROPHETS SPEAK

Thomas S. Monson:

> The call for courage comes constantly to each of us. It has ever been so, and so shall it ever be. The battlefields of war witness acts of courage. Some are printed on pages of books or contained on rolls of film, while others are indelibly impressed on the human heart. (*Live the Good Life* [Salt Lake City: Deseret Book, 1988], 66)

Stephen L Richards:

> Those who have convictions must have courage; the courage to state their convictions of the truth as it has come to them—not to attain supremacy in an argument, but to perform a service and a duty—the service of a brother to a brother and a duty to God. (*Where Is Wisdom?* [Salt Lake City: Deseret Book, 1955], 123–24)

Boyd K. Packer:

> Leaders must be courageous. One of the highest qualities of all true leadership is a high standard of courage. When we speak of courage and leadership we are using terms that stand for the quality of life by which men determine consciously the proper course to pursue and stand with fidelity to their convictions. There has never been a time in the Church when its leaders were not required to be courageous men; not alone courageous in the sense that they were able to meet physical dangers, but also in the sense that they were steadfast and true to a clear and upright conviction. (*The Holy Temple* [Salt Lake City: Bookcraft, 1980], 179)

IDEAS FOR DAILY LIVING

Here are three points that may help you develop courage in your life:

1. Courage grows from within, rooted in factors such as the following:
- *A higher cause*—Courageous people usually have a value or a cause that they believe in that motivates them. Our cause is the kingdom of God and the welfare of Heavenly Father's children.
- *Sound values and principles*—The first true act of courage is to decide to base your life on gospel values and principles. Examples of such principles are love, respect for life, honesty, and forgiveness. James Freeman Clarke said it this way: "Conscience is the root of all true courage. If a man would be brave, let him obey his conscience."
- *Self-discipline*—In self-mastery, we develop a sense of integrity and conviction; we learn to be courageous in small ways, and to stand firm when tested.
- *Decisiveness*—Courage often has roots in the decisions you make within yourself, such as: "Whatever happens today, I promise myself that I will act according to the principles I have accepted for my life—no matter what." Such a decision will lead to courageous acts.
- *Learning*—Courage can be cultivated. You can say to yourself, looking back on the day, "How might I have acted with more courage? How can I do better tomorrow?"
- *An everyday opportunity*—Remember, situations that require courage are found in everyday life, such as courage to be honest, kind, and full of integrity.

2. Courage and love go together.
- *Positives reinforce each other*—Your respect and love for others can often give you the strength of courage you need to help them, support them, snatch them from harm's way, and stand up for

their dignity and their well-being in the face of life's challenges. The more you act on your love, the more courageous you become.

- *There are built-in rewards*—Courageous acts always bless—both the giver and the receiver.
- *Teaching others brings joy*—You can help others (family members, friends, coworkers) cultivate courage by recognizing and reinforcing the courageous decisions and acts they make on a daily basis.
- *Self-worth fosters courage*—Courage is rooted in respect for self. Thus self-worth and self-confidence are necessary when being courageous in the presence of peer pressure.

3. Courage opens up channels of strength.

- *Physical strength*—When you act on courage, your body produces adrenaline and energy that allow you to rise beyond your ordinary abilities.
- *Spiritual strength*—When you act with spiritual courage to uphold correct principles, you are strengthened by the Lord and His Spirit.
- *Higher perspective*—Courage gives you the strength to see from a higher perspective; not the fleeting moment of pleasure that comes from an act of self-gratification, but the enduring sense of peace that comes from courage over time. Courageous acts often require time to be validated, while self-gratification is immediate but has no lasting value.
- *You can choose*—Many people have great sorrow for their failure to be courageous in moral and civil decisions. This is unnecessary, because they *can* find the power within themselves, and access the spiritual power beyond themselves, to act with courage and grow in confidence and self-worth.

ILLUSTRATIONS FOR OUR TIMES

President Gordon B. Hinckley relates an experience from his mission that taught him the value of courage and obedience.

Willing and Obedient

Years ago I was on a mission in England. I had been called to labor in the European Mission office in London under President Joseph F. Merrill of the Council of the Twelve, then president of the European Mission. One day three or four of the London papers carried reviews of a reprint of an old book, snide and ugly in tone, indicating that the book was a history of the Mormons. President Merrill said to me, "I want you to go down to the publisher and protest this." I looked at him and was about to say, "Surely not me." But I meekly said, "Yes, sir."

I do not hesitate to say that I was frightened. I went to my room and felt something as I think Moses must have felt when the Lord asked him to go and see Pharaoh. I offered a prayer. My stomach was churning as I walked over to the Goodge Street station to get the underground train to Fleet Street. I found the office of the president and presented my card to the receptionist. She took it and went into the inner office and soon returned to say that the president was too busy to see me. I replied that I had come five thousand miles and that I would wait. During the next hour she made two or three trips to his office; then finally he invited me in. I shall never forget the picture when I entered. He was smoking a long cigar with a look that seemed to say, "Don't bother me."

I held in my hand the reviews. I do not recall what I said after that. Another power seemed to be speaking through me. At first he was defensive and even belligerent. Then he began to soften. He concluded by promising to do something. Within an hour word went out to every book dealer in

England to return the books to the publisher. At great expense he printed and tipped in the front of each volume a statement to the effect that the book was not to be considered as history, but only as fiction, and that no offense was intended against the respected Mormon people. Years later he granted another favor of substantial worth to the Church, and each year until the time of his death I received a Christmas card from him.

I came to know that when we try in faith to walk in obedience to the requests of the priesthood, the Lord opens the way, even when there appears to be no way. (Gordon B. Hinckley, "If Ye Be Willing and Obedient," *Ensign,* July 1995, 2)

SUMMARY

Courage is not only manifest on the battlefield. In today's world we need people with the fortitude and valor to stand for truth and righteousness. Courage to do what one knows is right requires integrity of the soul. The histories of war record countless acts of valor. We should be more valiant in our war against crime, misery in the family, and dishonesty. Everyone knows that we all need to be more courageous in standing for truth and a righteous value system. We have marvelous examples to follow in our own rich heritage. Let us be like Nephi, willing to follow his priesthood leaders and embark on a new life; or like Alma the Younger, not recoiling from the pain of necessary repentance to overcome sin. Let us be like Joseph Smith, unwavering in our testimony, despite ridicule and persecution. Finally, let us be like our Savior, unflinching in the face of tribulation until we have fulfilled our own divine mission.

COVENANTS

Eternal covenants are binding agreements between God and His children. God gives the covenants through revelation to His prophets. We, with our moral agency, can agree to and enter into these covenants if we are worthy. There are many covenants and ordinances we can participate in within the Church. The essential covenants and ordinances are baptism, receiving the gift of the Holy Ghost through confirmation as a member of the Church, priesthood covenants, and temple covenants and ordinances, which include washings and annointings, the endowment, and temple sealings. These eternal covenants provide the means whereby we can receive the blessings of exaltation from our Heavenly Father.

THE SCRIPTURES TEACH US

Mosiah 18:8–10. *And it came to pass that he said unto them: Behold, here are the waters of Mormon (for thus were they called) and now, as ye are desirous to come into the fold of God, and to be called his people, and are willing to bear one another's burdens, that they may be light; Yea, and are willing to mourn with those that mourn; yea, and comfort those that stand in need of comfort, and to stand as witnesses of God at all times and in all things, and in all places that ye may be in, even until death, that ye may be redeemed of God, and be numbered with those of the first resurrection, that ye may have eternal life—Now I say unto you, if this be the desire of your hearts, what have you against being baptized in the name of the Lord, as a witness before him that ye have entered into a covenant with him, that ye will serve him and keep his commandments, that he may pour out his Spirit more abundantly upon you?*

The covenant and ordinance of baptism is necessary to enter into the Church and kingdom of God. It is also the gateway into the celestial kingdom. We covenant to be members of His fold, witnessing of Him and lifting His children (see James 1:27). If we are faithful to our covenants by always remembering the suffering of our Savior, by taking His name upon us, by always remembering Him (see D&C 20:37, 77, 79) by keeping the commandments to the end of our mortal lives (see 2 Ne. 31:19–20), we can enjoy the blessings of eternal life. This should be our goal.

Doctrine and Covenants 52:15–16. *Wherefore he that prayeth, whose spirit is contrite, the same is accepted of me if he obey mine ordinances. He that speaketh, whose spirit is contrite, whose language is meek and edifieth, the same is of God if he obey mine ordinances.*

We must pray with a broken heart and a contrite spirit, but this in itself is not enough. Drawing near Deity with our lips when our hearts are not focused on keeping the covenants is not acceptable to the Lord (see JS–H 1:19). The Lord is displeased and the earth is defiled by the breaking and changing of the ordinances and covenants (see Isa. 24:5). Obedience to our covenants is the true expression of our love; in this we can stand approved of the Lord and draw near unto Him.

Doctrine and Covenants 84:33–40. *For whoso is faithful unto the obtaining these two priesthoods of which I have spoken, and the magnifying their calling, are sanctified by the Spirit unto the renewing of their bodies. They become the sons of Moses and of Aaron and the seed of Abraham, and the church and kingdom, and the elect of God. And also all they who receive this priesthood receive me, saith the Lord; For he that receiveth my servants receiveth me; And he that receiveth me receiveth my Father; And he that receiveth my Father receiveth my Father's kingdom; therefore all that my Father hath shall be given unto him. And this is according to the oath and covenant which belongeth to the priesthood. Therefore, all those who receive the priesthood, receive this oath and covenant of my Father, which he cannot break, neither can it be moved.*

The "oath and covenant" of the priesthood is among the most sublime bestowals of honor, blessing, and sacred obligation granted by God unto His children on earth. Everything the Father has is to be shared with the faithful and elect holders of the priesthood of the Almighty, and those women who sustain and honor the priesthood, based on covenant obedience and righteousness. The Lord makes clear that this blessing—an integral part of the Abrahamic Covenant—is given "not for your sakes only, but for the sake of the whole world" (D&C 84:48). It is through our faithfulness to our covenants that the Lord blesses not just us, but all His children.

Doctrine and Covenants 132:6–7. *And as pertaining to the new and everlasting covenant, it was instituted for the fulness of my glory; and he that receiveth a fulness thereof must and shall abide the law, or he shall be damned, saith the Lord God. And verily I say unto you, that the conditions of this law are these: All covenants, contracts, bonds, obligations, oaths, vows, performances, connections, associations, or expectations, that are not made and entered into and sealed by the Holy Spirit of promise, of him who is anointed, both as well for time and for all eternity, and that too most holy, by revelation and commandment through the medium of mine anointed, whom I have appointed on the earth to hold this power . . . are of no efficacy, virtue, or force in and after the resurrection from the dead; for all contracts that are not made unto this end have an end when men are dead.*

Only those covenants made with God through God's authority are eternal. Receiving and honoring the new and everlasting covenant of marriage is necessary for the highest degree of exaltation. It is necessary for eternal increase (see D&C 131:2–4). We must be true and faithful to this covenant so that it can be sealed by the Holy Spirit of Promise.

MODERN PROPHETS SPEAK

James E. Faust:

> If you keep the covenants and commandments of God, you will have the joy promised by the Savior when he walked upon the earth. You will have "peace in this world, and eternal life in the world to come." (D&C 59:23.) (*Reach Up for the Light* [Salt Lake City: Deseret Book, 1990], 69)

Howard W. Hunter:

> This question may appear as a play on the words of the Lord when he said this is the true and living church. When I ask, "Am I a true and living member?" my question is, Am I deeply and fully dedicated to keeping the covenants I have made with the Lord? Am I totally committed to living the gospel and being a doer of the word and not a hearer only? Do I live my religion? Will I remain true? Do I stand firm against Satan's temptations? He is seeking to cause us to lose our way in a storm of derision and a tide of sophistry. We can have victory, however, by responding to that inner voice calling, "Stand firm!" (*That We Might Have Joy* [Salt Lake City: Deseret Book, 1994], 149)

Gordon B. Hinckley:

> The priest at the sacrament table places all in the congregation under sacred covenant. The offering of the prayer is not a ritual to be thoughtlessly spoken. It is, rather, the voicing of an obligation and a promise. Cleanliness of hands, as well as purity of heart, should be taught to the priests who officiate at the sacrament table. (*Teachings of Gordon B. Hinckley* [Salt Lake City: Deseret Book, 1997], 484)

IDEAS FOR DAILY LIVING

Some ideas on how we can better understand and keep our covenants:

1. Understanding and appreciating our covenants.

- *Careful study*—An in-depth study of the doctrines, principles, ordinances, and covenants of the Church requires searching the scriptures and the words of our living prophets (see D&C 84:43–45; D&C 21:4–6). The more we learn of our covenants, the more we know how to keep them.
- *Pray for understanding*—Knowledge comes to us from our Heavenly Father by the Holy Spirit. He can reveal to us eternal truths that bring a comprehension of those things we seek to know and understand and appreciate (see Prov. 3:5; Alma 17:2). Many times we need to pray and accept things on faith, and in time we will have a witness (see Ether 12:6). We will be filled with gratitude, which will give us a desire to keep our covenants.
- *Keep the covenants*—We will know the truth of, and receive the benefit of, the covenants of God primarily by living the doctrines and commandments of God (see John 7:17). We can and will receive the blessings of eternal life by keeping the covenants and enduring to the end (see 2 Ne. 33:4; D&C 101:38–40).
- *Temple worship*—The more we return to the temple, the more our understanding is deepened. Revelation to many truths can come as we seek enlightenment within the walls of the house of the Lord (see D&C 97:13–16).

2. Keeping our covenants.

- *Plan to remember*—A system for remembering is the key to not forgetting. It is easy to forget due to the busyness of life and the ease of the way (see Hel. 12:2–3). Many covenants include a command to "always remember" (see D&C 20:77, 79). A sign, a note, a friend to help, a regular happening (the ring of the doorbell, the telephone, etc.)—such simple things can awaken within us a remembrance of our covenant promises.

- *Prayer*—Earnest, sincere prayer is absolutely essential to receive the strength necessary to keep the commandments.
- *Exercise your faith*—In faith, all things can be done (see Moro. 7:33). Faith moves us to action and gives the power to do all things. Remember, the Lord will provide a way to do what He commands (see 1 Ne. 3:7).
- *Write a mission statement*—Your mission statement could include references to the covenants you have made, including the commitments of obedience involved and reminders of the great spiritual benefits that accrue therefrom. Take the time to review your mission statement on a regular basis.

ILLUSTRATIONS FOR OUR TIMES

Author Richard J. Allen uses an example from early Church history to illustrate the importance of missionary work in keeping our covenants with the Lord.

Honoring the Abrahamic Covenant

The Lord promised Abraham: "in thy seed after thee . . . shall all the families of the earth be blessed, even with the blessings of the gospel, which are the blessings of salvation, even of life eternal" (Abr. 2:11). According to this royal covenant, Israel was assured a homeland upon the earth and an inheritance in the mansions of the heavens, a bounteous earthly progeny, and (in keeping with the new and everlasting covenant of marriage) eternal increase in the hereafter. Israel is also promised the blessings of the fulness of gospel truth in the temporal sphere, followed by salvation and exaltation in the hereafter for the faithful and obedient. By divine decree, the obligation under this magnificent covenant was that Israel was to convey priesthood blessings to the entire world and spread the gospel of saving ordinances to the receptive children of God in all lands.

In keeping with this august commission, the Prophet Joseph Smith penned a letter on Thursday, May 14, 1840, to Orson Hyde and John E. Page, who were en route on their mission to the Jewish people in Europe and Palestine. Here is an excerpt: "Although [your mission] appears great at present, yet you have but just begun to realize the greatness, the extent and glory of the same. If there is anything calculated to interest the mind of the Saints, to awaken in them the finest sensibilities, and arouse them to enterprise and exertion, surely it is the great and precious promises made by our heavenly Father to the children of Abraham; and those engaged in seeking the outcasts of Israel, and the dispersed of Judah, cannot fail to enjoy the Spirit of the Lord and have the choicest blessings of Heaven rest upon them in copious effusions. Brethren, you are in the pathway to eternal fame, and immortal glory; and inasmuch as you feel interested for the covenant people of the Lord, the God of their fathers shall bless you. Do not be discouraged on account of the greatness of the work; only be humble and faithful. . . . He who scattered Israel has promised to gather them; therefore inasmuch as you are to be instrumental in this great work, He will endow you with power, wisdom, might, and intelligence, and every qualification necessary; while your minds will expand wider and wider, until you can circumscribe the earth and the heavens, reach forth into eternity, and contemplate the mighty acts of Jehovah in all their variety and glory" (*History of the Church,* 4:128–29). Thus the Prophet teaches the scope and significance of the mission of the Church in honoring and fulfilling its obligations under the Abrahamic Covenant. He also teaches that in honoring and fulfilling covenants, we are endowed with "power, wisdom, might, and intelligence, and every quality necessary." Although John

E. Page fell by the wayside, Orson Hyde continued with his mission and dedicated Palestine on Sunday, October 24, 1841, for the return of the Jewish people and the building of a future temple in Jerusalem.

—Richard J. Allen

SUMMARY

Keeping our sacred covenants is a matter of eternal life—our eternal life. Blessings are predicated upon our faithfulness to our covenants (see D&C 130:20–21). Nothing can bring about the ultimate blessings of God in our lives unless we are diligently keeping our covenants. Let us never forget or take lightly these promises we have made to our Heavenly Father. He will always honor us as we honor our commitments to the covenants of everlasting life.

DATING AND COURTSHIP

One of the most dynamic times in life is the dating and courting period. Those going through this adventure are faced with several challenges: understanding themselves, relating to people of the opposite sex, finding that "one and only" person, keeping up in schoolwork, cultivating job connections, fostering regular friendships, and participating in family life—all at the same time. People (including anxious parents) often say, "We're so glad we're through the dating and courting period. It was so pressure-packed. What a relief!" Recognizing that this is a challenging time, we would be well advised to follow some time-proven principles of survival and success as we navigate the white-water rapids of this critically important life phase. This is especially true in the context of the courting process as conducted in keeping with the principles and values of the gospel and preparing for temple marriage.

THE SCRIPTURES TEACH US

Authors' Note: As you can imagine, there are few specific ideas on dating and courtship in the scriptures as compared with other topics. In dating and courtship it seems that we should simply be our best selves and keep the commandments. Why? Because we want a worthy companion and a temple marriage.

Matthew 7:12. *Therefore all things whatsoever ye would that men should do to you, do ye even so to them: for this is the law and the prophets.*

Living the Golden Rule is the strategy that dating persons should live by. It covers a multitude of principles and commandments. If you follow this strategy, your relationship will be built upon love. Each will truly care for the other person and his or her well-being.

Mosiah 2:41. *And moreover, I would desire that ye should consider on the blessed and happy state of those that keep the commandments of God. For behold, they are blessed in all things, both temporal and spiritual; and if they hold out faithful to the end they are received into heaven, that thereby they may dwell with God in a state of never-ending happiness. O remember, remember that these things are true; for the Lord God hath spoken it.*

Righteousness has its reward—never-ending happiness in the presence of God. The timetable for marriage is different for everybody. Nevertheless, if we are righteous we can partake of all the blessings from our Heavenly Father.

Doctrine and Covenants 88:40. *For intelligence cleaveth unto intelligence; wisdom receiveth wisdom; truth embraceth truth; virtue loveth virtue; light cleaveth unto light; mercy hath compassion on mercy and claimeth her own.*

As we interact with others, we attract and are attracted to those who are like us in beliefs, values, and goals in life. Seek to be the kind of person you want your eternal companion to be.

MODERN PROPHETS SPEAK

Boyd K. Packer:

> Actually the loan of the car would not be as serious as you suppose, for should it be destroyed completely, it could be replaced. But there are some problems and some hazards with dating for which there is no such fortunate solution.
>
> When you are old enough you ought to start dating. It is good for young men and women to learn to know and to appreciate one another. It is good for you to go to games and dances and picnics, to do all of the young things. We encourage our young people to date. We encourage you to set high standards of dating.
>
> When are you old enough? Maturity may vary from individual to individual, but we are rather of the conviction that dating should not even begin until you are well into your teens. And then, ideal dating is on a group basis. None of this steady dancing, steady dating routine. Steady dating is courtship, and surely the beginning of courtship ought to be delayed until you are almost out of your teens.
>
> Dating should not be premature. You should appreciate your parents if they see to that. Dating should not be without supervision, and you should appreciate parents who see to that. . . .
>
> Be open with your parents. Communicate with them. Discuss your problems with them. Have prayer with them before a dating event.
>
> Stay in group activities. Don't pair off. Avoid steady dating. The right time to begin a courtship is when you have emerged from your teens.
>
> Heed the counsels from your bishop, from your priesthood and auxiliary teachers, from your seminary teacher. (*Memorable Stories and Parables of Boyd K. Packer* [Salt Lake City: Bookcraft, 1997], 56)

Harold B. Lee:

> Now, again, I would have you remember that the purpose of dating which leads to courtship and ultimately to marriage is a social process by which young people ultimately find their mates in marriage. It is a truism that we find our husband or wife among that company we frequent the most. (*The Teachings of Harold B. Lee,* edited by Clyde J. Williams [Salt Lake City: Bookcraft, 1996], 221)

Ezra Taft Benson:

> Clearly, right marriage begins with right dating. . . . Therefore, this warning comes with great emphasis. Do not take the chance of dating nonmembers, or members who are untrained and faithless. [You] may say, "Oh, I do not intend to marry this person. It is just a 'fun' date." But one cannot afford to take a chance on falling in love with someone who may never accept the gospel. (*Come, Listen to a Prophet's Voice* [Salt Lake City: Deseret Book, 1990], 8)

IDEAS FOR DAILY LIVING

1. Ideals to help you in your dating and courting experience.

- *Courtesy*—Good manners never go out of style. Young men: Be the perfect gentlemen. Young women: Be ladylike in every way. (And it doesn't matter how young or old you are.)
- *Respect*—Consideration for each other is simply a must.
- *Understanding*—Make sure you understand each other. An unrealized expectation usually results in negative feelings or responses.
- *Timeliness*—Always address concerns as soon as possible. If allowed to persist, they often become problems that are magnified, and hence the relationship suffers.
- *Problem-solving*—When experiencing concerns, never attack with words like, "You did . . ." or "It was your . . ." but rather, "I feel . . ." Feelings are usually less attacking in nature and express the idea of "I don't understand . . ." and "My perception is different than yours . . ." The "I feel" approach is an open-ended formulation that invites dialogue and fosters the process of sharing and finding common ground.
- *Standards*—The process of dating and courtship is just that—a process of exploring *promising* relationships and *potential* commitments. It should not involve the intimacy and responsibility of marriage. Keep your standards and appreciate the other person's good values as well.
- *Enjoyment*—Make dating and courting a fun and enjoyable experience. Seek to get to know each other. Do fun things together and in groups.
- *Consideration*—Always follow the Golden Rule.
- *Communication*—Seek to convey your feelings and ideas clearly. Often people complain about the "games" everyone plays in dating. Be open and honest with the person you are dating. Don't keep them guessing and wondering what you think.
- *Planning*—In planning dates it is important to consider both persons' likes and dislikes. Remember that if you're courting, you should consider a variety of activities, not all just playing, but working and serving together. This way you get to know the other person in different kinds of settings.

2. Ideas for parents of young people.

- *Be a good example*—The greatest gift that parents and leaders can give a dating son or daughter is to be loving with each other, and to demonstrate to the best of their ability how to cope with stress and solve problems—and still stay friends and devoted partners. This example gives the young person confidence and security to move forward. Single-parent homes can still teach the principles of coping with life's problems and overcoming challenges successfully, while fostering cherished and exemplary memories.
- *Help set boundaries*—Parents need to help the dating son or daughter establish wholesome boundaries and prudent protocols about what is appropriate and correct concerning hours to be kept and rules to be observed.
- *Help them build a strong foundation*—This is a period of intense consideration of values and principles for life. The dating son or daughter needs help in coming to terms with governing principles

such as honor, integrity, fidelity, commitment, selflessness, devotion to another, wholesome and healthful patterns of behavior, and cultivating a legacy for a new generation. This is the time to keep spiritual things in focus and remember the enduring gospel principles. Pray with and for your maturing children.

- *Encourage group dating*—As early dating begins, encourage group activities. Youth will avoid compromising situations, as well as get to know more people and develop stronger social skills.
- *Give guidance on feelings*—Parents can help the dating son or daughter sort out the tricky emotions and understand the difference between infatuation and commitment for the long term.
- *Teach self-reliance*—Parents need to balance their intense concern for the well-being of their son or daughter with the need to start to let him or her move through the transition toward self-determination and maturity.
- *Provide a welcome setting*—Make the home available to young people as they date and socialize. Make the home a gathering place where young people feel welcome to come as they crisscross the community in search of pleasant diversions and opportunities to explore wholesome relationships.

ILLUSTRATIONS FOR OUR TIMES

The following story tells us how a young couple searched diligently for the answer to an important question.

"The Answer": A Parable

Two young people, very much in love, were pondering the awesome step of marriage. Under such circumstances, it was the custom in their culture to seek out a certain wise man who lived high in the mountains, and ask for his advice. So one spring day, the young man took his truly beloved and hiked up the steep slope to the cabin of the venerated old grandfather.

"We have come, Sir," said the young man in hushed tones, "to hear your wisdom in our situation." The slender old patriarch said nothing, but beckoned the couple to enter and sit on the mat beside him. "We are very much in love," continued the young man, "and wonder if it is the correct thing for us to be married."

The old man remained silent. For an awkward moment, not a word was spoken among them. The young woman presently took courage, and repeated, "Honored Sir, our question is: Should we marry?"

Finally the old man smiled and, reaching for a weathered scroll nearby, unrolled it and handed it to the eager young couple. It was titled, "The Seven Deepest Questions."

The young man took the scroll and, in quiet reverence, slowly read aloud the words:

For the noble—Are you nobler together, than apart?
For the visionary—Are your eyes unseeing toward all others except this one special person?
For the quiet—Do you have joy in the silence, just being together?
For the selfless—Do you find no greater satisfaction in all the world than in making this one person happy?
For the free—Is your spirit free as the wind and free as the river—just to be in this person's presence?
For the peaceful—Does this companionship yield for you an ocean of harmony and a sky of peace?
For the living—Do you see in this person the doorway to an abiding family for the coming generation?

"If so, dear young people," said the old man, "then you have answered your own question."

For a long while, the two young people, hands held tightly interlocked, stared deeply into each other's eyes, entranced. Then, smiling and bowing, they thanked their aged teacher, and, hand in hand, made their way slowly down the mountain trail, oblivious to all else around them. They had their answer.

—Richard J. Allen

SUMMARY

Make dating and courting an enjoyable experience by following these simple ideas and remaining in tune with the Spirit. Seek those who share your dreams in life, and your beliefs in God. Find someone you cannot only laugh with, but work with too. When you "fall in love," keep your standards high. Create memories you can enjoy together.

DEATH

Life is full of things we do not understand. One of the most difficult is death. In our finite mortal minds, death is difficult and seemingly final. The sorrow is deep due to the loss of the loved one and the relationship. But let's remember: All who come to Earth must die, for it is part of the plan (see 2 Nephi 9:6). Temporal death is a temporary separation of our body and spirit, for the spirit never dies. Through the power of the resurrection, the soul is reunited and all mankind will live again. Given that knowledge, one should seek to live life to its fullest by keeping the commandments and preparing to meet God.

THE SCRIPTURES TEACH US

1 Corinthians 15:22. *For as in Adam all die, even so in Christ shall all be made alive.*

Mortality brings with it the promise of death as well as resurrection. This knowledge should fill us with hope as well as encourage us to live well while here upon the earth.

Alma 12:24. *And we see that death comes upon mankind, yea, the death which has been spoken of by Amulek, which is the temporal death; nevertheless there was a space granted unto man in which he might repent; therefore this life became a probationary state; a time to prepare to meet God; a time to prepare for that endless state which has been spoken of by us, which is after the resurrection of the dead.*

Life is a test, a time to see if we will keep the commandments (see Abr. 3:25). Death ends our mortal probation. In death we learn humility, knowing that God is over all. Death is a beginning of the transfer from one state of being (mortality) to another state (immortality). If we are true to our covenants and exercise our faith, death will not have so much sorrow. Sorrow in death comes from the knowledge of unrepentant sins (see Morm. 5:11).

Doctrine and Covenants 101:36. *Wherefore, fear not even unto death; for in this world your joy is not full, but in me your joy is full.*

Due to our gospel perspective regarding the afterlife, death is not something we should fear. While we should live life to its fullest, we know that it is in God that our joy is full. Whenever it is His will that we leave this earth, we can know that our life and progression will continue, and that if we are worthy, we will dwell with Him again.

MODERN PROPHETS SPEAK

Joseph Smith:

> The only difference between the old and young dying is, one lives longer in heaven and eternal light and glory than the other, and is freed a little sooner from this miserable, wicked world. Notwithstanding all this glory, we for a moment lose sight of it, and mourn the loss, but we do not mourn as those without hope. . . . It mattereth not whether we live long or short on the earth after we come to a knowledge of these principles [the principles of the gospel] and obey them unto the end. (*History of the Church*, 4:554, 555)

Spencer W. Kimball:

> Certainly it is not so much that men die, or when they die, but that they do not die in their sins.

> "Those that die in me shall not taste of death." (D&C 42:46.) I think that means they are not going into the other world feeling resentment and reticence. After they get past a certain point they go with happiness, peace and contentment. . . .

> Why should a young mother die? Why should her eight children be left motherless? Why did not the Lord heal her of her malady?

> A young man died in the mission field, and people critically questioned: "Why did not the Lord protect this youth while he was doing proselyting work?"

> I wish I could answer these questions fully. Sometime we'll understand and be reconciled.

> The following conclusions are my own, and I take full responsibility for them.

> . . . Could the Lord have prevented these tragedies? The answer is yes. The Lord is omnipotent, with all power to control our lives, save us pain, prevent all accidents, drive all planes and cars, feed us, protect us, save us from labor, effort, sickness, even from death. But is that what you want? Would you shield your children from effort, from disappointments, temptations, sorrows, suffering? The basic gospel law is free agency. To force us to be careful or righteous would be to nullify that fundamental law, and growth would be impossible.

> Should we be protected always from hardship, pain, suffering, sacrifice, or labor? Should the Lord protect the righteous? Should he immediately punish the wicked? If growth comes from fun and ease and aimless irresponsibility, then why should we ever exert ourselves to work or learn or overcome? If success is measured by the years we live, then early death is failure and tragedy. If earth life is the ultimate, how can we justify death, even in old age? If we look at mortality as a complete existence, then pain, sorrow, failure, and short life could be a calamity. But if we look upon life as an eternal thing stretching far into the pre-earth past and on into the eternal post-death future, then all happenings may be put in proper perspective.

Is there not wisdom in his giving us trials that we might rise above them, responsibilities that we might achieve, work to harden our muscles, sorrows to try our souls? Are we not permitted temptations to test our strength, sickness that we might learn patience, death that we might be immortalized and glorified?

. . . If mortality be the perfect state, then death would be a frustration, but the gospel teaches us there is no tragedy in death, but only in sin. (*The Teachings of Spencer W. Kimball,* ed. Edward L. Kimball [Salt Lake City: Bookcraft, 1982], 38)

Gordon B. Hinckley:

The pain of death is swallowed up in the peace of eternal life. Of all the events of the chronicles of humanity, none is of such consequence as this. . . .

Whenever the cold hand of death strikes, there shines through the gloom and the darkness of that hour the triumphant figure of the Lord Jesus Christ, He, the Son of God, who by his matchless and eternal power overcame death. He is the Redeemer of the world. He gave His life for each of us. He took it up again and became the firstfruits of them that slept. He, as King of Kings, stands triumphant above all other kings. He, as the Omnipotent One, stands above all rulers. He is our comfort, our only true comfort, when the dark shroud of earthly night closes about us as the spirit departs the human form. (*Teachings of Gordon B. Hinckley* [Salt Lake City: Deseret Book, 1997], 153)

IDEAS FOR DAILY LIVING

In dealing with the death of someone dear or the prospect of our own death, remember that we have not been left alone in our sorrow. Heavenly Father has given us many things to help us heal:

1. Spiritual help—Strength to overcome the hurt can come only from God (see Alma 7:11–12). Pray for understanding (see Ps. 119:169), comfort (see Ps. 142), and strength (see 1 Chron. 16:11).

2. Time—Time becomes your healing friend. Even though we are weak mortals, as we humble ourselves before the Lord we become stronger and the pain gradually lessens (see Ps. 73:26; Ether 12:27).

3. Service—When you lose a loved one, fill your life with increased service to others. When we love and serve others we are filled with the pure love of Christ, which never faileth (see Moro. 7:45–46), and are encircled in the arms of His love (see 2 Ne. 1:15). Being busy in a good cause does wonders to heal and lift the spirit.

4. Togetherness—Having family and friends around at times of loss helps immensely. In our baptismal covenants, we promise to "bear one another's burdens, . . . mourn with those who mourn; . . . and comfort those that stand in need of comfort" (see Mosiah 18:8–9). We can take comfort and hope in this community of the gospel where people will stand by us and strengthen us with their faith.

5. Renewal—Come to an understanding of the literal resurrection of mankind. This will fill your heart and mind with hope (see Moro. 7:41). Don't look back in sorrow on death, but forward to a future time of reuniting. The human spirit continues; death is not the final chapter of life, but a necessary experience in the flow of life.

6. Empathy—When helping others deal with death, be empathetic, sensitive, and caring, and above all, be there when needed (see D&C 108:7).

7. **Preparation**—Prepare your loved ones for the time when you will pass away. Keep a journal in which you record the positive, uplifting things in your life. Build relationships of love filled with memories that will comfort those you leave behind.

8. **Commitment**—Live each day, each moment, with a commitment to doing the very best you can (see D&C 4:2). We do not know when our opportunity to make a difference in life will be interrupted.

ILLUSTRATIONS FOR OUR TIMES

President Heber J. Grant reveals how his young daughter was able to receive peace from the Lord upon the death of her mother.

The Will of the Lord

I was thoroughly convinced in my own mind and in my own heart, when my first wife left me by death, that it was the will of the Lord that she should be called away. I bowed in humility at her death. The Lord saw fit upon that occasion to give to one of my little children a testimony that the death of her mother was the will of the Lord.

About one hour before my wife died, I called my children into her room and told them that their mother was dying and for them to bid her good-bye. One of the little girls, about twelve years of age, said to me: "Papa, I do not want my mamma to die. I have been with you in the hospital in San Francisco for six months; time and time again when mamma was in distress you [have] administered to her and she has been relieved of her pain and quietly gone to sleep. I want you to lay hands upon my mamma and heal her."

I told my little girl that we all had to die sometime, and that I felt assured in my heart that her mother's time had arrived. She and the rest of the children left the room.

I then knelt down by the bed of my wife (who by this time had lost consciousness) and I told the Lord I acknowledged His hand in life, in death, in joy, in sorrow, in prosperity, or adversity. I thanked Him for the knowledge I had that my wife belonged to me for all eternity, that the gospel of Jesus Christ had been restored, that I knew that by the power and authority of the Priesthood here on the earth that I could and would have my wife forever if I were only faithful as she had been. But I told the Lord that I lacked the strength to have my wife die and to have it affect the faith of my little children in the ordinances of the gospel of Jesus Christ; and I supplicated the Lord with all the strength that I possessed, that He would give to that little girl of mine a knowledge that it was His mind and His will that her mamma should die.

Within an hour my wife passed away, and I called the children back into the room. My little boy about five and a half or six years of age was weeping bitterly, and the little girl twelve years of age took him in her arms and said: "Do not weep, do not cry, Heber; since we went out of this room the voice of the Lord from heaven has said to me, 'In the death of your mamma the will of the Lord shall be done.'"

Tell me, my friends, that I do not know that God hears and answers prayers! Tell me that I do not know that in the hour of adversity the Latter-day Saints are comforted and blessed and consoled as no other people are! (Heber J. Grant, *Gospel Standards* [Salt Lake City: Deseret Book, 1981] 360–61)

SUMMARY

Everyone has been affected by death. When those who have lived a good, long life face death, they leave a sense of celebration of a life well lived. Our hearts seem to ache more for those who die in their youth because their lives are seemingly unfulfilled. Remember, with our finite minds we cannot see all the elements of the full picture of life. Tragic accidents and diseases seem difficult as we are haunted by the questions: Why? Why now? What could I have done? These questions bring us only negative feelings and memories of heartache, and lengthen the time for healing. Death hopefully brings one closer to God, expands our appreciation for the life of the deceased, and increases our commitment to better our own lives, as well as the lives of our families. We want to live worthy of the promises in our temple covenants, so that the love and relationships here will not end in death.

DESIRE

To desire is to wish for something earnestly, or to crave for a goal or object. Desire is often called the mother of change. It is the motivation from within. Its power can be seen in the lives of many successful and unsuccessful people—all depending upon their desires. The question in life is: How do you create righteous desires and keep them alive?

THE SCRIPTURES TEACH US

JST, Matthew 6:33. *Wherefore, seek not the things of this world but seek ye first to build up the kingdom of God, and to establish his righteousness, and all these things shall be added unto you.*

Our desires should be prioritized according to the principles of the gospel of Jesus Christ.

3 Nephi 14:7. *Ask, and it shall be given unto you; seek, and ye shall find; knock, and it shall be opened unto you.*

When we truly desire, we will take action. We will ask, we will seek, we will knock, and the Lord will answer us. The Lord is pleased with the righteous desires of our hearts and will grant them in His own way and in His own time.

Doctrine and Covenants 6:6–7. *Now, as you have asked, behold, I say unto you, keep my commandments, and seek to bring forth and establish the cause of Zion; Seek not for riches but for wisdom, and behold, the mysteries of God shall be unfolded unto you, and then shall you be made rich. Behold, he that hath eternal life is rich.*

When our desires are righteous, we will seek the cause of Zion and the wisdom of God, for they are eternal and of lasting value. Of all the gifts of our Heavenly Father that we could desire, eternal life is the greatest.

MODERN PROPHETS SPEAK

Russell M. Nelson:
> Elder Petersen addressed throngs assembled at the Mount of the Beatitudes to hear his discourse on the Sermon on the Mount. After he recited "Blessed are they which do hunger and thirst after

righteousness," he departed from the biblical text and pleaded this question: "Do you know what it is to be really hungry? Do you know what it is to really be thirsty? Do you desire righteousness as you would desire food under extreme conditions or drink under extreme conditions? [The Savior] expects us to literally hunger and thirst after righteousness and seek it with all our hearts!" (*The Power within Us* [Salt Lake City: Deseret Book, 1988], 21)

Dallin H. Oaks:

The scriptures say that when we desire righteousness our "heart is right" with God. The Psalmist condemned the people of ancient Israel because "their heart was not right with [God]" (Psalms 78:37). When King Solomon blessed the people at the dedication of the temple, he concluded with these words: "Let your heart therefore be perfect with the Lord our God, to walk in his statutes, and to keep his commandments, as at this day" (1 Kings 8:61). (*Pure in Heart* [Salt Lake City: Bookcraft, 1988], 4)

IDEAS FOR DAILY LIVING

Here are three strategies for creating and maintaining righteous desires:

1. Lay the right foundation.

- *Take stock*—We should regularly take an inventory of our lives. What is our heart set on now? What do we want to have happen? What do we enjoy and why? From these questions we can make a list of righteous and positive desires and how we want to work toward these goals. For example, if we want to develop charity, we will seek ways we can be kinder to others, get involved in service projects, pray to develop the attribute (see Moro. 7:45), and other such goals. We must recognize the value of each good desire and prioritize the desires so that we can focus most on those that will help us best realize our goals.
- *Create a positive environment*—We can adjust our environment at home and at work so that it reinforces good desires. By surrounding ourselves with objects that remind us of positive goals and with the kinds of people who are constructive, helpful, and upbeat, we are more likely to maintain our focus on these desires and be more successful.
- *Prepare our minds for success*—Remember, as we think in our hearts, our desires are created, and so we become (see Prov. 23:7). Understanding how desire creates outcome makes us dwell on the good. Know that what we desire and dwell on will come to pass. Therefore, be wise about what we allow our minds to think about.
- *Have an eye single to the glory of God*—When we seek the glory of God, we will be filled with light and, needless to say, our desires will be righteous (see D&C 88:67).

2. Exercise positive desires on a daily basis.

- *Be consistent*—Think positive thoughts, pray for positive thoughts, say positive things, sing positive songs, make positive plans, and be with positive people (see Alma 37:36).
- *Go to positive places*—Spend time in nature, in great museums, in places of worship, in community service projects—anyplace that will reinforce good and noble desires.
- *Be active*—Be actively engaged in positive things, rather than predominantly passive (see D&C 58:27–28). Let us limit our idle time with television, empty music, needless computer games, and poor literature. Idleness, along with procrastination, undermines and destroys desire (see 1 Tim. 5:13; Alma 34:33; Alma 38:13).
- *Help others*—Teach others to have the best desires. Make an environment of positive momentum for all our loved ones and colleagues. They, in turn, will help keep us upbeat. It's a self-reinforcing

cycle. As we strengthen other peoples' resolve to do and seek better, our own desire to do the same will be increased.

- *Take charge of your inner life*—Practice affirmative self-talk. Keeping the desire alive is as important as generating the desire in the first place.
- *Reward yourself*—Have a clear view of the positive outcomes of your good desires. Where possible and appropriate, have a commensurate reward or personal acknowledgment to help keep the desire alive. Remember that to keep the end result in mind adds forward motion to your plans.

3. Nip negative desires in the bud.

- *Shift gears*—When you feel the presence of negative desires, make the choice to shift your mind to your important lifelong objectives. Hum a happy tune; think of your obligations to loved ones; fill your heart with renewed commitment.
- *Do a switch*—Replace the allure of unwholesome outcomes with thoughts of the more desirable consequences to your positive goals, and then use that forward vision to motivate yourself to do the daily actions that will make the goals come true.
- *Stoke the fires*—If the good desire wanes, stop and evaluate and determine the cause, then rekindle the fire within. Recommit to your desires by setting new goals and redoubling your efforts.

ILLUSTRATIONS FOR OUR TIMES

Consider in the following story how righteous desire led one man and his family to the truth.

Story of a Military Chaplain

I remember the story of one of our LDS chaplains, a man of great faith, devotion, and courage. For a year or more he had been in the central highlands of South Vietnam during the war there some 30 years ago. He had been where the fighting was bitter and the losses as tragic as in any area of Vietnam. On two occasions he was wounded. He saw a tragically large percentage of his brigade become casualties, many of them killed in action. The men of his unit loved and respected him. His superior officers honored him.

He was not always a member of this Church. As a boy in the southern U.S. he grew up in a religious home where the Bible was read and where the family attended the little church of the community. He desired the gift of the Holy Ghost of which he had read in the scriptures but was told that it was not available. The desire never left him. He grew to manhood. He served in the U.S. Army. He searched but never found the thing he most wanted. Between military enlistments, he became a prison guard. While sitting in the gun tower of a California prison, he meditated on his own deficiencies and prayed to the Lord that he might receive the Holy Ghost and satisfy the hunger which he felt in his soul. That hunger had not been fully satisfied with sermons to which he had listened.

One day two young men knocked at his door. His wife invited them to return when her husband would be at home. These two young men taught that family by the Holy Spirit. In two and a half weeks they were baptized. I have heard this man testify to the effect that as he was taught by the power of the Holy Spirit, he was edified and rejoiced with those who taught him. Out of that marvelous beginning, with the gift of the Holy Ghost, came a shedding forth of light and truth that gave peace to the dying, comfort to the bereaved, blessings to the wounded, courage to the timid, and faith to those who had scoffed. Sweet are the fruits of teaching done under the inspiration of the Holy Spirit. They feed the spirit and nourish the soul. (Gordon B. Hinckley, "Feed the Spirit, Nourish the Soul," *Ensign,* October 1998, 2)

SUMMARY

If all would have the desire to fulfill their important eternal roles within the great plan of happiness, life would be magnificent. The problem is that worldly pressure and goals get our attention, hence our desires are channeled toward them. Thoughts dwelt upon germinate desires, which start us on the path to achieving our goals. The question should echo in our soul: *What* do we desire?—for eventually our thoughts and desires will take us there. But we must also consider, will our desires take us to happiness? As we answer that question, let us remember the counsel of the Lord to Hyrum Smith, given through his brother, the Prophet Joseph: "Verily, verily, I say unto you, I will impart unto you of my Spirit, which shall enlighten your mind, which shall fill your soul with joy; And then shall ye know, or by this shall you know, all things whatsoever you desire of me, which are pertaining unto things of righteousness, in faith believing in me that you shall receive" (D&C 11:13–14).

DISCIPLESHIP

As baptized members and followers of the Lord Jesus Christ, we are His disciples. We have a belief and testimony of the doctrines and teachings of the gospel of Jesus Christ and of the Church and kingdom of God here upon the earth. We seek to be obedient to the commandments, to stand as witnesses at all times and in all places (see Mosiah 18:8–9), and to share the gospel with all mankind (see Morm. 9:22). We seek to become like Him (see 3 Ne. 27:27). We truly become His disciples as we love and serve our fellowman (see John 13:34–35) and seek always to do the will of God.

THE SCRIPTURES TEACH US

John 13:34–35. *A new commandment I give unto you, That ye love one another; as I have loved you, that ye also love one another. By this shall all men know that ye are my disciples, if ye have love one to another.*

Love, the great commandment, is truly a symbol of one's discipleship of the Lord Jesus Christ. Remember that love is the most righteous motive for all that is good, and it is expressed through service.

Doctrine and Covenants 41:5. *He that receiveth my law and doeth it, the same is my disciple; and he that saith he receiveth it and doeth it not, the same is not my disciple, and shall be cast out from among you.*

Discipleship requires action. We must be doers of the word and not hearers only (see James 1:22).

Doctrine and Covenants 103:28. *And whoso is not willing to lay down his life for my sake is not my disciple.*

True discipleship requires total and complete sacrifice of all things. While we may never be called upon to die for the gospel, as Christ's disciples, we are called upon to live for it.

MODERN PROPHETS SPEAK

Bruce R. McConkie:

> Scriptural tests establishing true discipleship include: 1. Believing the true doctrines of Christ (Ether 4:10–12); 2. Obeying the principles of the gospel (John 8:31); 3. Having "love one to another" (John 13:35); 4. Accepting the message and aiding the work of the missionaries (D&C 84:87–91); and 5. Bringing forth works of righteousness (John 15:4–8.) (*Mormon Doctrine,* 2nd ed. [Salt Lake City: Bookcraft, 1966], 198)

Neal A. Maxwell:

> Heavenly power can be accessed only by those who are Christlike; it is a power whose continued availability is maintained by meekness along with the other virtues. Nor can we have the loving empathy or understanding mercy necessary for true discipleship without meekness. (*Meek and Lowly* [Salt Lake City: Deseret Book, 1987], 85)

> Discipleship is not simply surviving and enduring; discipleship is a pressing forward, a creative Christianity. Discipleship does not wait to be acted upon, but instead acts upon men and circumstances to make things better. . . .

> True discipleship is for volunteers only. Only volunteers will trust the Guide sufficiently to follow Him in the dangerous ascent which only He can lead. (*The Neal A. Maxwell Quote Book,* ed. Cory H. Maxwell [Salt Lake City: Bookcraft, 1997], 91)

IDEAS FOR DAILY LIVING

Here are seven ideas to help us be true disciples of the Lord Jesus Christ:

1. Express our love—Let us express love in a pure and meaningful way to all those with whom we come in contact.
- Do a good deed (see Mosiah 5:15).
- Show empathy and concern through service (see Mosiah 18:8–9).
- Share the gospel as directed by the Spirit (see 3 Nephi 5:13).
- Listen to others—someone always needs a listening ear (see 1 Pet. 3:1–8).

2. Set a good example.
  Our good works not only help others, but glorify God (see 3 Ne. 12:16).
- Remember that someone is always watching (see 3 Ne. 15:12; 27:21).
- What we are and do speak more powerfully than our words (see Alma 39:11).

3. Share the gospel.
- Pray for those who do not know God (see Alma 6:6).
- Set a date to have someone taught the gospel (see D&C 88:81; 123:12).
- Go on splits with the full-time missionaries.
- Open your mouth. Start a friendly conversation; place a copy of the Book of Mormon; hand out a pass-along card or introduce someone to the Church with a video, TV program, or other appropriate activity in their area (see D&C 33:8–11).
- Contribute to the missionary fund.

4. As in all things, persevere in living the gospel.
- Search the scriptures (see 2 Ne. 32:3; D&C 84:43–45).
- Fast and pray to do the will of the Father (see D&C 10:5; 19:38; 32:4; 61:39; 88:126; 90:21).
- Keep the commandments (see John 14:15; D&C 93:1).

5. Magnify our callings.
- Learn your duty (see D&C 107:99–100)
- Be accountable for your responsibilities (see Jacob 1:19; 2:2).

6. Follow the Spirit.
- Yield to the enticings of the Spirit (see Mosiah 3:19).
- Yield your heart to God (see Hel. 3:35).

7. Endure to the end.
- Persevere (see Eph. 6:18).
- Never give up (see 2 Ne. 31:20).
- Dedicate and devote everything we can to the Lord (see Hel. 10:4–5; D&C 4:2).

ILLUSTRATIONS FOR OUR TIMES

Richard J. Allen tells us how Elder Neal A Maxwell's humble acceptance of his failing health due to leukemia stands as an example of faithful discipleship.

The Higher Perspective

In the first of the worldwide priesthood training sessions conducted by satellite on January 11, 2003, Elder Neal A. Maxwell taught a precious lesson in discipleship when recounting his challenges with leukemia. As he spoke on the subject of revelation and how the "mind and heart, intellect and feeling" are to be in tune with the Spirit, he shared with the audience that he had pleaded one day with the Lord concerning matters of health and continued service in the kingdom. He was concerned that due to his failing health he could not serve the Savior of His people as an effective disciple. As Elder Maxwell recounted it, the answer came to him in a thirteen-word statement: "I have given you leukemia that you might teach my people with authenticity." What a transcendent expression concerning the nature of true discipleship and how each of us—despite the adversities of life placed in our pathway of progress—can rise to all occasions for service in the spirit of humility and acceptance, always viewing things from a higher, more spiritual perspective.

—Richard J. Allen

SUMMARY

Devoted followers of the Lord Jesus Christ are true disciples. The sacrifice is great; the reward is eternal life. We live His doctrine and precepts. We preach and teach His word and His gospel. We all can be His true disciples. There is no comparison by title, position, or station; there is no competition with others. There is only one question: Do we do the will of God?

DUTY

When one assumes or agrees to assume a responsibility, it becomes one's duty to follow through. Often duties are simply inherent within the office you occupy or the role you play. There are often moral and legal issues in doing one's duty. In the Scout Oath, the words "On my honor I will do my best to do my duty to God and my country" cast a guiding light over the full range of our human endeavor. These words should echo in our hearts and remind us of our duties at home, at school, in the workplace, in the Church, and throughout all of society. We, as a Christian people, have many rights and many duties to uphold. The family and the workplace would be so much better if all people would simply do their duty. Honoring one's duty is an enduring principle upon which society as a whole—and family life in particular—must be based.

THE SCRIPTURES TEACH US

Ecclesiastes 12:13. *Let us hear the conclusion of the whole matter: Fear God, and keep his commandments: for this is the whole duty of man.*

When we reverence our Heavenly Father and keep His commandments, we are doing our duty in all things. You cannot separate doing your duty at work or at home from living the gospel of Jesus Christ. Performing your duty with honor in any venue is honoring your integrity. It is using your time wisely; it is gaining more knowledge; it is blessing others.

Moroni 9:6. *And now, my beloved son, notwithstanding their hardness, let us labor diligently; for if we should cease to labor, we should be brought under condemnation; for we have a labor to perform whilst in this tabernacle of clay, that we may conquer the enemy of all righteousness, and rest our souls in the kingdom of God.*

Things were not going well at the time for Mormon and Moroni in regard to helping the Nephites repent and keep the commandments. In this verse we learn a transcending truth: regardless of the situation we find ourselves in, we all have duties relating to our different roles. We are duty bound to do our best at all times and in all things lest we be brought under condemnation. We owe it to God, our fellowmen, and ourselves to do our best.

MODERN PROPHETS SPEAK

Ezra Taft Benson:

> We have many responsibilities, and a person cannot expect the full blessings of the kind Providence if he neglects any major duty. A man has duties to his church, to his home, to his country, and to his profession or job. . . .

> Our great benefactor, Brigham Young, understood the basic principle that you cannot help a man permanently by doing for him what he could do and should do for himself. Shrink not from duty as it is made known. Accept responsibility. Be grateful for work. Hesitate not to do your full share of it. (*The Teachings of Ezra Taft Benson* [Salt Lake City: Bookcraft, 1988], 292, 293)

Joseph F. Smith:

> If I do my duty, according to my understanding of the requirements that the Lord has made of me, then I ought to have a conscience void of offense; I ought to have satisfaction in my soul, in the consciousness that I have simply done my duty as I understand it, and I will risk the consequences. With me it is a matter between me and the Lord; so it is with every one of us. (*Gospel Doctrine: Selections from the Sermons and Writings of Joseph F. Smith,* comp. John A. Widtsoe [Salt Lake City: Deseret Book, 1939], 249)

IDEAS FOR DAILY LIVING

Here are three strategies to help us do our duties in all aspects of life:

1. Start with success in mind.

- *Recognition*—Accept the principle of duty as a sacred part of your life. Recognize the various duties within your life and commit to making a plan to do them.
- *Alignment*—Commit only to those tasks that align with your principles and values.
- *Team work*—Involve your family and loved ones in your commitments so that they, too, can be part of the decision and the performance. A key element in following through is to keep in mind how your performance will affect the lives of others.
- *Capacity*—Do not commit beyond your capacity or resources.
- *Balance*—What are our greatest duties? To God, to family, to self, to the community, to the nation. We cannot perform well our duty to family or country without performing well our duty to God. Build duty into all aspects of your life: family, professional, personal, spiritual. Keep balance in your commitments.
- *Honor*—Make your word your fortress. When you give your word, keep it. Honor is the partner of duty. When you commit, honestly do your best to fulfill the commitment.

2. Have a plan for honoring your duties.

- *Total commitment*—When you give your word, you also commit your resources. Enlist all available resources to do your duty—including your time, talents, and material goods.
- *Training*—When you accept a responsibility, insist on and obtain proper training and instruction, but remember it is your responsibility to learn your duty.
- *Management*—Make a timeline for fulfilling your duty. Divide things into daily performance tasks. Keep to your schedule or routine so you will not be overwhelmed.
- *Measurement*—Build measurement into assignments. Create agreement and understanding as to how your performance will be evaluated. When possible, make target dates for completion, with intermediate checkpoints to stay on track.
- *Motivation*—Come to terms with motivation. Duty is motivated by a variety of influences, including love, the hope for reward, or fear. Love is the highest form of motivation. Rewards should be appropriate and in keeping with the natural consequences of the behavior. Fear is often induced by the leader, and it is sometimes also generated by the individual out of anxiety for failure. Threats of punishment have only short-term effect and are not nearly as powerful as the motive of love. We should avoid the motive of fear at all costs. Always remember that self-motivation in regard to one's duty is best.

3. Do your duty to teach duty to others.

- *Delegation*—In giving assignments to others, include quality criteria and a performance schedule. Always arrange for follow-up. Build accountability into the duty process.

- *Kindness*—Teach others the importance of duty through persuasion and kindness. Give regular assignments to children and younger workers. Carefully guide them to success. As you inspire others to do their duties, it is important to remember that persuasion with love is essential.

ILLUSTRATIONS FOR OUR TIMES

President Thomas S. Monson relates a story of how a pair of home teachers faithfully fulfilled their duty, thus greatly blessing the life of a German brother.

Duty Calls

Should we feel [any] assignment too arduous or time-consuming, let me share with you the experience of a faithful home teacher and his companion in what was then East Germany.

Brother Johann Denndorfer had been converted to the Church in Germany, and following World War II, he found himself virtually a prisoner in his own land—the land of Hungary in the city of Debrecen. How he wanted to visit the temple! How he desired to receive his spiritual blessings! Request after request to journey to the temple in Switzerland had been denied, and he almost despaired. Then his home teacher visited. Brother Walter Krause went from the northeastern portion of Germany all the way to Hungary. He had said to his home teaching companion, "Would you like to go home teaching with me this week?"

His companion said, "When will we leave?"

"Tomorrow," replied Brother Krause.

"When will we come back?" asked the companion.

"Oh, in about a week—if we get back then!"

And away they went to visit Brother Denndorfer. He had not had home teachers since before the war. Now, when he saw the servants of the Lord, he was overwhelmed. He did not shake hands with them; rather, he went to his bedroom and took from a secret hiding place his tithing that he had saved from the day he became a member of the Church and returned to Hungary. He presented the tithing to his home teachers and said: "Now I am current with the Lord. Now I feel worthy to shake the hands of servants of the Lord!"

Brother Krause asked him about his desire to attend the temple in Switzerland. Brother Denndorfer said: "It's no use. I have tried and tried. The government has even confiscated my Church books, my greatest treasure."

Brother Krause, a patriarch, provided Brother Denndorfer with a patriarchal blessing. At the conclusion of the blessing, he said to Brother Denndorfer, "Approach the government again about going to Switzerland." And Brother Denndorfer submitted the request once again to the authorities. This time approval came, and with joy Brother Denndorfer went to the Swiss Temple and stayed a month. He received his own endowment, his deceased wife was sealed to him, and he was able to accomplish the work for hundreds of his ancestors. He returned to his home renewed in body and in spirit. (Thomas S. Monson, "Duty Calls," *Ensign,* May 1996, 43)

SUMMARY

As we come to realize the importance of doing our duty in our lives, we begin to realize a great number of associated benefits: growth, order, self-respect, self-confidence, service, greater happiness. If duty is simply modified behavior without principle and without focus, we can never find the joy in our work. All duties, in their most unlimited sense of being honorable undertakings and worthy acts of performance, ultimately bless lives—especially the life of the one doing the duty.

EDUCATION

This topic has been written with the young student in mind. Gaining knowledge and skill through education should be the goal for everyone, but especially for the rising generation. The lack of formal education limits one's choices by restricting the acquisition of knowledge and skills. Education allows one to choose a rewarding occupation based upon preferences and aptitudes. In today's society one's capacity to provide financially is directly tied the amount of education one receives.

Nevertheless, income should not be the sole motivating force behind our education, since learning in general opens the door to a myriad of opportunities in the quest for a fulfilling, rewarding, and productive life. It expands the mind, feeds the soul, and provides enjoyment and excitement for life. There is still so much to learn about God, His children, and all of creation.

THE SCRIPTURES TEACH US

2 Nephi 28:30. *For behold, thus saith the Lord God: I will give unto the children of men line upon line, precept upon precept, here a little and there a little; and blessed are those who hearken unto my precepts, and lend an ear unto my counsel, for they shall learn wisdom; for unto him that receiveth I will give more; and from them that shall say, We have enough, from them shall be taken away even that which they have.*

Learning is a process that builds on each concept we internalize. We are encouraged to learn by study and by faith (see D&C 88:118). We are to seek knowledge in many things, especially an understanding of different peoples and their countries so that we can better prepare for the building up of the kingdom of God through missionary labors (see D&C 93:53).

2 Nephi 9:29. *But to be learned is good if they hearken unto the counsels of God.*

Let us remember to balance secular education with gospel learning. All worthy learning is a reflection of the light and truth imbued in us through the Creator. Learning isolated unto itself stands in risk of fostering pride; learning in a spirit of gratitude to our Father in Heaven, and in accordance with principles of truth, is ennobling.

Alma 37:35. *O, remember, my son, and learn wisdom in thy youth; yea, learn in thy youth to keep the commandments of God.*

The more education we receive, and the earlier we receive it, the better off we will be. We should learn and incorporate the gospel as early in life as we can to stay near our Savior and avoid sin. We are also admonished to help our children learn in their youth, and especially to educate them to keep the commandments (see D&C 68:25–28).

Doctrine and Covenants 88:118. *And as all have not faith, seek ye diligently and teach one another words of wisdom; yea, seek ye out of the best books words of wisdom; seek learning, even by study and also by faith.*

We are a church of learners and teachers; we are all called to teach one another, and so must seek to better understand truth. The Lord has provided us with scriptures, words of the prophets, as well as a world of great literature and textbooks, from which to gain knowledge. It is our job to seek this knowledge from all good sources (see A of F 1:13) through faith, that we can learn what God has to teach us and what the Holy Ghost can testify of (see Moro. 10:5).

Doctrine and Covenants 93:36–37. *The glory of God is intelligence, or, in other words, light and truth. Light and truth forsake that evil one.*

As we seek to become like our Savior and Heavenly Father, let us aspire to partake of Their wisdom and glory— that is, Their divine intelligence. Light and truth will educate us eternally and give us power to overcome evil.

MODERN PROPHETS SPEAK

Ezra Taft Benson:
> Knowledge is power, but the most vital and important knowledge is a knowledge of God—that He lives, that we are His children, that He loves us, that we are created in His image, that we can in faith pray to Him and receive strength and inspiration in time of need.
>
> Such knowledge is priceless. True, "man is saved no faster than he gains knowledge" (*Teachings of the Prophet Joseph Smith,* p. 217). Knowledge of what? Knowledge of God! Knowledge of His purpose and plans for the welfare, blessing, and eternal exaltation of us, His children. All useful knowledge is of value. The seeking of such knowledge is, therefore, commendable and rewarding. But in all of our searching for truth, we must remember that the knowledge of God, our Father, and His plans for us, His children, is of supreme importance. (*The Teachings of Ezra Taft Benson* [Salt Lake City: Bookcraft, 1988], 294)

Gordon B. Hinckley:
> Each day we are made increasingly aware of the fact that life is more than science and mathematics, more than history and literature. There is need for another education, without which the substance of our secular learning may lead only to our destruction. I refer to the education of the heart, of the conscience, of the character, of the spirit—these indefinable aspects of our personalities which determine so certainly what we are and what we do in our relationships one with another. (*Teachings of Gordon B. Hinckley* [Salt Lake City: Deseret Book, 1997], 167–68)
>
> Be smart about training your minds and hands for the future. Each of you is a member of The Church of Jesus Christ of Latter-day Saints. . . . You have an obligation to make the most of your life. Plan now for all the education you can get, and then work to bring to pass a fulfillment of that plan. . . .

I am not suggesting that all of you should become professional men. What I am suggesting is this: whatever you choose to do, train for it. Qualify yourselves. Take advantage of the experience and learning of those who have gone before you in whatever field you choose. Education is a shortcut to proficiency. It makes it possible to leapfrog over the mistakes of the past. . . .

Begin early in exposing children to books. The mother who fails to read to her small children does a disservice to them and a disservice to herself. It takes time, yes, much of it. It takes self-discipline. It takes organizing and budgeting the minutes and hours of the day. But it will never be a bore as you watch young minds come to know characters, expressions, and ideas. Good reading can become a love affair, far more fruitful in long term effects than many other activities in which children use their time. It has been estimated that "the average child on this continent has watched something like 8,000 hours of TV before he or she even starts school." A very large part of that is of questionable value.

Parents, work at the matter of creating an atmosphere in your homes. Let your children be exposed to great minds, great ideas, everlasting truth, and those things which will build and motivate for good. (*Teachings of Gordon B. Hinckley* [Salt Lake City: Deseret Book, 1997], 169)

IDEAS FOR DAILY LIVING

Here are four things to remember in seeking and gaining a meaningful education:

1. Keep your motivation high.

- *Increased financial security*—Derek Bok, former president of Harvard University, put it well: "If you think education is expensive, try ignorance." There is no greater place to invest your time, energy, and resources than in a meaningful education.
- *Enhanced communication skills*—In our world, so much depends on interpersonal skills, and a well-educated person is simply more comfortable with a wider range of people.
- *Staying up-to-date*—The constant influx of knowledge in our time means that education on a continuing basis is the only way you can succeed.
- *Self-respect*—It is more than just a case of earning more money; education will add depth and breadth to your life. Do your best in school. Help your children succeed in school. You will give them—and yourself—the gift of self-respect.
- *Quality of life*—"It's learning what to do with a living after you earn it that counts" (Abraham Lincoln).

2. Have an educational strategy in mind and follow it.

- *Develop good study and learning habits.*
  Study in a place where distractions are minimal.
  Read lecture material prior to the teacher's lecture.
  Take good notes.
  Have a study partner or study group.
  Make a timeline for completing assignments.
  Take a memory course, which will help in all of your classes.
  Budget your time wisely so that each subject is covered.
  In preparation for tests be sure you cover the teacher's prescribed material.
- *Follow your preferences*—Do those worthwhile and noble things that you love to do, and build the best education around them.

- *Be practical*—It is not just facts and figures that matter, but rather it is the wise and judicious use of information to bless lives that really counts.
- *Balance*—You don't need to give up *all* your television and recreation time—but make education a top priority. Don't forget your spiritual education.
- *Preparation*—Prepare well for college or other forms of higher learning and training. Research what you need to do to qualify for these opportunities, and then follow through.
- *Informal learning*—There is also continuing, informal education that is important—networking with others, newspapers, books, the internet, internships, non-credit courses, seminars, and workshops.

3. Do it for others as well.
- *Consequences*—Your education has consequences for your children, for your whole family, for the community. Therefore, it's not just for you that you are educated. Remember your loved ones.
- *Responsibility*—Take responsibility for the education of your children. Make education a family goal.

4. Never give up.
- *Be persistent*—Whatever you do, never quit high school. It will plague you forever. And never quit learning. "The education of a man is never completed until he dies" (Robert E. Lee).

5. Always seek gospel knowledge.
- *We cannot be saved in ignorance*—Let us seek the word of God in all that we do. This is the knowledge that saves our souls if we will follow the counsel of the Lord (see D&C 131:6).
- *Never sacrifice the testimony of God to gain secular knowledge*—Let us never put our trust in the arm of flesh and the reasoning of the secular world. The world's knowledge is always in flux, whereas the laws of God are eternal verities (see 2 Ne. 9:28–29).

ILLUSTRATIONS FOR OUR TIMES

This story recounts a time in the author's life when he discovered that the majority of troubled youth in his city were illiterate, and how this experience impressed upon him the great value of education.

The Root Cause

I was serving on the children and youth committee for our city years ago. We, like other cities, had concerns for the well-being of our youth. Dropouts from high school were on the rise, delinquency was increasing, and truancy and misguided behavior in school were affecting too many children. We had a problem. We enlisted PTA help. Parents became not only concerned but also highly involved. Things began to change. We started to help the troubled youth. When they knew we cared, it affected their desire and behavior in a positive way. It was surprising the change, but it was wonderful. As we began to receive feedback from the youth, we soon realized a common denominator among all the troubled and delinquent youth—more than 80 percent of them had difficulty in reading. They could not read! That was it. That was the root cause. Their education was so limited that they could not and would not "fit in" with their peers. Low self-esteem and self-confidence had lead them to withdraw. They sought acceptance in gangs. Birds of a feather really do flock together. How could all this start? Education gives freedom, increases abilities, and gives self-confidence and self-esteem. Remember, don't shortchange yourself or your family—help everyone achieve in life by getting a good education.

—Ed J. Pinegar

* * *

The following story discusses how knowledge is of little value until it is helpfully and wisely applied.

The Hidden Wisdom

It began as a routine statement about education but ended as a life-changing demonstration about wisdom. The presenter, a representative of one of the large publishing houses in America, stood on the stage before a vast audience of educators and writers. Behind him was a gigantic banner than stretched from wall to wall, emblazoned with the words "Education is the Acquisition of Knowledge." As he intoned his message about acquiring learning, it seemed that he was preaching to the choir, restating the age-old message about the need for expanding one's inventory of facts and figures. The audience was on the verge of getting sleepy.

But then, just at the right moment, he raised the question about whether his thesis, in fact, was really true. That caught our attention. At the same time, he did something uncommon. He walked back to the banner and pointed out a fold midway in the material. With the help of several assistants, he then caused this fold to be opened up, revealing the hidden text contained within. Now the expanded statement read: "Education is the acquisition of the art of the utilization of knowledge." The audience gasped at the implication. The statement, a quote from the British philosopher Alfred North Whitehead, was a clear reminder that education for its own sake, without application, was a shallow exercise. What truly counts is learning that can profitably be applied to good ends.

I will never forget that demonstration in applied learning. In a memorable way it reminded me (and all of the other attendees at the conference) that knowledge, isolated unto itself, is of little value. Only when learning is turned to helpful and wise applications of service can it be deemed useful. In fact, applied learning leads, in time, to that most desirable quality—wisdom. It was King Benjamin who stated the case most succinctly: "And behold, I tell you these things that ye may learn wisdom; that ye may learn that when ye are in the service of your fellow beings ye are only in the service of your God" (Mosiah 2:17). The paragon and prototype of this kind of applied learning was the Savior Himself, whom Isaiah characterized in this manner: "And the Spirit of the Lord shall rest upon him, the spirit of wisdom and understanding, the spirit of counsel and might, the spirit of knowledge and of the fear of the Lord" (2 Ne. 21: 2). It is this kind of proactive and goal-centered learning that constitutes wisdom, concerning which Solomon assured us: "Happy is the man that findeth wisdom, and the man that getteth understanding" (Prov. 3:13).

—Richard J. Allen

SUMMARY

The ideas and suggestions in this article are designed to help you and your children succeed in acquiring more education—in school, in college, in the workforce, and in personal study. Society has learned by sad experience that illiteracy and poor school performance are often a common denominator for juvenile delinquency. In light of this, it is important to create an atmosphere of learning in the home. Let us strive to make it exciting and rewarding to learn. One of the most noble things a parent can do to bless the life of a child is to help him or her have a desire to learn. Education in all of its ramifications should ultimately be the quest for truth. The gospel encompasses all truth; understanding and appreciating knowledge will help us live a Christlike life and lead us back into the presence of our Heavenly Father.

ENDURING TO THE END

Enduring to the end is the process of continuing on the straight and narrow course, serving God and our fellowmen to the end of our mortal lives. By enduring, we are persistent in doing our duty with unwavering steadfastness. We walk in the ways of the Lord by keeping the commandments. Enduring to the end is proof of our faith and confirmation of the depth of our conversion to the gospel of Jesus Christ. This becomes the true test of life: Will we endure to the end?

THE SCRIPTURES TEACH US

Matthew 24:13. *But he that shall endure unto the end, the same shall be saved.*

Salvation and exaltation are the reward for all those who endure to the end. If we do not endure to the end we are damned (see 2 Ne. 9:24).

2 Nephi 31:20. *Wherefore, ye must press forward with a steadfastness in Christ, having a perfect brightness of hope, and a love of God and of all men. Wherefore, if ye shall press forward, feasting upon the word of Christ, and endure to the end, behold, thus saith the Father: Ye shall have eternal life.*

Enduring with a "steadfastness in Christ" means we remain faithful to our covenants with the Lord, and stay active in His Church and His gospel. To endure we should continue with hope, love, and feasting upon the word of God. This will give us power to endure to the end. We will seek the cause of Zion, publish peace, and be lifted up at the last day (see 1 Ne. 13:37).

Alma 1:25. *Now this was a great trial to those that did stand fast in the faith; nevertheless, they were steadfast and immovable in keeping the commandments of God, and they bore with patience the persecution which was heaped upon them.*

Merely enduring is not enough. We must endure well by standing fast in the faith, being steadfast and immovable, abiding in patience even when persecution is upon us.

Doctrine and Covenants 127:4. *And again, verily thus saith the Lord: Let the work of my temple, and all the works which I have appointed unto you, be continued on and not cease; and let your diligence, and your perseverance, and patience, and your works be redoubled, and you shall in nowise lose your reward, saith the Lord of Hosts. And if they persecute you, so persecuted they the prophets and righteous men that were before you. For all this there is a reward in heaven.*

It is not enough to just go to church once, or participate in a family home evening once, or read the Book of Mormon once. We are to carry out the works of the Lord *unceasingly.* As Saints of the Most High God, our devotion is expressed in our diligence in keeping the commandments—even when persecution rages against us. We never give up, never give in, never give out.

MODERN PROPHETS SPEAK

Jeffrey R. Holland:

> Often one hears trite, sometimes consciously apologetic references to "enduring to the end" as an addition to the first principles and ordinances of the gospel. Nevertheless, the doctrine of faithful endurance is infinitely serious, and it is here [2 Ne. 31:15–16] declared to be a basic principle of the gospel by the God and Father of us all. "Enduring to the end" is an integral element in the doctrine of Christ, and without it, it would have been better not to have known him. (*Christ and the New Covenant: The Messianic Message of the Book of Mormon* [Salt Lake City: Deseret Book, 1997], 54)

> This is another "first principle" beyond the four usually listed, taught by the Father himself. Nephi wrote, "I heard a voice from the Father, saying: Yea, the words of my Beloved are true and faithful. He that endureth to the end, the same shall be saved." Nephi then added his own witness, saying, "And now, my beloved brethren, I know by this that unless a man shall endure to the end, in following the example of the Son of the living God, he cannot be saved." [2 Nephi 31:15–16.] (*Christ and the New Covenant: The Messianic Message of the Book of Mormon* [Salt Lake City: Deseret Book, 1997], 398)

Neal A. Maxwell:

> Enduring affliction is certainly part of enduring to the end, but the word enduring also means to last, to continue, and to remain (see 2 Nephi 33:9). This emphasis on staying the course appears at so many points in the scriptures (for examples, see D&C 20:29; 2 Nephi 9:24). We could scarcely become "finished" or "completed" if we did not finish and complete all of life's assigned course! (*Lord, Increase Our Faith* [Salt Lake City: Bookcraft, 1994], 45)

Joseph B. Wirthlin:

> I know that each of us has much to do. Sometimes we feel overwhelmed by the tasks we face. But if we keep our priorities in order, we can accomplish all that we should. We can endure to the end regardless of temptations, problems, and challenges. Those who remain faithful will receive God's greatest blessing—eternal life—and the privilege of living with our Heavenly Father and his Beloved Son in the celestial kingdom. (*Ensign,* Nov., 1990, 64)

Marion G. Romney:

> When earth life is over, and things appear in their true perspective, we shall more clearly see . . . that the fruits of the gospel are the only objectives worthy of life's full effort. (Conference Report, October 1949, 39)

IDEAS FOR DAILY LIVING

Here are four ideas to help us endure to the end:

1. Maintain your vision of the plan of happiness.
- *Understand the rewards*—Knowing the rewards for keeping the commandments and enduring well will keep us focused on living the gospel (see D&C 14:7).
- *Understand the doctrine*—When we understand and appreciate the saving principles and ordinances, we will want to partake of them and keep them (see 1 Ne. 16:29).

- *Keep service as the center of our mission*—The true purpose of life is not in the accumulation of things, but in serving God and our fellowmen to the end of our mortal lives (see Mosiah 18:13).
- *Transcend adversity*—Recognize that trials, tribulation, and even persecution are part of the test (see 2 Nephi 2:11; 4:27; Abr. 3:25). We must overcome and endure well in order to pass the test of life (see D&C 121:8).
- *Know the Lord's expectations*—We must never forget that where much is given much is expected (see Luke 12:48), and never-ending happiness is our reward if we endure well our time on earth (see Mosiah 2:41).

2. Cultivate the vision of your role in the plan of happiness.

- *Focus on eternal roles*—Each of us has eternal roles within the family unit that have eternal consequences in relation to how well we magnify them. We have callings within the Church that require a similar accounting as to our performance. Enduring to the end has everything to do with the fulfilling these two kinds of roles.
- *Remember the obligation to build up the kingdom*—We are to seek to build up the kingdom of God (see JST, Matt. 6:38) by helping people come unto Christ (see D&C 15:6).
- *Seek to bless others*—We are disciples of Christ. We love one another (see John 13:34–35). We serve with all our heart, might, mind, and strength (see D&C 4:2), strengthening one another in all we do (see D&C 108:7).

3. Be totally and completely converted.

- *Conversion is the key to power*—The depth of our conversion gives us power to serve with all diligence (see Alma 36:24).
- *Conversion brings a commitment to serve others*—When one is converted, one's first concern is for the welfare of others (see Enos 1:9, 11; Mosiah 28:3). This gives us enduring power to serve when things are difficult. The sons of Mosiah are perfect examples.
- *Conversion leads to the gift of the Holy Ghost*—With conversion comes the gift of the Holy Ghost (see 2 Ne. 31:12), who will comfort, teach, and strengthen us in our times of need (see D&C 36:2), helping us to endure to the end.
- *Service opens the way for obedience*—As we seek to serve the Lord, He will always provide us a way to keep the commandments (see 1 Ne. 3:7).

4. Seek strength in the Lord.

- *Covenant valor brings strength*—The Lord Jesus Christ gives us strength and support as we remain faithful to our covenants.
- *Humility brings strength*—When we recognize that our strength is in the Lord, and not in ourselves, we will have the power given us through Him to endure (see Alma 26:12).

ILLUSTRATIONS FOR OUR TIMES

Told by Leon R. Hartshorn, the following story provides a witness that enduring to the end is a lifelong pursuit.

Endure to the End

Authorization, as many of you know, has been given by the Brethren for Relief Societies, under specified circumstances, to be organized in nursing or residential homes for older sisters. One day I visited such a Relief Society. The members were between seventy-five and ninety years of age. They were ambulatory, bright of mind, and enthusiastic over their society. The lesson was from the Doctrine and Covenants and was followed by testimony bearing. The sisters contributed intelligently to the lesson discussions. Their offerings reflected a knowledge of Church doctrine and familiarity with the gospel, as well as rich life experiences. It was a delightful meeting. Then came the testimony period. Each sister who spoke, one by one, prayed that she would endure to the end. As I contemplated their intelligent understanding of the gospel as demonstrated in the discussion, and as I considered how late in life it was for most of them, I thought, why would they pray that they might endure to the end? Surely they have already proved themselves.

Later, however, in private conversation with some of them, I was made aware that they were not entirely above reproach, that they had a tendency to excuse themselves for failures to comply with the laws of the gospel because of age and circumstances.

These are a few comments made by these sisters as I talked with them:

One sister said, "We have sacrament meeting here at the home, as well as Relief Society, but I never go to sacrament meeting. I am too old to be preached to." I inquired, "Don't you feel a need to partake of the sacrament?" "No," the sister indifferently replied. "I don't think it matters at my age."

Another sister said, "I want to move to a little better home.

"I have enough money to do so. I have no one on whom to spend my money but myself. My family does not need it, and I am no longer interested in doing things for others that cost money. I don't even pay tithing. I don't think the Lord expects it of one my age."

Still another sister, who was drinking tea as I called, said, "I almost live on tea. When I was a younger woman, you couldn't have hired me to drink a cup of tea, but I don't think it will be held against me now."

Yet another said, as we heard footsteps near the door, "I hope that's not my daughter. She only comes because she fears criticism if she doesn't. She has very little love for me, and I have very little for her." One more comment: "I seem to be growing weaker every day, suffering as I do with pain. I used to have the elders administer to me, but I don't believe in that anymore."

Attendance at sacrament meeting, partaking of the sacrament, renewing one's covenants, the payment of tithing, observance of the Word of Wisdom, love of family, priesthood administration—all basic laws of the gospel—had been abandoned by one or the other of these sisters with a feeling of justification; yet each had earnestly prayed that she might endure to the end.

Sympathetic as we may be toward these sisters and toward their circumstances, and understanding as we may be of their actions, yet we must recognize that with clear minds they were justifying the nonobservance of God's laws. I am led to ask also, Has the Lord ever set a retirement age for keeping his commandments? (as told by Leon R. Hartshorn, comp., *Remarkable Stories from the Lives of Latter-day Saint Women,* 2 vols. [Salt Lake City: Deseret Book, 1973], 1:231)

SUMMARY

The reward for enduring to the end is eternal life—the greatest gift of God (see D&C 14:7). Recognizing the blessings of eternal life should increase our desire and motivation to persevere with all diligence. Enduring requires steadfastness rooted in Christ and a willingness to sacrifice all for the gospel cause. It is not an easy road and it wasn't intended to be so, but the joy of the work will carry us forward (see Alma 36:24), even to eternal life, a state of never-ending happiness (see Mosiah 2:41). Our goal is set: Endure to the end.

ETERNAL PROGRESSION

In premortal life we lived as the children of God the Eternal Father. Heavenly Father's plan was presented and we accepted it, under the leadership of Jesus Christ, the Son of the Almighty. We were valiant in our premortal estate and were sent here to Earth as mortals to work out our salvation through the gospel plan. Earth life is a test (see Abr. 3:25) to see if we will continue in our progression, which began long before we were born. We are given enabling power through the grace of God to grow and progress through the difficulties and challenges we face. This is why Christ's atoning sacrifice was the center of the plan of happiness and the very core of the gospel of Jesus Christ. His Atonement makes possible not only forgiveness of our sins if we repent, but provides for immortality and eternal life. Each of these aspects of the Atonement is a way for us to progress. Eternal life is given to those who qualify by entering into sacred covenants and ordinances and remaining true and faithful to them. This is eternal progression. We then can enjoy the blessings of exaltation.

THE SCRIPTURES TEACH US

Romans 8:16. *The Spirit itself beareth witness with our spirit, that we are the children of God.*

The knowledge that we are the children of God should give us magnificent self-worth and confidence. We are created in His image and have the potential to become like Him if we are faithful to our covenants.

2 Nephi 28:30. *For behold, thus saith the Lord God: I will give unto the children of men line upon line, precept upon precept, here a little and there a little; and blessed are those who hearken unto my precepts, and lend an ear unto my counsel, for they shall learn wisdom; for unto him that receiveth I will give more; and from them that shall say, We have enough, from them shall be taken away even that which they have.*

Here on earth we grow one step at a time. When we receive and hearken to the Lord's counsel and commandments, the Lord gives us more. We continue to grow and to become like Him.

Alma 13:3. *And this is the manner after which they were ordained—being called and prepared from the foundation of the world according to the foreknowledge of God, on account of their exceeding faith and good works; in the first place being left to choose good or evil; therefore they having chosen good, and exercising exceedingly great faith, are called with a holy calling, yea, with that holy calling which was prepared with, and according to, a preparatory redemption for such.*

We not only accepted the plan of salvation premortally but we also proved our worthiness through our obedience and loyalty. Thus we became foreordained to continue this progression in performing covenant duties and services upon the earth.

Doctrine and Covenants 81:6. *And if thou art faithful unto the end thou shalt have a crown of immortality, and eternal life in the mansions which I have prepared in the house of my Father.*

The blessings of following Christ and keeping His commandments are beyond comprehension (see D&C 76:114). Surely the reward that the Lord has prepared for us should help us in our desire and effort in progressing to become like Him.

Abraham 3:25–26. *And we will prove them herewith, to see if they will do all things whatsoever the Lord their God shall command them; And they who keep their first estate shall be added upon; and they who keep not their first estate shall not have glory in the same kingdom with those who keep their first estate; and they who keep their second estate shall have glory added upon their heads for ever and ever.*

We kept our first estate in the pre-earth life (meaning we were faithful) and are now here upon the earth to be tested to prove ourselves worthy of returning to the presence of our Heavenly Father. This is the time to prepare to meet God (see Alma 34:32). We have the blessing of moral agency which God gave so we could choose for ourselves—liberty and eternal life (progression) or captivity and death (digression) (see 2 Ne. 2:27).

MODERN PROPHETS SPEAK

Gordon B. Hinckley:
> The Church is the great teacher and builder of values. Its precepts are designed to lead men and women along the way of immortality and eternal life, to make their lives more complete, more rich and happy while moving through this vale of tears, and in preparing them for the beauties and wonders of that which lies ahead. Keep faith with the Church. It is true. It is divine. (*Teachings of Gordon B. Hinckley* [Salt Lake City: Deseret Book, 1997], 116)

Neal A. Maxwell:
> Discipleship need not be hectic. The gospel suggests to us ultimate perfection, but eternal progression rests on the assumption of gradual but regular improvement in our lives. In the city of Enoch the near perfection of this people occurred "in process of time" over many, many years. This is also the case with us. (*Deposition of a Disciple* [Salt Lake City: Deseret Book, 1976], 70)

> It is much easier to believe in eternal progression than to practice daily improvement. Likewise, the need for humility is easy to assent to, but it is so difficult to receive corrective counsel humbly. The hard doctrines . . . are more keys to personal growth. This scripture could well be their theme: "He that *refuseth* instruction *despiseth his own soul*: but he that *heareth reproof* getteth *understanding*." (Proverbs 15:32. Italics added.) (*All These Things Shall Give Thee Experience* [Salt Lake City: Deseret Book, 1979], 71)

IDEAS FOR DAILY LIVING

Here are some ideas concerning premortality, mortality, and immortality and eternal life that will help us in our understanding and progression.

1. **The foundation for eternal progression was laid in the premortal existence.**
   - *Heritage*—We are the divine spirit children of God the Eternal Father (see Rom. 8:16).
   - *First estate*—We made good choices in our first estate (see Alma 13:3).
   - *Commitment to the plan*—We joyfully accepted the plan of salvation (see Job 38:7) and agreed to come to Earth to work out our salvation according to the gospel plan (see Abr. 3:26).
   - *Memory*—We have had a veil placed over our memories of the first estate so that we can progress in our faith.

2. **The time of probation and proving is the mortal years.**
   - *Preparation to meet God*—This is the time to prepare to meet God (see Alma 34:32).
   - *Agency*—We have the God-given power to make correct choices that will bring us closer to our goal (see 2 Ne. 2:27).
   - *The Spirit*—We can be directed by the Spirit in our progression (see 2 Ne. 32:5).
   - *Proactive engagement*—Progression is not measured just in the big milestones, but in moving forward every day. We should always be "anxiously engaged in a good cause" (see D&C 58:27–28).
   - *Line upon line*—We learn and progress line upon line and precept upon precept (see 2 Ne. 28:30). This is not a race for the swift but for those who endure to the end (see 2 Ne. 31:20). We need not be overwhelmed, for the Lord will help us (see 1 Ne. 3:7).
   - *Vision*—Keep the vision, desire, preparation, and commitment for living a Christlike life foremost in your minds.

3. **The rewards and promised glory come with immortality and eternal life.**
   - *Gratitude*—The blessings of immortality and eternal life come from our Heavenly Father through His Son Jesus Christ as He worked out the infinite and eternal sacrifice we call the Atonement (see 2 Ne. 9:10–13). Progression is not possible without the Atonement. Gratitude for this transcending sacrifice surely should inspire us to keep the commandments.
   - *Grace*—With the grace of God through the Atonement, all that remains is for us to work out our salvation by keeping the commandments (see 2 Ne. 25:23). He has made our progression possible despite our mortal shortcomings.
   - *Exaltation*—Immortality is given to all who kept their first estate, but exaltation is reserved for those who have entered into the lifesaving covenants and ordinances, progressing in faith to the end (see D&C 63:20; 84:33–44; 131).

ILLUSTRATIONS FOR OUR TIMES

This experience demonstrates the importance of everyday choices to our eternal progression:

The Great Divide

A few miles west of magnificent Lake Louise in Banff National Park, Alberta, there is a small stream that flows down the western slope of the mountain ridge and passes underneath the Trans Canada Highway, where it soon encounters an outcropping of rocks and divides into two tiny streamlets, each one barely a foot across. One of them flows northward into the Bow River, and then eastward via major waterways into the Hudson Bay. The other flows southward into the Kicking House River, and from thence into the Columbia River and eventually into the Pacific Ocean. A droplet of water flowing down that stream would face the prospect, at the seemingly small Great Divide, of going either toward the frozen expanse of the North, or toward the more hospitable waters of the Pacific. Either direction is as likely as the other for the water in these streamlets.

As a young man, I used to drive tour a tour bus in that area to earn money for college. One of the most compelling sights for tourists was that stop near the large sign spanning the highway that identified "The Great Divide." The visitors would walk down a path along the small stream and peer with fascination at the spot where it divided into two. On one of the tours, I noticed a woman staring engrossed at the dividing stream for several minutes. "Why are you so interested in that stream?" I asked her. "Because," she said quietly, "that's life." And so it is. Life is a series of small daily choices that define our ultimate progression. Out of the small choices of today will flow the mighty downstream rivers of tomorrow. In life the small often defines the large; the seemingly insignificant frequently determines the big picture. The milestones of our eternal progression consist of even the simple decisions we make—day by day—that define our character, align us with cherished and proven principles, and ultimately convey us toward perfection.

All too often, though, we fail to see what greatness is possible from such simplicity. The Syrian Naaman was told by Elisha to bathe himself seven times in the waters of the Jordan and be freed of his leprosy—and Naaman almost relinquished the reward of well-being out of contempt for the simplicity of the solution (2 Kgs. 5:8–14). Centuries before, Moses instructed the Israelites, plagued and tormented by poisonous snakes, simply to look upon the elevated brazen serpent and live (Num. 21:7–9; 2 Ne. 25:20). Yet many would not even do that. In all of the complexity of modern life, in all of the sophistication of modern society, we also overlook the elegant simplicity of the gospel plan, the supremely straightforward and unobtrusive counsel of the prophets to direct our vision to the Master. "And as many as should look upon that serpent should live, even so as many as should look upon the Son of God with faith, having a contrite spirit, might live, even unto that life which is eternal" (Hel. 8:15). All of us come to the Great Divide every day of our lives. With the help of God, we can make those daily decisions that comprise fixing our gaze upon the Savior. We can decide to do the simple deeds of righteousness, kindness, and service that lead to eternal life. Eternal progression is accomplished line upon line, here a little and there a little, one day at a time, one step at a time—but ever toward that transcendent example set by the Savior as marked by His footprints in the spiritual sands of time.

—Richard J. Allen

SUMMARY

The joy and opportunity of becoming like our Heavenly Father and our Savior is the essence of life. The plan has been given, the Atonement has been wrought, and it is left up to us to choose. The only way we can truly grow is by making choices that lead to eternal life. Our Heavenly Father seeks our happiness—our immortality and eternal life. If we fail it is because we have broken ourselves against the commandments and have not practiced the lifesaving principle of repentance. We can enjoy the blessings of exaltation and become perfect—simply by repenting perfectly. This will bring joy to us and to our Heavenly Father and our Savior (see D&C 18:13).

EXAMPLE

An example is a model or pattern for living, and it is one of life's most powerful teachers. Its power is often greater than that of words. We follow examples, and we act as examples to others for good or for ill nearly every moment of our lives, and even after we are gone.

THE SCRIPTURES TEACH US

John 13:15. *For I have given you an example, that ye should do as I have done to you.*

Whenever we have a doubt or concern as to how to act or treat others, remember we have our perfect example in the Lord Jesus Christ. Our goal should be to do as He has done (see 3 Ne. 27:27).

Acts 13:47. *For so hath the Lord commanded us, saying, I have set thee to be a light of the Gentiles, that thou shouldest be for salvation unto the ends of the earth.*

It is important that we set a worthy example for everyone, especially those who have not heard the gospel. The Lord has commanded us to do so, and the Spirit will direct us.

Jacob 2:35. *Behold, ye have done greater iniquities than the Lamanites, our brethren. Ye have broken the hearts of your tender wives, and lost the confidence of your children, because of your bad examples before them; and the sobbings of their hearts ascend up to God against you. And because of the strictness of the word of God, which cometh down against you, many hearts died, pierced with deep wounds.*

Just as good examples have the power to bless lives, so do bad examples have the power to hurt lives. One must never forget that someone is watching and will be affected by what we do.

MODERN PROPHETS SPEAK

Ezra Taft Benson:

> How many parents in the Church today owe their membership in the Church largely to the example of one of their own children, one of their children who first came in contact with the Church through the Primary, through a Scout troop or some other unit. When you teach them, often your lessons are carried into homes where parents may not be members of the Church, or may be in-active. The power of example in the life of a child is most potent indeed. (*The Teachings of Ezra Taft Benson* [Salt Lake City: Bookcraft, 1988], 158)

Harold B. Lee:

> In all leadership situations in which we seek to improve human behavior, it is difficult to overestimate the power of example—whether it consists of parents both showing and telling their children about the value of temple marriage or a returned missionary who shines forth as a result of the changes and maturation the gospel has wrought in him. (*The Teachings of Harold B. Lee,* ed. Clyde J. Williams [Salt Lake City: Bookcraft, 1996], 508)

Gordon B. Hinckley:

> Behold your little ones and teach them. I need not remind you that your example will do more than anything else in impressing upon their minds a pattern of life. It is always interesting to meet the children of old friends and to find in another generation the ways of their fathers and mothers. (*Be Thou an Example* [Salt Lake City: Deseret Book, 1981], 38)

IDEAS FOR DAILY LIVING

Listed below are three ideas to remember as part of being an example:

1. Make a conscious decision to be the best possible example.
- *Recognition*—Recognize the power of example and seek to become an example you would be pleased to have others follow. Remember that every moment someone, somewhere, is being affected by the power of your example (see 1 Tim. 4:12).
- *Choice*—We cannot choose *not* to be an example, for we are an example in spite of ourselves—but we can choose to be a good one.
- *Values*—Establish the gospel of Jesus Christ as the standard for behavior. Establish a pattern, even a routine, for living an exemplary life.
- *Love*—Think of your life as a garden of love. Through your example, you are planting good seeds for the coming generation. What you cultivate in your garden will grow into plants that will bear good fruit and nourish the lives of others.
- *Total commitment*—Your example is projected in your thoughts, in your speech, in your deportment, in your habits, in your actions. Like a television medium, there are many channels to your example that people will tune into, whether or not you are aware of it. Make a commitment that *each* channel of your life will be an example worthy of emulation.

2. Have an action plan for being a good example on a daily basis.
- *Write it down*—Make a specific plan to do exemplary things for your children and loved ones each day. Make a list of the values you would like your family to cultivate, and then set a goal to exemplify each of those values in some specific way on a regular basis.
- *Be patient*—Don't force it. Look for the teaching moments, rather than being preachy or coercive.
- *Praise others*—Recognize and praise others gratefully for their good example to you.
- *Have heroes*—Select good role models for yourself and your family. Identify a few people who have contributed exemplary patterns for your life and point out their good example to your loved ones and children. Point out to your family the good examples of forebears. Encourage your children to pick out good role models as well.
- *Look to God*—Look to the Savior's examples for comfort and encouragement. The greatest patterns for life are found in the scriptures and in the lives of those who follow the teachings therein (see John 13:15).

3. You're not perfect—but you can keep trying. When you slip and fall short of the expectations you have set for yourself, frankly admit it and do better. Set an example of someone who is humble, teachable, and committed to improving day-by-day.

ILLUSTRATIONS FOR OUR TIMES

The following story illustrates how we are always being an example, whether we choose to be or not.

Like Father, Like Son

In my life I have been affected tremendously by the power of example, just as you have. For good or ill, example is always there. I'll never forget the day when I took my two youngest sons, ages eight and six, to look at new cars. We casually walked through the car lot. As we passed a car, I kicked the tire as we all sometimes do. I looked back to check my sons to see if they were close to me. I watched in awe as each son walked by the car and kicked the tire just like their dad did. It hit me with such impact—*I must be a good example for my children. They will do what I do.* I'd best consider my ways and choose always to be a good example in all things. Take the time to be an example at all times and in all places.

—Ed J. Pinegar

* * *

Elder Packer relates how a Latter-day Saint family positively influenced the image of the Church in Russia:

Latter-day Saint Influence Endures

> One Sunday, Sister Packer and I were returning from an assignment in Europe, the last three days of which were spent in St. Petersburg, Russia. There we met the missionaries with the members and attended a fireside for members and investigators. We held two days of meetings with the leaders of the priesthood of the district and the branches there. While that is a different world, it is the same world. I was reminded of how important the little things are in our lives.

> We were invited to the office of Vladimir P. Yakovlev, who is the deputy mayor of St. Petersburg, to have lunch with him. The first thing he said through an interpreter was: "You don't need to tell me about your church or about your beliefs. I know about you, your people. Thirty years ago," he said, "I was on a cultural exchange in Pittsburgh, Pennsylvania, and I stayed for two months in the home of Timothy and Dorthea Smith. I saw them and their family. I went to the meetings with them."

> He said, "I just read the reports." It happens, incidentally, that in that city of five million, among his other duties he has the responsibility for advising on all matters relating to religion. He said, "The reports show that you will do something, you will do it. When you say you will not do something, you will not do it. You are a people who can be trusted."

> I told him we would try to find Timothy and Dorthea Smith. I haven't as yet had the opportunity. He said he would like to get in touch with them again.

> Who would have supposed that thirty years ago in that chance encounter members of the Church, just behaving themselves, would influence a man who now is in a very crucial position to affect the onrolling of the work of the Lord in that great city which only a short time ago was behind the Iron Curtain? (Boyd K. Packer, *Memorable Stories with a Message* [Salt Lake City: Deseret Book, 2000], 69–70)

SUMMARY

When the Savior visited the Saints in ancient America following His Resurrection, He provided His disciples with the consummate counsel for the unending process of self-perfection and covenant service:

"Therefore, what manner of men ought ye to be? Verily I say unto you, even as I am" (3 Ne. 27:27). We are to emulate His perfect example. It is the pinnacle of the "godly walk and conversation" (D&C 20:69) we are striving to acquire and practice. Let us all be committed to the process of improving our lives in conformity with divine example. Let us also strive to exhibit the best possible example to others.

FAITH

Faith is the first principle of the gospel of Jesus Christ. We learn that it is impossible to please God except with faith (see Heb. 11:6). Faith, then, becomes that which we must possess in order not only to gain eternal life, but also to do the will of God while we are on the earth. In Hebrews 11 and Alma 32 we learn that faith is a hope for something that we do not see. Too often we end faith in this hopeful and believing stage. The Prophet Joseph Smith, in the *Lectures on Faith,* described the three degrees of faith. The first degree is the substance of things hoped for (see *Lectures on Faith,* 1:7–8). Of the second degree, the Prophet Joseph said, "Faith is the moving cause of all action in intelligent beings" (*Lectures on Faith,* 1:12). The third degree of faith is the principle and source of power (see *Lectures on Faith,* 1:15). When all three degrees are applied, faith is exercised to its fullest. The Prophet went on to say: "Faith, then, is the first great governing principle which has power, dominion, and authority over all things; by it they exist, by it they are upheld, by it they are changed or by it they remain agreeable to the will of God" (*Lectures on Faith,* 1:24).

THE SCRIPTURES TEACH US

Luke 17:5. *And the apostles said unto the Lord, Increase our faith.*

Not only is our faith *in* Christ, but it comes from Him. As did the early Apostles, we can approach the Lord and ask Him to strengthen our faith. If the Apostles of the Lord needed an increase in faith, how much more do we need more faith in our lives?

Hebrews 11:6. *But without faith it is impossible to please him: for he that cometh to God must believe that he is, and that he is a rewarder of them that diligently seek him.*

As the children of God, our desires are to please Him and do His will. Recognizing this fact makes having and exercising faith in God and the Lord Jesus Christ paramount in our lives.

Mosiah 18:20. *Yea, even he commanded them that they should preach nothing save it were repentance and faith on the Lord, who had redeemed his people.*

In the Book of Mormon the prophets urged the teachers to preach the doctrine of faith and repentance to the point that this was the emphasis in their teaching (see also Mosiah 25:22).

Alma 32:27. *But behold, if ye will awake and arouse your faculties, even to an experiment upon my words, and exercise a particle of faith, yea, even if ye can no more than desire to believe, let this desire work in you, even until ye believe in a manner that ye can give place for a portion of my words.*

As stated above, the first part of faith is hope, a desire to believe. Following the analogy given in Alma 32 of planting a seed, as we nurture and cultivate this hope and desire, it will grow into a powerful conviction.

Alma 34:15–17. *And thus he shall bring salvation to all those who shall believe on his name; this being the intent of this last sacrifice, to bring about the bowels of mercy, which overpowereth justice, and bringeth about means unto men that they may have faith unto repentance. And thus mercy can satisfy the demands of justice, and encircles them in the arms of safety, while he that exercises no faith unto repentance is exposed to the whole law of the demands of justice; therefore only unto him that has faith unto repentance is brought about the great and eternal plan of redemption. Therefore may God grant unto you, my brethren, that ye may begin to exercise your faith unto repentance, that ye begin to call upon his holy name, that he would have mercy upon you.*

Faith can allow us to do all things according to the will of God. The most important thing we will ever do in our lives is to repent and come unto Christ with full purpose of heart. The thing that will be of most worth to us and bring us true joy is to help others repent (see Alma 29:9–10; D&C 15:6; 18:10–16).

Hebrews 11, Alma 32, Ether 12, Moroni 7.

All the scriptures (as we search and feast upon the word) will increase our faith. The chapters cited above are rich in the doctrine and principle of faith in God and the Lord Jesus Christ. Search the Topical Guide for additional scriptures specific to faith.

MODERN PROPHETS SPEAK

Joseph Fielding Smith:
> Let it be uppermost in your minds, now and at all times, that Jesus is the Christ, the Son of the living God, who came into the world to lay down his life that we might live. That is the truth and is fundamental. Upon that our faith is built. It cannot be destroyed. (*Doctrines of Salvation,* 3 vols., edited by Bruce R. McConkie [Salt Lake City: Bookcraft, 1954–1956], 2:302)

Ezra Taft Benson:
> Now let me describe to you what faith in Jesus Christ means. Faith in Him is more than mere acknowledgment that He lives. It is more than professing belief. Faith in Jesus Christ consists of complete reliance on Him. As God, He has infinite power, intelligence, and love. There is no human problem beyond His capacity to solve. Because He descended below all things, He knows how to help us rise above our daily difficulties. (*The Teachings of Ezra Taft Benson* [Salt Lake City: Bookcraft, 1988], 66)

Gordon B. Hinckley:
> If there is any one thing you and I need in this world it is faith, that dynamic, powerful, marvelous element by which, as Paul declared, the very worlds were framed (Hebrews 11:3). . . . Faith—the kind of faith that moves one to get on his knees and plead with the Lord and then get on his feet and go to work—is an asset beyond compare, even in the acquisition of secular knowledge. (*Teachings of Gordon B. Hinckley* [Salt Lake City: Deseret Book, 1997], 186)

IDEAS FOR DAILY LIVING

Here are five ideas to consider as we study and seek to increase our faith:

1. **Faith is a doctrine of principle and power.**
   - *Creative power*—The earth was created by the power of faith (see Heb. 11:3).
   - *Priesthood power*—The power of the priesthood is faith (Thorpe B. Isaacson, Conference Report, April 1954, 126). The powers of the priesthood are inseparably connected with the powers of heaven, and can be worked only through the principles of righteousness (see D&C 121:36).
   - *The power to achieve righteousness*—Faith is the foundation of all righteousness (see *Lectures on Faith* 1:10).
   - *Godly power*—Faith is an attribute of God and dwells independently in Him (see *Lectures on Faith* 2:2).

2. **Faith is the governing principle in the lives of all just men and women.**
   - *Faith as the compass of life*—Just men and women live by faith (see Hab. 2:4; Rom. 1:16; Gal. 3:11).
   - *Faith as the key to perfection*—We learn that "just" or faithful men are made perfect (see D&C 76:69).
   - *Faith as the partner of grace*—We are justified by our faith by the Spirit through the grace of our Savior Jesus Christ and His atoning sacrifice (see Rom. 3:28; 5:1).

3. **Remember that faith is the source of myriad blessings in our lives.**
   - *Shield against evil*—Faith is the shield of protection from the fiery darts of the adversary (see Eph. 6:16).
   - *Key to good works*—Faith is evidenced by our works (see James 2:18).
   - *Deliverance from guilt*—Enos, the great prophet, exercised faith unto repentance, and his guilt was swept away (see Enos 1:8).
   - *The doorway to receiving the Spirit*—By faith the prophet Lehi received the blessing and the gift of the Holy Ghost. Living by the Spirit comes through faith (see 1 Ne. 10:17).
   - *Instrumentality of miracles*—Healing the sick and similar miracles occur by the power of faith (see James 5:15; 2 Ne. 26:13).
   - *Divine guidance*—The Liahona worked by faith, diligence, and giving heed to the word. Receiving direction in life depends on the faith we exercise (see 1 Nephi 16:28).
   - *Strength*—Faith gives us strength (see Alma 2:30; 14:26), and with it we can do all things.
   - *Spiritual vitality*—We are alive in Christ through faith (see 2 Ne. 25:25).
   - *Power of expression*—We become mighty in word, able to preach the word through faith in the Lord Jesus Christ (see Ether 12:23).
   - *Communion with God's messengers*—Angels appear through faith on the Lord Jesus Christ; miracles are wrought through faith (see Moro. 7:37).
   - *Power of learning*—Learning comes through faith (see D&C 88:118).
   - *Fulfilling God's will*—By faith we can do all things that are expedient in the Lord (see 2 Nephi 1:10; Moroni 7:33).
   - *Divine assistance*—We pray, exercising faith with real intent, and the Lord will send angels (see Mosiah 27:13–14), whether mortal or immortal.
   - *Power of conversion*—It was faith that Nephi and Lehi used to cause a great change among the Lamanites (Ether 12:14).
   - *Key to the ministry*—We must remember that faith is necessary in order that God the Father and Jesus Christ can work through us, for They work only with those who exercise faith (Ether 12:30).
   - *Power of goodness*—Faith is that principle that moves us to do good always (Alma 29:4).

4. **The Lord opens the way for us to acquire and increase our faith.**
   - *Hearing the word*—Faith comes by hearing the word of God (see Rom. 10:17). We hear the word of God from living prophets, by the power of the Holy Ghost (see D&C 68:3–4), and from

searching the word of God in the scriptures. We must ponder and meditate upon the scriptures. In studying and searching the word of God, we gain faith.

- *Fasting and prayer*—Second, faith comes by fasting and prayer: "They did fast and pray oft, and did wax stronger and stronger in their humility, and firmer and firmer in the faith" (Hel. 3:35). Faith is a great blessing, but we must pay a price of fasting and prayer. We can fast every fast Sunday and on other special occasions that we might increase in our faith.
- *Love*—Faith comes and works through love, which is the motivating cause of all righteous deeds. The motivation of God's work is His love for us (see John 3:16). The motivation for Christ's Atonement and His great service is His love for us (see 2 Ne. 26:24). Faith works according to our love (see Gal. 5:6). Not only is love the great commandment (see Matt. 22:36–40), it motivates faith, which is a gift from God through righteousness (see 1 Cor. 12:9).
- *Humility*—All spiritual growth begins with humility. Humility is having and understanding our relationship to God the Father and Jesus Christ and our dependence upon Them. They are the objects upon which our faith rests, the figures in whom our faith is centered (see *Lectures on Faith* 2:23).

5. Remember that faith grows as we exercise it in our daily living. How can we now use this power that can move mountains, this power that brought the mighty change among the Lamanites, this power that created the earth, this power that causes us to move to action? We must use our faith to accomplish our purpose here upon the earth.

6. Develop a plan of action based on faith—We need goals and a plan of action. We need to exercise faith in practice, not just in concept. As we learn in Alma 32, we need to cultivate our desire to have faith, to have a testimony. We should set our course to include goals that will increase our faith (studying the word of God, paying tithes, praying, etc.). As we cultivate this faith, it will take root and deepen (see John 7:17).

7. Move our minds in faithful channels—Having our mind focused on the values and purposes of God, we begin to exercise faith to accomplish our goals. How does this happen? The Prophet Joseph Smith said that faith is exercised through mental exertion (*Lectures on Faith* 7:3). In mentally thinking on these things, exerting the power of our minds, acting with every fiber of our being, we exert so much power that when we speak, things come to pass (see Jacob 4:9). The power of God is exercised by the word of God as inspired by the power of the Holy Ghost. Mental exertion requires pondering and focusing of our minds and hearts with real intent. It is through this effort that our prayers are heard and answered, and we are forgiven of our sins (see Enos 1:3–8).

ILLUSTRATIONS FOR OUR TIMES

In the following story, told by Hugh B. Brown, we see the courage and steadfastness of a woman who had unshakeable faith. This woman's testimony and eternal perspective lifted her in her time of need.

Are You in Trouble?

> I should like to introduce a story coming out of the first world war. I had a companion, a fellow officer, who was a very rich man, highly educated. He was a lawyer, had great power, was self-sufficient, and he said to me as we often talked of religion (because he knew who I was), "There is nothing in life that I would like to have that I cannot buy with my money."

Shortly thereafter he and I with two other officers were assigned to go to the city of Arras, France, which was under siege. It had been evacuated, and upon arrival there we thought there was no one in the city. We noted that the fire of the enemy was concentrated on the cathedral. We made our way to that cathedral and went in. There we found a little woman kneeling at an altar. We paused, respecting her devotion. Then shortly she arose, wrapped her little shawl around her frail shoulders, and came tottering down the aisle. The man among us who could speak better French said, "Are you in trouble?"

She straightened her shoulders, pulled in her chin, and said, "No, I'm not in trouble. I was in trouble when I came here, but I've left it there at the altar."

"And what was your trouble?"

She said, "I received word this morning that my fifth son has given his life for France. Their father went first, and then one by one all of them have gone. But," straightening again, "I have no trouble; I've left it there because I believe in the immortality of the soul. I believe that men will live after death. I know that I shall meet my loved ones again."

When the little soul went out, there were tears in the eyes of the men who were there, and the one who had said to me that he could purchase anything with money turned to me and said, "You and I have seen men in battle display courage and valor that is admirable, but in all my life I have never seen anything to compare with the faith, the fortitude and the courage of that little woman."

Then he said, "I would give all the money I have if I could have something of what she has." (Hugh B. Brown, Conference Report, October 1969, 106–107)

SUMMARY

The Lord cautions us to not be of the world. We cannot do the work of the Lord when we are worried about worldly things. We must be focused on the Lord's work, which is the welfare of His children. That is why we exercise our faith unto repentance, that we might be saved. That is why we exercise our faith in behalf of others, that they might be blessed.

Let us not strive to move all the mountains today; let us just have faith to follow the prophet. Let us not go about trying to heal the entire world or raise the dead; let us have faith enough to move ourselves to action by being a loving parent, a devoted and obedient child, a sensitive neighbor. Let us not exercise our faith to gain the whole world, but rather for the building up of the kingdom of God through love and service to our fellow beings. Through small and simple things, great things come to pass—simply through the exercising of faith (see D&C 64:33). Let us start today with some goals and a plan to increase in our faith that we might be an instrument in the hands of the Lord to bless our family and all mankind.

FAMILY

The basic unit of the Church and society is the family. Whenever civilization struggles, it is often a result of broken homes where values are neither lived nor taught. In today's world, the family is at risk. Too many people do not protect the rights and values of the family. Families can be successful with committed parents and children. As the gospel teaches, families are forever.

THE SCRIPTURES TEACH US

Colossians 3:20. *Children, obey your parents in all things: for this is well pleasing unto the Lord.*

Parents are to lead and teach (see D&C 68:25–28), while children are to learn and obey. These roles need to be understood and appreciated so that everyone's attitude will be positive and all family members will be respectful to each other.

Mosiah 4:15. *But ye will teach them to walk in the ways of truth and soberness; ye will teach them to love one another, and to serve one another.*

Parents are to teach love within the family. Parents have countless duties (see Mosiah 4:4), but among the greatest is the responsibility to show love to their children.

3 Nephi 18:21. *Pray in your families unto the Father, always in my name, that your wives and your children may be blessed.*

Prayer is the strength of the family. It is a blessing and a protection to all members of the family. Heavenly Father wants families to succeed, and with His help they can.

Doctrine and Covenants 130:2. *And that same sociality which exists among us here will exist among us there, only it will be coupled with eternal glory, which glory we do not now enjoy.*

If we are not loving families now, we will not be in the eternities. The same sociality will exist there. It is important that we develop a celestial family now if that is what we want in eternity.

MODERN PROPHETS SPEAK

First Presidency and Quorum of the Twelve Apostles:
> The family is ordained of God. Marriage between man and woman is essential to His eternal plan. Children are entitled to birth within the bonds of matrimony, and to be reared by a father and a mother who honor marital vows with complete fidelity. Happiness in family life is most likely to be achieved when founded upon the teachings of the Lord Jesus Christ. Successful marriages and families are established and maintained on principles of faith, prayer, repentance, forgiveness, respect, love, compassion, work, and wholesome recreational activities. By divine design, fathers are to preside over their families in love and righteousness and are responsible to provide the necessities of life and protection for their families. Mothers are primarily responsible for the nurture of

their children. In these sacred responsibilities, fathers and mothers are obligated to help one another as equal partners. Disability, death, or other circumstances may necessitate individual adaptation. Extended families should lend support when needed. ("The Family: A Proclamation to the World," *Ensign,* Nov. 1995, 102)

Gordon B. Hinckley:

We are a church which bears testimony of the importance of the family—the father, the mother, the children—and of the fact that we are all children of God our Eternal Father. Parents who bring children into the world have a responsibility to love those children, to nurture them and care for them, to teach them those values which would bless their lives so that they will grow to become good citizens. If there is less trouble in the homes, there will be less trouble in the nations. I want to emphasize that which is already familiar to you, and that is the importance of binding our families together with love and kindness, with appreciation and respect, and with teaching the ways of the Lord so that your children will grow in righteousness and avoid the tragedies which are overcoming so many families across the world. (*Teachings of Gordon B. Hinckley* [Salt Lake City: Deseret Book, 1997], 208)

Ezra Taft Benson:

Remember, the family is one of God's greatest fortresses against the evils of our day. Help keep your family strong and close and worthy of our Father in Heaven's blessings. As you do, you will receive faith and strength, which will bless your lives forever. (*Come, Listen to a Prophet's Voice* [Salt Lake City: Deseret Book, 1990], 2)

Spencer W. Kimball:

The gospel has been a family affair. By committing ourselves to having the regular and inspirational family home evening and by carefully planning the content of that evening, we are sending a signal to our children which they will remember forevermore. When thus we give our children of our own time, we are giving of our presence, a gift that is always noticed. (*The Teachings of Spencer W. Kimball,* edited by Edward L. Kimball [Salt Lake City: Bookcraft, 1982], 344)

IDEAS FOR DAILY LIVING

Incorporating the following can make a difference in your family:

1. **Priorities**—Make your family your number-one priority in time and effort.

2. **Decisions**—Equate everything you do with this standard: "Will what I do bless my family?" If it won't, don't do it.

3. **Service**—Look for ways daily to help each member of the family.

4. **Praise**—Seek to praise and compliment every day.

5. **Guidance**—Never criticize or condemn a family member—separate the behavior from the person. Help them understand and appreciate what they should do; then their attitude and behavior will change.

6. **Cooperation**—Competition often breeds problems; therefore, emphasize cooperation.

7. Family council—Meet together in family council regularly to discuss concerns, standards, needs, and solutions and to plan a calendar of things to do together.

8. Safety—Make your home a safe place, a refuge from the world, where love abounds and peace is a hallmark. Your home should not only be a place of physical safety, but of emotional and spiritual safety as well.

9. Learning—Make your home a place of learning—values and standards, life skills, and pursuit of a quality education begin at home. Establish family learning on a bedrock of enduring principles such as trust, love, honesty, accountability, and spiritual truth.

10. Family prayer—Spend time kneeling together in prayer. Implore Heavenly Father for the blessings of heaven to be on your family.

11. Family scripture time—Set a regular time each day to search (not just read) the scriptures together as a family.

12. Family home evening—Hold regular family home evening on Monday nights. Involve the entire family in all of the activities.

13. Family interviews—On a monthly basis visit with each child individually to listen to his or her concerns. Take time to teach, train, nurture, give blessings, and help each child in every way possible.

14. Family traditions—Create special times and places to establish righteous and enjoyable activities that have lasting value in the lives of family members.

15. Being a wise media gatekeeper—Parents have a sacred obligation to ensure that their children are exposed to only those media influences that are uplifting and conducive to righteous patterns of living. (See Elder Ballard's talk in the November 2003 *Ensign* for some helpful counsel on the issue of media in the home.)

ILLUSTRATIONS FOR OUR TIMES

The following excerpt from an *Ensign* article by Rex D. Pinegar emphasizes the importance of home and family:

Home First

> The Lord, through His prophets, has taught us of the divine power and influence of the home. "There is no substitute for the home," said President Joseph F. Smith. "Its foundation is as ancient as the world, and its mission has been ordained of God from the earliest times. . . .
>
> "There can be no genuine happiness separate and apart from the home, and every effort made to sanctify and preserve its influence is uplifting to those who toil and sacrifice for its establishment. There is no happiness without service, and there is no greater service than that which converts the home into a divine institution, and which promotes and preserves family life." (*Gospel Doctrine,* 5th ed., Salt Lake City: Deseret Book, 1939, p. 300.)

On the night of September 21, 1989, Hurricane Hugo passed with all its fury over the beautiful city of Charleston, South Carolina. My good friend Alvie Evans lived in a low-lying area near the water, where the maximum strength of the storm was headed. He gathered his family together and moved to higher ground, to the home of his mother.

Late in the night, 150-mile-per-hour winds raged around them, uprooting trees and ripping away parts of the house. The storm became so severe they began to fear they would experience physical harm. Alvie, with his wife and children, his mother and his brothers and sister and their families, knelt together in the entrance hall of the home and prayed humbly to the Lord, asking for protection and for safety.

The next morning they viewed the devastation. Of the fifty or more large, strong oak trees that had been growing in his mother's yard, only eight remained standing. There was damage to the house, the cars, the entire city, but the family was safe. The Lord had heard their prayers and had protected them through the storm. Alvie said, "I didn't know then if we would have a house to return to, but I knew we would always have a home, because our family was intact and secure."

President David O. McKay once said, "There is nothing temporary in the home of the Latter-day Saint." (In Conference Report, June 1919, p. 77.)

He also stated: "[One] can have a beautiful house with all the decorations that modern art can give or wealth bestow. [It] can have all the outward forms that will please the eye and yet not [be] a home. . . . It may be a hovel, a log hut, a tent, a wickiup, if you have the right spirit within, the true love of Christ, and love for one another—fathers and mothers for the children, children for parents, husband and wife for each other—you have the true life of the home that Latter-day Saints build and which they are striving to establish." (*Gospel Ideals,* Salt Lake City: Improvement Era, 1953, pp. 480–81.)

Today, evil forces are challenging the home as never before. If our homes are to endure, parents and children must dedicate themselves to the gospel ideals that ensure preservation of home and family. (Rex D. Pinegar, "Home First," *Ensign,* May 1990, 9)

SUMMARY

The number of things one can do to strengthen the family is limitless. However, the only things that are truly *essential* to strengthen the family are the proper desire, attitude, work ethic, and values—all of which are based on love. We all have observed this in families that are well adjusted and happy. It is up to us to make our families the best they can be, and to never give up in this endeavor. There is no more important mission than to leave behind for your family a legacy of love, harmony, peace, and righteous principles for living.

FASTING

Purposely going without food and drink for a period of time is fasting. In a religious sense, fasting is never complete without prayer—hence the phrase "fasting and prayer" is commonly used in relation to this principle. We are counseled always to align our fast with a spiritual purpose, such as improving ourselves in righteousness, seeking a worthy blessing, expressing our love and gratitude, or serving our God and our fellowman. Bruce R. McConkie has stated the following:

> Fasting, with prayer as its companion, is designed to increase spirituality; to foster a spirit of devotion and love of God; to increase faith in the hearts of men, thus assuring divine favor; to encourage humility and contrition of soul; to aid in the acquirement of righteousness to teach man his nothingness and dependence upon God; and to hasten those who properly comply with the law of fasting along the path to salvation.

> Many specific reasons for fasting are found in the scriptures. It is a general obligation imposed by revelation upon church members in good standing. (D&C 59:13–14; 88:76; Luke 5:33–35; 2 Cor. 6:5; 11:27.) It is itself a form of the true worship of God. (Luke 2:37; Acts 9:9; Alma 45:1; 4 Ne. 12.) It is proper to fast for the sick (2 Sam. 12:16); for special blessings (Mosiah 27:22–23); to gain a testimony (Alma 5:46); to gain revelation (Alma 17:3; 3 Ne. 27:1; Ex. 34:28; Deut. 9:9, 18); for the conversion of nonmembers to the truth, (Alma 6:6; 17:9); for guidance in the choice of church officers (Acts 13: 3); as an accompaniment of righteous mourning and sorrow (Alma 28:2–6; 30:2; Hel. 9:10); as a means of sanctifying one's soul (Hel. 3: 35); and for guidance along the path leading to salvation. (Omni 26.) Temples are houses of fasting. (D&C 88:119; 95:16; 109:8, 16.) To be acceptable fasting must conform to the Lord's law and not be done for hypocritical reasons. (Matt. 6:16–18; 3 Ne. 13:16–18.) (Bruce R. McConkie, *Mormon Doctrine*, 2nd ed. [Salt Lake City: Bookcraft, 1966], 276)

THE SCRIPTURES TEACH US

Alma 5:46. *Behold, I say unto you they are made known unto me by the Holy Spirit of God. Behold, I have fasted and prayed many days that I might know these things of myself. And now I do know of myself that they are true; for the Lord God hath made them manifest unto me by his Holy Spirit; and this is the spirit of revelation which is in me.*

Great blessings flow from God to the faithful who sincerely practice a prayerful fast, whether the blessings are strengthening, healing, or an increase of understanding. In this instance, Alma refers to gaining his testimony. This prophet, who had seen an angel, received his witness through the same process we do—fasting and prayer.

Alma 17:3. *But this is not all; they had given themselves to much prayer, and fasting; therefore they had the spirit of prophecy, and the spirit of revelation, and when they taught, they taught with power and authority of God.*

The blessings of the Spirit and the power to teach by that same Spirit come through fasting and prayer (see Alma 17:9).

Helaman 3:35. *Nevertheless they did fast and pray oft, and did wax stronger and stronger in their humility, and firmer and firmer in the faith of Christ, unto the filling their souls with joy and consolation, yea, even to the purifying and the sanctification of their hearts, which sanctification cometh because of their yielding their hearts unto God.*

The blessings of faith and humility, even unto sanctification by the Holy Spirit, can come through fasting and prayer.

MODERN PROPHETS SPEAK

Joseph F. Smith:

> The Lord has instituted the fast on a reasonable and intelligent basis, and none of his works are vain or unwise. His law is perfect in this as in other things. Hence, those who can are required to comply thereto; it is a duty from which they cannot escape; but let it be remembered that the observance of the fast day by abstaining twenty-four hours from food and drink is not an absolute rule, it is no iron-clad law to us, but it is left with the people as a matter of conscience, to exercise wisdom and discretion. Many are subject to weakness, others are delicate in health, and others have nursing babies; of such it should not be required to fast. Neither should parents compel their little children to fast. I have known children to cry for something to eat on fast day. In such cases, going without food will do them no good. Instead, they dread the day to come, and in place of hailing it, dislike it; while the compulsion engenders a spirit of rebellion in them, rather than a love for the Lord and their fellows. Better teach them the principle, and let them observe it when they are old enough to choose intelligently, than to so compel them.
>
> But those should fast who can, and all classes among us should be taught to save the meals which they would eat, or their equivalent, for the poor. None are exempt from this; it is required of the Saints, old and young, in every part of the Church. It is no excuse that in some places there are no poor. In such cases the fast donation should be forwarded to the proper authorities for transmission to such stakes of Zion as may stand in need.
>
> So shall we gain favor in the sight of God, and learn the acceptable fast before him. (*Gospel Doctrine: Selections from the Sermons and Writings of Joseph F. Smith,* comp. John A. Widtsoe [Salt Lake City: Deseret Book, 1939], 243)

Gordon B. Hinckley:

> It is not a burden to refrain from two meals a month and give the value thereof to assist in caring for the poor. It is, rather, a blessing. Not only will physical benefits flow from the observance of this principle, but spiritual values also. Our program of the fast day and the fast offering is so simple and so beautiful that I cannot understand why people everywhere do not take it up. Hearings have recently been held in the Congress of the United States on a proposal to recommend to the president a day of fasting to raise funds for the starving people of Africa. Our own experience last spring was so easy of execution and so tremendously productive that our consecrations have blessed thousands without causing any of us to suffer in the least. (*Teachings of Gordon B. Hinckley* [Salt Lake City: Deseret Book, 1997], 217–18)

IDEAS FOR DAILY LIVING

Here are some ideas to help us as we live the law of the fast:

1. Cultivate a spiritual attitude about fasting.

- *Humility*—Fast with a spirit of humility, never begrudgingly (see Isa. 58).
- *Joy*—Fast with a cheerful countenance and not to be seen of men (see Matt. 16:16–18).
- *With purpose*—Fast with a purpose. Fasting, like prayer, must be purposeful—acting with faith and real intent (see Alma 5:46). Look at fasting as an opportunity, not just something required of you.
- *According to need*—Some blessings of the Lord require fasting and prayer. We need to do more than merely ask for the blessing (see Matt. 17:21).
- *Using wisdom*—There are times, such as when we are under a doctor's care or experiencing special medical conditions, where fasting would not be wise or prudent. This does not prevent one from fasting in the spiritual sense: "If I could, I would."

2. Share the blessings of the fast with others.

- *Use patience*—When teaching your children the law of the fast, it is important to explain the *purpose* of fasting. Be patient with your children as they learn. This often takes time and requires much more than an announcement stating, "Today we fast."
- *Bear testimony*—As the Spirit directs, bear solemn and humble witness of the truth of the gospel during fast and testimony meeting and in family gatherings.
- *Contribute fast offerings*—Remember that on our monthly fast Sunday we use the money or goods that would otherwise have been used for food for the blessing of the poor and needy.

ILLUSTRATIONS FOR OUR TIMES

The following story discusses the doctrine of fasting and its significance in the early years of the restored Church:

The Hidden Gem

On May 17, 1845, nearly a year after the martyrdom of Joseph and Hyrum, the Twelve issued a general letter to the Church to convey special instructions:

> *Beloved Brethren:* Our whole souls bless you; and we are happy in the privilege of communicating to you a few thoughts. Much more would we rejoice were it our privilege to be in your midst the coming Sabbath and tell you all that is in our hearts; but we are pilgrims in a world of sorrow and woe. In our journeyings to proclaim the gospel and bring about salvation to the honest in heart, God is with us and we prosper; though weary, we are not cast down nor discouraged, for we know that victory is with the upright.
>
> We are happy to hear of the great union and love manifested at your recent fast, which also the Spirit bore witness of to us, and of your liberality towards the poor, and may the abundance which you have so liberally contributed in your penury in dealing your bread to the hungry be the omen of an abundant harvest of the fruits of the earth into your granaries the present and all future seasons.
>
> Since we commenced our journey we have discovered some letters from Brother Joseph Smith to Bishop Partridge from which we extract the following for your edification and instruction: . . .
>
> The Principle of Fasts Defined—Let this be an ensample to all saints, and there will never be any lack for bread: When the poor are starving, let those who have, fast one day and give what they

otherwise would have eaten to the bishops for the poor, and every one will abound for a long time; and this is one great and important principle of fasts approved of the Lord. And so long as the saints will all live to this principle with glad hearts and cheerful countenances they will always have an abundance. (*History of the Church,* 7: 412–13)

In discovering and publishing the missing letters from the Prophet, including the choice statement about the law of the fast, the Twelve had retrieved a hidden gem of wisdom for the enrichment of the spiritual life of the Saints. There is a type and an emblem to this discovery, for the law of the fast is itself a means to unearth hidden wisdom and spiritual truth. As we participate in fasting and prayer, we are often blessed to find within ourselves hidden strength and unexpected insight to facilitate our journey through mortal life. The word "fast" itself comes from a Middle English antecedent word meaning "firm" or "fixed." As we remain firm in the faith, with our eye "fixed" upon the goal of spiritual perfection, our fasting and prayer will edify our natures and lift us higher toward our quest for perfection as servants of God.

—Richard J. Allen

SUMMARY

The law of the fast, when practiced sincerely, empowers the individual with spiritual power. As we fast, we literally overcome the flesh. When we pay our fast offerings, we practice the great commandment of love. The Lord is explicit as to our spiritual status if we fail to care for the needy. The Lord has said through His servant Amulek, "And now behold, my beloved brethren, I say unto you, do not suppose that this is all; for after ye have done all these things, if ye turn away the needy, and the naked, and visit not the sick and afflicted, and impart of your substance, if ye have, to those who stand in need—I say unto you, if ye do not any of these things, behold, your prayer is vain, and availeth you nothing, and ye are as hypocrites who do deny the faith" (Alma 34:28). The regular practice of fasting and prayer is a dynamic power in our lives; it allows us to tap into the power of God to enrich our lives and make us more valiant servants.

FATHERHOOD

Of all the roles a man can have, nothing supersedes the role of father. A father should be a provider, a leader, and a teacher. Undoubtedly, society has suffered because so many fathers have abdicated their roles and responsibilities in the family. Why do some fathers feel that success somehow lies *outside* the home? Why do we think that things and money make up for not spending time with our children? It is time to evaluate our lives and recognize what matters most. We simply cannot let the world take us away from our greatest treasure—our marriage and family.

THE SCRIPTURES TEACH US

Ephesians 6:4. *And, ye fathers, provoke not your children to wrath: but bring them up in the nurture and admonition of the Lord.*

As we lead and teach our children, we should use a loving yet firm manner. One cannot afford to generate resentment or anger in his or her children in the teaching process. Such would render the process of being good no longer enjoyable for the children, which might result in rebellion rather than obedience.

1 Timothy 3:4–5. *One that ruleth well his own house, having his children in subjection with all gravity; (For if a man know not how to rule his own house, how shall he take care of the church of God?)*

As parents, one of our roles is to lead in righteousness so that our children might be willing to follow and obey. There is nothing more crucial to a family than to realize the importance of each other's roles and how we fit within the family. Fathers and mothers are to lead and teach. Children are to learn and obey—then they will be prepared to do the same thing when they are parents. Raising children is serious business because the consequences are so great.

Hebrews 12:9. *Furthermore we have had fathers of our flesh which corrected us, and we gave them reverence: shall we not much rather be in subjection unto the Father of spirits, and live?*

Giving correction is one of the most difficult things we do as fathers. It is our duty to correct, as moved upon by the Holy Ghost, early on and with clarity so that there is no misunderstanding, always in love (see D&C 121:41–44). In correcting children, we must ensure that they always feel that it is done in love. They need to know that the only reason we correct them is because we care for them and love them. As this scripture shows, it is through these family relationships that we come to understand our relationship with our Heavenly Father—how and why He loves, chastens, and blesses us.

3 John 1:4. *I have no greater joy than to hear that my children walk in truth.*

There is no greater joy than the joy you have in your posterity. Their righteous lives are the joy of a parent's life. We, as parents—and particularly as fathers—are responsible for the teaching of our family (see D&C 68:25–28; Moses 5:12).

Doctrine and Covenants 93:42–43. *You have not taught your children light and truth, according to the commandments; and that wicked one hath power, as yet, over you, and this is the cause of your affliction. And now a commandment I give unto you—if you will be delivered you shall set in order your own house, for there are many things that are not right in your house.*

In the early days of the restored Church, Frederick G. Williams and all the members of the First Presidency, including the Prophet Joseph Smith, were counseled to do better with their families. This teaches a transcending doctrine concerning responsibilities associated with our eternal roles. We can never delegate our duties as fathers. We are responsible and accountable, and nothing is more important. Our responsibility is to be loving husbands and devoted fathers. We must ask ourselves, How am I doing in my eternal role as husband and father within the Church and kingdom of God?"

MODERN PROPHETS SPEAK

Ezra Taft Benson:

> Our homes should be havens of peace and joy for our families. Surely no child should fear his own father, especially a priesthood father. A father's duty is to make his home a place of happiness and joy. He cannot do this when there is bickering, quarreling, contention, or unrighteous behavior.

As fathers of our homes, we have a serious responsibility to assume leadership in the home. We must create homes where the Spirit of the Lord can abide. We must always remember the statement of the Savior that "the spirit of contention is not of [Him], but is of the devil." (3 Nephi 11:29.) We must not allow the adversary to be an influence in our homes.

We must be more Christlike in our attitude and behavior than what we see in the world. We should be as charitable and considerate with our loved ones as Christ is with us. He is kind, loving, and patient with each of us. Should we not reciprocate the same love to our wives and children? (*Come unto Christ* [Salt Lake City: Deseret Book, 1983], 53.)

Fathers cannot delegate their duty as head of the home. They must train up their children in righteousness. (*The Teachings of Ezra Taft Benson* [Salt Lake City: Bookcraft, 1988], 524)

Gordon B. Hinckley:

You men who are husbands and fathers should have had kindled in your hearts tonight . . . a resolve so to conduct yourselves in your homes as to be worthy of the love, the respect, the honor, the companionship of your wives and your children. Holding the priesthood does not give any man the right to domineer over those for whom he should show the greatest of love and the greatest of consideration. Each of us should go home this night with a stronger resolve in our hearts to live worthy of the companionship of those who love us most and whom we should love and honor and respect without reservation.

I repeat that plea to all fathers. Yours is the basic and inescapable responsibility to stand as head of the family.

That does not carry with it any implication of dictatorship or unrighteous dominion. It carries with it a mandate that fathers provide for the needs of their families. Those needs are more than food, clothing, and shelter. Those needs include righteous direction and the teaching, by example as well as precept, of basic principles of honesty, integrity, service, respect for the rights of others, and an understanding that we are accountable for that which we do in this life, not only to one another but also to the God of heaven, who is our Eternal Father. . . . With the obligation to beget goes the responsibility to nurture, to protect, to teach, to guide in righteousness and truth. Yours is the power and the responsibility to preside in a home where there is peace and security, love and harmony. (*Teachings of Gordon B. Hinckley* [Salt Lake City: Deseret Book, 1997], 219–20)

IDEAS FOR DAILY LIVING

Here are five things we can do to help us be better fathers:

1. Be a father with all your heart, mind, and soul.

- *Never forget*—Constantly remind yourself of your non-transferable role as father. You can't delegate it. You can't transfer it. It is your work. It is your joy and glory.
- *Attend "fatherhood school"*—Take time to learn of the things you need to do to be a good father. Search the scriptures, fast and pray, attend the temple, and study Church manuals that can assist you. Read good books, ask others, study good role models, confer with your wife, and attend parenting courses.

2. Establish your family on a foundation of enduring gospel principles.

- *Have standards for the family*—Help them understand and appreciate the standards. When values and standards are agreed upon, there will be unity in the family.
- *Be loving*—Enthrone love as the governing principle of family life. Remember that the greatest gift you can give your family is your love and your time. Love your wife. Show her every courtesy and kindness. Show that romance has perpetuity. Say the magic words frequently to your wife and your children. "I love you" never goes out of style.
- *Be honest*—Always keep your word. Never lie to your wife or children.
- *Be humble*—Be quick to ask forgiveness when you're not at your best.
- *Be honorable*—Never, ever abuse your family in any way—emotionally, verbally, physically, or sexually.

3. Teach by example.

- *Strive for excellence*—Excel in your profession to set an example of how to raise the bar of excellence in personal development and self-mastery.
- *Learn continuously*—Study and read. Take courses. Limit passive television time. Be prudent in how much time you devote to outside interests. Even sports can be done to excess. Set an example of lifelong growth and learning.
- *Be a role model*—Be an exemplar of honesty, integrity, and upright character.

4. Foster harmony and unity.

- *Cultivate balance in family goals and activities*—Include work and play, personal growth and development, health and fitness, and spiritual growth.
- *Worship together*—Follow all the things mentioned in the *Family* section of this book regarding things you can do to be an eternal family.
- *Eat together as a family*—Make dinnertime a fun time to enjoy one another's conversation and company, not a time to watch TV and ignore one another.
- *Play together*—Play games with your children. Get down on the floor with the younger children and the grandchildren. Things look different from that perspective—a lot less stuffy and strict.
- *Create memories*—Plan and carry out memorable outings together. Balance recreation and work.
- *Cultivate a sense of humor*—Have a bright twinkle in your eye to offset the sometimes-gloomy disappointments that children can go through. A funny song, a spontaneous joke, a clever one-liner, a clownish antic—all these go a long way to warm up the atmosphere.

5. Use appropriate leadership principles. Aim high.

- *Think big*—Have a family "vision" and mission that can be written down and discussed. Set goals together and review them often.
- *Listen*—Sit down next to the kids frequently and just listen. Be interested in what interests them. You will be amazed at how they will open up. Nothing will enhance their self-esteem more than sincerely listening to them.
- *Reinforce good behavior*—Catch children doing good things. Sincerely praise and compliment them on a regular basis.
- *Be grateful*—Do not take for granted the chance you have to raise your children. Appreciate every moment you have with them.
- *Manage skillfully*—Manage your time and your money carefully, and involve the children in the process so that they learn how to invest precious resources wisely.
- *Foster teamwork within the family*—Teach your children about planning and organizing, evaluation, and follow-through. Let them help in this process.

- *Train and educate your children*—Help them excel at family assignments. Cultivate talents and productive hobbies. Allocate funds for lessons. Help them with schoolwork. Make learning a process of discovery rather than a chore. Become the rehearsal audience. Give constructive feedback.
- *Evaluate progress*—Count the milestones. Celebrate the successes. Teach the process of carrying out mid-course corrections as needed. Have family councils to conduct the family's business and showcase the progress.

ILLUSTRATIONS FOR OUR TIMES

"Father Smith," as Joseph Smith Sr. was affectionately known, exemplified faith and compassion throughout his life, and was rewarded by the Lord upon his death. As discussed in the following, his support of his son left an indelible impression:

A True Patriarch

Fourth months after Joseph Smith Sr. had passed away, his son, the Prophet Joseph, received a revelation, now known as Section 124 of the Doctrine and Covenants, in which there is reference to "my aged servant Joseph Smith, Sen., who sitteth with Abraham at his right hand, and blessed and holy is he, for he is mine" (verse 19). The funeral for the ailing patriarch had taken place in Nauvoo on Tuesday, September 15, 1840, he having died the previous day at age 69 of consumption (tuberculosis) contracted during the expulsion of the Saints from Missouri. Of his father the Prophet remembers: "He was the first person who received my testimony after I had seen the angel, and exhorted me to be faithful and diligent to the message I had received. . . . He was one of the most benevolent of men; opening his house to all who were destitute. While at Quincy, Illinois, he fed hundreds of the poor saints who were flying from the Missouri persecutions, although he had arrived there penniless himself" (*History of the Church*, 4:190–91).

Elder Robert B. Thompson, private secretary to Joseph Smith Jr., delivered an eloquent eulogy, during which he stated: "The man whom we have been accustomed to look up to as a Patriarch, a Father, a Counselor is no more an inhabitant of mortality; he has dropped his clay tenement, bid adieu to terrestrial scenes, and his spirit now free and unencumbered, roams and expatiates in that world where the spirits of just men made perfect dwell, and where pain and sickness, tribulation and death cannot come" (*History of the Church*, 4:192). Elder Thompson ends with this admonition: "May we, beloved friends, who survive our venerable Patriarch, study to prosecute those things which were so dear to his heart, and pray that a double portion of his spirit may be bestowed on us, that we may be the humble instruments in aiding the consummation of the great work which he saw so happily begun" (*History of the Church*, 4:196–97). Such leadership in the home is what our world needs. May we all draw from the lives of our own fathers those noble traits and qualities that may serve as a pattern for us to follow in fulfilling our own commission to be faithful servants of the Lord.

—Richard J. Allen

SUMMARY

The list could go on. Take time to make some goals and plans to be the best father for your family. There is no need for comparisons. You can be uniquely successful at it. No one can take our place as fathers. It is up to us to fulfill this magnificent role.

FOREORDINATION

In premortal life many children of God were foreordained (called and set apart) to future assignments prior to coming here to the earth (see Jer. 1:5; Alma 13:3–7; D&C 138:53–57; Abr. 3:22–23). Those foreordained had exhibited exceeding faith and good works. While it is true that we have all been sent to the earth with a purpose, foreordination does not override the agency of man—we are free to choose if we will fulfill our mission in life or not.

THE SCRIPTURES TEACH US

Alma 13:3–4. *And this is the manner after which they were ordained—being called and prepared from the foundation of the world according to the foreknowledge of God, on account of their exceeding faith and good works; in the first place being left to choose good or evil; therefore they having chosen good, and exercising exceedingly great faith, are called with a holy calling, yea, with that holy calling which was prepared with, and according to, a preparatory redemption for such. And thus they have been called to this holy calling on account of their faith, while others would reject the Spirit of God on account of the hardness of their hearts and blindness of their minds, while, if it had not been for this they might have had as great privilege as their brethren.*

We had agency in the premortal world. Those spirits who chose the good, exercising much faith, were called to holy callings. Unfortunately, some of us will harden our hearts and therefore not obtain the holy callings to which we were foreordained in the premortal existence.

Doctrine and Covenants 138:53–56. *[I saw] The Prophet Joseph Smith, and my father, Hyrum Smith, Brigham Young, John Taylor, Wilford Woodruff, and other choice spirits who were reserved to come forth in the fulness of times to take part in laying the foundations of the great latter-day work, Including the building of the temples and the performance of ordinances therein for the redemption of the dead, were also in the spirit world. I observed that they were also among the noble and great ones who were chosen in the beginning to be rulers in the Church of God. Even before they were born, they, with many others, received their first lessons in the world of spirits and were prepared to come forth in the due time of the Lord to labor in his vineyard for the salvation of the souls of men.*

While this scripture refers specifically to certain Church leaders, the phrases "other choice spirits" and "with many others" reveal what our prophets have since stated: that anyone who has a calling in the kingdom of God was foreordained to that very assignment. We may be assured that we each had a life and a relationship with God before we came to Earth.

Abraham 3:22–23. *Now the Lord had shown unto me, Abraham, the intelligences that were organized before the world was; and among all these there were many of the noble and great ones; And God saw these souls that they were good, and he stood in the midst of them, and he said: These I will make my rulers; for he stood among those that were spirits, and he saw that they were good; and he said unto me: Abraham, thou art one of them; thou wast chosen before thou wast born.*

Abraham, like so many others, was called to his position prior to coming to Earth due to his righteousness. We too have a plan for our lives that began in premortality, and as we live the gospel we will come to understand our own purpose and mission.

MODERN PROPHETS SPEAK

Joseph Smith:

> I believe in the fall of man, as recorded in the Bible; I believe that God foreknew everything, but did not foreordain everything; I deny that foreordain and foreknow is the same thing. He foreordained the fall of man; but all merciful as He is, He foreordained at the same time, a plan of redemption for all mankind. (*History of the Church*, 4:78)

Harold B. Lee:

> But now there is a warning: Despite that calling which is spoken of in the scriptures as "foreordination," we have another inspired declaration: "Behold, there are many called, but few are chosen." (D&C 121:34.)

> This suggests that even though we have our free agency here, there are many who were foreordained before the world was to a greater state than they have prepared themselves for here. Even though they might have been among the noble and great, from among whom the Father declared He would make His chosen leaders, they may fail of that calling here in mortality. Then the Lord poses this question: "And why are they not chosen?" (D&C 121:34.)

> Two answers were given: First, "Because their hearts are set so much upon the things of this world." And second, they "aspire to the honors of men." (D&C 121:35.) (*The Teachings of Harold B. Lee*, ed. Clyde J. Williams [Salt Lake City: Bookcraft, 1996], 185)

Ezra Taft Benson:

> To fulfill the purpose of His omniscient design, our Heavenly Father foreordained certain valiant spirit children and assigned them to come to earth at specific times and places to fulfill their appointments. The greatest of these spirits He reserved to come as prophets and priesthood leaders in His kingdom. "Every man," said the Prophet Joseph Smith, "who has a calling to minister to the inhabitants of the world was ordained to that very purpose in the Grand Council of Heaven before this world was."

> Other good and valiant spirits were foreappointed to lay the foundation for man's liberty through their service in political matters. The Founding Fathers of this American nation were in this category. (*The Teachings of Ezra Taft Benson* [Salt Lake City: Bookcraft, 1988], 21)

IDEAS FOR DAILY LIVING

Here are six ideas to help us understand and appreciate the doctrine of foreordination:

1. Our spiritual success depends on righteousness. We are blessed and called according to our righteousness (see 2 Ne. 27:23; Alma 13:3).

2. Agency is the overriding principle. Foreordination does not and cannot override the agency of man (see 2 Ne. 2:27). If we are not worthy, the Lord will choose another to fulfill His purposes (see D&C 121:34).

3. Learning is universal and unending. We learn and grow in the premortal world, in mortality, and in the worlds to come. At the center of this process of learning and growing is that we come to know and receive all the knowledge and blessings of God (D&C 84:38).

4. Our patriarchal blessing is a compass for our personal life. Our patriarchal blessing can help us understand and appreciate some of the blessings we were endowed with prior to coming to Earth as well as those we might receive in the future, if we remain worthy.

5. From the divine perspective, all is done in order. In the context of the plan of salvation, and according to the foreknowledge of God, He can foreordain one to an assignment, but He never "predestines" anyone. The agency of man is always operative.

6. We have a divine destiny. Remember that we are the children of Heavenly Father. He loves us and seeks our happiness and eternal life. He has a purpose for us here upon His earth. We have a mission. We cannot be casual in regard to our assignments, for they are part of a grand design for the immortality and eternal life of man (Moses 1:39).

ILLUSTRATIONS FOR OUR TIMES

President Harold B. Lee explained foreordination, its relation to our agency, and the importance of our lineage as follows:

Understanding Who We Are Brings Self-Respect

> A further truth is clearly set forth in that scripture [Abr. 3:22–23], that many were chosen, as was Abraham, before they were born, as the Lord told Moses and also Jeremiah. This was made still more meaningful by the Latter-day prophet, Joseph Smith, who declared, "I believe that every person who is called to do an important work in the kingdom of God, was called to that work and foreordained to that work before the world was." Then he added this, "I believe that I was foreordained to the work that I am called to do." (See *Documentary History of the Church,* vol. 6, p. 364.)

> But now there is a warning: Despite that calling which is spoken of in the scriptures as "foreordination," we have another inspired declaration: "Behold, there are many called, but few are chosen. . . ." (D&C 121:34.)

> This suggests that even though we have our free agency here, there are many who were foreordained before the world was, to a greater state than they have prepared themselves for here. Even though they might have been among the noble and great, from among whom the Father declared he would make his chosen leaders, they may fail of that calling here in mortality. Then the Lord poses this question: ". . . and why are they not chosen?" (D&C 121:34.)

> Two answers were given—First, "Because their hearts are set so much upon the things of this world. . . ." And second, they ". . . aspire to the honors of men." (D&C 121:35.)

> Now then, to make a summary of what I have just read, may I ask each of you again the question, "Who are you?" You are all the sons and daughters of God. Your spirits were created and lived as organized intelligences before the world was. You have been blessed to have a physical body because of your obedience to certain commandments in that premortal state. You are now born into a family to which you have come, into the nations through which you have come, as a reward for the kind of lives you lived before you came here and at a time in the world's history, as the

apostle Paul taught the men of Athens and as the Lord revealed to Moses, determined by the faithfulness of each of those who lived before this world was created.

Hear now the significant words of that powerful sermon to "The Unknown God" preached by the apostle Paul, to those who were ignorantly worshipping images of stone and brass and wood, and I quote:

"God that made the world and all things therein, seeing that he is Lord of heaven and earth, dwelleth not in temples made with hands;

"And hath made of one blood all nations of men for to dwell on all the face of the earth [now mark you this], and hath determined the times before appointed, and the bounds of their habitation;

"That they should seek the Lord, if haply they might feel after him, and find him, though he be not far from every one of us." (Acts 17:24, 26–27.)

Here then again we have the Lord making a further enlightening declaration to Moses as recorded in the Book of Deuteronomy:

"When the most High divided to the nations their inheritance, when he separated the sons of Adam, he set the bounds of the people according to the number of the children of Israel." (Deut. 32:8.)

Now, mind you, this was said to the children of Israel before they had arrived in the "Promised Land," which was to be the land of their inheritance.

Then note this next verse: "For the Lord's portion is his people; Jacob is the lot of his inheritance." (Deut. 32:9.)

It would seem very clear, then, that those born to the lineage of Jacob, who was later to be called Israel, and his posterity, who were known as the children of Israel, were born into the most illustrious lineage of any of those who came upon the earth as mortal beings.

All these rewards were seemingly promised, or foreordained, before the world was. Surely these matters must have been determined by the kind of lives we had lived in that premortal spirit world. (Harold B. Lee, "Understanding Who We Are Brings Self-Respect," *Ensign,* January 1974, 2)

SUMMARY

Foreordination is part of the plan of salvation according to the foreknowledge of God and the righteousness of certain individuals in premortal life. Everyone who comes to this earth has the capacity to receive the blessings of exaltation according to his or her obedience to the laws and commandments of God. The status or hierarchical position of one's calling does not exalt; only individual righteousness and the grace of God can lift one to a state of exaltation and eternal life.

FORGIVENESS

The capacity to forgive is one of the most divine attributes we can possess. It is a commandment of God to forgive others (see Matt. 6:15). Forgiveness brings peace to the forgiver as well as those forgiven. Without a doubt, true forgiveness is one of the most difficult aspects of human behavior to perfect. It is an expression of godliness; as God is forgiving and merciful, so we ought to be. Forgiveness of one's sins is covered in this volume under *Repentance*.

THE SCRIPTURES TEACH US

Matthew 6:12, 14–15. *And forgive us our debts, as we forgive our debtors. For if ye forgive men their trespasses, your heavenly Father will also forgive you: But if ye forgive not men their trespasses, neither will your Father forgive your trespasses.*

Forgiving others is a commandment of God (see 3 Ne. 13:14–15). Through the Atonement, we are forgiven as we forgive others, because only as we forgive others do we show that we are truly repentant and humble before the Lord. We do not purchase our forgiveness from the Lord; rather, we prove our complete devotion to Him by exhibiting a forgiving spirit.

Matthew 18:32–35. *Then his lord, after that he had called him, said unto him, O thou wicked servant, I forgave thee all that debt, because thou desiredst me: Shouldest not thou also have had compassion on thy fellowservant, even as I had pity on thee? And his lord was wroth, and delivered him to the tormentors, till he should pay all that was due unto him. So likewise shall my heavenly Father do also unto you, if ye from your hearts forgive not every one his brother their trespasses.*

If we do not forgive others, having pleaded for our own forgiveness from the Lord, we must suffer even as the man in this scripture who had to pay for his unwillingness to forgive. Simply put, if we forgive others, we can be forgiven of the Lord (see Luke 6:37).

3 Nephi 12:23–24. *Therefore, if ye shall come unto me, or shall desire to come unto me, and rememberest that thy brother hath aught against thee—Go thy way unto thy brother, and first be reconciled to thy brother, and then come unto me with full purpose of heart, and I will receive you.*

Before we seek forgiveness from our Heavenly Father, we must first resolve our concerns and misgivings with our fellowmen. Then our hearts will be pure, we will have peace of conscience, and the Lord will receive us.

Doctrine and Covenants 64:9–10. *Wherefore, I say unto you, that ye ought to forgive one another; for he that forgiveth not his brother his trespasses standeth condemned before the Lord; for there remaineth in him the greater sin. I, the Lord, will forgive whom I will forgive, but of you it is required to forgive all men.*

Forgiveness is tied to our righteousness to such an extent that we are condemned of the Lord and we have the greater sin if we fail to forgive others. We may wonder how this can be so when we are sometimes victims.

However, the Lord was the greatest victim of all and yet He uttered, "Father, forgive them; for they know not what they do" (Luke 23:34). Christ was forgiving by nature: though the soldiers crucified Him, He forgave them. We are commanded to be like Him (see 3 Ne. 27:27), so we ought to be forgiving like He is.

MODERN PROPHETS SPEAK

Spencer W. Kimball:
> Do we follow that command [to be reconciled with our brother] or do we sulk in our bitterness, waiting for our offender to learn of it and to kneel to us in remorse?
>
> And this reconciliation suggests also forgetting. Unless you forget, have you forgiven? A woman in a branch in the mission field where there had been friction finally capitulated and said, "Yes, I will forgive the others, but I have an eternal memory." Certainly she had not fulfilled the law of forgiving. She was meeting the letter but not the spirit. Frequently we say we forgive, then permit the grievance to continue to poison and embitter us.
>
> The Lord forgets when he has forgiven, and certainly must we. He inspired Isaiah to say: "I, even I, am he that blotteth out thy transgressions for mine own sake, and will not remember thy sins." (Isaiah 43:25.)
>
> No bitterness of past frictions can be held in memory if we forgive with all our hearts. So long as we are bitter, hold grudges, and are unrepentant ourselves and unforgiving to others, how can we partake of the sacrament? (*Faith Precedes the Miracle* [Salt Lake City: Deseret Book, 1972], 194)
>
> He who will not forgive others breaks down the bridge over which he himself must travel. This is a truth taught by the Lord in the parable of the unmerciful servant who demanded to be forgiven but was merciless to one who asked forgiveness of him. (See Matt. 18:23–35.) (*The Miracle of Forgiveness* [Salt Lake City: Bookcraft, 1969], 269)

Joseph Smith:
> Meekly persuade and urge everyone to forgive one another all their trespasses, offenses and sins, that they may work out their own salvation with fear and trembling. Brethren, bear and forbear one with another, for so the Lord does with us. Pray for your enemies in the Church and curse not your foes without: for vengeance is mine, saith the Lord, and I will repay. To every ordained member, and to all, we say, be merciful and you shall find mercy. (*Discourses of the Prophet Joseph Smith,* comp. Alma P. Burton [Salt Lake City: Deseret Book, 1977], 213)

Gordon B. Hinckley:
> What a glorious and wonderful season of year this is. Our hearts change. Our attitudes change. Our way of thinking changes. There is a little more forgiveness in us. A little more of kindness. A little more of love. A little more of patience. A little more of understanding at the Christmas season of the year. (*Teachings of Gordon B. Hinckley* [Salt Lake City: Deseret Book, 1997], 60–61)

IDEAS FOR DAILY LIVING

Here are three things to remember to help us show forgiveness:

1. Forgiveness is not just something you *do*—it is something you *are*.
- Character—Forgiveness shows qualities of a Christlike character, becoming even as He is.
- *Charity*—For the forgiving person, the pure love of Christ serves as the foundation of life. Forgiveness is a sign of that love.
- *Strength*—Forgiveness is a sign of true strength, based on empathy and understanding.

2. Forgiveness brings a host of values and benefits in its wake.
- *Peace*—We will experience more peace if we forgive others. As we do so, we are free from the guilt of holding a grudge, and from allowing others' actions to have power over us.
- *Liberty*—Forgiveness frees us of hurt, anger, and the desire for vengeance and retaliation. We are free of the burden of someone else's sin.
- *Productivity*—Forgiveness will increase our ability to be creative and productive. An unforgiving attitude will sap our creativity and productivity and cause us do be trapped in a downward spiral.
- *Self-confidence*—Forgiving ourselves by learning from our mistakes and going on with our lives will increase our understanding of others and increase our wisdom.
- *Unity*—When comments are expressed to another in the spirit of understanding and forgiveness, relationships can be healed and strengthened.

3. Forgiveness is a divine process.
- *Know yourself*—We must acknowledge that we are capable of making mistakes ourselves. Therefore, forgiveness is a better choice than judging others.
- *Communicate*—If we feel offended, we must clarify the situation with the offending party. Perhaps we simply did not understand what he or she meant to say or do.
- *Realize that the other person must act too*—Forgiving another doesn't give absolution for the perpetrator. That person is ultimately responsible for his or her own actions and must make peace with his or her own past.
- *Keep learning*—Forgiveness does not mean we will forget, but rather that we can find peace and freedom from guilt. The goal is to learn from the past and try to use it to help ourselves and others.

ILLUSTRATIONS FOR OUR TIMES

An example from the Prophet Joseph Smith's life explains the nature of true forgiveness.

Unconditional Forgiveness

Many have experienced the feeling of being condemned by others unjustly or accused of unkind motives that they have never harbored. The Prophet Joseph Smith was repeatedly subjected to the most vile derision and persecution without cause or provocation. His response was consistent. He forgave. He fought for the right and defended the Church and its doctrines indefatigably in the face of the most outrageous lies and malicious attacks. He fought valiantly and forcefully, but he forgave nonetheless.

Consider his behavior toward those who inflicted serious bodily harm upon him on Saturday, March 24, 1832. At that time, he and his family were staying at the home of John Johnson in Hiram, Ohio. Suddenly, a mob of some two dozen drunken men tore Joseph from the side of his ailing son, eleven-month-old Joseph Murdock Smith (one of two adopted twins), dragged him from the house, stripped him of his clothes, beat him brutally, and tarred and feathered him. All during that night friends and family removed the skin-searing tar from his body, taking up large areas of skin in the process. Sidney Rigdon had been dragged feet-first from his home, sustaining a concussion as his head thumped down the steps and along the frozen ground. He was beaten and left comatose in the snow. Young Joseph Murdock, already suffering with measles, contracted pneumonia from the exposure that night, and died a few days later. On the morning of Sunday, March 25, the day after the brutal attack, Joseph delivered a sermon before the gathering of Saints. What was his theme? Forgiveness. A number of individuals were baptized that afternoon. Three of the mobsters present at the Prophet's sermon on forgiveness were converted and joined the Church. (See *History of the Church*, 1:261–65.)

It was a remarkable instance of unconditional forgiveness and a lasting memorial to the Prophet's understanding and embracing of the Lord's injunction to cultivate a forgiving heart and practice forgiveness every day: "Ye have heard that it hath been said, Thou shalt love thy neighbor, and hate thine enemy. But I say unto you, Love your enemies, bless them that curse you, do good to them that hate you, and pray for them which despitefully use you, and persecute you; That ye may be the children of your Father which is in heaven" (Matt. 5:43–45). It is clear that children of God are in their very essence the epitome of unconditional forgiveness.

—Richard J. Allen

SUMMARY

As we consider the act of forgiveness, let us remember that mercy begets mercy. Forgiveness leads to a literal renewal of the emotional and spiritual state. The Lord requires all of us to forgive, and He requires the offender to change and repent. We can attain a remarkable degree of freedom and peace as we forgive others. Forgiveness is truly akin to godliness and one of the defining characteristics of the children of God.

GODLINESS

Godliness implies those qualities associated with our Heavenly Father and our Savior Jesus Christ. We should be devout in our worship of God and seek to be Christlike in our everyday behavior: We seek to be like the Father and the Son by acting in a godly manner. Indeed, we seek to be even as They are (see 3 Ne. 12:48; 27:27). This is part of the process of taking upon ourselves the divine nature of Christ (see 2 Pet. 1:3–12). As we do so, our life takes on a new vision. We have an eye single to His glory, a perception born of love for all mankind, an overwhelming desire to seek to do as He would do in all things. Godliness should be our goal in everything we do and in everything we say.

THE SCRIPTURES TEACH US

1 Timothy 4:7–8. *But refuse profane and old wives' fables, and exercise thyself rather unto godliness. For bodily exercise profiteth little: but godliness is profitable unto all things, having promise of the life that now is, and of that which is to come.*

In his letter to Timothy, Paul emphasizes the importance of acquiring the attributes of godliness, as it relates to both mortality and to our life to come.

2 Peter 3:10–11. *But the day of the Lord will come as a thief in the night; in the which the heavens shall pass away with a great noise, and the elements shall melt with fervent heat, the earth also and the works that are therein shall be burned up. Seeing then that all these things shall be dissolved, what manner of persons ought ye to be in all holy conversation and godliness?*

Our greatest preparation for the last days is developing the attributes of godliness. We should learn to interact with others in a godly manner.

Doctrine and Covenants 84:20–21. *Therefore, in the ordinances thereof, the power of godliness is manifest. And without the ordinances thereof, and the authority of the priesthood, the power of godliness is not manifest unto men in the flesh.*

It is through the priesthood that we are able to fully develop and experience the power of godliness.

MODERN PROPHETS SPEAK

Joseph Smith:

> When I contemplate the rapidity with which the great and glorious day of the coming of the Son of Man advances, when he shall come to receive his Saints unto himself, where they shall dwell in his presence and be crowned with glory and immortality, when I consider that soon the heavens are to be shaken and the earth tremble and reel to and fro and that the heavens are to be unfolded as a scroll when it is rolled up, that every mountain and island are to flee away—I cry out in my heart, ". . . What manner of person ought I to be in all holy conversation and godliness!" (2 Peter 3:11). (*Joseph Smith's Commentary on the Bible,* Kent P. Jackson, comp. and ed. [Salt Lake City: Deseret Book, 1994], 210)

Lorenzo Snow:

> Be upright, just, and merciful, exercising a spirit of nobility and godliness in all your intentions and resolutions—in all your acts and dealings. Cultivate a spirit of charity, be ready to do for others more than you would expect from them if circumstances were reversed. Be ambitious to be great, not in the estimation of the worldly minded, but in the eyes of God, and to be great in this sense: "Love the Lord your God with all your might, mind and strength, and your neighbor as yourself." You must love mankind because they are your brethren, the offspring of God. Pray diligently for this spirit of philanthropy, this expansion of thought and feeling, and for power and ability to labor earnestly in the interest of Messiah's kingdom. (*The Teachings of Lorenzo Snow,* ed. Clyde J. Williams [Salt Lake City: Bookcraft, 1984], 10)

Charles W. Nibley:

> What power, then, what mysterious power is it that had led and guided them [the Latter-day Saints] and that still leads and guides them and holds them together as they are held? Let me tell you what it is. I will read from the book of Doctrine and Covenants, Section 84: [vs. 19–21, quoted.]

> That is what holds these people together—the power of the priesthood. And in the administration of it we have seen and do see the power of godliness; not a form of godliness, mind you, but the power of godliness. Paul said that in the latter days men would be "having a form of godliness but denying the power thereof" [2 Tim. 3:5]; but what I refer to is the power of godliness. Have you ever seen it manifested in your lives? We heard of it this morning from the leader of the

Church as manifested in the healing of the sick. We see it in the temples of the Lord; we see it in the sick rooms; we see it manifested in presidencies of stakes, bishoprics of wards.

In all the leadership of the priesthood you see that same power of godliness. . . . It is the power of godliness, of godly lives. It is the power of godly men and godly women, through the ordinances of the priesthood made manifest; and everyone shares in it. (*Latter-day Prophets and the Doctrine and Covenants,* comp. Roy W. Doxey [Salt Lake City: Deseret Book, 1978], 3:74)

IDEAS FOR DAILY LIVING

Here are seven ideas to help us acquire the attributes of godliness:

1. Ponder the word. Study the word of God as given in the scriptures and through the voice of the living prophets. Herein are the attributes of godliness identified, clarified, and put forward for emulation (see Jacob 3:2; Alma 32:28; D&C 138:1–11).

2. Choose the best patterns. Organize and structure your life after the best models and examples—the Lord's prophets and servants, righteous neighbors and family members. Especially seek to follow in the footsteps of the Savior (see Matt. 16:24).

3. Be clean. Cleanliness is next to godliness as reflected in purity of thought (see Prov. 23:7) and actions (see Mosiah 5:15; James 1:22).

4. Be obedient. Godliness entails righteousness (see D&C 27:14; 98:30). Faith is the foundation of righteousness (see Rom. 3:22; 9:30–32); hence it is most important as we seek godliness (see 2 Pet. 1:3–12; Moro. 10:32–33; D&C 4:6).

5. Be a leader in all walks of life. Godliness entails being a good example. Through our example we can lift and bless others (1 Tim. 4:12; Alma 17:11; 3 Ne. 12:16).

6. Be prepared—Recognize that those who lead a godly life will suffer persecution (see 2 Tim. 3:12). Understand the blessings and the challenges.

7. Remember—Create a way to remember the things that are required in taking upon oneself the attributes of godliness. Surround yourself with reminders: pictures, charts, posters, notes—anything that will bring the principles of godliness to mind throughout the day. Guard against forgetting due to the ease of the way (see Hel. 12:1–2), but remember the goodness and mercy of the Lord in all things (see Mosiah 4:11).

ILLUSTRATIONS FOR OUR TIMES

Apostle Russell M. Nelson discusses the attribute of godliness in the following excerpt from a general conference address:

Examples of Godliness

Godliness is an attribute that seems as difficult to define as it is to attain. Scriptures refer to "the mystery of godliness." (1 Tim. 3:16; D&C 19:10.) . . .

Simon Peter counseled us "to be in all holy conversation and godliness, looking for and hasting unto the coming of the day of God." (2 Pet. 3:11–12.)

"The power of godliness is manifest" in the ordinances of the priesthood. (D&C 84:20.) Godliness is not a product of perfection; it comes of concentration and consecration.

Godliness characterizes each of you who truly loves the Lord. You are constantly mindful of the Savior's atonement and rejoice in His unconditional love. Meanwhile you vanquish personal pride and vain ambition. You consider your accomplishments important only if they help establish His kingdom on earth.

The Mormon Tabernacle Choir's songs helped to convey their uncommon spirit of godliness. From their hearts the choir sang one number which bore testimony of love so amazing, so divine. Tears moistened the faces of more than a few as they expressed personal feelings of conversion and commitment to godliness. This song which the choir will soon sing includes these verses penned by Isaac Watts:

When I survey the wondrous cross
On which the Prince of glory died,
My richest gain I count but loss,
And pour contempt on all my pride.

Forbid it, Lord, that I should boast,
Save in the death of Christ, my God!
All the vain things that charm me most,
I sacrifice them to his blood. . . .

Were the whole realm of nature mine,
That were a present far too small;
Love, so amazing, so divine,
Demands my soul, my life, my all!

Such are lessons taught by those who "serve unto the example and shadow of heavenly things." (Heb. 8:5.) Unitedly members of the Mormon Tabernacle Choir testify of the living Lord and of His Church restored in these latter days, as do I. May God bless us to lift our lives by their example, I pray in the name of Jesus Christ, amen. (Russell M. Nelson, "These . . . Were Our Examples," *Ensign*, November 1991, 59ff)

SUMMARY

Godliness follows faith, virtue, knowledge, temperance, patience, and brotherly kindness in our development of our divine nature (see 2 Pet. 1:3–12). Godliness precedes charity, the pure love of Christ. As we begin to think and act in a godly manner, we begin to understand charity—we begin to possess this ultimate attribute. Thus we see the utmost importance of godliness in our efforts to be like and be one with God. When we develop godliness, our hearts are set on the things of God.

GOOD WORKS

Good works can be defined in many ways. Ultimately, "good works" pertains to those things we do to build up the kingdom of God. Good works include living up to the covenants we make and doing all we can to further the work of the gospel. Good works involve being like Christ, serving as He would have us serve in the kingdom. True service is based on love, and nothing is as fulfilling as service. Serving those who cannot help themselves is a vicarious act and one of the greatest expressions of love. We lose ourselves in the service of others, and we find our true power in doing so. We overcome all feelings of selfishness, and as we serve others, they will have a desire to serve. Service is not just contagious, but exponential in its power to affect lives throughout the world.

THE SCRIPTURES TEACH US

Matthew 25:40. *And the King shall answer and say unto them, Verily I say unto you, Inasmuch as ye have done it unto one of the least of these my brethren, ye have done it unto me.*

Mosiah 2:17. *And behold, I tell you these things that ye may learn wisdom; that ye may learn that when ye are in the service of your fellow beings ye are only in the service of your God.*

As we serve others, we truly serve our Savior. When we believe this, we will serve others automatically and will find great joy in doing so. We will share the goodness that we have found in life with others.

James 2:26. *For as the body without the spirit is dead, so faith without works is dead also.*

The Lord Himself warns us that faith alone is not enough. We cannot just believe; we have to be sincere in *living* our beliefs, in doing what we know is right. At the same time, good works alone do not qualify us for the blessings of salvation and eternal life. None of us is perfect, and therefore none of us can be justified by the law without the atoning sacrifice of the Savior (see 2 Ne. 2). In addition to the good works and service we perform, we need the grace of God to carry us the remaining distance back to our heavenly home.

Mosiah 4:15. *But ye will teach them to walk in the ways of truth and soberness; ye will teach them to love one another, and to serve one another.*

As we walk in the ways of the Lord, we will do the things that He would do. All of the work of our Savior is motivated by love (see 2 Ne. 26:24). When we truly love others, we will serve them and perform good works of charity and compassion.

Doctrine and Covenants 81:5. *Wherefore, be faithful; stand in the office which I have appointed unto you; succor the weak, lift up the hands which hang down, and strengthen the feeble knees.*

As Saints of the latter days we have been given a great work to do. Fulfilling the callings and opportunities extended to us is part of keeping our baptismal covenant to help people with their burdens, and to comfort them in their hour of need (see Mosiah 18:8–9). The Lord commands us to reach down and lift up those around us that they too may enjoy happiness and eternal life.

MODERN PROPHETS SPEAK

Jeffrey R. Holland:

> The spiritual impact of that doctrine of restoration is sobering for those who may have believed that Christ's atonement and their resurrection would somehow bring something more than was deserved. Alma made it very clear that if our works are good in this life, and the desires of our hearts are good, then in the Resurrection we will be restored to that which is good. But, by the same token, if our works are evil, then our reward will be the restoration of evil in the Resurrection. To Corianton, who apparently was taking casually some of these "points of doctrine," Alma expressed strongly that no one should fallaciously assume that the restorative powers of the Resurrection could restore one "from sin to happiness." That can never be, for "wickedness never was happiness." (*Christ and the New Covenant: The Messianic Message of the Book of Mormon*, [Salt Lake City: Deseret Book, 1997], 242)

L. Tom Perry:

> Consider your ways. Is religion an active, vital part of your life? Are you looking for or hiding from opportunities to serve? Are you anxiously engaged in good works? (*Living with Enthusiasm* [Salt Lake City: Deseret Book, 1996], 45)

Ezra Taft Benson:

> Reach out to others. Rather than turning inward, forget self and really serve others in your Church callings, in personal deeds of compassionate service, in unknown, unheralded personal acts of kindness. (*Come, Listen to a Prophet's Voice* [Salt Lake City: Deseret Book, 1990], 59)

Gordon B. Hinckley:

> Those who are engaged in this service know that out of it all comes a sweet and satisfying feeling. This sweet blessing of the Spirit becomes literally a medicine to cure many of the ailments of our lives. From such experiences we come to realize that only when we serve others do we truly serve the Lord. (*Faith: The Essence of True Religion* [Salt Lake City: Deseret Book, 1989], 40)

David O. McKay:

> Live in all things outside yourself by love. As you serve others, the children around you, your father, your mother, your associates, ever striving to make yourself and the world better, then will your souls grow in wisdom. Therein you will find the guide to the happy life. (*Pathways to Happiness* [Salt Lake City: Bookcraft, 1957], 161)

IDEAS FOR DAILY LIVING

Here are four things to consider in performing good works, and in loving and serving your fellowmen:

1. Do good with no thought of personal reward.

- *Service is unconditional*—When you serve, do not look for rewards or bonuses. Instead, do good works without any expectation of recognition or return.
- *Don't keep score*—When doing good works, don't keep track. "[Love] is to be all made of faith and service," said Shakespeare. Don't compare your works to others; just do the best you can.
- *Goodness is timeless*—Momentary pleasures are fleeting and leave no traces; service and other good works leave behind an influence for good that never fades.

- *Service is inner satisfaction*—Notice the feelings you have after you do a good deed. You can enjoy those feelings of inner peace by simply doing good, and that should be reward enough.

2. Adopt the service "habit."
- *Follow the universal rule of service*—Use the Golden Rule as your guiding principle: Treat others in the same way you wish to be treated.
- *Service and duty are partners*—Recognize the inherent duties of service within your roles in the family.
- *Plan to do good*—Plan to be regularly involved in good activities and to give service regularly. But don't forget to be spontaneous, serving whenever you discern a need.
- *Serve proactively*—Service does not say, "Let me know if you need any help." Service takes appropriate action *now*.
- *Do it with a smile*—When you serve, do it with a willing smile and never condescendingly. Always attempt to make the person feel glad he or she came to you or allowed you to help.

3. Teach good works through example.
- *Goodness is the most enduring legacy*—There is no greater example to leave behind for your family than a life of goodness and service to your children and others.
- *Service is contagious*—Service offers the receiver motivation to give in a like manner, generating exponential blessings.
- *Encourage through gratefulness*—Receive kindness and service with gratitude and thanksgiving. There is nothing that reinforces and teaches service more effectively.

4. Balance your service.
- *Be generous in scope*—Remember that service is multifaceted. It can be an expression of concern, love, or gratitude, where emotions and feelings are served. On the other hand, service can be intellectual, fostering learning and growth, or it can be social, as in being a friend. It can be temporal as to things and deeds.
- *Follow the tracks of need*—Service is especially appropriate on behalf of widows, the infirm, the fatherless, the hungry, the homeless, the cold—any place where fundamental human needs are wanting.
- *Remember to feed your own soul*—If you want to truly help others, you must nourish your soul through the good works of prayer, church attendance, scripture study, temple worship, and so on. In doing these good things you are helping others by building up the kingdom.

ILLUSTRATIONS FOR OUR TIMES

President Thomas S. Monson recounts the reorganization of a stake where he was prompted to recognize the good works and influence of the outgoing stake president.

Twenty-three Years of Service

Some years ago I was in Star Valley, Wyoming, to effect a reorganization of the stake presidency there. The stake president at the time was the late E. Francis Winters. He had served faithfully for the lengthy term of twenty-three years. Though modest by nature and circumstance, he had been a perpetual pillar of strength to everyone in the valley. On the day of the stake conference, the building was filled to overflowing. Each heart seemed to be saying a silent thank-you to this noble leader who had given so unselfishly of his life for the benefit of others.

As I stood to speak following the reorganization of the stake presidency, I was prompted to do something I had not done before. I stated how long Francis Winters had presided in the stake; then I asked all whom he had blessed or confirmed as children to stand and remain standing. Then I asked all those persons whom President Winters had ordained, set apart, personally counseled, or blessed to please stand. The outcome was electrifying. Every person in the audience rose to his feet. Tears flowed freely—tears that communicated better than could words the gratitude of tender hearts. I turned to President and Sister Winters and said, "We are witnesses today of the prompting of the Spirit. This vast throng reflects not only individual feelings but also the gratitude of God for a life well-lived." (Thomas S. Monson, *Inspiring Experiences That Build Faith: From the Life and Ministry of Thomas S. Monson* [Salt Lake City: Deseret Book, 1994], 45)

SUMMARY

Perhaps the most succinct and memorable statement about service in the kingdom of God is this: "Pure religion and undefiled before God and the Father is this, To visit the fatherless and widows in their affliction, and to keep himself unspotted from the world" (James 1:27). To be wholly devoted to the welfare of others is our religion. "There is no higher religion than human service. To work for the common good is the greatest creed," observed Albert Schweitzer, himself a devoted practitioner of good works and charity. When we become a service-oriented people, life's greatest blessing will come to us: happiness. Good works and service are the by-products of love, and life offers us an endless variety of ways to assist and bless others. Let us magnify our callings and rise to the challenge of being a Zion people by giving our life in service and good works on behalf of all those within our circle of influence.

GOSPEL OF JESUS CHRIST

The gospel or the "good news" is best defined in the Savior's own words: "Behold I have given unto you my gospel, and this is the gospel which I have given unto you—that I came into the world to do the will of my Father, because my Father sent me. And my Father sent me that I might be lifted up upon the cross; and after that I had been lifted up upon the cross, that I might draw all men unto me, that as I have been lifted up by men even so should men be lifted up by the Father, to stand before me, to be judged of their works, whether they be good or whether they be evil—And for this cause have I been lifted up; therefore, according to the power of the Father I will draw all men unto me, that they may be judged according to their works" (3 Ne. 27:13–15).

The gospel is the foundation of the Church (see 3 Ne. 27:8–11). The doctrine of Christ—including all of the principles and ordinances of the gospel—is what we accept and apply in order to make the Atonement of Jesus Christ active in our lives. We must remember that the fulness of the gospel becomes efficacious as we *live* the gospel of Jesus Christ, not merely acknowledge it. Knowing is not enough: we must live it. The gospel, just like all of the associated doctrines, principles, covenants, ordinances, and priesthoods, is centered in Christ.

THE SCRIPTURES TEACH US

Ether 4:18. *Therefore, repent all ye ends of the earth, and come unto me, and believe in my gospel, and be baptized in my name; for he that believeth and is baptized shall be saved; but he that believeth not shall be damned; and signs shall follow them that believe in my name.*

All mankind must not only believe in the gospel of Jesus Christ, but repent and be baptized in order to be saved. Again, just knowing is not enough; we must *do*.

Doctrine and Covenants 76:40–42. *And this is the gospel, the glad tidings, which the voice out of the heavens bore record unto us—That he came into the world, even Jesus, to be crucified for the world, and to bear the sins of the world, and to sanctify the world, and to cleanse it from all unrighteousness; That through him all might be saved whom the Father had put into his power and made by him.*

The gospel is centered in the Atonement of the Lord Jesus Christ. Every individual must be sanctified and cleansed through Christ's Atonement. It is only through our Savior that all mankind can be saved by obedience to the principles and ordinances of the gospel.

Moses 5:58. *And thus the gospel began to be preached, from the beginning, being declared by holy angels sent forth from the presence of God, and by his own voice, and by the gift of the Holy Ghost.*

The gospel of Jesus Christ has been preached since the beginning of time. It didn't start with Christ's birth, or with the law of Moses, or even with Adam's Fall. It is eternal. It is our duty not only to believe it, but to preach it to all the world (see Matt. 24:14; Mark 16:15; Morm. 9:22; D&C 18:28).

MODERN PROPHETS SPEAK

Gordon B. Hinckley:

> I want to thank you for living the gospel, for doing what is right, for keeping the commandments and living in faith. I want to thank you for the goodness of your lives. You are the kind of people who keep the Church going. You pay your tithing and your fast offerings, you observe the Word of Wisdom. You try to do the right thing. You have family home evening. You try to help one another. You read the scriptures. You are my kind of people—good people, faithful people. Thank you for being the kind of people you are.

> I encourage you to go forward and live the gospel and love the gospel. Make it a part of your lives—this great and glorious thing which has come to us through the providence of the Almighty. Live the gospel. Love the gospel. Read the scriptures. You won't get a testimony of the Book of Mormon unless you read the Book of Mormon. You won't get a testimony of the Doctrine and Covenants unless you read the Doctrine and Covenants. Faith comes of drinking at the fountain of eternal truth.

> The gospel of Jesus Christ is the only thing that will bless the lands of the world. Many people live in poverty and ignorance. They have a long way to go, and the gospel provides a bridge over which they walk, as it were, from their present situation to a brighter future. (*Teachings of Gordon B. Hinckley* [Salt Lake City: Deseret Book, 1997], 245)

Joseph Fielding Smith:

> The Church has two great responsibilities, that is the members of the Church have these responsibilities. . . . It is our individual duty to preach the gospel by precept and by example among our neighbors. In section 88 of the Doctrine and Covenants we are informed that even those who are warned are under the obligation to receive the message and also to warn their neighbors.
>
> The people who are living are entitled to hear the message, so this responsibility to teach the world is an outstanding one. We cannot get away from this obligation. The Lord declared that his coming is nigh at hand and that he would cut short his work in righteousness. It is our duty, then, to do all we can, and the Lord will bring to our aid other forces besides our missionaries that his work may advance and his words be fulfilled.
>
> I speak of this responsibility at this time for fear there may be some who think the work they are doing is the great work of this dispensation. The people engaged in the Relief Society, the Sunday School, and the Mutual work, feel that they have great responsibilities, and they have, but their work does not overshadow this great duty of preaching the gospel to the world.
>
> The other great responsibility which is placed upon each of us individually is to seek after our dead. (*Doctrines of Salvation,* 3 vols., ed. Bruce R. McConkie [Salt Lake City: Bookcraft, 1954–1956], 1:307)

IDEAS FOR DAILY LIVING

As is obvious from the size of this book, the gospel of Jesus Christ encompasses a great deal, and there is much we can do to improve how we live the gospel. Here are just a few general ideas to help you understand and live the gospel of Jesus Christ:

1. Search the scriptures. They contain the written word of the gospel of Jesus Christ, and we are to live by that word (see D&C 84:43–44).

2. Pray. Pray and ponder to better understand and appreciate the gospel so that it will become part of your life (see 3 Nephi 17:3; D&C 138:1–11).

3. Plan. Set some goals and develop a plan (see D&C 88:119) to live the principles and ordinances of the gospel on a daily basis. Let us not just exist; we need to be anxiously engaged (see D&C 58:27–29), with a goal and a path.

4. Cultivate charity. Understand the worth of souls. They are precious to our Heavenly Father and our Savior, and they are our brothers and sisters (see John 3:16; 2 Ne. 26:24; Mosiah 28:3; D&C 18:10–16; Moses 1:39). Learn to love others as He does.

5. Be active in temple work. Attend the temple regularly to refresh your mind concerning your covenants and to be involved in the redemption of the dead (see D&C 128:15; 138:53–54).

6. Proclaim the gospel. Set a date for missionary activity, open your mouth (see D&C 33:8–11), assist the missionaries in every possible way, pray for those who do not know God (see Alma 6:6), place copies of the Book of Mormon, use pass-along cards, and so forth. Share this marvelous gift you've been blessed with.

7. **Remind yourself to remember.** Have a method to remember the Savior (see D&C 20:77, 79), to remember your covenants, to keep the commandments, to search and apply the scriptures to your life, to do good on a daily basis, and especially to remember who you really are. Use pictures, posters, notes, photos, desk objects—anything that will bring the gospel to mind throughout the day (see Mosiah 4:11).

8. **Focus on the Atonement.** Understand and appreciate the Atonement. When we understand and appreciate the Atonement, we will be filled with gratitude, which is a catalyst for change and a motivator to action. Feeling grateful and acting upon those feelings is essential to living the gospel on a daily basis (see 2 Ne. 9; D&C 19:15–19; review *Atonement* in the book).

ILLUSTRATIONS FOR OUR TIMES

The following story illustrates the personal nature of the gospel of Jesus Christ:

Timeless Gospel

Something my widowed Aunt Viola said to me when I was only ten or eleven years of age was life changing. She took me aside not long after my mother had passed away in giving birth to my younger brother, Robert, and shared with me the following experience. During a dream one night it seemed to her as though my mother had come to her and requested solemnly and with tenderness that she help care for her three bereaved children. So real was the impact of this experience that my aunt took it most seriously. In fact, throughout the rest of my early years, she found every occasion to provide special service and guidance, much like a mother would do. It was as if the hand of charity was being extended from the unseen world to bless and nurture those still plying the pathways of mortality.

What more fitting description could there be of the nature of the gospel of Jesus Christ? It is a boundless, all-pervasive program of heavenly nurture, transcending the limits of space and the confines of time to endow individuals, in whatever phase of spiritual progress they might find themselves, with the blessings essential for eternal growth and vitality. The Savior extends His hand of charity to all mankind in a gesture of divine redemption that began in the premortal realm, continues throughout mortality, reaches the pinnacle of atoning advocacy with the judgment—when He is to draw all individuals to the Father "to stand before me, to be judged of their works, whether they be good or whether they be evil" (3 Ne. 27:14)—and extends on into the eternities. Just as mothers give life to their children and continue to yearn for their well-being, even beyond the veil, the Father and the Son give life to all mankind and, through the gospel of Jesus Christ, bestow upon all individuals a persistent, enduring, and longsuffering blessing of compassion and love. Such is the nature of the timeless gospel.

—Richard J. Allen

SUMMARY

The fulness of the gospel was restored in these the latter days. The gospel of Jesus Christ is the foundation of the Church and kingdom of God. The Atonement of Jesus Christ is the core of the gospel. All things in the plan of salvation are centered in Jesus Christ. This is why "we talk of Christ, we rejoice in Christ, we preach of Christ, we prophesy of Christ, and we write according to our prophecies, that our children may know to what source they may look for a remission of their sins" (2 Ne. 25:26). We live this gospel as we practice its first four principles and ordinances: faith (in Jesus Christ), repentance (through Jesus Christ), baptism (by means of which we take upon us the name of Jesus Christ), and then receiving the gift of the Holy Ghost from the Father (because of Jesus Christ), and then enduring to the end. It is our duty to know and live the gospel, and to take it unto all the world.

GRACE

The grace of God is manifested by His great love, mercy, and kindness to His children. From the creation, to the Atonement, the resurrection, and on to eternal life, His grace is evident. It is the grace of God that makes up for all our weaknesses and fulfills the law of justice after all we can do (see 2 Ne. 25:23). Through His grace, we become justified and sanctified (see D&C 20:30–32). The grace of our Heavenly Father and our Savior is sufficient for all those who love Them and keep Their commandments.

THE SCRIPTURES TEACH US

1 Corinthians 15:10. *But by the grace of God I am what I am: and his grace which was bestowed upon me was not in vain; but I laboured more abundantly than they all: yet not I, but the grace of God which was with me.*

Let us never forget that without the grace of God we are nothing. Our Heavenly Father expects us to labor abundantly in the cause of Christ in gratitude, but we cannot save ourselves. It is through God that we can do all and fulfill our potential.

Ephesians 2:8–10. *For by grace are ye saved through faith; and that not of yourselves: it is the gift of God: Not of works, lest any man should boast. For we are his workmanship, created in Christ Jesus unto good works, which God hath before ordained that we should walk in them.*

This well-known scripture is sometimes incorrectly used to indicate that we need not do good works to be exalted, but verse 10 makes it clear that we are expected to do good and not merely rely on the goodness of our Savior. Again, it is through the grace of God that we *can* do good works and progress.

2 Nephi 10:24. *Wherefore, my beloved brethren, reconcile yourselves to the will of God, and not to the will of the devil and the flesh; and remember, after ye are reconciled unto God, that it is only in and through the grace of God that ye are saved.*

When we reconcile ourselves to Christ, we accept Him, we submit ourselves to His will, and we are in total harmony with His commandments, doing all in our power to be obedient and Christlike. Then, through the grace of God we are saved.

2 Nephi 25:23. *For we labor diligently to write, to persuade our children, and also our brethren, to believe in Christ, and to be reconciled to God; for we know that it is by grace that we are saved, after all we can do.*

We are commanded to do all that we can in order to qualify for the eternal blessings of the grace of God and thus return to the presence of our Heavenly Father.

Doctrine and Covenants 20:30–34. *And we know that justification through the grace of our Lord and Savior Jesus Christ is just and true; And we know also, that sanctification through the grace of our Lord and Savior Jesus Christ is just and true, to all those who love and serve God with all their mights, minds, and strength. But there is a possibility that man may fall from grace and depart from the living God; Therefore let the church take heed and pray always, lest they fall into temptation; Yea, and even let those who are sanctified take heed also.*

As we repent, we are justified and sanctified through the grace of God; however, if we do not continue in good works, we can lose the blessings of the grace of God. It behooves us to continue on the straight and narrow course, thus qualifying for the grace of God.

MODERN PROPHETS SPEAK

Dallin H. Oaks:

> We are not saved *in* our sins, as by being unconditionally saved through confessing Christ and then, inevitably, committing sins in our remaining lives (see Alma 11:36–37). We are saved *from* our sins (see Hel. 5:10) by a weekly renewal of our repentance and cleansing through the grace of God and His blessed plan of salvation (see 3 Ne. 9:20–22). ("Have You Been Saved?" *Ensign*, May 1998, 55)

James E. Faust:

> The nature of the Atonement and its effects is so infinite, so unfathomable, and so profound that it lies beyond the knowledge and comprehension of mortal man. I am profoundly grateful for the principle of saving grace. Many people think they need only confess that Jesus is the Christ and then they are saved by grace alone. We cannot be saved by grace alone, "for we know that it is by grace that we are saved, *after* all we can do." ("The Atonement: Our Greatest Hope," *Ensign*, November 2001, 18)

Spencer W. Kimball:

> One of the most fallacious doctrines originated by Satan and propounded by man is that man is saved alone by the grace of God; that belief in Jesus Christ alone is all that is needed for salvation. . . . One passage in the Book of Mormon, written perhaps with the same intent as Paul's statement above—to stress and induce appreciation for the gracious gift of salvation offered on condition of obedience—is particularly enlightening: "For we labor diligently to write, to persuade our children, and also our brethren, to believe in Christ, and to be reconciled to God; for we know that it is by grace that we are saved, after all we can do." [2 Nephi 25:23.] . . .
>
> However good a person's works, he could not be saved had Jesus not died for his and everyone else's sins. And however powerful the saving grace of Christ, it brings exaltation to no man who does not comply with the works of the gospel.
>
> Of course we need to understand terms. If by the word salvation is meant the mere salvation or redemption from the grave, the "grace of God" is sufficient. But if the term salvation means returning to the presence of God with eternal progression, eternal increase, and eventual godhood, for this one certainly must have the "grace of God," as it is generally defined, plus personal purity, overcoming of evil, and the good "works" made so important in the exhortations of the Savior and his prophets and apostles. (*The Teachings of Spencer W. Kimball*, ed. Edward L. Kimball [Salt Lake City: Bookcraft, 1982], 71)

Ezra Taft Benson:

> As a Church, we are in accord with Nephi, who said, "it is by grace that we are saved, after all we can do" (2 Nephi 25:23). Grace consists of God's gift to His children wherein He gave His Only Begotten Son that whosoever would believe in Him and comply with His laws and ordinances would have everlasting life.
>
> By grace, the Savior accomplished His atoning sacrifice so that all mankind will attain immortality. By His grace, and by our faith in His atonement and repentance of our sins, we receive the strength to do the works necessary that we otherwise could not do by our own power. By His grace we receive an endowment of blessing and spiritual strength that may eventually lead us to eternal life if we endure to the end. By His grace we become more like His divine personality. Yes, it is "by grace that we are saved, after all we can do" (2 Nephi 25:23).
>
> What is meant by "after all we can do"? "After all we can do" includes extending our best effort. "After all we can do" includes living His commandments. "After all we can do" includes loving our fellowmen and praying for those who regard us as their adversary. "After all we can do" means clothing the naked, feeding the hungry, visiting the sick and giving "succor [to] those who stand in need of [our] succor" (Mosiah 4:15)—remembering that what we do unto one of the least of God's children, we do unto Him (see Matthew 25:34–40; D&C 42:38). "After all we can do" means leading chaste, clean, pure lives, being scrupulously honest in all our dealings and treating others the way we would want to be treated. (*The Teachings of Ezra Taft Benson* [Salt Lake City: Bookcraft, 1988], 353–54)

IDEAS FOR DAILY LIVING

Here are seven ideas to help us understand the doctrine of grace and to apply it to our lives:

1. Gratitude. The doctrine of the grace of God is founded upon His goodness toward, and love of, His children. When we come to realize this truth, we will be filled with gratitude. Gratitude is the catalyst for obedience, change, and growth. Gratitude is an essential quality in those seeking the reconciling grace of God (see 1 Cor. 1:4).

2. Love begets love. When we feel the love of our Heavenly Father, we want to reciprocate. We want to show our love by keeping the commandments (see John 14:15; 21:15–17).

3. Atonement. The love and grace of Heavenly Father (see John 3:16) and our Savior Jesus Christ (see 2 Ne. 26:24) were the motivating forces empowering the atoning sacrifice of our Lord. The accompanying effects continually bless us in all facets of our lives: He takes upon Himself our pains, sicknesses, and infirmities, and He succors us continually (see Alma 7:11–12).

4. Diligence and hard work. The Lord gives us everything; therefore, it is because of His grace that we receive temporal and spiritual blessings here upon the earth. However, the law of the harvest is part of the magnificent plan: we must prepare the earth (which is the Lord's); we must plant the seeds (which were created by the Lord as a gift to us); we must nurture the seeds (water and the nutrients are the Lord's), and we must recognize that the vitality within the seeds (from the Lord) is empowered by the sun (which power is from the Lord). We can therefore look forward to the seeds bringing forth their fruit. The same law of the harvest applies to humankind and our spiritual growth: we plant the seeds of the word of God through faith, diligence, and patience (see Alma 32:40–43); we receive the blessings of the fruit because of His grace and mercy towards us; and we cultivate our spiritual blessings through obedience and valor according to our Heavenly Father's plan. Thus it is true that we prosper and bear fruit by grace after all we can do (see 2 Ne. 25:23).

5. Recognize our weaknesses. When we recognize our weaknesses, we become humble. Then we are strengthened through the grace of God (see Ether 12:27).

6. Understand the doctrine of the Fall of Adam. We are in a fallen state, which involves both spiritual and temporal separation from God. Only through the grace of God can this separation be bridged, provided we repent (see Mosiah 4:5–11).

7. Repentance. The process of repentance requires that we seek the grace of God in order to be forgiven (see Hel. 12:24).

ILLUSTRATIONS FOR OUR TIMES

The following explores the grace and mercy of our Savior in our own lives:

Without Grace We Are Nothing

Elder Boyd K. Packer had presided over the reorganization of our Stake, and now it was time for the new leadership to be installed during a special session. The brother whom the Lord had called to be patriarch took his place on the designated chair and the Apostle laid his hands on his head and began the ordination and setting apart with the words, "Brother [mentioning his name], you are *nothing.* . . ." This last word received considerable emphasis, followed by a long pause—which gave everyone present the motivation for deep soul-searching. Then Elder Packer continued: ". . . without the Lord." It was a profoundly powerful teaching moment about leadership. No matter what our callings in the Church from time to time, we are truly "nothing without the Lord." It is the Lord, through His Spirit, who energizes our service. It is the Lord who kindles our desire, hope, and love—all essential for meaningful service. It is the Lord who activates within us the gifts and talents we must draw upon in order to contribute effectively our modest donation to the building up of His kingdom. It is the Lord, through His Spirit, who sustains us, empowers us, guides us, and teaches us the correct way to proceed. It is the Lord, through His grace, who brings us the blessings of redemption and reconciliation with the Father, "after all we can do" (2 Ne. 25:23).

The Atonement of Jesus Christ transforms our nothingness to a potentiality of spiritual grandeur based on hope, faith, and obedience. This process depends on the merits, mercy, and grace of the Savior. There is only one verse in Holy Writ that contains all three of these key words of redemption, and it occurs in the Book of Mormon in the remarkable discourse of Lehi in which he instructs his son Jacob about the dynamic process of the Atonement (see 2 Ne. 2:8). However, just before he explains this idea, Lehi reminds Jacob: "And men are instructed sufficiently that they know good from evil. And the law is given unto men. And by the law no flesh is justified; or, by the law men are cut off. Yea, by the temporal law they were cut off; and also, by the spiritual law they perish from that which is good, and become miserable forever" (2 Ne. 2:5). The Apostle Paul was to say something very similar some four centuries later: "Therefore by the deeds of the law there shall no flesh be justified in his sight: for by the law is the knowledge of sin" (Rom. 3:20).

To say that no flesh is justified by the law is to confirm that no individual can ascend to a state of reconciliation with God on the basis of obedience alone. No individual in the world, save the Savior Himself, has ever lived the law to perfection, or ever will do so. Thus there remains always a deficit in the nature and works of man that can be bridged only through an infinite sacrifice and atonement based on grace. The key to closing the spiritual gap in the progress of mankind is summarized by Lehi in the extraordinary verse alluded to earlier: "Wherefore, how great the importance to make these things known unto the inhabitants of the earth, that they may know that there is no flesh that can dwell in the presence of God, save it be through the merits, and mercy, and grace of the Holy Messiah, who layeth down his life according to the flesh, and taketh it again by the power of the Spirit, that he may bring to pass the resurrection of the dead, being the first that should rise. Wherefore, he is the firstfruits unto God, inasmuch as he shall make intercession for all the children of men; and they that believe in him shall be saved" (2 Ne. 2:8–9).

It is the intercession of the Holy Messiah that lifts mankind from a state of nothingness to a state of redeeming hope in Christ, after all they can do. It is through grace that the balance is made up. "Wherefore, redemption cometh in and through the Holy Messiah; for he is full of grace and truth" (2 Ne. 2:6).

—Richard J. Allen

SUMMARY

Understanding and appreciating the grace of God increases our love for God and helps us recognize our total dependence upon Him. This encourages us to be full of gratitude and maintain a sense of humility, which is required in order to receive the grace of God. Let us remember and keep in mind the goodness and grace of God every day of our lives. Focusing on the atoning grace of the Savior is key to keeping the commandments.

GRATITUDE

One of the cardinal virtues of life is gratitude. Gratitude is how you feel when you understand and appreciate someone or something. There is nothing quite so moving and wholesome as the experience of gratitude. It blesses both the giver and the receiver. An "attitude of gratitude" really enhances your life, for it helps you see the things that matter most.

THE SCRIPTURES TEACH US

Ephesians 5:20. *Giving thanks always for all things unto God and the Father in the name of our Lord, Jesus Christ.*

We should always give thanks to our Heavenly Father. Nothing offends God as much as not showing gratitude (see D&C 59:21), and this gratitude should include thankfulness for all things that we receive here upon the earth (see Alma 7:23).

Mosiah 2:20. *I say unto you, my brethren, that . . . you should render all the thanks and praise which your whole soul has power to possess, to that God who has created you, and has kept and preserved you, and has caused that ye should rejoice, and has granted that ye should live in peace one with another.*

It is impossible to comprehend all that we have been given. Therefore, we should strive to show our gratitude with all our strength. Nevertheless, in giving thanks unto God for all things, we are still indebted to Him (see Mosiah 2:21). God blesses us beyond the measure of our performance because He loves us.

Alma 34:38. *That ye contend no more against the Holy Ghost, but that ye receive it, and take upon you the name of Christ; that ye humble yourselves even to the dust, and worship God, in whatsoever place ye may be in, in spirit and in truth; and that ye live in thanksgiving daily, for the many mercies and blessings which he doth bestow upon you.*

When we live in thanksgiving daily, our minds are filled with gratitude for all things. Every part of our life is a blessing from God: to see, to hear, to smell, to touch, to taste, to breathe—everything we are able to do. The earth in all its beauty pleases the eye and gladdens the soul: the mountains, the rivers, the lakes, the magnificent formations, the flowers, the trees, and everything that dwells here on earth, including the animals in all their beauty and splendor.

Doctrine and Covenants 78:19. *And he who receiveth all things with thankfulness shall be made glorious; and the things of this earth shall be added unto him, even an hundred fold, yea, more.*

We receive a multitude of blessings for being grateful, and with a grateful heart we will recognize more and more of what God has given us. Gratitude expressed causes us to have an attitude of hope and faith, which moves us to action. Therefore, gratitude is a catalyst for action.

MODERN PROPHETS SPEAK

Gordon B. Hinckley:

> The grateful man sees our society is afflicted by a spirit of thoughtless arrogance unbecoming those who have been so magnificently blessed. How grateful we should be for the bounties we enjoy. Absence of gratitude is the mark of the narrow, uneducated mind. It bespeaks a lack of knowledge and the ignorance of self-sufficiency. It expresses itself in ugly egotism and frequently in wanton mischief. . . .
>
> Where there is appreciation, there is courtesy, there is concern for the rights and property of others. Without appreciation, there is arrogance and evil. (*Teachings of Gordon B. Hinckley* [Salt Lake City: Deseret Book, 1997], 247)

Joseph F. Smith:

> The grateful man sees so much in the world to be thankful for, and with him the good outweighs the evil. Love overpowers jealousy, and light drives darkness out of his life. Pride destroys our gratitude and sets up selfishness in its place. How much happier we are in the presence of a grateful and loving soul, and how careful we should be to cultivate, through the medium of a prayerful life, a thankful attitude toward God and man! (*Gospel Doctrine: Selections from the Sermons and Writings of Joseph F. Smith,* comp. John A. Widtsoe [Salt Lake City: Deseret Book, 1939], 263)

Ezra Taft Benson:

> The Prophet Joseph is reported to have said at one time that one of the greatest sins for which the Latter-day Saints would be guilty would be the sin of ingratitude. . . .
>
> Sometimes I feel we need to devote more of our prayers to expressions of gratitude and thanksgiving for blessings already received. (*The Teachings of Ezra Taft Benson* [Salt Lake City: Bookcraft, 1988], 363)

Brigham Young:

> I do not know of any, excepting the unpardonable sin, that is greater than the sin of ingratitude. (*Discourses of Brigham Young,* ed. John A. Widtsoe [Salt Lake City: Bookcraft, 1998], 228)

IDEAS FOR DAILY LIVING

Here are four things you can do to feel and show more gratitude:

1. Remember that gratitude spreads under its own power.

- *Contagious desire*—When you show gratitude to others, their hearts are touched. You induce in them, in turn, a willingness and desire to be grateful in their homes and communities.
- *Infectious joy*—Gratitude sows joy in the receiver and the giver.
- *Transferable goodness*—When you help others see their blessings, they will have a greater desire to do good. That is one way you can leverage your contributions to family, community, and society.
- *Antidote to smallness*—Gratitude disarms envy, shames selfishness, and renders jealousy without effect.

2. Remember that gratitude brings its own rewards.

- *Confidence*—Far from showing weakness and generating dependency, gratitude, if practiced on a consistent basis, helps build feelings of confidence and self-worth.
- *Togetherness*—Gratitude builds togetherness and unity in families and groups.
- *Stature*—Gratitude enhances stature because it shows that you have greater capacity to appreciate the good. Your character is enlarged and radiates to those around you.
- *Leadership*—Gratitude is an element of leadership that attracts others to follow your example. Nothing is so needed as appreciation for a job well done.
- *Blessings of the Spirit*—Blessings of the Spirit are often felt as gratitude is expressed or received. True gratitude is expressed and received by the Spirit, and the fruits of the Spirit are felt (see D&C 11:12–13).

3. Remember that gratitude starts with the little things.

- *Look around*—Open your vision to the good in things and look for the best in others. Often by just looking for things to be grateful for, you will find that you have blessings in abundance.
- *Catch others doing good*—By catching others doing good and expressing gratitude to them for it, you not only enforce the good being done, but you open the way for greater happiness and joy in life. It's all too easy to see the negative, but it takes a strong spirit to see the positive and be grateful for it.
- *Say it*—Express gratitude on a regular basis to your family, friends, and coworkers. Everyone will be blessed.
- *Write it*—Write a thank-you note every month (or more frequently if you can) to someone who has blessed your life.
- *Ask for it*—Desire a grateful heart. Remember the prayer: "Give me one more thing, Lord—a grateful heart."

4. The Lord expects us to feel and express thanksgiving and gratitude.

- *Remember to thank God always*—We are to thank God in all things (see Eph. 5:20).
- *We offend God as we fail to give thanks*—When we fail to acknowledge God in all things, we offend Him (see Mosiah 26:39; D&C 59:21).

- *Receive all things with thanksgiving*—When we receive all things—every experience and opportunity—with thanksgiving to our God, we are exceedingly blessed (see Mosiah 2:19–21; D&C 78:19).
- *How we do things makes a difference*—Do all things with an attitude of gratitude and thanksgiving (see D&C 59:15–16).
- *Live with a mindset of a grateful heart*—Gratitude and thanksgiving should be our walk and our talk in our daily lives (see Alma 34:38).
- *Pray and offer thanksgiving*—We can rejoice in gratitude at the end of each day as we thank the Lord for all our blessings (see 2 Ne. 9:52).
- *Offer thanks through sacrifice*—In the Old Testament and early times in the Book of Mormon, the Lord's servants offered sacrifice in gratitude and thanksgiving for their blessings (see Amos 4:5; 1 Ne. 2:7; 5:9). Our true offering of thanksgiving and gratitude can be a sacrifice of our whole soul (see Jacob 1:26) and a broken heart and contrite spirit (see 2 Ne. 9:20).

ILLUSTRATIONS FOR OUR TIMES

In one of his last general conference addresses, Apostle David B. Haight provided wonderful counsel regarding the importance of expressing gratitude to our Heavenly Father.

Were There Not Ten Cleansed?

As recorded in Luke, one day the Savior entered a village where there were 10 lepers. Now, those of us who have grown up in the last few years know very little about lepers. Leprosy was a terrible, dreaded disease anciently. These 10 lepers came to the Savior and said, "Master, have mercy upon us; have mercy upon us who have that terrible ailment of leprosy." And He said to the 10 lepers, "Go visit your priest, and he will take care of you"—which they did. They went to see their priests, and they were cleansed, all 10 of them. A short time later, one of them returned to the Savior and fell on his face and his hands and his knees, thanking the Savior for blessing him and making him well from that terrible disease. And the Savior said to that one man: "Weren't there 10? What has happened to the other nine? Where are they?" (See Luke 17:11–19.)

As I've read that story again and again, it's made a great impression upon me. How would you like to be part of the "nine society"? Wouldn't that be something—to be numbered among those who failed to return and acknowledge the Savior for the blessings He had given them? Only one returned.

It's so easy in life for us to receive blessings, many of them almost uncounted, and have things happen in our lives that can help change our lives, improve our lives, and bring the Spirit into our lives. But we sometimes take them for granted. How grateful we should be for the blessings that the gospel of Jesus Christ brings into our hearts and souls. I would remind all of you that if we're ever going to show gratitude properly to our Heavenly Father, we should do it with all of our heart, might, mind, and strength—because it was He who gave us life and breath. He gave us the opportunity to live as we are, to have the gospel in our lives, to have the example of good people like President Hinckley leading the Church throughout the world today and the opportunity for the young people to look to him with pride and gratitude for a leader who looks and acts the part and demonstrates what the Spirit of Christ can bring into our heart and soul. As that gratitude is magnified and developed and expanded, it can bless our hearts and our minds and our souls to where we'd like to continue to carry on and do those things that we are asked to do. (David B. Haight, "Were There Not Ten Cleansed?" *Ensign*, November 2002, 24)

SUMMARY

Gratitude can be a catalyst for growth and change in our lives. We heard a young man express with great sincerity his gratitude for a certain blessing in his life. He came to understand and appreciate that blessing, and his new state of mind, in turn, changed his life. The principle is clear. When you feel grateful, you will desire to show it through service. And you will be amazed at how others follow your example. That is the miracle of gratitude. Certainly one of the hallmarks of a disciple of the Savior is a lifestyle that reflects gratitude and thanksgiving.

GRIEF

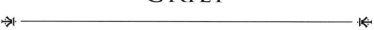

Dealing with grief is one of the great challenges in life. The feelings of agony, heartache, misery, regret, sorrow, and suffering are part of life—a very difficult part, to be sure, yet essential to the learning process. Grief is unpleasant to experience and to endure. Still, the law of opposition in all things requires that we have a measure of grief in our lives (see 2 Ne. 2:11). We will have grief in death, in sin, and in our everyday trials and tribulations, especially for those we love who have strayed from the gospel path. The Lord suffered all these things so that He might know better how to succor us in our grief (see Alma 7:11–12). He will heal us and continue to bear our grief. He will give us peace (see D&C 19:23).

THE SCRIPTURES TEACH US

Matthew 5:4. *Blessed are they that mourn: for they shall be comforted.* (Compare 3 Ne. 12:4; D&C 101:14.)

The power of the gospel is a healing and comforting power. Whatever the source of our grief, whether through bereavement or disappointment or the effects of impenitence—we can find in the gospel the means to overcome grief through the operation of the Spirit and through striving to do the will of the Father.

Mosiah 18:9. *Yea, and are willing to mourn with those that mourn; yea, and comfort those that stand in need of comfort, and to stand as witnesses of God at all times and in all things, and in all places that ye may be in, even until death, that ye may be redeemed of God, and be numbered with those of the first resurrection, that ye may have eternal life.*

As part of our baptismal covenants we promise to comfort and mourn with those who grieve. In addition, we must remember in our own times of grief that we have a community of Saints to comfort us.

Mosiah 25:11. *And again, when they thought upon the Lamanites, who were their brethren, of their sinful and polluted state, they were filled with pain and anguish for the welfare of their souls.*

Our grief for the sins of others shows our love and concern for the welfare of our brothers and sisters (see Mosiah 28:3).

Alma 38:8. *And it came to pass that I was three days and three nights in the most bitter pain and anguish of soul; and never, until I did cry out unto the Lord Jesus Christ for mercy, did I receive a remission of my sins. But behold, I did cry unto him and I did find peace to my soul.*

Sorrow and grief for sin is real. The Lord can and will heal us through His atoning sacrifice and give us peace as we repent and redirect our lives.

MODERN PROPHETS SPEAK

Thomas S. Monson:

> God in His infinite mercy has not left grieving loved ones to wonder. He has provided truth. He will inspire an upward reach, and His outstretched arms will embrace you. Jesus promises to one and all who grieve, "I will not leave you comfortless: I will come to you." ("Think to Thank," *Ensign,* November 1998, 17)

Russell M. Nelson:

> Dealing with grief occasioned by the passing of a loved one is made more tolerable because of the Lord, who provided sublime gifts of comfort and peace. He offered "the Comforter, which is the Holy Ghost, whom the Father will send" in his name. "He shall teach you all things," the Lord said, "and bring all things to your remembrance, whatsoever I have said unto you."
>
> Then the Master added: "Peace I leave with you, my peace I give unto you: not as the world giveth, give I unto you. Let not your heart be troubled, neither let it be afraid." (John 14:26–27.)
>
> Comfort and peace! What divine and priceless gifts!
>
> Remarkably reassuring for those who encounter grief is the promised visitation of the Holy Ghost—the divine Comforter—who will provide hope and perfect love. And when nourished by prayer, that hope and love will endure until the end, when all saints shall dwell with God. (See Moroni 8:26.)
>
> These gifts extend to all who truly believe in him, and are granted because of his infinite love for us. His peace comes as we comprehend his grace and act according to his will. It comes from faith founded upon his infinite atonement. To find that hope, that reassurance, and the ability to carry on, the bereaved person will seek to know the Lord and to serve him. It is his atonement that will make our future bright, regardless of the dark days inevitably encountered on life's journey. (*The Gateway We Call Death* [Salt Lake City: Deseret Book, 1995], x)

Marvin J. Ashton:

> It is expedient for all of us, particularly those who may be weighed down by grief because of acts of misconduct or misfortune, to recall that even the Prophet Joseph Smith had hours of despair because of his very trying experiences in the Liberty Jail. Perhaps he too was entitled to question, "What did I do wrong? What have I done to displease Thee, O Lord? Where have I failed? Why are the answers to my prayers and pleas withheld?" In response to the feelings of his heart and mind he cried out:
>
> "O God, where art thou? And where is the pavilion that covereth thy hiding place?" (D&C 121:1.)
>
> The reassuring response came:
>
> "My son, peace be unto thy soul; thine adversity and thine afflictions shall be but a small moment; "And then, if thou endure it well, God shall exalt thee on high; thou shalt triumph over all thy foes." (D&C 121:7–8.)

The promise God gave to Joseph Smith is a promise for all of us: "If thou endure it well, God shall exalt thee on high; thou shalt triumph over all thy foes," and also over heartaches caused by misconduct of loved ones.

As we are called upon to suffer we need to ask ourselves the question:
"The Son of Man hath descended below them all. Art thou greater than he?" (D&C 122:8.) (*Be of Good Cheer* [Salt Lake City: Deseret Book, 1987], 18)

IDEAS FOR DAILY LIVING

Here are four ideas to help us understand and deal with grief:

1. Seek to understand.
- *Grief comes with the mortal experience*—Opposition in all things is part of the plan of happiness (see 2 Ne. 2:11).
- *Grief provides an opportunity to grow*—Growth comes from overcoming and enduring well the challenges of life (see Eccl. 1:18).

2. Reach out for help—do not remain in isolation.
- *Depend on a support team*—Loved ones who can show empathy and understanding can strengthen and give hope to one who is in the midst of grief and misery. They can lighten the burden and help lift the heart to God, for He is our greatest support (see Prov. 3:5–6).
- *Priesthood power can assist*—Blessings from the priesthood can heal us both physically and spiritually (see D&C 107:18). This is one way we can invite the power of God into our lives.
- *The Savior can lighten the burden*—We must apply the Atonement to our lives in all things. All things that we bear can be laid at the feet of the Savior, and He will help us bear our burdens and make them light (see Mosiah 24:14–15; Alma 33:23).

3. Choose an affirmative perspective.
- *Faith dispels grief in time*—Remember that sooner or later things will be better as we rely on the Lord and do all that lies within our power (see D&C 123:17).
- *Be positive*—Hope in the Savior will give us strength to carry on (see Moro. 7:41). Have faith and trust in God (Alma 36:3). In virtually all cases someone somewhere will have it worse than we do. In every case, the situation is far easier than what the Savior went through during His atoning sacrifice (see D&C 19:15–19; 122:8).

4. Take active steps to dispel or dilute grief.
- *Pray*—Do not forget that prayer is always part of living the gospel. Prayer has the power to bring down the blessings of heaven (see Ps. 102).
- *Maintain a proactive attitude*—We can choose how to deal with each situation. We can be positive and move forward or we can be negative by asking, "Why me?" by fixing fault and laying blame and thus wallowing in misery. It is our choice.
- *Face it head on: be of strong courage*—Don't deny grief, but seek to overcome and accept comfort. Talk to a loved one or dear friend. Remember, it is all right to shed tears. Recognize your feelings and how they need to be addressed (see Ps 31:24).
- *Seek to serve*—When we turn ourselves outward, looking to bless and serve, we receive the comfort of the Holy Spirit, and our pain can be lightened or relieved (see Moro. 8:26).

- *Exercise foresight whenever possible*—Hindsight is always 20/20. If we are careful and count the costs and weigh each decision carefully, relying on the Lord, we can often avoid the grief and misery that come from poor decisions and behavior.
- *Be tolerant*—Everyone is different. Every person will not proceed at the same recovery rate, nor will their perception be the same. We should simply be supporting, loving, and nonjudgmental. We can never know the depths of another's feelings. We musn't compare ourselves with others who have gone through a similar experience.

ILLUSTRATIONS FOR OUR TIMES

In the following portion of a general conference address, Elder Lance B. Wickman tells the touching story of he and his wife's bereavement, and the comfort they find in the gospel:

But If Not

Grief is the natural by-product of love. One cannot selflessly love another person and not grieve at his suffering or eventual death. The only way to avoid the grief would be to not experience the love; and it is love that gives life its richness and meaning. Hence, what a grieving parent can expect to receive from the Lord in response to earnest supplication may not necessarily be an elimination of grief so much as a sweet reassurance that, whatever his or her circumstances, one's child is in the tender care of a loving Heavenly Father. . . .

I offer this as profound conviction born in the fiery crucible of life's experience. Our second son, Adam, entered our lives when I was far away in the jungles and rice paddies of Vietnam. I still have the joyful telegram announcing his birth. Adam was a blue-eyed, blond-haired little fellow with an impish personality. As he turned five years old, Adam eagerly looked forward to starting school. Then a common childhood illness blanketed our southern California community, and Adam contracted the disease. Aside from concern for his comfort, we were not worried. He even seemed to have a light case. Suddenly one morning he did not arise from his bed; he was in a deep coma. We rushed him to the hospital, where he was placed in intensive care. A constant cadre of devoted doctors and nurses attended him. His mother and I maintained a ceaseless vigil in the waiting room nearby.

I telephoned our dear stake president, a childhood friend and now a beloved colleague in the Seventy, Elder Douglas L. Callister, and asked if he would come to the hospital and join me in giving Adam a priesthood blessing. Within minutes he was there. As we entered the small, cramped space where Adam's lifeless little body lay, his bed surrounded by a bewildering maze of monitoring devices and other medical paraphernalia, the kind doctors and nurses reverently stepped back and folded their arms. As the familiar and comforting words of a priesthood blessing were spoken in faith and earnest pleading, I was overcome by a profound sense that Someone else was present. I was overwhelmed by the thought that if I should open my eyes I would see the Savior standing there! I was not the only one in that room who felt that Spirit. We learned quite by chance some months later that one of the nurses who was present that day was so touched that she sought out the missionaries and was baptized.

But notwithstanding, Adam made no improvement. He lingered between this life and the next for several more days as we pleaded with the Lord to return him to us. Finally, one morning after a fitful night, I walked alone down a deserted hospital corridor. I spoke to the Lord and told Him that we wanted our little boy to return so very much, but nevertheless what we wanted most was for His will to be done and that we—Pat and I—would accept that. Adam crossed the threshold into the eternities a short time later.

Frankly, we still grieve for our little boy, although the tender ministering of the Spirit and the passage of the years have softened our sadness. His small picture graces the mantel of our living room beside a more current family portrait of children and grandchildren. But Pat and I know that his path through mortality was intended by a kind Heavenly Father to be shorter and easier than ours and that he has now hurried on ahead to be a welcoming presence when we likewise eventually cross that same fateful threshold.

When through the deep waters I call thee to go,
The rivers of sorrow shall not thee o'erflow,
For I will be with thee, thy troubles to bless, . . .
And sanctify to thee thy deepest distress.
When through fiery trials thy pathway shall lie,
My grace, all sufficient, shall be thy supply.
The flame shall not hurt thee; I only design . . .
Thy dross to consume and thy gold to refine. . . .
The soul that on Jesus hath leaned for repose I will not,
I cannot, desert to his foes;
That soul, though all hell should endeavor to shake, . . .
I'll never, no never, no never forsake!
("How Firm a Foundation," *Hymns,* no. 85)
(Lance B. Wickman, "But If Not," *Ensign,* Nov. 2002, 30)

SUMMARY

Experiencing grief and all of its companions (including misery, woe, despair, and sorrow) is essential to our growth here upon the earth. All of us will suffer grief. The questions are: How will we deal with it? How can we grow from it? How can we help others using the lessons we have learned? All things we experience on the earth are part of our learning process and will help us become perfect as Heavenly Father and His Son are perfect. Just as Job, Joseph Smith, and many of God's choice servants suffered, so must we all suffer in our own way, remembering that Christ suffered for all mankind more than we can comprehend. Let us go forward knowing the goodness of God and maintaining our hope through Christ as we look forward to a better time and place.

HEAVENLY FATHER

Our Heavenly Father loves us. We are His children. He is all-powerful (omnipotent, see Ether 3:4). He is all-knowing (omniscient, see 2 Ne. 9:20). He is in and through all things (omnipresent, see D&C 88:41). The Doctrine and Covenants teaches us: "By these things we know that there is a God in heaven, who is infinite and eternal, from everlasting to everlasting the same unchangeable God, the framer of heaven and earth, and all things which are in them" (D&C 20:17). Heavenly Father is not only unchangeable in His role and dealings with His children, He is also no respecter of persons (see Moro. 8:18; D&C 38:16). He loves all His children infinitely and equally. His work and His glory are to bring to pass the immortality and eternal life of all of His children (see Moses 1:39). All can ask Him and He will give according to our needs and faith, for He seeks to help us return to His presence. Having a relationship with God is what life is all about. "And this is life eternal, that they might know thee the only true God, and Jesus Christ, whom thou hast sent" (John 17:3). We are totally dependent upon our Heavenly Father. We love Him and our Savior. We will seek the will of God in all things.

THE SCRIPTURES TEACH US

Psalm 111:10. *The fear of the Lord is the beginning of wisdom: a good understanding have all they that do his commandments: his praise endureth for ever.* (See also Prov. 9:10.)

There are many references in the scriptures concerning "the fear of the Lord," meaning that we should always reverence God and keep His commandments with complete resolve and obedience. Fearing God brings great blessings into our lives, including wisdom and understanding.

John 3:16. *For God so loved the world, that he gave his only begotten Son, that whosoever believeth in him should not perish, but have everlasting life.*

Our Heavenly Father loves us so much that He was willing to sacrifice His Son for our eternal welfare. This should move us to such gratitude that we not only love Heavenly Father (see Matt 22:36–40), but we have an overwhelming desire to keep His commandments (see John 14:15).

2 Nephi 9:20. *O how great the holiness of our God! For he knoweth all things, and there is not anything save he knows it.*

When we realize that God in fact knows all things, we are more anxious to call upon Him for help. We can trust that following His counsel will lead us to happiness.

Alma 26:35. *Now have we not reason to rejoice? Yea, I say unto you, there never were men that had so great reason to rejoice as we, since the world began; yea, and my joy is carried away, even unto boasting in my God; for he has all power, all wisdom, and all understanding; he comprehendeth all things, and he is a merciful Being, even unto salvation, to those who will repent and believe on his name.*

Should we not rejoice, like Amulek did in this scripture, in the greatness of our Heavenly Father? We should recognize and remember the goodness of God in all things. This will move us to such gratitude that we will want to be good and do good and trust in His knowledge and mercy.

Doctrine and Covenants 88:41. *He comprehendeth all things, and all things are before him, and all things are round about him; and he is above all things, and in all things, and is through all things, and is round about all things; and all things are by him, and of him, even God, forever and ever.*

The knowledge, power, and omnipresence of God the Father bring comfort to our soul. Confidence in Him inspires our faith and obedience, knowing as we do that He is in control. Because of His eternal perspective, He is full of justice and mercy and judges us perfectly (see Mosiah 29:12).

Doctrine and Covenants 130:22. *The Father has a body of flesh and bones as tangible as man's; the Son also; but the Holy Ghost has not a body of flesh and bones, but is a personage of Spirit. Were it not so, the Holy Ghost could not dwell in us.*

"Our Father in Heaven has a resurrected body of tangible substance. He is an exalted man. The prophet Lorenzo Snow said, "As man now is, God once was; as God now is, man may be" (Lorenzo Snow, *The Teachings of Lorenzo Snow,* ed. Clyde J. Williams [Salt Lake City: Bookcraft, 1984], 2). We can claim this amazing promise through righteousness.

MODERN PROPHETS SPEAK

Henry B. Eyring:
> How can you and I remember, always, the goodness of God, that we can retain a remission of our sins? The Apostle John recorded what the Savior taught us of a gift of remembrance which comes through the gift of the Holy Ghost: "But the Comforter, which is the Holy Ghost, whom the Father will send in my name, he shall teach you all things, and bring all things to your remembrance, whatsoever I have said unto you." (John 14:26.) (*To Draw Closer to God: A Collection of Discourses* [Salt Lake City: Deseret Book, 1997], 77–78)

Neal A. Maxwell:
> Just as the love of God for us is unconditional, one day ours for Him will be likewise. This is what the first commandment is all about. But even then, the adoration and awe we have developed for God will take humble and eternal notice of the vital fact stressed by John—that God loved us first. (1 John 4:19.) Indeed, while God's great plan of redemption was made *feasible* by His omniscience and His omnipotence, it was made *inevitable* because of His perfect love for us! (*All These Things Shall Give Thee Experience* [Salt Lake City: Deseret Book, 1979], 128)

Gordon B. Hinckley:
> *God has given us the power of love.* Love of what? Love for the Lord; love for his work, his cause, and his kingdom; love for people; love for one another. I have seen, time and again, how the love of God can bridge the chasm of fear. (*Faith: The Essence of True Religion* [Salt Lake City: Deseret Book, 1989], 16)

IDEAS FOR DAILY LIVING

Here are some ideas for knowing, loving, and obeying God:

1. Knowing God.
- *Through Jesus Christ*—We not only learn of God the Father through our Savior, but we come to Him through the Savior as well (see Ether 5:5).
- *The earth testifies of God*—The handiwork of God's creation witnesses of His presence and His power (see Alma 30:44).
- *Scriptures and written records testify of God*—From the beginning of time the written record has spoken of God the Father and has revealed Him to mankind through His holy prophets (see Matt. 3:17; John 3:16).
- *Revelation and prayer*—Adam, the Prophet Joseph, and others have witnessed His presence (JS–H 1:17). Through prayer, we can come to know of our Heavenly Father and His goodness (see D&C

67:10). The Holy Ghost will testify to our spirit that there is a God in the heavens who is our Father and who loves us (2 Ne. 31:18; 3 Ne. 28:11).

2. Increasing our love for God.

- *Recognize and remember the goodness of God*—There are many examples from the Book of Mormon: Nephi and his brothers were protected from Laban and enabled to obtain the records (see 1 Ne. 7:11). Lehi's family was led through the wilderness by the Liahona (see Alma 9:9). God preserved them in their voyage across the ocean (see 2 Ne. 4:20). In our own lives we can enumerate examples of when Heavenly Father has preserved us, strengthened us, and supported us. Once we recognize the grace of God in all things, we receive His enabling power.
- *Appreciate the gift of His Only Begotten Son*—When we comprehend the magnificence of the sacrifice of our Savior, our gratitude toward our Heavenly Father will deepen. This gratitude magnifies our love of God (see John 3:16; 16:27), and then our lives are changed because we have the love of God in our hearts (see 4 Ne. 1:15–16).
- *Be aware of the blessings of life*—To see, hear, smell, taste, and feel brings joy to our lives. To breathe and to have our bodies function properly are all blessings from our Heavenly Father (Alma 34:38). When we recognize that these blessings and all other blessings come from Heavenly Father, our love is intensified (see Mosiah 4:5–6).
- *Have concern for the work of God*—When we care about the things that Heavenly Father cares about (see Moses 1:39; JST, Matt. 6:38), we will seek to serve Him and our brothers and sisters (see Mosiah 28:3; Alma 36:24; Hel. 10:4–5; D&C 18:10–16). An interesting thing occurs as we serve: we learn to love those we serve. The more we serve Heavenly Father, the more we will love Him (see John 13:34–35; D&C 42:29).

3. Obeying God.

- *The greater the love, the greater the obedience*—The scriptures have taught us clearly that if we love God we will keep His commandments (see John 14:15). Love is the motive for every righteous act.
- *Understand and appreciate the doctrines, principles, and covenants*—Once we can comprehend the truth and power of the doctrines, principles, and covenants, we are filled with gratitude. We understand how careful God was and is in creating a wonderful plan for us to be able to return to Him. Through the gospel of His Son, with our covenants, we can draw nearer to God. This becomes the catalyst for change. Our attitudes, even our hearts, are full of faith and hope, resulting in a change of behavior (see 3 Ne. 27:13–15).
- *Loving the law*—There is an excitement in the gospel of Jesus Christ when we joy in the privilege of keeping the commandments—the joy of loving and serving our God and our fellowmen (see Matt. 22:36–40). The fruits of loving others are truly enjoyable; hence we love the great commandment of love. The list goes on as we come to love our Heavenly Father and the commandments that are designed to bless our lives.

ILLUSTRATIONS FOR OUR TIMES

In a general conference talk, Elder Jeffrey R. Holland gives a beautiful testimony of God the Father, as follows:

The Grandeur of God

I make my own heartfelt declaration of God our Eternal Father this morning because some in the contemporary world suffer from a distressing misconception of Him. Among these there is a tendency to feel distant from the Father, even estranged from Him, if they believe in Him at all. And if they do believe, many moderns say they might feel comfortable in the arms of Jesus, but they are uneasy contemplating the stern encounter of God. Through a misreading (and surely, in some cases, a mistranslation) of the Bible, these see God the Father and Jesus Christ His Son as operating very differently, this in spite of the fact that in both the Old Testament and the New, the Son of God is one and the same, acting as He always does under the direction of the Father, who is Himself the same "yesterday, today, and forever." . . .

Of course the centuries-long drift away from belief in such a perfect and caring Father hasn't been helped any by the man-made creeds of erring generations which describe God variously as unknown and unknowable—formless, passionless, elusive, ethereal, simultaneously everywhere and nowhere at all. Certainly that does not describe the Being we behold through the eyes of these prophets. Nor does it match the living, breathing, embodied Jesus of Nazareth who was and is in "the brightness of his glory, and the express image of his [Father]."

In that sense Jesus did not come to improve God's view of man nearly so much as He came to improve man's view of God and to plead with them to love their Heavenly Father as He has always and will always love them. The plan of God, the power of God, the holiness of God, yes, even the anger and the judgment of God they had occasion to understand. But the love of God, the profound depth of His devotion to His children, they still did not fully know—until Christ came.

So feeding the hungry, healing the sick, rebuking hypocrisy, pleading for faith—this was Christ showing us the way of the Father, He who is "merciful and gracious, slow to anger, long-suffering and full of goodness." In His life and especially in His death, Christ was declaring, "This is God's compassion I am showing you, as well as that of my own." In the perfect Son's manifestation of the perfect Father's care, in Their mutual suffering and shared sorrow for the sins and heartaches of the rest of us, we see ultimate meaning in the declaration: "For God so loved the world, that he gave his only begotten Son, that whosoever believeth in him should not perish, but have everlasting life. For God sent not his Son into the world to condemn the world; but that the world through him might be saved."

I bear personal witness this day of a personal, living God, who knows our names, hears and answers prayers, and cherishes us eternally as children of His spirit. I testify that amidst the wondrously complex tasks inherent in the universe, He seeks our individual happiness and safety above all other godly concerns. We are created in His very image and likeness, and Jesus of Nazareth, His Only Begotten Son in the flesh, came to earth as the perfect mortal manifestation of His grandeur. In addition to the witness of the ancients we also have the modern miracle of Palmyra, the appearance of God the Father and His Beloved Son, the Savior of the world, to the boy prophet Joseph Smith. I testify of that appearance, and in the words of that prophet I, too, declare: "Our heavenly Father is more liberal in His views, and boundless in His mercies and blessings, than we are ready to believe or receive. . . . God does not look on sin with [the least degree of] allowance, but . . . the nearer we get to our heavenly Father, the more we are disposed to look with compassion on perishing souls; we feel that we want to take them upon our shoulders, and cast their sins behind our backs."

I bear witness of a God who has such shoulders. And in the spirit of the holy apostleship, I say as did one who held this office anciently: "Herein [then] is love, not that we loved God, but that he loved us, and sent his Son to be the propitiation for our sins. Beloved, if God so loved us, we ought also to love one another"—and to love Him forever, I pray. In the sacred name of Jesus Christ, amen. (Jeffrey R. Holland, "The Grandeur of God," *Ensign,* November 2003, 70)

SUMMARY

We cannot say enough about the greatness and goodness of our Heavenly Father. His work is to help us return to His presence and enjoy a state of never-ending happiness. As we seek to know Him and love Him, we will find a joy in life that is consuming. Life will take a different course as we realize why we came to Earth and what Heavenly Father has in store for His faithful children: all that He has, including eternal life.

HOLY GHOST

The Holy Ghost is a personage of Spirit and is the third member of the Godhead. His influence and power can be felt throughout the earth. He has different functions and powers, including the many gifts of the Spirit (see Moro. 10:4–19; D&C 46:10–33). He is the Spirit of Truth and the Holy Spirit of Promise. He comforts, testifies, sanctifies, and acts as the constant companion of those who have received the gift of the Holy Ghost and live worthy of it. The gift of the Holy Ghost is the greatest gift we receive from our Heavenly Father to help us in our sojourn here upon the earth. The Holy Ghost will show us all things we should do (see 2 Ne. 32:5). To live worthy of this blessing, we must repent and be baptized, receive the Holy Ghost by the laying on of hands, and then keep the commandments (see D&C 20:77, 79).

THE SCRIPTURES TEACH US

2 Nephi 31:13. *By following your Lord and your Savior down into the water, according to his word, behold, then shall ye receive the Holy Ghost; yea, then cometh the baptism of fire and of the Holy Ghost; and then can ye speak with the tongue of angels, and shout praises unto the Holy One of Israel.*

When we are confirmed as members of the Church, we receive the Holy Ghost (baptism of fire). We become sanctified (holy) by the Spirit (see 3 Ne. 27:20). With the gift of the Holy Ghost, we become clean and pure. We can testify of Christ and His goodness (see John 15:26).

John 14:26. *But the Comforter, which is the Holy Ghost, whom the Father will send in my name, he shall teach you all things, and bring all things to your remembrance, whatsoever I have said unto you.*

The Spirit will console and encourage us in our times of need. The Spirit will also instruct us to do good, walk humbly, do justly, and judge righteously, and He will enlighten our souls (see D&C 11:12–13) and help us to feel love, peace, joy, and faith (see Gal. 5:22–23).

Moroni 6:9. *And their meetings were conducted by the church after the manner of the workings of the Spirit, and by the power of the Holy Ghost; for as the power of the Holy Ghost led them whether to preach, or to exhort, or to pray, or to supplicate, or to sing, even so it was done.*

Everything we do, from major life decisions to the conduct of our meetings, should be directed by the Spirit. As we do this, our actions will be fruitful and bring about righteous purposes (see D&C 43:8–10).

Moroni 10:5. *And by the power of the Holy Ghost ye may know the truth of all things.*

The Holy Ghost will witness the truth of all things to us in answer to our prayers (see D&C 6:23; 9:8–9). This is why the Nephites were so eager to receive the Holy Ghost and prayed for this special blessing (see 3 Ne. 19:9).

Doctrine and Covenants 46:11–12. *For all have not every gift given unto them; for there are many gifts, and to every man is given a gift by the Spirit of God. To some is given one, and to some is given another, that all may be profited thereby.*

According to the Lord, we have all been given gifts of the Spirit that we can use to bless people's lives. He gives us these gifts according to needs and worthiness. As we study the blessings of having the Holy Ghost with us, we come to realize the great blessing it is to feel His presence in our lives. We should ever live worthy of this blessing. (See Moro. 10:4–25 and D&C 46:10–33 for a listing of gifts of the Spirit.)

Search the Topical Guide for additional scriptures concerning the Holy Ghost.

MODERN PROPHETS SPEAK

Marion G. Romney:
> The Holy Ghost is not only a witness to the truth; he is also a great revealer and teacher of truth. ("The Holy Ghost," *Ensign,* May 1974, 90)

Neal A. Maxwell:
> In a "wheat and tares" world, how unusually blessed faithful members are to have the precious and constant gift of the Holy Ghost with reminders of what is right and of the covenants we have made. "For behold, . . . the Holy Ghost . . . will show unto you all things what ye should do." (2 Ne. 32:5.) Whatever the decibels of decadence, these need not overwhelm the still, small voice! Some of the best sermons we will ever hear will be thus prompted from the pulpit of memory— to an audience of one! ("Behold, the Enemy Is Combined," *Ensign,* May 1993, 76)

Joseph B. Wirthlin:
> As with all gifts, this gift must be received and accepted to be enjoyed. When priesthood hands were laid upon your head to confirm you a member of the Church, you heard the words, "Receive the Holy Ghost." This did not mean that the Holy Ghost unconditionally became your constant companion. Scriptures warn us that the Spirit of the Lord will "not always strive with man." When we are confirmed, we are given the *right* to the companionship of the Holy Ghost, but it is a right that we must continue to earn through obedience and worthiness. We cannot take this gift for granted. ("The Unspeakable Gift," *Ensign,* May 2003, 26)

James E. Talmage:
> As already pointed out, the special office of the Holy Ghost is to enlighten and ennoble the mind, to purify and sanctify the soul, to incite to good works, and to reveal the things of God. But, beside these general blessings, there are certain specific endowments promised in connection with the gifts of the Holy Ghost. The Savior said: "These signs shall follow them that believe; In my name shall

they cast out devils; they shall speak with new tongues; They shall take up serpents; and if they drink any deadly thing, it shall not hurt them; they shall lay hands on the sick, and they shall recover." Mark 16:17, 18; D&C 84:65–73. (*Articles of Faith* [Salt Lake City: Deseret Book, 1981], 151)

John A. Widtsoe:

Only those who conform to the first ordinances of the gospel are connected officially with the powers of the Holy Ghost in such a way as to secure added help. A distinct and real power comes to the individual who receives the Holy Ghost. It is as if he had been given a key to a vast and wonderful building which he may enter at his pleasure. However, if the key be unused, the gift is of no value. Man must seek help from the Holy Ghost, if the gift shall be real. The gift of the Holy Ghost also represents a general law, for it is evident that all who have faith made active by repentance, and show obedience to law, will be in such harmony with intelligent forces as to receive much light from them if desired or needed. (*A Rational Theology* [Salt Lake City: Deseret Book, 1937], 96–97)

Henry B. Eyring:

To me, the best directions about how to get the help of the Holy Ghost, directions that I have tested and know to be true, were given by President Marion G. Romney. I will give you his instructions in his own words. Then together let us see if we can figure out how we can work to prepare for that Sunday School teacher or quorum leader or sacrament meeting speaker to whom we will listen next Sunday.

Here are President Romney's instructions: "If you want to obtain and keep the guidance of the Spirit, you can do so by following this simple four-point program. One, *pray.* Pray diligently. Pray with each other. Pray in public in the proper places. . . . Learn to talk to the Lord; call upon his name in great faith and confidence. Second, *study* and learn the gospel. Third, *live righteously;* repent of your sins by confessing them and forsaking them. Then conform to the teachings of the gospel. Fourth, *give service* in the Church." And then President Romney concludes this way: "If you will do these things, you will get the guidance of the Holy Spirit and you will go through this world successfully, regardless of what the people of the world say or do." (*To Draw Closer to God: A Collection of Discourses* [Salt Lake City: Deseret Book, 1997], 14–15)

IDEAS FOR DAILY LIVING

Here are some of the doctrines, principles, and covenants that will help us understand the Holy Ghost, as well as some ideas to help us obtain and retain His guidance:

1. Faith. Faith, the foundation of all righteousness, is key to having the blessing and power of the Holy Ghost in our lives (see 1 Ne. 10:17).

2. Love. The motive for every righteous act is love (see John 3:16; 2 Ne. 26:24). The blessings and power of the Holy Spirit can come only to those who love God (see D&C 76:11).

3. Obedience. The law is decreed for receiving blessings (see D&C 130:20–21). The Lord has made this doctrine clear through the sacramental prayers. If we keep the commandments we can enjoy the companionship of His Spirit (see D&C 20:77, 79), and if not, we lose the blessing (see 2 Ne. 26:11; Morm. 1:14).

4. Gratitude for receiving the Holy Ghost. The gift of the Holy Ghost is received by the laying on of hands. It is a precious gift from God that brings direction and power to our lives (see Acts 8:17; D&C 20:41–43). In our gratitude for this wonderful gift, we become humble and more easily entreated by His guidance.

5. Being born again. Following baptism one receives the Holy Ghost, making complete the process of being born again (see Mosiah 27:25), becoming a new creature (see Mosiah 27:26), and being sanctified by reception of the Holy Ghost (see 3 Ne. 27:20). Remember, to be born again is essential to enter the kingdom of God as well as the Celestial Kingdom.

6. Mighty prayer. Pray and fast for the blessing of the Holy Ghost (see 3 Ne. 19:9, 21). We must literally plead for the Spirit, for without it we are left to ourselves with no comfort, no guide, no teacher, and no knowledge of truth.

7. Searching the scriptures. Faith comes by hearing the word (see Rom. 10:17). The word is given by the power of the Holy Ghost (see 2 Ne. 32:3), and it "shall be scripture, shall be the will of the Lord, shall be the mind of the Lord, shall be the word of the Lord, shall be the voice of the Lord, and the power of God unto salvation" (D&C 68:4). This is why we must live by the word of God (see D&C 84:44–46).

8. Understanding and seeking the blessings and fruits of the Spirit. When we exercise our faith, keep the commandments, show love, and are pure before the Lord, we are blessed with the Spirit. We trust in the Spirit, which leads us to do good, to do justly, to walk humbly, and to judge righteously. Thus our minds are enlightened and we feel joy (see D&C 11:12–13). We also receive the fruits of the Spirit: "love, joy, peace, longsuffering, gentleness, goodness, faith, meekness, temperance" (Gal 5:22–23).

9. Understanding and seeking the gifts of the Spirit. The gifts of the Spirit can be ours according to our needs and our stewardship responsibilities, that we in turn might be able to bless others. We should prepare to be worthy of these gifts that are given for the benefit of the children of God. Therefore, in order that we might be instruments in the hand of the Lord to bless our brothers and sisters, we should seek earnestly those gifts (see D&C 46:8). In addition, we should always give thanks for the blessings of the Spirit that we enjoy (see D&C 46:10–33).

10. Church service. Through the Holy Ghost, our efforts in the Church are magnified. We can teach effectively only by the Spirit (see D&C 42:14), and our meetings should be directed by the Spirit (see Moro. 6:9). In all of our Church service we rely on the Spirit in every facet of the work, whether it is to testify (see 3 Nephi 28:11) or do the work of the ministry (see Acts 13:2–4; 16:6). As disciples we have the joy of the Spirit (see Acts 13:52).

ILLUSTRATIONS FOR OUR TIMES

Apostle Bruce R. McConkie reveals how he was saved from serious injury, even death, when his father listened to the prompting of the Holy Ghost. In addition, Elder McConkie relates instances where righteous individuals listened to the voice of the Spirit.

Hearkening to the Voice

> I was once saved from death or serious accident because my father hearkened to the voice of the Spirit. If he had not responded instantly to the whisperings of the still small voice, my life might have ended then or had its course totally changed.

One of my earliest childhood recollections is of riding a horse through an apple orchard. The horse was tame and well broken, and I felt at home in the saddle.

But one day something frightened my mount, and he bolted through the orchard. I was swept from the saddle by the overhanging limbs, and one leg slipped down through the stirrup. I desperately hung to an almost broken leather strap that a cowboy uses to tie a lariat to his saddle. My weight should have broken the strap, but somehow it held for the moment. Another lunge or two of the stampeding horse would have broken the strap or wrenched it from my hands and left me to be dragged to injury or death with my foot entangled in the stirrup.

Suddenly the horse stopped, and I became aware that someone was holding the bridle tightly and attempting to calm the quivering animal. Almost immediately I was snatched up into the arms of my father.

What had happened? What had brought my father to my rescue in the split second before I slipped beneath the hoofs of my panic-driven horse?

My father had been sitting in the house reading the newspaper when the Spirit whispered to him, "Run out into the orchard!"

Without a moment's hesitation, not waiting to learn why or for what reason, my father ran. Finding himself in the orchard without knowing why he was there, he saw the galloping horse and thought, *I must stop this horse.*

He did so and found me. And that is how I was saved from serious injury or possible death.

The Spirit told Wilford Woodruff to move his team away from the tree where he had tied them. He did so, and almost immediately the tree was uprooted and destroyed by a whirlwind.

The Spirit told President Joseph F. Smith to leave the platform on the rear of a train and to go inside and sit down. He did so, and almost immediately the train was involved in an accident.

I know an army pilot who was flying a military plane through a dense cloud over Vietnam when the Spirit told him to turn right. The pilot made an instant turn and another plane flashed by. He missed a head-on collision by inches.

When we are baptized, we receive the gift of the Holy Ghost, which is the right to the constant companionship of this member of the Godhead based on faithfulness. This is the greatest gift possible to receive in mortality.

There is nothing any of us need as much as the guiding and preserving care of the Holy Spirit—the Spirit that is given by the prayer of faith to those who love and serve the Lord.

I testify that if we love the Lord, keep His commandments, and seek His Spirit, we shall be blessed beyond our fondest hopes. (Bruce R. McConkie, "Friend to Friend: Hearken to the Spirit," *Friend,* September 1972, 10)

SUMMARY

The Holy Ghost is the source of great blessings in our lives. We could not carry out the mission of the Church without the Holy Ghost and the supernal gifts of inspiration provided by Him. In all things the Spirit is the key to understanding and living the gospel of Jesus Christ. The Spirit will indeed show us all things to do. Our duty is to live worthy of the companionship of the Spirit so we can serve the Lord and build up the kingdom of God here upon the earth.

HOME TEACHING

Home teaching is the Lord's way of watching over His flock (see D&C 20:53–55, 59). It is a program organized through the priesthood that allows us, as disciples, to show charity and love (see John 13:34–35), to strengthen and help others (see D&C 81:5; 108:7), and to nurture the Saints (see Moro. 6:4). Home teachers serve the people they visit. They counsel with the head of the home to understand the family's needs and concerns. They pray for strength and wisdom as they represent the Lord and Church leaders in this important assignment. Surely the home teacher, acting as an undershepherd of the Lord, is the first line of defense for the flock.

THE SCRIPTURES TEACH US

Psalms 142:4. *I looked on my right hand, and beheld, but there was no man that would know me: refuge failed me; no man cared for my soul.*

There is nothing worse than feeling unloved and uncared for. We should be certain that the families in our stewardship feel that we love and care for them.

James 1:27. *Pure religion and undefiled before God and the Father is this, To visit the fatherless and widows in their affliction, and to keep himself unspotted from the world.*

This is what the gospel is all about—caring for and uplifting one another, seeking each other's welfare and salvation.

Doctrine and Covenants 20:53–55. *The teacher's duty is to watch over the church always, and be with and strengthen them; And see that there is no iniquity in the church, neither hardness with each other, neither lying, backbiting, nor evil speaking; And see that the church meet together often, and also see that all the members do their duty.*

According to the Lord, it is our duty to ensure that the members who have been entrusted to our stewardship are watched over. They must be spiritually nurtured and fed by their home teachers, and, if necessary, physically nurtured and fed by their home teachers.

Doctrine and Covenants 20:59. *They are, however, to warn, expound, exhort, and teach, and invite all to come unto Christ.*

As home teachers, we are to teach our assigned families the word of God by the Spirit (see D&C 42:14; 50:17–23) and to strengthen them in all that we do (see D&C 108:7).

Doctrine and Covenants 81:5. *Wherefore, be faithful; stand in the office which I have appointed unto you; succor the weak, lift up the hands which hang down, and strengthen the feeble knees.*

We are called to lift and succor one another, even as the Savior lifts and succors us (see Alma 7:11–12).

Doctrine and Covenants 108:7. *Therefore, strengthen your brethren [and sisters] in all your conversation, in all your prayers, in all your exhortations, and in all your doings.*

When we build caring relationships with those we home teach, we are better able to strengthen them both temporally and spiritually.

MODERN PROPHETS SPEAK

Anthony W. Ivins:
> It is my duty, as a shepherd of the flock of Christ, to warn them of the danger which threatens; and if I fail in my duty and the danger comes upon them and they perish, the Lord has said that he will require their blood at my hands, and at the hands of every other shepherd of the flock, who, knowing his duty fails to perform it. (Conference Report, October 1928, 18)

Ezra Taft Benson:
> Shepherds—home teachers:
> Are you watching over your families as you should?
> Are you ministering to their needs?
> Do you care enough about your families' welfare that you find out their interests, that you remember birthdays and special events, and that you continually pray for them?
> Are you the first one to the home when the family needs assistance?
> Does the head of the household call on you first?
> Are you attentive to the needs of each member of the family?
> When one of your assigned families moves, do you know where they have moved? Do you make an effort to obtain their new address? Do you check with neighbors, friends, and relatives? (*Come unto Christ* [Salt Lake City: Deseret Book, 1983], 64)

Gordon B. Hinckley:
> You have a responsibility, an inescapable responsibility to go out into the homes of the people and teach them the gospel. See that there is no iniquity or backbiting or evil speaking, and build their faith. See that they are getting along temporally. It is a big responsibility. . . . We do not do as well with our home teaching as we ought to. We could do a great deal better than we do.

> Home teaching isn't a lot of work, it just takes a little faith.

> I hope that home teachers and visiting teachers will experience two things: first, the challenge of the responsibility that is in their great calling, and second, the sweetness of results from their work, particularly with those among us who are less active. I hope that these teachers will get on their knees and pray for direction, and then go to work to bring these wandering prodigals back into

the fold of the Church. If home and visiting teachers respond to this challenge, I honestly believe that they will taste the sweet and wonderful feeling which comes of being an instrument in the hands of the Lord in leading someone back into activity in His church and kingdom.

Our people need help. They have so many problems—social problems, domestic problems, marital problems—so much of it. We need to help. We need to get home teachers out more among them, to strengthen them, to listen to them, to lift them and encourage them and help them with their complicated lives. (*Teachings of Gordon B. Hinckley* [Salt Lake City: Deseret Book, 1997], 263)

IDEAS FOR DAILY LIVING

Here are four ideas that will help us to perform our home teaching duties more effectively:

1. Be a true shepherd as described in John 10:1–16.
- *Watchman*—Shepherds watch for enemies to the flock. Similarly, home teachers should remain vigilant for anything that could hurt the family.
- *Protector*—Shepherds protect the flock from the enemy. Do anything and everything that can protect and strengthen the family.
- *Nurturer*—Shepherds lead the flock to pasture and to water. Teach and nurture the family with love and with the word of God, and serve them with all your heart, might, mind, and strength.
- *Friend*—Shepherds know the names of their sheep and the sheep recognize the shepherd's voice. Know the names of family members, their hopes and dreams, the things they enjoy, and their concerns.
- *Trusted guide*—The flock trusts the shepherd because he has demonstrated love for them and he cares for their welfare. As home teachers show their love and respect for family members, they will love and trust them.
- *Devoted servant*—Shepherds will give their lives to protect their flocks because they have unconditional, godlike love for their flocks. Faithful home teachers truly love and nurture those they have been assigned to teach.

2. Remember the doctrines, principles, and covenants that will inspire us and help us do our duty.
- *Keep in mind the purposes and goodness of God*—Remember that God's goodness, mercy, and covenants are all centered in His children—their happiness, immortality, and eternal life (see Moses 1:39).
- *Make charity the central strategy*—Realize the power of love. As disciples we are to love one another (see John 13:34–35), and as undershepherds we are to feed His sheep, because we love Him and them (see John 21:15–17).
- *Seek understanding*—Seek to understand the doctrines and principles of the gospel. First, obtain the word (see D&C 11:21), then teach the word of God and testify as to its power, which in turn can and will change lives (see Alma 31:5).
- *Be converted*—Acknowledge the power of true conversion. Only when we are truly converted can we teach and lift others. When we are truly converted, we will have an overwhelming desire to bless and serve others (see Enos 1:9, 11, 16; Mosiah 28:3).
- *Recognize the value of your assigned families*—Understand the worth of souls (see D&C 18:10–16). We are responsible and accountable for the teaching and nurturing of our families (see Moro. 6:4). We are the agents for the bishop and the Lord. We are on the Lord's errand, and must seek to help these souls to return to the presence of our Heavenly Father.
- *Build them up*—We must recognize the power of positive self-image. By giving genuine and honest praise, we can encourage those we teach to do good and keep the commandments.

- *Apply faith*—Our power to bless others in and through the strength of the Lord is dependent upon our increasing and exercising our own faith (see Moro. 7:33).
- *Pray*—We can pray regularly for the well-being of those we are blessed to serve (see 1 Ne. 1:5).

3. Ask ourselves these questions concerning our attitude and devotion as home teachers:

- *Caring*—Do we truly show that we care for our families? When you care about things they care about, they will know you care about them.
- *God's representatives*—Do we recognize that we are on the errand of the Lord? As priesthood representatives we act with the authority of God—and to do what? To bless and nurture God's children according to His will and pleasure. This is our honor, privilege, responsibility, and joy (see D&C 20:46–47, 51, 53–55).
- *Actual needs*—Do we seek to understand the needs of family members and attempt to fulfill them? We must seek to become men of a sound understanding so as to be better able to bless the people we serve (see Alma 17:2).
- *Supplication*—Do we really pray for the families we teach and their well-being? When we fast, do we fast and pray for our home teaching families? The prayers of the righteous are answered in behalf of others (see 2 Chron. 30:18; Enos 1:9, 11, 16; Mosiah 27:14; Alma 6:6; 10:23; 3 Ne. 12:44).
- *Follow through*—Do we look for specific ways to serve and then follow through with initiative, or do we use the old cliché, "Let me know if I can help in any way." You can evaluate your very soul and determine things you need to do to be a good shepherd for those you teach. The Lord holds us accountable to learn our duty to fulfill our stewardships (see Jacob 1:19; D&C 72:3; 107:99–100). Let us be anxiously engaged, not casually involved (see D&C 58:27–28).

4. Seek to make home teaching an act of joy for ourselves and our assigned families.

- *Be early*—Call and make appointments early in the month. This shows caring.
- *Note the milestones*—Remember birthdays and special days in the lives of family members. Simple gestures and treats can have a wonderful effect.
- *Recognize accomplishments*—Find out about successes or honors that each family member has received and seek to praise and encourage each one so honored.
- *Know their preferences*—Learn of their favorite foods, hobbies, and things they like to do, and then surprise them with a simple gift of relevance.
- *Follow the Spirit*—Above all, invite the Spirit to direct you and in turn bless family members according to their needs.
- *Use initiative*—As home teachers, we don't have to limit ourselves to only one formal visit a month. We can fellowship our assigned families in other ways, such as inviting them over for dinner, or planning a game night or outdoor activity together. Companionships may want to make a list of fun activities or ways to serve assigned families.

ILLUSTRATIONS FOR OUR TIMES

In a general conference talk, John H. Vandenberg tells how a woman joined the Church because of the perseverance of her husband's faithful home teachers.

A Letter on Home Teaching

So wrote one sister: She, having been born and raised in another church, states that she and her Mormon husband lived the first years of their marriage without any religious activity. One evening two pleasant fellows appeared at their door and introduced themselves as home teachers. With little encouragement, they kept coming, month after month. Then the husband began, for the first time, to read such church books as he had.

The sister said that when they moved to another town she packed the books away where she hoped her husband would never find them again. Sure enough, the couple again forgot about religion until other home teachers arrived at their new home.

After the first visit of these new teachers, her husband searched for his books until he found them. The sister states that the one teacher was so friendly that they couldn't help liking him, and when he began inviting them to church affairs, they accepted because he seemed to really want them there, and they didn't want to disappoint him.

"Finally," said the sister, "after calling for many months, he asked if he could offer a prayer in our home, and we didn't know how to refuse. So the first prayer ever offered in our home was by this home teacher.

"About this time our teenage son began to complain at being sent to my church while neither his father nor I was attending church ourselves. So we compromised by attending the Mormon Church and my church on alternate Sundays.

"Our home teachers had been calling on us for about two years when they asked if the missionaries might call. (We had had them in our former town, but I had refused to listen to them.) This time I agreed to hear the missionaries but failed to make any effort to listen or understand and refused to read any of the material that was given to me. After the fourth call, the missionaries handed me more pamphlets and suggested that I read fifty more pages in the Book of Mormon (I had read none of the book yet); then one of them said good-naturedly, 'Now you can get further behind.'

"Suddenly I was ashamed of my attitude and determined to read the entire Book of Mormon before his next visit. I carried out this promise, and when the missionaries returned I told them I wanted to be baptized." As a result of these efforts by the priesthood brethren, the family was unified and is now enjoying the true purpose of life in harmony with the principles and teachings of the gospel. (John H. Vandenberg, Conference Report, October 1970, 11)

* * *

The following details how the Savior's visit to America in Third Nephi serves as a model for the visits we make as servants in the Church.

The Visit

We are a visiting church. Several years ago, it occurred to me that the Savior's visit to America established the model and standard for home teachers, visiting teachers, priesthood and Relief Society leaders, missionaries, and families—all of whom use visits to strengthen the Church and enlarge the kingdom of God. As a result, I fashioned a little bookmark to remind all of us in the high priests group, in which I was serving as group leader, to raise the bar of excellence in our home teaching. The bookmark featured the following pattern practiced by the Savior in His extraordinary visit to the ancient American Saints (all references from Third Nephi):

The Savior bore testimony—"Behold, I am Jesus Christ the Son of God" (9:15).

The Savior taught only the fundamentals of the gospel—See 11:31–41; 17:20; 27:13–21; 15:1.

The Savior brought enduring gifts to the people—Peace, light, love, and life (17:21–25).

The Savior brought a life-changing influence—"Old things are done away, and all things have become new. Therefore, I would that ye should be perfect even as I, or your Father who is in heaven is perfect" (12:47–48; 27:27).

The Savior taught us who we are—"The sons of God" (9:17); "the children of your Father who is in heaven" (12:45); "the children of the prophets . . . the children of the covenant" (20:25–26).

The Savior taught us how to gain a fulness of truth—"[G]o ye unto your homes. and ponder upon the things which I have said, and ask of the Father, in my name, that ye may understand, and prepare your minds for the morrow" (17:3).

The Savior taught us how to participate in the ultimate fulfilling of the Father's covenant with the house of Israel—"And then will I gather them in from the four quarters of the earth; and then will I fulfil the covenant which the Father hath made unto all the people of the house of Israel" (16:5).

The Savior taught us how to endure to the end—"Give heed unto the words of these twelve" (12:1); the sacrament (18:1–14); "watch and pray always" (18:15); "pray in your families" (18: 21); "meet together oft" (18:22); "hold up your light that it may shine unto the world" (18:24); read the scriptures (23:1, 5; 23:8–14); and pay tithing (24:10).

No visit could be as perfect as the visit of the Savior to His Saints. But we can strive to follow His pattern and improve day by day.

—Richard J. Allen

SUMMARY

Home teaching can be a fulfilling and enjoyable experience as we catch the vision and importance of this sacred work to bless the lives of our brothers and sisters. Once the vision is clear in our minds and we seek to fulfill it, our desire will increase. We will prepare every needful thing in order to be good home teachers. We will be full of enthusiasm and we will make and keep our priesthood covenant to "watch over the church always, and be with and strengthen them" (D&C 20:53). We will honor our priesthood and be devoted servants of the Lord. We will be true undershepherds to our home teaching families.

HONESTY

Defined as "fairness and straightforwardness of conduct" (Merriam-Webster's 11th Collegiate Dictionary), honesty is the expression of one's true character. It "implies a refusal to lie, steal, or deceive in any way" (ibid.), and is the core of integrity. This character trait is of utmost importance in our relationships. When based on honesty and truthfulness, communication can be trusted. Thus in the family, school, and workplace—in all of life—honesty becomes a principle that governs, the principle of trust. This is why we must be honest with ourselves and with our God. With trust, all relationships can be built and maintained.

THE SCRIPTURES TEACH US

Exodus 20:16. *Thou shalt not bear false witness against thy neighbour.*

The Lord commands us to be honest in our dealings. This is reiterated in the temple recommend interview. If we are not honest with our fellowmen and with the Lord, we are not worthy to enter His house.

2 Nephi 9:34. *Wo unto the liar, for he shall be thrust down to hell.*

No unclean thing can enter into the presence of the Lord. Therefore, no dishonest person, without full repentance, can achieve exaltation.

Alma 27:27. *For they were perfectly honest and upright in all things; and they were firm in the faith of Christ, even unto the end.*

The converted Ammonites followed the teachings of Christ without compromise. They were in all respects upright and honest. True conversion brings with it personal righteousness, of which honesty is an integral part.

Doctrine and Covenants 51:9. *And let every man deal honestly, and be alike among this people, and receive alike, that ye may be one, even as I have commanded you.*

Honesty is crucial to being united and to building Zion. Zion cannot be built without trust. Honesty is the principle on which trust and unity are built.

Doctrine and Covenants 98:10. *Wherefore, honest men and wise men should be sought for diligently, and good men and wise men ye should observe to uphold; otherwise whatsoever is less than these cometh of evil.*

When selecting those who will govern us, we should consider character above all else. If integrity is compromised then trust is destroyed. This is of primary concern for us not only in electing government officials, as this scripture indicates, but in all our dealings. We should seek to associate with those who are honest, and strive to be honest ourselves.

MODERN PROPHETS SPEAK

Joseph F. Smith :
> And above all things one must be honest and sincere in the performance of his religious duties. On these lines we are dealing with our conscience and with our God, but in every phase of life strict honesty is the "best policy." (*From Prophet to Son: Advice of Joseph F. Smith to His Missionary Sons,* comp. Hyrum M. Smith III and Scott G. Kenney [Salt Lake City: Deseret Book, 1981], 108–109)

Gordon B. Hinckley:
> Be strong . . . with the strength of simple honesty. How easy it is to "lie a little, take the advantage of one because of his words, dig a pit for thy neighbor" (2 Ne. 28:8). Nephi so describes the

people of his day, as he also describes so many of our day. How easy it is for us to say, "We believe in being honest, true, chaste, benevolent" (A of F 1:13). But how difficult for so many to resist the temptation to lie a little, cheat a little, steal a little, bear false witness in speaking gossipy words about others. Rise above it, brethren. Be strong in the simple virtue of honesty.

Simple honesty is so remarkable a quality. It is of the very essence of integrity. It demands that we be straightforward, unequivocal, in walking the straight and narrow line of what is right and true. It is so easy to cheat. At times it is so enticing to do so. Better a poor grade than a dishonest act. (*Teachings of Gordon B. Hinckley* [Salt Lake City: Deseret Book, 1997], 269)

IDEAS FOR DAILY LIVING

Here are four ideas to help us be honest:

1. Honesty is the foundation upon which you can build your future.

- *Honesty is the first principle*—A person should build his or her life upon principle, and the place to start is honesty. A life built on dishonesty will crumble in due time. A life built upon honesty will have endurance, resilience, and vitality. (See also A of F 1:13.)
- *Honesty is a personal decision*—If you decide to build your character, relationships, and life's vision on the principle of honesty, then you have just spared yourself the task of making ten thousand and more future decisions—for you only need to decide once to be honest (see Job 27:5; Mal. 2:6).

2. Honesty has consequences that are highly desirable.

- *Think results*—In all of your decisions, weigh the consequences. Always look forward with gratitude to the positive consequences of being honest. Always remember that dishonesty bears no good fruit (see 2 Ne. 9:34).
- *Honesty generates trust*—To be trusted requires total honesty. You cannot expect honesty in others if you're not totally honest yourself. If you lack honesty, you'll also be unable to trust others, because you will question their honesty. That is not a circle of consequences to be desired (see Alma 27:27; D&C 51:9).
- *Honesty is a creative force*—Honesty builds friendship and unity. Dishonesty tears down. The results of dishonesty can destroy personal friendships, families, and even society itself. All of your relationships depend upon your honesty (see Eph. 4:25).
- *Honesty brings peace*—Total honesty allows your conscience to be at peace (see 1 Tim. 2:2).
- *Honesty is like a magnet*—Honesty attracts; dishonesty repels. Anyone who wants to be attractive, to display effective leadership, to unite and bring people together, must build a life of honesty and integrity.
- *Honesty pays dividends*—Honesty in a business is the one trait that will do the most to ensure the vitality of that business. Customers will return to an honest enterprise that provides quality products and services; workers will flourish in an honest work environment; shareholders will be loyal where management is honest and forthright. So it is in other aspects of our lives: family, friends, and stewardships.
- *Honesty has staying power*—Honesty is an enduring, perennial source of vitality; dishonesty is like a weed—it grows up quickly but is soon scorched in the sun of disclosure and blown away in the winds of discontent.
- *Honesty liberates*—The honest person has nothing to fear from the light of truth. Dishonesty enslaves. A dishonest act can lead to others in an attempt to cover the first. It is not difficult to

discern the virus of dishonesty: If people will cheat in small things, they will cheat in big things, for they are slaves to their addiction.

3. Honesty is the backbone of leadership.

- *Honesty is congruent*—Be consistently honest. Authentic honesty is impartial to the situation. It operates always and in every case the same way: with truth and integrity.
- *Honesty is a way to show love*—You can teach honesty in the home by gentle persuasion, kindness, and love—honesty is a soul mate of love. You are honest with people out of love for them as children of God, and you teach honesty because it will generate the highest degree of harmony, peace, and unity among those you love, and among all people.
- *Draw a line in the sand*—Stand up for the principle of honesty. The most odious patron of dishonesty is the liar, the gossiper, the twister of truth. When you discern the operation of a liar in your community or in your workplace, take steps immediately to make truth the basis for decision making and policy formulation.

4. Honesty is the heart and soul of one's covenant with God.

- *Honesty is the soul of law*—Is there another quality that better reflects the core essence of each of the Ten Commandments? If we are honest and true in our thoughts, our desires, our relationships, our speech, our service, and our devotion, we are on the straight and narrow.
- *Honesty has roots in the Golden Rule*—Honesty will always be enhanced if we remember the Golden Rule—to treat others as we would have them treat us. We want honesty from others, so we should expect it of ourselves.
- *Honesty is the absolute of character qualities*—Honesty is not only the best policy, it is the *only* policy. Let us pray that we will always be honest.

ILLUSTRATIONS FOR OUR TIMES

In the following excerpt from Hartman Rector Jr., we learn that seemingly insignificant choices regarding honesty can set a pattern for our lives, and that honesty is always the right choice.

He Really Passed the Test

I had a friend, one time, who went to take a test in school, a test for which he had not studied. Of course he had prayed pretty hard about it. He had asked the Lord to help him remember something he had not bothered to learn. There are some things the Lord cannot do. Other things he can, but he will not. And praying will not work in these cases. I know; I have tried it. But as this friend went in to take this test, he found he was sitting right next to the smartest girl in the class. He said, "Well, this must be the answer to my prayer. Here she is. The Lord provided her, right here." But he was a returned missionary. He had been preaching honesty for two years. It is very difficult to go against that which you have been preaching and for which you have had a witness of the Spirit. While he was arguing with himself about what he was going to do on this test, he flunked the test. But as a matter of fact he really passed.

You see, he had passed the Lord's test, and that is the test that we have to pass here upon this earth. Tests are all around us. Fifty years from the day that he took the test he would not remember what his grade was, and it really would not make any difference so long as it was honest. But if he cheated on the test, he would remember that, for it makes an indelible imprint on the spirit. It also makes it easier the next time we are faced with a temptation where our honesty is in question to go down that "broad road." Lucifer would not dare tempt you with a sin as grievous as robbing a bank with your first experience with dishonesty. That would turn you off. You would not dare do that. So he will start with something small, something little, something that seems insignificant. If you flunk that one, he will see to it that you get a larger one and then a larger one, until it reaches the point where some people can sit down and methodically work out a plan to rob a bank. Oh, they will rationalize some justification for it, such as, "It is insured by the government so nobody is losing anything." Or, "Well, I really have it coming to me; I have not had the breaks that other people have." This is called rationalization, which is a form of lying to yourself. But it is lying, nevertheless. As Nephi said: ". . . And thus the devil cheateth their souls, and leadeth them away carefully down to hell." (2 Nephi 28:21.) (Hartman Rector Jr., "Get Up and Glow," *Speeches of the Year,* January 5, 1971, 7)

SUMMARY

The little exaggerations, the silent tongue when things need to be said, the so-called misrepresentations—all these are forms of dishonesty. Dishonesty within the bonds of matrimony is without doubt the most destructive force; families are devastated and the effects are so long lasting. In all situations, honesty is pivotal in maintaining a level of communication built on trust. Honesty is the best policy, or rather, the *only* policy—and should become our quest in all things. In our dealings with others and with the Lord, let us make honesty the flywheel of personal progress and the central principle of spiritual growth and vitality.

HOPE

Our anticipation and expectation for things to be better in our lives is called hope. True hope is based upon the Lord Jesus Christ and upon the concept of eternal life, which God promised to the faithful before the world began (see Titus 1:2). Hope provides us with a sense of confidence in looking forward in righteousness. When we lose hope, life becomes difficult in every sense. We then fail to enjoy life or to do anything to build a better future. A life without hope is empty, but a life filled with hope is a life filled with light and meaning. We can start with faith in Jesus Christ and confidence in the plan of redemption. Let us cultivate an attitude of being optimistic and use practical wisdom to develop a lifestyle based on uplifting hope.

THE SCRIPTURES TEACH US

Proverbs 10:28. *The hope of the righteous shall be gladness: but the expectation of the wicked shall perish.*

Hope gives one strength to deal with life. With hope we are positive. We know that sooner or later things will be better. Hope is integrally connected to faith. We cannot have one without the other.

Jeremiah 17:7. *Blessed is the man that trusteth in the Lord, and whose hope the Lord is.*

True hope is centered in Christ. Through Christ we can obtain a forgiveness of sins through repentance, and anticipate a glorious resurrection. Christ is our Rock upon whom we build. We cannot fall when our hope and trust is in Him.

1 Corinthians 15:19. *If in this life only we have hope in Christ, we are of all men most miserable.*

Our hope in Christ is not just here in mortality; through Him we have hope for the eternities. That is why we should be filled with gladness. The hope for life eternal is in Christ.

2 Nephi 31:20. *Wherefore, ye must press forward with a steadfastness in Christ, having a perfect brightness of hope, and a love of God and of all men. Wherefore, if ye shall press forward, feasting upon the word of Christ, and endure to the end, behold, thus saith the Father: Ye shall have eternal life.*

When we build our lives upon our Savior Jesus Christ, we have hope—a perfect brightness of hope which fills us with light. Hope is an attitude that can create a power and motivation to go forward and endure.

Ether 12:4. *Wherefore, whoso believeth in God might with surety hope for a better world, yea, even a place at the right hand of God, which hope cometh of faith, maketh an anchor to the souls of men, which would make them sure and steadfast, always abounding in good works, being led to glorify God.*

In order for us to have the power to cope with adversity, our lives must be riveted to hope, which is an anchor for our souls. Hope is not a platitude of simply having a positive attitude; rather, it is rooted in Christ, which gives us the strength to go forward doing good works. We are to seek hope through understanding the gospel plan and living its teachings.

Ether 12:32. *And I also remember that thou hast said that thou hast prepared a house for man, yea, even among the mansions of thy Father, in which man might have a more excellent hope; wherefore man must hope, or he cannot receive an inheritance in the place which thou hast prepared.*

The promises of our Heavenly Father concerning eternal life give us a desire that is so compelling that we want to return to His presence. Such is the essence of a more excellent hope.

Moroni 7:42–44. *Wherefore, if a man have faith he must needs have hope; for without faith there cannot be any hope. And again, behold I say unto you that he cannot have faith and hope, save he shall be meek, and lowly of heart. If so, his faith and hope is vain, for none is acceptable before God, save the meek and lowly in heart; and if a man be meek and lowly in heart, and confesses by the power of the Holy Ghost that Jesus is the Christ, he must needs have charity; for if he have not charity he is nothing; wherefore he must needs have charity.*

The fabric of a saintly life is woven out of the threads of hope, faith, meekness, and charity. These qualities combine to form the essence of discipleship. They are the indispensable qualities upon which an individual can build a lifetime of valor and obedience.

Moroni 8:26. *And the remission of sins bringeth meekness, and lowliness of heart; and because of meekness and lowliness of heart cometh the visitation of the Holy Ghost, which Comforter filleth with hope and perfect love, which love endureth by diligence unto prayer, until the end shall come, when all the saints shall dwell with God.*

Hope is a gift of the Spirit conveyed to all who have a broken heart and a contrite spirit and are willing to sacrifice pride and selfishness in favor of a better way, the way of Christ.

Doctrine and Covenants 12:8. *And no one can assist in this work except he shall be humble and full of love, having faith, hope, and charity, being temperate in all things, whatsoever shall be entrusted to his care.*

As we seek to build up the kingdom of God, we should remember that in order to be an instrument in the hands of the Lord we must first fulfill certain prerequisites. The foregoing scripture is a formula for service. Hope is so closely connected to faith and charity that it cannot be separated. When we depend upon God and exhibit the fruits of humility, exercise our faith, have an attitude of hope, and aspire to be full of charity, we will then be able to assist the Lord in His glorious work.

MODERN PROPHETS SPEAK

Russell M. Nelson:

> The gospel of Jesus Christ provides hope for all in this wailing world. "Now, what do we hear in the gospel which we have received? A voice of gladness! A voice of mercy from heaven; and a voice of truth out of the earth; glad tidings for the dead; a voice of gladness for the living and the dead; glad tidings of great joy." (D&C 128:19.) (*The Gateway We Call Death* [Salt Lake City: Deseret Book, 1995], 108–109)

Neal A. Maxwell:

> Real hope, said Paul, is a hope for things that are not seen that are true. (See Romans 8:24.) Paul accurately linked hopelessness and godlessness as he wrote of those "having no hope, and without God in the world." (Ephesians 2:12.) Christ-centered hope, however, is a very specific and particularized hope. It is focused on the great realities of the resurrection, eternal life, a better world, and Christ's triumphant second coming "things as they really will be." (Jacob 4:13.) (*Notwithstanding My Weakness* [Salt Lake City: Deseret Book, 1981], 40–41)

Gordon B. Hinckley:

> Ours is truly a message of hope and reconciliation. It is a word of hope for all mankind, a beacon of eternal truth to which men may look as they lift their eyes and souls to their Creator and in the process come to recognize their common brotherhood. (*Teachings of Gordon B. Hinckley* [Salt Lake City: Deseret Book, 1997], 373)

Spencer W. Kimball:

> We have a hope in Christ here and now. He died for our sins. Because of him and his gospel, our sins are washed away in the waters of baptism; sin and iniquity are burned out of our souls as though by fire; and we become clean, have clear consciences, and gain that peace which passeth understanding. (See Philip. 4:7.) . . .

> We have also a hope in Christ for the eternity that lies ahead; otherwise, as Paul said, we would be "of all men most miserable" (1 Cor. 15:19). ("An Eternal Hope in Christ," *Ensign,* November 1978, 71)

IDEAS FOR DAILY LIVING

Here are three strategies for developing and maintaining an attitude of hope:

1. Understand that hope is power.
- *Hope gets things done*—Hope, like faith, is a self-fulfilling prophecy; it brings about the conditions to realize the vision that it sees for the future. Therefore, hope is an indispensable ally (see D&C 18:19).

- *Hope is centered in Jesus Christ*—The opportunity to repent and gain eternal life is made possible through the Savior, who wrought the magnificent Atonement and brought about the resurrection. Once we have this hope, we can repent, bettering ourselves and our lives.
- *Hope is connected to faith*—The power of faith is increased with an attitude of hope (see Ether 12:4).
- *Hope is a guide for life*—Through the eyes of hope, you see opportunities that would otherwise be invisible and therefore lost. Therefore, look at life from the perspective of hope (see 2 Ne. 31:20).

2. Identify and do those key actions that generate hope.
- *Count your blessings*—In particular, counting the blessings we receive from the gospel—and all those associated with eternal life—will fill us with hope. We can choose to look at the bright and optimistic side of life.
- *Spend time with the hopeful*—Which of your family members or friends would you characterize as being full of hope, optimistic, cheerful, eagerly working toward meaningful goals? Spend more time with those people when you need to recharge your spiritual and emotional batteries. Seek out a friend or associate who will help you see things clearly, and avoid pessimism. Read about exemplary people who have made hope a key part of their lives.
- *Plan your agenda around hope*—You can create a feeling of hope in life as you take the initiative to plan and carry out things that are enjoyable and uplifting.
- *Be a problem-solver*—If you begin to feel dejected or hopeless, it becomes imperative to study the situation and make decisions to solve the problem. Try to think of hope, rather than feeling despair. Remember that challenges are opportunities for growth.
- *Work on long-range goals*—Hope is a partner of action: the more you do the right kinds of things to attain your goals, the more hope you will have.
- *Ask for hope*—Look to God for help and comfort. The highest form of hope is one based on deep spiritual awakenings, especially as it relates to the Atonement (see Moro. 7:41). Therefore, pray for hope each day.
- *Think positively*—It is your choice. You can do all things with faith (see Moro. 7:33) and in the strength of the Lord (see Alma 26:12). He will provide the way (see 1 Ne. 3:7). Live hopefully and cheerfully do all you can, and the arm of the Lord will be extended to you (see D&C 123:17).

3. Give hope to others, and it will expand in your own life.
- *Make it a regular gift*—Hope is a gift you give to others who depend on you; therefore, cultivate hope and then help others to have it.
- *Be a leader of hope*—A leader shows the vision of the future and then helps generate the hope-filled actions that bring it about. Without hope, there is no leadership; with hope, leadership is empowered to lift and inspire.
- *Be a teacher of hope*—In every lesson, in every teaching moment, it is vital to give hope to those you teach. With hope people can carry on. Without hope, sin and discouragement, even despair, are at the door.

ILLUSTRATIONS FOR OUR TIMES

In the following story, told by Heidi S. Swinton, we learn that the Lord blesses those who faithfully pray to Him in hope—not only with a better life in mortality, but with eternal life.

Seven Times the Note Said Yes

Those who have lived in Bulgaria speak of the stunning countryside, the grand Balkan Mountains, and the choice resorts edging the Black Sea. Picturesque though it is, however, the dramatic scenery did not make bearable the oppressive social and political conditions imposed by the Communist government. Bulgarians feared the government, their associates, and even their "friends." Yet getting out of the country was virtually impossible. To do so would take a miracle.

Kiril and Nevenka Kiriakov, a young dental technician and his wife, had long been praying for a way to leave Bulgaria to rear their children in freedom. A slim chance came in 1963 when Algeria became independent of France. The new country approached the Bulgarian government for assistance in restructuring its economy. The state laboratory was asked to furnish one dental technician for a two-year assignment. Kiril, like each of his six colleagues, hoped to be chosen. He later wrote in his personal history, "My chances were not good. Most of my colleagues had a contact or a relative who held a high position in the government, someone they could rely on for help. I knew of no one who could help me, so I put my entire faith and hope in our Heavenly Father. My wife and I decided that only our fervent prayers to the Lord could open the door to the free world."

Everyone at the lab recognized that the position in Algeria was a passport to freedom. When the day of the selection came, "one of my colleagues proposed that we decide the matter by drawing lots, placing seven folded pieces of paper in a hat, six of which would have no written on them and one would contain the word yes."

This seemed fair, and all agreed. The slips of paper were prepared and placed in the hat. Kiril drew his and opened it. "I could not believe my eyes," he said, "the piece of paper I had drawn had yes written on it."

Immediately his associates protested the outcome because he had been in the laboratory only eight months, and many of them had worked there for a lifetime. They insisted on another drawing. A second time Kiril drew the yes. Again they refused to accept the results. He returned the slip and drew another time but with the same astonishing result. Four more times the group drew from the hat. Each time, Kiril opened his slip of paper to find the yes. Finally, instead of objecting, the amazed group gathered around him. Although the Bulgarian government had outlawed all religious conviction, his associates agreed that the only way he could have drawn the yes slip seven times in a row was with the help of God. They had witnessed a miracle.

The Kiriakov family spent the next two years in Algeria. For them it was "like living in paradise." At the end of their assignment, when Kiril was expected to return with his family to Bulgaria, he petitioned his government to return by way of France. Usually the procedure was to force the family to return separately to limit the possibility of defection. Kiril recalled, "The idea presented itself to add the words 'and family' on my exit permit and we were successful in obtaining tourist visas to France for the entire family." The Kiriakovs defected in France.

Fifteen days later a bloody coup d'etat toppled the Communist government in Algeria, and all Bulgarians were rounded up and flown home en masse. But the Kiriakov family was safe in Marseilles.

About two years later, this Bulgarian family learned the reason the Lord had said yes to their leaving their homeland. Two missionaries of The Church of Jesus Christ of Latter-day Saints knocked on their door, "something that never would have happened in Bulgaria." The Lord had opened the way for them to come to Zion.

"In their affliction they will seek me early." (Hosea 5:15.) (Heidi S. Swinton, *Pioneer Spirit: Modern-Day Stories of Courage and Conviction* [Salt Lake City: Deseret Book, 1996], 32)

SUMMARY

In our society, many people appear to be dejected, depressed, and in a state of hopelessness. Without hope, sin is often at the door, waiting to enter our lives. The causes vary, but the solution is always possible through our Savior Jesus Christ. If we do not build upon the rock of our Redeemer, we cannot have lasting hope. Through the application of gospel principles, things always get better sooner or later. Jesus assured us: "with God all things are possible" (Matt. 19:26).

HUMILITY

Humility is critical to our growth and learning. When we understand and acknowledge our relationship to and dependence upon God, we begin to be humble. In the state of humility—being submissive, easily entreated, and teachable—we receive the blessings of humility, including peace, inspiration, hope, and the guidance of the Lord. Humility involves having a broken heart and a contrite spirit, and it causes one to relate to God in gratitude and love.

THE SCRIPTURES TEACH US

Matthew 18:4. *Whosoever therefore shall humble himself as this little child, the same is greatest in the kingdom of heaven.*

The Lord puts considerable emphasis on humility. We truly must become "as a child, submissive, meek, humble, patient, full of love, willing to submit to all things which the Lord seeth fit to inflict upon [us], even as a child doth submit to his father" (Mosiah 3:19).

James 4:10. *Humble yourselves in the sight of the Lord, and he shall lift you up.*

We become empowered by God by virtue of our relationship and dependence upon Him. He can use us as instruments in His hands if we are malleable and teachable.

Alma 32:16. *Therefore, blessed are they who humble themselves without being compelled to be humble; or rather, in other words, blessed is he that believeth in the word of God, and is baptized without stubbornness of heart, yea, without being brought to know the word, or even compelled to know, before they will believe.*

When we humble ourselves before God we are blessed more than if we are compelled to be humble with trials, tribulations, famine, or pestilence. We grow much more quickly in the state of humility because we are open and teachable.

Doctrine and Covenants 12:8. *And no one can assist in this work except he shall be humble and full of love, having faith, hope, and charity, being temperate in all things, whatsoever shall be entrusted to his care.*

In magnifying our callings and fulfilling our eternal roles, we simply cannot do the work effectively without humility. Remember that in the Church and kingdom of God, we are doing the Lord's work, not our own.

MODERN PROPHETS SPEAK

Ezra Taft Benson:
> Humility responds to God's will—to the fear of His judgments and the needs of those around us. To the proud, the applause of the world rings in their ears; to the humble, the applause of heaven warms their hearts. ("Cleansing the Inner Vessel," *Ensign,* May 1986, 4)

Dallin H. Oaks:
> How, then, do we prevent our strengths from becoming our downfall? The quality we must cultivate is humility. Humility is the great protector. Humility is the antidote against pride. Humility is the catalyst for all learning, especially spiritual things. Through the prophet Moroni, the Lord gave us this great insight into the role of humility: "I give unto men weakness that they may be humble; and my grace is sufficient for all men that humble themselves before me; for if they humble themselves before me, and have faith in me, then will I make weak things become strong unto them" (Ether 12:27). ("Our Strengths Can Become Our Downfall," *Ensign,* October 1994, 11)

Gordon B. Hinckley:
> Be humble. Don't be arrogant. The world is full of arrogant people. Oh, how obnoxious they are! How obnoxious is an arrogant man. Girls, isn't that so? And how obnoxious, likewise, is an arrogant girl. Be humble. There is no place for arrogance with any of us. There is no place for egotism with any of us. There is no place for cross pride.
>
> People ask me frequently what is my favorite verse of scripture. I have many and this is one of them, "Be thou humble; and the Lord thy God shall lead thee by the hand, and give thee answer to thy prayers" (D&C 112:10). (*Teachings of Gordon B. Hinckley* [Salt Lake City: Deseret Book, 1997], 265)

Spencer W. Kimball:
> Humble and meek properly suggest virtues, not weaknesses. They suggest a consistent mildness of temper and an absence of wrath and passion. Humility suggests no affectation, no bombastic actions. It is not turgid nor grandiloquent. It is not servile submissiveness. It is not cowed nor frightened. No shadow or the shaking of a leaf terrorizes it.
>
> How does one get humble? To me, one must constantly be reminded of his dependence. On whom dependent? On the Lord. How remind oneself? By real, constant, worshipful, grateful prayer. . . .

Humility is teachableness—an ability to realize that all virtues and abilities are not concentrated in oneself. . . .

Humility is gracious, quiet, serene—not pompous, spectacular, nor histrionic. It is subdued, kindly, and understanding—not crude, blatant, loud, or ugly. Humility is not just a man or a woman but a perfect gentleman and a gentlelady. It never struts nor swaggers. Its faithful, quiet works will be the badge of its own accomplishments. It never sets itself in the center of the stage, leaving all others in supporting roles. Humility is never accusing nor contentious. It is not boastful.

When one becomes conscious of his great humility, he has already lost it. When one begins boasting of his humility, it has already become pride—the antithesis of humility.

Humility is repentant and seeks not to justify its follies. It is forgiving others in the realization that there may be errors of the same kind or worse chalked up against itself. . . .

It is not self-abasement—the hiding in the corner, the devaluation of everything one does or thinks or says; but it is the doing of one's best in every case and leaving of one's acts, expressions, and accomplishments to largely speak for themselves. (*The Teachings of Spencer W. Kimball*, ed. Edward L. Kimball [Salt Lake City: Bookcraft, 1982], 233)

IDEAS FOR DAILY LIVING

Here are five ideas for developing, maintaining, and exhibiting humility:

1. Humility is the beginning of spirituality.
- *Fast and pray often*—Pray and fast for humility (see Hel. 3:35). The essence of humility is the prayer in which you say with sincerity, "Thy will be done."
- *See from a higher perspective*—Remember that all are of equal value in the sight of God, no one greater than another (see Alma 1:26).
- *Listen to spiritual input*—Be easily entreated; be teachable and then you will always be learning (see Alma 7:23; 13:28).
- *Acknowledge your dependence upon God*—Recognize and remember your relationship to God and your total dependence upon Him (see Mosiah 4:5).
- *Receive the grace of God*—When you acknowledge your dependence on God in all humility, you are then able to receive the goodness and grace of God in your life and overcome humankind's weak nature through Him (see Ether 12:27).

2. Humility is a quality of strength. Humility is not a weakness; we become strong in our humility (see Hel. 3:35). Humility says of an individual that he or she is willing to learn, willing to work with others, willing to admit mistakes and improve, willing to operate under the principle that only God is perfect, omniscient, and omnipotent.
- *Make humility part of your nature*—Be "clothed in humility," or humble in everything you do and say (see 1 Pet. 5:5).
- *Choose to be humble*—Seek to be humbled by the word of God and His goodness rather than being compelled to be humble due to the difficult situations (see Alma 32:16; 48:20).
- *Humility is required of those who serve*—We must be humble in order to receive direction from the Lord and assist in the work (see D&C 12:8).

3. Humility belongs in the family.
- *Grow together*—Humility in a family setting means listening to every voice, having family councils to make plans and decisions that bless the lives of everyone, and suppressing any manifestation of anger, sarcasm, or abuse of any kind.
- *Foster a childlike nature*—Get down on the floor and play with some children. Learn from their innocent delight in learning and frolicking. Learn from their zest for life. Learn from their candor and honesty. Be humble like a child and life will suddenly be filled with the wonder of endless learning and growth.

4. Humility belongs in the workplace.
- *Value all alike*—Humility in the workplace means a willingness to listen to good ideas from everyone—superiors and subordinates alike.
- *Listen to learn*—Humility presupposes a willingness to listen without judgment until there is clarity of thought and direction.

5. Humility belongs in society.
- *Humility makes society flow*—Humility is a cousin to courtesy and a sibling of forgiveness. It is that oil that renders interpersonal relationships smooth and wholesome.
- *Humility is the foundation for respect*—Treat all persons with kindness, love, and respect. Never put down another to elevate yourself.
- *Compete for self-mastery*—Competition to beat someone else often creates pride unless within the competition we recognize the real challenge: to react with dignity and humility, regardless of whether we win or lose.

ILLUSTRATIONS FOR OUR TIMES

The following story, related by Eldred G. Smith, former Church Patriarch, demonstrates the greatest lessons we learn in life are studies in humbling ourselves before the Lord.

He Had Quit Several Times

All the requirements of living the gospel become easier through humility.

A young man told me his experience in becoming a member of the Church, which is typical of many in their activities of investigating the Church. He said the missionaries came to the lesson on the Word of Wisdom. He and his wife were both users of tobacco. After the meeting was over and the missionaries had left, they talked it over with each other and decided among themselves, "Well, if that is what the Lord wants and if this is the Lord's Church, we will try it." He said that he was not particularly concerned about himself, he thought he could do it easily. He was worried about his wife; she had never tried to quit before. On the other hand, he had quit several times. After proving to himself that he could quit, of course, he went back to the use of cigarettes again. But he said in this case it was just the reverse.

His wife quit without any apparent difficulty, but he had tremendous difficulty. He became nervous and irritable. He could not rest. He was cranky among his fellow workers. He could not sleep at night. But inasmuch as his wife had quit, he was not going to be outdone by her. So, one night, he became so restless, so disturbed that he could not sleep, and his wife suggested to him that he pray about it. He thought that was a good joke. He ridiculed the idea of prayer; he said, "This is something I have to do. Nobody can help me with this. I can do this." But as the night passed and he had done everything he could to stimulate sleep and rest without any success, finally in despair, he humbled himself enough to kneel at the side of the bed and pray vocally.

According to his own testimony, he said that he got up from his prayer, got into bed, went to sleep, and has never been tempted by cigarettes since. He has absolutely lost his taste for tobacco. He said, "The Word of Wisdom was not a health program for me. It was a lesson of humility." He said, "I had to learn humility." That is what it meant to him. As it is with many of the requirements of the Church, we have to demonstrate humble obedience. (Eldred G. Smith, Conference Report, April 1955, 42)

SUMMARY

This world boasts men of great wisdom, women of great worth, and people with outstanding accomplishments, but no one stands as tall as the one who is humble in all of his or her achievements. Humility not only enables us to do good but blesses all of mankind. When we are humble, we are constantly reminded of our dependence upon God in all things. Humility provokes us to pray, an act demonstrating we know our lowly place in the grand scheme of things. Humility gives us strength in the Lord. This strength gives us self-worth and the self-confidence to do significant things. President Ezra Taft Benson teaches us: "With humility, there come many blessings. For example, 'Be thou humble; and the Lord thy God shall lead thee by the hand, and give thee answer to thy prayers' (D&C 112:10). The humble will 'be made strong, and blessed from on high, and receive knowledge' (D&C 1:28). The Lord is 'merciful unto those who confess their sins with humble hearts' (D&C 61:2). Humility can turn away God's anger (see Helaman 11:11)." (*The Teachings of Ezra Taft Benson* [Salt Lake City: Bookcraft, 1988], 370).

HUSBAND

The role of husband should be the most prominent one in every man's life. The greatest fulfillment in life really lies within the family unit. In today's society, many men abdicate their role as husband, and both their wife and their children suffer. Husbands must realize that their role can have no substitute, that no one can take that place. Make a commitment to be the best husband for your wife.

THE SCRIPTURES TEACH US

1 Corinthians 7:3. *Let the husband render unto the wife due benevolence: and likewise also the wife unto the husband.*

When we make our first concern the well-being of our mate, we will show compassion and empathy. We will be warm-hearted and understanding. Indeed, we will be charitable in all things.

Ephesians 5:23–28. *For the husband is the head of the wife, even as Christ is the head of the church: and he is the saviour of the body. Therefore as the church is subject unto Christ, so let the wives be to their own husbands in every thing. Husbands, love your wives, even as Christ also loved the church, and gave himself for it; That he might sanctify and cleanse it with the washing of water by the word, That he might present it to himself a glorious church, not having spot, or wrinkle, or any such thing; but that it should be holy and without blemish. So ought men to love their wives as their own bodies. He that loveth his wife loveth himself.*

When we realize as husbands that we are responsible for the well-being of our wife in all things, we will express our love and concern for her. In turn, she will want us to preside and take care of things even as Christ did for the Church. Christ did everything for us because He loved us, and yet we are stewards of our own lives. Likewise we should do everything we can for our sweetheart. "Husband and wife have a solemn responsibility to love and care for each other and for their children" ("The Family: A Proclamation to the World," 1995).

Colossians 3:19. *Husbands, love your wives, and be not bitter against them.*

Love is the feeling and action that we show people we care about. It is a "devoted concern," if you will, that brings about righteous service on behalf of others. Within the marital relationship, this cannot be done merely as a duty but rather should be done with emotion and passion for the happiness of your companion. If we do things with a bad attitude, begrudgingly, harboring resentment in any form, we are indeed "bitter" and not pure in our actions. We should truly love our wife with all of our hearts (see D&C 42:22).

Jacob 2:31. *For behold, I, the Lord, have seen the sorrow, and heard the mourning of the daughters of my people in the land of Jerusalem, yea, and in all the lands of my people, because of the wickedness and abominations of their husbands.*

We must be completely faithful in our marriage. Infidelity brings immeasurable sorrow and devastation to families. We must make the commitment to keep our marriage covenants at all times.

Doctrine and Covenants 75:28. *And again, verily I say unto you, that every man who is obliged to provide for his own family, let him provide, and he shall in nowise lose his crown; and let him labor in the church.*

As husbands, we are responsible for the temporal welfare of our wife and family. This is part of our eternal role—we are the providers. The consequences are clear if we do not fulfill our duty towards our family.

MODERN PROPHETS SPEAK

Joseph Smith:

> It is the duty of a husband to love, cherish, and nourish his wife, and cleave unto her and none else; he ought to honor her as himself, and he ought to regard her feelings with tenderness, for she is his flesh, and his bone, designed to be an help unto him, both in temporal, and spiritual things; one into whose bosom he can pour all his complaints without reserve, who is willing (being designed) to take part of his burden, to soothe and encourage his feelings by her gentle voice. It is the place of the man, to stand at the head of his family, and be lord of his own house, not to rule over his wife as a tyrant, neither as one who is fearful or jealous that his wife will get out of her place, and prevent him from exercising his authority. It is his duty to be a man of God (for a man of God is a man of wisdom,) ready at all times to obtain from the scriptures, the revelations,

and from on high, such instructions as are necessary for the edification, and salvation of his household. (*Encyclopedia of Joseph Smith's Teachings,* ed. Larry E. Dahl and Donald Q. Cannon [Salt Lake City: Bookcraft, 1997], 410–11)

Brigham Young:

Let the husband and father learn to bend his will to the will of his God, and then instruct his [wife] and children in this lesson of self-government by his example as well as by precept, and his neighbors also, showing them how to be brave and steadfast, in subduing the rebellious and sinful disposition. Such a course as this will eventually subdue that unhallowed influence which works upon the human heart. (*Discourses of Brigham Young,* sel. John A. Widtsoe [Salt Lake City: Deseret Book, 1954], 198)

Ezra Taft Benson:

The Apostle Paul points out that "the husband is the head of the wife, *even as* Christ is the head of the church" (Eph. 5:23; italics added). That is the model we are to follow in our role of presiding in the home. We do not find the Savior leading the Church with a harsh or unkind hand. We do not find the Savior treating His Church with disrespect or neglect. We do not find the Savior using force or coercion to accomplish His purposes. Nowhere do we find the Savior doing anything but that which edifies, uplifts, comforts, and exalts the Church. Brethren, I say to you with all soberness, He is the model we must follow as we take the spiritual lead in our families. ("To the Fathers in Israel," *Ensign,* November 1987, 48)

Gordon B. Hinckley:

The most important decision of life is the decision concerning your companion. Choose prayerfully. And when you are married, be fiercely loyal one to another. Selfishness is the great destroyer of happy family life. I have this one suggestion to offer. If you will make your first concern the comfort, the well-being, and the happiness of your companion, sublimating any personal concern to that loftier goal, you will be happy, and your marriage will go on through eternity. (*Teachings of Gordon B. Hinckley* [Salt Lake City: Deseret Book, 1997], 328–29)

IDEAS FOR DAILY LIVING

Here are some ideas that can help husbands fulfill their most significant role:

1. Build from within.

- *Establish gospel principles*—Build your marriage and family relationship on a foundation of honor, honesty, service, and harmony. These principles will help your relationship endure.
- *Put your priorities in order*—Make being husband and father the highest priority and goal in your life. Your wife will rise to the level of your love for her. Treat her as a princess and she will be a princess. Treat her as a queen and she will be a queen. Treat her as a goddess and she will someday be a goddess. It is your choice.

2. Use constructive strategies with long-term benefits.

- *Be a loyal provider*—Provide for your wife and family in the best possible way so that your wife can be a true homemaker.
- *Honor your wife's role*—Recognizing the role of your wife as your sweetheart and the mother of your children is of quintessential importance in the home. Women are simply more sensitive and nurturing by nature. This does not mean that you cannot show these qualities as well in your role as the husband or father, but she is the wife and mother.

- *Use tenderness*—Be tender in your intimacy with your wife.
- *Be forgiving*—Do not expect perfection from your wife and family. We should all try to progress together.
- *Be an example of love*—Confirm the old saying, "The best thing you can do for your children is to love their mother."
- *Recognize the differences*—Women have different needs; help them fulfill them.

3. Find common ground and common purpose. Have many common goals: health, companionship, spiritual growth, and leaving a legacy of honor and harmony for your children. Here are some of the mutually important things for husband and wife to keep in mind:

- *Fidelity in all things*—Even "harmless" flirtation with others can lead to adultery, which destroys families.
- *Loyalty*—Be loyal to and supportive of your wife.
- *Selflessness*—Think of her first, before yourself.
- *Overcoming selfishness*—Selfishness is the cause of virtually all marital discord. It is evidenced in the inability to communicate and reason together, leading to misunderstandings, unrealized expectations, and demanding behavior, among other things.
- *Communication*—Be willing to counsel together. Discuss *all* things relating to your marriage, your family, and your lives.
- *Happiness*—Channel and sublimate your efforts for the well-being and happiness of your wife.
- *Togetherness*—Do things together: dining, vacationing, fun activities, domestic chores—simply everything where possible. Take time to plan a fun vacation together.
- *Empathy*—If you practice empathy and understanding, then you will appreciate your wife. Gratitude will abound. Your attitudes toward each other will change, as will your behavior. If it's important to your wife, it should be important to you.
- *Service*—Look for ways to serve each other and your children.
- *Uniqueness*—Recognize that each of you has unique roles in your marriage. Be understanding and supportive.
- *Praise*—Genuinely praise your sweetheart. Write her love notes. Give her sweet surprises.
- *Privacy*—Give her space, for friends, hobbies, etc.
- *Affection*—Be affectionate. Children need to know that you like to show affection to your wife and accept the same from her.
- *Worship together*—Search the scriptures together. Pray together. Genuinely seek spiritual growth with your wife. Nothing will add a more lasting glow to the relationship.

ILLUSTRATIONS FOR OUR TIMES

Elder L. Tom Perry relates a touching exchange between David O. McKay's wife and a young boy who noticed President McKay's adoration of his spouse.

I Guess that Man Loves You

Let me tell you an experience related by Emma Rae McKay, wife of President David O. McKay:

"Last summer on reaching Los Angeles, we decided to have our car washed by one of those 'Quickies' on Wilshire Boulevard.

"As I was watching the last part of the operation from a bench, to my surprise a tiny voice at my elbow said, 'I guess that man over there loves you.'

"I turned and saw a beautiful little curly-haired child with great brown eyes who looked to be about seven years of age.

"'What did you say?' I asked.

"'I said, I guess that man over there loves you.'

"'Oh, yes, he loves me; he is my husband. But why do you ask?'

"A tender smile lighted up his face and his voice softened as he said, ''Cuz, the way he smiled at you. Do you know I'd give anything in this world if my pop would smile at my mom that way.'

"'Oh, I'm sorry if he doesn't.'

"'I guess you're not going to get a divorce,' he [questioned me].

"'No, of course not; we've been married over fifty years. Why do you ask that?'

"''Cuz everybody gets a divorce around here. My pop is getting a divorce from my mom, and I love my pop and I love my mom. . . .'

"His voice broke and tears welled up in his eyes, but he was too much of a little man to let them fall.

"'Oh, I'm sorry to hear that!'

"And then he came very close and whispered confidentially into my ear, 'You'd better hurry out of this place or you'll be getting a divorce too!'" (The Savior, the Priesthood and You, Melchizedek Priesthood Manual, 1973–74, p. 207.)

Husbands, are your actions at all times a reflection of your love for wife? If that had been you at the carwash, would that little boy have noticed the same tender love in so much abundance? (L. Tom Perry, "Father—Your Role, Your Responsibility," *Ensign,* November 1977, 62)

* * *

In the following personal account, a woman tells of her appreciation for her husband's vigilant attendance at her hospital bedside during a serious illness.

A Face in the Night

I remember a woman recounting a personal experience. She was a sensitive wife who was paying tribute to the role of husband on a special Father's Day program. There was deep, responsive quiet in the audience as this woman spoke. She explained: "One of my most memorable, beautiful experiences happened while I was in the hospital's intensive care section the first night after surgery for cancer. Momentarily I regained consciousness, opened my eyes, and there, leaning over the foot of my bed, was a heavenly face, radiant, anxious, beautiful! 'What time is it?' I inquired. (Always concerned about the time—but why? I wasn't going anywhere.) 'Three A.M.' he replied. Conscious enough to make a strong judgment, I answered, 'Not many husbands would come at that hour in the morning.' And then I was gone again. As long as I live, I need only to close my eyes to see that most transparent, handsome face—showing concern, his interest, his love for me. How disappointing it must have been for him to see me close my eyes again after that brief communion! He sat in a chair in my room the remainder of the night, and several other nights—just to be near me." Oh, husbands are important to wives!

—Ed J. Pinegar

SUMMARY

The husband is to be the protector, the provider, and stabilizing influence in the home. This is the doctrine of Jesus Christ. It is essential for a strong marriage and happy family. "By divine design, fathers are to preside over their families in love and righteousness and are responsible to provide the necessities of life and protection for their families. Mothers are primarily responsible for the nurture of their children. In these sacred responsibilities, fathers and mothers are obligated to help one another as equal partners" ("The Family: A Proclamation to the World," 1995). Cherish your wife, appreciate her in all facets of life, and she will show gratitude. Be her best friend and confidant. Counsel together. Make your role as husband fulfilling in every way. Value it and treasure it and you will become the man your wife always wanted to marry.

JESUS CHRIST

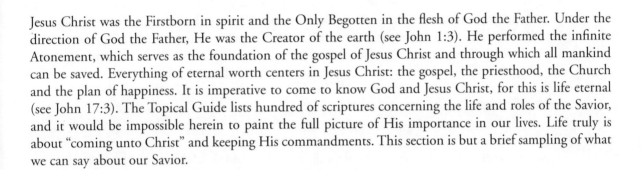

Jesus Christ was the Firstborn in spirit and the Only Begotten in the flesh of God the Father. Under the direction of God the Father, He was the Creator of the earth (see John 1:3). He performed the infinite Atonement, which serves as the foundation of the gospel of Jesus Christ and through which all mankind can be saved. Everything of eternal worth centers in Jesus Christ: the gospel, the priesthood, the Church and the plan of happiness. It is imperative to come to know God and Jesus Christ, for this is life eternal (see John 17:3). The Topical Guide lists hundred of scriptures concerning the life and roles of the Savior, and it would be impossible herein to paint the full picture of His importance in our lives. Life truly is about "coming unto Christ" and keeping His commandments. This section is but a brief sampling of what we can say about our Savior.

THE SCRIPTURES TEACH US

Deuteronomy 32:4. *He is the Rock, his work is perfect: for all his ways are judgment: a God of truth and without iniquity, just and right is he.*

This perfect and just God, Jesus Christ, must be our foundation. Because of His perfection, we can trust in Him and build our lives on the foundation of His gospel (see Hel. 5:12).

1 Timothy 2:5–6. *For there is one God, and one mediator between God and men, the man Christ Jesus; Who gave himself a ransom for all, to be testified in due time.*

Christ's mission, simply put, was to come and make it possible for us, imperfect beings, to return to our perfect Father in Heaven. He is the Mediator who bridges the gap our imperfection creates. He atoned for our sins so we could be made pure to dwell with God (see Moro. 10:32).

2 Nephi 31:16. *And now, my beloved brethren, I know by this that unless a man shall endure to the end, in following the example of the Son of the living God, he cannot be saved.*

We should follow Christ's example in all things. Because He wants us to return to His Father, He showed us the way, and then commanded us to be even as He is (see 3 Ne. 27:27).

Mosiah 3:8. *And he shall be called Jesus Christ, the Son of God, the Father of heaven and earth, the Creator of all things from the beginning; and his mother shall be called Mary.*

Jehovah, the premortal Christ, is the Creator. When we see the beauty of the earth and mankind, we should reflect on the goodness of God.

Doctrine and Covenants 93:9. *The light and the Redeemer of the world; the Spirit of truth, who came into the world, because the world was made by him, and in him was the life of men and the light of men.*

The light of the Lord is in and through all things (see D&C 88). Christ is the Light that we should hold up (see 3 Ne. 18:24). He redeems us through His atoning sacrifice and by the power of the resurrection (see Mosiah 18:2). All of this causes an overwhelming feeling of gratitude that inspires us to do the will of God.

MODERN PROPHETS SPEAK

Spencer W. Kimball:

> Men may know Christ. The ultimate and greatest of all knowledge, then, is to know God and his program for our exaltation. We may know him by sight, by sound, by feeling. While relatively few ever do really know him, everyone may know him, not only prophets—ancient and modern—but, as he said: "Every soul who forsaketh his sins and cometh unto me, and calleth on my name, and obeyeth my voice, and keepeth my commandments, shall see my face and know that I am." (D&C 93:1.) (*The Teachings of Spencer W. Kimball,* edited by Edward L. Kimball [Salt Lake City: Bookcraft, 1982], 7)

Gordon B. Hinckley:

> Believe in Jesus Christ, the Savior and Redeemer of the world. It is He who stands at the head of this Church to which you belong. This Church is not mine. It belongs to the Lord Jesus Christ. It bears His holy name. He stands at the head of this great work. He stands to assist us with our problems. He stands to bless us in our time of need. (*Teachings of Gordon B. Hinckley* [Salt Lake City: Deseret Book, 1997], 199)

Marion G. Romney:

> Latter-day Saints know that much pain and suffering could be avoided if people would accept and follow the Savior. Our mission as a church is to bring people to a knowledge of Christ and thus avoid all unnecessary suffering. (*Look to God and Live* [Salt Lake City: Deseret Book, 1971], 241)

IDEAS FOR DAILY LIVING

Here are some ideas to help us increase our testimonies of Jesus Christ, and to help us love and follow Him:

1. Know and accept that Jesus is the Christ, the Savior and Redeemer of the world.
- *Search the scriptures, for they testify of Christ*—The word of God testifies of Christ (see John 5:39). Indeed, we refer to our books of scripture as "testaments." In studying Christ's words, we not only learn to know Him, but to love Him and His teachings. As we learn of Christ through His words, we will enjoy His peace (see D&C 19:23).
- *Seek revelation from God*—We can know that Jesus is the Christ by the power of revelation (Matt. 16:17), for the Holy Ghost will give us this knowledge (see 1 Cor. 12:3). Through prayer and inspiration, we can learn the truth of all things (see Moro. 10:4–5).
- *Do the will of God to know of the truthfulness of the doctrine of Christ*—When we live the doctrine of Christ, we will know the Author (see John 7:17).

- *All things testify of God and Christ*—Every blessing in our lives, every good thing, and the magnificent creations show us there is a God and that He loves us (see Alma 30:44).
- *Seek the testimonies of the prophets, especially in the Book of Mormon*—The prophets and the scriptures speak of God and His Son Jesus Christ (see Alma 30:44). The Book of Mormon is to convince the world that Jesus is the Christ (see Title Page of the Book of Mormon). A prophet's greatest desire is for others to believe in Christ (see 2 Ne. 33:10).

2. Love our Savior Jesus Christ.

- *Remember the goodness of our Savior at all times*—Everything the Lord has done for us, including the infinite Atonement, is because He loves us (see 2 Ne. 26:24). We should love Him because He first loved us (see 1 Jn. 4:19).
- *Remember that He succors us in all things*—The Savior suffered our sins and sorrows so He would be able to help us according to the flesh (see Alma 7:11–12). We truly are indebted to the Savior for our very lives (see Mosiah 2:21), and this should inspire us to keep the commandments (see Mosiah 2:22). When we realize His love for us, we will come to love Him, and when we love Him we will keep the commandments (see John 14:15).

3. Follow our Savior Jesus Christ.

- *Accept the invitation of Jesus Christ to "come unto Him"*—Through faith, repentance, baptism, and receiving the Holy Ghost, we take upon ourselves the name of Jesus Christ; we become His sons and daughters (see Mosiah 5:7). These are the first steps in following our Savior. As we endure to the end, we can be perfected and enter into our exaltation (see 3 Ne. 12:48; Moro. 10:32).
- *Live by the word of God*—We are to live by every word of our Lord and Savior (see D&C 84:43–46), because the word will tell us all things we should do (see 2 Ne. 32:3). The Lord will guide us through life if we let Him.
- *Seek to build up the kingdom of God*—As members of the Church and followers of Christ, we seek to build up His kingdom (see JST, Matt. 6:38). We do this by sharing our joys and bringing souls unto Christ (see Alma 29:9–10; Alma 36:24), strengthening our brothers and sisters (see D&C 108:7), and entering into our temple covenants and redeeming the dead (see D&C 128:15).

ILLUSTRATIONS FOR OUR TIMES

The following experience makes us stop and ponder what it will be like to see our Savior face-to-face after this life.

That Was Christ

I was attending the celebrated Passion Play at Oberammergau in Southern Germany in 1960, along with a number of other missionaries. It was interesting to walk the streets of this quaint and beautiful village and observe the townsfolk, virtually all of whom participated on stage during the performances. They looked as though they had just stepped out of a period of time millennia old. At one point we entered the bookstore near the theater to purchase a copy of the text for the performance next day. As we were considering our purchase, we noticed a distinguished gentleman walk in. He had a pleasant countenance, with a prepossessing smile, a well-trimmed beard, and long, neat tresses. Everyone in the store fell silent at his approach. He made a purchase and then left. Noting our puzzled looks, the saleswoman leaned over and whispered to us in hushed tones, "Das war der Christus" ("That was Christ.") It gave us a chill to think that we had come so close to "Christus"—even though in this case he was only an actor, albeit one who commanded great respect in the village, even reverence. Then we pondered the lesson flowing out of this brief encounter: "Beloved, now are we the sons of God, and it doth not yet appear what we shall be: but we know that, when he shall appear, we shall be like him; for we shall see him as he is" (1 Jn. 3:2). There will come a time, for all mankind, when the encounter with the Son of God will be literal—for the faithful and obedient, a moment of glory and peace; for the disobedient and nonvaliant, a moment of profound remorse. And when we see Him, we will also see the Father, for Christ is "the brightness of his glory, and the express image of his person" (Heb. 1:3). As we are created in the image of God and His Son, we are reminded to honor this heritage and rise spiritually to meet the awesome potential that is upon us.

—Richard J. Allen

* * *

In a personal story, Elder Marion D. Hanks demonstrates the necessity of sharing our testimonies of Jesus Christ with others.

Say, Hanks, Do You Believe in Jesus Christ?

The Christmas story that I want to mention occurred in the middle of the summer some years ago, at a naval training center. The man opposite me in the room had the many stripes on his arm that signified long and distinguished service; I was an apprentice seaman in boot camp. Nonetheless, Commander Hamilton, as he greeted me at the door, was most gracious—called me "Mr. Hanks," seated me with cordiality, and we talked as equals. He had invited me to discuss the possibility of a chaplaincy. I was quick to tell him that because of a mission, I had not finished an academic degree and didn't qualify under the Navy's standards. He as quickly responded that he felt he could do something about getting that requirement waived, all things else being favorable. After a little more conversation, this rangy, fine looking man, who had been over the bow of the Yorktown on a line when she was sunk shortly before, who had everything about him that was manly and attractive to a man and was a chaplain and servant of the Lord, not of our faith, said to me, "Before I recommend you to the Chief of Chaplains, do me a favor, please. Talk to me about your experience in your Church, about what you think may help me recommend you as qualified to represent the Lord in the military chaplaincy."

And so I began, and, I want to protest, with earnestness and honesty, to try to tell him what I felt, out of our common experience in the Church, might qualify me to serve in that very significant role. He who had been so courteous and so kind began to be fidgety, and I quickly knew, as we do when we seek to communicate person-to-person, that I wasn't making it, that I was losing. And I became a little more anxious, trying to tell him what there is, this stage-by-stage opportunity in the Church for a young person to develop the quality to be a servant of God. I told him from the beginning—the early two and a half minute talks, the scouting, the deacon opportunity, the Sunday School teaching, and the mission.

After a time his demeanor completely changed. He finally interrupted me. He said, "Say, Hanks, do you believe in Jesus Christ?"

I said, "Yes, sir. Everything I believe relates to Jesus Christ. The name of the Church that I belong to is his name. My faith revolves around him as my Savior."

He, looking at his watch, said, "Well, you have been talking seven minutes and you haven't said so." I think I have not made that mistake again. (Marion D. Hanks, "Was He Relevant?" *BYU Speeches of the Year,* December 17, 1968, 2–3)

SUMMARY

Our Savior's purpose is to bring about our immortality and eternal life. Our purpose should be to center our lives on the Savior and His gospel plan. As we live the gospel and receive the sacred ordinances of the temple, we come to know our Savior and can receive the blessings of exaltation. We hope and pray for all mankind to come unto Christ that they may partake of His goodness and dwell with Him and our Heavenly Father in the celestial kingdom.

JOY

Everyone seeks happiness; it is the object of our existence. It is important to realize the difference between short-term pleasure and lasting joy. Pleasure-seeking tends to be short term in nature and must be re-experienced continually because it is not happiness. We can feel good, but it is not true happiness. This does not preclude us having an enjoyable time or doing fun things with friends and associates. To be truly happy, however, we must have the love of God in our hearts (see 4 Ne. 1:15–16), which will result in a myriad of blessings in our lives. The state of happiness comes from righteousness (see Mosiah 2:41).

THE SCRIPTURES TEACH US

Psalms 146:5. *Happy is he that hath the God of Jacob for his help, whose hope is in the Lord his God.*

Joy can be found only in our God and our Savior Jesus Christ, for in and through Them we are sustained, blessed, and given hope of eternal life, which God promised before the world began (see Titus 1:2).

Proverbs 29:18. *Where there is no vision, the people perish: but he that keepeth the law, happy is he.*

When we don't see life with proper perspective, or the "vision" of the gospel, we dwell in confusion and uncertainty. Obedience is the only sure way to happiness and joy. Obedience leads us to righteousness, through which we can enjoy a state of never-ending happiness.

3 John 1:4. *I have no greater joy than to hear that my children walk in truth.*

As mortals, we feel joy in our family as we see our family members progress on the path to eternal life. This provides a glimpse of the joy of the Lord over a soul that repents (see D&C 18:13) and over those who show an increase in faith (see 3 Ne. 17:20). Truly our joy lies in living the gospel and helping others to do so.

1 Nephi 8:10. *And it came to pass that I beheld a tree, whose fruit was desirable to make one happy.*

The fruit of the tree Lehi speaks of is the love of God. The love of God was expressed through the gift of

His Only Begotten Son, who would redeem the world and provide an opportunity for all to enjoy eternal life. We should hold to the iron rod and stay on the straight and narrow path and partake of His goodness; therein is joy.

Mosiah 2:41. *And moreover, I would desire that ye should consider on the blessed and happy state of those that keep the commandments of God. For behold, they are blessed in all things, both temporal and spiritual; and if they hold out faithful to the end they are received into heaven, that thereby they may dwell with God in a state of never-ending happiness. O remember, remember that these things are true; for the Lord God hath spoken it.*

Obedience to the commandments of God and enduring to the end will lead us back to the presence of God, to a state of never-ending happiness. Obedience—exact, immediate, and courageous obedience—should be our quest. We can find joy through keeping the commandments.

Alma 29:9–10. *I know that which the Lord hath commanded me, and I glory in it. I do not glory of myself, but I glory in that which the Lord hath commanded me; yea, and this is my glory, that perhaps I may be an instrument in the hands of God to bring some soul to repentance; and this is my joy. And behold, when I see many of my brethren truly penitent, and coming to the Lord their God, then is my soul filled with joy; then do I remember what the Lord has done for me, yea, even that he hath heard my prayer; yea, then do I remember his merciful arm which he extended towards me.*

We find joy in serving the Lord by helping others repent and come unto Him. Joy can only be found in serving and helping others grow (see D&C 18:10–16).

MODERN PROPHETS SPEAK

Ezra Taft Benson:
> If you really want to receive joy and happiness, then serve others with all your heart. Lift their burdens, and your own burdens will be lighter. Truly in the words of Jesus of Nazareth: "He that findeth his life shall lose it: and he that loseth his life for my sake shall find it." (Matt. 10:39.) (*Come, Listen to a Prophet's Voice* [Salt Lake City: Deseret Book, 1990], 59–60)

> Missionary work provides us the happiest years of our lives. I know whereof I speak. I have tasted the joy of missionary work. There is no work in all the world that can bring an individual greater joy and happiness. Like Ammon of old, our joy can be full because of seeing others come into the kingdom of God. (*Come unto Christ* [Salt Lake City: Deseret Book, 1983], 95)

David O. McKay:
> It is the duty of parents and of the Church not only to teach but to demonstrate to young people that living a life of truth and moral purity brings joy and happiness, while violations of moral and social laws result only in dissatisfaction, sorrow, and, when carried to extremes, in degradation. (*Steppingstones to an Abundant Life* [Salt Lake City: Deseret Book, 1971], 93)

> Joy is sweeter than pleasure. Joy is an emotion excited with the acquisition or expectation of good. Pleasure is a state of gratification of the senses or mind and may be sensuous. It may be self-indulgence. It is nearly always transitory. Joy and happiness are permanent. Joy is pleasure not to be repented of. (*Steppingstones to an Abundant Life* [Salt Lake City: Deseret Book, 1971], 219)

IDEAS FOR DAILY LIVING:

Here are four ideas to help us find happiness.

1. Happiness and joy depend on how we relate to God.
- *Obedience*—Happiness comes through obeying God, keeping His commandments (see Prov. 29:18), and blessing others (see Alma 36:24).
- *Receiving the love of God*—God's love expressed through the gift of His Beloved Son (see John 3:16–17) is the source of our joy, and is represented by the fruit of the tree of life (see 1 Ne. 8:10). This love, when it dwells in our hearts, causes us to live righteously and to enjoy happiness (4 Ne. 1:15–16).
- *Separation from God brings sorrow*—We separate ourselves from God through wickedness and lose the Spirit because of our disobedience (see 2 Ne. 26:11; Morm. 1:14). We cannot enjoy true happiness in wickedness, because wickedness never was happiness (see Alma 41:10).
- *Blessings*—Knowing that by keeping the commandments we can dwell with God in a state of never-ending happiness (see Mosiah 2:41), we are motivated and drawn forward in our desire to repent and humbly seek and pursue happiness (see Alma 27:18).
- *Peace*—Happiness is inner peace that endures because of righteousness. It is a gift from the Lord. It is peace that transcends mortality (see D&C 59:23).

2. Happiness and joy depend on how we deal with ourselves.
- *Attitude*—An attitude of faith and hope attracts us to joy and happiness, and that is the way we choose to live (see 2 Ne. 5:27). Our attitudes will affect our level of happiness more than almost anything else, because as we think, so are we (see Prov. 23:7). "Most people are about as happy as they make up their minds to be" (Abraham Lincoln).
- *Principles*—Happiness is knowing that we have aligned our lives with gospel principles and values that are not momentary and fleeting, but have endurance. Our "contentment level" must come from adherence to values and standards that are designed to bring us happiness. We cannot be happy doing things that hurt ourselves and others.
- *Rejoicing in success*—Happiness is knowing that we have overcome our trials and temptations, our weaknesses and mortal frailties.
- *Being*—Happiness is a state of being, not a state of ownership or worldly attainment. We should not let success and happiness depend on possessions, positions, or comparisons.

3. Happiness and joy depend on how we deal with others.
- *Service*—Happiness is the perception that we have enriched the lives of others in ways that bring them lasting joy and peace (see Alma 36:24).
- *Togetherness*—Happiness is togetherness with those we love. When we have someone to share our happiness with, we are infinitely more happy.
- *Discernment*—Happiness is the capacity to discern in every person, if not the creativity of a Michelangelo or the brilliance of an Einstein or the compassion of a Florence Nightingale, then at least the capacity of a child of God who is striving, growing, and reaching to become like Him.

4. Happiness and joy depend on how we deal with life.
- *Meaning*—Happiness is an assurance that we have gained the vision of eternal life sufficient to infuse us with purpose, meaning, and the hope of an eternal family living in the presence of God.

- *Simplicity*—Happiness is the ability to see in any given moment the purpose of life, goodness, and joy—all because you are alive and can choose your steps in life. Don't look beyond the mark. Enjoy the journey of life. Find joy in the simple things of life along the way.
- *Beauty*—Happiness is the thrill of experiencing the beauties of life and nature in all its wondrous variety and abundance, and realizing that it is a gift from God because He loves us.

ILLUSTRATIONS FOR OUR TIMES

This narrative about the personal search for happiness reveals the timeless truth—that true joy is what we do and what we are, not what we have.

The Dream Home

As young students in graduate school, we weren't very wealthy. In fact, we struggled. I borrowed in order to get through school. And for our dates, we would buy graph paper and draw our future dream house. This went on for nine years as we began our lives, did a stint in the military, and came back again. And after nine years of marriage and moving ten times, it looked like we were finally going to be in our dream home. My sweetheart drew the plans. All those days we'd taken that graph paper and said, "When we move into our house then we can really be happy. Then we can really be happy."

Well, around the tenth year, we began to move into our new home. It was beautiful, located on a mountain crest looking over the valley, under the shadows of the mountain peaks. It was wonderful, on a half-acre of land. Oh, our dreams came true. As we were moving in that day, I thought back, "Wait, isn't this the day? Yes, this is the day we start being happy. We finally get to have our own home—our very own home." I was reflective, and I realized this physical presence of our house did not bring happiness. I had sought happiness in a possession that I thought would bring happiness.

As my wife walked downstairs while we were moving some furniture and some items, I said, "How do you feel?"

"Fine," she said.

"Do you feel any different than yesterday?" I said.

"No, it's just fun to move in."

Yes, we had both missed the point. It's not moving into a new home that brings us happiness. Happiness is a journey of living a life according to principles based on happiness, not on things that are possessed, not on positions, or titles, or stations. Happiness is in the living, not in the getting. Do not wait to be happy, do not put it off.

—Ed J. Pinegar

SUMMARY

For many, happiness in mortality is fleeting because the perceived source of happiness is rooted in a worldly value system. As we seek joy in mortality, we will never find it without the eternal perspective of the plan of happiness uppermost in our mind. The eternal perspective gives credence to mortality as part of an eternal landscape. Life can be wonderful as we seek eternal truths and then choose to keep the Lord's commandments.

To be humble and devout players on this grand stage of life makes of us seekers of happiness rather than simply participants in the mortal experience. "Men are, that they might have joy," stated the prophet Lehi (2 Ne. 2:25). That joy flows from seeking the will of the Father and following in the footsteps of the Son.

JUDGMENT

Judgment entails coming to a decision or conclusion about something. We will not discuss personal choices or decisions, but rather judging other people as individuals. The process of making judgments about others is an ongoing part of our lives. Some questions include, When is judging others appropriate? What is my criteria for judging? These questions are important because they deal with perception in our relationships, and because they affect the way we will be judged in our own lives.

THE SCRIPTURES TEACH US

John 7:24. *Judge not according to the appearance, but judge righteous judgment.*

We must be careful and wise in our judgments, using the discernment of the Spirit in our evaluations of ourselves and others (see Moro. 7:15–17).

3 Nephi 14:1–5. *Verily, verily, I say unto you, Judge not, that ye be not judged. For with what judgment ye judge, ye shall be judged; and with what measure ye mete, it shall be measured to you again. And why beholdest thou the mote that is in thy brother's eye, but considerest not the beam that is in thine own eye? Or how wilt thou say to thy brother: Let me pull the mote out of thine eye—and behold, a beam is in thine own eye? Thou hypocrite, first cast the beam out of thine own eye; and then shalt thou see clearly to cast the mote out of thy brother's eye.*

In this part of the Sermon on the Mount, our Savior provides the standard for judging. The Joseph Smith translation of Matthew 7:1 adds that we are not to judge *unrighteously*. We are judged according to how we judge, so let us do so righteously and with mercy. When judging, let us make sure that we know all the pertinent facts, and that we seek to help, not condemn.

MODERN PROPHETS SPEAK

Bruce R. McConkie:
> Judging the brethren and evil speaking against the saints is in effect judging the gospel and evil speaking against its laws, for the gospel reserves judgment to the Lord. Thus, those who presume to judge others usurp the prerogatives of Deity, of him only who has power to impose sentence, that is, "to save and to destroy." (*Doctrinal New Testament Commentary*, 3 vols. [Salt Lake City: Bookcraft, 1965–1973], 3:267)

Boyd K. Packer:
> Don't be too anxious to call yourself a failure or to judge others as failures. When all accounts are settled, you will find that no effort to teach righteousness is ever completely lost. Nothing you do in the way of trying to convey the gospel of Jesus Christ is ever futile. (*Teach Ye Diligently* [Salt Lake City: Deseret Book, 1975], 339)

Mark E. Petersen:

>It is the simple gospel of the Lord Jesus Christ, which teaches mankind to be true brethren and sisters, to love our neighbors as ourselves, to go the extra mile, to turn the other cheek, to forgive—even seventy times seven—to do unto others as we would be done by, to seek reconciliation wherein we have offended others, to avoid judging others, that we ourselves may not be judged; to be kind, patient, long-suffering, charitable, temperate, humble and God-like. (*The Way to Peace* [Salt Lake City: Bookcraft, 1969], 24)

James E. Faust:

>There are three sources of guidance for making moral judgments. First is the guidance of the Holy Ghost. This is always a sure compass for those who have been baptized and received this supernal gift. The second source is the wise counsel of priesthood leaders whom the Lord has put in place to guide us. Third, the constant demonstration of love should temper all our judgments. Sometimes this means discipline. ("The Weightier Matters of the Law: Judgment, Mercy, and Faith," *Ensign,* November 1997, 53)

IDEAS FOR DAILY LIVING

Here are five ideas to help us make righteous judgments and avoid unrighteous ones:

1. First decide whether a judgment is needed.
- *Live and let live*—In most cases, we can live in peace with our fellowmen without the need to subject them to our constant judgment. We have our hands full just keeping ourselves on the straight and narrow path, let alone worrying about keeping score for the world.
- *Focus on need*—Is there a need to judge or voice an opinion? If not, don't (see Matt. 7:1–3). On occasion, of course, there may be a need to make a judgment of others—people we are considering for hire, people who want to open a business relationship with us, people who want to enter public office, people we may be interacting with as part of our stewardship in the gospel, or people who would like to be a part of our family circle. If there is a genuine need to make a judgment, do it in righteousness.

2. Place the emphasis on positive things. Is our philosophy to catch people doing wrong or to catch people doing right? We will have greater peace and joy in life if our prevailing philosophy is to find the good in people and bring out their best qualities.

3. Establish a firm foundation for informed and correct judgment.
- *Get the facts*—Do you have reliable and accurate information for making a judgment? Always get *all* the applicable facts before making a judgment.
- *Take into account your own bias*—Is your perception of reality objective or is it skewed by the situation, past experiences, attitudes, or values? Seek the opinion of someone you trust to give you a second opinion and offer a more objective view.
- *Consider the circumstances*—Do the people behave as they do because of unique or unusual circumstances?
- *Be a careful observer*—It is exceedingly difficult to determine the inner motivation of people with any degree of accuracy. Therefore, it is best to observe how people *act* in different circumstances and then fashion an opinion about the person's patterns of belief and standards of behavior.

- *Look for patterns*—Everyone slips up occasionally, but how does a person act after a misstep or lapse? Does that person quickly make amends, or is there an observable pattern that betrays a deficit of character and sounds a warning signal?
- *Look for the little things*—When we need to form an opinion of someone, we must first understand if that person is aligned with lasting principles of honesty and integrity and if that person's word can be trusted implicitly. How do we make that kind of judgment? By looking at the small and simple indicators. If someone will cheat in little things, beware of the implications for larger things. If someone is uncompromisingly honorable in the little things, chances are that he or she will come through successfully in the big things.

4. Show leadership in judgment.
- *Start in the family*—As parents, we are faced with the ongoing problem of helping our children choose good, moral friends. This involves a judgment call that is difficult but necessary.
- *Teach the principle of giving the benefit of the doubt*—A true leader in the family, in the workplace, or in the community is quick to be magnanimous and slow to condemn. Set measurable standards of quality performance and enforce them rigorously. But always give people a second chance to rise above their mistakes and learn from their experiences.
- *Go directly to the person involved*—If someone's actions result in disharmony in your life or harm to you or those you care about, go to that person and state clearly what you have observed. Then give that person a chance to respond and, if needed, correct the situation.
- *Keep confidences*—Following the process of judgment, never share feelings or information that would discredit or hurt another when the whole truth is not known. As the saying goes about gossiping, "Picking up feathers is awfully hard in a windstorm."

5. Be forgiving and understanding.
- *Judgment is tempered by mercy*—Always give the benefit of the doubt in regard to judgment. If there is a question as to the accuracy of the information or opinions involved, always err on the side of mercy.
- *Judgment is always two-sided*—The same standard you use in judging others will be used in how they judge you. Often the faults we see in others are simply mirror images of the faults we would like to deny within ourselves. When you are tempted to condemn another, quickly see if you are not really referring to yourself.
- *Seek higher-level assistance*—Pray and seek inspiration from the Almighty in understanding the hearts of others and in rendering righteous judgment.
- *Use wisdom*—Leave to God the role of being the ultimate judge of lives.

ILLUSTRATIONS FOR OUR TIMES

Elder N. Eldon Tanner gives us important counsel regarding unrighteous judgment, something we must all guard against.

Judge Not, That Ye Be Not Judged

Let me give you one or two examples of unjust criticism and judging without the facts.

There is a little story about Sister McKay, the wife of President David O. McKay, when she began teaching school. As the principal introduced her to the class, he pointed to a certain boy and said he was a troublemaker. She sensed the boy's embarrassment and feared he would live up to his reputation, so she wrote a note and slipped it to him as she passed his desk. It said, "Earl, I think the principal was mistaken about your being a bad boy. I trust you, and know that you are going to help me make this room the best in the school." Earl not only became a paragon of scholastic virtue but also one of the town's most important people.

I should like to give you another example. One of our most respected community-minded citizens began to act as though his feelings had been hurt and to stay away from socials where, in the past, he had gone and taken a most active part. People started accusing him of being a sorehead, a poor sport, antisocial, etc., and even evaded him whenever possible. Later, a medical diagnosis showed he was suffering from a brain tumor, which had been the cause of his lack of interest in activities that he had previously attended and even sponsored.

Let me give you another example or two of what I would call unrighteous judgment. First, a bishop who needs additional officers sees a member of his ward who, though not active, seems to have ability, but he says to himself, "Oh, he wouldn't be interested. He wouldn't want to accept a position." So he does not approach him, and the man remains inactive for years.

A new bishop is called to the ward, asks the man if he would be willing to accept a position, and finds that he is really ready and anxious to work.

Don't prejudge, but give the person an opportunity. Let him decide for himself to accept or decline.

On the other hand, we hear a man say to his family and to others, "I don't see why the bishop does this or that. You would think he would know better." Here he is judging the bishop without the facts, which, if known to him, would be full justification for the action taken. The man's judgment was not only unrighteous, but it had probably prejudiced his children and caused them to lose respect for the bishop and had weakened their faith.

These examples show how important it is that we do not judge, but encourage rather than denounce. (N. Eldon Tanner, "Judge Not, That Ye Be Not Judged," *Ensign,* July 1972, 34)

SUMMARY

As we come to realize the crucial nature of judging, we will understand the caution and care we must give to this important aspect of our lives. People can make mistakes resulting in misbehavior or trying situations. Remember, though, that people can change, and the ultimate judge is God. Let us always keep in our hearts the divine dictum: "I, the Lord, will forgive whom I will forgive, but of you it is required to forgive all men" (D&C 64:10).

JUSTICE AND MERCY

Justice connotes righteous judgment as it relates to mankind in keeping the commandments of God. Justice demands payment for sins. On the other hand, mercy forgives the debt required by justice. Mercy is the benevolent kindness and grace of God shown to His children through the infinite Atonement that pays the debt for our sins, if we repent. In this way, God is both just and merciful. His mercy fulfills the demands of justice, providing the way for mankind to exercise faith unto repentance (see Alma 34:15–17) and be forgiven.

THE SCRIPTURES TEACH US

Alma 12:15. *But this cannot be; we must come forth and stand before him in his glory, and in his power, and in his might, majesty, and dominion, and acknowledge to our everlasting shame that all his judgments are just; that he is just in all his works, and that he is merciful unto the children of men, and that he has all power to save every man that believeth on his name and bringeth forth fruit meet for repentance.*

We will all stand before the Lord on Judgment Day. If we are righteous, it will be a pleasant experience. Moroni calls judgment "the pleasing bar of the great Jehovah" (Moro. 10:34). By contrast, if we have sinned without repenting, we may feel like Alma did prior to his repentance: "The very thought of coming into the presence of my God did rack my soul with inexpressible horror" (Alma 36:14). The key is to repent with full purpose of heart—then is the Lord's mercy extended towards us, and we will be judged worthy to enter His kingdom.

Alma 42:24–25. *For behold, justice exerciseth all his demands, and also mercy claimeth all which is her own; and thus, none but the truly penitent are saved. What, do ye suppose that mercy can rob justice? I say unto you, Nay; not one whit. If so, God would cease to be God.*

Let us never forget that to qualify for mercy we must repent, else we must suffer the consequences of our sins (see D&C 19:15–19). It is profitable to read the entire explanation that Alma gave to his son Corianton on this vital subject (see Alma 42:1–31).

Alma 41:3. *And it is requisite with the justice of God that men should be judged according to their works; and if their works were good in this life, and the desires of their hearts were good, that they should also, at the last day, be restored unto that which is good.*

Remember that we are a result of all our thoughts and desires. We do eventually act upon many of them, and they become our works. Justice demands that we receive the consequences of our works. If we are good, the doctrine of restoration is clear: we receive good for being good (see Alma 41:3–15).

MODERN PROPHETS SPEAK

Boyd K. Packer:

> Those who make one serious mistake tend to add another by assuming that it is then too late for them. It is never too late! Never! While your temptations are greater than were ours, that

will be considered in the judgments of the Lord. He said that "his mercies [are suited] according to the conditions of the children of men" (D&C 46:15). That is only just. A great contribution to Christian doctrine is the explanation in the Book of Mormon of how *justice* and *mercy* and *repentance* and *forgiveness* work together to erase transgressions (see Alma 42). The discouraging idea that a mistake (or even a series of them) makes it everlastingly too late does not come from the Lord. He has said that *if* we will repent, not only will He forgive us our transgressions but He will also forget them, will remember our sins no more (see Isaiah 43:25; Hebrews 8:12; 10:17; D&C 58:42; Alma 36:19). (*Let Not Your Heart Be Troubled* [Salt Lake City: Bookcraft, 1991], 51)

Neal A. Maxwell:

Part of the basis for demonstrating the perfection of God's justice and mercy will thus be the cumulative record which we ourselves will have made (see Alma 41:7). Out of this we can be justly judged, a judgment that will include our compliance with outward gospel ordinances with all their respective covenants. (*Lord, Increase Our Faith* [Salt Lake City: Bookcraft, 1994], 75)

Dallin H. Oaks:

The laws of God achieve their purposes through justice, mercy, and the atonement of Jesus Christ. Church discipline is concerned with all of these, but most particularly with mercy and the atonement. . . . In its relationship to justice and mercy, *the atonement* is the means by which justice is served and mercy is extended. For this purpose, the Messiah "offereth himself a sacrifice for sin, to answer the ends of the law, unto all those who have a broken heart and a contrite spirit; and unto none else can the ends of the law be answered." (2 Ne. 2:7; see also Rom. 5:18–19.) In one of the greatest of all scriptural declarations, Alma explains that because of the atonement, "mercy claimeth the penitent, and mercy cometh because of the atonement." (Alma 42:23.) (*The Lord's Way* [Salt Lake City: Deseret Book, 1991], 216–18)

IDEAS FOR DAILY LIVING

Here are three ideas to help us understand the principles of justice and mercy:

1. Cultivate a broken heart and a contrite spirit.
- *Remember that we are nothing without the Lord*—"I am the vine, ye are the branches: He that abideth in me, and I in him, the same bringeth forth much fruit: for without me ye can do nothing" (John 15:5). Mercy comes to those who are humble and teachable. Mercy eschews the proud and the haughty, which must necessarily be caught in the web of justice if they do not repent.
- *Remember that we are everything* with *the Lord*—"In his strength I can do all things," declared Ammon (Alma 26:12). By leaning on the arm of the Lord, we bring ourselves within the embrace of mercy, "which overpowereth justice, and bringeth about means unto men that they may have faith unto repentance" (Alma 34:15). Because the Lord can exercise mercy and forgive the debt that justice exacts on our works, we need to rely on Him to overcome sin and obtain salvation.
- *Receive our prophets and leaders*—When those inquiring about the Church willingly receive the missionaries, and when Church members similarly receive the counsel of ecclesiastical leaders, they can obtain blessings and mercy from the Lord (D&C 99:3). It is through the Lord's mercy that we have the gospel and leaders raised up to teach it. If we fail to embrace the message of our prophets and leaders, we cannot qualify for the Lord's mercy further.

2. View justice and mercy as attributes of our Father in Heaven.

- *In God are blended perfectly the qualities of justice and mercy*—Our daily thoughts and deeds should always be placed in the context of our relationship with a just and merciful God. We forsake evil and sin so that justice is not constrained to condemn us; we embrace the principles of the gospel of Jesus Christ that mercy can have hold on our being.

- *We "fear" God's justice*—The fear of God, as this term is used in the scriptures, implies that we obey God out of reverence and respect, knowing that He cannot "look upon sin with the least degree of allowance" (D&C 1:31). We shall be judged according to our works according to the justice of God (see Alma 41:3).

- *We have hope in God's mercy*—Knowing of our nothingness before the Lord (see Mosiah 4:11), we reach out in humble contrition to ask for a blessing of mercy. Such should be the essence of our daily prayers. God is a God of mercy and will show mercy unto the meek (see D&C 97:2). His mercy is extended to us through His Only Begotten Son (see Alma 12:33). As we exercise faith unto repentance (see Alma 34:16) and as the demands of justice are satisfied through Christ's atoning sacrifice (see 2 Ne. 9:26), we receive the mercy of God.

3. Treat others with mercy and charity. We can learn more about mercy and its operation by acting in mercy toward others; we can learn more about justice and its operation by withholding judgment and criticism of our fellowmen.

- *Let God be the Judge*—Rather than judging and holding grudges, forgive others their trespasses (see D&C 64:10). Take upon yourself the divine essence by practicing understanding and forbearance.

- *Extend mercy unconditionally*—Without condoning misdirected and hurtful behavior in others, we can nonetheless reach out in the spirit of mercy, giving others the benefit of the doubt and allowing them the chance to rise to the level of their potential (see D&C 88:40). As we are merciful, we shall obtain mercy (see Matt. 5:7).

- *Teach by principle*—In dealing with others (especially our own children), we need to amplify for them the principles to follow and the consequences that flow naturally from our compliance or lack thereof. Often the greatest application of mercy is to teach with clarity and precision the operation of principles and values in one's life. As every parent knows, the greatest joy comes from seeing children "walk in truth" (3 Jn. 1:4). Likewise, the greatest sorrow comes from seeing children suffer the ill consequences of violating the laws of God.

ILLUSTRATIONS FOR OUR TIMES

We learn from the Prophet Joseph Smith the necessity of showing mercy to one another in the following:

The Allowance of Mercy

On Thursday, June 9, 1842, the Prophet Joseph Smith delivered an address regarding mercy to the sisters of the Female Relief Society in Nauvoo—one filled with delicious spiritual food. Here is a sampling of his wisdom: "Nothing is so much calculated to lead the people to forsake sin as to take them by the hand, and watch over them with tenderness. When persons manifest the least kindness and love to me, O what power it has over my mind, while the opposite course has a tendency to harrow up all the harsh feelings and depress the human mind" (*History of the Church,* 5:23–24). And also, "God does not look on sin with allowance, but when men have sinned, there must be allowance made for them. All the religious world is boasting of righteousness: it is the doctrine of the devil to retard the human mind, and hinder our progress, by filling us with self-righteousness. The nearer we get to our heavenly Father, the more we are disposed to look with compassion on perishing souls; we feel that we want to take them on our shoulders, and cast their sins behind our backs . . . if you would have God have mercy on you, have mercy on one another" (*History of the Church,* 5:24). And finally: "How oft have wise men and women sought to dictate Brother Joseph by saying, 'O, if I were Brother Joseph, I would do this and that;' but if they were in Brother Joseph's shoes they would find that men or women could not be compelled into the kingdom of God, but must be dealt with in long-suffering, till God shall bring such characters to justice. There should be no license for sin, but mercy should go hand in hand with reproof" (*History of the Church,* 5:24).

The message is clear: we are to feed God's sheep with mercy and long-suffering. The best way for us to bring others to Christ is not by harsh criticism and judgment, but by encouragement and love. This not only shows them the love of the Lord, but extends it to us as well. The Savior declared: "Blessed are the merciful: for they shall obtain mercy" (Matt. 5:7).

—Richard J. Allen

SUMMARY

What greater statement can there be regarding justice and mercy than the one that Alma the Younger—himself a firsthand authority in the operation of these principles—gives to his sometimes-deviant son Corianton: "O my son, I desire that ye should deny the justice of God no more. Do not endeavor to excuse yourself in the least point because of your sins, by denying the justice of God; but do you let the justice of God, and his mercy, and his long-suffering have full sway in your heart; and let it bring you down to the dust in humility" (Alma 42:30). Then Alma gives to Corianton the same counsel that applies to us all: Repent and go and serve in the kingdom of God, teaching others the doctrines of justice and mercy, that they might make covenants of salvation with the Lord and honor them, even unto the end.

JUSTIFICATION

To be justified means that we have been approved of the Lord and absolved of all wrongdoing. We stand guiltless and blameless before the Lord, justified by the Spirit (see Moses 6:60), which ratifies the righteous (see 1 Ne. 16:2), and we stand approved and exonerated. Justification by the Spirit is made possible through the Atonement of the Lord Jesus Christ (see Mosiah 14:11), for as in all things it is by the grace of God that we are saved (see D&C 20:30).

THE SCRIPTURES TEACH US

1 Nephi 16:2. *And it came to pass that I said unto them that I knew that I had spoken hard things against the wicked, according to the truth; and the righteous have I justified, and testified that they should be lifted up at the last day; wherefore, the guilty taketh the truth to be hard, for it cutteth them to the very center.*

We must be worthy of all blessings from the Lord, showing forth faith, good works, and righteousness, and then the Spirit justifies us and makes us acceptable before the Lord. Through justification, our souls become guiltless and therefore subject to grace and mercy.

2 Nephi 2:5, 8. *And men are instructed sufficiently that they know good from evil. And the law is given unto men. And by the law no flesh is justified; or, by the law men are cut off. Yea, by the temporal law they were cut off; and also, by the spiritual law they perish from that which is good, and become miserable forever. . . . Wherefore, how great the importance to make these things known unto the inhabitants of the earth, that they may know that there is no flesh that can dwell in the presence of God, save it be through the merits, and mercy, and grace of the Holy Messiah, who layeth down his life according to the flesh, and taketh it again by the power of the Spirit, that he may bring to pass the resurrection of the dead, being the first that should rise.*

In this counsel to his son Jacob, Lehi makes clear that no mortal is justified by the law; that is, no mortal achieves perfection by virtue of complete obedience to the law. Being imperfect, we all are dependent upon the "merits, and mercy, and grace of the Holy Messiah" to make up the difference, justifying us through the Atonement, "for we know that it is by grace that we are saved, after all we can do" (2 Ne. 25:23).

Mosiah 14:11. *He shall see the travail of his soul, and shall be satisfied; by his knowledge shall my righteous servant justify many; for he shall bear their iniquities.*

Using this quotation from Isaiah, the prophet Abinadi teaches wicked King Noah and his subjects about the Savior's atoning sacrifice ("travail") and how it can justify those who live the gospel and honor their covenant. They are justified when the demands of justice are met through the merciful Atonement of our Savior.

Doctrine and Covenants 20:30. *And we know that justification through the grace of our Lord and Savior Jesus Christ is just and true.*

The Lord justifies us through His Atonement as He bears our iniquities, all because of His loving grace towards us.

Moses 6:60. *For by the water ye keep the commandment; by the Spirit ye are justified, and by the blood ye are sanctified.*

Through baptism we accept Christ and promise to keep His commandments. We are justified by the Holy Ghost because of our righteousness and the goodness of God. When we repent, we become pure and clean (sanctified) through the atoning blood of the Lord Jesus Christ.

MODERN PROPHETS SPEAK

Bruce R. McConkie:

> To be justified is to be made righteous and therefore to be saved. Men are justified in what they do when their deeds conform to divine standards. Righteous acts are approved of the Lord; they are ratified by the Holy Ghost; they are sealed by the Holy Spirit of Promise; or, in other words, they are justified by the Spirit. Such divine approval must be given to "all covenants, contracts, bonds, obligations, oaths, vows, performances, connections, associations, or expectations"—that is, to all things—if they are to have "efficacy, virtue, or force in and after the resurrection from the dead." (D&C 132:7.) Such a requirement is part of the terms and conditions of the gospel covenant. (*The Promised Messiah* [Salt Lake City: Deseret Book, 1978] 344)

Joseph Smith:

> Dear Brethren:—It is a duty which every Saint ought to render to his brethren freely—to always love them, and ever succor them. To be justified before God we must love one another: we must overcome evil; we must visit the fatherless and the widow in their affliction, and we must keep ourselves unspotted from the world: for such virtues flow from the great fountain of pure religion. Strengthening our faith by adding every good quality that adorns the children of the blessed Jesus, we can pray in the season of prayer; we can love our neighbor as ourselves, and be faithful in tribulation, knowing that the reward of such is greater in the kingdom of heaven. What a consolation! What a joy! Let me live the life of the righteous, and let my reward be like this!" (*History of the Church,* 2:229).

Spencer W. Kimball:

> "And such were some of you: but ye are washed, but ye are sanctified, but ye are justified in the name of the Lord Jesus, and by the Spirit of our God." (1 Cor. 6:11.)

> This is the great secret. Some of those who inherit the kingdom may have committed one or more of these grievous sins, but they are therefore no longer in those categories. They are *no longer unclean,* having been washed, sanctified, and justified. Paul's hearers had been in those despicable categories, but having now received the gospel with its purifying, transforming powers, they were changed. The cleansing process had been applied and they were washed clean and had become eligible for the first resurrection and for exaltation in God's kingdom. ("God Will Forgive," *Ensign,* March 1982, 2)

IDEAS FOR DAILY LIVING

Here are five ideas to help us understand and prepare to receive the blessings of justification:

1. Justification is a gift of grace. Recognize that all blessings of exaltation are tied to the grace of God and the Atonement of the Lord Jesus Christ. On our own merits, we cannot become justified through obedience to the laws and commandments, since we will fall short of the mark through our imperfections. Thus the sublimating and redeeming grace of the Lord is required to elevate and justify the righteous. We should be grateful for the Lord's grace and mercy in opening up the pathway to immortality and eternal life (see D&C 20:30).

2. Justification is accomplished through the instrumentality of the Holy Ghost. Justification is a sacred function of the Holy Spirit acting to bless the righteous children of our Father in Heaven. Let us therefore live in worthiness for the blessings of the Spirit. We must think and act in accordance with spiritual principles in order to invite the Spirit into our lives at all times (Moses 6:60).

3. Justification is accomplished "after all we can do" (2 Ne. 25:23). Justification before God requires covenant righteousness. Righteousness is a prerequisite for all blessings from the Lord with the exception of the resurrection which comes as a pure gift of unconditional grace (see *Righteousness* for additional ideas).

4. Justification comes about through faith. It is by the power of faith that mortals embark upon the pathway of ultimate justification before God. We cannot be justified unless we have faith to live the gospel and to repent. Let us do all in our power to increase and strengthen our faith daily (see Rom. 3:28). (See *Faith* for additional ideas.)

5. Justification is an act of charity. Just as the Atonement was enacted and empowered through divine love, we too can sustain and strengthen our case for individual justification on the basis of our unconditional love and charity toward our fellow beings. Each day we can memorialize our gratitude to Heavenly Father and His Son through our own works of charity that bless the lives of our families and all those around us.

ILLUSTRATIONS FOR OUR TIMES

The following story compares a lesson about the law of justification to how the Lord Jesus Christ feels about humankind.

They Don't Have to Be Perfect—They Just Have To Come

Some time ago one of the families in our high priests group came forward with a challenge. Home teaching visits to their home had become somewhat sporadic, and the family was sensing a deficit in the priesthood encouragement and support that can come from the faithful discharge of home teaching responsibilities. The wife's characterization of the job description of a home teacher was a classic: "They don't have to be perfect—they just have to come." Her memorable comment was the ideal metaphor for the greater human condition as viewed in the context of the plan of salvation and the law of justification. The Lord said: "Come unto me, all ye that labour and are heavy laden, and I will give you rest. Take my yoke upon you, and learn of me; for I am meek and lowly in heart: and ye shall find rest unto your souls. For my yoke is easy, and my burden is light" (Matt. 11:28–30). It is in the "coming" that mortals begin the journey toward justification through the Spirit. The Lord, through His infinite sacrifice, prepared the way; but we must embark thereon, in all our imperfections, if His merits and mercy and grace (2 Ne. 2:8) are to be efficacious in lifting us beyond our nothingness to a realization of the divine potential within.

Jacob expounded on this theme of coming to the font of grace and mercy when he taught: "Come, my brethren, every one that thirsteth, come ye to the waters; and he that hath no money, come buy and eat; yea, come buy wine and milk without money and without price. Wherefore, do not spend money for that which is of no worth, nor your labor for that which cannot satisfy. Hearken diligently unto me, and remember the words which I have spoken; and come unto the Holy One of Israel, and feast upon that which perisheth not, neither can be corrupted, and let your soul delight in fatness. Behold, my beloved brethren, remember the words of your God; pray unto him continually by day, and give thanks unto his holy name by night. Let your hearts rejoice. And behold how great the covenants of the Lord, and how great his condescensions unto the children of men; and because of his greatness, and his grace and mercy, he has promised unto us that our seed shall not utterly be destroyed, according to the flesh, but that he would preserve them; and in future generations they shall become a righteous branch unto the house of Israel" (2 Ne. 9:50–53).

As mortals, we are never justified before God on the basis of perfect obedience to all the laws and commandments. Lehi made that clear when he said, "And by the law no flesh is justified" (2 Ne. 2:5). Only through the divine Atonement can mankind hope to be justified—"after all we can do" (2 Ne. 25:23). In effect, the Lord says: "They don't have to be perfect—they just have to come." It is in the "coming" before Him with a broken heart and a contrite spirit, in faith and obedience, that we can aspire to the essential state of justification through grace, and thus enter into His presence once again.

—Richard J. Allen

SUMMARY

Living the gospel and accepting Jesus Christ as our Savior is the only thing that can free us of the sins of the world. We can only be justified because our Savior sacrificed Himself to atone for these sins. If we accept His Atonement and seek righteousness in all that we do, the Holy Spirit can ratify our lives and we can become justified. This should be our goal: to realize these precious blessings by becoming a "just" person—one who lives by faith and does good works.

KINDNESS

In kindness, one shows the qualities of gentleness, thoughtfulness, sympathy, cordiality, pleasantness, and benevolence. Kind persons will experience inner peace as they show love and respect to others. Kindness requires a character based on gospel principles. It becomes an outward expression of our love of God, a manifestation of a pure heart and genuine concern for others.

THE SCRIPTURES TEACH US

Ephesians 4:32. *And be ye kind one to another, tenderhearted, forgiving one another, even as God for Christ's sake hath forgiven you.*

Kindness is a facet of the virtue of charity (see Moro. 7:45). When we express kindness we are exhibiting the pure love of Christ and the qualities of godliness (see 2 Pet. 1:3–12).

Doctrine and Covenants 121:41–42. *No power or influence can or ought to be maintained by virtue of the priesthood, only by persuasion, by long-suffering, by gentleness and meekness, and by love unfeigned; By kindness, and pure knowledge, which shall greatly enlarge the soul without hypocrisy, and without guile.*

In any aspect of life, when seeking to influence or to persuade another person, we should act out of a central disposition to be kind. Whether we seek to influence or not, kindness seems to be the best policy in every case.

MODERN PROPHETS SPEAK

Gordon B. Hinckley:

> Let us as Latter-day Saints cultivate a spirit of brotherhood in all of our associations. Let us be more charitable in our judgments, more sympathetic and understanding of those who err, more willing to forgive those who trespass against us. Let us not add to the measure of hatred that periodically sweeps across the world. Let us reach out in kindness to all men, even toward those who speak evil of us and who would, if they could, harm us. (*Teachings of Gordon B. Hinckley* [Salt Lake City: Deseret Book, 1997], 661)

George Albert Smith:

> *The gospel is a gospel of love and kindness.* I pray that the love of the gospel of our Lord will burn in our souls and enrich our lives, that it will cause husbands to be kinder to wives, and wives to be kinder to husbands, parents to children, and children to parents because of the gospel of Jesus

Christ, which is a gospel of love and kindness. It will cause us, if we are living as we should, to love our neighbors as ourselves, and go out of our way, if possible, to help them understand better the purpose of life. These are some of our privileges. (*The Teachings of George Albert Smith,* ed. Robert McIntosh and Susan McIntosh [Salt Lake City: Bookcraft, 1996], 136)

IDEAS FOR DAILY LIVING

Here are four ideas that can help you to be more kind to others:

1. Kindness operates on the basis of charitable principles.
- *Dignity of life*—Kindness sees value and worth in all living things: people, animals, and the living environment of our world.
- *Freedom of choice*—Kindness is not preemptive, but creates choices and options for people, honoring the principle that everyone is free to make choices in life.
- *Love of God*—Kindness is the mirror of the infinite, being the earthly embodiment of the eternal charity we see in the Creator. Thus kindness operates on the principle that we must honor the highest potential within us to do good.

2. Kindness reflects the best human qualities.
- *Tolerance*—Kindness is not quick to judge or condemn, but stops to listen and encourage. "Gently to hear, kindly to judge" is how Shakespeare put it.
- *Evenhandedness*—Kindness is consistent, respecting the needs of even the stranger whose path one crosses.
- *Authenticity*—Kindness is not strategic or calculating, but genuinely benevolent and charitable.
- *Quiet*—Kindness is quiet and often invisible, operating behind the scenes, whereas the ostentatious and the boastful compete openly for the admiration of the public. They have their reward in the praise of men, rather than the peace of the Lord (see Matt. 6:1–4).
- *Love*—Kindness is all too rare in our society, and it flourishes best in the seedbed of love.
- *Gratitude*—Kindness always shows gratitude for anything received.

3. Kindness has the power to transform.
- *Attraction*—Kindness attracts kindness, for even the most hard-hearted person is disarmed in the presence of a kind soul.
- *Warmth*—Kindness is the warm breeze that dispels the frost of anger, resentment, greed, and envy.
- *Humor*—Often using the heart-warming effects of mild humor, kindness recognizes graciously that everyone has weaknesses and imperfections, but extends the hand of love and fellowship nevertheless.
- *Service*—Kindness quietly transforms the landscape of home, workplace, and community by lifting, strengthening, giving hope, and teaching the principles of self-improvement.

4. Kindness can be cultivated.
- *Take the initiative*—Look for ways to be thoughtful and gracious.
- *Monitor your speech*—Be genuine in your expressions.
- *Monitor your behavior*—Make your demeanor appropriate to the act of kindness, avoiding any display of boastfulness or self-aggrandizement.
- *Do the simple things*—Remember that simple and small acts of kindness are often the most precious.
- *Smile*—It always lifts another's spirit and is contagious too.
- *Show leadership*—Diffuse difficult situations with a cordial and pleasant attitude.
- *Keep them guessing!*—Enjoy doing random and anonymous acts of kindness.

ILLUSTRATIONS FOR OUR TIMES

President Thomas S. Monson shares a letter received at Church headquarters that provided a wonderful example of kind service given to a stranger by members of the Church.

Good Samaritans

We have no way of knowing when our privilege to extend a helping hand will unfold before us. The road to Jericho each of us travels bears no name, and the weary traveler who needs our help may be one unknown.

Genuine gratitude was expressed by the writer of a letter received some time ago at Church headquarters. No return address was shown, no name, but the postmark was from Portland, Oregon:

"To the Office of the First Presidency:

"Salt Lake City showed me Christian hospitality once during my wandering years.

"On a cross-country journey by bus to California, I stepped down in the terminal in Salt Lake City, sick and trembling from aggravated loss of sleep caused by a lack of necessary medication. In my headlong flight from a bad situation in Boston, I had completely forgotten my supply.

"In the Temple Square Hotel restaurant, I sat dejectedly. Out of the corner of my eye I saw a couple approach my table. 'Are you all right, young man?' the woman asked. I raised up, crying and a bit shaken, related my story and the predicament I was in then. They listened carefully and patiently to my nearly incoherent ramblings, and then they took charge. They spoke with the restaurant manager, then told me I could have all I wanted to eat there for five days. They took me next door to the hotel desk and got me a room for five days. Then they drove me to a clinic and saw that I was provided with the medications I needed—truly my basic lifeline to sanity and comfort.

"While I was recuperating and building my strength, I made it a point to attend the daily Tabernacle organ recitals. The celestial voicing of that instrument from the faintest intonation to the mighty full organ is the most sublime sonority of my acquaintance. I have acquired albums and tapes of the Tabernacle organ and the choir which I can rely upon any time to soothe and buttress a sagging spirit.

"On my last day at the hotel, before I resumed my journey, I turned in my key; and there was a message for me from that couple: 'Repay us by showing gentle kindness to some other troubled soul along your road.' That was my habit, but I determined to be more keenly on the lookout for someone who needed a lift in life.

"I wish you well. I don't know if these are indeed the 'latter days' spoken of in the scriptures, but I do know that two members of your church were saints to me in my desperate hours of need. I just thought you might like to know."

What an example of caring compassion. (Thomas S. Monson, "Compassion," *Ensign,* May 2001, 18)

* * *

In this story from his life, President James E. Faust reveals his deep regret for a kind act left undone.

The Weightier Matters

> I fear that some of our greatest sins are sins of omission. These are some of the weightier matters of the law the Savior said we should not leave undone (Matthew 23:23). These are the thoughtful, caring deeds we fail to do, and feel so guilty for having neglected them.
>
> As a small boy on the farm during the searing heat of the summer, I remember my grandmother, Mary Finlinson, cooking our delicious meals on a hot woodstove. When the wood box next to the stove became empty, Grandmother would silently pick up the box, go out to refill it from the pile of cedar wood outside, and bring the heavily laden box back into the house. I was so insensitive and so interested in the conversation in the kitchen, I sat there and let my beloved grandmother refill the kitchen wood box. I feel ashamed of myself and have regretted my omission for all of my life. I hope someday to ask for her forgiveness. (James E. Faust, *Stories from My Life* [Salt Lake City: Deseret Book, 2001], 57–58)

SUMMARY

When we receive an act of kindness, whether material or verbal, we feel gratitude. This feeling in turn causes us to desire to be kind to others; kindness truly is contagious. Volumes of literature have been written about wonderful acts of kindness that have affected the lives of others. Make a goal today to do a random act of kindness and feel the joy it can bring to your life and the lives of others.

KNOWLEDGE

We gain knowledge as we come to an understanding of truth or evident facts. Mankind has gained a great deal of knowledge and learning through observation and experience. Worldly knowledge often changes according to scientific progress and advances. Knowledge of secular matters is good but has no direct saving or exalting power, although we have been commanded to obtain knowledge to help and lift others. Gospel knowledge deals with eternal truths given by God to man, and this kind of knowledge can save us. Such knowledge never changes, but is the same yesterday, today, and forever. When we gain a clear understanding of the doctrines, principles, and covenants pertaining to the gospel and the kingdom of God, we are enlightened. We increase in our intelligence, for we have acquired light and truth. This pure knowledge comes by the power of the Holy Ghost, for "by the power of the Holy Ghost ye may know the truth of all things" (Moro. 10:5).

THE SCRIPTURES TEACH US

Proverbs 15:14. *The heart of him that hath understanding seeketh knowledge: but the mouth of fools feedeth on foolishness.*

When we genuinely understand life and possess an eternal perspective, we will hunger and thirst after righteousness; that is, we will seek knowledge from the Holy Ghost concerning true principles.

2 Nephi 9:28–29. *O that cunning plan of the evil one! O the vainness, and the frailties, and the foolishness of men! When they are learned they think they are wise, and they hearken not unto the counsel of God, for they set it aside, supposing they know of themselves, wherefore, their wisdom is foolishness and it profiteth them not. And they shall perish. But to be learned is good if they hearken unto the counsels of God.*

Let us remember that the learning (knowledge) of man is desirable and useful to the extent that it accords with enduring principles and brings about worthwhile purposes. However, learning for the sake of prideful elevation can lead us to believe more in our own abilities than in the power of God. We must remember that the knowledge given to us by God is composed of saving truths of an eternal nature.

Doctrine and Covenants 131:6. *It is impossible for a man to be saved in ignorance.*

Let us aspire to seek and gain knowledge that will help us live righteously, thus qualifying ourselves for eternal life.

MODERN PROPHETS SPEAK

Gordon B. Hinckley:
> You cannot afford to stop. You must not rest in your development. . . . There is so much to learn and so little time in which to learn it. I confess I am constantly appalled by the scarcity of my knowledge, and the one resentment I think I carry concerns the many pressing demands which limit the opportunity for reading. As we talk of reading, I should like to add a word concerning that which we absorb not only out of the processes of the mind, but something further which comes by the power of the Spirit. Remember this promise given by revelation: "God shall give unto you knowledge by his Holy Spirit, yea, by the unspeakable gift of the Holy Ghost. . . ." (D&C 121:26.) . . .
>
> There is . . . incumbent upon you, you who are members of The Church of Jesus Christ of Latter-day Saints, the responsibility to observe the commandment to continue to study and to learn. Said the Lord: "Seek ye out of the best books words of wisdom; seek learning, even by study and also by faith" (D&C 88:118). (*Teachings of Gordon B. Hinckley* [Salt Lake City: Deseret Book, 1997], 303)

Bruce R. McConkie:
> Worldly wisdom and knowledge gained by intellectual talents are available to all men. But the knowledge of God and his eternal laws—gospel knowledge, saving knowledge, the hidden wisdom that comes from on high, the wisdom of those to whom the wonders of eternity are an open book, divine wisdom—all these are gifts of the Spirit. "The things of God knoweth no man, but the Spirit of God." (1 Corinthians 2:11.)
>
> Among the true saints are those endowed with divine knowledge and heavenly wisdom "that all may be taught to be wise and to have knowledge." (D&C 46:17–18. See also Moroni 10:9–10; 1 Corinthians 12:8.) Of those so endowed, Paul says: "We have received, not the spirit of the world, but the spirit which is of God; that we might know the things that are freely given to us of God. Which things also we speak, not in the words which man's wisdom teacheth, but which the Holy Ghost teacheth." (1 Corinthians 2:12–13.) (*A New Witness for the Articles of Faith* [Salt Lake City: Deseret Book, 1985], 372)

IDEAS FOR DAILY LIVING

Here are three ideas to assist you in your quest for gospel knowledge:

1. Cultivate a learning attitude.

- *Willingly accept God's commandment to seek learning*—The Lord commands, "learn of me, and listen to my words; walk in the meekness of my Spirit, and you shall have peace in me" (D&C 19:23), and further, "seek ye out of the best books words of wisdom; seek learning, even by study and also by faith" (D&C 88:118). The Lord has blessed us with a world abundant in knowledge so that we can fulfill this divine mandate.

- *Learn by faith*—Know that God will open the way for you to acquire saving knowledge if you diligently seek the truth. "If any of you lack wisdom, let him ask of God, that giveth to all men liberally, and upbraideth not; and it shall be given him. But let him ask in faith, nothing wavering. For he that wavereth is like a wave of the sea driven with the wind and tossed" (James 1:5–6). Follow the example of the Prophet Joseph and inquire of the Lord.

- *Enjoy the benefits*—Remember that your attitude and behavior improve as you come to understand (gain knowledge of) the doctrines and principles of the gospel. You will be edified, broadened in wisdom, comforted through the Spirit, and given a feeling of peace and confidence as you seek to learn in a framework of obedience: "Let thy bowels also be full of charity towards all men, and to the household of faith, and let virtue garnish thy thoughts unceasingly; then shall thy confidence wax strong in the presence of God; and the doctrine of the priesthood shall distil upon thy soul as the dews from heaven" (D&C 121:45).

- *Be easily entreated*—Go to Church and other types of meetings with an attitude of humility and learning, having prepared your heart and mind to learn.

2. Go to the correct sources.

- *Pray*—Seek knowledge from the Lord in earnest and faithful prayer, remembering that the Holy Ghost can reveal the truth of all things (see Moro. 10:5).

- *Hearken to the prophets*—Study the words of the living oracles of God (see 3 Ne. 28:34–35; D&C 1:38; 21:4–6).

- *Search the scriptures*—Remember the choice words from the Psalmist: "Thy word is a lamp unto my feet, and a light unto my path" (Ps. 119:105), As well as the words of our modern-day prophet: "I would encourage my people to read the scriptures, to read the Book of Mormon, to read the New Testament. I would urge them with all the capacity I have to read quietly and thoughtfully and introspectively" (Gordon B. Hinckley, "Inspirational Thoughts," *Ensign*, October 2003, 4). The word of God as contained in the scriptures will tell us all things to do (see 2 Ne. 32:3), will invoke change in us (see Alma 31:5), and will give us the instruction we should live by (see D&C 84:43–46).

- *Enjoy group-learning environments*—Commitment to effective learning practices is often strengthened when we learn in groups. Regularly attend Church, seminary, and institute classes, as well as other worthwhile offerings for continued gospel learning.

- *Family learning*—Make family home evening and family councils exciting opportunities to learn together and reinforce gospel truths in the family. Always search the scriptures together as a family.

3. Organize your learning strategy.

- *Goal-setting*—Set a goal and make a plan to seek gospel knowledge diligently and with devotion.

- *Consistency*—Be consistent in your study. Follow through on your study goals and plans.

- *Eternal perspective*—Remember that we never cease to learn. Seek every opportunity to learn and grow (see D&C 109:7).

ILLUSTRATIONS FOR OUR TIMES

The following illustrates the emphasis of gospel knowledge over secular knowledge in the lives of two great scholars: James E. Talmage and Theodore M. Burton.

Prepared in All Things

Years ago as a graduate student at the Johns Hopkins University in Baltimore, I was searching through the library card index files one day and happened to come upon a number of entries under the authorship of James E. Talmage. It was a startling reminder of the range of knowledge that encompasses the human condition. Elder Talmage (1862–1933) did advanced work at Johns Hopkins in geology and related fields, going on later to serve as president of the University of Utah from 1894 to 1897. He was called as a member of the Quorum of the Twelve Apostles in 1911. While rising to preeminence in secular knowledge, he became a celebrated scholar of sacred knowledge as well, authoring such perennial classics as *Articles of Faith* (1899), *House of the Lord* (1912), and *Jesus the Christ* (1915). The example of Elder Talmage and his commitment to worthwhile teaching and learning of all kinds is a salient illustration of the Lord's commandment to be prepared in all things and seek a breadth of knowledge as a fundamental means of preparation in building up the kingdom of God on earth: "And I give unto you a commandment that you shall teach one another the doctrine of the kingdom. Teach ye diligently and my grace shall attend you, that you may be instructed more perfectly in theory, in principle, in doctrine, in the law of the gospel, in all things that pertain unto the kingdom of God, that are expedient for you to understand; Of things both in heaven and in the earth, and under the earth; things which have been, things which are, things which must shortly come to pass; things which are at home, things which are abroad; the wars and the perplexities of the nations, and the judgments which are on the land; and a knowledge also of countries and of kingdoms—That ye may be prepared in all things when I shall send you again to magnify the calling whereunto I have called you, and the mission with which I have commissioned you" (D&C 88:77–80). While the quest for knowledge is to be broad and all-encompassing, the central goal for God's servants is to serve as well-prepared instruments in advancing the cause of the gospel and its saving principles.

This preeminence of gospel knowledge over secular knowledge was illustrated by Elder Theodore Burton, under whom I served as a missionary in Germany many years ago. He would on occasion speak of his career as a chemistry professor of note, drawing attention to his numerous honors and publications in that field. However, he would emphasize that his purpose was not to boast, but rather to provide evidence that he had been blessed with a searching and inquiring mind, well-trained to detect error and falsehood. Then he would bear fervent testimony of the truth of the gospel and the restored Church, saying that if the rationale of logic and meaning attached to the Church and its teachings were in any way suspect, he would have long ago detected such discontinuities and exposed them as misguided. However, such was not the case, he would emphasize, reporting that the gospel was not only logically true, but confirmed in its spiritual veracity through the power of the Holy Ghost. Thus Elder Burton used his secular accomplishments as an adjunct to the higher or more important knowledge that comes through divine revelation.

—Richard J. Allen

SUMMARY

Knowledge is power. Gospel knowledge gives one the power to do good and overcome the trials, tribulations, and temptations of the world. Let us seek diligently to know and understand the things of God, and then live by this higher knowledge day by day. Just as we nourish our body with food, so likewise we must nourish our spirit with saving knowledge. Every day is an opportunity to gain knowledge, become closer to God, and live as He would have us live.

LOVE

Love is a word we use frequently in the English language. It means affection, passion, and strong heartfelt feelings. Additionally, we often use the word *love* colloquially to express feelings of affection for things or events. The Greek language contains words that represent three different forms of love: *eros*—physical love; *philia*—brotherly and reciprocatory love; and *agape*—godly love. Since we use only one English word to express love, we might suggest a broader meaning: "ultimate concern that brings about righteous service." Love is about caring, empathy, and service.

THE SCRIPTURES TEACH US

Matthew 22:37–38. *Jesus said unto him, Thou shalt love the Lord thy God with all thy heart, and with all thy soul, and with all thy mind. This is the first and great commandment.*

The first great commandment is to love God with all our heart, might, mind, and soul. This fulfills all the law and the prophets, as obeying this commandment will cause us to love our fellowmen as well (see Matt 22:40; Rom. 13:8). Love is the purest motive of obedience (see John 14:15).

Matthew 22:39. *And the second is like unto it, Thou shalt love thy neighbour as thyself.*

We cannot love God and hate our fellowmen (see 1 Jn. 4:20), because loving God will engender feelings of love in us for all mankind. As we love and serve our neighbor, we are loving and serving our God (see Mosiah 2:17). Fulfilling this command shows the world that we are indeed the disciples of Jesus Christ (see John 13:34–35).

John 15:12–13. *This is my commandment, That ye love one another, as I have loved you. Greater love hath no man than this, that a man lay down his life for his friends.*

Christ gave His life because He loved us (see 2 Ne. 26:24). A life of service for our fellowmen proves our love for them.

Galatians 5:6. *For in Jesus Christ neither circumcision availeth any thing, nor uncircumcision; but faith which worketh by love.*

Faith, the moving cause of all action, is motivated by love. The greatest command the Lord has given to us is to love. When our love is strong enough we will obey the Lord's commands (see John 14:15). We will be motivated to do good as our Heavenly Father and our Savior do (see John 3:16; 2 Ne. 26:24).

1 John 4:7–11. *Beloved, let us love one another: for love is of God; and every one that loveth is born of God, and knoweth God. He that loveth not knoweth not God; for God is love. In this was manifested the love of God toward us, because that God sent his only begotten Son into the world, that we might live through him. Herein is love, not that we loved God, but that he loved us, and sent his Son to be the propitiation for our sins. Beloved, if God so loved us, we ought also to love one another.*

The expression of love from God is an expression of His very being. Just as faith dwells in God as part of His nature and power, so likewise does love. It is the nature of God not only to possess love but to demonstrate it on behalf of His children. Our Heavenly Father has shown ultimate concern for us through His Only Begotten Son. This is how love begets love. As we love people, it will draw them toward us, even as we are drawn toward the Savior because He loves us (see 3 Ne. 27:13–14).

3 Nephi 12:44. *But behold I say unto you, love your enemies, bless them that curse you, do good to them that hate you, and pray for them who despitefully use you and persecute you.*

Loving our enemies is one of the most difficult commandments of life. Do we actually love them and care for their well-being? The sons of Mosiah not only cared for their Lamanite brethren, they went to them and served them, that they might bring them unto Christ. Why? Because "they could not bear that any soul should perish . . . the very thoughts that any soul should endure endless torment did cause them to quake and tremble" (Mosiah 28:3). This is true charity, the highest form of love.

Moroni 8:26. *And the remission of sins bringeth meekness, and lowliness of heart; and because of meekness and lowliness of heart cometh the visitation of the Holy Ghost, which Comforter filleth with hope and perfect love, which love endureth by diligence unto prayer, until the end shall come, when all the saints shall dwell with God.*

When we live by the Spirit, we will be blessed with a perfect love—love that has no bounds, love that is unconditional, love that is shown to our fellowmen, love that serves God and causes us to keep the commandments (see D&C 42:29).

MODERN PROPHETS SPEAK

Thomas S. Monson:

> If you or I were there, we might then have asked, "Master, how might we best show our love?" Perhaps we would have heard the words, "He that hath my commandments, and keepeth them, he it is that loveth me." (John 14:21.) Or, "If ye love me, keep my commandments." (John 14:15.)

> Another question: "How might I best show my love for my fellowmen?" And the words of King Benjamin could well apply: "When ye are in the service of your fellow beings ye are only in the service of your God." (Mosiah 2:17.) Service is the best measuring stick of love. (*Be Your Best Self* [Salt Lake City: Deseret Book, 1979], 193–94)

> Love is the catalyst that causes change. Love is the balm that brings healing to the soul. ("The Doorway of Love," *Ensign*, October 1996, 2)

Joseph Smith:

> It is a time-honored adage that love begets love. Let us pour forth love—show forth everlasting increase; cast our bread upon the waters and we shall receive it after many days, increased to a hundredfold. (*Teachings of the Prophet Joseph Smith,* sel. Joseph Fielding Smith [Salt Lake City: Deseret Book, 1938], 316)

Marvin J. Ashton:

> *Love* is such a vague word. To reap the benefits of loving, specific actions must be taken. The hungry man must not be pitied—he must be fed. The lonesome young woman needs not just a quick smile—she needs someone to walk with her, arm in arm. The tired mother needs not just a valentine saying "I love you"—she needs to be given help with daily tasks. We are told to love our neighbors. There are many ways to show love: a compliment, a kind word, a loaf of bread, a visit, a listening ear. "As I have loved you . . . love one another." (*Ye Are My Friends* [Salt Lake City: Deseret Book, 1972], 23)

Gordon B. Hinckley:

> This must be the foundation of our instruction: love of God and love for and service to others—neighbors, family, and all with whom we have association. That which we teach must be constantly gauged against these two standards established by the Lord. If we shall do so, this work will continue to roll forward. (*Teachings of Gordon B. Hinckley* [Salt Lake City: Deseret Book, 1997], 316–17)

IDEAS FOR DAILY LIVING

Here are six suggestions to help us show more love:

1. Love is a choice.

- *Choose a vision of love*—Love takes a certain kind of vision: the vision that sees in every person, regardless of his or her present condition or circumstances, an abundant measure of value and a limitless potential for good.
- *Choose the principle of love*—We can choose to build our lives on a foundation of love. Love can inform our every thought and deed—if we choose to let it do so.
- *Choose to keep the commandment of love*—Remember that love is a commandment: love God (see Deut. 6:5; Matt 22:37); love our enemies (see Matt 5:44; 3 Nephi 12:44); love our neighbor (see Matt. 19:19; 22:39); love one another (see John 13:34–35); the law is fulfilled in love (see Gal 5:14); and love is of God (see 1 Jn. 4:7). We cannot assist in the work of the kingdom without love (see D&C 12:8).

2. Love is many small kindnesses added together.

- *Take the initiative to be kind*—Do simple acts of kindness that show how much you care.
- *Show respect*—Love allows people room to grow. Ask questions without prying into others' feelings.
- *Smile*—Congeniality and friendliness in our comments and behavior with others are important keys to showing and developing love.
- *Be genuinely interested in others*—We can show empathy by caring about things that are important to those we love.
- *Find the good*—Catch people doing good and compliment and praise them for it. Send a note of appreciation or praise. Be ready to praise rather than criticize or find fault.
- *Say the magic words*—Wherever appropriate (and it's almost always appropriate), tell someone that you love them. Verbally express the words "I love you" with sincerity.

- *Be a loving cheerleader*—Discern in people their special talents, and do things to encourage them to cultivate and share those talents. Praise them and recognize their progress.
- *Listen*—Love listens with patience. Love sees through the eyes of others, hears through their ears, feels with their hearts.
- *Be open to love*—Show appreciation when you receive love from others. Receive kindness graciously and openly.

3. Love is multifaceted.
- *Cultivate a well-rounded love*—Show love in the family, in the neighborhood, in the workplace, and in the community.
- *Love everyone*—Love them because they are children of God. Defend the rights of all people, regardless of gender, age, cultural background, or national origin.
- *Have special love for your family*—Focus the main beam of your love on your family—your spouse, your children, your grandchildren, and others in your extended family.

4. Love takes effort.
- *Pay the price willingly*—Love often requires sacrifice because of your concern for those you love—but they are worth it.
- *Give love without strings attached*—Be ready and willing to give service with no thought of reward.
- *Use active love*—Love is not passive. Sometimes action is called for to make the world a better place for the coming generation. It takes action to root out bigotry, defeat discrimination, neutralize hatred, dissipate anger, and overcome greed.
- *Love sometimes chastens*—Withholding correction from a loved one who is falling by the wayside is withholding love. Love is a teaching tool, a power for change (see D&C 121:41–44).

5. Love can be cultivated.
- *Take the initiative to serve*—If you do not feel love toward certain people in your circle of acquaintance, even family members, find ways to serve them—not for the reward or recognition (which may not be forthcoming anyway), but only to kindle within you the right kinds of feelings. These people have good in them, and perhaps only you can illuminate that good and reveal it.
- *Be forgiving*—Love cannot flourish in an atmosphere of rancor or grudges. You can make room for love by forgiving others and by evicting hatred and ill will from your life.
- *Understand the circle of love*—Live to learn; learn to love; then you will love to live.

6. Go to the source of all love.
- *Know who you are*—Don't forget to put yourself on your list of people to love. Your talents and abilities have a divine source; your potential and capacity come from God. You must love yourself as part of your preparation to love others.
- *Become a student of love*—Love flows from Heavenly Father and our Savior. To obtain more love, go to the Source. Pray. Study the scriptures. Attend church. Meditate on spiritual things. Practice spiritual love, then put it to work in real life.
- *Love God*—Feeling genuine, soul-deep love for Heavenly Father is one of the hallmarks of a balanced and complete life. To learn to love God is to learn to love all of His children.

ILLUSTRATIONS FOR OUR TIMES

As the following illustrates, there is an amazing power in expressed love.

The Power of Love

I was teaching high school in 1966. We were covering the subject of love and expressing love. The students all seemed to be anxiously engaged in the conversation of the day. I got the idea of asking for a volunteer to do a special homework assignment. I stopped the class and said, "Who will do me a favor?" The hands all flew up. A young boy near the back of the room named Dennis Dunn seemed quite anxious. I called him up to the front and I said, "Dennis, do you really want to do this favor for me?"

He said, "Sure!"

"This is really hard."

"I can do it. That's no problem. I can do it," he said.

"Well, this is really going to take some effort," I said.

In exasperation he said, "I'll do it. Just what do you want me to do?"

"This is it. When you go home tonight, you call out for your mother. When your mother comes to you, you take her in your arms and give her a big embrace. Yes, Dennis, a big kiss. And then you whisper in her ear, 'Oh, Mommy, I love you.'"

He stopped, looked at me and said, "No way! No way can I do that."

"Dennis, do you love your mother?"

"Of course I do."

I said, "Then, why don't you do it?"

He replied, "You just don't do things like that."

"Dennis, if you love her you should tell her."

"No way!"

Well, Dennis and I were pretty good friends, and so I said to him, "Dennis, I think I can hear a chicken clucking in this class." The class all started to laugh and Dennis felt uneasy. "In fact, Dennis, I think there's a yellow stripe coming right up your back." Now everyone was laughing—even Dennis.

We played around for a minute and finally he relented and said, "Okay, okay, I'll do it. Just let me go back to my seat." So Dennis went back to his seat. The class period ended, and life went on.

The next day as I was greeting the members of the class as they came in, I said, "Dennis, how did it go last night?"

He looked at me and said, "Oh, it was wonderful!"

"Can you tell me about it?"

"Can I tell the whole class?"

"You're on," I said. So, after the introductory remarks to the class, I said, "We have a special report today from Dennis."

Dennis came up in front—the big junior in high school, but something was different. His lips began to quiver, and his eyes began to fill up with tears, then he blurted out, "Oh, you guys, it was the greatest day of my life. My mom cried for two hours. I can't believe it." They all laughed. Then he said, "You don't realize what we've done to our parents. We've locked them out of our lives. They've done everything for us, and we treat them like dirt. We should be ashamed. They're starved for our love just like we're starved for their love. But you've gotta say it. You've gotta tell 'em." Well, the class was just on fire. And he said, "You've all gotta go home and do it just like I did." At that moment in class, silent commitments were made, and needless to say, they went home and did it.

A couple of weeks went by, and we had what is known as "parents' night," when the parents come back and have visits with the teachers. In our class, we had all of the parents sit in the chairs of their children. I stood up in front and told them how we were discussing different things in class. One parent said, "What do you do in this class?" I attempted to explain again. She said, "No, you don't understand. My son's nice to me now. He even told me he loved me. And the only thing I can think of that's been different in his life lately is this class." Other hands came up. "Yes, that happened to me, too." Well, the class was on fire. The parents all of a sudden felt so good about their children.

When I responded I merely said, "Oh, it's just their goodness. You've just learned just how good your children really are." Well, lives were changed by that experience of Dennis Dunn. He made a difference in all those young people's lives, for he had set an example and challenged them. They took the challenge, made the commitment, and families were blessed. Parents were happy, families were happy, and life was beautiful. Yes, the power of love, expressed, can make all the difference in the world.

—Ed J. Pinegar

SUMMARY

Remember, love is more than an emotion: it is a choice to give and receive. The most important thing we should remember is the command to "love one another." When we love one another, we learn the ultimate secret about love—that it is not just an emotion, but a principle of action, like faith. Love causes things to happen. It is a power of good, an energy that brings about enduring growth and lasting vitality.

MAGNIFYING YOUR CALLING

We all receive callings here upon the earth—some of limited time span and some of eternal scope. The question that will be asked of each of us by the Lord Jesus Christ is this: "Did you magnify your callings?" Each calling or role honorably fulfilled ultimately blesses someone's life; therefore, when we magnify our calling, we strengthen the people we serve. Blessing and serving our fellowmen help to build up the kingdom of God (see JST, Matt. 6:38), in that we invite all to come unto Christ and strengthen those who have made covenants (see D&C 108:7). Magnifying our callings in this way is serving our God (see Mosiah 2:17) and assisting in His work (see Moses 1:39). Each role and calling is important within the stewardship and framework in which we serve. Everyone is needed and everyone is important in his or her callings—for we all have need of each other (see 1 Cor. 12:14–27). President Gordon B. Hinckley has stated, "We magnify our calling, we enlarge the potential of our priesthood when we reach out to those in distress and give strength to those who falter" (*Teachings of Gordon B. Hinckley* [Salt Lake City: Deseret Book, 1997], 478). Let us therefore diligently seek to magnify our eternal roles and callings, thus qualifying ourselves to return to the presence of our Heavenly Father.

THE SCRIPTURES TEACH US

2 Timothy 1:6–7. *Wherefore I put thee in remembrance that thou stir up the gift of God, which is in thee by the putting on of my hands. For God hath not given us the spirit of fear; but of power, and of love, and of a sound mind.*

In order for us to magnify our callings, we must be worthy of inspiration by the Holy Ghost and then follow the spiritual promptings that come. The Lord has made us equal to the task by making accessible to the faithful and valiant all of His power and gifts. He will support us (see D&C 84:85–88), and if we are prepared, we shall not fear (see D&C 38:30).

Jacob 1:19. *And we did magnify our office unto the Lord, taking upon us the responsibility, answering the sins of the people upon our own heads if we did not teach them the word of God with all diligence; wherefore, by laboring with our might their blood might not come upon our garments; otherwise their blood would come upon our garments, and we would not be found spotless at the last day.*

When we magnify our calling, we labor with all our might, mind, and strength so that we can stand blameless before the Lord (see D&C 4:2). Let us never forget that we have duties that no one else can perform. Our calling or stewardship is for us to magnify—regardless of the situation—or else we stand condemned before the Lord (see Moroni 9:6).

Alma 17:2–3. *Now these sons of Mosiah were with Alma at the time the angel first appeared unto him; therefore Alma did rejoice exceedingly to see his brethren; and what added more to his joy, they were still his brethren in the Lord; yea, and they had waxed strong in the knowledge of the truth; for they were men of a sound understanding and they had searched the scriptures diligently, that they might know the word of God. But this is not all; they had given themselves to much prayer, and fasting; therefore they had the spirit of prophecy, and the spirit of revelation, and when they taught, they taught with power and authority of God.*

To magnify our callings we must pay the price of preparation. The sons of Mosiah exemplify this: they searched the scriptures and fasted and prayed, and they were consequently endowed with the power of God to teach by the Spirit. We must obtain His Word (see D&C 11:21) and seek His counsel in all things (see Alma 37:37) as we diligently magnify our callings. This formula of searching the scriptures and fasting and prayer should be part of our personal preparation to magnify our callings.

Doctrine and Covenants 81:5. *Wherefore, be faithful; stand in the office which I have appointed unto you; succor the weak, lift up the hands which hang down, and strengthen the feeble knees.*

In every office and calling, let us never forget that people matter more than anything else. People are the reason we serve. Every person is important in his or her calling in the Lord's kingdom here upon the earth (see D&C 84:109–110). We should seek to bless and strengthen others in all things (see D&C 108:7).

Doctrine and Covenants 84:33. *For whoso is faithful unto the obtaining these two priesthoods of which I have spoken, and the magnifying their calling, are sanctified by the Spirit unto the renewing of their bodies.*

Sanctification comes to those who yield their hearts to the Lord (see Hel. 3:35) and who magnify their priesthood. We can be sanctified as we do the will of God with all of our hearts. Having an eye single to His glory in all that we do will allow Him to magnify us with His light so that we can comprehend all things (see D&C 88:67).

MODERN PROPHETS SPEAK

Matthew Cowley:

> God bless us all that we may have strength and endure to the end, to run the race and run it well. Be loyal and faithful and sustain one another in our work in the Church. Magnify our calling. Be humble before the Lord and in our humility God will magnify us as he always does beyond our own experience, our own age, and our own natural ability to do things. (*Matthew Cowley Speaks* [Salt Lake City: Deseret Book, 1954], 429)

George Q. Cannon:

> God blesses those who magnify callings. He is ready to bless every man in His Church who will magnify His office and calling. (*Gospel Truth: Discourses and Writings of President George Q. Cannon,* ed. Jerreld L. Newquist [Salt Lake City: Deseret Book, 1987], 183)

Thomas S. Monson:

> How well do we obey his bidding? How do we magnify our calling from the Lord? The Prophet Joseph was often asked, "Brother Joseph, what do you mean by magnifying a calling?" Joseph replied: "What does it mean to magnify a calling? It means to build it up in dignity and importance, to make it honorable and commendable in the eyes of all men, to enlarge and strengthen it, to let the light of heaven shine through it to the view of other men. And how does one magnify a calling? Simply by performing the service that pertains to it. An elder magnifies the ordained calling of an elder by learning what his duties as an elder are and then by doing them." (*Pathways to Perfection* [Salt Lake City: Deseret Book, 1973], 146)

Howard W. Hunter:

> The Lord never calls a man to any office in his Church but what he will by revelation help that man to magnify his calling. (*The Teachings of Howard W. Hunter,* ed. Clyde J. Williams [Salt Lake City: Bookcraft, 1997], 215)

George Albert Smith:

> Now, while we live and labor let us magnify our calling. Let no man be found recreant to his opportunities. Let us not turn our backs upon the blessings of the Lord, but day by day go faithfully on blessing our father's children. (*The Teachings of George Albert Smith,* ed. Robert McIntosh and Susan McIntosh [Salt Lake City: Bookcraft, 1996], 95)

IDEAS FOR DAILY LIVING

Here are some ideas to help us magnify our callings:

1. Learn your duty.
- Search the scriptures for direction (see 2 Ne. 32:3; Alma 37:37–47).
- Seek counsel from the Lord (see Jacob 4:10; James 1:5–6).
- Study the Church manuals (see D&C 88:118).
- Attend the temple with a prayer in our heart (see D&C 97:13–14).
- Seek direction from the prophet and other Church leaders (see D&C 21:4–5; 38:23).
- Attend all the training meetings for your calling (see D&C 43:8–10).
- Learn and do your duty so as to not be a slothful servant (see D&C 107:99–100).

2. Be directed by the Spirit
- Be worthy of the Spirit with faith (see 1 Ne. 10:17), love and purity (see D&C 76:116), and obedience (see D&C 20:77, 79).
- The Spirit will show you all things to do (see 2 Ne. 32:5).
- The Spirit will give you at the very moment the things you need to say (see D&C 100:5–6).
- The Spirit will direct you even if you don't always know the things to do (see 1 Ne. 4:6).

3. Understand the needs of those you serve.
- Get acquainted with those we serve.
- Build relationships of trust so that you can understand them and have credibility with them.
- Number and name those you have a responsibility for and, according to their needs, nurture them with the word of God (see Moro. 6:4).

4. Pray for understanding and direction (see James 1:5–6).
- Pray for special help (Mosiah 27:14).
- Pray to have success in blessing others (see Alma 31:34–35).

5. Diligently seek to serve and bless your fellowmen.
- Labor with all your might within your stewardship (see Moro. 9:6).
- Seek the one who struggles or who is lost (see D&C 81:5; Luke 15:6).
- Remember that when you are helping another person you are helping the Lord (see Matt. 25:40; Mosiah 2:17).
- Serve with all your heart that you may stand blameless before the Lord (see D&C 4:2).

ILLUSTRATIONS FOR OUR TIMES

The following personal account illustrates how the members of one ward learned to magnify many callings, developing new skills and talents, touching several lives, and reaching a new level of understanding of working today in the kingdom of God.

Quickening the Pace

Some callings, like those of father, mother, husband, or wife, extend for eternity. Other callings are subsets of a greater and never-ending mission to help build the kingdom of God. Our family lived one time in a ward where the bishopric used an unusual strategy that seemed to help the members focus with an uncommon degree of devotion on their callings. Each December, all of the callings in the ward were changed; that is, each member received a new calling, of precisely one year's duration. The entire ward family was therefore reorganized once each year. This had several consequences, apart from adding considerably to the leadership responsibilities of the bishopric: (1) the interest in roles and duties increased; (2) people tended to accelerate the pace of learning their new duties, since they had a shorter time in which to have a positive impact; (3) the energy level seemed to be higher; and (4) a great deal of networking and discussion occurred behind the scenes regarding correlation and cooperation. I am not sure the bishopric continued the practice for more than several cycles, as we moved into to another ward, but during the time the yearly organization took place, people certainly lengthened their stride and gained a keener sense of unity.

Undoubtedly, we are a unified body of Christ where talents, gifts, and resources must be shared interdependently and with unwavering commitment if there is to be an optimization of the gospel "harvest." What if we regarded each calling as if it lasted only one day—today—and thus made every day an example of magnifying our calling and building the kingdom? Amulek stated bluntly: "And now, as I said unto you before, as ye have had so many witnesses, therefore, I beseech of you that ye do not procrastinate the day of your repentance until the end; for after this day of life, which is given us to prepare for eternity, behold, if we do not improve our time while in this life, then cometh the night of darkness wherein there can be no labor performed" (Alma 34:33). It is interesting that the word "day" is singular, thus implying that we can improve our lot faithfully one day at a time.

—Richard J. Allen

SUMMARY

As we magnify our callings, we do the will of God, and we act as instruments in His hands for good. When we magnify our callings, we are building up the kingdom of God. The kingdom of God is composed of Heavenly Father's children, so by magnifying our callings, we bless our brothers and sisters. This is the greatest good, and the purpose of the priesthood and every calling within the Church. Let us make a commitment to magnify our callings and find joy in the work.

MARRIAGE

The union of man and woman in marriage brings together God's greatest creations. Marriage and sealing in the temple of our Lord is for time and all eternity. This is the ultimate ordinance and covenant that makes possible exaltation and eternal lives. If we are true and faithful to the new and everlasting covenant of marriage, we can have eternal increase (see D&C 131; 132:19). Each spouse should make his or her primary concern the well-being and happiness of the companion. In this union, the purpose is to create a family. The family should live in love and harmony so as to help each member become a disciple of Jesus Christ and build up the kingdom of God here upon the earth.

THE SCRIPTURES TEACH US

Moses 3:24. *Therefore shall a man leave his father and his mother, and shall cleave unto his wife; and they shall be one flesh.*

The unity of husband and wife brings a oneness like unto the Godhead—one in purpose, cause, and action. President Marion G. Romney provided the following commentary on the meaning of one flesh: "They [husband and wife] should be one in harmony, respect, mutual consideration. Neither should plan or follow an independent course of action. They should consult, plan and decide together" (*Ensign*, December 1978, 2). Unity is the key. If we are not one, we are not the Lord's (see D&C 38:27).

Doctrine and Covenants 49:15–16. *And again, verily I say unto you, that whoso forbiddeth to marry is not ordained of God, for marriage is ordained of God unto man. Wherefore, it is lawful that he should have one wife, and they twain shall be one flesh, and all this that the earth might answer the end of its creation.*

Marriage is not only ordained of God, but is the very institution without which the plan of salvation and the purpose for which the earth was created would have been in vain. The earth is for the physical creation and testing of Heavenly Father's children.

Doctrine and Covenants 131:2–4. *And in order to obtain the highest, a man must enter into this order of the priesthood [meaning the new and everlasting covenant of marriage]; And if he does not, he cannot obtain it. He may enter into the other, but that is the end of his kingdom; he cannot have an increase.*

Only those who are married for time and all eternity in the temple and honor their covenants can have the blessings of eternal increase.

Doctrine and Covenants 132:19–20. *And again, verily I say unto you, if a man marry a wife by my word, which is my law, and by the new and everlasting covenant, and it is sealed unto them by the Holy Spirit of promise, by him who is anointed, unto whom I have appointed this power and the keys of this priesthood; and it shall be said unto them—Ye shall come forth in the first resurrection; . . . and shall inherit thrones, kingdoms, principalities, and powers, dominions, all heights and depths . . . and if ye abide in my covenant, and commit no murder whereby to shed innocent blood, it shall be done unto them in all things whatsoever my servant hath put upon them, in time, and through all eternity; and shall be of full force when they are out of the world; and they shall pass by the angels, and the gods, which are set there, to their exaltation and glory in all things, as hath been sealed upon their heads, which glory shall be a fulness and a continuation of the seeds forever and ever. . . . Then shall they be gods, because they have all power, and the angels are subject unto them.*

These verses explain all the blessings of the Lord to those who are faithful to their temple marriage vows. These include the blessings of the first resurrection, thrones, kingdoms, principalities, powers, dominions, exaltation, glory in all things, continuation of the seeds forever and ever (eternal increase), becoming gods (Abraham, Isaac and Jacob have already entered into this state; see D&C 132:37), and having all power (see D&C 84:38). These are our blessings if we are faithful in keeping our covenants. Understanding and appreciating these magnificent blessings should give us the desire and commitment to make and keep these sacred covenants.

MODERN PROPHETS SPEAK

Gordon B. Hinckley:

> Perhaps our greatest concern is with families. The family is falling apart all over the world. The old ties that bound together father and mother and children are breaking everywhere. We must face this in our own midst. There are too many broken homes among our own. The love that led to marriage somehow evaporates, and hatred fills its place. Hearts are broken, children weep. Can we not do better? Of course,

we can. It is selfishness that brings about most of these tragedies. If there is forbearance, if there is for-giveness, if there is an anxious looking after the happiness of one's companion, then love will flourish and blossom. ("Look to the Future," *Ensign*, November 1997, 67)

If you will make your first concern the comfort, the well-being, and the happiness of your companion, sublimating any personal concern to that loftier goal, you will be happy, and your marriage will go on through eternity. (*Teachings of Gordon B. Hinckley* [Salt Lake City: Deseret Book, 1997], 328–29)

Ezra Taft Benson:

Marriage, designed to be an eternal covenant, is the most glorious and most exalting principle of the gospel of Jesus Christ. Faithfulness to the marriage covenant brings the fullest joy here and glorious rewards hereafter. The abuse of this sacred ordinance despoils the lives of individuals, wrecks the basic institution of the home, and causes the downfall of nations.

Marriage, the home, and family are more than mere social institutions. They are divine, not man-made. God ordained marriage from the very beginning. In the record of that first marriage recorded in Genesis, the Lord makes four significant pronouncements: first, that it is not good for man to be alone; second, that woman was created to be a helpmeet for man; third, that they twain should be one flesh; and fourth, that man should leave father and mother and cleave unto his wife. (See Genesis 2:18, 24.) (*The Teachings of Ezra Taft Benson* [Salt Lake City: Bookcraft, 1988], 534)

Howard W. Hunter:

There is no more powerful principle of life to promote love, forbearance, and devotion in the home than that of eternal marriage. Good adjustment and performance in adult life depend largely on the quality of home life. The principle of eternal marriage is a most powerful stabilizing influence in promoting the kind of home needed to rear children who are happy and well adjusted. (*The Teachings of Howard W. Hunter*, ed. Clyde J. Williams [Salt Lake City: Bookcraft, 1997], 131)

Harold B. Lee:

You young men must ever keep in mind that your lovely companion is possessed of finer sensibilities than you, and if your private conduct is brutal or beastly, bitterness and even disgust may drive out of her heart the affection and regard she once held for you. Both of you must remember that the prime purpose of your marriage under God's command is to build the bridge from the eternity of spirits to mortality, over which God's spirit children might come into mortal bodies. Your failure to remember that revealed truth will be your failure to attain the highest bliss in married life. (*The Teachings of Harold B. Lee,* ed. Clyde J. Williams [Salt Lake City: Bookcraft, 1996], 239)

IDEAS FOR DAILY LIVING

Here is a list of ten helpful hints for a successful marriage:

1. Love—Show your love, both verbally and by your actions.

2. Vision—Share with your spouse a common vision for your marriage. Counsel together often.

3. Flexibility—Always be willing to accommodate each other. Remember, if it is important to your mate, it is important to you.

4. Respect—Always remember that selfishness is the destroyer of all relationships. Mutual respect is built on trust, commitment, and love.

5. Togetherness—Do things together. Pray together, search the scriptures together, eat together, read together, play together, shop together, work together, raise your children together—in essence, whenever possible, do all things together.

6. Admiration—Look for the good in each other. You might even write a love letter listing all the reasons why you love your spouse.

7. Enjoyment—Go on a weekly date and have fun together.

8. Communication—Talk to each other. Communicate your needs, desires, and wishes rather than experiencing unrealized expectations, which often results in negative feelings.

9. Joy—There is nothing more joyful than a happy marriage and family. Write a list of things you and your spouse can do that will bring joy and happiness to your marriage.

10. Goals—Set some goals and make some plans to achieve the "vision" of your marriage, making it one worthy to be called celestial.

ILLUSTRATIONS FOR OUR TIMES

Author Richard J. Allen discusses the importance of eternal vision and perspective in making our marriages celestial.

The Mirror of Majesty

In our neighborhood is a venerated senior couple whose manner of living reflects the epitome of the "godly walk and conversation" (D&C 20:69) to which all Saints should aspire. The friendly glow in their countenances is consistently the same, whether they are seen in public places or in the privacy of their home. They are a celestial pair who have devoted their years to service—service to others as well as to each other. In visiting them one day, I was favored with an explanation of the unusual mirror mounted high on the wall of the entrance to their home opposite a lofty upper window. The man of the house explained that his wife was unable to view the majestic nearby mountain peak from the lower windows of the house; thus he had mounted the large mirror so that, in passing, she could look up and view the towering summit of the mountain. Similarly, in the small fenced garden behind the house, he had mounted another large mirror at just the right angle so that his wife could look through the window facing the garden and catch a glimpse of a second inspiring mountain vista and thus feel edified and liberated from the confines of the condo walls.

Celestial marriage is like that—each partner taking every opportunity to discover ways of lifting the other, strengthening faith, illuminating the pathway, giving encouragement, and opening the view to higher aspirations and blessings of a heavenly nature. When the Prophet Isaiah looked forward with visionary eyes to see the latter-days, he used the image of the mountain as an emblem of the house of the Lord: "Come ye, and let us go up to the mountain of the Lord, to the house of the God of Jacob; and he will teach us of his ways, and we will walk in his paths" (Isaiah 2:3). Similarly, speaking of the faithful, "Even them will I bring to my holy mountain, and make them joyful in my house of prayer" (Isaiah 56:7). Every couple who makes sacred covenant vows at the altars of the holy temple embarks on a straight and narrow pathway leading to the lofty and sublime spiritual domain of the Lord characterized as eternal rest, "which rest is the fulness of his glory" (D&C 84:24).

Both partners in a celestial marriage have the transcendent commission of helping one another keep in view the future goal of glory and eternal lives promised to the valiant and obedient. With the eyes of faith, the covenant pair can view in the mirror of the majesty of truth "the things which God hath prepared for them that love him" (1 Cor. 2:9). What is seen now with but limited, earthly vision shall eventually be viewed in resplendent actuality, for the righteous shall transition "to their exaltation and glory in all things, as hath been sealed upon their heads, which glory shall be a fulness and a continuation of the seeds forever and ever. Then shall they be gods, because they have no end" (D&C 132:19–20).

—Richard J. Allen

SUMMARY

The list of helpful hints could go on and on but the main thing is to care for each other. The world is full of separation and divorce, which always bring sadness to those involved. The world is also full of happy marriages and families, invariably based on commitment, tireless effort, courtesy, charity, and spiritual unity. Celestial marriage is heavenly: it is eternal marriage sanctioned and commissioned by the Almighty, anchored in covenant fidelity, vitalized by the Holy Spirit, infused with lasting bonds of love, and edified by the saving and enduring principles of the gospel of Jesus Christ.

MISSIONARY WORK

Why is missionary work emphasized so much in the Church? Why do we have over 60,000 missionaries in the field sharing the gospel of Jesus Christ? The answer is simply that souls are precious, and that in the dispensation of the fulness of times we have a duty to proclaim the gospel of Jesus Christ to every nation, kindred, tongue, and people (see Morm. 9:22). The Prophet Joseph reminds us, "After all that has been said, the greatest and most important duty is to preach the gospel" (*Teachings of the Prophet Joseph Smith,* sel. Joseph Fielding Smith [1976], 113). Proclaiming the gospel is part of the three-fold mission of the Church to invite all to "come unto Christ." The work and glory of Heavenly Father and our Savior is to bring about the immortality and eternal life of mankind (see Moses 1:39). As disciples of Jesus Christ, we have been foreordained to assist with this work (see Jacob 5:70–75; Alma 13:3–7; D&C 138:53–57).

THE SCRIPTURES TEACH US

Mark 16:15. *And he said unto them, Go ye into all the world, and preach the gospel to every creature.* (See also Matt. 28:19; 2 Cor. 4:5; Rev. 14:7; Alma 29:8; Morm. 9:22; D&C 39:15; 84:87; 90:11; Moses 8:19.)

We have been called to take the gospel to all the earth by the resurrected Savior Himself. We are witnesses of Christ, His gospel, and His kingdom, wherever we are (see Mosiah 18:9).

Mosiah 28:3. *Now they were desirous that salvation should be declared to every creature, for they could not bear that any human soul should perish; yea, even the very thoughts that any soul should endure endless torment did cause them to quake and tremble.*

When we realize the value of the souls of mankind, we will have an overwhelming desire to share the gospel of Jesus Christ, which effort will bring us eternal satisfaction, glory, and joy (see Alma 29:9–10). Sharing the gospel and bringing souls unto Christ is the work that is of most worth to us and to God (see D&C 15:6).

Doctrine and Covenants 11:21. *Seek not to declare my word, but first seek to obtain my word, and then shall your tongue be loosed; then, if you desire, you shall have my Spirit and my word, yea, the power of God unto the convincing of men.*

To be good missionaries, we need to first know the word of God, to be prepared. As we treasure up the word, the Lord can give us access to it at the very moment we need it (see D&C 84:85). When we open our mouths with courage and faith, the Holy Spirit will inspire us to say the words the Lord would have us say (D&C 33:8–11; 100:5–6).

Doctrine and Covenants 31:3–5. *Lift up your heart and rejoice, for the hour of your mission is come; and your tongue shall be loosed, and you shall declare glad tidings of great joy unto this generation. You shall declare the things which have been revealed to my servant, Joseph Smith, Jun. You shall begin to preach from this time forth, yea, to reap in the field which is white already to be burned. Therefore, thrust in your sickle with all your soul, and your sins are forgiven you, and you shall be laden with sheaves upon your back, for the laborer is worthy of his hire. Wherefore, your family shall live.*

When we serve as member missionaries, ward missionaries, or full-time missionaries, we will declare glad tidings to all those with whom we come in contact. As we help people come unto Christ by teaching and bearing testimony, they are converted by the Spirit and we are both blessed—our joy is great (see Alma 36:24), our sins are forgiven (see James 5:20; D&C 31:5; 62:3), and our friends have the blessing of the gospel in their lives.

MODERN PROPHETS SPEAK

Spencer W. Kimball:
> The gospel of Jesus Christ is a gospel for all the world and for all people. We proclaim the fatherhood of God and the brotherhood of all mankind. We proclaim the divine sonship of Jesus Christ and him crucified, that his divine sacrifice was a ransom for all mankind. We bear witness of his resurrection and that he lives today, standing at the right hand of God, to guide the affairs of his earthly kingdom. ("The Stone Cut without Hands," *Ensign*, May 1976, 4)

Gordon B. Hinckley:
> It is our duty, divinely imposed, to continue urgently and militantly to carry forward our missionary work. We must continue to call missionaries and send them out to preach the gospel, which was never more needed than now, which is the only remedy for the tragic ills that now afflict the world, and which alone can bring peace and brotherly love back amongst the peoples of the earth. . . .
>
> I think every member of the Church has the capacity to teach the gospel to nonmembers. I was told the other day of a crippled woman, homebound, who spends her days in a wheelchair, who

has been the means of bringing thirty-seven people into the Church. . . . We need an awareness, an everyday awareness of the great power that we have to do this thing. . . .

It is an inspiring experience . . . to witness the manner in which the Lord is weaving the tapestry of his grand design in those foreign parts of the earth. He is gathering his children there as elsewhere— "one of a city and two of a family." He is remembering the promises made of old as he works among those who have seen so much of poverty and misery and evil and oppression. He is answering the prayers of those who have gone before, and who struggled to establish a foothold for the gospel in those distant places. . . .

The work is becoming very much enlarged. It does require a commensurate accumulation of men and means. It requires an expansion of mind and energy, ability and perseverance. Let us prepare ourselves more diligently for the great assignment which God has laid upon us to carry this work to the children of the earth wherever we may be permitted to go. (*Teachings of Gordon B. Hinckley* [Salt Lake City: Deseret Book, 1997], 367)

IDEAS FOR DAILY LIVING

Here are three ideas to help us understand the importance of missionary work and our role as missionaries:

1. Souls are precious.
- *God's work is centered in His children*—All of the work of our Heavenly Father and our Savior centers in us. Their work and their glory is to bring to pass our immortality and eternal life (see Moses 1:39). They joy in a soul that repents, as should we.
- *Share the gospel*—Put yourself on the line and bear your testimony to someone you know. Do this because you love all of God's children and want them to have the same blessings you have.

2. Prepare well to be an instrument in the hand of the Lord.
- *Search the scriptures*—Learn the word of God. Make a plan to study the scriptures and other helpful material regularly in preparation for missionary service (see D&C 11:21).
- *Strengthen your faith*—Fast and pray to become strong in humility and firm in your faith (see Hel. 3:35).
- *Experience the mighty change of heart*—Repent so you can be a clean instrument in the hands of the Lord, genuinely worthy of the Spirit. If you are not truly converted and devoted to the Lord's cause, you cannot help convert others.
- *Build your testimony*—Gain a strong testimony of the gospel and the Church through study, prayer, keeping the commandments, and bearing your testimony often.
- *Develop a good work ethic*—Missionary work requires industry, devotion, energy, and productive effort.
- *Prepare every needful thing*—Make an additional list of things you can do personally to better prepare for missionary service.

3. Take action.
- *Missionary work is the work of the Lord's disciples*—Disciples of Christ help in the conversion, retention, and activation process. Remember, you are a disciple wherever you go (see Mosiah 18:9).
- *Use the proven system*—Missionary work involves finding, teaching, baptizing, and fellowshipping new converts into the Church. We find by opening our mouths; the Lord will help us identify those who are willing to listen (see D&C 84:85–88). We teach by the Spirit (see Alma 17:2–3;

D&C 50:17–22). We baptize those who are prepared and willing to make the commitment (D&C 20:37). We fellowship and love them into the Church by being a friend and strengthening them (see Moro. 6:4; D&C 108:7).

- *Be systematic*—As members, we can set goals to help people come into the Church as follows: (1) Set a date to have one or more prospective converts prepared to hear the gospel; (2) prayerfully select a person or persons; (3) build a relationship of trust so that they will be willing to listen to you; (4) prepare them to hear the missionaries; (5) invite them to hear the missionaries and pray that they will receive a witness of the truthfulness of the gospel.

- *Remember to pray*—As members of the Church, we should always pray for those who do not know God that a way might come about for them to receive the word (see Alma 6:6).

ILLUSTRATIONS FOR OUR TIMES

The following discusses the importance of the Book of Mormon in converting souls to the truthfulness of the restored gospel.

Sprouting Seeds

The Book of Mormon is the textbook of conversion. One of its principal figures and teachers, Alma the Younger, compares faith to a seed and inspires his listeners to undertake a most practical strategy in spiritual horticulture: "But behold, if ye will awake and arouse your faculties, even to an experiment upon my words, and exercise a particle of faith, yea, even if ye can no more than desire to believe, let this desire work in you, even until ye believe in a manner that ye can give place for a portion of my words" (Alma 32:27). He then gives his memorable counsel for understanding how the Lord cultivates within us the power to rise to our divine potential based on faith. Thus the Book of Mormon contains the inspired instructions according to which it is to be applied as an instrument of faith in the lives of its readership.

From the earliest days of the Restoration, the Book of Mormon has served as a magnet to draw truth-seekers into the fold. Take the story of Joseph Smith's younger brother, Samuel Harrison Smith, who as a twenty-two-year-old returned from his mission somewhat discouraged with the results. But look what came of his labors: On Saturday, April 14, 1832, Brigham Young, "the Lion of the Lord" (*History of the Church*, 7:435), was baptized after two years of intensive study and prayer centered on the Book of Mormon, a copy of which his brother Phineas had given him. Phineas had purchased the copy from the Prophet's younger brother, Samuel Harrison, in April 1830, during the latter's early missionary labors. Samuel also provided a copy to Reverend John P. Greene, husband of Phineas' sister, Rhoda. Both were subsequently converted. Brigham Young had given his copy of the Book of Mormon to his sister, Fanny Young Murray, the mother-in-law of Heber C. Kimball, who, along with his family, also became converted because of it. These families were thus brought into the Church through the Book of Mormon. And the Book of Mormon became accessible to them as a result of the devoted missionary labors of the twenty-two-year-old Samuel Harrison Smith. Young Samuel had returned home discouraged from this early mission to upstate New York—unaware at the time that his labors would eventually yield such extraordinary fruit. (See *Church History in the Fulness of Times*, 74–75.)

The sprouting seeds that come from a sincere study of the Book of Mormon lead to the growth and maturation of a tree of faith: "[B]ehold, by and by ye shall pluck the fruit thereof, which is most precious, which is sweet above all that is sweet, and which is white above all that is white, yea, and pure above all that is pure; and ye shall feast upon this fruit even until ye are filled, that ye hunger not, neither shall ye thirst" (Alma 32:42).

Is it any wonder that the Lord has commanded us to share the Book of Mormon with our friends and colleagues so that they, too, can learn divine truth through spiritual confirmation (see Moro. 10:4)? It is our greatest missionary tool. As Nephi confirmed, the coming forth of the Book of Mormon is concrete, indisputable evidence that the Lord will fulfill His solemn promise to bring the gospel to His children: "And it shall come to pass that my people, which are of the house of Israel, shall be gathered home unto the lands of their possessions; and my word also shall be gathered in one. And I will show unto them that fight against my word and against my people, who are of the house of Israel, that I am God, and that I covenanted with Abraham that I would remember his seed forever" (2 Ne. 29:14).

—Richard J. Allen

SUMMARY

The vision of the worth of souls and the covenant commitment to do missionary work go hand in hand. As members of the Lord's true Church, we need to set goals and make plans to do our member missionary work. Let us set some dates for being member-missionaries now, and plan to serve a full-time mission for the Lord. We have been repeatedly counseled by the Brethren about serving missions as young adults and as seniors. Remember that as we serve the Lord, He will help us and we will have the joy of helping build up the kingdom of God here upon the earth.

MORALITY

Morality is the key to a righteous society and a sustained civilization. History bears the sad stories of empires, kingdoms, and civilizations being destroyed through immorality and wickedness. The fundamental principles of morality do not change, but how such principles are applied by individuals and cultures can, unfortunately, evolve and degrade over time through the misguided decisions of individuals and society as a collective body.

As a society, we must change for the better—one person at a time, standing for and defending virtue. William Penn wrote: "Right is right, even if everyone is against it; and wrong is wrong, even if everyone is for it." Stephen L Richards counseled: "There is no spiritual progress or excellence without moral purity." Our children, and in turn, society, will suffer if we are permissive and apathetic regarding moral values and conduct. Our standard is the gospel of Jesus Christ. Let us uphold it and teach it to our children with devotion and love."

THE SCRIPTURES TEACH US

2 Corinthians 7:1. *Having therefore these promises, dearly beloved, let us cleanse ourselves from all filthiness of the flesh and spirit, perfecting holiness in the fear of God.*

The standard of the gospel of Jesus Christ is chastity, decency, goodness, honesty, and in all things seeking the righteousness of a Christlike life. We must not be carnally minded, for that brings spiritual death (Rom. 8:6). A moral and chaste person is completely true to all gospel standards.

Doctrine and Covenants 3:4. *For although a man may have many revelations, and have power to do many mighty works, yet if he boasts in his own strength, and sets at naught the counsels of God, and follows after the dictates of his own will and carnal desires, he must fall and incur the vengeance of a just God upon him.*

The price of immorality is captivity by sin and by the devil. We must realize that all immoral behavior has consequences. We will be held accountable for every immoral and unjust act we commit, just as we will receive a spiritual benefit from upholding the standards of the gospel with resolute obedience and righteousness.

MODERN PROPHETS SPEAK

Ezra Taft Benson:

> The plaguing sin of this generation is sexual immorality. This, the Prophet Joseph said, would be the source of more temptations, more buffetings, and more difficulties for the elders of Israel than any other. (See Journal of Discourses, 8:55.)

> President Joseph F. Smith said that sexual impurity would be one of the three dangers that would threaten the Church within—and so it does (see Gospel Doctrine, pp. 312–13). It permeates our society. (*The Teachings of Ezra Taft Benson* [Salt Lake City: Bookcraft, 1988], 277)

Gordon B. Hinckley:

> The Lord has made it clear, and the experience of centuries has confirmed it, that happiness lies not in immorality, but rather in abstinence. The voice of the Church to which you belong is a voice pleading for virtue. It is a voice pleading for strength to abstain from that which is evil. It is a voice declaring that sexual transgression is sin. It is contrary to the will of the Lord. It is contrary to the teachings of the Church. It is contrary to the happiness and well-being of those who indulge in it. (*Teachings of Gordon B. Hinckley* [Salt Lake City: Deseret Book, 1997], 48)

Spencer W. Kimball:

> That the Church's stand on morality may be understood, we declare firmly and unalterably, it is not an outworn garment, faded, old-fashioned, and threadbare. God is the same yesterday, today, and forever, and his covenants and doctrines are immutable; and when the sun grows cold and the stars no longer shine, the law of chastity will still be basic in God's world and in the Lord's church. Old values are upheld by the Church not because they are old, but rather because through the ages they have proved right. It will always be the rule. . . . The world may countenance premarital sex experiences, but the Lord and his church condemn in no uncertain terms any and every sex relationship outside of marriage. (*The Teachings of Spencer W. Kimball*, ed. Edward L. Kimball [Salt Lake City: Bookcraft, 1982], 265)

IDEAS FOR DAILY LIVING

The following ideas can help each of us to be a moral person and contribute to the building up of a moral society:

1. Morality begins within.

- *Understand the process of moral development*—Morality begins with our thoughts, takes root in our character, flows outwardly through our deeds, and crystallizes in our patterns of life. How carefully, therefore, should we guard our very thoughts, for they are the crucible of our destiny.
- *Base your life on gospel principles*—There is much talk today of "relative values"—suggesting that there is no absolute compass of decency. But there are indeed moral values that do not change, and we find these principles in the gospel.
- *Follow your conscience*—Recognize your internal moral standard of attitudes and behavior: your conscience. Don't compromise.

2. Morality pays high dividends.

- *Enjoy the fruits of proper conduct*—Living a virtuous and moral life has innate rewards: good health, a clear conscience, providing a good example to your children, and enjoying lasting feelings of well-being and vitality.
- *Attract lasting friendships*—Our language is a mirror to our inner values. Sarcasm, snide remarks about others, ethnic slurs, off-color stories—all these are clear symptoms of a value system in need of reexamination. Such behavior repels all principled minds. On the other hand, honesty and virtue in discourse and social interaction attract lasting friendships and earn the respect of all principled minds.
- *Sow the seeds of harmony and peace*—Moral behavior fosters harmony and unity. Immorality, selfishness, greed, and envy foster divisiveness, acrimony, anger, and distrust.

3. You can be a moral leader.

- *Respect every person*—Never take advantage of another. Morality is anchored in honoring the dignity of every soul, regardless of circumstances. Morality sees potential more than condition.
- *Illuminate better pathways*—The leader in moral decency does not simply draw a line in the sand, but provides better options and alternatives. "Let's do this instead" is a powerful antidote to the plethora of debasing options being touted as "cool" in today's relativistic society.
- *Uphold the freedom to choose*—A leader always honors one's freedom to choose. Coercion and peremptory heavy-handedness are themselves immoral. Remember, with morality, everyone has God-given rights that no one else has the right to take away.
- *Leadership starts at home*—Morality is best taught in the home. How great is the responsibility placed on parents and older children to model behavior that teaches growing children correct choices based on true principles. Every father and every mother need to place the well-being of the family and the children uppermost.

4. Morality is a spiritual enterprise.

- *Know yourself*—The essence of morality is the wondrous insight that you are a child of God. Knowing that you bear the image of the Creator should lift your view to a higher plane, elevate your vision to higher possibilities, and instill within you the desire—the responsibility—to act according to the highest standards of decency and honor.
- *Know God*—Study the principles of morality in the scriptures. Pray for moral courage and strength.

ILLUSTRATIONS FOR OUR TIMES

The heartbreaking story of an unwed, pregnant girl demonstrates the devastating consequences of sexual immorality.

"If Only I Had Known Five Minutes Before"

We will never forget that sweet young girl of sixteen who came to live with us one summer for the remaining months of her unwed pregnancy. My husband is an attorney and was handling the adoption of her baby. She hadn't wanted to marry the boy who was the father of her unborn child. She had been beguiled and had partaken of the bitter fruit.

In September she gave birth to a beautiful little boy, and the day she was to leave the hospital, Dean and I had to go to Salt Lake City. We stopped at the hospital long enough to meet the couple who were adopting the baby. Under hospital rules, this young mother, sixteen years old, had to take her beautiful nine-pound boy from the arms of the nurse and hand him over to my husband, who then stepped outside the room and gave the baby to the adopting parents. It tore me apart to watch her and to see that young couple leave with her baby.

She said to me, "Sister Payne, he lied to me when he said nobody would get hurt, and that because we loved each other, anything we did was alright. He didn't really love me. That is why I didn't marry him, because he wasn't worthy to be the father of my little boy. It's all a great big lie, and I don't want to live a lie!

"Oh, if only I had known five minutes before I was immoral how I would feel five minutes after I gave my baby away!"

For this girl not to have thought ahead about the consequences of her actions and not to have realized that lust is the mere image of love is indeed heartbreaking. It is so important to keep in tune, keep in touch, to receive the Spirit each and every day. We never know what is going to happen; and if we make the commitment in our private rooms, by the side of our beds, to our Father in heaven, of what we want to be in life—what we will do and what we won't do—and then ask for his help in keeping our commitments, he will help us in public and private. (Jaynann Payne in *Remarkable Stories from the Lives of Latter-day Saint Women,* comp. Leon R. Hartshorn [Salt Lake City: Deseret Book, 1973], 2:203)

SUMMARY

The blessings of morality are long lasting. Immorality may give "moments of pleasure" that are fleeting—but enduring joy and happiness cannot be drawn from this well. "For what is a man profited, if he shall gain the whole world, and lose his own soul?" (Matthew 16:26). Integrity is required to maintain a state of morality—individually and collectively. The gospel standard is our moral law. There are universal moral laws that all should conform to. In society as a whole, one must be courageous in fighting for that which is morally right. When the majority have no concern for morality, all suffer. Standards are not upheld. Wickedness is the result—all because of the lack of society's integrity in upholding high moral standards. "We whittle away our heritage unless we conform to the moral laws," is how one anonymous source put it, and correctly so. By embracing and sustaining a moral lifestyle, you can make a difference—for yourself, your family, your community, and even the world.

MORTALITY

The work of Heavenly Father and our Savior Jesus Christ is to bring to pass our immortality and eternal life (see Moses 1:39). There are many phases in our existence, but we will focus here on the phase of mortality and all of its trials and joys. To make life beautiful, enjoyable, and fulfilling we must remember to build a value system around the gospel of Jesus Christ, for this life is the time to prepare to meet God (see Alma 34:32). Keeping the commandments leads to righteousness, and in righteousness we find happiness as our reward for a good life.

THE SCRIPTURES TEACH US

Matthew 16:25–26. *For whosoever will save his life shall lose it: and whosoever will lose his life for my sake shall find it. For what is a man profited, if he shall gain the whole world, and lose his own soul? or what shall a man give in exchange for his soul?*

The Lord commands us to spend our lives in His service and in the service of our fellowmen in building up the kingdom of God (see JST, Matt. 6:38). Our souls are precious (see D&C 18:10), and as such we should not jeopardize them for things of the world or momentary pleasures. The price our Savior paid for us was terribly great, and His death should not be in vain in regard to our personal lives. We should claim the blessing of eternal life through repentance. If we do not, we must suffer as Christ did (see D&C 19:15–19).

Romans 6:12. *Let not sin therefore reign in your mortal body, that ye should obey it in the lusts thereof.*

According to the scriptures, life is a test (see Abr. 3:25). We must endure temptation and opposition in all things as part of the test of life. We should not succumb to the flesh, but rather let our spirit dictate to our body. The questions to ask ourselves are: Do we yield our hearts to the enticings of the Holy Spirit (see Mosiah 3:19)? Do we love God totally and completely? If we don't, we will become carnal, sensual, and devilish (see Moses 5:13).

Alma 12:24. *And we see that death comes upon mankind, yea, the death which has been spoken of by Amulek, which is the temporal death; nevertheless there was a space granted unto man in which he might repent; therefore this life became a probationary state; a time to prepare to meet God; a time to prepare for that endless state which has been spoken of by us, which is after the resurrection of the dead.*

Life on earth is a temporary proving ground for our eternal destiny. It is a trial period for us to prove our worthiness to come back into the presence of God. We should not procrastinate the day of our repentance, lest we lose the blessings of eternal life (see Alma 34:33–35).

Doctrine and Covenants 84:44. *For you shall live by every word that proceedeth forth from the mouth of God.*

We should live life according to the word of God, our compass for life (see Alma 37:37–47). Life can be wonderful as we hold to the iron rod and stay on the straight and narrow path to partake of the precious fruit. The love of God will bring us back to His presence as we partake of the Atonement of Christ.

Moses 3:7. *And I, the Lord God, formed man from the dust of the ground, and breathed into his nostrils the breath of life; and man became a living soul, the first flesh upon the earth, the first man also; nevertheless, all things were before created; but spiritually were they created and made according to my word.*

Heavenly Father is the Father of our spirits. In mortality we begin life as a living soul (both spirit and body). We are eternal beings, divine children of God, having an earthly experience we call mortality. Just as He gave Adam life, so does the Lord give us the breath of life (see Mosiah 2:21).

MODERN PROPHETS SPEAK

Ezra Taft Benson:

> Life has a fourfold purpose. First of all, we come to this mortal life to receive a physical, mortal body. Without a physical body man is limited in his progression and only with a spirit and a body united

together permanently can man receive a fulness of joy; so we are living today part of eternity. We accepted that plan in the spirit world before we came here, and we rejoiced at the opportunity of coming here.

Second, we came here to gain experience—experience with a physical, mortal world.

The third purpose of life is to give us an opportunity to prove ourselves (Abraham 3:25). To prove that even in the presence of evil and sin we can live a good life. To prove that in spite of temptation that we have the strength and the character to adhere to the principles of the gospel.

And fourth, this life is intended to provide an opportunity to help our Father in Heaven with His great plan, and we do that through honorable parenthood. We cooperate with our Heavenly Father in helping to prepare tabernacles to house spirits of His other children. (*The Teachings of Ezra Taft Benson* [Salt Lake City: Bookcraft, 1988], 27)

Marvin J. Ashton:
> In whatever circumstance we may find ourselves, whether in the midst of tragedy, the pain of misconduct, or merely the daily struggle to live the life of a faithful Latter-day Saint, we must remember "the race is not to the swift, nor the battle to the strong, but he that endureth to the end shall be saved." (*Be of Good Cheer* [Salt Lake City: Deseret Book, 1987], 21)

Gordon B. Hinckley:
> Life is a mission, not just the sputtering of a candle between a chance lighting and a gust of wind that blows it out forever. . . .
>
> While here, we have learning to gain, work to do, service to give. We are here with a marvelous inheritance, a divine endowment. How different this world would be if every person realized that all of his actions have eternal consequences. How much more satisfying our years may be if in our accumulation of knowledge, in our relationships with others, in our business affairs, in our courtship and marriage, and in our family rearing, we recognize that we form each day the stuff of which eternity is made. . . . Life is forever. Live each day as if you were going to live eternally, for you surely shall. (*Teachings of Gordon B. Hinckley* [Salt Lake City: Deseret Book, 1997], 174)

Thomas S. Monson:
> We are the sons and daughters of Almighty God. We have a destiny to fulfill, a life to live, a contribution to make, a goal to achieve. The future of our country in these rapidly changing times awaits our mark of influence. The growth of the kingdom of God upon the earth will, in part, be aided by our devotion. (*Be Your Best Self* [Salt Lake City: Deseret Book, 1979], 119)

Neal A. Maxwell:
> Determining whether we will live myopically and selfishly or live now for eternity is a fundamental decision that colors every day of daily life. To live a life of "thanksgiving daily" (Alma 34:38) while in the midst of adversity and its tutorials is impossible without a degree of meekness. (*Meek and Lowly* [Salt Lake City: Deseret Book, 1987], 4)

IDEAS FOR DAILY LIVING

Here are four ideas to remember for getting the most out of life:

1. Life is what you choose to make it.

- *Choose wisely*—Remember that you have the power to choose your responses to life and all your governing attitudes (see 2 Ne. 2:27). Have an attitude of hope—sooner or later things can and will be better.
- *Be positive*—Try not to be negative. A negative outlook sometimes becomes self-fulfilling.
- *Uphold your standards*—Live up to your values and principles. If you don't, you will suffer from guilt, and your credibility in the eyes of your children and your friends could be lost.
- *Think long term*—Cultivate a vision for life, set some goals and make some plans. Seek lasting joy rather than short-term pleasures. When they become an end in themselves, short-term pleasures can fill life with emptiness and an insatiable hunger for something higher.

2. Life is this very moment.

- *Don't wait to enjoy life*—Enjoy the journey today.
- *Life is now*—Realize that life is not "out there." It is "in here," or inside yourself—how you respond to the moment-by-moment feelings, events, and opportunities that make up your world. You can think of each moment as a special act of living or as a burden; it's all in how you respond.
- *Life is a miracle*—Experience the vitality of life, a feeling of "aliveness" that has its own miraculous, self-sustaining energy. Even at times of illness and malaise, the life-adoring individual holds onto each moment of living as one more opportunity to watch the sunset, marvel at nature's handiwork, or hold the hand of a loved one.
- *Keep it simple*—Don't over-program or over-commit yourself. Too many "things" make life hectic and sometimes unbearable.
- *Stay healthy*—Take care of yourself: eat well, get adequate rest, and exercise regularly. To some extent, health is your choice.

3. Life is enriched through service to others.

- *Life is togetherness*—Enjoy togetherness. Everyone can have togetherness, even the person whom circumstances have deprived of immediate family and relatives. That person can still help and serve others out of a deep commitment to humanity, out of a deep sense of obligation to make this a better world.
- *Look beyond yourself*—Always take time to look outside yourself. Your worst days will be when you are overly concerned with your own well-being. Selfishness destroys the beauties in life.
- *Seek to build up the kingdom of God*—Be an instrument in the hand of the Lord to help people come unto Christ (see JST, Matt. 6:38; Alma 29:9–10).
- *Seek to serve others*—Serve others, and your joy will be exquisite (see Alma 36:24).

4. Life is an exhilarating climb upward, one step at a time.

- *Rise to your potential*—Work toward your highest prospects and possibilities. Life is an opportunity to rise on the wings of self-transcendence and self-mastery to the highest level of which one is capable.
- *Prepare well*—Organize yourself for life's journey. Part of the joy in life is getting ready to climb higher (see D&C 88:119).
- *Communicate with care*—Be true to your promises, and you will avoid hurting others.
- *Do it now*—Don't procrastinate! Procrastination causes you to waste more energy being frustrated than you would spend just getting the job done in the first place. It also makes you feel discouraged.
- *Savor the good consequences*—Reward yourself for goals achieved and things well done.
- *Make life a spiritual experience*—Remember that life on earth is a training ground for a better life to come. Nothing quells the narrow appetites of a mortal nature more than the desire, hope, and

faith to qualify for an eternal life in which the cares of this world are replaced with the glories of eternal lives in the celestial kingdom (see 2 Ne. 9:39).

ILLUSTRATIONS FOR OUR TIMES

In the following story by Milton R. Hunter, we learn about the length of time we exist in the mortal sphere as compared to our eternal existence.

The Dot Is Very, Very Small

The Prophet Joseph Smith termed it this way, that the purpose of our existence is that we might have happiness. We want to be happy today, tomorrow, next week, next year, ten years from now, a hundred years from now, a thousand years from now, a million years from now.

I was in a stake conference one time, and I made a remark similar to the statement I just made. There were several little boys sitting on the front row. One little chap spoke aloud what he was thinking. He said, "Oh, we won't live that long!"

This gave me a fine opportunity to make an explanation. I said, "Young man, we will live that long. We live forever and ever."

Permit me to give you a little illustration. If we take a pencil and put a dot on the wall over there, we could call that dot mortality. Then if we take that pencil and run a line clear around this big fieldhouse in which we are meeting, we could call that line the eternal existence or life we shall live. Notice that the dot is very, very small in comparison to the line; and yet it is most important, extremely important, because the joy that we have throughout the eternities or the sorrow that we have throughout the eternities is determined by the choices we make during our mortal lives. Also, the status of our life or existence, the future world in which we live, will be determined by what happens in this little dot, or, in other words, in this short span of life that we live here in mortality. (Milton R. Hunter in *Outstanding Stories by General Authorities,* comp. Leon R. Hartshorn [Salt Lake City: Deseret Book, 1974], 3:171–72)

* * *

This counsel from Thorpe B. Isaacson reminds us of the precious nature of this mortal life and that the line between life and death is exceedingly thin.

Not Yet, Dear Lord, Not Yet

Today, if I may, I would like to take just one sentence from President McKay's beautiful dedicatory prayer offered at the London Temple, and may I quote from that one sentence. Speaking to the Lord, he said: "May we express overwhelming gratitude just to be alive."

I have a personal reason this morning for repeating this sentence from President McKay's dedicatory prayer, because today I am truly grateful just to be alive. A few months ago I became critically ill, and I learned then, as I have never learned before, that the line between life and mortality and death and immortality is very thin indeed. It only takes a few seconds—yes, a very few seconds—to change from life and mortality to death and immortality, and I saw how close one can get to the pale of death. I thought I was passing from this life to the other, and I am truly grateful to the Lord that he permitted me to live. I fully realized then that I was not prepared or ready for that passing, and it brought to my mind a few words that I have read in a poem that goes something like this:

"There is no time that we could set for parting. Ever our prayer would be [as mine was], Not yet, dear Lord, not yet, just another day."

I realized then more than ever before how dependent we are upon God, our Eternal Father, even for the preservation of our lives. When one faces such a change, and we are all going to face it, when we come close to it, many things come to our minds. I wonder if you are ready for that change. I wonder if you are prepared to change from life to death. I believe that we can become prepared and ready, and I concluded then that if the Lord would permit me to live longer, I intended to live better so that I could die better. (Thorpe B. Isaacson in *Outstanding Stories by General Authorities,* comp. Leon R. Hartshorn [Salt Lake City: Deseret Book, 1974] 3:194)

SUMMARY

Life is a gift from God, and our righteous lives can be our gift to God. You are in charge of your life, and you can choose to be "even as [He is]" (see 3 Ne. 27:27). Be understanding and kind, treating people with consideration. You can make a difference in the life of every person you meet, as well as your own life. As you do this, you will feel fulfilled and life will be sweet. Make a commitment to live life to the fullest and enjoy your time on earth.

MOTHERHOOD

Motherhood is the most dynamic and powerful role on the earth. Mothers give life, the most precious gift of all, to each child. Mothers nurture the family, give love, and serve. They constantly do things for their children that their children can't do for themselves—they love them, teach them, serve them, and perform a myriad of other things only mothers can do. Society undeniably rests on the contributions and sacrifices of mothers. Elder ElRay L. Christiansen stated: "So far, no worthy substitute has been found for good mothers. Without them, civilization is doomed to decay." According to a Jewish proverb: "God could not be everywhere; therefore, he made mothers." Abraham Lincoln articulated the sentiments of virtually all mankind when he said, "All that I am, or hope to be, I owe to my angel mother."

May we thank Heavenly Father always for our mothers and pay homage to them. May we respect them, honor them, and praise them for their sacrifices on our behalf. May we strive to lift them up and appreciate them for who they are: an embodiment of the godly principles of life, love, and leadership.

THE SCRIPTURES TEACH US

Genesis 3:16. *Unto the woman he said, I will greatly multiply thy sorrow and thy conception; in sorrow thou shalt bring forth children; and thy desire shall be to thy husband, and he shall rule over thee.*

Women experience great hardship and difficulty in pregnancy and childbirth. Just as the Savior gave birth to our immortality in a magnificent vicarious act, so likewise do mothers bring forth mortality in a magnificent act of service. Christ sorrowed for our sins in His anguish and suffering, and mothers sorrow on behalf of their children. Mothers should have a desire to be one with their husbands, as the Savior commands His Church to be. In all families, groups, and organizations, there is one who presides. In the case of eternal matters, God the Father Elohim presides over our Savior and over all of mankind. In mortal families, the father holds that responsibility. In the Godhead, there is unity; likewise, in a family the parents should be united in purpose, cause, and action, being equally yoked together in bringing forth a righteous family.

Alma 57:21. *Yea, and they did obey and observe to perform every word of command with exactness; yea, and even according to their faith it was done unto them; and I did remember the words which they said unto me that their mothers had taught them.*

Just as the mothers of the sons of Helaman taught their sons, so likewise do all mothers, who are the great nurturers, teach and bless their children. The greatest service one can give to another is to teach and nourish them with the word of God. Remember, the word of God has the power to lead people to do what is right (see Alma 31:5).

MODERN PROPHETS SPEAK

Spencer W. Kimball:
> Relief Society leaders and teachers should ask, how can we help the wife and mother understand the dignity and worth of her role in the divine process of motherhood? How can we help her make her home a place of love and learning, a place of refuge and refinement? How can we strengthen her to assume an added family leadership role when her husband is away from the home, or in those homes without a father? (*The Teachings of Spencer W. Kimball,* ed. Edward L. Kimball [Salt Lake City: Bookcraft, 1982], 435)

Gordon B. Hinckley:
> The true strength that is America's, the true strength of any nation, lies in those qualities of character that have been acquired for the most part by children taught in the quiet, simple, everyday manner of mothers. What Jean Paul Richter once declared of fathers is even more true of mothers—and I paraphrase it just a little to make the point—"What a mother says to her children is not heard by the world, but it will be heard by posterity." . . .

> It is my opinion that the very situation of an ever-increasing number of mothers out of the home and in the workplace is a root cause of many of the problems of delinquency, drugs, and gangs, both male and female. Why then do women leave families to work? A recently published newspaper article pointed out some of the problems family heads face which dictate this move. . . . Not only are we exacting a terrible slice of income for taxes and family-required goods and services, but concomitantly we are exacting a terrible price in the weakening of the family which occurs when a mother absents herself from the home each working day while latchkey children wait for her return. When she does return, too often she is tired and under such stress and frustration that in all too many cases she cannot give to her children the attention and the affection which they so much crave and need. (*Teachings of Gordon B. Hinckley* [Salt Lake City: Deseret Book, 1997], 386, 389)

David O. McKay:

> Motherhood is the greatest potential influence either for good or ill in human life. The mother's image is the first that stamps itself on the unwritten page of the young child's mind. It is her caress that first awakens a sense of security; her kiss, the first realization of affection; her sympathy and tenderness, the first assurance that there is love in the world. True, there comes a time when Father takes his place as exemplar and hero of the growing boy; and in the latter's budding ambition to develop manly traits, he outwardly seems to turn from the more gentle and tender virtues engendered by his mother. Yet that ever-directing and restraining influence implanted during the first years of his childhood linger with him and permeate his thoughts and memory as distinctively as perfume clings to each particular flower. (*Gospel Ideals: Selections from the Discourses of David O. McKay* [Salt Lake City: Improvement Era, 1953], 452)

Spencer W. Kimball

> Motherhood is a holy calling, a sacred dedication for carrying out the Lord's work, a consecration and devotion to the rearing and fostering, the nurturing of body, mind, and spirit of those who kept their first estate and who came to this earth for their second estate to learn and be tested and to work toward godhood.
>
> Mothers have a sacred role. They are partners with God, as well as with their own husbands, first in giving birth to the Lord's spirit children, and then in rearing those children so they will serve the Lord and keep his commandments. Could there be a more sacred trust than to be a trustee for honorable, well-born, well-developed children? (*The Teachings of Spencer W. Kimball,* ed. Edward L. Kimball [Salt Lake City: Bookcraft, 1982], 326)

IDEAS FOR DAILY LIVING

Here is a brief list of the acts and attributes of mothers—and the list could go on forever:

- *Giving life*—Mothers give life. They instantly love their children, for they have already served and sacrificed by giving birth.
- *Caring*—Mothers tenderly care for their children and tend to all their physical and emotional needs.
- *Leading*—Mothers patiently lead their children through their early years.
- *Teaching*—Mothers begin the teaching process—from language to proper behavior—and carry it on with love and patience.
- *Listening*—Mothers listen with focus, without distraction, without impatience, without crossness or unkindness.
- *Understanding*—Mothers seek to understand their children's needs and concerns.
- *Wisdom*—Mothers separate behavior from the individual. They always respect the individual child, even if the child's behavior needs to be channeled into more appropriate patterns.
- *Serving*—Mothers are always there in times of routine as well as in moments of crisis. Someone said, "Every mother is a working woman."
- *Devotion*—Mothers know that their role is non-transferable.
- *Praising*—Mothers honestly and generously praise their children regularly.
- *Honoring*—Mothers never abuse or make light of their children in any way.
- *Fostering enjoyment*—Mothers try to make family time fun and enjoyable, even if it is a little hectic.
- *Humility*—Mothers seek forgiveness of their children when the mothers are not at their best.

- *Honesty*—Mothers always keep their word. They are trustworthy, just as they are trusting.
- *Giving*—Mothers always give their love and their time. Their children always know that they are loved and important to their mothers.

ILLUSTRATIONS FOR OUR TIMES

An anonymous parable reminds us of the great sacrifices made by mothers, and of the crown they receive for faithful motherhood.

The Crown from Heaven—A Parable

At the door of the Angel of Life there sounded a knocking, at first very faint, then growing louder and more insistent. Opening the door, the angel saw on the threshold a woman pale with pain, but with a look of expectant joy in her eyes.

"I am here," she said triumphantly. "I have come for my child. Give it to me quickly for it is a long journey and a hard one, and my strength may be exhausted before I return."

"Wait," said the angel slowly. "Your child is here—a beautiful boy. But first you must pay for him."

"Pay you?" faltered the woman. "But I have very little money and we shall need that for him."

"I have no use for money," answered the angel. "But I must have a little of your health, a great deal of your time, some of your peace of mind, and at least half of your heart."

Without hesitating the woman handed him the things for which he asked, and the angel turned away and returned with the child. The woman clasped him eagerly in her weak arms, then bravely set out for the land from which she came. As she turned to go, the angel placed on her head a crown. She turned in surprise.

"This is my gift to you," said the Angel of Life. "It is the crown of motherhood, which will recompense you for the things you have given up."

—Anonymous

* * *

In an inspirational account, a blind woman tells of her mother's devotion to and sacrifice for her children, and of the lasting effects in her own life.

My Guiding Light

My mother was so quiet and unassuming that many of her closest neighbors never really learned to know her; yet she was truly a friend to the friendless and a comfort to the lonely-hearted.

My early childhood would have been desolate indeed without her love and devotion. How clearly I remember a conversation that went something like this: "Mamma, will you read to me now? Just a few pages, Mamma."

I would carry a book into the kitchen where my mother was ironing or to the dining room where she sat at her sewing machine. Sometimes I followed her to the back porch where she scrubbed clothes on a washboard. Her explanations that she must first finish her work were always gentle and patient. Never did she raise her voice in anger or impatience. More often than not, she would leave her work only to finish it later in the evening when I was tucked safely into bed. Due to her kindness and tact, I was eight years old before I realized that I was blind.

When a teacher was found to teach me Braille, Mother learned Braille with me. Since we could see the teacher only once a week, Mother felt that my progress would be too slow with so little help, so my education became another of her many tasks. When I did enter a day school for the blind, I was able to go into the fifth grade with the children in my own age group. Had she merely been the traditional busy housewife, this would have been noteworthy enough, but since she was the sole provider for four children, it was remarkable. By taking in washing and sewing, working in the homes of neighbors, and remaking second-hand clothing that friends and relatives contributed, we were able to manage.

My mother was often asked why she did not send me away to school. In those days, practically all blind children attended special state institutions. To such questions Mother would say, "I want Lucile to have the same love and care that my other children have. . . ." . . .

I could never have finished high school and college without Mother's help. In the late twenties and early thirties, there were very few textbooks to be had in Braille. Mother did most of my reading. She also spent long hours dictating French to me, and I transcribed page after page of it into Braille. . . .

Because of her, I have never known a world of darkness. Because of her, I have been able to live a busy and happy life. With her as my inspiration, I shall continue to do so. As she always has been, she always will be my guiding light. (Lucile Tournear in *Remarkable Stories from the Lives of Latter-day Saint Women,* comp. Leon R. Hartshorn, [Salt Lake City: Deseret Book, 1973], 2:233–35)

SUMMARY

The list of what mothers accomplish could go on forever, but the point seems clear: a mother's influence is critical to the lives of her children. We are all indebted to our mothers for life itself and for their love and kindness expressed through service. It is interesting to see the gratitude of a young mother for her own mother after she has given birth to a child. Undoubtedly, we all owe to our angel mothers a righteous life of service and charity, so that their lives will have not been in vain. Mothers today need to remember that there is no success outside the home that can equate to the success of raising a child with love and devotion. Mothers are truly the queens of the earth, and within their realm lies the heavenly commission to bring up their children in truth and see to their nurture and well-being. Motherhood is the essence of life. May life be sweet for all families as mothers and fathers and children work together in harmony and love.

OBEDIENCE

According to the Lord, learning to obey is the principal test of life (see Abr. 3:25). Through obedience, we become the sons and daughters of God. In this regard, James E. Faust counseled: "The price of discipleship is obedience." Obedience, in fact, is the first law of heaven, and all blessings are predicated on this law (see D&C 130:20–21). One of the great blessings of keeping the commandments is that the Spirit attends us when we do so (see D&C 20:77, 79). On the other hand, when we disobey, we lose the blessing of the Spirit in our lives (see Morm. 1:13–14). When we gain mastery over our conduct through obedience to the Lord, our spiritual nature desires that which is good, and we comport ourselves in a Christlike manner. Thus St. Augustine taught: "Obedience is in a way the mother of all virtues."

The scriptures provide abundant evidence of the power that comes through obedience. The sons of Helaman, for example, were full of faith and exactly obedient, and this acted as a protection and a shield to them. Sometimes, however, we are not at our best—we fall short of exact, immediate, and courageous obedience. The children of Adam and Eve were taught the plan of redemption, and then Satan came among them, commanding them "to believe it not," and some of them "believed it not, and they loved Satan more than God." The result was that they became carnal, sensual, and devilish (see Moses 5:11–13). They were willfully disobedient by nature and suffered the consequences. They did not obey God completely when they ceased to love Him completely (see John 14:15).We all claim to love God—and we do love Him. The question is: Do we love Him deeply enough? We cannot love God and mammon and be obedient to the laws of God. The blessing of obedience is righteousness, which leads us to a state of happiness, the ultimate desire of our heart.

THE SCRIPTURES TEACH US

1 Samuel 15:22. *And Samuel said, Hath the Lord as great delight in burnt offerings and sacrifices, as in obeying the voice of the Lord? Behold, to obey is better than sacrifice, and to hearken than the fat of rams.*

By sacrificing, we please the Lord and learn that obedience is the supreme law. We do not pick and choose which commandments to keep or select those sacrifices that we want to make. To demonstrate our obedience, we must strive with all our might to keep all of the commandments and to sacrifice all things the Lord commands us.

John 7:17. *If any man will do his will, he shall know of the doctrine, whether it be of God, or whether I speak of myself.*

It is through obedience that we learn the truth of the doctrines of Christ and receive the blessings associated with each doctrine.

1 Nephi 22:31. *Wherefore, if ye shall be obedient to the commandments, and endure to the end, ye shall be saved at the last day.*

The simple truth of life is that if we lovingly obey the commandments of God and endure to the end, we will be exalted.

Doctrine and Covenants 130:19–21. *And if a person gains more knowledge and intelligence in this life through his diligence and obedience than another, he will have so much the advantage in the world to come. There is a law, irrevocably decreed in heaven before the foundations of this world, upon which all blessings are predicated—And when we obtain any blessing from God, it is by obedience to that law upon which it is predicated.*

The law of the harvest is simple: We are blessed by practicing true principles and obeying the commandments of God.

MODERN PROPHETS SPEAK

Brigham Young:

> Every son and daughter of God is expected to obey with a willing heart every word which the Lord has spoken, and which he will in the future speak to us. It is expected that we hearken to the revelations of his will, and adhere to them, cleave to them with all our might; for this is salvation, and any thing short of this clips the salvation and the glory of the Saints. 2:2. (*Discourses of Brigham Young,* selected and arranged by John A. Widtsoe [Salt Lake City: Deseret Book, 1954], 220)

Howard W. Hunter:

> Obedience must always precede knowledge. You will remember when Adam was driven from the Garden of Eden he offered sacrifices. "An angel of the Lord appeared unto Adam, saying: Why dost thou offer sacrifices unto the Lord? And Adam said unto him: I know not, save the Lord commanded me." (Moses 5:6.) Then the angel explained to him the meaning of sacrifices. Obedience must always precede knowledge. If we are obedient to our assigned responsibility, knowledge will follow. We are prone to discount things we cannot understand. (*The Teachings of Howard W. Hunter,* ed. Clyde J. Williams [Salt Lake City: Bookcraft, 1997], 22)

Spencer W. Kimball:

> The way to perfection is through obedience. Therefore, to each person is given a pattern—obedience through suffering, and perfection through obedience. Let each person learn obedience of faith in all things and thus exemplify the attributes of the Master. (*The Teachings of Spencer W. Kimball,* ed. Edward L. Kimball [Salt Lake City: Bookcraft, 1982], 168)

IDEAS FOR DAILY LIVING

Here are three strategies that can motivate all of us to be more obedient:

1. Realize that obedience is a reflection of your faith and love.
- *A choice*—With increased faith and abundant love in God, you will choose to obey Him. If you align yourself with lasting values and principles, little, everyday rules have a way of taking care of themselves.
- *A journey*—Obedience should be an exciting journey, not a restricting requirement of behavior.
- *A matter of faith*—When you understand a doctrine or principle through your faith, you will be eager to obey.

2. Understand the essence of the commandments, laws, and rules.
- *Freedom*—Look at obedience as a doorway to more freedom, rather than a straitjacket on your behavior. Laws and rules are made to enhance freedom to the highest degree for the greatest number of people. Recognize that obeying laws must be seen as a way to freedom rather than as a restriction.

- *Consequences*—All laws have consequences. For example, obedience to the laws of health and well-being is simply in your best interest. Learn the benefits of obedience to the law. The natural upholding of laws brings the blessings of safety, peace, and security to your family and society.
- *Knowledge*—Know the doctrines and principles of the gospel. Know the laws and rules of the government. Protect yourself from the effects of your own ignorance as well as from the designs of those who would exercise unrighteous power by perverting the laws and rules to their own advantage.

3. Take the initiative to foster obedience in family, community, and society.

- *Example*—Teach obedience to others through example and love rather than through the exercise of power and control. Help others understand and appreciate the reasons for laws. This will help them change their behaviors and attitudes.
- *Leadership*—A good leader must also understand how to be a good follower, since all must answer to someone above them in the chain of leadership. Therefore, regard obedience to proper and meaningful assignments as the energy that keeps the team functioning well.
- *Quest*—Make obedience a quest in your life, both for yourself and for your family. Obedience raises self-confidence and increases self-discipline, which has its own rewards.
- *Love*—Overcome fear through your love of God and your desire to obey His commandments. Aristotle taught: "Wicked men obey for fear, but the good for love."

ILLUSTRATIONS FOR OUR TIMES

The following personal account shows how obedience to parents in childhood can lead to blessings later in life.

Cooked Spinach, Cabbage, and Cauliflower

We lived on a farm during World War II. While we had plenty of food, we still had to go to the store for additional items. During the war, everyone had a little ration book. The ration book allowed each family to purchase so much food for each member of the family. We were no different. I can still remember going to the store and helping my mother. We could buy only the amount of food we had coupons for, because there was only so much food for every family. So food was important. That's where the story begins.

You see, my father was a big man—six foot three and 250 pounds—and when he spoke, we obeyed. When he said eat, we ate. I remember my parents liked to eat cooked cauliflower, cooked spinach, and cooked cabbage—and I couldn't stand any of them. I learned something as an eight-year-old boy. I could chew these offensive items while holding my breath and taking a big drink of milk—and I wouldn't even taste them. I was able to cope with all this horrible food my parents were eating. My angel mother always gave me just a small portion knowing of my great dislike. Yet we had to eat what was rationed to us, and we had to obey.

Years went by and I was married. My wife asked me if I would go to the store and buy the groceries. She gave me the list, and I was off to the store. On the list was "cooking vegetables." I could choose anything I wanted—corn, peas, artichokes, squash. Consider this—I was the big man in the market: I could buy what I wanted. I was alone with the list and the money. As I walked down through the produce section, I noticed a beautiful head of cabbage, which I took, a beautiful bag of spinach, and a large, white head of cauliflower. I stopped in amazement. I couldn't believe it. I had bought the very food I thought I hated. I learned to love these foods through obedience. Even to this day, I think of spinach steamed and hot with a little butter, a twist of lemon, and sprinkles of pepper—and I feel like Pavlov's dogs. I love cooked spinach, cabbage, and cauliflower, and I learned to love them as a child through obedience. I would hate to think of never being able to enjoy these foods. Certainly, obedience to any rule or law always has a blessing.

—Ed J. Pinegar

* * *

The following story, related by Elder Joseph B. Wirthlin, illustrates how exact obedience is required for the desired results.

Live in Obedience

Let me share an experience from my own youth, an experience that taught me the importance of obedience in doing even small things well. I loved to play football in high school and at the university. I wanted to be a good athlete. I especially remember one game. Our university team faced the University of Colorado in a contest for the conference championship. We were well coached and really well prepared.

The star of the Colorado team was Byron "Whizzer" White, an all-American who was a tremendous athlete. He was a fast, versatile, and powerful quarterback. His athletic prowess was legendary. . . .

Our wise coach was Ike Armstrong. His warnings before the game included two simple instructions: one, do not kick off or punt the ball to Whizzer White, and two, never let him get past the line of scrimmage.

We followed his instructions and held Colorado scoreless throughout the first half. Early in the second half, however, Whizzer White kicked a field goal. We answered with a touchdown and kicked the extra point. We were ahead seven to three at the end of the third quarter.

On the second play of the fourth quarter, we punted. The ball sailed deep into the corner of the field, near their end zone. Whizzer White plucked the tumbling ball out of the air at his fifteen-yard line and dropped back to his five-yard line to evade the first of our tacklers. Then with the speed, strength, and agility that had built his reputation, he started upfield and sidestepped every player of our team. I managed only to touch him with my little finger. He ran the entire length of the field for a touchdown—thrilling for Colorado, but disappointing for us.

Later in the fourth quarter, Whizzer dashed around his own right end and beyond the line of scrimmage and ran fifty-seven yards for another touchdown. The game ended with a score seventeen to seven. Colorado won the game and the conference championship.

Though we lost, I learned the importance of constant obedience to detailed instructions of our leader. Failure to obey our coach's two pregame warnings for just two plays—two brief lapses in an otherwise outstanding effort—cost us the game and the conference championship. That is all it took for us to lose something we had worked so hard to achieve.

I testify to you, my brethren, that your Heavenly Father loves you and wants you to receive and enjoy every blessing He has for His children, including the blessings of happiness and peace. We, the leaders of the Lord's church, love you. We pray for you earnestly and constantly. Your leaders in your wards and branches and in your stakes and districts likewise love you and pray for you. Your parents' prayers and love for you are beyond measure. We all want you to succeed in this life and to qualify for the greatest of God's gifts—eternal life in the celestial kingdom. To achieve your goals in this mortal life and prove yourselves worthy of eternal blessings, learn to obey. There is no other way. Obedience brings great strength and power into your lives. (Joseph B. Wirthlin, "Live in Obedience," *Ensign,* May 1994, 39)

SUMMARY

In life, we are free to choose, but we must remember that there are rewards or consequences for all decisions. Every person has experienced the blessings of obedience to principles and laws. That kind of experience brings mounting conviction that obedience to fundamental principles of truth is for our best good. As we go about our daily lives, let us always remember that the laws of the gospel are given by God in love, for He knows that obedience will bring great blessings to us—blessings of joy, happiness, and salvation. We can begin today making correct choices and thus enjoy more fully the success brought about by obedience. "You cannot be a true man until you learn to obey," said Robert E. Lee. Even more important than that: we cannot be true disciples of Christ until we learn to obey. Consider His supernal example: "Though he were a Son, yet learned he obedience by the things which he suffered; And being made perfect, he became the author of eternal salvation unto all them that obey him" (Heb. 5:8–9). Let us strive each day to honor His atoning sacrifice by accepting Him as our Savior and obeying with faith every word with which He has blessed us.

PATIENCE

Patience involves being calm and understanding during difficult times and is usually demonstrated by equanimity and composure. Webster defines *patience* as:

1. The suffering of afflictions, pain, toil, calamity, provocation or other evil, with a calm, unruffled temper; endurance without murmuring or fretfulness. *Patience* may spring from constitutional fortitude, from a kind of heroic pride, or from Christian submission to the divine will.
2. A calm temper which bears evils without murmuring or discontent.
3. The act or quality of waiting long for justice or expected good without discontent.
4. Perseverance; constancy in labor or exertion.
5. The quality of bearing offenses and injuries without anger or revenge (*An American Dictionary of the English Language,* Noah Webster, 1828, electronic ed. [Salt Lake City: Deseret Book, 1998]).

Apostle Joseph B. Wirthlin taught: "We will have genuine joy and happiness only as we learn patience," and Ralph Waldo Emerson wrote: "The years teach much which the days never knew." Developing patience is of primary importance in becoming like our Savior Jesus Christ, for patience is part of His divine nature. People will be blessed as we emulate the Savior's example of patience and radiate a spirit of peace and tranquility. Being patient does not equate with being permissive, easily manipulated, or readily taken advantage of. Rather, patience signifies a level of maturity that ennobles one's character. Patience, like perseverance, is a governing virtue of success in all facets of life.

THE SCRIPTURES TEACH US

Luke 21:19. *In your patience possess ye your souls.*

The virtue of patience gives us mastery over our very being. Patience is part of the attribute of charity (see Moro. 7:45), and is a virtue that helps us nurture the word of God (see Alma 31:40–43).

Mosiah 3:19. *For the natural man is an enemy to God, and has been from the fall of Adam, and will be, forever and ever, unless he yields to the enticings of the Holy Spirit, and putteth off the natural man and becometh a saint through the atonement of Christ the Lord, and becometh as a child, submissive, meek, humble, patient, full of love, willing to submit to all things which the Lord seeth fit to inflict upon him, even as a child doth submit to his father.*

Patience is of critical importance in becoming a saint. It is also part of the divine nature of the Lord Jesus Christ (see 2 Pet. 1:3–12), leading us to brotherly kindness and eventually to charity.

Doctrine and Covenants 24:8. *Be patient in afflictions, for thou shalt have many; but endure them, for, lo, I am with thee, even unto the end of thy days.*

Enduring our trials and tribulations with patience is part of the test of life. Learning patience is part of the perfecting process (see D&C 67:13), and the Lord will be with us as we patiently endure.

MODERN PROPHETS SPEAK

Ezra Taft Benson:
> Patience is another form of self-control. It is the ability to postpone gratification and to bridle one's passions. In his relationships with loved ones, a patient man does not engage in impetuous behavior that he will later regret. Patience is composure under stress. A patient man is understanding of others' faults.
>
> A patient man also waits on the Lord. We sometimes read or hear of people who seek a blessing from the Lord, then grow impatient when it does not come swiftly. Part of the divine nature is to trust in the Lord enough to "be still, and know that [he] is God" (D&C 101:16). A priesthood holder who is patient will be tolerant of the mistakes and failings of his loved ones. Because he loves them, he will not find fault nor criticize nor blame. (*The Teachings of Ezra Taft Benson* [Salt Lake City: Bookcraft, 1988], 446)

Gordon B. Hinckley:
> Let us be more compassionate, gentler, filled with forbearance and patience and a greater measure of respect one for another. In so doing, our very example will cause others to be more merciful, and we shall have greater claim upon the mercy of God who in His love will be generous toward us. (*Teachings of Gordon B. Hinckley* [Salt Lake City: Deseret Book, 1997], 338)

IDEAS FOR DAILY LIVING

Here are four ways to increase our level of patience in all situations:

1. Plan for patience.

- *Make it a goal to be patient*—You might consider placing signs in the home, your workplace, and in your car to remind you to be patient.
- *Look ahead*—Anticipate situations that will test your patience and change the environment or conditions to prevent any blowup or confrontation.
- *Control your time*—Make time your ally by preparing in advance so that a few minutes here or there are not so critical in your life. Even bad traffic won't bother you if you leave early.

2. Always look from a higher vision.

- *Discern potential*—See people not for what they are at this moment, but for what they can become. Recognize that all are learning. Not everyone may be as astute as you may be.
- *Learn from adversity*—Look at disappointments as opportunities to redirect your life in meaningful ways. For every door that shuts, there may be several of a different nature that open for you. In patience, you will be able to discern such opportunities.
- *Envision your legacy*—Do you want your spouse, children, and associates to remember you for your anger or for your patience? Remember to consider the future as you control yourself in the present. Leave behind the seeds of harmony, peace, balance, and unity for the coming generations.

3. Use peacemaker strategies of leadership.

- *Nurture young people*—With children it is vital to be patient. Children are so fragile that anger or impatience on the part of adults often frustrates them. Impatience can damage your relationship with children, while patience can generate lasting relationships.
- *Work in teams*—With the desire to be patient, you will often find it helpful to enlist the support and cooperation of others. When all work together toward a common goal, there is less chance for patience-threatening situations to arise.
- *Commiserate with people*—Rather than respond to emotional outbursts with preaching, simply go along with the emotion ("I can see how you would be upset over that . . .") and guide the person gradually into a state of greater composure so that you can teach better behavior at the appropriate time.
- *Be tolerant*—Use the patience of the farmer. Teach others through a soft voice, and learn to wait and watch others grow. The law of the harvest calls for you to practice patience as you nurture others.
- *Break the pattern*—When people act out, it sometimes helps to break the pattern by doing something unexpected to force the person to look at the situation differently. Using appropriate humor in tense situations can often dispel ill feelings.
- *Make time the common ally*—Use the tested formula: "Let's give it a few more minutes [hours, days]."
- *Teach consequences*—Patiently guide an impatient person through the exercise of seeing the ultimate consequence of his or her behavior. You might say, "And if you continue with this, what will be the result?" Let the person figure it out on his own or her own.

4. Cultivate the patience necessary to become more Christlike.

- *Pray for patience*—Consider how patient Heavenly Father is with His children, in view of how we sometimes fall short of our potential. Therefore, pray often that the Lord will enrich your spiritual life with patience.
- *Make hope your governing principle*—Cultivate hope that is stronger than the forces of discouragement. Remember, you can *become* patient as you *practice* patience. Time is on your side.

ILLUSTRATIONS FOR OUR TIMES

In this oriental parable, we learn of the remarkable rewards of patience.

The Tiger's Whisker—A Parable

A young man of the Far East fell deeply in love with a beautiful young girl who lived in a valley nearby. He did all in his power to win her affection, but to no avail. No matter what gifts he brought her, no matter how many poems he wrote for her, no matter how many songs he sang for her—she remained aloof and distant.

Discouraged, he went to visit a wise old man who lived high in the mountains. "What can I do?" asked the youth. "I am so much in love, but nothing seems to turn her eye toward me or warm her heart."

The old man only smiled and said. "This kind of case requires a special love potion made from the whisker of a wild tiger."

"A wild tiger!" exclaimed the young man. "How shall I acquire a whisker of a wild tiger and still live to tell the tale?"

"Do what you must in all patience," responded the wise old man. "And when you have the whisker, come back to me, and I promise you shall see a happy outcome to your problem."

So the young man, dejected, went down into the market square where he sat on a wooden bench to think. "How ever shall I get a tiger's whisker and still survive?" he asked himself. Almost as an afterthought, he bought a piece of meat at the butcher's stall and wrapped it in paper and set off for the mountains where the tigers lived. After many hours, he came to a clearing before a large cave, and there in the distance was a huge tiger, sleeping in the sun outside the cave. The young man watched quietly from behind a tree, and then decided to leave the piece of meat just a few feet into the clearing. He then retreated far away and watched from behind a bush. After an hour, the tiger slowly got up and went over to the place where the meat was lying, and ate it down in a gulp. The young man swallowed hard, thinking to himself, "I am very glad that it was not I who served as the tiger's meal today."

Every day for the next month, the young man took a piece of meat up to where the tiger lived and left it for the huge beast, each time a foot or two closer to the tiger's lair. Finally, after being so patient and careful, he found that he could get quite close to the tiger without hearing any growls or snarls. At last the tiger allowed the young man to come right up to him and leave the meat directly under his mouth. After many weeks of repeating this ritual, the young man ventured to reach out and actually touch the tiger. The tiger just purred and licked his hand, and thereafter the two were able to take a nap side by side as if they were the best of friends.

Then one day, after feeding the tiger, the young man waited until the great animal was sound asleep. He could feel his own heart beating within him as he watched the tiger breathing deeply. Then he quietly took a pair of scissors and reached out and clipped off one of the tiger's whiskers. He was overjoyed! Finally, he had the solution to his most important challenge in life.

He fairly raced to the hut of the wise old man and proudly handed him the extraordinary prize—a genuine tiger's whisker. The old man smiled, received the whisker graciously, then threw it into the fire where— poof—it vanished in a puff of smoke.

The young man was horrified! He saw his dreams going up in smoke. "What have you done?" he shrieked. "How can I ever win the heart of my maiden now?"

The wise old man just smiled. "Any man," he said, "with the patience and courage to retrieve a tiger's whisker and live to tell of it, has the patience and courage to win this young lady's heart. You have the secret within you. Go now, and you will triumph."

—Richard J. Allen (based on an old Korean tale)

SUMMARY

Demonstrating patience towards others and toward yourself provides the opportunity, space, and time to grow. Mothers provide incredible examples of patience, since the successful nurturing and caring for children requires great patience. From the patience shown to us, we gain the strength to show patience toward others. Patience can thus become a self-perpetuating power. To show patience at all times is difficult, but it is a virtue all must strive to cultivate. "Patience and perseverance have a magical effect before which difficulties disappear and obstacles vanish," observed John Quincy Adams. Above all, patience is a virtue grounded in faith, as Alma confirmed through his grand metaphor of the seed sprouting up as a tree of life: "Then, my brethren, ye shall reap the rewards of your faith, and your diligence, and patience, and long-suffering, waiting for the tree to bring forth fruit unto you" (Alma 32:43).

PATRIARCHAL BLESSINGS

A patriarchal blessing is a priesthood blessing by an ordained patriarch that provides specific revelation for the individual recipient. It is a blessing given primarily to identify one's lineage in the house of Israel. It also contains promised blessings to the recipient if he or she is faithful to sacred covenants. A patriarchal blessing serves as a message of hope regarding eternal life, as well as a reminder of responsibilities to which the recipient has committed. Patriarchal blessings are unique to the individual, identifying him or her as a descendant of a specific tribe of Israel, and indicating his or her gifts and duties in the kingdom of God. These blessings are prophetic counsel for each Church member's life based on his or her worthiness to participate in the promised blessings.

THE SCRIPTURES TEACH US

Genesis 49:22–26. *Joseph is a fruitful bough, even a fruitful bough by a well; whose branches run over the wall: The archers have sorely grieved him, and shot at him, and hated him: But his bow abode in strength, and the arms of his hands were made strong by the hands of the mighty God of Jacob; (from thence is the shepherd, the stone of Israel:) Even by the God of thy father, who shall help thee; and by the Almighty, who shall bless thee with blessings of heaven above, blessings of the deep that lieth under, blessings of the breasts, and of the womb: The blessings of thy father have prevailed above the blessings of my progenitors unto the utmost bound of the everlasting hills: they shall be on the head of Joseph, and on the crown of the head of him that was separate from his brethren.*

This statement from the blessing given by the patriarch Israel (Jacob) to his son Joseph enumerates the extraordinary promises bestowed by the Lord upon the lineage of Joseph, through his sons Ephraim and

Manasseh. Blessings flow likewise to other Israelite tribes as part of the patriarchal heritage of the Abrahamic covenant. (Compare Father Lehi's blessing upon his son Joseph, who was of the lineage of Israel's son Joseph—2 Nephi 3:3–7.)

Ephesians 4:11–13. *And he gave some, apostles; and some, prophets; and some, evangelists; and some, pastors and teachers; For the perfecting of the saints, for the work of the ministry, for the edifying of the body of Christ: Till we all come in the unity of the faith, and of the knowledge of the Son of God, unto a perfect man, unto the measure of the stature of the fulness of Christ.*

Articles of Faith 1:6. *We believe in the same organization that existed in the Primitive Church, namely, apostles, prophets, pastors, teachers, evangelists, and so forth.*

Consider the magnificent organization of the kingdom of God, with the several offices and functions of the priesthood designed by the Lord to provide blessings, protection, and saving ordinances for the Saints. Among these is the office of evangelist—or patriarch—which serves as the channel for extraordinary prophetic blessings to the faithful, including the declaration of lineage and other grand views into the future of one's possibilities. The Prophet Joseph Smith taught: "An Evangelist is a Patriarch, even the oldest man of the blood of Joseph or of the seed of Abraham. Wherever the Church of Christ is established in the earth, there should be a Patriarch for the benefit of the posterity of the Saints, as it was with Jacob in giving his patriarchal blessing unto his sons, etc." (*Teachings of the Prophet Joseph Smith,* sel. Joseph Fielding Smith [Salt Lake City: Deseret Book, 1976], 151)

Authors' Note: Little is said in the scriptures about patriarchal blessings. Perhaps it is because of the personal and sacred nature of these blessings that we have so few scriptural records of actual blessings. But as indicated above, we know such blessings were given and were important in the early Church, as they are in the latter days. The office of patriarch and the offering of such blessings were a part of the Restoration of the Church (see D&C 124:92).

MODERN PROPHETS SPEAK

Gordon B. Hinckley:

> I hope that we are encouraging those who are mature enough to understand the importance of a patriarchal blessing to receive one. I count my patriarchal blessing as one of the great sacred things of my life. A patriarchal blessing is a unique and sacred and personal and wonderful thing that may be given to every member of this Church who lives worthy of it. I hope, brethren, that you men of the bishoprics, particularly, are counseling your people concerning this. . . .

> I hope we encourage our people to live worthy to receive a patriarchal blessing, and to make the effort to get one. It's a rare privilege to have a patriarchal blessing. It's unique from all other things in this world. There is nothing like it, to have a man speak on an individual basis and pronounce blessings in authority of the Holy Priesthood. (*Teachings of Gordon B. Hinckley* [Salt Lake City: Deseret Book, 1997], 424)

Thomas S. Monson:

> A blessing you can qualify to receive is your patriarchal blessing. Your parents and your bishop will know when the time is right for you to receive it. A patriarchal blessing contains chapters from your life's book of possibilities. To you it will be as a lighthouse on a hill, warning of dangers, and direct-

ing you to the tranquility of safe harbors. It is a prophetic utterance from the lips of one called and ordained to provide you such a blessing. ("Your Celestial Journey," *Ensign,* May 1999, 96)

Joseph Fielding Smith:

A blessing given by a patriarch is intended to point out the path which the recipient should travel. It should be given by the spirit of revelation and should be a great comfort and incentive to the recipient to continue on in faithfulness to the end. The patriarch also holds the key by which the lineage of those whom he blesses may be made known. It is a very important and most holy and sacred calling. (*Doctrines of Salvation,* 3 vols., ed. Bruce R. McConkie [Salt Lake City: Bookcraft, 1954–1956], 3:170)

Ezra Taft Benson:

I would encourage you . . . to receive a patriarchal blessing. Study it carefully and regard it as personal scripture to you—for that is what it is. A patriarchal blessing is the inspired and prophetic statement of your life's mission together with blessings, cautions, and admonitions as the patriarch may be prompted to give. . . . receive your patriarchal blessing under the influence of fasting and prayer, and then read it regularly that you may know God's will for you. (*The Teachings of Ezra Taft Benson* [Salt Lake City: Bookcraft, 1988], 214)

IDEAS FOR DAILY LIVING

Some things to understand regarding patriarchal blessings:

1. Every member of the Church should receive a patriarchal blessing. Heavenly Father loves each of His children dearly and wants to bless them. He has provided patriarchs as one means of doing so. When we are ready for this spiritual counsel, we should take advantage of the opportunity.

2. Live worthy of receiving a patriarchal blessing. We must prepare ourselves spiritually to receive this blessing. Patriarchal blessings and the promises therein are contingent on our own worthiness in life, so we must be worthy when we receive these blessings and responsibilities.

- *Seek to have your blessing at the appropriate age*—You should be mature enough to understand and appreciate it and young enough that many of life's decision are still in the future.
- *Prepare spiritually to receive it*—This may include coming in a humble attitude of prayer, and even fasting if you so desire.

3. Remember that your patriarchal blessing is personal and sacred. Your blessing is for you, not all your friends and family. If you seek understanding, discuss it with the patriarch, bishop or trusted family member.

4. Never compare blessings with another person. If you choose to share your blessing with someone close to you (such as your spouse or parents), do not worry that your blessing is different than theirs. Remember, each blessing is unique, and the Lord knows best what blessings you need.

5. Apply your patriarchal blessing to your daily life with faith and thanksgiving.

- *Your potential*—Examine any attributes and qualities mentioned in your blessing and seek to become the glorious person presented in this spiritual portrait of your potential. Cultivate and apply the talents and gifts the Lord has granted you, "that all may be profited thereby" (D&C 46:12).

- *Gifts and blessings*—Receive with joy and gratitude the promised blessings revealed to you through the patriarch and live in such a manner that they can be granted to the full extent, based on your faithfulness and devotion.
- *Admonitions and exhortations*—Be easily entreated in following the counsel and guidance given in your blessing. Let your blessing serve as a spiritual compass for your life, keeping you firmly on the straight and narrow pathway of righteousness.
- *Cautions and concerns*—Where specific cautions might be given regarding the course of your life, prayerfully heed this divine guidance and warning.
- *Lineage and responsibility to it*—Give praise to the Lord that He has anchored you securely within the fold of His covenant people. Give thanks that you can serve with devotion to help build the kingdom of God and carry the message of salvation to many others in keeping with the responsibilities of the Abrahamic covenant.
- *Joys and blessings in fulfillment*—View your blessing as a spiritual passport to the realization of divine promises that the Lord, in His mercy and loving-kindness, has bestowed upon you personally through one of His chosen priesthood servants.

ILLUSTRATIONS FOR OUR TIMES

Eldred G. Smith, in a general conference address, tells a memorable story of a young woman who acted on counsel received in her patriarchal blessing and was greatly blessed for it.

What a Patriarchal Blessing Can Do

An example of what a patriarchal blessing can do came to me in a story which I have repeated many times, which a woman told me. As a young woman she lived in a small town. When she finished high school, there was no further opportunity to continue her education. There was no further opportunity to get work so that she could be independent, so she came to Salt Lake City where she found herself a job. As time came for registration at the University, she became very anxious to go to school again, and knowing that there was not a possibility, under present conditions, she felt quite disheartened. She went to the patriarch and received her patriarchal blessing, and in the blessing he promised her that she should receive a good education. She was elated, and she went out of the office feeling very happy. Before she had gone half a block, she said, she fell to earth out of her cloud with a realization that going to college cost money, and she did not have any, nor the means to get it. The opportunity and possibility of going to college at present did not seem to be at all possible, which made her very downhearted again. And the thought came to her to go visit her aunt, who was living in Salt Lake City. Without stopping to analyze that impression she turned, and instead of going back to work she went to visit her aunt and told her aunt of her experience—cried on her shoulder. And her aunt said to her, "I know an elderly woman who lives down the street a few blocks. She has at various times helped young girls get through college in return for the help the girls can give to her. I do not know whether she has help now or not, but," she said, "this woman knows who I am. Go down and see her and tell her I sent you."

She went on the run to this elderly woman's home, and within two weeks from the time she received her patriarchal blessing, she registered at the University of Utah, signed a promissory note to pay for her education, and eventually paid for it. She said if she had stopped to question the first impression she got to go visit her aunt, she would have said to herself, "Why should I go visit my aunt and tell her my troubles? I came to Salt Lake City to be independent; why not be independent? She cannot help me with my troubles; she has enough of her own. She doesn't have space in her home to let me sleep there, let alone board me or help me. Why need I go and bother my aunt?" But she did not stop to analyze that impression; she acted on it. (Eldred G. Smith, Conference Report, April 1952, 39–40)

SUMMARY

Never forget that your patriarchal blessing is a gift that will help you return to the presence of Heavenly Father. As you seek to understand and appreciate your patriarchal blessing, you will feel grateful for your blessings and you will be filled with a desire to change. You will have a different attitude about yourself and about life, knowing that you can become like our Savior Jesus Christ. Your patriarchal blessing can be a tremendous source of inspiration in your life.

PEACE

We all seek the feeling of peace. Peace is a sense of well-being, a feeling of harmony, tranquility, and amity with God, yourself, and others. Peace is knowing that you please God and live up to your values and standards. When you feel peace, there is no discord or contention; your conscience is clear and you are free from inner conflict. When individuals and societies do not enjoy peace due to immorality and impiety, the result is contention, discord, and eventually even war. On a large scale, we experience war throughout our world in different places and at different times due to the violation of the principles of peace. On a smaller scale, the effects of losing inner peace can also be devastating to individuals and families. Beginning today, let us seek to become at peace with Heavenly Father, our Savior, ourselves, our family, and our circle of influence. Peace in the world begins with each of us.

THE SCRIPTURES TEACH US

Alma 38:8. *And it came to pass that I was three days and three nights in the most bitter pain and anguish of soul; and never, until I did cry out unto the Lord Jesus Christ for mercy, did I receive a remission of my sins. But behold, I did cry unto him and I did find peace to my soul.*

As Alma was in the process of repentance, he experienced the pain and sorrow of sin. There can be no peace through sin, only through the forgiveness empowered by the Atonement of Christ. When we come unto Christ through repentance, we will find true peace—there is no other way. The surrogate feelings of well-being generated through the philosophies and practices of the world are all short term. True peace can only come from living the gospel.

Matthew 5:9. *Blessed are the peacemakers: for they shall be called the children of God.*

Peacemakers are full of empathy and love. They spread the gospel of Jesus Christ in all that they do, for this is the source of peace. As we seek peace, we should help people come into the kingdom of God. By so doing they too become the sons and daughters of Christ (see Mosiah 5:7) and members of the eternal family of God. Remember that contention is of the devil (see 3 Ne. 11:28–29).

John 14:27. *Peace I leave with you, my peace I give unto you: not as the world giveth, give I unto you. Let not your heart be troubled, neither let it be afraid.*

One of the ultimate purposes of life is to find that "peace of God, which passeth all understanding" (Philip. 4:7). The peace of the Lord is different from that outer calm the world calls peace. His peace can dwell in our hearts despite our circumstances or the influences of the outside world. We should seek peace in righteous living and sow peace in our conscience (see Ps. 34:14). Peace of mind and heart should be one of our main goals as we seek happiness here and in the hereafter.

Psalms 34:14. *Depart from evil, and do good; seek peace, and pursue it.*

Peace comes by coming unto Christ with full purpose of heart. Through repentance our guilt is taken away—we have peace of conscience (see Enos 1:6–8; Mosiah 4:3). We love the laws and commandments of God and in them we find peace (see Ps. 119:165). We have only the desire to bless others and live peaceably with our fellowmen (see Mosiah 4:13).

MODERN PROPHETS SPEAK

Marvin J. Ashton:

> At such times external events make it even more imperative that we seek peace within ourselves. It is futile to seek it from outward sources.
>
> It was George C. Marshall who wisely said, "We must take the nations of the world as they are, the human passions and prejudices of people as they exist, and find some way to secure . . . a peaceful world."
>
> Peace must be a triumph of principles. Selfishness and lack of patience seem to block the way. (*Be of Good Cheer* [Salt Lake City: Deseret Book, 1987], 90)

Howard W. Hunter:

> Because of the difference in definitions, those who seek peace may be searching for unrelated conditions. The peace for which the world longs is a time of suspended hostilities; but men do not realize that peace is a state of existence that comes to man only upon the terms and conditions set by God, and in no other way.
>
> In a psalm in the book of Isaiah are these words: "Thou wilt keep him in perfect peace, whose mind is stayed on thee: because he trusteth in thee" (Isaiah 26:3). This perfect peace mentioned by Isaiah comes to one only through a belief in God. This is not understood by an unbelieving world. (*The Teachings of Howard W. Hunter,* ed. Clyde J. Williams [Salt Lake City: Bookcraft, 1997], 171)

Gordon B. Hinckley:

> The satisfying thing is that obedience brings happiness; it brings peace; it brings growth—all of these to the individual, and his good example brings respect for the institution of which he is a part. (*Be Thou an Example* [Salt Lake City: Deseret Book, 1981], 12)
>
> On billboards in some of our cities a statement read, "A nation at prayer is a nation at peace." I believe this. I hope this is more than a catchy motto. I am satisfied that we shall not have peace

unless and until we request it in the name of the Prince of Peace. (*Be Thou an Example* [Salt Lake City: Deseret Book, 1981], 32)

IDEAS FOR DAILY LIVING

Here are four ideas to remember as we become seekers of peace:

1. Peace comes through living the gospel of Jesus Christ.

- *Be true to your standards*—Outer peace is a function of inner peace. And inner peace can come only if we are living in harmony with the gospel principles by which peace is generated and maintained. Peace is a byproduct of righteous behavior.
- *Invite all to come unto Christ*—The source of peace is the plan of happiness, which is centered in Jesus Christ. Sharing this plan is the best way we can promote peace in the world.
- *Repentance*—We can receive peace only when we are free from guilt. This necessitates the process of repentance. "A peace above all earthly dignities, is a still and quiet conscience," said Shakespeare.
- *Pray for peace*—Seek confirmation from God. He wants to bless us, but we must ask and be willing to do what it takes to receive these blessings.
- *Be patient*—Time is your friend. Some things take time, often more than we would like. Pray for strength. Sooner or later, you will find peace.
- *Be honest with yourself and all others*—Peace comes through honesty, an inner assurance that there are no misguided shortcuts to integrity that you need to account for.
- *Live by a long-term perspective*—Peace does not come in the endless quest for more variety, titillation, and pleasure. Such things are ephemeral and fade as the foam on the sea. Peace comes by planting the seeds of harmony, respect, love, and balance in the family and the community.
- *Leave a legacy of honor*—Peace comes through the knowledge that you are leaving behind a strong legacy of honor and love for your children and your posterity.

2. Peace comes through self-mastery.

- *Do your best*—Your confidence will increase if you know you've done your best. This will help eliminate anxiety and worry.
- *Optimize your health*—Peace comes through taking care of your physical body through proper diet, exercise, adequate rest, and wholesome living habits.

3. Peace comes through leadership.

- *Foster goodwill*—Avoid contention while maintaining your integrity. Being a peacemaker is not being permissive—it is not being silent when your voice should be raised. Stand up for your values while still fostering peace and unity in your circle of influence.
- *Foster communication*—When people find fault or choose to contend with you, start a dialogue to resolve the conflict. If peace is your goal and others feel it, peace will eventually abound.
- *Mobilize behind a mutual vision*—Within the family or group, peace will exist when everyone agrees upon the same values, purposes, and goals. Such unity of purpose brings peace. The German poet Goethe stated: "He is happiest, be he king or peasant, who finds peace in his home."
- *Uphold the law*—In family, group, or society settings let us ensure peace through strict enforcement of the prevailing rules and laws (see Alma 1:33). This serves to foster peace as all learn to understand the blessings and consequences of their choices.

4. Peace comes through preparation.

- *Be self-reliant*—Establish financial goals that will provide sufficient means for your family's well-being and security. Have enough money set aside for a rainy day. Educate yourself so that you can take care of yourself and your family. True peace of mind can come when we rely solely on the Lord and ourselves.
- *Stay out of debt*—Peace comes through being debt-free, so far as possible, and living within your means. The anxiety and stress of debt defeats peace. Peace can only come through righteous living, not through bigger or better things.

ILLUSTRATIONS FOR OUR TIMES

This account shows how peace can come from the Lord as we seek His comfort and follow His commandments.

A Higher Peace

We were living in England and our son Cory had returned home to America for school. He was living with our son Steve and his family. Cory was full of life. He was good. He was sensitive, and he was a tough outside linebacker on the football team. The big Provo High School Bulldogs had just beaten the great cross-town rival Timpview Thunderbirds. Cory had "sacked" the quarterback, blocked a punt, and in general had an awe-inspiring game.

Following the game, Cory had a date with his girlfriend. As they were driving along, in the excitement of the night, Cory started to drive a little faster. It was dark, and the road was not well lit. All of a sudden, the road curved. Cory overcorrected and the car rolled over, and he was thrown from the car. The ambulance came and took them to the hospital. The girl was bruised, but had no major injuries and was okay. Cory had suffered a concussion. The doctors didn't give him any hope of survival. They put him on life-support machines. We were reached in London and returned home immediately. I can still remember looking down at my son, his eyes closed and his body still. The machines breathed for him and helped his body function, but his brain waves were flat. We prayed and pleaded, but the answer that came was no. Cory was to die. I felt as if my insides had been ripped from my body. I hurt. My sweetheart and children cried—our beloved son and brother was dead. As those who have experienced this pain know—at that moment you wonder if you can ever feel happy or at peace again because the hurt is so deep.

Something happened as we turned it over to the Lord. We turned to Him in our grief and received His comfort by the Spirit and through our knowledge of the gospel. It was miraculous. Our hearts began to heal. Life was bearable, and a power came into our lives that transcended life itself. I know, because it happened to me. This was a power greater than mortals can exhibit. It was a power from on high. Peace filled my soul. I could go on. We all will live again through the miracle of the Atonement and the resurrection. This peace filled me with hope, and life was not only livable, but became wonderful.

We still remember Cory. In fact, we celebrate his life on his birthday every year with the family. My sweetheart prepares Cory's favorite dinner, and then we all talk about Cory and his wonderful life. Our family is at peace. We are at peace because we have hope that through the mercy of the Lord, and through our worthiness, we can all be together again. There is a peace that transcends our earthly trials and tribulations and our heartaches and heartbreaks, and the reason is clear through the words of the Savior: "Peace I leave with you, my peace I give unto you: not as the world giveth, give I unto you. Let not your heart be troubled, neither let it be afraid" (John 14:27).

—Ed J. Pinegar

SUMMARY

Peace should be the quest for all of mankind. Peace is lost because of the lack of righteousness within. The solution in our quest for peace is to place Christ at the center of our lives. "Do as He would do" is a worthy universal motto for achieving a peaceful life. The microcosm of individual lives is expressed in the macrocosm of the world—and wickedness brings war and destroys peace. Peace begins with the individual, with each of us. Let us become the champions of peace by living in accordance with the example of the Prince of Peace.

PERSONAL IMPROVEMENT AND PERFECTION

We are all familiar with the command to be perfect (see Matt. 5:48). However, we also know that this goal is virtually unobtainable in this life. But we must not give up hope. Our goal should be to constantly work toward perfection, gradually but consistently improving ourselves. We all seek to improve our condition and progress toward our goal of becoming like and dwelling with God. As we seek to become more Christlike, we want to improve in kindness, courtesy, patience, wisdom, and love. We desire to be the best we can for the sake of our family and our friends.

Personal improvement is by definition all about *you*. However, in focusing on yourself, you will find that there cannot be significant improvement unless you bless the lives of others. Essentially, personal improvement is about increasing your capacity to bless and serve others. That is why the quest for perfection is logically anchored in spiritual improvement, which is sustained by the exercise of charity and emulation of the example of the Savior.

THE SCRIPTURES TEACH US

3 Nephi 27:27. *Therefore, what manner of men ought ye to be? Verily I say unto you, even as I am.*

We have the perfect example in our Savior Jesus Christ. As we strive to be like Him, we must remember that we grow line upon line and precept upon precept (see 2 Ne. 28:30). Perfection does not happen in great leaps, but in small, achievable steps.

Moroni 10:32. *Yea, come unto Christ, and be perfected in him, and deny yourselves of all ungodliness; and if ye shall deny yourselves of all ungodliness, and love God with all your might, mind and strength, then is his grace sufficient for you, that by his grace ye may be perfect in Christ; and if by the grace of God ye are perfect in Christ, ye can in nowise deny the power of God.*

It is only through Christ that we can be perfected—by *His* grace and mercy, through *His* Atonement. Our role in our own perfection is to come to Him and let Him perfect us and purify us through the trials and opportunities we receive.

Doctrine and Covenants 58:27–28. *Verily I say, men should be anxiously engaged in a good cause, and do many things of their own free will, and bring to pass much righteousness; For the power is in them, wherein they are agents unto themselves. And inasmuch as men do good they shall in nowise lose their reward.*

Although the Lord has commanded us to become perfect (see 3 Ne. 12:48)—a seemingly impossible task—this is not meant to be overwhelming. The Lord did not require a timetable of us, except that we should use this probationary phase of life to demonstrate our unwavering devotion and obedience to His commandments. Our Savior did not prescribe perfection overnight; He simply wants us on the straight and narrow path doing good and keeping the commandments. He wants us anxiously engaged in becoming better and lifting others. As we serve Him with all our heart, might, mind, and strength, He will help us rise progressively to our greatest potential.

Doctrine and Covenants 75:29. *Let every man be diligent in all things. And the idler shall not have place in the church, except he repent and mend his ways.*

The Lord expects us to work hard. Diligence is one of the important aspects of self-improvement. To truly improve, we must always be thinking of and serving others (see Matt 25:40; D&C 15:6; 18:10).

MODERN PROPHETS SPEAK

Joseph B. Wirthlin:

We don't have to be perfect today. We don't have to be better than someone else. All we have to do is to be the very best we can.

Though you may feel weary, though you sometimes may not be able to see the way, know that your Father in Heaven will never forsake His righteous followers. He will not leave you comfortless. He will be at your side, yes, guiding you every step of the way. ("One Step after Another," *Ensign,* November 2001, 26–27)

Spencer W. Kimball:

It is true of all of us that, as we progress spiritually, our sense of belonging, identity, and self-worth increases. Let us create a climate in which we encourage the sisters of the Church to have a program of personal improvement. It ought to be a practical and realistic program, one that is determined personally and not imposed upon them. Yet it ought to cause them to reach for new levels of achievement. We are not asking for something spectacular but rather for our sisters to find real self-fulfillment through wise self-development in the pursuit of righteous and worthy endeavors. (*My Beloved Sisters* [Salt Lake City: Deseret Book, 1979], 20–21)

Accept the reality that personal improvement on the part of each priesthood holder is expected by our Father in Heaven. We should be growing and we should be developing constantly. If we do, others will sense the seriousness of our discipleship and can then more easily forgive us our frailties which we sometimes show in the way in which we lead and manage. (*The Teachings of Spencer W. Kimball,* ed. Edward L. Kimball [Salt Lake City: Bookcraft, 1982], 175)

Marvin J. Ashton:

The Savior has taught us, "Blessed are they which do hunger and thirst after righteousness: for they shall be filled."

May God help us to involve ourselves in people's lives, involve ourselves in personal improvement, involve ourselves in work, and involve ourselves in his business, and thereby reap the rewards that come from such commitments. (*The Measure of Our Hearts* [Salt Lake City: Deseret Book, 1991], 120)

IDEAS FOR DAILY LIVING

As stated previously, perfection can only come through our Savior Jesus Christ. But there is much we can do in our efforts to come unto Christ and become more like Him. Here are five ideas to help us improve ourselves and work toward perfection:

1. Personal improvement starts within.
- *Choices*—You can improve yourself through personal choices. Personal improvement is itself a choice of monumental importance. Leo Tolstoy observed: "Everybody thinks of changing humanity and nobody thinks of changing himself." It is up to you to set goals, make plans, and then implement them. "Our own progress can be enhanced if we can look for solutions instead of being critical of those around us and blaming external conditions for our lack of progress," counseled Apostle Marvin J. Ashton ("Straightway," *Ensign,* May 1983, 30).
- *Foundation*—You can improve yourself by improving the foundation upon which you build. Instead of building on the sands of shifting pleasures and fads, build on the rock of the Lord Jesus Christ (see Hel. 5:12), and develop the qualities of honesty, integrity, harmony, peace, and service.
- *Vision*—You can improve yourself by adopting a vision for the future that will lead you and your loved ones to a state of happiness. Make sure your vision clearly details the things you want to become or accomplish. Follow the word of God, taking your guidance from the prophets.
- *Thoughts*—You can improve yourself by controlling your thoughts, filling your mind with ideas and dreams that are positive, affirmative, wholesome, and full of hope.

2. Personal improvement continues with good personal habits.
- *Health*—You can improve yourself by optimizing your health through proper diet, regular exercise, uncompromising personal hygiene, and adequate rest.
- *Environment*—You can improve yourself by improving your environment to reflect order, cleanliness, and elements that are uplifting and inspiring.
- *Language*—You can improve yourself by improving your language so that it is not only grammatically correct but also positive, supportive, lucid, encouraging, and structured to promote understanding.
- *Education*—You can improve yourself through education—reading, studying, taking courses, and seeking advice and counsel from knowledgeable people who can help you to be more effective and productive.
- *Conversion*—Above all, you can improve yourself by coming unto Christ with full purpose of heart. Identify concerns and behaviors in yourself and then work to overcome or improve them with all diligence.

3. Personal improvement is a social matter.
- *Family*—You can improve yourself by devoting your life to your family and loved ones. As they grow and improve, they lift you up and give meaning and purpose to your life. The legacy you leave behind for them is the measure of your own stature.
- *Friends*—You can improve yourself by surrounding yourself with friends who have noble goals and aspirations. Make appropriate commitments to your friends. Enlist their support.

4. Personal improvement is a matter of careful life-management.
- *Measurement*—You can improve yourself by taking the time to regularly measure and assess your progress. Chart it out, set goals, make plans, implement them, evaluate, and begin again. Follow up periodically and make mid-course corrections as needed.

- *Discipline*—You can improve yourself by maintaining self-respect, self-confidence, and the discipline to keep at it. If setbacks occur, start again. Oliver Wendell Holmes reminds us: "I find the great thing in this world is not so much where we stand, as in what direction we are moving."

5. Personal improvement is a spiritual matter.

- *Gratitude*—You can improve yourself by meditating on your blessings and on your relationship with Heavenly Father and our Savior, from whom all blessings flow. Be grateful for your blessings, including the help you receive in your efforts to improve.
- *Spiritual growth*—You can improve yourself spiritually. Search the scriptures. Fast and pray. Practice the principles of the gospel of Jesus Christ. Do your duty. Above all, serve your fellowmen in love.
- *Pursuit of excellence*—The pamphlet *Pursuit of Excellence,* published by the Church, is a wonderful aid for personal improvement. (You may order it from Church Distribution, or ask your ward leaders how to obtain a copy.)

ILLUSTRATIONS FOR OUR TIMES

Author and scholar Robert L. Millet shares a personal story about his quest for perfection and his realization that we cannot become perfect without the Lord's help.

Becoming Perfect in Our Generation

I remember the Sunday afternoon I turned to my wife and made a very serious commitment. We had been married but a few months and were very happy. In a sincere moment I indicated that I had every intention of being perfect by the age of thirty. She smiled kindly and wished me well, and the matter was dropped. I really believed in what I was doing. I determined to read and study and pray and labor for the next several years, and then, after attaining the notable plateau, I would work to help others reach the same spiritual height.

I suppose it isn't necessary to admit at this point that my goal was never quite achieved. Oh, I think I was a better man at thirty than I was at twenty-three, but I certainly wasn't perfect. Now almost twenty years after passing my initial goal, I still am not perfect in the sense I had originally intended to be, but I think I understand the process a little better now.

I supposed, in my naivete, if I just held my tongue, squelched my bitter feelings, blocked my thoughts, gritted my teeth, pushed myself to do my duty, and gripped the rod of iron white-knuckled-like for a sufficient time, that eventually such things would become quite natural and second nature to me. And I admit that many of what were once quite labored actions are now a bit more spontaneous. Over the years, however, I came to know that perfection in this life is not only difficult but impossible, at least as we usually define perfection.

It is one thing to attend all my church meetings, pay a full tithing and generous offerings, live the Word of Wisdom, and visit my home teaching families regularly. In a sense, I suppose, we can keep these laws perfectly if we simply do them and do them for the right reason. But at what point in my progression will I be able through sheer willpower to love my neighbor perfectly, evidencing in my attitudes and my actions such fruits of the Spirit as patience, long-suffering, gentleness, meekness, kindness, and the pure love of Christ? Where along the road to perfection will I no longer take offense, blame others, or harbor bitterness? One need not ponder on these matters for a lifetime before it becomes clear that becoming Christlike is a continuing pursuit that we simply cannot accomplish on our own. (Robert L. Millet, *Within Reach* [Salt Lake City: Deseret Book, 1995], 56–59)

SUMMARY

Personal improvement can be most fulfilling as we seek to become more Christlike. It is interesting to note that as we better ourselves, we always end up helping others. Personal improvement brings us self-confidence and an understanding of our self-worth, which in turn enhances our sphere of influence. As you analyze your life, select one or two areas where you need to improve and carefully set some goals to become better. You can do it, in the strength of the Lord.

The Apostle John clearly saw the potentiality of our discipleship in Christ: "Behold, what manner of love the Father hath bestowed upon us, that we should be called the sons of God: therefore the world knoweth us not, because it knew him not. Beloved, now are we the sons of God, and it doth not yet appear what we shall be: but we know that, when he shall appear, we shall be like him; for we shall see him as he is. And every man that hath this hope in him purifieth himself, even as he is pure" (1 Jn. 3:1–3). Let us all therefore strive to perfect ourselves one step at a time, every day coming a little closer to our goal of being like the Savior.

PLAN OF HAPPINESS

The plan of happiness is known by a variety of titles, including the plan of redemption, the plan of salvation, and the plan of exaltation. The commonality of all these titles is that life is a *plan,* a set order for Heavenly Father's children to accomplish their objective of being tested and progressing to return to Him in worthiness. As spirits in the premortal realm, we accepted the all-encompassing plan of our Heavenly Father. Jesus Christ is the center and pivotal point in the plan as the Creator, Redeemer, and Savior of the world through His infinite Atonement and His glorious Resurrection. If we are obedient to the laws and ordinances of the gospel, we are fulfilling our part of the plan and can, through grace, can partake of the blessings of eternal life, the greatest gift of God (see D&C 14:7).

THE SCRIPTURES TEACH US

Titus 1:2. *In hope of eternal life, which God, that cannot lie, promised before the world began.*

In the premortal life, Heavenly Father presented His plan to His spirit children. Because we have a physical body here on the earth, we know we accepted that plan. We had hope in the plan then, and we can still hope in it now. We can trust our Heavenly Father to hold true to His promise from the beginning—that if we remain faithful, we can return to Him.

Alma 34:9. *For it is expedient that an atonement should be made; for according to the great plan of the Eternal God there must be an atonement made, or else all mankind must unavoidably perish; yea, all are hardened; yea, all are fallen and are lost, and must perish except it be through the atonement which it is expedient should be made.*

The gospel plan is that Jesus Christ would come to Earth to atone for our sins, that He might draw all mankind to Him (see 3 Ne. 27:13–14). This is the core and center of the plan, as well as the foundation of the Church (see 3 Ne. 27:8–11). Without the Atonement, all souls would perish and become subject to the devil (see 2 Ne. 9:6–10). We should be filled with gratitude for the plan of redemption of our Heavenly Father and the goodness of our Savior, who paid the price for our sins so that we might live again with Him and our Father (see John 3:16; 2 Ne. 26:24).

Alma 42:13–16. *Therefore, according to justice, the plan of redemption could not be brought about, only on conditions of repentance of men in this probationary state, yea, this preparatory state; for except it were for these conditions, mercy could not take effect except it should destroy the work of justice. Now the work of justice could not be destroyed; if so, God would cease to be God. And thus we see that all mankind were fallen, and they were in the grasp of justice; yea, the justice of God, which consigned them forever to be cut off from his presence. And now, the plan of mercy could not be brought about except an atonement should be made; therefore God himself atoneth for the sins of the world, to bring about the plan of mercy, to appease the demands of justice, that God might be a perfect, just God, and a merciful God also. Now, repentance could not come unto men except there were a punishment, which also was eternal as the life of the soul should be, affixed opposite to the plan of happiness, which was as eternal also as the life of the soul.*

Justice demands payment for our sins. God's plan of happiness does not ignore or preclude this justice, yet neither does it defy mercy: the plan beautifully allows for both. In His great mercy, Christ made the infinite sacrifice and atoned for our sins so that justice can be paid by Him and He can grant mercy to us. To fulfill the law of justice and mercy, we must repent in order to receive the full blessings of Christ's atoning sacrifice.

MODERN PROPHETS SPEAK

Neal A. Maxwell:

> Fundamental to a man's understanding about his identity and purpose upon this planet is to know that God has a plan of salvation also called a plan of happiness, a plan of mercy, etc. (Alma 24:14; 42:8; 42:15). . . .
>
> One has only to ponder what a striking difference the gospel fulness would make for so many mortals who now view themselves and this life so existentially and provincially. How glorious if these individuals were willing to understand that (1) God has a plan of salvation of which this second estate—or mortality—is a key part; (2) "men are that they might have joy;" (3) we are truly accountable for our thoughts, words, and deeds while here; (4) the resurrection is a reality; and (5) a loving Father is seeing us through this mortal schooling as our Schoolmaster.
>
> Such knowledge and understanding would not put an end to human imperfection, but it would put an end to ultimate uncertainty on the pathway to salvation, making possible tremendous shifts in attitudes and behavior for immense numbers of people on this planet. (*But for a Small Moment* [Salt Lake City: Bookcraft, 1986], 62)

Our happiness is the intent of God's plan of happiness.

The more we come to understand the plan of happiness, the more we come to understand how incomplete and unfinished we were in our first estate and how much we needed this difficult mortal experience. We finally realize that there is no other way. Remembering this reality helps, especially when the only way is so difficult and discouraging at times and when we experience sadness as participants in the great plan of happiness. (*Lord, Increase Our Faith* [Salt Lake City: Bookcraft, 1994], 49)

Joseph B. Wirthlin:

The Father's plan gave us our agency to choose right or wrong, good or evil so we can learn, develop, and progress. As part of the plan, Jesus offered to atone for the sins of all mankind and bear the suffering for those sins, satisfying the law of justice, if the sinners repent. Otherwise, they have to suffer and pay the penalty for their transgressions. (*Finding Peace in Our Lives* [Salt Lake City: Deseret Book, 1995], 116)

Gordon B. Hinckley:

Reach out to bless others in all that you do, that, because of your efforts, someone may live a little closer to the Lord and have a little greater happiness in his or her life. That is the end of our existence, when all is said and done: to build happiness in the lives of people, because the thing we teach is the Lord's plan of happiness. (*Teachings of Gordon B. Hinckley* [Salt Lake City: Deseret Book, 1997], 255)

IDEAS FOR DAILY LIVING

Here are several ideas to help us understand and appreciate the plan of happiness and put it into practice in our daily lives:

1. The Father's plan should instill enduring gratitude in our hearts. Consider the unfolding of the Lord's blessings to us in a great panorama: the plan of happiness from premortal life, mortality with the opportunity to prove ourselves worthy, the Savior's Atonement that makes salvation possible through the grace of God, the glorious resurrection, and the reward of a degree of glory according to our faithfulness. All of this was designed for our welfare and happiness. Considering everything our Heavenly Father and Savior do for us that we might have immortality and eternal life should fill our hearts with gratitude and thanksgiving.

2. The Atonement is the center of the plan of happiness. The Savior's Atonement is the most important event in all of human history. Without the Atonement, the plan of happiness would be for naught, as we would be unable to return to the presence of our Heavenly Father (see Alma 11:37; 3 Ne. 27:19).

3. Obedience is crucial. In order for the plan of happiness to be efficacious in our lives, we must keep the laws and commandments upon which the blessings of the plan are predicated.

4. Sacrifice is required. The Lord asks us to offer to Him a broken heart and a contrite spirit (see 3 Ne. 9:20). In other words, we are to turn our full devotion to Him, recognizing our dependence on His mercy.

5. Remember that trials and tribulations are part of the plan. Opposition in all things is an eternal verity and is indispensable to our learning and progression (see 2 Ne. 2:13). This life is intended to be a test, a proving ground of our faith and obedience (see Abr. 3:25).

6. Temple blessings and vicarious service are essential. Part of the reason for temple work is to bring eternal blessings to other generations, that all will have the opportunity to participate in the fulness of the plan. Regular attendance at the temple will help us understand the plan and the blessings associated with it.

7. **Prayer and study help us accept Father's plan.** As we pray about and study gospel principles, we will come to understand and appreciate the plan of happiness. This acceptance will give us the desire to live the plan by keeping the Lord's commandments and serving others.

ILLUSTRATIONS FOR OUR TIMES

Often we make life more complicated than it has to be. The following is an experience of how one of the Lord's servants clarified and simplified in a very matter-of-fact way how the plan of happiness works in our lives.

Simple Truth

My wife was so pleased to accompany her friend to the stand where Ezra Taft Benson, then President of the Quorum of the Twelve, was receiving visitors. He had just spoken to a special gathering of Saints in the Washington, D.C. area, and my wife wanted her friend to meet him. This young woman had just that day—in the same stake center—been baptized a member of the Church, after many months of learning and being fellowshipped by my wife. So we stood in line waiting for our turn to meet Elder Benson. When we finally reached the place where the Apostle was standing, we greeted him, and then my wife introduced her friend as a new convert. He held the friend's hand and looked her straight in the eye. With a spirit of great kindness, but also soberness and firmness, he bore a simple testimony to her: "The gospel is true. If you live it, you will be happy. If you don't, you won't." What a rare blessing for a new convert to hear a personal witness from an Apostle of the Lord and receive such direct and penetrating counsel. My wife and I have spoken of this incident many times since, and the words echo in our minds and hearts as advice concerning this great plan set in order that all can benefit from: "If you live it, you will be happy. If you don't, you won't." And so it is.

—Richard J. Allen

SUMMARY

Heavenly Father's plan of happiness is His work and His glory, for it brings about the salvation of His children (see Moses 1:39). His Beloved Son, our Savior Jesus Christ, is the center of the plan. This divine and eternal plan embraces man's existence and his eternal destiny. Let us make it our lifelong goal to conform to the plan of happiness—even the teachings and guidance found in the gospel of Jesus Christ. Obedience to this plan will bring us eternal life, which is a state of never-ending joy and happiness (see Mosiah 2:41). Through scripture study, prayer, worship, temple attendance, and righteousness, we will come to understand the power of the plan of happiness in our lives.

PLANNING

Planning is an important aspect of the gospel. The gospel itself is God's plan for us—the "great plan of happiness" (Alma 42:8; see also Alma 12:25, 30; 34:9; 42:15). We have been commanded to plan, to "organize [our]selves; prepare every needful thing" (D&C 88:119). The old adage "If you fail to plan, you plan to fail" is true. Planning to complete our goals is a key step toward success. One cannot underestimate the power of preparation through proper planning. In the Church, family, school, and workplace, planning should be part of your everyday life. Vision and planning go hand in hand: without vision, planning is an exercise in futility; without planning, vision remains but a dream. Similarly, faith and planning go hand in hand: without faith, planning is impoverished; without planning, faith remains only belief. Where vision, planning, faith, and action interact consistently, goals and objectives are more readily attained.

THE SCRIPTURES TEACH US

Doctrine and Covenants 38:30. *But if ye are prepared ye shall not fear.*

Our planning and preparation will give us confidence in the Lord and confidence in His guidance and protection. We will be ready for whatever comes our way—good or bad.

Moses 6:62. *And now, behold, I say unto you: This is the plan of salvation unto all men, through the blood of mine Only Begotten, who shall come in the meridian of time.*

From before the foundation of the world, the Father and the Son planned every detail of the plan of happiness (see Alma 18:39). Central to this plan is the part the Savior plays in the infinite Atonement (see Alma 34:9). Similarly, we are to plan our lives in such a way that our families will have the maximum chance of achieving the goals of righteousness and exaltation.

Abraham 3:17. *And there is nothing that the Lord thy God shall take in his heart to do but what he will do it.*

Abraham Chapter 4 Preface. *The Gods plan the creation of the earth and all life thereon—Their plans for the six days of creation are set forth.*

We learn here that when Heavenly Father plans to do something, He does it. Our planning ought to follow that pattern of consistency and integrity.

MODERN PROPHETS SPEAK

Joseph B. Wirthlin:
> Most people manage their lives by crises. They are driven by external events and circumstances. As each problem arises, they focus on the problem. However, effective time managers are not problem-minded. They are opportunity-minded. They think preventably by using long-range planning. They set their priorities, organize themselves to accomplish these priorities, and then execute their tasks. In other words, they *prepare*, then *perform* their tasks to *improve* on their time. (*Finding Peace in Our Lives* [Salt Lake City: Deseret Book, 1995], 224)

Spencer W. Kimball:
> Such planning must begin early. It has been said that "even the very longest journey begins with a single first step." So when that first step is made it must be on a properly charted course. Otherwise, habits come upon us unawares, and sin has us in its clutches before we realize it.
>
> As well as establishing worthy goals, charting the course prevents one from living an unplanned, haphazard life—a tumbleweed existence. (*The Miracle of Forgiveness* [Salt Lake City: Bookcraft, 1969], 233–34)

IDEAS FOR DAILY LIVING

Here is a checklist of ten things to consider when you plan:

1. Be specific. Evaluate your situation and ask, "What are my objectives?" Make specific plans with immediate and long-term results specified, and set appropriate target dates. Time-management expert Alan Lakein counsels that "Planning is bringing the future into the present so that you can do something about it now."

2. Be flexible. Plan from the outset to be resilient, flexible, accommodating, and willing to adjust as you go—firmness of purpose is essential, but rigidity of process is a mistake.

3. Strive for balance. Plan with balance in mind, including personal, family, professional, and community service, plus spiritual goals.

4. Look for a chain of successes. Plan for now, not just the distant future. Plan for milestones along the way, starting with today. Plan for a chain of small successes that add up to a superhighway of achievement.

5. Be cooperative. Plan as a team. The people who are affected by important decisions you make need to be involved in the planning process. Be sure that all who are part of the planning process understand your goals. In planning sessions with groups, involve everybody, delegate properly, have adequate accountability, and then follow through.

6. Focus on the benefits. Plan to accomplish your end goals and benefit from the positive consequences. Plan to reap the harvest of hard work and effort. Planning is fun if you keep the rewards in mind.

7. Chart it out. Plan in writing, preferably with a chart that makes details, relationships, and timelines clear.

8. Review often. Plan to review your plan frequently in order to keep it dynamic and alive. Abraham Lincoln confirmed: "We must ask where we are and whither we are tending." Remember that planning is a process, not an event.

9. Back it up with resources. Put teeth in your plan by arranging to provide adequate knowledge, training, and resources to assure success.

10. Teach others to plan. Remember that planning is a function of leadership, so teach your children and dependents how to plan. Their world needs planning and organizing just like yours does. The home is the perfect schoolhouse for teaching correct principles of planning. Family home evening and family councils provide a wonderful forum for teaching planning skills and following through with tasks and assignments.

ILLUSTRATIONS FOR OUR TIMES

This story shows what can occur when we fail to plan, and how this applies to our goal to achieve eternal life.

The New Testament Came Very Forcefully to My Mind

> One morning as I made a tour through the northern part of our fair city, I went down a street which I had not traveled before. Lo and behold! there was under construction one of the finest

looking homes I had ever seen! This house struck my fancy because it was almost identical to a plan which my wife had hoped that we would one day build. Working for the Church, we realized it would not be possible, but we dreamed about it.

I found myself, more often than not, going that way just to see the progress of the home that was not even mine. I am sure you do things like this in your own way. A month or two had gone by; and as the house was about two-thirds completed, one morning as I passed that way I noticed that the workmen had ceased their labors. No work was being accomplished.

The days grew into weeks. The thing that gave me the most concern, as I am sure it did the owner, was that the once bright, shiny, new lumber was now starting to fade because it was not yet painted. It turned first to a light brown, a darker brown, and then to kind of an off-yellowish, indicating that the deterioration process had set in. I thought, as I made one of my frequent trips by that way, how unfortunate more insight and vision hadn't gone into the planning.

Then, one morning as I passed by to see if there had been any progress, one of the eternal truths of the New Testament came very forcefully to my mind as I viewed the situation. It is one I am sure you are familiar with. We all have read it many times in New Testament courses and studies. Luke records it this way. He tells about an incident in the life of the Savior when a great multitude gathered, and as they frequently did, commenced to ask questions in an attempt to trap him. In this particular setting the Savior makes a very profound observation, so profound that it is just as applicable here today as it was in the time in which he uttered it. He said, as he turned to meet the multitude:

> For which of you, intending to build a tower, sitteth not down first, and counteth the cost, whether he have sufficient to finish it?

> Lest haply, after he hath laid the foundation, and is not able to finish it, all that behold it begin to mock him,

> Saying, This man began to build, and was not able to finish.

Then he goes on to suggest another possibility:

> Or what king, going to make war against another king, sitteth not down first, and consulteth whether he be able with ten thousand to meet him that cometh against him with twenty thousand? (Luke 14:28–31.)

Now his logic here makes pretty good sense, doesn't it?

We could make application to the tower the Savior refers to as it might apply to eternal life. We can say, in essence, "For which of us, intending to build eternal lives, sitteth not down first and consulteth whether we will have sufficient to complete the task?" The process of educating the body, the mind, and the spirit is the foundation on which this can be achieved. (Paul H. Dunn, as quoted in *Outstanding Stories by General Authorities* [Salt Lake City: Deseret Book, 1971], 2:122–124)

SUMMARY

In planning, it is always prudent to examine the costs involved in any worthwhile project—time, money, resources, and people. An architect is the perfect example of a planner, for without his or her plans, there will be no structure or finished product. In any situation, one can usually tell when poor planning has occurred: there are many observable faults within the project. Obviously, it would be good for all of us to consider our lives and plan for a better tomorrow. The ultimate model in such planning is the Lord, who has shared with us the essential points of doctrine having to do with His incomparable plan of happiness: "And the great God has had mercy on us, and made these things known unto us that we might not perish; yea, and he has made these things known unto us beforehand, because he loveth our souls as well as he loveth our children; therefore, in his mercy he doth visit us by his angels, that the plan of salvation might be made known unto us as well as unto future generations" (Alma 24:14). With an eternal model of planning communicated to us in such clarity, we have the prototype for all our myriad projects and undertakings. Above all, let us ensure that our own planning remains in alignment with the principles of honor and truth reflected by our Maker in His timeless designs for our good.

PRAISE

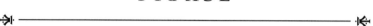

Some of the greatest blessings in life lie in the expression of approval for something someone else has done. People need approval. People need to feel accepted. People need to know they are all right. People need to know that they are of worth and can do meaningful things. Genuine praise and encouragement become some of the greatest motivating tools in the world. Let us say something good about our family, friends, and coworkers. It will bless our lives as well as theirs. If we are in a leadership position, we should praise, instruct, and then encourage. We will have a better relationship and all involved will find joy in the work.

THE SCRIPTURES TEACH US

Psalms 9:1–2. *I will praise thee, O Lord, with my whole heart; I will shew forth all thy marvellous works. I will be glad and rejoice in thee: I will sing praise to thy name, O thou most High.*

For all the good that we have and do in life, the glory belongs to God. In all our praising we should always praise and thank God for His goodness and mercy towards us.

Matthew 25:21. *His lord said unto him, Well done, thou good and faithful servant: thou hast been faithful over a few things, I will make thee ruler over many things: enter thou into the joy of thy lord.*

In the Savior's parable we catch a glimpse of the grand feelings of satisfaction we will experience if we can endure to the end in valor and righteousness, being at last welcomed by the Lord and Master with acceptance and rejoicing. In smaller but still significant measure, we can lift up and encourage others along the highways and byways of life by recognizing their good desires and efforts frequently and praising them with sincerity and genuine respect.

MODERN PROPHETS SPEAK

Howard W. Hunter:

> We enjoy life when we have the ability to praise others for their good works. George Matthew Adams said: "He who praises another, enriches himself more than he does the one praised. To praise is an investment in happiness. The poorest human being has something to give that the richest cannot buy." (*BYU Speeches of the Year*, 1961, 3)

Neal A. Maxwell:

> So often we can serve by bathing the wounded and bruised egos of others in the warm waters of deserved commendation. (*The Neal A. Maxwell Quote Book,* ed. Cory H. Maxwell [Salt Lake City: Bookcraft, 1997], 260)

Gordon B. Hinckley:

> We have such an obligation to those who are baptized into the Church. We cannot neglect them. We cannot leave them to stand alone. They need help as they become accustomed to the ways and culture of this Church. And it is our great blessing and opportunity to afford that help. . . . A warm smile, a friendly handshake, an encouraging word will do wonders. ("Inspirational Thoughts," *Ensign,* October 2003, 3)

IDEAS FOR DAILY LIVING

Consider the following five points when offering praise:

1. When

- *Do it without delay*—Procrastinated praise or delayed encouragement loses its power. Do it in a timely manner, while it is still fresh in your mind.
- *Each day*—Praise or encourage someone honestly and openly every day. Do it regularly. Make it a habit.

2. How

- *Be specific*—Identify the precise behavior or result that has elicited your appreciation, and refer to it directly.
- *Do it with enthusiasm*—It's not always what you say, but how you say it, that conveys the true feelings.
- *Be genuine*—True praise is never maudlin or affected in any way, but is always sincere and honest.
- *Use variety*—Spoken words are effective, but there are other ways that can work just as well: an appropriate small gift, a related news clipping, an e-mail message, or a favor returned—all of these can be effective. Write a complimentary note whenever possible to family, friends, and coworkers.
- *With gratitude*—Remember to receive praise from others with graciousness and appreciation. Don't turn it back, but accept it as a genuine gift.

3. What. Praise small things, not just great achievements. Praise improvements and courage for other efforts.

4. Where. Don't hesitate to do it in public, as long as it doesn't embarrass the person. "Advise your friends in private, but praise them openly" (Publilius Syrus).

5. Who

- *Your spouse*—We often forget to give encouragement to the one closest to us. Don't take the ones so dear for granted.
- *Especially children*—Remember that children grow and improve much faster with praise than criticism.
- *Even your "enemies"*—There is good in everyone. It will amaze you, oftentimes, what effect genuine praise—direct or indirect—will have on those you consider not entirely your friends.
- *Everyone*—Do it to strangers as well as friends. Look for something good about everyone you come in contact with.
- *Don't forget Heavenly Father*—Let God, "from whom all blessings flow," also have your daily praise and thanks.

ILLUSTRATIONS FOR OUR TIMES

Give Vision and Encouragement

Some years ago I was near our front gate splitting rails for a fence. A young man came to make a delivery. He had recently returned from overseas combat duty. He had falsified his age and left school to join the Marines. When I asked about his future plans, he didn't know. Jobs were scarce; he had no skills to offer.

I counseled him to go back to high school and get his diploma. He thought he couldn't do that; he was too old now. "If you do it," I told him, "you probably will not exactly fit in. And the students will call you the 'old man' or 'grandpa.' But you faced an enemy in combat; surely you've got the courage to face that."

The lesson is this: I only spent ten minutes with him, sitting on a log by our front gate. I did not build a school or ask the Church to build one. I did not pay his tuition or prepare his lessons. What he needed was some direction, some counsel, some encouragement, and some vision. In this case he took the counsel and returned to school. Now he has a family and an occupation.

I only gave him the vision and encouragement. It does not take additional Church budget to do that. That is the responsible role of every priesthood leader in counseling members on careers. We must help people to help themselves. (Boyd K. Packer, *Memorable Stories with a Message,* [Salt Lake City: Deseret Book, 2000], 34–35)

SUMMARY

Honest and genuine praise and encouragement can change the soul. Thanksgiving and gratitude expressed bring so much joy to the receiver as well as the giver. As you look to see good in others, you will live the thirteenth Article of Faith. We surely should seek after praiseworthy things and bring joy to others as we practice the principle of praise and encouragement.

PRAYER

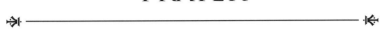

Prayer is truly the yearning of the soul to reach God. Sincere prayer reaches to the heavens and is often a two-way communication between us and Heavenly Father. A passage from the Bible Dictionary explains prayer as follows:

> As soon as we learn the true relationship in which we stand toward God . . . then at once prayer becomes natural and instinctive on our part (Matt. 7:7–11). Many of the so-called difficulties about prayer arise from forgetting this relationship. Prayer is the act by which the will of the Father and the will of the child are brought into correspondence with each other. The object of prayer is not to change the will of God, but to secure for ourselves and for others blessings that God is already willing to grant, but that are made conditional on our asking for them. . . . Prayer is a form of work, and is an appointed means for obtaining the highest of all blessings. (Bible Dictionary, "Prayer," 752–53)

We are strengthened by prayer, we worship through it, and we receive instructions from it. Alfred Lord Tennyson observed: "More things are wrought by prayer than this world dreams of." Confirmed President Gordon B. Hinckley: "Heavenly Father . . . has invited [all] to come unto Him in prayer, to speak with Him, with the promised assurance that He will hear and respond" (*Teachings of Gordon B. Hinckley*, [Salt Lake City: Deseret Book, 1997] 238).

To make our prayers more efficacious, we should pray often and regularly, with real intent and faith, willing to accept the Lord's will, and willing to do our part.

THE SCRIPTURES TEACH US

James 1:5–6. *If any of you lack wisdom, let him ask of God, that giveth to all men liberally, and upbraideth not; and it shall be given him. But let him ask in faith, nothing wavering. For he that wavereth is like a wave of the sea driven with the wind and tossed.*

Heavenly Father will freely give wisdom—with no condemnation—to His children as they ask. He wants us to ask. We must pray in humility and in faith, as did the Prophet Joseph Smith.

2 Nephi 32:9. *But behold, I say unto you that ye must pray always, and not faint; that ye must not perform any thing unto the Lord save in the first place ye shall pray unto the Father in the name of Christ, that he will consecrate thy performance unto thee, that thy performance may be for the welfare of thy soul.*

Prayer is not just a single moment when we are on our knees. It is an attitude of humility and submission to God. The Lord commands us to pray always, either on our knees or in our hearts. This continual communication with God draws us close to Him, shielding and fortifying us against temptation. This is why Satan tries to teach us not to pray, while the Spirit teaches us we must pray (see 2 Ne. 32:8).

Alma 13:28. *Humble yourselves before the Lord, and call on his holy name, and watch and pray continually, that ye may not be tempted above that which ye can bear, and thus be led by the Holy Spirit, becoming humble, meek, submissive, patient, full of love and all long-suffering.*

Prayer should be continual and consistent. It offends our Heavenly Father if we don't pray (see Ether 2:14). Through prayer, we can gain the power to overcome and avoid temptation (see 3 Ne. 18:18). Frequent prayer will ensure us the Holy Spirit's guidance in our lives (see 3 Ne. 19:9; D&C 42:14).

Alma 17:3. *But this is not all; they had given themselves to much prayer, and fasting; therefore they had the spirit of prophecy, and the spirit of revelation, and when they taught, they taught with power and authority of God.*

The blessings of prayer and fasting can empower us to do all things. We can teach with the power and authority of God, seek forgiveness of sins (see Enos 1:4), gain knowledge of the truth (see Alma 5:46), help people who do not know God (see Alma 6:6), and bless others through our righteous prayers (see Mosiah 27:14; Alma 10:23). Through prayer, we can also counsel with the Lord and receive direction from Him (see Alma 37:37), become stronger in our humility and firmer in our faith (see Hel. 3:35), and receive the blessing of charity (see Moro. 7:48).

MODERN PROPHETS SPEAK

Gordon B. Hinckley:

> Be prayerful. You can't do it alone. You know that. You cannot make it alone and do your best. You need the help of the Lord . . . and the marvelous thing is that you have the opportunity to pray, with the expectation that your prayers will be heard and answered. . . . The marvelous thing about prayer is that it is personal, it's individual, it's something that no one else gets into, in terms of your speaking with your Father in Heaven in the name of the Lord Jesus Christ. Be prayerful. Ask the Lord to forgive your sins. Ask the Lord for help. Ask the Lord to bless you. Ask the Lord to help you realize your righteous ambitions. . . . Ask the Lord for all of the important things that mean so much to you in your lives. He stands ready to help. Don't ever forget it. (*Teachings of Gordon B. Hinckley* [Salt Lake City: Deseret Book, 1997], 468)

Ezra Taft Benson:

> Prayer will bring solace and comfort. It has healed sickness, comforted those distressed, and has continued the faithful in paths of righteousness. The value of a man is evidenced in part by the dust on his knees. His willingness to believe in and accept a being greater than himself as evidenced by his prayer has increased his moral stature, refined his understanding, and has brought him along the road of his eternal development. Our great example in prayer is our Lord and Master Jesus Christ who knew that only through constant supplication and obedience would God the Father manifest His will and release the power for its attainment through man. Truly there is power in prayer. (*The Teachings of Ezra Taft Benson* [Salt Lake City: Bookcraft, 1988], 422)

Harold B. Lee:

> The four essentials that the missionaries teach to one who has never prayed before are: he first must thank; he next must ask; he must do it in the name of Jesus Christ; and then he must conclude it with amen. And with that simple instruction the beginning inquirer after truth is taught to pray. In praying, he is enjoined as the father said to his son, after listening to his son's prayers, "Son, don't give the Lord instructions. You just report for duty." (*The Teachings of Harold B. Lee*, ed. Clyde J. Williams [Salt Lake City: Bookcraft, 1996], 126)

IDEAS FOR DAILY LIVING

Here are five ideas to help us with our prayers:

1. Prayer can have many forms.

- *Choose what is appropriate for the needs of the occasion*—Note the rich variety of prayers: As thoughts or as words, silent and within or spoken and audible, expressed alone or as part of a group, as feelings and yearnings or as established patterns of communication, even as song (see D&C 25:12). There are as many kinds of prayer as there are individuals and circumstances.
- *Consider what is most important*—There are many important aspects of prayer—the manner, the language, the appropriate form. But the most important thing is for the prayer to be sincere and genuine.

2. Prayer operates on specific, enduring principles. Some of the key principles of prayer are: vision, love, gratitude, humility, faith, and patience.

- *Vision*—Allow your vision to open up fully. See yourself not as an isolated, alienated being in the darkness, but as a child of God in a divine relationship governed by light and love. Know that He cares and will answer your prayers.
- *Love*—Allow love to take over your soul: love for God, love for the creation and plan of happiness, love for the potential within you planted there by God, and love for family and friends.
- *Gratitude*—Allow gratitude to supplant any feelings of selfishness or envy, anger, or pride. Always express your gratitude to Heavenly Father on a daily basis.
- *Humility*—Allow humility to take root in your soul—a willingness to accept the will of God and see opportunity in adversity, purpose in trials, and meaning in suffering and sacrifice. Let dependence on His higher will replace the self-sufficiency that so often turns to arrogance and ego-driven desires in mortals. Come before God with a broken heart and a contrite spirit: "The Lord is nigh unto them that are of a broken heart; and saveth such as be of a contrite spirit" (Ps. 34:18).
- *Faith*—Allow faith to unfold within you; allow the hope for worthy things to develop even though you cannot see them at present. Remember that exercising faith is essential to efficacious prayers.
- *Patience*—Allow patience to temper impetuous insistence on immediate solutions. Let the peace of patience comfort you.

3. There are simple ways to magnify the power of prayer.

- *Pray frequently*—Remember daily personal and family prayers. Regardless of how inadequate or seemingly unworthy you feel, *always pray*. Be as worthy as possible—but always pray. Satan would encourage you not to pray (see 2 Ne. 32:8).
- *Be prepared*—Always do your part. If you pray for solutions, first study things out in your mind and come to a conclusion and then take it to the Lord. Listen for confirmation or the urge to seek further (see D&C 9:7–9).
- *Focus on others, not always on yourself*—Always pray for the welfare of others (see Alma 6:6).
- *Consider attitude*—The proper attitude of prayer is a broken heart, a contrite spirit, real intent, the exercise of hope and faith, and knowing that a loving Heavenly Father is waiting to bless your life.
- *Seek unity*—In a group setting, it enhances the feelings of accord and unity if the participants respond to the prayer of the spokesperson by echoing the word *amen* at the end. The word *amen* (with similar-sounding Greek, Latin, and Hebrew roots) means "truly" and suggests "may it become true" or "so be it."

4. Prayer and wisdom go hand in hand.

- *Pray for the right kinds of things*—Be wise in your requests. Don't ask for unrighteous things or merely your desires of the moment. Ask for things that matter most: wisdom, understanding, health and strength, power to do good, and the well-being of loved ones. Pray for strength rather than to have a challenging situation change or disappear. The Lord will give you strength to overcome all things as you act in faith.
- *Ask forgiveness*—Make prayer an opportunity to humbly express your weaknesses before the Lord, asking His forgiveness and His blessing that you may do better in the future. Thomas Guthrie put it this way: "Unless your prayers stop your sins, your sins will stop your prayers."
- *Be thankful*—Always give credit to God for all your blessings. Wisdom knows that all good flows from God.

5. Prayer is a gift to your family.

- *Teach children how to pray*—Teach prayer by example within the family circle. Pray as a family frequently. Pray to bless the food at mealtime. Pray as you arise in the morning and as you retire in the evening. Express love for your spouse and children during prayer.
- *Give guidance early on*—Give suggestions to very young children to help them feel their way through the patterns of prayer. In most cases, prayer comes very naturally to children, and they will have a spontaneous and beautiful way of expressing themselves before God. Praise them sincerely for their prayers. In fact, learn from your children: "little children do have words given unto them many times, which confound the wise and the learned" (Alma 32:23).
- *Show leadership*—Often the momentum within a family is toward action and carrying out the hurried tasks of the day. Remember to pause for prayer. You can teach compelling lessons in harmony, peace, and service if you step forward and say, "Let's take time to have our prayer before we continue."

ILLUSTRATIONS FOR OUR TIMES

In this story told by Lucy Mack Smith, her fervent prayers helped preserve the lives of her sons Joseph and Hyrum.

Faith and Prayers of a Mother

On the first of August [1834], Joseph and Hyrum returned [from Zion's Camp]. They were overjoyed to meet us again in health, more especially on account of the perils which they had passed through during their absence. Joseph and Hyrum sat down beside me, each holding one of my hands in his, while they related the following story:

"When we started on our journey, we made arrangements to have everyone made as comfortable as possible; but the sufferings which are incident to such an excursion made some of the brethren discontented, and they began to murmur against us, saying, The Lord never required them to take such a tiresome journey, and that it was folly for them to suffer such fatigue and inconvenience just to gratify us. We warned them, in the name of the Lord, to stop their murmuring; for, if they did not, the displeasure of the Almighty would be manifested in judgments in their midst. But many of them paid no attention to what we said, until one morning when they went out to harness up their horses, and found them all so lame as to be unable to travel. We then told them that this was a curse which had come upon them because of transgression; but, if they would repent, it might be removed—if not, a greater curse would come upon them. They believed what we said and repented of their folly. . . . It was not long, however, till the spirit of dissension arose again. . . .

"Soon after arriving at the point of destination, the cholera broke out in our midst; the brethren were so violently attacked that it seemed impossible to render them any assistance. They immediately sent for us to lay hands on them, but we soon discovered that this, also, was a judgment from the Almighty; for, when we laid our hands upon them, in the name of the Lord, the disease immediately fastened itself upon us and in a few minutes we were in awful agony. We made signals to each other . . . in order to join in prayer to God that he would deliver us from this dreadful influence. . . . We were hardly able to stand upon our feet, and we feared that we should die in that western wilderness without the privilege of blessing our children, or giving them one word of parting counsel. We . . . fell upon our knees and cried unto the Lord that he would deliver us from this awful calamity, but we arose worse than before. We kneeled down the second time, and when we commenced praying the cramp seized us, gathering the cords in our arms and legs in bunches and operating equally severe throughout our system. We still besought the Lord, with all our strength, to have mercy upon us, but all in vain. It seemed as though the heavens were sealed against us. . . . We then kneeled down the third time, concluding never to rise to our feet again until one or the other should get a testimony that we should be healed; and that the one who should get the first intimation of the same from the Spirit, should make it known to the other."

They stated further, that after praying some time the cramp began to release its hold; and, in a short time, Hyrum sprang to his feet and exclaimed, "Joseph, we shall return to our families. I have had an open vision, in which I saw mother kneeling under an apple tree; and she is even now asking God, in tears, to spare our lives, that she may again behold us in the flesh. The Spirit testifies, that her prayers, united with ours, will be answered."

"Oh, my mother!" said Joseph, "how often have your prayers been the means of assisting us when the shadows of death encompassed us." (Lucy Mack Smith, as quoted in *Best-Loved Stories of the LDS People,* eds. Jack M. Lyon, Linda Ririe Gundry, and Jay A. Parry [Salt Lake City: Deseret Book, 1997], 132)

* * *

This family story demonstrates the power of a prayer offered in a child's simple faith.

The Needle

As parents we had always prayed together as a family and encouraged our children to pray for all things—for help and in gratitude. Karie Lyn, our oldest daughter, was six years old and wanted to sew with a needle and thread with her friend Cindy. My sweetheart, Pat, had suggested that if they played with a needle and thread they must be careful, because Karie's little sister, Kristi, was playing in the same room and was learning to crawl. Karie continued to plead, so finally Pat relented and warned them to be very careful, because if Kristi swallowed the needle it would be horrible.

They were excited and began to sew. As fate would have it, within a minute the tiny needle was lost. Karie Lyn was panicked. She quickly went to her bedroom and pleaded with the Lord, "Please help me find the needle." Hurrying back to the sewing area, she and Cindy began to search. Her prayer was answered—

through another, as the Lord often does. Cindy exclaimed, "I've found it! I've found it!" Joy was felt—the needle and thread and material were returned to Mother, and Karie went directly to her bedroom and offered a prayer of gratitude. Yes, prayers are answered; even the simplest and smallest prayers are important to Heavenly Father.

—Ed J. Pinegar

SUMMARY

Obviously, there will be times when we don't receive the answers to prayer that we anticipate. We don't always receive the immediate or long-lasting relief that we seek. Patience and long-suffering are part of the growth process of our earthly existence. Recognizing this is a key part of prayer. We must also come to realize that we are always receiving blessings from God—though we may not always have the discernment to see them. The time will come when we will understand all things (see Alma 12:10–11; D&C 121:26–32); meanwhile, let us make prayer an enduring part of our lives. Abraham Lincoln said: "I have been driven many times to my knees by the overwhelming conviction that I had nowhere else to go. My own wisdom, and that of all about me, seemed insufficient for the day." When we pray, we will gain wisdom, our lives will be enriched, and we will have greater power to do good.

PRIDE

Pride, the universal sin, is at the crux of almost every other sin. Pride is expressed in arrogance, haughtiness, self-love, vanity, and egotism. Because pride involves man setting his will against God's, it creates enmity between God and man. The sin of pride is directly opposed to the Christlike quality of humility. In the Book of Mormon, pride was the downfall of the Jaredite and Nephite peoples, and pride can be our downfall as well if we are not careful. Prideful thoughts are so powerful that they can lead to sinful thoughts and behavior, such as selfishness, greed, lust, jealousy, power-seeking, envy, and a whole host of related sins. This is why the Lord continually counsels us against pride (see Prov. 16:18; D&C 23:1).

THE SCRIPTURES TEACH US

James 4:6. *Wherefore he saith, God resisteth the proud, but giveth grace unto the humble.*

Pride separates us from God. If we exercise humility, the opposite of pride, our lives will be enhanced through the mercy and kindness of God. Through the grace of the Lord, we can do all things (see Alma 26:11–12).

1 Nephi 11:36. *And it came to pass that I saw and bear record, that the great and spacious building was the pride of the world; and it fell, and the fall thereof was exceedingly great. And the angel of the Lord spake unto me again, saying: Thus shall be the destruction of all nations, kindreds, tongues, and people, that shall fight against the twelve apostles of the Lamb.*

As the spacious building in Lehi's dream had no foundation, those who separate themselves from God have no foundation. They are left to themselves, and their pride will be their downfall, for they will receive no strength from God in pride.

2 Nephi 9:28–29. *O that cunning plan of the evil one! O the vainness, and the frailties, and the foolishness of men! When they are learned they think they are wise, and they hearken not unto the counsel of God, for they set it aside, supposing they know of themselves, wherefore, their wisdom is foolishness and it profiteth them not. And they shall perish. But to be learned is good if they hearken unto the counsels of God.*

When we become learned in the things of the world, the egotism of self-sufficiency can develop in our hearts. The punishment for such haughtiness, such disregard for our need of the Lord, is severe (see 2 Ne. 28:15). Knowledge we gain is of worth only when we listen to and counsel with the Lord (see Jacob 4:10).

Jacob 2:16. *O that he would rid you from this iniquity and abomination. And, O that ye would listen unto the word of his commands, and let not this pride of your hearts destroy your souls!*

Pride has destroyed great nations, and it can destroy us as individuals. Remember that pride separates us from God and leads us to a multitude of sins. Most sins begin with some form of pride (see Alma 1:32).

3 Nephi 25:1. *For behold, the day cometh that shall burn as an oven; and all the proud, yea, and all that do wickedly, shall be stubble; and the day that cometh shall burn them up, saith the Lord of Hosts, that it shall leave them neither root nor branch.*

Being prideful carries with it consequences and resulting punishments. We cannot take lightly the sin of pride.

4 Nephi 1:24. *And now, in this two hundred and first year there began to be among them those who were lifted up in pride, such as the wearing of costly apparel, and all manner of fine pearls, and of the fine things of the world.*

Following the advent of the Savior in the New World, there ensued a period of several generations where the people were of one heart and one mind, living in love and harmony according to the Savior's teachings. But the first instance of the breaking of this pattern of obedience was the introduction, once again, of pride. A small incursion of pride eventually led to the downfall of an entire nation. Pride is the poison that can dissipate charity and righteousness to the destruction of millions of lives.

Doctrine and Covenants 121:37. *That they may be conferred upon us, it is true; but when we undertake to cover our sins, or to gratify our pride, our vain ambition, or to exercise control or dominion or compulsion upon the souls of the children of men, in any degree of unrighteousness, behold, the heavens withdraw themselves; the Spirit of the Lord is grieved; and when it is withdrawn, Amen to the priesthood or the authority of that man.*

Any form of prideful behavior can be our downfall as it relates to the exercise of the priesthood. The priesthood is not given to us as a means of lifting ourselves above others. We must be humble before the Lord, depend upon Him, and recognize that He is the source of all power.

MODERN PROPHETS SPEAK

Ezra Taft Benson:

> In the scriptures there is no such thing as righteous pride. It is always considered as a sin. We are not speaking of a wholesome view of self-worth, which is best established by a close relationship with God. But we are speaking of pride as the universal sin, as someone has described it. Mormon writes that "the pride of this nation, or the people of the Nephites, hath proven their destruction" (Moroni 8:27). The Lord says in the Doctrine and Covenants, "Beware of pride, lest ye become

as the Nephites of old" (D&C 38:39). Essentially, pride is a "my will" rather than "thy will" approach to life. The opposite of pride is humbleness, meekness, submissiveness, or teachableness (see Alma 13:28). . . .

Pride does not look up to God and care about what is right. It looks sideways to man and argues who is right. Pride is manifest in the spirit of contention. Was it not through pride that the devil became the devil? Christ wanted to serve. The devil wanted to rule. Christ wanted to bring men to where He was. The devil wanted to be above men. Christ removed self as the force in His perfect life. It was not my will, but thine be done (see Mark 14:36; Luke 22:42).

Pride is characterized by "What do I want out of life?" rather than by "What would God have me do with my life?" It is self-will as opposed to God's will. It is the fear of man over the fear of God. (*The Teachings of Ezra Taft Benson* [Salt Lake City: Bookcraft, 1988], 435)

Pride is a sin that can readily be seen in others but rarely admitted in ourselves. . . . It is manifest in so many ways, such as faultfinding, gossiping, backbiting, murmuring, living beyond our means, envying, coveting, withholding gratitude and praise that might lift another, and being unforgiving and jealous. . . .

Pride affects all of us at various times and in various degrees. . . .

Pride is the universal sin, the great vice.

The antidote for pride is humility—meekness, submissiveness.

We can choose to humble ourselves by conquering enmity towards our brothers and sisters, . . . by receiving counsel and chastisement, . . . by forgiving those who have offended us, . . . by rendering selfless service, . . . by going on missions and preaching the word that can humble others, . . . by getting to the temple more frequently, . . . [and] by confessing and forsaking sins and being born of God.

Pride is the great stumbling block to Zion. ("Beware of Pride," *Ensign*, May 1989, 4)

Gordon B. Hinckley:
> And so I repeat, do not let pride stand in your way. The way of the gospel is a simple way. Some of the requirements may appear to you as elementary and unnecessary. Do not spurn them. Humble yourself and walk in obedience. I promise that the results that follow will be marvelous to behold and satisfying to experience. (*Be Thou an Example* [Salt Lake City: Deseret Book, 1981], 68)

Dallin H. Oaks:
> Humility is the opposite of and the antidote for the pride of self-satisfaction. To counter pride we need to cultivate humility. . . . The pride of comparison is also a matter of attitude. It is also rooted in pre-occupation with self. One antidote for that preoccupation is service. Service to others swings our spotlight of priorities outward, away from ourselves. To counter pride we need to give unselfish service.

> The prophet Jacob prescribed another remedy, a thought and an action that can be taken by those afflicted with the pride of comparison because of their riches: "Think of your brethren

like unto yourselves, and be familiar with all and free with your substance, that they may be rich like unto you" (Jacob 2:17). To counter this kind of pride we need to be "familiar with all and free with [our] substance."

Differences in knowledge, prominence, or position can also be sources of the pride of comparison. The prophet Alma describes how those Nephites who were "steadfast and immovable in keeping the commandments of God" resisted this kind of pride. . . .

"And . . . the priest, not esteeming himself above his hearers, for the preacher was no better than the hearer, neither was the teacher any better than the learner; and thus they were all equal, and they did all labor, every man according to his strength." (Alma 1:26.)

No matter how prominent or praised, the preacher is no better than the hearer, the teacher is no better than the learner. To avoid pride, preachers and teachers and others in prominent positions must struggle not to esteem themselves above their hearers. (*Pure in Heart* [Salt Lake City: Bookcraft, 1988], 144)

IDEAS FOR DAILY LIVING

Here are four ideas to help us overcome pride:

1. Tune our attitudes to the Spirit.
- *Listen for warning signs*—The Spirit will guide us away from the temptation to assume a vertical relationship toward others (as if we were somehow superior) and remind us, as King Benjamin did, that we are truly nothing without the Lord and His goodness and strength: ". . . I would that ye should remember, and always retain in remembrance, the greatness of God, and your own nothingness, and his goodness and long-suffering towards you, unworthy creatures, and humble yourselves even in the depths of humility, calling on the name of the Lord daily, and standing steadfastly in the faith of that which is to come, which was spoken by the mouth of the angel" (Mosiah 4:11).
- *Cultivate gratitude*—A worthy antidote to pride is a sense of gratitude toward the Lord for His blessings. Count your blessings; write them into your journal. Dismiss pride and a feeling of self-sufficiency before the Lord.
- *Let charity abound in our minds and thoughts*—When we keep charity at the forefront of our hearts and minds, we have little room left for prideful interests and thoughts.

2. Set up a system of regular defenses.
- *Pray for protection against pride*—Infuse daily prayers with an invocation to the Lord that He help us cleanse our souls of pride and our daily walk of any semblance of haughtiness or arrogance. Praying for humility and meekness is a noble antidote to pride.
- *Cultivate modesty*—How we comport ourselves in daily life, how we dress, how we manage our surroundings—these are opportunities to practice humility and put the brakes to conceit and ego-centered habits.
- *Read the word of God*—Daily scripture study is a powerful remedy for the effects of pride. The word of God renews our perspective of how we fit into the grand design of the Lord's plan of salvation: Pondering the scriptures prayerfully kindles a sense of humility about self and love of, and dependence on, God.

- *Pay tithes and offerings*—What a splendid reminder of the fact that everything we have comes from God as a gift to us. Let us have joy in returning that portion to Him that He asks of us to support the cause of building the kingdom.
- *Visit the temple often*—The sacred precincts of the Lord's house offer the world's greatest instruction in humility, meekness, and love unfeigned. Pride is literally purged from our being as we participate worthily in temple service.

3. Serve with devotion.
- *Focus on the family*—When we immerse ourselves in devoted family service, practicing unselfish love toward our spouse, our children, our grandchildren, and our extended family—giving of our ourselves: our time, our listening ear, our talents, our counsel—there is little time for pride to creep in.
- *Magnify Church callings*—What a grand opportunity for humble service is afforded by our callings. Let us learn our duty in all diligence and humbly give ourselves to the Lord to be instruments in His hands for much good. Pride has no place in an environment of devoted service.
- *Serve in the community*—Our neighbors and our communities need our service as well. Often such opportunities can be accomplished quietly in the background, even anonymously. Sometimes we can step forward in leadership roles to serve our fellows, but always by cultivating teamwork and promoting worthy causes, never for self-aggrandizement.

4. Embrace humility as a way of life. (See *Humility* for detailed steps on how to apply each of the following principles.)
- *Humility is the beginning of spirituality*—Recognizing our own nothingness before the Lord is where we begin our worship and dependence on Him (see Mosiah 2:20–25).
- *Humility is a quality of strength*—Sometimes it takes more strength of character to be meek (see 3 Ne. 12:5).
- *Humility belongs in the family, in the workplace, in society*—When we begin to lift ourselves above others, we plant the seeds of contention and strife. Humility is the basis of genuine service and charity, a quality that cannot exist with pride.

ILLUSTRATIONS FOR OUR TIMES

Apostle Marvin J. Ashton counsels us to remember that all of our blessings come from our Heavenly Father, and that we should be grateful, not boastful.

Neither Boast of Faith Nor of Mighty Works

> Our Savior, Jesus Christ, to whose Church we belong, would be disappointed if we ever created the impression that the efforts and the hard work put forth to build his kingdom were based only on the wisdom and power of man.
>
> Recently during a special women's conference, a speaker told about how he'd been quite successful in land development and how everything he'd touched had turned to gold. He'd also tried to live a faithful life and had been a very active servant in the gospel. Then he'd been called as a mission president. He had apparently been a very effective mission president and had subsequently returned to his home state. Throughout his life he'd experienced one success after another—he was a recognized leader in his community, had built a prosperous business. Being called as a mission president had sort of cemented in his mind that he'd "made it"—that he was an all-around success.

When he returned from his mission, a combination of changing interest rates and other business factors caused his once-prosperous business to plummet. In fact, he'd lost nearly everything. Telling the story, this man said, "I realized that I'd become quite boastful—that while I felt I had a testimony of Jesus Christ, in my mind I had brought about all of these wonderful things through my hard work, intelligence, and so forth. But when hard times hit, I began to realize how offensive I must have been to others and to my Heavenly Father to assume that I had brought all of these good things on my own. I felt like I'd lived a life of arrogance and boasting."

Helaman's advice to his sons, Nephi and Lehi, can give us strength today:

"Therefore, my sons, I would that ye should do that which is good. . . .

"And now my sons, behold I have somewhat more to desire of you, which desire is, that ye may not do these things that ye may boast, but that ye may do these things to lay up for yourselves a treasure in heaven, yea, which is eternal." (Hel. 5:7–8.)

Helaman wanted his sons to do good for the right reasons—not to boast, but to lay up treasures in heaven.

"Let not thy left hand know what thy right hand doeth" is counsel often stated. (Matt. 6:3.) This is especially true when we have had the opportunity to comfort, console, or counsel any fellow-men who are confused, troubled, or weary. Whatever success we might have had as we have tried to help should usually not be discussed, let alone boasted about. Humble, quiet, compassionate service is so soul-rewarding; who would need to point out the subject or location of kindly deeds?

"For although a man may have many revelations, and have power to do many mighty works, yet if he boasts in his own strength, and sets at naught the counsels of God, and follows after the dictates of his own will and carnal desires, he must fall and incur the vengeance of a just God upon him." (D&C 3:4.)

How easy it is for man to believe that temporal success has been achieved by his own skills and labor. Everything good comes from the Lord.

Consideration for the feelings of others should always be important to worthy Latter-day Saints. Rightfully we may be happy about the number of children with which we have been blessed, the missionaries who have served, the temple marriages of our offspring, and the accomplishments of family members; but others who are not so fortunate may have feelings of guilt or inadequacy. They may have been praying long and hard for the same blessings about which we are boasting. These people may feel that they are out of favor with God.

For this reason our appreciation should be sincerely felt and gratitude expressed frequently to our Father in Heaven—but not too vocally to the world.

May we all be gratefully aware of the source of our blessings and strengths and refrain from taking undue credit for personal accomplishments. (Marvin J. Ashton, "Neither Boast of Faith Nor of Mighty Works," *Ensign,* May 1990, 65)

SUMMARY

Of all the barriers that prevent us from doing the will of God, pride is the most common. Once we realize the devastating effect pride has on us, we will avoid it like a plague. The great historian Plutarch wrote: "Five great enemies to peace inhabit with us: viz., avarice, ambition, envy, anger, and pride. If those enemies were to be banished, we should infallibly enjoy perpetual peace." We must come unto Heavenly Father always acknowledging our unworthiness before Him (see Alma 38:14). In humility, we will find the answer to many of our problems, because we will rely upon the Lord and not boast in our own strength. Let us make a resolute, conscious effort to overcome pride and gain a sense of humility.

PRIESTHOOD

The priesthood, the authority and power of God, is given to mankind here upon the earth to act for the blessing and salvation of God's children. Though men bear the responsibility of the priesthood, women who are faithful and sustain the priesthood are likewise recipients of its miraculous blessings and saving ordinances. The priesthood—the power by which the earth was created—is the power by which all things are done. Two grand divisions—the Aaronic and the Melchizedek—compose the priesthood, which gives direction to the Church and kingdom of God on the earth under the leadership of Jesus Christ through His holy prophets. The underlying purpose of the priesthood is to bless people's lives.

THE SCRIPTURES TEACH US

Doctrine and Covenants 13:1. *Upon you my fellow servants, in the name of Messiah I confer the Priesthood of Aaron, which holds the keys of the ministering of angels, and of the gospel of repentance, and of baptism by immersion for the remission of sins; and this shall never be taken again from the earth, until the sons of Levi do offer again an offering unto the Lord in righteousness.*

The Lord has seen fit to bless the worthy young men of the Church with the Aaronic Priesthood—the lesser priesthood. Though the "lesser," it entails many important responsibilities concerning the welfare of the Church and its members. Bearers of this priesthood should not take the call lightly, and should remember that they are preparing for the Melchizedek Priesthood and all its accompanying opportunities to serve. Each Aaronic Priesthood bearer should understand his mission in the Aaronic Priesthood: to become converted to the gospel, to magnify his priesthood callings, to give of himself in service, and to prepare to receive the Melchizedek Priesthood, serve a mission, receive the blessings of the temple, and become a righteous husband and father.

Doctrine and Covenants 84:19–21. *And this greater priesthood administereth the gospel and holdeth the key of the mysteries of the kingdom, even the key of the knowledge of God. Therefore, in the ordinances thereof, the power of godliness is manifest. And without the ordinances thereof, and the authority of the priesthood, the power of godliness is not manifest unto men in the flesh.*

The Melchizedek Priesthood allows mankind the privilege of receiving the gospel, understanding the mysteries of God (see D&C 42:61), and receiving the ordinances of salvation: baptism, the reception of the Holy Ghost, and all of the temple blessings, which ordinances manifest the power of godliness and the keys to the knowledge of God.

Doctrine and Covenants 84:33–41. *For whoso is faithful unto the obtaining these two priesthoods of which I have spoken, and the magnifying their calling, are sanctified by the Spirit unto the renewing of their bodies. They become the sons of Moses and of Aaron and the seed of Abraham, and the church and kingdom, and the elect of God. And also all they who receive this priesthood receive me, saith the Lord; For he that receiveth my servants receiveth me; And he that receiveth me receiveth my Father; And he that receiveth my Father receiveth my Father's kingdom; therefore all that my Father hath shall be given unto him. And this is according to the oath and covenant which belongeth to the priesthood. Therefore, all those who receive the priesthood, receive this oath and covenant of my Father, which he cannot break, neither can it be moved. But whoso breaketh this covenant after he hath received it, and altogether turneth therefrom, shall not have forgiveness of sins in this world nor in the world to come.*

The oath and covenant of the priesthood (which also includes verses 42 through 44) carries with it eternal blessings if we are true and faithful: sanctification, a renewal of the body, becoming the seed of Abraham and the elect of God, and receiving all that the Father has. For those who turn away from this great covenant, severe punishments await. When one is given the opportunity to serve with priesthood authority, he must remember that where much is given much is required (D&C 82:3).

Doctrine and Covenants 121:36. *That the rights of the priesthood are inseparably connected with the powers of heaven, and that the powers of heaven cannot be controlled nor handled only upon the principles of righteousness.*

To exercise the priesthood we must be worthy, inspired by the Holy Ghost, and committed to do only the will of the Lord. Faith is the foundation of all righteousness. Therefore, the principle of power by which the priesthood operates is faith—faith in our God and our Savior Jesus Christ (see *Lectures on Faith* [Salt Lake City: Deseret Book, 1985], Q&A 1:3).

MODERN PROPHETS SPEAK

Brigham Young:

> The Priesthood of the Son of God, which we have in our midst, is a perfect order and system of government, and this alone can deliver the human family from all the evils which now afflict its members, and insure them happiness and felicity hereafter. (*Discourses of Brigham Young,* sel. John A. Widtsoe [Salt Lake City: Deseret Book, 1954], 130)

Gordon B. Hinckley:

> The priesthood is here. It has been conferred upon us. We act in that authority. We speak as sons of God in the name of Jesus Christ and as holders of this divinely given endowment. We know, for we have seen, the power of this priesthood. We have seen the sick healed, the lame made to walk, and the coming of light and knowledge and understanding to those who have been in darkness. . . .

> I want to speak a little about blessing the people, placing our hands upon their heads and blessing them. Brethren, how great is our opportunity, how tremendous our responsibility, to live worthy to be, as it were, a conduit between the powers of heaven and those upon the earth on whose heads we lay our hands. I suppose every man here who holds the Melchizedek Priesthood has had the opportunity to bless. And I suppose that, when called on to do so, he has prayed within his heart that he

might be a worthy instrument to bestow a blessing upon the heads of those who come in faith. Bless the people when you set them apart and under other circumstances, in times of sickness. You fathers bless your children. Lay your hands upon their heads and bless them. You cannot do a greater thing for them. (*Teachings of Gordon B. Hinckley* [Salt Lake City: Deseret Book, 1997], 473, 480–81)

Harold B. Lee:

Some have speculated that the strength of this church lies in the tithing system; some have thought in the missionary system; but those who understand rightly the word of the Lord understand full well that the strength of the Church is, fundamentally, in neither of these. The strength of the Church is not in a large membership, but the real strength of this church lies in the power and authority of the holy priesthood which our Heavenly Father has given to us in this day. If we exercise properly that power and magnify our callings in the priesthood, we will see to it that the missionary work shall go forward, that the tithing shall be paid, that the welfare plan shall prosper, that our homes shall be safe, and that morality among the youth of Israel shall be safeguarded. (*The Teachings of Harold B. Lee,* ed. Clyde J. Williams [Salt Lake City: Bookcraft, 1996], 487)

Ezra Taft Benson:

A priesthood holder is kind. One who is kind is sympathetic and gentle with others. He is considerate of others' feelings and courteous in his behavior. He has a helpful nature. Kindness pardons others' weaknesses and faults. Kindness is extended to all—to the aged and the young, to animals, to those low of station as well as the high. . . .

An imperative responsibility, if you would lead more righteous lives, is to govern righteously in your priesthood stewardships. The revelation pertaining to this responsibility is in section 121 of the Doctrine and Covenants. Three phrases claim our attention: "the rights of the priesthood," "the powers of heaven," and "the principles of righteousness." (*The Teachings of Ezra Taft Benson* [Salt Lake City: Bookcraft, 1988], 216)

Bruce R. McConkie:

What, then, is the doctrine of the priesthood? And how shall we live as the servants of the Lord?

This doctrine is that God our Father is a glorified, a perfected, and an exalted being who has all might, all power, and all dominion, who knows all things and is infinite in all his attributes, and who lives in the family unit.

It is that our Eternal Father enjoys this high status of glory and perfection and power because his faith is perfect and his priesthood is unlimited.

It is that priesthood is the very name of the power of God, and that if we are to become like him, we must receive and exercise his priesthood or power as he exercises it.

It is that he has given us an endowment of heavenly power here on earth, which is after the order of his Son and which, because it is the power of God, is of necessity without beginning of days or end of years.

It is that we can enter an order of the priesthood named the new and everlasting covenant of marriage (see D&C 131:2), named also the patriarchal order, because of which order we can create for ourselves eternal family units of our own, patterned after the family of God our Heavenly Father.

It is that we have power, by faith, to govern and control all things, both temporal and spiritual; to work miracles and perfect lives; to stand in the presence of God and be like him because we have gained his faith, his perfections, and his power, or in other words the fulness of his priesthood.

This, then, is the doctrine of the priesthood, than which there neither is nor can be anything greater. This is the power we can gain through faith and righteousness.

Truly, there is power in the priesthood—power to do all things! ("The Doctrine of the Priesthood," *Ensign,* May 1982, 32)

IDEAS FOR DAILY LIVING

Here are three ideas to help us understand the blessings of the priesthood:

1. Worthiness to exercise the priesthood comes through living a righteous life.
- *Repentance*—The priesthood operates on the principle of righteousness (see D&C 121:36). We must purify ourselves through repentance and sanctify ourselves by yielding our heart unto God (see Hel. 3:35).
- *Following the will of the Lord*—We are to seek the Lord's will and not our own as we utilize His priesthood power.
- *Inspiration*—When we are pure and clean, we can receive direction from the Holy Ghost.
- *Preparation*—Let us commit to be spiritually prepared to exercise our priesthood whenever we are called upon to do so.
- *Gratitude*—We show our gratitude for the priesthood and its blessings by living worthy of it and by using it when called upon.

2. Blessings of the priesthood flow from God.
- *The process of returning to the presence of God*—We can be brought back into the presence of God only by receiving and keeping the covenants and ordinances of the priesthood.
- *Worthiness*—Receiving the blessings of the priesthood is always predicated upon our worthiness.
- *Sacred blessings*—In every possible situation, lives have been blessed by the power of the priesthood, from raising the dead to healing the sick, from giving comfort to giving direction in life. The responsibility lies with us to ask for the blessings of the priesthood, to be worthy to receive them, and to exercise our faith.
- *Patriarchal blessings*—Everyone should prepare for, and be worthy of, receiving a patriarchal blessing. This is a powerful blessing that gives invaluable guidance and instruction to the recipient.
- *Power of God*—Let us never forget that everything good here upon the earth comes from the blessings of the power of God. The priesthood is this power of God on the earth.

3. The purpose of the priesthood has been taught by the prophets of every dispensation.
- *Direction for the kingdom of God*—In all dispensations of time, the priesthood has been here on the earth to direct the kingdom of God and bless Heavenly Father's children.
- *Sealing power*—The priesthood provides the sealing power to enable families to endure forever, and to bring about the gathering of Israel (see D&C 110:11–13).
- *Covenant power*—The priesthood provides for the governing of the Church and all the priesthood covenants and ordinances that manifest the power of godliness (see D&C 84:21).
- *Opening the way to return home*—The priesthood is here to help Heavenly Father's children return to His presence.

ILLUSTRATIONS FOR OUR TIMES

President Wilford Woodruff relates a personal experience that demonstrates the importance and power of the offices of the priesthood, the Aaronic priesthood specifically.

Honoring the Priesthood

I was once moved upon to go and warn old Father Hakeman, living on Petty-John Creek, Arkansas. He had been in Jackson County during the persecution period. His wife died there. His family consisted of five sons, all over six feet tall. Most of them had been whipped with hickory gads by mobs, and he went south into Arkansas, taking his sons with him. We went a good deal out of our way for the purpose of visiting Father Hakeman. I had a vision the night previous, in which was manifested to me the trouble that lay before us, but that the Lord would deliver us. We arrived at his house on Sunday morning. He was taking breakfast. We had had breakfast at the place where we stayed overnight. I saw a Book of Mormon on the shelf. He did not seem to pay any attention to us, or to take any interest in us. I took up the Book of Mormon, and said, "You have a very good book here."

"Yes," said he, "but it is a book that came from the devil."

That opened my eyes. He had been an elder; he had been in Zion; had been persecuted there and driven out; but I found that he had apostatized, and he was our enemy. I saw he would do anything he could against us.

We left him and went to Brother Hubbard's and stayed with him three weeks, during which we took our axes and cleared some land for him. I was strongly impressed three times to go up and warn Father Hakeman. At last I did so, according to the commandment of God to me. The third time I met with him, his house seemed to be full of evil spirits, and I was troubled in spirit at the manifestation. When I finished my warning, I left him. He followed me from his house—with the intention of killing me. I have no doubt about his intention, for it was shown to me in vision. When he came to where I was, he fell dead at my feet, as if he had been struck with a thunderbolt from heaven. I was then a priest, but God defended me and preserved my life. I speak of this because it is a principle that has been manifest in the church of God in this generation as well as in others. I had the administration of angels while holding the office of a priest. I had visions and revelations. I traveled thousands of miles. I baptized men, though I could not confirm them because I had not the authority to do it.

I speak of these things to show that a man should not be ashamed of any portion of the priesthood. Our young men, if they are deacons, should labor to fulfill that office. If they do that, they may then be called to the office of a teacher, whose duty it is to teach the people, visit the Saints and see that there is no evil or iniquity carried on. God has no respect for persons in this priesthood any further than as they magnify their callings and do their duty. (Wilford Woodruff, in *Best-Loved Stories of the LDS People,* eds. Jack M. Lyon, Linda Ririe Gundry, and Jay A. Parry [Salt Lake City: Deseret Book, 1997], 304–305)

SUMMARY

Heavenly Father allows us, through His Son Jesus Christ, to exercise His power and authority here upon the earth for the blessing and salvation of mankind. For this, we should be eternally grateful, and we should reverence our Heavenly Father by honoring the priesthood and by keeping our covenants. If we do so, through charity and virtue, magnificent blessings await us and our families: "Then shall thy confidence wax strong in the presence of God; and the doctrine of the priesthood shall distil upon thy soul as the dews from heaven. The Holy Ghost shall be thy constant companion, and thy scepter an unchanging scepter of righteousness and truth; and thy dominion shall be an everlasting dominion, and without compulsory means it shall flow unto thee forever and ever" (D&C 121:45–46).

PURITY

The dictionary definition of the term *purity* implies being free from moral or physical defilement, to be chaste, free from pollution, being absolute, blameless—even sinless. This seems a bit overwhelming, as we have been commanded to be perfect. How can we be completely pure and virtuous, when we are still mortal and subject to sin? The answer is that we can aspire to absolute purity in the strength of the Lord and through the help of the Spirit. We can repent and practice spiritual endurance. We can tell the story of the nature and blessings of moral goodness. We can testify to it and can live it and can make a difference. We can stand for purity and virtue. As we strive for purity, we may fall short, but we are on the path to perfection, and we are becoming more like our Savior.

THE SCRIPTURES TEACH US

Matthew 5:8. *Blessed are the pure in heart: for they shall see God.*

Purity of heart is reflected in our behavior, our thoughts, our intentions, and through our affections toward God. When we have a change of heart and follow through with a change in the way we comport ourselves—cultivating a "godly walk and conversation" (D&C 20:69)—we become pure and receive the blessings of the Spirit, being worthy to be in the presence of God.

Philippians 4:8. *Finally, brethren, whatsoever things are true, whatsoever things are honest, whatsoever things are just, whatsoever things are pure, whatsoever things are lovely, whatsoever things are of good report; if there be any virtue, and if there be any praise, think on these things.* (See also A of F 1:13.)

We should control our minds and think of good and virtuous things. Thoughts dwelled upon create a desire that, if encouraged, results in action. This is why we are commanded to "let virtue garnish [our] thoughts unceasingly" (D&C 121:45). There is great power in worthy mental exertion that activates faith! We are commanded to think about just, pure, and lovely things, and to practice virtue and holiness before the Lord (see D&C 46:33).

1 Peter 1:22. *Seeing ye have purified your souls in obeying the truth through the Spirit unto unfeigned love of the brethren, see that ye love one another with a pure heart fervently.*

We become pure and sanctified by the Spirit as we yield our hearts to God (see Hel. 3:35). As we do this, we will choose to be obedient and show love to one another, because a pure heart is always full of love.

Moroni 7:48. *Wherefore, my beloved brethren, pray unto the Father with all the energy of heart, that ye may be filled with this love, which he hath bestowed upon all who are true followers of his Son, Jesus Christ; that ye may become the sons of God; that when he shall appear we shall be like him, for we shall see him as he is; that we may have this hope; that we may be purified even as he is pure. Amen.*

If we seek charity (the pure love of Christ) with all the energy of our hearts through prayer, we will eventually be filled with charity, like our Savior. In this process, we become pure and virtuous (see 2 Pet. 1:5–7).

MODERN PROPHETS SPEAK

David O. McKay:

> That is the mission of every man, from the President of the Church down to the latest convert in the Church. Every officer holds his position to build up, to bless; and, as President Joseph F. Smith has said, to establish righteousness, purity, and virtue among mankind. (*Gospel Ideals: Selections from the Discourses of David O. McKay* [Salt Lake City: Improvement Era, 1953], 143)

Ezra Taft Benson:

> We covenant to live the law of chastity. The law of chastity is virtue and sexual purity. This law places us under covenant to live this commandment strictly. (*The Teachings of Ezra Taft Benson* [Salt Lake City: Bookcraft, 1988], 278)

Gordon B. Hinckley:

> The temple is a place of covenants. . . . In the house of the Lord, as all of you know who have been to a temple, we take upon ourselves covenants and obligations regarding lives of purity and virtue and goodness and truth and unselfishness to others. (*Teachings of Gordon B. Hinckley* [Salt Lake City: Deseret Book, 1997], 148)

> Moral cleanliness. Cleanliness before the Lord in matters of morality and virtue and purity. There is so much of pornography in the world. There is so much of evil, enticing evil, in the world. Shun it, my brothers and sisters. Avoid it. (*Teachings of Gordon B. Hinckley* [Salt Lake City: Deseret Book, 1997], 405)

IDEAS FOR DAILY LIVING

Here are six ideas to help us to be pure and virtuous and encourage purity and virtue in others:

1. Make a commitment to purity and virtue.
- *Set a high standard*—We must establish a moral and upright standard of behavior based on the principles of the gospel. Make a commitment to be clean in all ways—emotionally, physically, intellectually, and spiritually. Do not put anything into your body or mind that is unclean. Said Hippocrates: "With purity and with holiness I will pass my life and practice my art."
- *Be honest in our dealings with our fellowmen*—We can cultivate honorable motives as we go about our professional lives. We can be honest and forthright. We can add genuine value to our associates,

our customers, and all our fellow human beings. We can pay an honest tax, and honest tithe, and take an honest reward for our contributions.

- *Strive for optimum health*—Understand and appreciate the principles of morality as they relate to good health.
- *Be wise*—Seek the qualities of love and charity, for they are the foundation of virtue. Remember that a moment's pleasure is often paid for with months' or years' worth of sorrow and misery.

2. Transform your environment.

- *Control your setting*—Choose an edifying environment. Read uplifting books; watch ennobling television shows and movies; use the Internet to expand your mind rather than debase it; speak in positive and honorable terms with others.
- *Watch your step*—Keep yourself out of situations that lead to promiscuity. Few active Church members plan to be immoral—it just happens because they end up in situations they are not prepared to handle.
- *Decorate and beautify your home with uplifting things*—We can have a clean and wholesome home and workplace. We can purify the environment so that it reflects the kind of order that will encourage good ideas, clear thinking, and decent behavior.

3. Purity and virtue are not merely good advice; they are the gateway to eternal life.

- *Freedom*—Remember that virtue is liberating, while immorality is enslaving. Virtue is your gateway to freedom, for virtue leads to harmony, peace, balance, and long-term rewards. If you capitulate to the never-ceasing hunger for momentary pleasures and titillation, if you do not fear captivating addictions, if you choose to ignore the alienation that comes from self-intoxicating lasciviousness or blatant dishonesty, then immorality is your gateway.
- *Strength*—Virtue is strong, while immorality is weak. It takes strength of character to lead a life of virtue and integrity, while living a life of lax morals and pandering to appetite shows shallowness and weakness. If strength is a principle you want to live by, virtue is your gateway. If you find happiness in caving in to shallow desires or abusing others, then immorality is your gateway.
- *Honor*—Virtue attracts respect and honor, while immorality repels respect. People of virtue garner honor and esteem (even though dissenters may snivel and act condescendingly). If you wish to cultivate respect and honor, virtue is your gateway. If you wish to leave behind a legacy of selfishness and loneliness, then immorality is your gateway.

4. Make it a family effort.

- *Do it for them*—We keep our lives pure for the sake of our loved ones—our spouse and our children—because that gives them a life and a legacy they can build on. The Savior said, in His grand intercessory prayer, "And for their sakes I sanctify myself, that they also might be sanctified through the truth" (John 17:19). We leave behind for the coming generations the good seeds of wholesome behavior, harmony, peace, and love.
- *Keep marriage sacred*—Honor the sacred bonds of matrimony. Never do anything before or during marriage that would violate that relationship.
- *Make a promise*—As many parents do with their children, sign an agreement of chastity. Make a covenant to be pure. "Who knows what sort of life would result if we attained to purity?" mused Thoreau. And, indeed, if we attained to absolute purity, it would be a different world.
- *Make the home a school of virtue*—Teach your children and family members to practice principles of upright virtue, and convey to them the promised blessings of harmony and peace. The great composer Beethoven declared: "Recommend to your children virtue; that alone can make happiness, not gold."

5. Purity is a quality of leadership. Purity, or virtue, does not just refer to sexual purity; it also implies living with integrity, doing only good and lifting others.

- *Show leadership in purifying conversation*—Do not tolerate vulgar language, and do not give in to crude and offensive discourse. Be exemplary in your manner of speech—be perfectly pure in that regard.
- *Purity leverages your leadership*—Purity blends well with all aspects of leadership—at church, at home, in the workplace, and in the community. Virtue supports creativity, wisdom, planning, organizing, and managing. It is not an isolated quality, but an integral part of leadership. If we get ahead in life without virtue, we will have hurt many, including ourselves. "All virtue is summed up in dealing justly," said Aristotle.
- *Teach virtue skillfully*—Do not act "holier than thou" in practicing virtuous principles. At a moment of choice where you let virtue prevail, you can simply say to those who may disagree, "We choose to differ on this matter. I believe I will take this particular course, and leave to others the right to choose their way."
- *Be exemplary*—Virtue is best taught with deeds, not words. An example of virtuous and upright living illuminates the landscape of human behavior in a way that preaching can scarcely accomplish.
- *Be patient*—Remember that becoming a virtuous person takes time—it is a lifetime goal. Be patient with yourself and improve a step at a time. Likewise, be patient with others as they learn this principle. Be a leader of influence who is modest, patient, kind, and long-suffering.

6. Draw strength from the Lord in becoming pure and virtuous.

- *Make a fresh start*—Repent. We can do all in our power to correct the mistakes of the past and go forward with new resolve and a clean slate. We can apologize to any we have wronged and do everything possible to make restitution. We can go before God and confess our wrongdoings and ask for forgiveness.
- *Pray for strength*—Purity and virtue flow from God. Seek the direction of the Holy Spirit to rise to the challenge of being pure and chaste.
- *Practice virtue to bless others*—Remember that the purpose of virtue is to bless others; the by-product is your virtuous life and the harmony and peace that flow from it. Start the day with uplifting thoughts and ideas, and the day will unfold with greater peace and success.

ILLUSTRATIONS FOR OUR TIMES

An anonymous story by a concerned parent clearly demonstrates the wisdom of sexual purity.

What About Abstinence?

> I was holding a notice from my thirteen-year-old son's school announcing a meeting to preview the new course in sexuality. Parents could examine the curriculum and take part in an actual lesson presented exactly as it would be given to the students.
>
> When I arrived at the school, I was surprised to discover only about a dozen parents there. As we waited for the presentation, I thumbed through page after page of instructions in the prevention of pregnancy or disease. I found abstinence mentioned only in passing. When the teacher arrived with the school nurse, she asked if there were any questions. I asked why abstinence did not play a noticeable part in the material.

What happened next was shocking. There was a great deal of laughter, and someone suggested that if I thought abstinence had any merit, I should go back to burying my head in the sand. The teacher and the nurse said nothing as I drowned in a sea of embarrassment. My mind had gone blank, and I could think of nothing to say.

The teacher explained to me that the job of the school was to teach facts, and the home was responsible for moral training. I sat in silence for the next 20 minutes as the course was explained. The other parents seemed to give their unqualified support to the materials.

"Donuts, at the back," announced the teacher during the break. "I'd like you to put on the name tags we have prepared—they're right by the donuts—and mingle with the other parents."

Everyone moved to the back of the room. As I watched them affixing their name tags and shaking hands, I sat deep in thought. I was ashamed that I had not been able to convince them to include a serious discussion of abstinence in the materials. I uttered a silent prayer for guidance.

My thoughts were interrupted by the teacher's hand on my shoulder. "Won't you join the others, Mr. Layton?" The nurse smiled sweetly at me. "The donuts are good."

"Thank you, no," I replied.

"Well, then, how about a name tag? I'm sure the others would like to meet you."

"Somehow I doubt that," I replied.

"Won't you please join them?" she coaxed. Then I heard a still, small voice whisper, "Don't go." The instruction was unmistakable. "Don't go!"

"I'll just wait here," I said.

When the class was called back to order, the teacher looked around the long table and thanked everyone for putting on name tags. She ignored me. Then she said, "Now we're going to give you the same lesson we'll be giving your children. Everyone please peel off your name tags."

I watched in silence as the tags came off. "Now, then, on the back of one of the tags, I drew a tiny flower. Who has it, please?"

The gentleman across from me held it up. "Here it is!"

"All right," she said. "The flower represents disease. Do you recall with whom you shook hands?"

He pointed to a couple of people. "Very good," she replied. "The handshake in this case represents intimacy. So the two people you had contact with now have the disease."

There was laughter and joking among the parents. The teacher continued, "And whom did the two of you shake hands with?"

The point was well taken, and she explained how this lesson would show students how quickly disease is spread. "Since we all shook hands, we all have the disease." It was then that I heard the still, small voice again. "Speak now," it said, "but be humble."

I noted wryly the latter admonition, then rose from my chair. I apologized for any upset I might have caused earlier, congratulated the teacher on an excellent lesson that would impress the youth, and concluded by saying I had only one small point I wished to make. "Not all of us were infected," I said. "One of us . . . abstained." (Author unknown)

SUMMARY

We should continually strive to attain a state of purity in our lives. In the strength of the Lord, we can become persons of noble character, exemplary behavior, integrity, and moral goodness. May we make a commitment to stand for virtue and to make a difference in the world by promoting a moral environment in our community. Consider the magnificent blessings that flow to the pure in heart: "But behold, I, Jacob, would speak unto you that are pure in heart. Look unto God with firmness of mind, and pray unto him with exceeding faith, and he will console you in your afflictions. . . . O all ye that are pure in heart, lift up your heads and receive the pleasing word of God, and feast upon his love; for ye may, if your minds are firm, forever" (Jacob 3:1–2).

REACTIVATION

Since the beginning of time, many souls have lost their way through poor choices, sins of omission, apathy, taking offense, or willfully going against God's commandments, among other things. They have separated themselves and become lost from Heavenly Father, the Savior, the Holy Spirit, the Church and kingdom of God, and often their precious families. Our duty is to find and feed the Lord's "sheep" (see John 21:15–17) and especially to seek after the lost sheep (see Luke 15).

THE SCRIPTURES TEACH US

Luke 15:4–7. *What man of you, having an hundred sheep, if he lose one of them, doth not leave the ninety and nine in the wilderness, and go after that which is lost, until he find it? And when he hath found it, he layeth it on his shoulders, rejoicing. And when he cometh home, he calleth together his friends and neighbours, saying unto them, Rejoice with me; for I have found my sheep which was lost. I say unto you, that likewise joy shall be in heaven over one sinner that repenteth, more than over ninety and nine just persons, which need no repentance.*

Every soul is precious to our Heavenly Father and our Savior, as it should be to us (see Moses 1:39; Mosiah 28:3; D&C 18:10–16). We must make every possible effort to find and reclaim, through love, our brothers and sisters who have strayed (see Matt. 18:14). (For further study of the role of shepherds in the Lord's kingdom, see Ezekiel 34.)

John 21:15–17. *So when they had dined, Jesus saith to Simon Peter, Simon, son of Jonas, lovest thou me more than these? He saith unto him, Yea, Lord; thou knowest that I love thee. He saith unto him, Feed my lambs. He* *saith to him again the second time, Simon, son of Jonas, lovest thou me? He saith unto him, Yea, Lord; thou knowest that I love thee. He saith unto him, Feed my sheep. He saith unto him the third time, Simon, son of Jonas, lovest thou me? Peter was grieved because he said unto him the third time, Lovest thou me? And he said unto him, Lord, thou knowest all things; thou knowest that I love thee. Jesus saith unto him, Feed my sheep.*

Prior to the Savior's ascension, His last instructions were to feed His lambs and His sheep. When the Savior gave these instructions to Peter, He used a word referring to the highest form of love, *agape* or *agapao*, which means a perfect, godlike, unconditional, and unfailing love (see *The Interlinear Greek-English New Testament* [Basingstoke, Hants, UK: Samuel Bagster and Sons Ltd., 1987], 460). Peter responded with the word *philia*, which refers to brotherly, friendly, or reciprocating love, which is not fully adequate in order to truly feed the Lord's sheep—hence the Lord inquires of Peter three times. The lesson and application seem to be that in order to truly feed the Lord's sheep we must love with the pure love of Christ, which will never fail.

1 Corinthians 12:25–26. *That there should be no schism in the body; but that the members should have the same care one for another. And whether one member suffer, all the members suffer with it; or one member be honoured, all the members rejoice with it.*

The Apostle Paul describes the body of Christ as "one," stating that each member is an important part (see 1 Cor. 12:12–24). Verses 25–26 emphasize the oneness and unity that our Savior seeks for us in His kingdom. We should not to be separated in the body of Christ, but rather we should care for each other, and when one is suffering or struggling, we too should sorrow because of our love and concern for them. Likewise, we will rejoice with others when there is cause to rejoice.

Alma 31:34–35. *O Lord, wilt thou grant unto us that we may have success in bringing them again unto thee in Christ. Behold, O Lord, their souls are precious, and many of them are our brethren; therefore, give unto us, O Lord, power and wisdom that we may bring these, our brethren, again unto thee.*

Our prayers, like Alma's, should be to seek out our struggling brothers and sisters with a hope, through our service and by the power of the Spirit, of assisting them and bringing them back into the fold.

MODERN PROPHETS SPEAK

N. Eldon Tanner:

> Every bishop, every stake president, every leader of any organization knows someone who needs attention, and you and we have the responsibility of going to find that lost sheep. If we had knowledge tonight that some young man was lost, if anyone knew of someone who was drowning, we wouldn't hesitate one minute to do all in our power to save that individual, to save the one who was lost, the one who was drowning, the one who was in need of our help. These young men and these older men who are inactive in the Church, who have strayed away from the Church because of inactivity or for any reason, need our help and need our attention just as much. They need our prayers and our consideration, and nothing will bring us greater joy and happiness than to see one come back into activity.

> By saving one, we might save a family. We might even save a generation. By losing one, we may lose not only the individual but a family and his posterity. The responsibility is great. ("Search for the Wanderers," *Ensign*, June 1971, 59)

Marvin J. Ashton:

> When I think of the Savior's admonition to do cheerfully all things that lie in our power, I think of the father of the prodigal son. The father was heartbroken by the loss and conduct of his way-ward son. Yet we have no mention of his lamenting, "Where did I go wrong?" "What have I done to deserve this?" Or, "Where did I fail?"
>
> Instead he seemed to have endured without bitterness his son's misconduct and welcomed him back with love. "For this my son was dead, and is alive again; he was lost, and is found. And they began to be merry." (Luke 15:24.)
>
> When family members disappoint us, we especially need to learn endurance. As long as we exercise love, patience, and understanding, even when no progress is apparent, we are not failing. We must keep trying. (*Be of Good Cheer* [Salt Lake City: Deseret Book, 1987], 18)

IDEAS FOR DAILY LIVING

Here are some ideas to consider as we strive to serve those who are lost or struggling:

1. Love everyone. According to the Lord, we should love everyone with the pure love of Christ (see John 13:34–35). It is a commandment (see John 15:12) with a precious blessing (see 2 Pet. 1:10).

- *The pure love of Christ is necessary*—In order to love unfailingly, we must seek to possess the pure love of Christ (see Moro. 7:48), which will provide strength as we seek to bless those who have strayed (see D&C 4:6).
- *Find them*—We must have an overwhelming desire to seek out the lost sheep (see John 21:15–17). Then we can number them and name them so they can be nurtured with the good word of God (see Moroni 6:1–4).
- *Understand their situation*—Each person comes with different perceptions and challenges. Be careful not to judge, except righteously (see JST, Matt. 7:1–2). Seek to understand how others feel and why they struggle. Then show forth love with empathy and patience.
- *Determine and clarify others' needs*—Once others' needs are identified, we are better able to assist them—we can offer our love in a way that will best help fill their needs. Sometimes the lost sheep do not perceive their own needs, and this kind of situation takes time, patience, and total reliance upon the Lord (see Prov. 3:4–5).
- *Seek counsel and strength from the Lord and the Spirit*—Seek direction through prayer (see 3 Nephi 14:7), from the Spirit (see 2 Ne. 32:5), from the Lord (see 2 Ne. 9:29; Jacob 4:10), from the scriptures (see 2 Ne. 3:23), and from your leaders (see D&C 108:1). Remember, the Lord is always there to help us and strengthen us in all things (see Alma 26:11–12).
- *Help others feel your love and caring spirit*—The old adage holds true that people don't care how much you know until they know how much you care. We must be a true friend. When people feel our love, they are drawn by its motivating power (see John 3:16; 2 Ne. 26:24; 3 Ne. 27:13–15).
- *There must be a concerted effort on their part*—As we become involved, it is imperative that those we are working with accept responsibility and make some form of commitment to change. Real growth requires commitment. A regularly scheduled class where they can be taught might be appropriate.
- *Utilize all the resources available*—Use the person's family, friends, ward leaders, ward council, and every other resource that the Lord inspires you to employ. This must be done in wisdom, at the proper pace according to the person's capacity to change.

2. Seek to strengthen their faith in Christ. The Savior must become a struggling person's rock (see Hel. 5:12), and we must do all we can to increase his or her faith in Him (see Luke 17:5) so that this faith might become perfect (2 Ne. 9:23). This helps a person become spiritually sufficient in the Lord.

- *Focus on the one*—As directed by the Spirit, one-on-one contact can be very effective, even as the Savior demonstrated His love for the Nephite people one by one (see 3 Ne. 11:15).
- *Never give up, never give in, and never give out*—Enduring to the end in all things is the key, especially as we act as instruments in the hands of the Lord to bless those struggling Saints who desperately need help. We must press forward with unwearyingness (see Hel. 10:4–5), acknowledging that lost souls may take a long time to learn to nourish their own budding faith.
- *Hope in all things*—Through exercising our faith, we can have hope in all things through the Atonement of our Savior Jesus Christ (see Moro. 8:26). We can have hope that a lost lamb's faith will grow and lead him or her to repentance. As our hope is centered in Christ, so a fallen soul's will ultimately be.

ILLUSTRATION FOR OUR TIMES

In a general conference address, Elder Joseph B. Wirthlin gives examples of the success we can have in seeking lost souls and bringing them back to full activity in the Church and kingdom of God.

Reclaiming the Lost Sheep

> This work of reclaiming the lost sheep, as Jesus so vividly expressed it, must receive top priority by every stake, ward, branch, and quorum leader. All inactive members should be considered candidates for activation regardless of their response to any previous approach. We must use kindness, patience, long-suffering, love, faith, and diligence. . . .

> Recently, I attended a stake conference and heard a story of member activation that moved me deeply. The bishop of one of the wards in the stake took a keen interest in arousing inactive brethren to Church activity. He knew that the first step was one of communication, that he must have a meaningful visit with each inactive brother.

> So he began by telephoning one of them. The wife answered the phone and said, "Bishop, I surely appreciate your call. My husband is outside, but I will have him come to the phone."

> When the husband heard that it was the bishop that wished to speak to him, his reaction was as expected. He attempted to sidestep this phone call and responded, "Tell the bishop that I'm out sawing logs," and with a humorous touch, "Tell him I'm dead."

> The brother spoke the truth more literally than he realized. It was true. He was sawing logs, and tragically, he was dead to the spiritual things of his life.

> A good wife, however, is a mighty force in any man's life, and, in a kindly manner, she persuaded her husband to come to the phone.

> Then the bishop, using the power of suggestion and in a friendly voice, said, "I should very much appreciate having a visit with you for a few moments this evening in my office." The brother couldn't refuse so warmhearted an invitation, and a meeting took place.

The testimony of the bishop and his deep concern kindled a fire in the heart of the inactive brother, and he agreed to join the temple preparation class that was about to begin.

Each session, taught by a tactful teacher with a great knowledge of the truth and an inspiring testimony, motivated the inactive brother. He resolved to strengthen his family and bind them together eternally through the blessings of the temple.

This good brother may still be sawing logs, but there is now much more. He has added for himself an indescribable dimension of happiness, as well as joy to the lives of each and every family member.

In another ward, the bishop assigned his two best home teachers to work with one specially selected inactive family. The husband and father had been inactive for many years, even though he held the office of elder in the Melchizedek Priesthood. The couple was approached and asked if the special teachers could come and teach them the gospel in weekly visits to their home. The family agreed, and the teachers proceeded to bring gospel lessons tailored to the needs and desires of the family.

The bishop also helped by interviewing the couple every few weeks. The husband usually went golfing on Sundays and had no desire to change his life-style at first. During one interview, the bishop said to the husband, "You've got to get going on spiritual matters so that you won't lose your fine family." This caused the inactive brother to think deeply about important issues, and within a couple of weeks he asked for another interview with the bishop and said that he had started paying tithing and that he and his wife wanted to set a goal of being sealed in the temple.

As this family became active, their whole attitude changed, and they seemed to be very happy to embrace the gospel principles and make the necessary change in life-style. . . .

The president of an elders' quorum in one of our outstanding stakes in Brazil—I love that great people, our members in Brazil—reported phenomenal success in reactivating fifteen elders in his quorum last year. I asked the question, "How did you accomplish this?" He said, "We and the home teachers visited them often. These inactive elders knew that we really cared for them." Their testimonies were strengthened. They and their families are now active members of the Church.

The Lord has promised great rewards for those who reach out to strengthen their brothers and sisters.

The Lord has said in modern revelation, "And if it so be that you should labor all your days in crying repentance unto this people, and bring, save it be one soul unto me, how great shall be your joy with him in the kingdom of my Father!" (D&C 18:15.)

I wish I could engrave on every heart what I so keenly know and feel. I bear unwavering testimony that our Heavenly Father and His Divine Son, Jesus Christ, rule and reign, and that we must all understand that the gospel is everlasting. It is forever and applicable to all, and each of us is to be held accountable. (Joseph B. Wirthlin, "Restoring the Lost Sheep," *Ensign,* May 1984, 39)

SUMMARY

Souls are precious. Each person on the earth is a divine child of God. There can be no limit to our effort and desire to help everyone return to the presence of our Heavenly Father. This is our Savior's goal: to redeem all of God's children. The prophet Joseph F. Smith summed it up best when he said, "Jesus had not finished his work when his body was slain, neither did he finish it after his resurrection from the dead; although he had accomplished the purpose for which he then came to the earth, he had not fulfilled all his work. And when will he? Not until he has redeemed and saved every son and daughter of our father Adam that have been or ever will be born upon this earth to the end of time, except the sons of perdition. That is his mission. We will not finish our work until we have saved ourselves, and then not until we shall have saved all depending upon us; for we are to become saviors upon Mount Zion, as well as Christ. We are called to this mission" (Joseph F. Smith, *Gospel Doctrine: Selections from the Sermons and Writings of Joseph F. Smith,* comp. John A. Widtsoe [Salt Lake City: Deseret Book, 1939], 442). We are undershepherds with the task of finding and blessing those who have lost their way.

RELATIONSHIPS

Relationships are one of the most rewarding yet challenging aspects of life. The first and most important relationship is with our Heavenly Father and our Savior Jesus Christ. We must come to know, love, trust, respect, and reverence our God and His Only Begotten Son. Remember: "And this is life eternal, that they might know thee the only true God, and Jesus Christ whom thou hast sent" (see John 17:3). This will be the foundation of all other relationships.

Earth life and all of its joys are built upon relationships. Our association with others—spouse, family, friends, and associates—constitutes one of life's supreme values. Marriage, family, school, and the workplace become enjoyable when they involve positive, meaningful relationships. Life's enduring memories are usually associated with the people we care about and spend our time with. These relationships make life full and wonderful when they are joyful and vibrant, or empty and miserable when they are hurtful and incomplete.

Our actions and attitudes determine the fulfillment and success we enjoy in relationships. Successful relationships are a source of joy and happiness in this life, as well as in the life to come.

THE SCRIPTURES TEACH US

John 13:34–35. *A new commandment I give unto you, That ye love one another; as I have loved you, that ye also love one another. By this shall all men know that ye are my disciples, if ye have love one to another.*

Our involvement with our fellowmen should be based on love. Relationships not based on love do not have the depth of meaning or possibilities for growth that those centered in godly love do. True charity is expressed as we have concern for one another. We then build relationships based upon trust, respect, and love. This should be our highest goal: to love our fellowmen, as this also manifests our love for God (1 Jn. 4:20).

MODERN PROPHETS SPEAK

Jeffrey R. Holland:

> We should try to be more constant and unfailing, more longsuffering and kind, less envious and puffed up in our relationships with others. As Christ lived so should we live, and as Christ loved

so should we love. (*Christ and the New Covenant: The Messianic Message of the Book of Mormon* [Salt Lake City: Deseret Book, 1997], 336–37)

Ezra Taft Benson:

To be like Christ should be the righteous aspiration of every member of the Church. We should act as He would act in our relationships with others. (*Come unto Christ* [Salt Lake City: Deseret Book, 1983], 52)

The formula for successful relationships with others boils down to that divine code known as the Golden Rule:

"Therefore all things whatsoever ye would that men should do to you, do ye even so to them. . . ." (Matt. 7:12.)

It was the Master who said, ". . . whosoever will be chief among you, let him be your servant." (Matt. 20:27.)

Unselfish, willing service to others was the keynote of his relationship with men. (*God, Family, Country: Our Three Great Loyalties* [Salt Lake City: Deseret Book, 1974], 6)

Joseph B. Wirthlin:

I believe that the little things are of great importance in our relationship with ourselves, in our relationships with others, and in our relationship with God. . . . Do we take the time to remember the simple courtesies that are so important in building relationships with others? Do we remember the smile, the compliment, the positive note, and the word of encouragement? We should do these things without hesitation. They should be a part of our everyday manner. (*Finding Peace in Our Lives* [Salt Lake City: Deseret Book, 1995], 64)

IDEAS FOR DAILY LIVING

Listed below are some helpful hints for developing good relationships with others.

1. Relationships are like gardens: we must provide constant nurture.
- *Common vision*—We cultivate the soil of common ground and mutual interests.
- *Understanding*—We constantly clear back the weeds of misunderstanding and jealousy.
- *Hope*—We supply the nutrients of encouragement, hope, and positive support.
- *Love*—We add the cleansing moisture of forgiveness, compassion, and charity.
- *Enthusiasm*—We bring to the relationship the sunshine of enthusiasm and energy.
- *Harmony*—Together, we harvest the fruits of harmony, balance, peace, and joy.
- *Legacy*—We leave behind the good seeds of honesty and integrity for the coming generations.

2. Relationships are based on many small acts of initiative.
- *Trust*—Build relationships based on trust, love, dependability, and respect. Become a trustworthy person. Follow through on even the little things you say you will do.
- *Kindness*—Learn to be a loving person, both in giving and receiving. Thomas Aquinas counseled: "The happy man needs friends . . . namely, that he may do good to them, that he may delight in seeing them do good, and again that he may be helped by them in his good work."
- *Respect*—Respect all people in every way. Don't let the state of your relationship affect your respect.

- *Service*—Do things for others that enhance and build up the relationships.
- *Loyalty*—Never gossip. It will damage all your relationships as people will always wonder what you say behind their backs. "Now friendship may be thus defined: a complete accord on all subjects human and divine, joined with mutual goodwill and affection," declared Cicero.
- *Support*—Honestly compliment and praise others regularly.
- *Caring*—Do the little things that let people know you care. "Real friendship is shown in times of trouble; prosperity is full of friends," counseled Euripides.

3. Some relationships are sacred.
- *Parents*—We must do all in our power to honor our parents, no matter the circumstances.
- *Spouse*—Where the relationship between husband and wife is grounded in commitment, shared vision, forgiving tenderness, and abiding love, success and harmony are almost ensured.
- *Children*—No duty or commission in life is higher than the parents' sacred obligation to work for the good of their children.
- *God*—If our relationship with Heavenly Father and our Savior Jesus Christ is based on humility, gratitude, honor, and obedience, our lives will reflect peace and quiet joy.

ILLUSTRATIONS FOR OUR TIMES

The following, as told by F. Burton Howard in a general conference talk, emphasizes the point that beautiful relationships require great care and commitment.

Eternal Marriage

> I think eternal marriage cannot be achieved without a commitment to make it work. Most of what I know about this I have learned from my companion. We have been married for almost 47 years now. From the beginning she knew what kind of marriage she wanted.

> We started as poor college students, but her vision for our marriage was exemplified by a set of silverware. As is common today, when we married she registered with a local department store. Instead of listing all the pots and pans and appliances we needed and hoped to receive, she chose another course. She asked for silverware. She chose a pattern and the number of place settings and listed knives, forks, and spoons on the wedding registry and nothing else. No towels, no toasters, no television—just knives, forks, and spoons.

> The wedding came and went. Our friends and our parents' friends gave gifts. We departed for a brief honeymoon and decided to open the presents when we returned. When we did so, we were shocked. There was not a single knife or fork in the lot. We joked about it and went on with our lives.

> Two children came along while we were in law school. We had no money to spare. But when my wife worked as a part-time election judge or when someone gave her a few dollars for her birthday, she would quietly set it aside, and when she had enough she would go to town to buy a fork or a spoon. It took us several years to accumulate enough pieces to use them. When we finally had service for four, we began to invite some of our friends for dinner.

> Before they came, we would have a little discussion in the kitchen. Which utensils would we use, the battered and mismatched stainless or the special silverware? In those early days I would often vote for the stainless. It was easier. You could just throw it in the dishwasher after the meal, and

it took care of itself. The silver, on the other hand, was a lot of work. My wife had it hidden away under the bed where it could not be found easily by a burglar. She had insisted that I buy a tarnish-free cloth to wrap it in. Each piece was in a separate pocket, and it was no easy task to assemble all the pieces. When the silver was used, it had to be hand washed and dried so that it would not spot, and put back in the pockets so it would not tarnish, and wrapped up and carefully hidden again so it would not get stolen. If any tarnish was discovered, I was sent to buy silver polish, and together we carefully rubbed the stains away.

Over the years we added to the set, and I watched with amazement how she cared for the silver. My wife was never one to get angry easily. However, I remember the day when one of our children somehow got hold of one of the silver forks and wanted to use it to dig up the backyard. That attempt was met with a fiery glare and a warning not to even think about it. Ever!

I noticed that the silverware never went to the many ward dinners she cooked, or never accompanied the many meals she made and sent to others who were sick or needy. It never went on picnics and never went camping. In fact it never went anywhere; and, as time went by, it didn't even come to the table very often. Some of our friends were weighed in the balance, found wanting, and didn't even know it. They got the stainless when they came to dinner. . . .

For years I thought she was just a little bit eccentric, and then one day I realized that she had known for a long time something that I was just beginning to understand. *If you want something to last forever, you treat it differently.* You shield it and protect it. You never abuse it. You don't expose it to the elements. You don't make it common or ordinary. If it ever becomes tarnished, you lovingly polish it until it gleams like new. It becomes special because you have made it so, and it grows more beautiful and precious as time goes by. (F. Burton Howard, "Eternal Marriage," *Ensign,* May 2003, 92; italics in original)

SUMMARY

A list of helpful hints for good relationships could go on forever. The key elements seem to be caring for the other person and working together to make the relationship strong. Through faith and devoted effort, we can truly attain our worthy goals to have close and endearing relationships. We are told: "in the strength of the Lord thou canst do all things" (Alma 20:4). Undoubtedly, our enduring relationships of trust and love are of great enough importance to the Lord for Him to lend His strength to them.

REMEMBERING

The word *remember* or a form of the word occurs frequently throughout the scriptures—over 110 times in the Book of Mormon and Doctrine and Covenants alone. As we have made covenants with our Heavenly Father, it is clear that the power to do good and be good is tied to our ability to remember these covenants. The ability to keep sacred things in our minds is also a part of our covenants—to remember to recall and retain, and to think back upon these things, that we might remember the goodness of God and keep the commandments. To remember is more than just recollecting the thought periodically. It means always to have the principle, doctrine, and covenant in our mind. In remembering, we should think upon the things of the Lord and in particular our covenants. This is a key point in living the gospel: "For as he thinketh in his heart, so is he" (Prov. 23:7).

THE SCRIPTURES TEACH US

1 Nephi 17:45. *Ye are swift to do iniquity but slow to remember the Lord your God.*

When we fail to remember the Lord, we easily and quickly stray from Him. Therefore, we are counseled constantly throughout the scriptures to remember: the Lord (see Mosiah 4:11), covenants and commandments (see 1 Ne. 15:20), the word of God (see 1 Ne. 7: 15), our heritage (see Alma 5:6), and those around us (see D&C 18:10).

2 Nephi 10:20. *And now, my beloved brethren, seeing that our merciful God has given us so great knowledge concerning these things, let us remember him, and lay aside our sins, and not hang down our heads, for we are not cast off.*

As we ponder the things of the gospel, we recognize its goodness, and we increase our desire to live righteously. We forsake our sins only if we remember to do so; this is why we are ever working for, studying, and searching out the things of God.

Doctrine and Covenants 20:77. *O God, the Eternal Father, we ask thee in the name of thy Son, Jesus Christ, to bless and sanctify this bread to the souls of all those who partake of it, that they may eat in remembrance of the body of thy Son, and witness unto thee, O God, the Eternal Father, that they are willing to take upon them the name of thy Son, and always remember him and keep his commandments which he has given them; that they may always have his Spirit to be with them. Amen.* (See also D&C 20:79; Moro. 4:3; 5:2.)

The sacramental prayers command us to remember His sacrifice, His body, and His blood, and to always remember Him and keep His commandments. If we do, we are rewarded with the blessing of always having His Spirit to be with us. During the sacrament we renew our baptismal covenants. The key to living them is to "remember."

MODERN PROPHETS SPEAK

Spencer W. Kimball:
> When you look in the dictionary for the most important word, do you know what it is? . . . "Remember" is the word. ("Circles of Exaltation" [Address to religious educators, BYU, 28 June 1968], 8)

Henry B. Eyring:
> How can you and I remember, always, the goodness of God, that we can retain a remission of our sins? The Apostle John recorded what the Savior taught us of a gift of remembrance which comes through the gift of the Holy Ghost: "But the Comforter, which is the Holy Ghost, whom the Father will send in my name, he shall teach you all things, and bring all things to your remembrance, whatsoever I have said unto you." (John 14:26.) (*To Draw Closer to God: A Collection of Discourses* [Salt Lake City: Deseret Book, 1997], 77–78)

Neal A. Maxwell:

> Remembering and counting our many blessings can humble us by reminding us of all the reasons we have to be thankful to God; not just today's reasons, but those relating to all our yesterdays. Each week a sincere partaking of the sacrament can become part of this very process. We partake "in remembrance," so that we may "always remember" what Jesus has done for us (3 Nephi 18:11; Moroni 4, 5).
>
> If we fail to stir remembrance of blessings received, the human tendency is to say, in effect, whether to one's God or to one's fellows, "What have you done for me lately?" Indeed, prophets of the Lord have asked directly whether their people had "sufficiently retained in remembrance" His deliverances and blessings (Alma 5:6–7). It is best to cultivate our "remembering" capacity now and to be guided accordingly, since at judgment day we will have "perfect remembrance" (Alma 5:18). The important theme of remembrance occurs in one form or another in the Old Testament well over two hundred times. It appears in the Book of Mormon dozens of times, too. This parallelism is to be expected, since the Israelites in Palestine observed the law of Moses and the Nephites kept it "strictly" for many years (see Mosiah 13:30; Alma 30:3). Wherever the gospel is, there too is the call to remembrance. (*A Wonderful Flood of Light* [Salt Lake City: Bookcraft, 1990], 51)

IDEAS FOR DAILY LIVING

Here are some ideas to help us remember the important things in life:

1. Search the scriptures and feast upon the word of God.
- *Goals*—Make specific goals to search the scriptures regularly.
- *Study*—Review the words of the living prophets, including general conference addresses.
- *Standard works*—Read and study the standard works. As noted above, the scriptures themselves are a reminder.

2. Pray always.
- *When*—Pray morning, noon, and night (see Alma 34:21). Even when ceasing to pray formally, we should go with a prayer in our heart (see 3 Ne. 20:1). Prayer will keep us focused on the Lord and His will.
- *How*—We are to pray with all the energy of our hearts (see Moro. 7:48).
- *Worship*—Our prayers are themselves a form of worship (see Alma 33:3).

3. Count blessings.
- *Counting is part of remembering*—The process of counting is an important part of remembering—for it will keep us tuned to our dependence on the Lord and prevent us from becoming proud and self-sufficient.
- *Gratitude*—When we remember our blessings, we will be filled with gratitude and we will remember the Savior and Heavenly Father and all that They have done for us.

4. Use innovative and creative strategies.
- *Signs*—Place signs around the house and workplace (posters, cards, photos, sticky notes).
- *External sounds or sights*—Assign something ordinary and everyday to be a trigger for memory. Examples include hearing the sound of a bell (telephone, door bell, digital planning device), hearing an automobile horn honking, or seeing a light or stop sign at an intersection—anything to

remind you of commitments and covenant promises. You should make a list of sounds or sights that work well for you.

- *The creations of God*—Notice animals, plants, rivers and streams, mountains and valleys, the stars in the heavens. All of these can serve as reminders of the magnificent gift of the Creation and the power and glory of God. As Alma says, "All things denote there is a God" (Alma 30:43), and point us to Him.
- *Inventions*—View the things the Lord has inspired others to invent or build as gifts from God. These may include cars, planes, boats, farm equipment, medical devices, technology, etc.

ILLUSTRATIONS FOR OUR TIMES

The following personal story reveals that our hands can be a constant reminder of our duties and obligations in the Lord's Church.

The Lesson of the Hands

The Lord's special memory device for bringing to our minds the promises of obedience we make to Him under the covenant is the sacrament of the Lord's supper. To partake of the sacrament we must, of course, use our hands. Should we not also think of our hands as a constant, ever-present lesson in remembering who we are and how we should behave? I recall many years ago being assigned as a priesthood leader to visit the Hampstead Branch of the Baltimore Stake. Seated on the stand during sacrament meeting, I had a clear view of the deacons along the front row waiting to pass the emblems to the congregation. That day the sacrament hymn was the beautiful and tender song that begins "While of these emblems we partake, in Jesus' name and for his sake." As we continued with the words—"Let us remember and be sure our hearts and hands are clean and pure"—I happened at just that moment to be looking down at one of the young deacons. There he was, holding both of his open hands out in front of him, palms upward. He was gazing upon them intently as if to find reassurance that he was, indeed, a worthy servant of the Lord about to participate in a sacred ordinance. I shall never forget that image of the young man and his extended hands. Our hands are, indeed, a constant reminder that we should be continually engaged in the Lord's errand, ever intent on keeping His commandments, ever vigilant that our hearts and hands remain unsullied by the world's ungodly practices, ever committed to that which is ennobling and edifying. The Lord counseled: "Be ye clean, that bear the vessels of the Lord" (Isa. 52:11).

—Richard J. Allen

* * *

This story suggests a simple way to help us remember to keep the commandments.

The Penny

Years ago I would put up signs all over the house to help me remember to keep the commandments—on the mirrors, on the bulletin boards, and even in the dental office—displaying just one word: "Remember." Then one day I was walking along and realized I wasn't "remembering" with sufficient intensity because the signs were not always in front of me—so I put a penny in my shoe so I wouldn't forget. I wore one in my shoe for over six years. Then I started giving them out at firesides. Pretty soon people would come up to me and say, "Brother Ed, I still have your penny in my shoe—it's really helping me remember." One night I was speaking at a "Know Your Religion Series" up in Oregon, and a man who taught institute came up to me, took off his shoe, removed a penny, and said, "I have had this penny for five years since you gave it to me when I was teaching at Orem High School Seminary—it really works." We reminisced and agreed that "remembering" is indeed the key to assisting us in keeping the commandments.

—Ed J. Pinegar

SUMMARY

Remembering is imperative in living the gospel of Jesus Christ and enduring to the end. When we forget God and are swallowed up in the temptations of the world, sin will easily beset us. Each Sabbath day we make covenants to remember our Savior and all He has done for us. We should try to remember each day to do the things the Lord has commanded us. If we do so, we will be happy, and through our righteousness and the grace of God, we can enjoy never-ending joy (see Mosiah 2:41).

REPENTANCE

The Atonement of Jesus Christ makes possible the miracle of repentance and forgiveness. Repentance, the process of becoming clean from sin, is necessary to our salvation (see D&C 20:29). It is the first principle of the gospel (see A of F 1:4), as it is through repentance that progression is even possible. Through repentance and faith on Jesus Christ, we can be forgiven and our guilt can be swept away (see Enos 1:6–8). Therefore, faith and repentance are preached continually throughout the scriptures and by our living prophets. Repentance and baptism are the gateway into the kingdom of God and a prerequisite for entrance into the celestial kingdom (see D&C 20:71). All must repent, for all have sinned (see 1 Jn. 1:8). The consequences for failing to repent are severe; if we do not repent, we must suffer even as our Savior Jesus Christ did (see D&C 19:15–19).

THE SCRIPTURES TEACH US

Acts 3:19. *Repent ye therefore, and be converted, that your sins may be blotted out, when the times of refreshing shall come from the presence of the Lord.*

The commandment is clear: the Lord wants people to repent and be converted to the gospel, come unto Him through baptism, and receive remission of their sins. We should thank our Heavenly Father for this great privilege and keep His commandments, with the fervent hope of returning to His presence.

Alma 5:31–33. *Wo unto such an one, for he is not prepared, and the time is at hand that he must repent or he cannot be saved! Yea, even wo unto all ye workers of iniquity; repent, repent, for the Lord God hath spoken it! Behold, he sendeth an invitation unto all men, for the arms of mercy are extended towards them, and he saith: Repent, and I will receive you.*

Let us never forget the necessity of repentance; it is through repentance that can we be saved. In fact, if we do not repent, and if we fail to believe in Christ and be baptized, we will be damned (see 3 Ne. 11:34). If we repent, He will receive us. Perfection is not so much about living a perfect life as it is in living a life of perfect repentance. Lehi taught that "by the law no flesh is justified"—meaning that no mortal can perfectly live every aspect of the law of God (see 2 Ne. 2:5)—hence the need for a Savior to extend the arms of mercy to all who repent and offer to Him a broken heart and a contrite spirit.

Alma 34:15–17. *And thus he shall bring salvation to all those who shall believe on his name; this being the intent of this last sacrifice, to bring about the bowels of mercy, which overpowereth justice, and bringeth about means unto men that they may have faith unto repentance. And thus mercy can satisfy the demands of justice, and encircles them in the arms of safety, while he that exercises no faith unto repentance is exposed to the whole law of the demands of justice; therefore only unto him that has faith unto repentance is brought about the great and eternal plan of redemption. Therefore may God grant unto you, my brethren, that ye may begin to exercise your faith unto repentance, that ye begin to call upon his holy name, that he would have mercy upon you.*

Repentance begins with faith in the Lord Jesus Christ, whose Atonement provides payment for our sins if we but choose to repent. If we do not repent, we will face the whole law of the demands of justice, and we will suffer in the eternities for our sins. The overpowering of justice by mercy is possible because Jesus Christ satisfied the demands of the law by His infinite and eternal sacrifice. This is what is referred to by the plan of redemption. We must call upon God, seeking forgiveness of our sins and asking that He have mercy on us.

Doctrine and Covenants 19:15–17. *Therefore I command you to repent—repent, lest I smite you by the rod of my mouth, and by my wrath, and by my anger, and your sufferings be sore—how sore you know not, how exquisite you know not, yea, how hard to bear you know not. For behold, I, God, have suffered these things for all, that they might not suffer if they would repent; But if they would not repent they must suffer even as I.*

The Savior loves us and has suffered for our sins. However, we can only take advantage of His Atonement if we repent. If we choose not to repent, justice requires that we suffer for our own sins. The Savior Himself described these sufferings as exquisite, as so sore and hard to bear that our finite human minds cannot comprehend it. How wise we would be to repent rather than to be smitten by the wrath and anger of the Lord, who cannot look on sin with the least degree of allowance.

Doctrine and Covenants 58:42–43. *Behold, he who has repented of his sins, the same is forgiven, and I, the Lord, remember them no more. By this ye may know if a man repenteth of his sins—behold, he will confess them and forsake them.*

When we truly repent, the Lord forgives us and no longer remembers our sins. True repentance requires confession of sins and forsaking them, or abandoning and never returning to them. The joy of knowing that the Lord will not remember our sins and that our guilt is swept away should be motive enough for us to repent.

MODERN PROPHETS SPEAK

Harold B. Lee:
> In order for good to blossom it must be cultivated and exercised by constant practice, and to be truly righteous there is required a daily pruning of the evil growth of our characters by a daily repentance from sin. (*The Teachings of Harold B. Lee,* ed. Clyde J. Williams [Salt Lake City: Bookcraft, 1996], 113)

Gordon B. Hinckley:

> Repentance is one of the first principles of the gospel. Forgiveness is a mark of divinity. There is hope for you. Your lives are ahead, and they can be filled with happiness, even though the past may have been marred by sin. This is a work of saving and assisting people with their problems. This is the purpose of the gospel. (*Teachings of Gordon B. Hinckley* [Salt Lake City: Deseret Book, 1997], 548)

Ezra Taft Benson:

> Yes, one can repent of moral transgression. The miracle of forgiveness is real, and true repentance is accepted of the Lord. But it is not pleasing to the Lord to sow one's wild oats, to engage in sexual transgression of any nature and then expect that planned confession and quick repentance will satisfy the Lord. . . .
>
> The Prophet Joseph Smith taught: "God does not look on sin with allowance, but when men have sinned, there must be allowance made for them" (*Teachings of the Prophet Joseph Smith,* pp. 240–41). That is another way of saying God loves the sinner, but condemns the sin. . . .
>
> We all stand in need of change and reformation. We all need to rededicate ourselves to righteous, moral living. . . .
>
> True repentance must come to each individual. (*The Teachings of Ezra Taft Benson* [Salt Lake City: Bookcraft, 1988], 70, 86)

IDEAS FOR DAILY LIVING

Here are some steps to follow in the repentance process:

1. Recognize your sin. Become aware of your transgression to the point that you realize your need for repentance.

2. Feel godly sorrow for sin. Godly sorrow entails having a broken heart and a contrite spirit, which "worketh repentance" (see 2 Cor. 7:10). Godly sorrow is motivated by love of the Lord and not social pressures. A broken heart and a contrite spirit, or in other words, a sorrowful heart and a humbled spirit, are the offering we give the Lord as a sacrifice before Him (see 3 Ne. 9:20).

3. Forsake the sin. Stop committing the sin (see D&C 58:42–43) and turn away from it, even to the point of having no desire to sin, but to do good continually (see Mosiah 5:2). George Q. Cannon confirmed: "All are sinners and need repentance. We cannot commit sin and retain His Spirit" (*Gospel Truth: Discourses and Writings of President George Q. Cannon,* selected, ed. Jerreld L. Newquist [Salt Lake City: Deseret Book, 1987], 126).

4. Confess the sin. Confess your sins to Heavenly Father and, when necessary, to your bishop (see D&C 64:7). "Without sincere confession of sin repentance is impossible," (James E. Talmage, *The Vitality of Mormonism* [Boston: Gorham Press, 1919], 83).

5. Make restitution for the sin. Attempt to restore where possible that which was taken or destroyed. We often cannot make full restitution due to the nature of the sin. The power of the Atonement makes it possible to overcome our inadequacies through our Savior Jesus Christ (see Alma 7:11–12).

6. Forgive others. We must forgive everyone, especially those involved in any sin committed against us (see Matt. 6:14–15). Though a difficult, and often a lengthy process, it is as necessary for our repentance and salvation as it is to the one who sinned against us (see D&C 64:9–10). Only as we forgive others do we show the Lord that our hearts are right and that we merit His forgiveness.

7. Make a commitment not to sin again. Make a commitment—or a covenant in the case of baptism and partaking of the sacrament—to be obedient to all the commandments and endure to the end in righteousness (see 2 Ne. 31:19–21).

ILLUSTRATIONS FOR OUR TIMES

Elder William H. Bennett compares the course corrections necessary on the Apollo 13 mission to the repentance we must undertake in order to stay on the course to eternal life.

The Correction Was Made

> The gospel teaches the importance of obedience to law. . . . You will remember that the astronauts on one of the missions had an outward trip and a return trip. On the outward trip their goal was the moon. On the return trip their goal was the earth, their home base. They reached their goals both going and coming because they themselves, the engines and the instruments under their control, and those at mission control at home base were able to operate in accordance with law.
>
> Do you remember what happened on the Apollo 13 mission? As they made their return trip they were almost home when they found out that they were off course a bit. They had to make a correction. To do so, they had to fire their engine. If that engine hadn't fired, the correction could not have been made; they would have missed the earth by eighty miles, and we wouldn't have been able to bring them back. But the engine did fire, and the correction was made, and they returned to earth safe and sound.
>
> Is there not an important lesson there for us? Is it not true that we, too, had an outward trip when we left our Father in heaven in the spirit world and came to earth? Are we not now walking around on our earth, which might be likened to the astronaut's moon? And is it not true that whether or not we will be able sometime in the future to return to our Father in heaven, our home base, will be dependent on our willingness and our ability to observe the laws and keep the commandments that pertain thereto? And is it not true that the Lord has provided us with a way through repentance for making a correction to put us back on course when we have strayed because of sin?
>
> The gospel of Jesus Christ is the answer to all problems. However, men and women everywhere must be doers of the word, and not hearers only, if they would have peace in the world and would find joy and happiness in this life and in the life to come. This is our great and important test. (William H. Bennett, in *Outstanding Stories by General Authorities,* comp. Leon R. Hartshorn [Salt Lake City: Deseret Book, 1974], 3:5)

SUMMARY

The Lord has made it clear that in order for us to apply and live His gospel we must repent and come unto Him (see 3 Ne. 27:20–21). Now this is the time for us to repent. We should not procrastinate the day of our repentance, for we never know when the days of our mortal probation will come to an end (see Alma

34:31–35). Constant repentance is the key to exaltation. Through the Atonement and the grace of God, we truly can be saved. Therefore, let us choose to repent and become clean and free from sin. Unspeakable blessings await the repentant soul who valiantly endures to the end in faith and obedience.

REVELATION

Revelation is communication from God to His children. This communication takes many different forms, including personal visitations of Deity, angels, or the Holy Ghost; open visions; the voice of the Holy Ghost; dreams; a whispering in the mind and heart; or any similar inspiration from the Holy Ghost. Revelation can be of universal significance, as given through the prophets, or of personal application, as given to us in our personal lives and Church callings. As children of our Heavenly Father, we have the privilege to receive inspiration and direction in our lives, for God is no respecter of persons (see D&C 38:16). The Holy Ghost as the Revelator will give us revelation and direction according to our needs and worthiness (see 2 Ne. 32:5; Moro. 10:5). The blessings of revelation can be ours as we ask in faith, believing that we will receive (see D&C 8:1–3).

THE SCRIPTURES TEACH US

Amos 3:7. *Surely the Lord God will do nothing, but He revealeth His secret unto His servants the prophets.*

The Lord has set up an order whereby He gives revelation to His Church, and we can trust in that order. We can trust in our prophets because they do in fact receive revelations from our Heavenly Father to direct the Church (see D&C 1:4–6, 38; 107:92).

Proverbs 29:18. *Where there is no vision, the people perish: but he that keepeth the law, happy is he.*

Revelation is the pattern by which mankind has been shown the things of God, and in particular the plan of salvation. It is the rock upon which the Church and kingdom of God is built (see Matt 16:18). Continuing revelation sets us apart from other religions.

1 Corinthians 2:10. *But God hath revealed them unto us by his Spirit: for the Spirit searcheth all things, yea, the deep things of God.*

The Revelator is the Holy Ghost. He will show us the things we should do (see 2 Ne. 32:5), the things we should say (see D&C 100:5–6), and the truth of all things (see Moro. 10:5). We must live worthy of the Spirit by increasing our faith (see 1 Ne. 10:17), being full of love, purifying ourselves before God (see D&C 76:116), and cultivating exact obedience as we keep the commandments (see D&C 20:77, 79). The Lord will provide a way to do this if we do our best in faith and humility (see 1 Ne. 3:7).

Alma 5:46. *Behold, I say unto you they are made known unto me by the Holy Spirit of God. Behold, I have fasted and prayed many days that I might know these things of myself. And now I do know of myself that they are true; for the Lord God hath made them manifest unto me by his Holy Spirit; and this is the spirit of revelation which is in me.*

It is our right, along with the prophets, to know the things of God (see D&C 42:61; 76:7). We gain this revelation by the same means they do; by fasting and praying to be near the Spirit of the Lord. There is a price to pay in order to know the things of God, as Oliver Cowdery learned (see D&C 9:7). We must do our part: study the word of God, fast and pray, exercise our faith, and have a righteous reason for asking (see Alma 17:2–3).

Articles of Faith 1:7, 9. *We believe in the gift of tongues, prophecy, revelation, visions, healing, interpretation of tongues, and so forth. . . . We believe all that God has revealed, all that He does now reveal, and we believe that he will yet reveal many great and important things pertaining to the kingdom of God.*

For the Church to bless the lives of Heavenly Father's children, continuous revelation is absolutely essential. Indeed, as a church and as individuals, we should live by the word of God (see D&C 84:43–46). Revelation is imperative in keeping individuals on the straight and narrow path.

MODERN PROPHETS SPEAK

Joseph Smith:

> The spirit of revelation is in connection with these blessings. A person may profit by noticing the first intimation of the spirit of revelation; for instance, when you feel pure intelligence flowing into you, it may give you sudden strokes of ideas, so that by noticing it, you may find it fulfilled the same day or soon; (i.e.) those things that were presented unto your minds by the Spirit of God, will come to pass; and thus by learning the Spirit of God and understanding it, you may grow into the principle of revelation, until you become perfect in Christ Jesus. (*History of the Church,* 3:381)

Joseph B. Wirthlin:

> In our own lives today, we receive revelation through the still, small voice that whispers "Yes, that applies to me." The Prophet Joseph Smith received this kind of revelation when he read in James 1:5 that he should pray and ask God. It was in a similar circumstance that President Joseph F. Smith, after reading and contemplating the scriptures, had the vision of the redemption of the dead (D&C 138) opened to his mind. Regular study of the scriptures and meditating upon them is essential for continual revelation. (*Finding Peace in Our Lives* [Salt Lake City: Deseret Book, 1995], 173)

Gordon B. Hinckley:

> I believe in prayer, that prayer which is the practice of those who have been called to leadership in this Church and which brings forth inspiration and revelation from God for the blessing of his church and people. I believe in prayer, the precious and wonderful privilege given each of us for our individual guidance, comfort, and peace. (*Teachings of Gordon B. Hinckley* [Salt Lake City: Deseret Book, 1997], 467)

Boyd K. Packer:

> Revelation in the Church comes to those who have been properly called, sustained, ordained, or set apart. A bishop, for instance, will not receive any revelation concerning a neighboring ward, because that is out of his jurisdiction. (*Let Not Your Heart Be Troubled* [Salt Lake City: Bookcraft, 1991], 212)

IDEAS FOR DAILY LIVING

Here are some ideas to help us qualify for and receive revelation:

1. Become worthy.

- *Become purified*—Worthiness implies personal righteousness through repentance (see Moro. 8:26), as well as the need for revelation according to our stewardship and the will of God.
- *Have a righteous focus*—An eye single to the glory of God will help us understand all things that are taught and revealed to us (see D&C 88:67).
- *Live in humility*—Humility is absolutely essential in understanding and following the will of God in our lives.
- *Be open to inspiration*—As children of our Father in Heaven, we have the sacred right to call upon Him for inspiration: "And it is the right and privilege of every man, every woman, and every child who has reached the years of accountability, to enjoy the spirit of revelation, and to be possessed of the spirit of inspiration in the discharge of their duties as members of the Church" (Joseph F. Smith, *Gospel Doctrine: Selections from the Sermons and Writings of Joseph F. Smith,* comp. John A. Widtsoe [Salt Lake City: Deseret Book, 1939], 34).

2. Prepare every needful thing.

- *Ponder*—We should ponder and meditate regarding the situation we need revelation for, just as Nephi did (see 1 Ne. 11:1) and as the Prophet Joseph F. Smith did (see D&C 138:1, 11).
- *Seek out holy places*—There are sacred places that are conducive to receiving revelation, such as temples and other sacred spots that are free from the things of the world. Often nature and mountaintops can contribute to a feeling of receptiveness for inspiration (think of the Prophet Joseph in the Sacred Grove or Moses on Mount Sinai).

3. Ask in faith.

- *Pray for inspiration*—The words, "Ask, and it shall be given you; seek, and ye shall find; knock, and it shall be opened unto you" (Matt. 7:7) should be our frame of mind in regard to receiving inspiration and revelation from the Lord.
- *Exercise faith*—We must have faith that we can and will receive revelation, or our spirit will not be receptive when the revelation comes. Let us ask in faith, believing.
- *Fast as needed*—It is essential to fast and pray as required, in order to receive revelation (see Alma 5:46).
- *Do the work*—Remember that we must do specific things to receive an answer. These may include studying, meditating, cultivating possible solutions, reading the scriptures, and making a concerted effort to think things through.

4. Recognizing spiritual promptings.

- *Be discerning*—Recognize the feelings of the Spirit: peace, love, long-suffering, etc. (see Gal. 5:22–23), and a desire to do good, walk humbly, do justly, and feel enlightened (see D&C 11:12–13). "We must be guided by personal revelation and the counsel of the living prophet so we will not be deceived" (Ezra Taft Benson, *Come unto Christ* [Salt Lake City: Deseret Book, 1983], 115).
- *Be receptive to the Lord's means of communicating with you*—The Lord can reveal truth in a variety of ways. Sometimes answers to prayers or lessons in wisdom come through others, sometimes through the scriptures, sometimes as a still, small voice. Know when these experiences are happening and when they are counterfeit.

ILLUSTRATIONS FOR OUR TIMES

In a personal account, Orson F. Whitney shows us how the Holy Ghost will prompt us to seek the revelation we need.

Why Don't You Pray?

I found myself in an overworked, run-down condition, manifesting a decided lack of physical and mental vigor. . . . One morning I was endeavoring to write the usual editorial [for the *Millennial Star* in Liverpool], but could make no headway, and wore out the whole day in a vain attempt to produce something worth reading. At last I threw down my pen and burst into tears of vexation.

Just then the Good Spirit whispered: "Why don't you pray?"

As if a voice had addressed me audibly, I answered, "I do pray." I was praying five times a day—secret prayers, morning, noon and night; and vocal prayers, with the rest of the household, at breakfast and dinner time. "I do pray—why can't I get some help," I asked, almost petulantly, for I was heartsick and half-discouraged.

"Pray now," said the Spirit, "and ask for what you want."

I saw the point. It was a special not a general prayer that was needed. I knelt and sobbed out a few simple words. I did not pray for the return of the Ten Tribes nor for the building of the New Jerusalem. I asked the Lord in the name of Jesus Christ to help me write that article. I then arose, seated myself, and began to write. My mind was now perfectly clear, and my pen fairly flew over the paper. All I needed came as fast as I could set it down—every thought, every word in place. In a short time the article was completed to my entire satisfaction. (Orson F. Whitney, *Through Memory's Halls: The Life Story of Orson F. Whitney* [Independence, MO: Zion's Printing and Publishing, 1930], 151–52)

SUMMARY

The blessing and privilege of revelation is given to the children of God through the power of the Holy Ghost. We need to ask ourselves: Are we worthy and prepared to receive revelation? Do we seek revelation? Do we ask with a pure heart and exercise our faith? Without revelation, we cannot know the things of God, we cannot be directed in our lives, and we cannot be exalted. Revelation is the rock upon which the Church is built and it is a principle of knowledge and wisdom in our personal lives.

REVERENCE

Elder Bruce R. McConkie said of reverence, "The feelings of respect, awe, veneration, and love are part of being reverent. In the world today we too often fail to teach and demonstrate reverence to our children. Reverence is due not only to God and his holy name, but to his laws, his gospel, his covenants, his prophets, his ordinances, his temples, his priesthood, and all the things he has revealed and given for the salvation and blessing of his children" (*Mormon Doctrine*, 2nd ed. [Salt Lake City: Bookcraft, 1966], 651).

When we treat lightly sacred and important things we fail to revere God. We create and become part of a generation of disrespectful, cynical, and often rudely-behaving people. The lack of reverence results in a lack of respect for laws and rules designed to bring civility to society and salvation to mankind. We can see that reverence truly affects the quality of life we all want to enjoy. President David O. McKay taught, "Reverence is profound respect mingled with love" (Conference Report, Oct. 1956, 6). Marion G. Romney observed, "Reverence is the soul of true religion. Its seedbed is sincerity" ("The Beginning of Wisdom," *BYU Speeches of the Year, 1964*, 7).

THE SCRIPTURES TEACH US

Hebrews 12:9. *Furthermore we have had fathers of our flesh which corrected us, and we gave them reverence: shall we not much rather be in subjection unto the Father of spirits, and live?*

As we show respect to our earthly fathers, we should consider our relationship with our Heavenly Father, who has given us all things. We should not only show reverence and devotion to our Heavenly Father, but we should be willing to submit to all things He asks of us, thus demonstrating our love and respect (see Mosiah 3:19).

Hebrews 12:28. *Wherefore we receiving a kingdom which cannot be moved, let us have grace, whereby we may serve God acceptably with reverence and godly fear.*

Understanding the glory of God and having a desire to serve Him requires that we demonstrate reverence. The word *fear* (godly fear) as used in the Old and New Testaments refers to reverence (see Bible Dictionary, "Fear," 672).

Doctrine and Covenants 76:92–93. *And thus we saw the glory of the celestial, which excels in all things—where God, even the Father, reigns upon his throne forever and ever; before whose throne all things bow in humble reverence, and give him glory forever and ever.*

When the Prophet Joseph and Sidney Rigdon received the visions of the degrees of glory, they prepared the way for us to know these great truths. This particular revelation teaches us that we are to become humble (having a relationship with, and dependence upon, our Heavenly Father and our Savior) and show reverence in total submissiveness. In this way we give God the glory in all things. When we remember these truths and incorporate them into our lives, we are more sober minded and more sensitive to the Spirit.

Doctrine and Covenants 84:54. *And your minds in times past have been darkened because of unbelief, and because you have treated lightly the things you have received—*

The context of this scripture is that the people had treated lightly the Book of Mormon and some of the commandments. The best blood of the nineteenth century—that of the Prophet Joseph Smith and Hyrum Smith—was given to bring forth the word of God. We must reverence all the gifts of God, but especially the word of God, for that is how we learn to live our lives day-by-day (see D&C 84:43–46). When we fail to show reverence for sacred things, we do not have an eye single to the glory of God, and hence we are not filled with light so as to comprehend all things (see D&C 88:67).

MODERN PROPHETS SPEAK

Gordon B. Hinckley:

We need to strengthen our sacrament meetings and make them hours of worship in very deed. Cultivate a spirit of reverence, an attitude in which people come into the chapel and are quiet and reverent and thoughtful. There is too much noise. We are a sociable people, but I wish we would not keep it up so loudly in the chapel. . . .

I hope brethren and sisters, that we will do all we can to cultivate a spirit of reverence always in the House of the Lord. I regret to say that we have so little of it in our meetinghouses. There is little of it even in the homes of the people. The temple is the one place to which our people can go, many of them carrying very heavy burdens, and feel a quiet and wonderful spirit of communion with our Father in Heaven. (*Teachings of Gordon B. Hinckley* [Salt Lake City: Deseret Book, 1997], 558)

Harold B. Lee:

We need to nurture reverence in children. Reverence defined is profound respect, mingled with love and awe, for a holy being, place, or exalted thing. Now, may I give you four statements to summarize what has been presented:

First, there must be an opportunity given for children to practice being reverent.

Second, there are certain symbols which induce reverence: beautifully played and appropriate organ music . . . the light, the heat, the seating, the voice of the teacher, the dress of the teacher, her manner—symbols that induce reverence.

Third, children to be taught reverence need examples. Could you imagine reverent children from a home where they see no respect of father for mother or mother for father? . . . Could you imagine a reverent child from a home where he hears the constant criticism of Church authorities or where there is habitual resistance to counsel coming from Church leaders? . . . Parents cannot expect their children to be better than the example they set at home. They cannot practice all the things that are wrong and then expect the children to do all things that are right.

Fourth, we reverence that which we love, adore, or respect. Reverence is a quality of the soul which needs a proper climate in which to flourish. Closely relative to this subject is what we call good manners. Manners might be said to be behavior and good breeding. Real manners have a moral significance and find their basis in that true and deepest self-respect which is built upon respect for others. "Manners," someone has said, "do not make the man but manners reveal the man." (*The Teachings of Harold B. Lee,* ed. Clyde J. Williams [Salt Lake City: Bookcraft, 1996], 202)

IDEAS FOR DAILY LIVING

Listed below are three things we can do to focus on reverence and help others to do likewise:

1. Decide what and whom you truly revere in life.
- *Heavenly Father and our Savior*—Without reverence for God there is no reverence for life. Understand the goodness of God and you will reverence God.

- *The word of God*—We will reverence the word of God as we come to understand the blessing and power of the scriptures in our lives.
- *All things*—There is dignity in all of God's creations, which testify of Him and His goodness (see Alma 30:44). We should appreciate the earth and all good things therein. Above all, we must reverence life and the inborn freedom that all should enjoy.
- *Values and principles*—Do you hold dear values such as truth, integrity, honor, courage, unity, harmony, and peace? Let people know you revere and respect such values.
- *Meditation*—Take time to ponder, meditate, savor the peaceful silence, and cultivate a feeling of thanks in your heart for the blessings of life.

2. Set an example of reverence for others.

- *Reverent speech*—Demonstrate by your speech a reverence for others and their beliefs. Never belittle people or things.
- *Spirituality*—Do not make light of sacred things. Set an example of reverence for the spiritual aspects of life. You can do this through prayer, dignified worship, reading the scriptures regularly, and giving praise and thanks to God.
- *Service*—There is no greater way to show that you revere people than by serving them willingly.

3. Exercise leadership in cultivating reverence in society.

- *The community*—Wherever you detect reverence in the community, recognize it, reinforce it, and reward it. Catch young people being reverent and respectful and thank them for their courtesy.
- *The environment*—Be reverent toward the environment by doing your part to prevent pollution, and by caring for and beautifying your space on earth. Teach others to do the same.
- *The law*—Respect and obey the law. Revere the institutions and positions of government that secure to individuals their rights and privileges. You can do this by playing an active role in the community, studying the issues, contributing to civic dialogue, and voting regularly.
- *The home*—Make the home a place of reverence by cultivating courtesy and respect among family members, fostering uplifting discourse and music, limiting the incursions of raucous and debasing television programs, and maintaining an environment that is peaceful and clean.

ILLUSTRATIONS FOR OUR TIMES

The following story tells how a teacher involved her class in hatching and "growing" chickens in order to teach them reverence for life.

Little Chicks Teach a Powerful Lesson

Mrs. Jones, a teacher, was trying to help the children of her class gain some sort of respect and reverence for life. They seemed so cynical and lacked the common decency associated with respect and reverence. Bill, the class clown, was always making fun of somebody. Tom, the tough guy, was always trying to hurt somebody or something. Others in the class were just ambivalent about life and sacred things. They were apathetic, to say the least. The teacher struggled. She thought, "I was teaching the subject okay, but I wasn't teaching *them*." After all, the theme of "Character Counts" was part of the ongoing curriculum for her school.

That's when Mrs. Jones came upon the idea. She decided to give them a life-changing experience—a hands-on experience with life. So she set up a little box with a warm light in it and put fertilized chicken eggs in the box. The children voted and named the chickens that would hatch in their very own classroom.

They were all excited. "We are having little chicks in our class!" Even Bill and Tom got involved. "Hey, this is pretty neat. We are growing chickens."

Time passed, and the big day came. The little chicks hatched. Now the class had to take care of them. They were responsible. They became the "mothers" or "hens" for the little chicks. They had to be careful, for they couldn't handle them too much—the little chicks couldn't tolerate that. The students got water and grain and all the things the chicks needed. The class became different. The students began to think differently. Because they were a part of the chicks' lives, they actually cared for the chicks. Everyone exhibited a respect for life and tenderness. Mrs. Jones was so pleased. A reverence for life, a reverence for learning was the result. She realized then that people had to "feel" about things in order to be respectful and reverent. Reverence and respect for life and sacred things comes with hands-on experience, the kind of experience that makes you a participant in the unfolding drama of our living world.

—Ed J. Pinegar

SUMMARY

An anonymous writer recorded these persuasive words: "Reverence is a cloak of honor we wear to keep warm and secure the feelings of love and respect we have within us for our fellowmen and for the dignity of life." Morality, civility, and peace are the by-products of reverence. Personal growth is enhanced with a reverent attitude and behavior. We can readily see the power of true principles when we practice being reverent.

RIGHTEOUSNESS

Righteousness describes that state of being in which one is blameless, faithful, full of good works, and obedient to the commandments of the Lord. Righteousness is the oil in our lamps (see Matt 25:1–13), and righteousness is happiness (see 2 Ne. 2:13). The Prophet Joseph explains how we must be righteous in order to obtain happiness: "Happiness is the object and design of our existence; and will be the end thereof, if we pursue the path that leads to it; and this path is virtue, uprightness, faithfulness, holiness, and keeping all the commandments of God" (*History of the Church* 5:134–135).

THE SCRIPTURES TEACH US

2 Nephi 9:18. *But, behold, the righteous, the saints of the Holy One of Israel, they who have believed in the Holy One of Israel, they who have endured the crosses of the world, and despised the shame of it, they shall inherit the kingdom of God, which was prepared for them from the foundation of the world, and their joy shall be full forever.*

Righteousness entails believing God, obeying Him, and enduring all the trials, tribulations, and persecutions of this life. Our righteousness will prepare us to receive all the Lord's blessings.

Mosiah 2:36–37. *And now, I say unto you, my brethren, that after ye have known and have been taught all these things, if ye should transgress and go contrary to that which has been spoken, that ye do withdraw yourselves from the Spirit of the Lord, that it may have no place in you to guide you in wisdom's paths that ye may be blessed, prospered, and preserved—I say unto you, that the man that doeth this, the same cometh out in open* *rebellion against God; therefore he listeth to obey the evil spirit, and becometh an enemy to all righteousness; therefore, the Lord has no place in him, for he dwelleth not in unholy temples.*

Righteousness, the state of becoming like Christ, comes from keeping the commandments. When we are taught gospel truths, we are accountable for our actions. As we break the commandments, we withdraw ourselves from the blessings of the Spirit, losing our direction. Choosing to follow Satan makes us enemies to all righteousness. We should be righteous so that the Spirit of God can dwell within us.

Mosiah 2:41. *And moreover, I would desire that ye should consider on the blessed and happy state of those that keep the commandments of God. For behold, they are blessed in all things, both temporal and spiritual; and if they hold out faithful to the end they are received into heaven, that thereby they may dwell with God in a state of never-ending happiness. O remember, remember that these things are true; for the Lord God hath spoken it.*

Although those in the world who behave wickedly and mock righteousness may seem happy, we have been taught otherwise. Our efforts at righteousness are not vain, but lead to happiness. During difficult times, we must remember that keeping the commandments leads to righteousness and true happiness.

3 Nephi 12:6. *And blessed are all they who do hunger and thirst after righteousness, for they shall be filled with the Holy Ghost.*

This magnificent beatitude helps us set our priorities and tune our desires and actions in regard to righteousness: we are to yearn for righteousness the way our physical bodies yearn for food and water. Then we will be rewarded with the companionship of the Holy Ghost, who will indeed lead us in righteousness and show us all things to do (2 Ne. 32:5).

MODERN PROPHETS SPEAK

Spencer W. Kimball:

> Righteousness requires action. People tend often to measure their righteousness by the absence of wrong acts in their lives, as if passivity were the end of being. But God has created "things to act and things to be acted upon" (2 Nephi 2:14), and man is in the former category. He does not fill the measure of his creation unless he acts, and that in righteousness. "Therefore to him that knoweth to do good, and doeth it not," warns James, "to him it is sin." (James 4:17)
>
> To be passive is deadening; to stop doing is to die. Here then is a close parallel with physical life. If one fails to eat and drink, his body becomes emaciated and dies. Likewise, if he fails to nourish his spirit and mind, his spirit shrivels and his mind darkens. (*The Teachings of Spencer W. Kimball,* ed. Edward L. Kimball [Salt Lake City: Bookcraft, 1982], 148)

Harold B. Lee:

> *We must hunger and thirst after righteousness.* Did you ever hunger for food or thirst for water when just a crust of stale bread or a sip of tepid water to ease the pangs that distressed you would seem to be the most prized of all possessions? If you have so hungered, then you may begin to understand how the Master meant we should "hunger and thirst after righteousness" (Matthew 5:6). It's that hungering and thirsting that leads those away from home to seek fellowship with Saints in sacrament services and that induces worship on the Lord's Day wherever we are. It is that which

prompts fervent prayer and leads our feet to holy temples and bids us be reverent therein. (*The Teachings of Harold B. Lee,* ed. Clyde J. Williams [Salt Lake City: Bookcraft, 1996], 613)

Bruce R. McConkie:

> Salvation is a personal matter. It comes only to those who keep the commandments and whose souls are filled with the Holy Spirit of God. No man can keep the commandments for and on behalf of another; no one can gain the sanctifying power of the Holy Spirit in his life and give or sell that holy oil to another. Every man must light his own lamp with the oil of righteousness which he buys at the market of obedience. Few doctrines are more evil and wicked than the false doctrine of supererogation, which is, that the saints, by doing more than is necessary for their own salvation, build up an immense treasure of merit in heaven, which can be dispensed and assigned to others so they too can be saved. (*The Mortal Messiah: From Bethlehem to Calvary,* 4 vols. [Salt Lake City: Deseret Book, 1979–1981], 3:468)

IDEAS FOR DAILY LIVING

Here are several ideas to help us acquire and maintain a state of righteousness:

1. The scriptures. Live according to the word of God (see 2 Ne. 32:3; D&C 84:43–44). Hold to the iron rod so the temptations will not overpower you (see 1 Ne. 15:24; Hel. 3:29).

2. Prayer. Pray not only to avoid temptation and sin (see 3 Ne. 18:18), but to find ways to be *actively* righteous.

3. Obedience. Choose the freedom and happiness of righteous living (see 2 Ne. 2:27).

4. Remember. Remember the covenants you have made and live up to them (see Mosiah 5:5; D&C 42:78).

5. Preparation. Prepare daily to meet the Savior with your lamp full of the oil of righteousness (see Matt. 25:1–13). You fill your lamp drop by drop with your righteous deeds.

6. Love. Practice righteousness by loving and by showing mercy. The Prophet Joseph Smith declared: "To be righteous is to be just and merciful" (*The Words of Joseph Smith,* eds. Andrew F. Ehat and Lyndon W. Cook [Salt Lake City: Deseret Book, 1996], 206).

7. Honor. Righteousness is not just doing the right thing, but doing the right thing for the right reasons. Righteous motives make the deed clean and wholesome (see Moro. 7:6–11; D&C 88:67). The Prophet Joseph Smith taught: "Righteousness must be the aim of the Saints in all things, and when the covenants are published, they will learn that great things must be expected from them. Do good and work righteousness with an eye single to the glory of God" (*History of the Church,* 2:229).

8. Purity. Keep your thoughts pure, for they will become your words and your actions (see Prov. 23:7).

9. Associations. Associate with people with the same values (see Prov. 22:24; D&C 121:9). People who live the gospel will support and encourage you in righteousness.

10. Armor. Fortify yourself with righteousness. Put on the armor of God (see Eph. 6:11–17; D&C 27:15–19).

11. Service. Seek to serve and bless others (see Mosiah 2:17).

ILLUSTRATIONS FOR OUR TIMES

Insight from personal experience and the scriptures emphasizes the importance and safety of daily righteousness.

The Courage to Do What Is Right

When Captain Moroni rose in the majesty of inspired leadership to erect the title of liberty and energize his compatriots to take a stand for the right, he made a symbolic statement that continues to echo with vibrant power down through the centuries. That statement confirms the verity that universal principles and divinely-rooted covenants have eternal meaning and predominance in the face of worldly relativism and materialistically-defined tyranny. There is a time and a place where God-fearing men and women have to draw a line and stand up for truth—and that time is *every day*, and that place is *everywhere*.

I recall the training I went through as a young college student to qualify for summer work as a licensed tour-bus driver in the Canadian Rockies. We were taken on dangerous switchbacks to learn the skills needed for maneuvering a large passenger vehicle safely in the mountains. One day the trainer surprised us with an unexpected question: "Imagine that you are driving a fully-loaded bus on the outside lane of a mountain highway with a steep granite wall rising to your left and a deep precipice dropping to your right. Suddenly you round a curve and find that a car is racing toward you in the middle of the road. What would you do?"

Naturally one's instinct is to veer out of the way—but that is the wrong answer. Any attempt to reposition the moving bus might take you too close to the edge and place your 45 passengers in even greater danger—with the possibility of death. The answer our trainer was looking for was simply this: You hold to your lane and hit the oncoming car directly. Your enormous weight and size will give you a powerful advantage in competition with the much smaller car—and the chances of maximizing the safety for your passengers will thereby be secured. At the time, this strategy seemed drastic, but it soon sunk in as the only possible solution to such a crisis.

The collision of honor and principle with moral compromise presents a similar scenario. There are many times in every person's life where a sudden and unexpected confrontation with the oncoming dangers of evil and falsehood demand a head-on stand for what is right and what is true. At such times of choice there can be no compromise. To leave the well-marked pathway and veer to right or left to avoid potential offense or embarrassment that could result from taking a stand can only exacerbate the crisis and lead to tragic consequences.

When Moroni led his forces in a life-and-death battle against Amalickiah and his power-hungry hordes, he demonstrated how to meet life's challenges head-on. His cause was the greater cause: "In memory of our God, our religion, and freedom, and our peace, our wives, and our children" (Alma 46:12). In countless variations every day, we experience similar occasions, of greater or lesser scope, where we are engaged to address the challenges of evil and temptation head-on, veering neither to the right nor to the left. Our model is the Lord Himself: "For God doth not walk in crooked paths, neither doth he turn to the right hand nor to the left, neither doth he vary from that which he hath said, therefore his paths are straight, and his course is one eternal round" (D&C 3:2).

Our commission in life is much like that of the bus driver. We journey along the highways of life with the responsibility to guide our families safely to the destination of sanctity and righteousness. There are many dangerous curves to maneuver. There are countless distractions to divert our vision from the course straight ahead. Our duty and our honor demand constant vigilance and the perpetual exercise of correct principles. When on occasion we come upon a sudden challenge in the road, we are then prepared and ready to take a stand for the sake of our families, our church, our peace, our faith. We stay in tune with the Spirit and follow the promptings that come.

As the Savior expressed it in His intercessory prayer: "And for their sakes I sanctify myself, that they also might be sanctified through the truth" (John 17:19). To overcome the perils of temptation and the threat of evil in this world, we need only emulate the example of righteous figures like Moroni, of whom Mormon said: "Yea, verily, verily I say unto you, if all men had been, and were, and ever would be, like unto Moroni, behold, the very powers of hell would have been shaken forever; yea, the devil would never have power over the hearts of the children of men" (Alma 48:17).

—Richard J. Allen

SUMMARY

President Ezra Taft Benson counseled: "We represent Jesus Christ. How that thought ought to prompt us toward more righteousness and a desire to be more like Him!" (*The Teachings of Ezra Taft Benson* [Salt Lake City: Bookcraft, 1988], 344). We should seek to honor Christ's name through righteousness. Hungering and thirsting after righteousness should be our main goal in life. We must remember that salvation is an individual thing and that we cannot transfer righteousness to another person. In righteousness there is long-lasting joy, whereas in wickedness—though there may be moments of worldly pleasure—the eventual reward is only heartache and heartbreak.

SABBATH

Though the Sabbath is often referred to as the Lord's day, He actually made it for us. He knew we would need a time for our bodies and spirits to rest and renew, and a time dedicated to remembering Him. Therefore, as He took one day of seven to rest from creating the earth, He gave us a day of rest. The purpose of the Sabbath day is to worship God, rest from our daily labors, renew our covenants, receive gospel instruction, and receive edification to our spirits. The Sabbath is a day to magnify our callings, caring for those who need help or, in other words, to practice pure religion (see James 1:27). Sabbath observance is not only commanded by God, it also signifies our covenants with, and dependence on, Him. "Verily my sabbaths ye shall keep: for it is a sign between me and you throughout your generations; that ye may know that I am the Lord that doth sanctify you" (Ex. 31:13).

THE SCRIPTURES TEACH US

Exodus 20:8. *Remember the sabbath day, to keep it holy.*

This short and simple commandment of the Lord holds a depth of meaning and application in our lives. *Remember* is a significant word in relation to our covenants. Webster's 1828 dictionary defines the verb *remember:* "To have in the mind an idea which had been in the mind before, and which recurs to the mind without effort. . . . To preserve the memory of; to preserve from being forgotten. . . . To think of and consider; to meditate. . . . To bear in mind with praise or admiration; to celebrate. . . . To bear in mind with reverence; to obey" (*An American Dictionary of the English Language*, Noah Webster, 1828, electronic ed. [Salt Lake City: Deseret Book, 1998]). Part of our Sabbath observance is remembering the Lord in these ways—with ease, in meditation, and in praise.

Keeping the Sabbath day holy demonstrates our personal attitudes toward our Heavenly Father and our Savior. Webster's 1828 dictionary defines the word *holy* as: "Properly, whole, entire, or perfect, in a moral sense. . . . Hence, holy is used as nearly synonymous with good, pious, godly. . . . Hallowed; consecrated or set apart to a sacred use, or to the service or worship of God; . . . Proceeding from pious principles, or directed to pious purposes; as holy zeal. . . . Perfectly just and good; as the holy law of God. . . . Sacred; as a holy witness" (ibid). Let us apply these definitions to our understandings as we seek to keep the Sabbath holy.

Deuteronomy 5:12. *Keep the sabbath day to sanctify it, as the Lord thy God hath commanded thee.*

Sanctifying the Sabbath means making it holy and special by setting it apart from other days and ensuring that we do not desecrate it through our actions. Remember that the Savior is Lord of this day as well (see Matt. 12:8), and that His resurrection occurred on the Sabbath day.

Mark 2:27. *And he said unto them, The sabbath was made for man, and not man for the sabbath.*

Too often the Sabbath day is a day of "Don't do this" and "Don't do that." Such an approach makes the Sabbath day a day of negatives. Rather, the Sabbath day is a day of "We get to": We get to worship and pay homage to our Heavenly Father and our Savior; we get to rest from our daily labors; we get to bless our fellowmen; we get to be with family. Let us make the Sabbath a joyous and happy day.

Mosiah 18:23. *And he commanded them that they should observe the sabbath day, and keep it holy, and also every day they should give thanks to the Lord their God.*

The Lord's true Church is not a Sunday-only church. We are gospel-oriented Saints, and we should live the gospel on a daily basis. This can be our source of joy and happiness as we apply correct principles and doctrines to our lives. We must not become like the Zoramites in the Book of Mormon, who forsook the gospel on a daily basis and then polluted the Sabbath day with false worship. Our Sabbath worship is enhanced by righteous daily living.

Doctrine and Covenants 59:9–13. *And that thou mayest more fully keep thyself unspotted from the world, thou shalt go to the house of prayer and offer up thy sacraments upon my holy day; For verily this is a day appointed unto you to rest from your labors, and to pay thy devotions unto the Most High; Nevertheless thy vows shall be offered up in righteousness on all days and at all times; But remember that on this, the Lord's day, thou shalt offer thine oblations and thy sacraments unto the Most High, confessing thy sins unto thy brethren, and before the Lord. And on this day thou shalt do none other thing, only let thy food be prepared with singleness of heart that thy fasting may be perfect, or, in other words, that thy joy may be full.*

We reverence Heavenly Father and Jesus Christ as we keep the Sabbath day holy. Through renewing our covenants and being edified, we are strengthened and able to keep ourselves free from temptation and sin—unspotted from the world. We also pay our tithes and offerings (oblations) on the Sabbath. Our "sacraments" constitute the binding of ourselves to the Lord through covenants; this is why we partake of the sacrament on the Sabbath day.

MODERN PROPHETS SPEAK

Spencer W. Kimball:
> The Sabbath is a holy day in which to do worthy and holy things. Abstinence from work and recreation is important but insufficient. The Sabbath calls for constructive thoughts and acts, and if one merely lounges about doing nothing on the Sabbath, he is breaking it. To observe it, one will be on his knees in prayer, preparing lessons, studying the gospel, meditating, visiting the ill and distressed, sleeping, reading wholesome material, and attending all the meetings of that day to which he is expected. To fail to do these proper things is a transgression on the omission side. (*The Miracle of Forgiveness* [Salt Lake City: Bookcraft, 1969], 96–97)

Joseph B. Wirthlin:
> In our day, standards for keeping the Sabbath day holy are lowered a little at a time by some individuals until practically anything seems to become acceptable. The sign between the Lord and his covenant people is trampled underfoot as Latter-day Saints skip Sunday meetings to seek recreation at lakes and beaches, in the mountains, at sports arenas, and at theaters. Parking lots at supermarkets and discount stores often are full on Sundays. Many store owners feel compelled to open their doors on Sundays because of the demand for the merchandise and services. The people who misuse the Sabbath lose the blessings of spiritual food and growth promised to those who keep this commandment. (*Finding Peace in Our Lives* [Salt Lake City: Deseret Book, 1995], 16)

Gordon B. Hinckley:
> It appalls me to see Latter-day Saints who shop on Sunday. I cannot understand how they can go in the face of the direct word of the Lord that "thou shalt keep the Sabbath day holy." Shopping is not a part of keeping the Sabbath day holy. . . . On the first Sabbath in the Salt Lake Valley, Brigham Young said, "We will not work on Sunday, for those who do will lose five times as much as they gain." I believe God will honor and bless and magnify and be quick to help those who try to keep His commandments. The commandment on the Sabbath Day is the longest of the Ten Commandments. The Lord was very specific about it, very detailed about it. I can't help but believe that the merchants would not be open on Sunday if we did not patronize their stores. Therefore, that responsibility rests upon our shoulders. I hope you will not shop on Sunday. (*Teachings of Gordon B. Hinckley* [Salt Lake City: Deseret Book, 1997], 560)

IDEAS FOR DAILY LIVING

Here are some ideas to help us keep the Sabbath day holy:

1. Remember whose day it is.
- *Reverence*—We should pause to revere and worship our Heavenly Father in mind, heart, and action on His day. Our attitude on this day should be respectful of the Lord and His command of Sabbath worship.
- *Sacrament*—We should prepare mentally and spiritually to partake of the sacrament with renewed gratitude for the Atonement and dedication to keep the commandments.

- *Refreshment*—The Lord made this day for us so that we could rest from our daily labors and be renewed and refreshed.
- *Service*—We should seek to emphasize the positives of the Sabbath through service and family togetherness.

2. Some other things to remember on the Sabbath.
- *Meetings*—We must faithfully attend all of our meetings, with advance preparation and with a desire to learn and participate.
- *Sacrament*—We ought to consider the covenants we renew during the sacrament, and renew these covenants with a firm determination to always keep them.
- *Build the family*—On the Sabbath, we should pursue spiritual and family-building activities rather than purely amusement-type activities.
- *Be spiritually resourceful*—President Spencer W. Kimball suggested many things we can do to make the Sabbath special: meditate; serve others; read edifying material (the scriptures, conference reports, Church publications, and uplifting literature); study the prophets' lives and teachings; prepare Church lessons and family home evenings; visit relatives and friends; write in our journals or to missionaries and others; enjoy uplifting music and sing Church hymns together; read with a child; do family history research; develop appreciation for the cultural arts; friendship nonmembers; and visit the sick, the aged, and the lonely. (See *Teachings of Spencer W. Kimball*, 217.)
- *Stay close to the Lord*—Many activities are appropriate on the Sabbath, while many are not. How do we know the difference? The key is to do only those things on the Sabbath that help us feel close to Heavenly Father and Jesus Christ; the Holy Ghost will help us identify those things.

ILLUSTRATIONS FOR OUR TIMES

In a general conference address, Elder ElRay L. Christiansen discusses the inappropriateness of recreational activities on the Sabbath day.

The Sabbath Breaker

On a number of occasions when I have been returning from conferences, I have met on the highway a great number of automobiles. In many of these were families apparently returning to their homes on the early Sunday evening. Attached to a good number of these cars were beautiful boats. Now, ordinarily we do not take boats to church, so one must conclude that these fine people had not been to church, nor were they on their way to church.

I wonder if it is wise—well, I can say positively—it is *not* wise for parents to take their children away from their appointed places of worship on the Sabbath day where they may learn the gospel and where they may become fortified to face life through increased faith, trust, and confidence in the Lord, and require their children to go with them on the Sabbath day to spend the day on the reservoir or at some other place of amusement. Such practices may seriously impair and affect the lives of these children and perhaps the lives of their children. In fairness to our children and to ourselves, we must go to the house of prayer on His holy day as the commandment requires.

An acquaintance of mine had purchased a lovely boat and had just finished varnishing it and painting it. When I stopped by, he was admiring it. I surmised that he was getting it ready to take it, with his family, to the reservoir the next Sunday. He said, "It is complete and in readiness except for one thing." Then he asked me, "Could you suggest an appropriate name for the boat?"

I knew him very well. I thought for a moment, and then I said, "Well, perhaps you should name it *The Sabbath Breaker.*"

He looked at me, and he understood. (ElRay L. Christiansen, Conference Report, April 1962, 33)

SUMMARY

If someone in one of our Church circles were asked what he or she was aspiring to become, the answer would probably be: "I am seeking eternal life and to be like our Savior." Fortunately, the Lord provided an entire day each week for us to work on this goal. Our Sabbath days should be used to come closer to our Heavenly Father and our Savior. Therefore, we need to use the Sabbath to study and pray, and to acquire those attributes that will help us not only keep the commandments but become like our Savior. On the Sabbath, we should be about our Father's work—bringing to pass the immortality and eternal life of ourselves and others (see Moses 1:39). In this way, we can sanctify the Sabbath day and keep it holy for the betterment of all of Heavenly Father's children.

SACRAMENT

In the Old Testament, sacrifices were offered to remind the people of the future Atonement of the Lord Jesus Christ. Adam was taught that the sacrifices were in the similitude of the Only Begotten of the Father (see Moses 5:7). Today, we still remember the Atonement, but with a different form of commitment. During the sacrament, we remember the Atonement of our Savior, witnessing that we willingly take the name of Christ upon us, that we will always remember Him, that we will keep the commandments—thus renewing our baptismal covenant (see D&C 20:37; Mosiah 18:8–9; Moro. 6:1–4). This renewal not only revives our commitment to the Lord, but reminds us of His promise to us: if we do these things, we will always have His Spirit with us.

THE SCRIPTURES TEACH US

Matthew 26:26–28. *And as they were eating, Jesus took bread, and blessed it, and brake it, and gave it to the disciples, and said, Take, eat; this is my body. And he took the cup, and gave thanks, and gave it to them, saying, Drink ye all of it; For this is my blood of the new testament, which is shed for many for the remission of sins.*

The new testament or new covenant was instituted by the Savior that we might remember Him and apply the Atonement in our lives through repentance. As noted in the scripture above, prior to His atoning sacrifice—as He had not yet been "broken"—He blessed the bread first and then broke it. In 3 Nephi 18, the Lord broke the bread first—for now He had offered the atoning sacrifice—and then blessed it.

1 Corinthians 11:26–29. *For as often as ye eat this bread, and drink this cup, ye do shew the Lord's death till he come. Wherefore whosoever shall eat this bread, and drink this cup of the Lord, unworthily, shall be guilty of* *the body and blood of the Lord. But let a man examine himself, and so let him eat of that bread, and drink of that cup. For he that eateth and drinketh unworthily, eateth and drinketh damnation to himself, not discerning the Lord's body.*

In partaking of the sacrament, we acknowledge and witness the Lord's Atonement. The process of partaking is sacred and holy and should be done in utmost reverence. When partaking of the sacrament, we must be worthy. This implies that we have honored the Lord's Atonement: we have repented of our sins, resolving them with the Lord and, when necessary, with our priesthood leaders. We must not say to ourselves, "I am just not feeling well about a few things, so I had better not partake of the sacrament." The bishop is responsible for ensuring that only worthy Church members partake of the sacrament, so if there is a question in your mind, see the bishop (see 3 Ne. 18:28–29). Let us be cautious about refusing the Lord's atoning sacrifice unless we are moved by godly sorrow to refrain, biding the time when repentance is complete, or unless we have been so instructed by the bishop.

3 Nephi 18:12–13. *And I give unto you a commandment that ye shall do these things. And if ye shall always do these things blessed are ye, for ye are built upon my rock. But whoso among you shall do more or less than these are not built upon my rock, but are built upon a sandy foundation; and when the rain descends, and the floods come, and the winds blow, and beat upon them, they shall fall, and the gates of hell are ready open to receive them.*

Verses 1 through 13 of 3 Nephi chapter 18 speak of the sacrament and its significance. Verses 12 through 13 teach a principle and doctrine of power that we can have if we properly partake of the sacrament. If we build upon the rock of the Lord, we cannot fall (see Hel. 5:12).

Doctrine and Covenants 20:77; Moroni 4:3. *O God, the Eternal Father, we ask thee in the name of thy Son, Jesus Christ, to bless and sanctify this bread to the souls of all those who partake of it, that they may eat in remembrance of the body of thy Son, and witness unto thee, O God, the Eternal Father, that they are willing to take upon them the name of thy Son, and always remember him and keep his commandments which he has given them; that they may always have his Spirit to be with them. Amen.*

Doctrine and Covenants 20:79; Moroni 5:2. *O God, the Eternal Father, we ask thee in the name of thy Son, Jesus Christ, to bless and sanctify this wine to the souls of all those who drink of it, that they may do it in remembrance of the blood of thy Son, which was shed for them; that they may witness unto thee, O God, the Eternal Father, that they do always remember him, that they may have his Spirit to be with them. Amen.*

The sacrament prayers extend great promises to those who truly partake of the sacrament with a broken heart and a contrite spirit. The commitment to our covenants will bring the Holy Spirit into our lives, along with untold blessings. Remember that the Spirit is the key to following Christ and living a Christlike life.

MODERN PROPHETS SPEAK

Joseph B. Wirthlin:
> Windows must be washed regularly to clean away dust and dirt. . . . Just as earthly windows need consistent, thorough cleaning, so do the windows of our spirituality. . . . By partaking of the sacrament worthily to renew our baptismal covenants, we clarify our view of life's eternal purpose and divine priorities. The sacrament prayers invite personal introspection, repentance, and rededication as we pledge our willingness to remember our Savior, Jesus the Christ. (*Ensign,* Nov. 1995, 77)

Boyd K. Packer:

It is not an easy thing in this world to stay worthy, to stay clean and pure. Each day may bring little irritations and temptations and mistakes. Our Heavenly Father has provided a way that we can renew the covenants we made with him at the time of our baptism. Each week we can gather together to partake of the sacrament for that purpose.

It is not very likely that during the course of a week, between sacrament meetings, we will get so far off the path of righteousness that we will lose our way. There is always that still, small voice to guide us. (*Let Not Your Heart Be Troubled* [Salt Lake City: Bookcraft, 1991], 233)

David B. Haight:

As we partake of the sacrament and reflect upon his sacrifice for each of us, we make a solemn commitment to keep the commandments he has given us; by so doing, we might always have his spirit to be with us. By partaking of the sacrament each Sunday, we receive the encouragement and strength to keep the commandments of God, to live uprightly, virtuously, and honestly. He himself summed those commandments up as follows: "Love the Lord thy God with all thy heart, and with all thy soul, and with all thy strength, and with all thy mind; and thy neighbour as thyself" (Luke 10:27).

This is what every person who partakes of the sacrament is committed to do. Living God's commandments obligates each of us to a life of goodness and to exclude from our lives hatred, enmity, immorality, selfishness, drunkenness, jealousy, and dishonesty. . . .

The sacrament is one ordinance that allows us to experience a personal relationship with God and enlarges our knowledge and understanding of him and his Only Begotten Son.

Our personal reward for compliance with the covenants and obligations in the ordinance of the sacrament is companionship of God's Holy Spirit. This is the light that leads to eternal life. (*A Light unto the World* [Salt Lake City: Deseret Book, 1997], 176–77)

IDEAS FOR DAILY LIVING

Here are some ideas to help us make the sacrament more meaningful in our lives:

1. Review some of the significant scriptures.
- *The Atonement*—See 2 Nephi 9; Mosiah 3–4; Alma 7, 11, 34, 42; 3 Nephi 11, 18, 27; D&C 19:15–19; see also *Atonement* in this volume.
- *The baptismal requirements*—See D&C 20:37, 69; Mosiah 18:8–9; Moroni 6:1–4.
- *The sacramental prayers*—See D&C 20:77, 79; 3 Nephi 18; Moroni 4:3; 5:2.
- *Keeping the commandments*—See John 14:15; Matthew 22:36–40; 3 Nephi 12–14; see also *Commandments* and *Obedience* in this volume.
- *The blessings of the Spirit*—See 2 Nephi 32:5 and *Holy Ghost* in this volume.

2. Make all needful preparations before partaking of the sacrament.
- *Repentance*—Forsake and confess your sins to Heavenly Father and, when necessary, to your bishop.
- *Reverence*—Come with a reverent attitude and with a broken heart and a contrite spirit. Arrive early to sacrament meeting in order to have time to ponder and meditate.

- *Family instruction*—Plan a family home evening on the Atonement and the significance of the sacrament.
- *Remember*—At an appropriate time on Sunday prior to sacrament meeting, remind yourself and your family concerning the partaking of the sacrament and its sacred significance.

3. Make the sacrament experience a spiritual feast.

- *Singing*—Sing the sacrament hymn with a reverent attitude, paying careful attention to the words.
- *Covenant*—When saying *amen* to the sacramental prayers, remember that you are making a covenant with the Lord.
- *Meditating*—As the sacrament is passed, be as reverent as possible, pondering and meditating on the Savior and His atoning sacrifice. Think of the sacramental prayers and your personal covenants.
- *Resolve*—Make a firm resolution to be and do better in the coming week.
- *Patience*—Remember that little children are learning reverence and they don't always understand; you can therefore learn patience as you seek to keep them under control during sacrament meeting. The Lord is pleased knowing that you are trying to be your best.

4. Remember the sacramental prayers during the week.

- *Reading the word of God*—Scripture time can be a wonderful time to refresh your mind concerning the Atonement and the covenants you make when partaking of the sacrament.
- *Prayers*—Family and personal prayers can serve to remind you of your worthiness and your efforts to bring the Spirit into your life.
- *Planning*—Plan and prioritize your life to make the sacrament an important part. Make sacrament meeting attendance a priority, and prepare yourself early for it.

ILLUSTRATIONS FOR OUR TIMES

Elder John H. Groberg tells the story of a woman who could not partake of the sacrament for a time, and the joy she felt when she became worthy to partake of it again.

The Beauty and Importance of the Sacrament

Some years ago, a young couple we will call the Joneses visited with their bishop about a problem the wife had. The details are not important, but through the direction of the Spirit, the bishop's decision was that, among other things, Sister Jones would not partake of the sacrament for a period of time while she worked out some attitudes and problems.

With lots of love and support, she continued to attend meetings with her family, and few but her husband and the bishop were aware of the situation or even noticed that week after week she did not partake of the sacrament. At first she didn't feel much difference; but as time went on, she became more and more desirous to be worthy to partake of the sacrament. She thought she had repented before, but as the real soul-searching deepened and as her desire to worthily partake of the sacrament increased, true fundamental changes began to take place in her life and in her actions and in her thinking.

More time passed. Finally, during one sacrament meeting, the Spirit bore witness to the bishop and to Brother and Sister Jones that the time had come for her to again partake of the sacrament. "Next Sunday," the bishop said.

Next Sunday came, and Sister Jones sat again with her family, nervous, yet excited and full of anticipation. "Am I really worthy? How I want to be!" she thought. The sacrament hymn was more meaningful than ever. She sang with such feeling that it was difficult to hold back the tears. And the sacrament prayers—how profound! She listened so intently that every word sank deep into her soul—to take his name, always remember him, keep his commandments, always have his Spirit. (See D&C 20:77, 79.) "Oh, how I desire this," she thought.

The deacons began to move up and down the aisles, and the trays were passed from person to person across the rows. As one young deacon got closer and closer to her row, her heart began to pound harder and harder. Then the tray was coming down her very row. Now her husband was holding the tray in front of her! Tears streamed down her face. There was a barely audible sob of joy, "Oh!" as she reached for the emblem of the Lord's love for her. The congregation did not hear the sob, but they did notice the tears in the bishop's eyes.

Life and hope and forgiveness and spiritual strength had been given and received. No one could be more worthy. Sister Jones truly *wanted* to have his Spirit. She *wanted* to take his name upon her. With all her heart, she *wanted* to remember him and keep his commandments. She *wanted* to repent, to improve, and to follow the guidance of his Spirit.

Think of it. Think of what could and should happen in your life, in your ward, in your stake, in the whole Church, in the whole world, if every Sunday individuals—hundreds, thousands, even millions—under the authority of the priesthood of God, took the sacrament worthily and thus repented and sincerely determined to better follow the guidance of the Lord's Spirit. (John H. Groberg, "The Beauty and Importance of the Sacrament," *Ensign,* May 1989, 38)

SUMMARY

The sacrament is a vital part of Heavenly Father's plan to help us keep the commandments. The Atonement of our Savior draws us to Him (see 3 Ne. 27:14–15), and when we partake of the sacrament, we promise to remember Him and to keep His commandments. We mortals, with our finite minds, need constant reminders, and the sacrament is Heavenly Father's way to help us remember His Son's sacrifice. As we make partaking of the sacrament an important part of our life, we will keep the commandments and live by the Spirit.

SACRIFICE

Prior to the Atonement of our Savior, the children of God offered blood sacrifices as a symbol of their reverence and devotion to God (see Moses 5:5–7). Such sacrifices serve as both a similitude of the Savior's Atonement and an offering of something of great worth. Today, following the new commandment from our Savior, we offer a different kind of sacrifice: a broken heart and a contrite spirit (see 3 Ne. 9:20). To offer a broken heart and a contrite spirit is to offer one's very self, giving one's will and one's decisions to the will of God.

Through the spirit of sacrifice, we enter a condition of profound change: we are in a state of humility; we depend upon God; we are easily entreated; we have no pride or ego to uphold; and we are willing to learn and to change. In short, we fully accept the Lord's magnificent, infinite, and eternal Atonement. The law of sacrifice requires that we, as disciples of Jesus Christ, give all that we have—our time, our talents, and all that we possess—in order to build up the kingdom of God and to gain exaltation (see D&C 98:13–15).

THE SCRIPTURES TEACH US

1 Samuel 15:22. *And Samuel said, Hath the Lord as great delight in burnt offerings and sacrifices, as in obeying the voice of the Lord? Behold, to obey is better than sacrifice, and to hearken than the fat of rams.*

Sacrifice is important but can never override obedience. A sacrifice is only counted as righteous when it is required by the Lord, because obedience is the first law of heaven. All blessings are predicated upon obedience, and sacrifice is often part of obedience.

2 Nephi 2:7. *Behold, he offereth himself a sacrifice for sin, to answer the ends of the law, unto all those who have a broken heart and a contrite spirit; and unto none else can the ends of the law be answered.*

The demands of justice require an infinite Atonement. Through the grace and mercy of our Savior, we qualify ourselves for the blessings of the Atonement by offering a sacrifice of a broken heart and a contrite spirit.

3 Nephi 9:19–20. *And ye shall offer up unto me no more the shedding of blood; yea, your sacrifices and your burnt offerings shall be done away, for I will accept none of your sacrifices and your burnt offerings. And ye shall offer for a sacrifice unto me a broken heart and a contrite spirit. And whoso cometh unto me with a broken heart and a contrite spirit, him will I baptize with fire and with the Holy Ghost.*

The Lord commands us to offer the ultimate gift: a broken heart and a contrite spirit. We should give the thing that is of most worth to us—our very lives and our will—to our Savior and our Heavenly Father.

MODERN PROPHETS SPEAK

Joseph Smith:

> Let us here observe, that a religion that does not require the sacrifice of all things never has power sufficient to produce the faith necessary unto life and salvation; for, from the first existence of man, the faith necessary unto the enjoyment of life and salvation never could be obtained without the sacrifice of all earthly things. It was through this sacrifice, and this only, that God has ordained that men should enjoy eternal life; and it is through the medium of the sacrifice of all earthly things that men do actually know that they are doing the things that are well pleasing in the sight of God. When a man has offered in sacrifice all that he has for the truth's sake, not even withholding his life, and believing before God that he has been called to make this sacrifice because he seeks to do his will, he does know, most assuredly, that God does and will accept his sacrifice and offering, and that he has not, nor will not seek his face in vain. Under these circumstances, then, he can obtain the faith necessary for him to lay hold on eternal life. (*Lectures on Faith* [Salt Lake City: Deseret Book, 1985], 6:7)

Ezra Taft Benson:

> Elder Bruce R. McConkie said, "Sacrifice pertains to mortality; in the eternal sense there is none. Sacrifice involves giving up the things of this world because of the promises of blessings to be

gained in a better world. In the eternal perspective there is no sacrifice in giving up all things—even including the laying down of one's life—if eternal life is gained through such a course." (See D&C 98:13–15.) But, just as when one loses his life to God, he really finds the abundant life, so also when one sacrifices all to God then God in return shares all that He has with him. (*The Teachings of Ezra Taft Benson* [Salt Lake City: Bookcraft, 1988], 443)

Gordon B. Hinckley:

Sacrifice is the very essence of religion; it is the keystone of happy home life, the basis of true friendship, the foundation of peaceful community living, of sound relations among people and nations. . . .

Without sacrifice there is no true worship of God. I become increasingly convinced of that every day. "The Father gave his Son, and the Son gave his life," and we do not worship unless we give—give of our substance, give of our time, give of our strength, give of our talent, give of our faith, give of our testimonies. . . .

A religion which requires devotion, which asks for sacrifice, which demands discipline, also enjoys the loyalty of its membership and the interest and respect of others. (*Teachings of Gordon B. Hinckley* [Salt Lake City: Deseret Book, 1997], 565)

Lorenzo Snow:

The Saints must be willing to sacrifice all. We have found the treasure in the field, we have found the pearl of great price, and now we have got to give all that we have for it, at one time or another. The Lord has said that He will prove us even unto death, to see whether we will stand by the covenants we have made with Him. Some Latter-day Saints have things in their possession which are so valuable to them that they would prefer death to the loss of those things. We have to deal with facts, not a mere ideal. In one sense, it is a hard thing for us to sell all that we have that we may secure these glories that have been opened to our view; but it will pay us in the end. (*The Teachings of Lorenzo Snow*, ed. Clyde J. Williams [Salt Lake City: Bookcraft, 1984], 115)

IDEAS FOR DAILY LIVING

Here are four ideas to consider regarding sacrifice:

1. Sacrifice is a principle of exaltation.

- *Sacrifice is built on love of God*—Without love and selflessness, there can be no willing and genuine sacrifice. We can be deprived of possessions, life, limb, and liberty; but only when we willingly give up these things for a cause can we be said to have "sacrificed." Mother Teresa confirmed: "It's not how much we give but how much love we put into giving."
- *Sacrifice is a measure of commitment*—If we are committed to God, to the well-being of family, community, or country, then no sacrifice is too great to achieve that goal.
- *Sacrifice is nurtured by balance*—We must keep balance in life, striving for enduring goals—harmony, peace, unity, well-being, joy—rather than putting great store in worldly things that fade and lose their luster. We must willingly give up pleasures, personal interests, and a fixation on material wealth if these things get in the way of higher causes, such as the kingdom of God, family, and spiritual wealth.

2. Sacrifice brings great rewards.

- *Self-respect*—Through sacrifice, we can learn about our own character and gain self-respect.

- *Perspective*—Sacrifice is an uplifting experience because it puts things in perspective. Worldly goods pale in value next to enduring relationships and the blessings of God.
- *Joy*—We need to sacrifice for things that will bless others. The greatest joy comes in service to others.
- *Long-term success*—We need to sacrifice the shallow "now" pleasures for the enduring "later" benefits in life. Our priorities—the things we sacrifice for—should be eternal life, successful family life, providing for our family, health and longevity, education, debt-free lifestyle, etc.
- *Inner strength*—We receive inner strength through sacrificing for the Lord and His Church, knowing that our priorities are in order and that we are doing what is of the most worth.
- *Spiritual peace*—By offering sacrifices in the form of a broken heart and a contrite spirit, we receive peace as only the Lord can give it.

3. Attitude and motivation are paramount.

- *Take stock*—List the things you would consider your sacrifices. Was your attitude right in regard to these offerings? What did you gain by way of experience, enhanced self-respect, character-growth, and giving blessings to others? Would you do it again, even in greater measure?
- *Exercise your choice*—Have the right attitude toward sacrifice. Do it willingly and with no thought of commendation or recognition, simply because it is the correct thing to do.
- *Use wisdom*—Recognize the value of the sacrifice as it relates to time: you can often save time in the long run by sacrificing for worthwhile causes early on. "Wisdom invokes sacrifice, and sacrifice deepens wisdom," said one anonymous source.
- *Do it out of devotion*—Sacrifice in the attitude of love, dedication, and devotion—not as a martyr or to be seen of others.

4. Sacrifice is part of leadership.

- *Teach the principle of sacrifice*—Ask others to sacrifice appropriately for worthy causes. An important aspect of leadership is to know when and how to guide others into channels of noble sacrifice so that they might achieve greatness. Do not try to shield people completely from the pains and sacrifices of life, lest you deprive them of important lessons for growth and development.
- *Use discernment in what needs to be sacrificed*—Where can the greatest leverage be obtained in a given circumstance to do good through sacrifice? Is it through time, gifts, service, compassion, resources, or a combination of these?
- *Live and teach the principle of "mind over matter"*—Occasionally "fast" from things of the world for a while as a reminder that your will and spirit control your temporal being. Such experiences provide spiritual food for the soul and serve as reminders of our dependence upon God for our very existence. Our regular fast Sundays offer great opportunities in this regard.

5. The key is learning how to offer a broken heart and a contrite spirit.

- *Cultivate a humble spirit*—Seek humility by recognizing your total dependence upon God.
- *Submit yourself entirely to God*—Submit to the will of God in all things.
- *Cultivate true repentance*—Feel true sorrow for sin. Recognize the sins that could be sacrificed in order to draw nearer to the Lord.
- *Remember the covenants*—Remember that when you were baptized, you agreed to be part of this kingdom and to do whatever is required.
- *Seek the Spirit*—The Spirit will enlighten those who sacrifice.

ILLUSTRATIONS FOR OUR TIMES

The following account tells how a father's monetary sacrifice led to the success of a valiant missionary couple.

The Coat

On several occasions as a young boy, I can recall my father telling me the story about "the coat." He had been saving for a considerable length of time to buy a heavy winter coat for my mother so that she would have added protection against the stark Canadian weather. Finally the coat fund had grown to a sufficient size and the time was at hand. As he sat one Sunday with the family in sacrament meeting, he was pondering the planned gift and thinking of the joy it would bring to his wife.

The program that day centered on missionary work and the sacrifices that the Saints are called upon to make in order to carry the gospel message to others. My father's thoughts then shifted to a certain older couple in town—two fine and stalwart members who were preparing to go on a mission. Being of modest means, they were struggling to gather together sufficient resources for their mission, and the local Church leaders had sent word requesting the support of local Saints. My father could not suppress an idea that came into his mind—the coat. He had the impression that he should donate those funds (several hundred dollars—a goodly sum in those days) for the benefit of the missionary couple and their service to the Lord. But how would his wife feel about the shift in plans? Surely she would be supportive, and—moreover—he felt the need to do what he was sure the Lord was commanding him, and have faith that a way would be prepared to obtain a coat at a later time. After all, he had stated over and over again to his family that Nephi was one of his great scriptural heroes, and if Nephi had the faith to do as the Lord commanded (see 1 Ne. 3:7), then should not he exercise faith as well?

And that is precisely what happened. He donated the entire coat fund to the Church for the benefit of the missionary couple, and they were able to go on the Lord's errand. As it turned out, they were soon called upon as part of their missionary service to preside over a branch of the Church that was struggling to achieve greater cohesion and unity. Their efforts succeeded admirably, and the branch prospered under their leadership. My father later commented that it was a source of much satisfaction to him to know that the coat was having such a protective and benign influence in building the kingdom of God. As for my mother, an opportunity presented itself eventually to obtain a fine coat for her after all, and thus all were served well.

Many years later, as a member of a branch presidency at the Missionary Training Center, I noted with admiration that many of the young missionaries had sacrificed temporal opportunities of various kinds—in some cases valuable and irretrievable athletic scholarships—to respond to missionary calls. They were putting the Lord first when confronted with a choice. In my own experience I have noted repeatedly that blessings flow from making such choices in favor of the Lord. During one period of my life I found that my testimony was strengthened immeasurably when I willingly accepted a call to serve as a bishop, even though it meant that the completion of the graduate degree I was pursuing at the time would need to be postponed for a while. But everything eventually worked out, as always, "in the due time of the Lord" (D&C 158:56). The opportunity to participate actively in building the kingdom of God was the pearl of great price—not to be exchanged for any professional pursuit. As the Savior taught during His ministry: "But seek ye first the kingdom of God and his righteousness, and all these things shall be added unto you" (3 Ne. 13:33; cf. Matt. 6:33).

—Richard J. Allen

SUMMARY

Through sacrifice we receive many blessings—patience here and now, blessings of eternal life in the life to come, compassion for others, self-reliance, and the list can go on and on. Because of the value of sacrifice to the well-being of all concerned, it is important that we all learn to sacrifice in ennobling ways. We should also teach our children to sacrifice. The family will be strengthened and the world's instant gratification will gradually be replaced with the ethic of work and sacrifice for the betterment of self, family, and our fellow citizens in the kingdom of God. Ultimately, every sacrifice we make in the name of the Savior is but a shadow of the transcendent eternal sacrifice He willingly made to enable us, through repentance and obedience, to return to our heavenly home one day. We cannot sacrifice enough to repay what He has given us, but we can sacrifice to bring ourselves closer to Him, and to bring others to Him. Let us sacrifice for future generations just as our predecessors have sacrificed for us.

SANCTIFICATION

Sanctification is a process of purification before God. We are sanctified when we are actually purified through the atoning blood of Christ and made innocent and holy. Through the grace of God we can become sanctified in Christ, made clean and pure by the power of the Holy Ghost (see 3 Ne. 27:19–20; Moro. 10:32–33). This sanctification comes through the Atonement of Christ as we receive the principles and ordinances of His gospel. Sanctification is more than just doing: it is a "becoming" within our soul— a mighty change, a heart yielding to the enticings of the Spirit and to God (see Mosiah 3:19). Then we, being sanctified, are prepared, made holy, consecrated, and set apart for sacred service.

THE SCRIPTURES TEACH US

John 17:17–19. *Sanctify them through thy truth: thy word is truth. As thou hast sent me into the world, even so have I also sent them into the world. And for their sakes I sanctify myself, that they also might be sanctified through the truth.*

The Word is Jesus Christ (see John 1:1–3, 14; Rev. 19:13). He is the way, the truth, and the life by which all come unto the Father (see John 14:6). To be sanctified by the word and truth of God is to be sanctified by Christ.

1 Corinthians 1:2. *Unto the church of God which is at Corinth, to them that are sanctified in Christ Jesus, called to be saints, with all that in every place call upon the name of Jesus Christ our Lord, both theirs and ours.*

Though sanctification comes by the power of the Holy Ghost (see Alma 5:54; 13:12; 3 Ne. 27:20), we are sanctified in Christ and become His Saints (see Heb. 10:10; Moro. 10:32–33). This makes us one with Christ and unified in all things (see Heb. 2:11). Thus the Lord, in the great intercessory prayer, following the verses referring to sanctification (see John 17:17–19), prays that the Apostles might be one even as the Father and Son are one—in purpose, cause, and action. Then they can be pure and clean, and set apart for holy and sacred work (see John 17:20–26).

Doctrine and Covenants 43:9. *And thus ye shall become instructed in the law of my church, and be sanctified by that which ye have received, and ye shall bind yourselves to act in all holiness before me.*

When we receive the things of the Lord—take them into our lives and apply them—we become sanctified in Christ, and can act in holiness before Him.

Doctrine and Covenants 43:16. *And ye are to be taught from on high. Sanctify yourselves and ye shall be endowed with power, that ye may give even as I have spoken.*

In this scripture, the Lord tells us that if we are to be taught from on high as He commands, we must be sanctified and worthy to receive such teaching.

Doctrine and Covenants 133:62. *And unto him that repenteth and sanctifieth himself before the Lord shall be given eternal life.*

The greatest blessing of sanctification is eternal life. When we are sanctified, our bodies and spirits are renewed by the Holy Ghost (see D&C 84:33). Furthermore, as we are sanctified, our minds will become single to God and we can behold Him, according to His will (see D&C 88:68). We keep the commandments; we are justified (cleansed and purified) by the Spirit; and through the grace of God and Christ we are sanctified by His atoning sacrifice (see Moses 6:60).

MODERN PROPHETS SPEAK

Dallin H. Oaks:
> Most of us experience some measure of what the scriptures call "the furnace of affliction" (Isa. 48:10; 1 Ne. 20:10). Some are submerged in service to a disadvantaged family member. Others suffer the death of a loved one or the loss or postponement of a righteous goal like marriage or childbearing. Still others struggle with personal impairments or with feelings of rejection, inadequacy, or depression. Through the justice and mercy of a loving Father in Heaven, the refinement and sanctification possible through such experiences can help us achieve what God desires us to become. ("The Challenge to Become," *Ensign,* Nov. 2000, 32)

James E. Faust:
> Faithful members of the Church who are true to their covenants with the Master do not need every jot and tittle spelled out for them. Christlike conduct flows from the deepest wellsprings of the human heart and soul. It is guided by the Holy Spirit of the Lord, which is promised in gospel ordinances. Our greatest hope should be to enjoy the sanctification which comes from this divine guidance; our greatest fear should be to forfeit these blessings. ("Search Me, O God, and Know My Heart," *Ensign,* May 1998, 17)

Harold B. Lee:
> The Lord said, "Therefore, sanctify yourselves that your minds become single to God, and the days will come that you shall see him; for he will unveil his face unto you, and it shall be in his own time, and in his own way, and according to his own will" (D&C 88:68). You may ask me, how does one sanctify himself, and make himself holy so that he is prepared to walk in the presence of the Lord? In that same great revelation the Lord says this, "And again, verily I say unto

you, that which is governed by law is also preserved by law and perfected and sanctified by the same" (D&C 88:34). What law? The laws of the Lord as contained in the gospel of Jesus Christ, the keeping of which laws and ordinances are the ways by which we are purified and made holy. The keeping of every law that the Lord has given us is one step closer to receiving the right to enter one day into the presence of the Lord. He has given us in another revelation the formula by which we can prepare ourselves as the years pass. "Verily, thus saith the Lord: It shall come to pass that every soul who forsaketh his sins and cometh unto me, and calleth on my name, and obeyeth my voice, and keepeth my commandments, shall see my face and know that I am" (D&C 93:1). Simple, isn't it? But listen again. All you have to do is to forsake your sins, come unto Him, call on His name, obey His voice, and keep His commandments, and then you shall see His face and shall know that He is.

There it is. You read it again and again, if you want the key as to how you may prepare yourselves to be so sanctified that you can enter into the presence of the Lord. (*The Teachings of Harold B. Lee,* ed. Clyde J. Williams [Salt Lake City: Bookcraft, 1996], 166)

IDEAS FOR DAILY LIVING

Here are several ideas to help us become sanctified in the Lord:

1. Hold fast to the basic truths of sanctification.

- *The key to sanctification*—Understand and accept the first four principles and ordinances of the gospel: faith, repentance, baptism, and the gift of the Holy Ghost (see 3 Ne. 27:20).
- *Atonement*—Remember that it is only through the Atonement of our Savior Jesus Christ that sanctification is possible (see Moses 6:60).
- *Unity*—Seek to be one with the Father and the Son (see John 17:20–26).
- *Cherish eternal blessings*—Remember that the greatest blessing of sanctification is eternal life (see D&C 133:62).

2. Act in all diligence to cultivate the spirit of sanctification.

- *Give yourself to God*—Yield your heart to the Spirit (see Mosiah 3:19) and to God (see Hel. 3:35).
- *Follow the Spirit*—Seek to live by and be directed by the Spirit, for He will sanctify you (see Alma 13:12).
- *Pray for the blessing of sanctification*—Ask God, the Eternal Father, in the name of His Son, for help in attaining the goal of sanctification, and He will bless you.
- *Cultivate a righteous lifestyle*—When sanctified, you will act in all holiness before the Lord (see D&C 43:9).
- *Deny all ungodliness*—Refrain from anything that takes you away from God (see Moro. 10:32–33).
- *Be obedient*—Obedience to the laws and ordinances of the gospel is key to sanctification (see D&C 88:21).
- *Welcome chastening*—Be grateful for chastening, for in it we are able to be brought to repentance (see D&C 95:1–2) and be prepared, in worthiness, for sanctification (see D&C 101:5).

ILLUSTRATIONS FOR OUR TIMES

President James E. Faust counsels us regarding the importance of heeding the correction of the still, small voice of the Holy Ghost, as it leads us to become better, purer, even sanctified.

Unwanted Messages

Many modern professors of human behavior advocate as a cure to an afflicted conscience that we simply ignore the unwanted messages. They suggest that we change the standard to fit the circumstances so that there is no longer a conflict, thus easing the conscience. The followers of the divine Christ cannot subscribe to this evil and perverse philosophy with impunity. For the troubled conscience in conflict with right and wrong, the only permanent help is to change the behavior and follow a repentant path.

The prophet Isaiah taught, "Woe unto them that call evil good, and good evil; that put darkness for light, and light for darkness; that put bitter for sweet, and sweet for bitter!" (Isa. 5:20).

During all of my ministry, I have been fascinated by the manner in which Jesus hardened the bone and spirit of his chief Apostle, Peter. When Jesus told Peter that he had prayed that Peter's faith would strengthen, Peter affirmed that he would go with the Savior to prison or to death. Peter was then told that the "cock shall not crow this day, before that thou shalt thrice deny that thou knowest me" (Luke 22:34). After the predicted three denials, the powerful, unwelcome, but steel-hardening message came: Peter heard the cock crow. And he "went out, and wept bitterly" (Matt. 26:75), but this strengthened Peter to fulfill his calling and to die for the cause.

There is one unerring voice that is ever true. It can always be relied upon. It should be listened to, although at times this voice too may speak unwelcome warning messages. I speak of the still, small, inner voice which comes from the divine source. As the prophet Elijah learned, "the Lord was not in the wind: and after the wind an earthquake; but the Lord was not in the earthquake: "And after the earthquake a fire; but the Lord was not in the fire: and after the fire a still small voice" (1 Kgs. 19:11–12).

One single unwanted message may be a call to change our lives; it may lead to the specially tailored opportunity we need. I am grateful that it is never too late to change, to make things right, to leave old activities and habits behind.

I wish to testify that the prophetic messages of this conference will lead any who will listen—and follow the counsel given—to the promise of the Savior, which is peace in this life and eternal life in the world hereafter. (James E. Faust, "Unwanted Messages," *Ensign,* Nov. 1986, 8)

SUMMARY

Sanctification—becoming clean and pure before the Lord—should be our goal. The greatest blessing that flows from sanctification is eternal life. Through sanctification we become holy, and we become one with Christ and fully aligned with His purpose to bring about the immortality and eternal life of all of God's children. The joy and blessings of sanctification can be ours as we yield ourselves to the Spirit and the will of God in all things.

SCRIPTURES

So much can be said about the scriptures and their importance in the lives of Latter-day Saints. We have been taught that the key to eternal life is to live by every word that proceeds from the mouth of God (see D&C 84:43). This is because the word of God has power to change lives (see Alma 31:5).

One metaphor we find for the word of God is in Nephi's vision of the tree of life. In the vision, the iron rod represents the word of God. Nephi teaches us that holding to the iron rod is the only way to navigate through the mists of darkness to the tree of life, the fruit of which represents the love of God (see 1 Ne. 11:25). Those who lay hold on the word of God are able to avoid the snares of the devil and make it across the gulf of misery (see Hel. 3:29). Failing to focus our minds and hearts on the word of God subjects us to eternal peril. Elder Neal A. Maxwell taught: "If we do not search the scriptures, we will miss the needed and reminding truths that God has sent among us for that purpose" (*A Wonderful Flood of Light* [Salt Lake City: Bookcraft, 1990], 53).

Revelations from God came by the power of the Holy Ghost. Expressed truth of this kind is scripture, "the will of the Lord . . . the mind of the Lord . . . the word of the Lord . . . the voice of the Lord, and the power of God unto salvation" (D&C 68:4). The word of God is taught by the prophets, who truly act for the Savior Jesus Christ, under His direction. The phrase "Word of God" sometimes refers to the Lord Jesus Christ Himself (see John 1:1–5). The New Testament prophet John records, concerning Him, "and his name is called The Word of God" (Rev. 19:13). Therefore, we see the importance of the scriptures: they are our means of drawing near to our Savior, the Word.

When we come to understand the principles of salvation, we begin to hunger for "the word." We seek to know the word of God and to draw on the mighty power it holds. Eventually, we learn to liken the scriptures to our lives and we learn to love and live the word of God, that we might become more like the Word of God. The scriptures can change our lives. They are literally the power of God unto salvation (see D&C 68:4).

THE SCRIPTURES TEACH US

Romans 10:17. *So then faith cometh by hearing, and hearing by the word of God.*

We grow in faith as the word of God comes into our hearts and minds and takes root in our lives. Faith in Jesus Christ is the first principle of His gospel and the foundation of all righteousness. The word of God has power to motivate people to repent (see Alma 31:5). As we search the scriptures and pray for faith, our prayers will be answered through the word of God, and we will be firmer in our faith (see Hel. 3:35).

1 Nephi 19:23. *And I did read many things unto them which were written in the books of Moses; but that I might more fully persuade them to believe in the Lord their Redeemer I did read unto them that which was written by the prophet Isaiah; for I did liken all scriptures unto us, that it might be for our profit and learning.*

Nephi read and taught the scriptures for the purpose of helping his family believe in Christ. In addition, he likened the scriptures to them—he related the words to their daily lives so they could apply them. If we do the same, we will gain profit and learning from the scriptures. We will grow and become like the Savior as we apply His word to our lives.

2 Nephi 32:3. *Angels speak by the power of the Holy Ghost; wherefore, they speak the words of Christ. Wherefore, I said unto you, feast upon the words of Christ; for behold, the words of Christ will tell you all things what ye should do.*

As we feast daily on the priceless scriptures and study with real intent, the word of the Lord will tell us the things we need to do—not some, but *all* things to do pertaining to righteousness. This is truly a commandment with a promise.

Doctrine and Covenants 84:43–46. *And I now give unto you a commandment to beware concerning yourselves, to give diligent heed to the words of eternal life. For you shall live by every word that proceedeth forth from the mouth of God. For the word of the Lord is truth, and whatsoever is truth is light, and whatsoever is light is Spirit, even the Spirit of Jesus Christ. And the Spirit giveth light to every man that cometh into the world; and the Spirit enlighteneth every man through the world, that hearkeneth to the voice of the Spirit.*

Let us never forget the standard by which we have been commanded to live. It is the word of God, which will lead us in "a straight course to eternal bliss" (Alma 37:44). We must never forget to nurture the word with faith, diligence, and patience so that it will grow up into a mighty tree bearing fruit that will bring us joy and happiness (see Alma 32:40–43).

MODERN PROPHETS SPEAK

Gordon B. Hinckley:

> I am grateful for emphasis on reading the scriptures. I hope that for you this will become something far more enjoyable than a duty; that, rather, it will become a love affair with the word of God. I promise you that as you read, your minds will be enlightened and your spirits will be lifted. At first it may seem tedious, but that will change into a wondrous experience with thoughts and words of things divine. (*Teachings of Gordon B. Hinckley* [Salt Lake City: Deseret Book, 1997], 573–74)

Ezra Taft Benson:

> The two groups in the Book of Mormon that seemed to have the greatest difficulty with pride are the "learned, and the rich." (2 Nephi 28:15.) But the word of God can pull down pride. (See Alma 4:19.) (*A Witness and a Warning: A Modern-Day Prophet Testifies of the Book of Mormon* [Salt Lake City: Deseret Book, 1988], 79)

Howard W. Hunter:

> We hope that you are studying the gospel regularly. Read from the scriptures, especially the Book of Mormon, each day as individuals and as families. Study the word of the Lord, and your faith and testimony will increase. What could be a more profitable use of discretionary time than reading from the scriptural library, the literature that teaches us to know God and understand our relationship to him? . . .
>
> Not in this dispensation, surely not in any dispensation, have the scriptures—the enduring, enlightening word of God—been so readily available and so helpfully structured for the use of every man, woman, and child who will search them. The written word of God is in the most readable and accessible form ever provided to lay members in the history of the world. Surely we will be held accountable if we do not read them. (*Teachings of Howard W. Hunter,* ed. Clyde J. Williams [Salt Lake City: Deseret Book, 1997] 51)

Neal A. Maxwell:

> Therefore, as we search the scriptures, our focus should be upon that which will tell us what we must do (to become as He is) and upon that which will stir us so to do. And the very word *search* means from the beginning to the latest unfolding of Holy Writ. (*Even As I Am* [Salt Lake City: Deseret Book, 1982], 19)

IDEAS FOR DAILY LIVING

Here are several ideas to help us understand and apply the word of God in our lives:

1. The ultimate source of all things is Heavenly Father.

- *Revelation*—The Savior reveals His Father's will (the word of God) through revelation. This can be in the form of a dream, vision, inspiration, or other divine manifestation. In some cases the Lord gives His word in person to His chosen servants. Most often, the word comes by the power of the Holy Ghost. Worthy individuals—from prophets to rank-and-file members of the Church—receive the word of God by the power of the Holy Ghost to sustain them in their respective callings. The prophets record the revelation they receive and it becomes our scripture.
- *Church leaders*—Those called by authority to teach and preach speak as moved upon by the power of the Holy Ghost. What they speak as directed by the Lord in their stewardships is scripture (see D&C 68:3–6).
- *A testimony of the word*—Knowing the source of the word—our Savior—should cause us to seek it and follow it with every fiber of our being. Set a goal to feast upon the word.

2. The word of God holds power and blessings.

- *A force for change*—If we study the word, it can change our lives in dramatic and enduring ways (see Alma 31:5). When we teach the word by the Spirit, we can help others change.
- *The key to humility*—The word can pull down pride and make people humble (see Alma 4:19). The more we read and rely on the word, the stronger our humility can be.
- *A channel for divine power*—The word operates through the power of God when those in authority speak (see Jacob 4:9). Through priesthood blessings and when moved by faith, we can call down the power of God.
- *Direction*—The word will tell us all things to do (see 2 Ne. 32:3).
- *The path to eternal life*—The word will direct us on the straight course to eternal life (see Alma 37:37–47).
- *A way to soften hearts*—The word can subdue our hearts and help us be more submissive (see D&C 96:5).
- *A defense against temptation*—The word will help us resist temptation (see 1 Ne. 15:24; Hel. 3:29).
- *A course leading to the love of God*—The iron rod, or the word, will lead us to the tree of life so that we might partake of the fruit (the love of God), which is desirable above all else (see 1 Ne. 8:10–11, 19).
- *Spiritual nourishment*—The word is the source of our spiritual nourishment and sustenance (see Moro. 6:4).

3. We should apply the word of God to our lives.

- A method to apply the word of God might be stated in simple steps:
  Read the scriptures carefully.
  Ponder them as they relate to you.

Write down each scripture reference and its main idea.
Write a personal statement as to how you are going to live this scripture. Use "I will," "I must," "I shall," "I can." These firstperson commitment statements will make the scriptures live in your life.

As an example, consider 1 Nephi 3:7: "And it came to pass that I, Nephi, said unto my father: I will go and do the things which the Lord hath commanded, for I know that the Lord giveth no commandments unto the children of men, save he shall prepare a way for them that they may accomplish the thing which he commandeth them."

Here is a possible personal application of this passage of scripture: "I will keep the commandments because the Lord will help me by preparing a way." Other variations might be: "I will study my scriptures because the Lord has commanded it and He will help me learn and strive to fulfill His command," or "I will keep the commandment of the fast on fast Sunday because I know Heavenly Father will give me the strength to do so."

These simple statements lead us to apply the scriptures directly to our lives. This application is the key to our profit and learning. When the word is internalized in our heart, it becomes part of our character, our very being. With the word in our hearts, we apply it, we live it. We become not only hearers of the word, but doers of the word. When the word of God is understood and the doctrine is comprehended, behavior becomes automatic—it is a natural consequence. That is why we become Christlike when we live Christ's words.

ILLUSTRATIONS FOR OUR TIMES

President Thomas S. Monson shares memories of President J. Reuben Clark which portray President Clark's great love of the scriptures.

A Love of the Scriptures

Many years ago I received an invitation to meet with President J. Reuben Clark Jr. a counselor in the First Presidency, a statesman of towering stature, and a scholar of international renown. My profession then was in the field of printing and publishing. President Clark made me welcome in his office and then produced from his old roll-top desk a large sheaf of meticulous, handwritten notes on eight-and-a-half-by-fourteen-inch canary-colored sheets. Many of the notes had been made when he was a law student long years before. He proceeded to outline for me his goal of producing a harmony of the Gospels. This goal was achieved with his monumental work, *Our Lord of the Gospels.* Many years later I still treasure my personally inscribed, leather-bound copy of this classic treatment of the life and teachings of Jesus of Nazareth.

I asked President Clark during one of our many conversations, "Which of the Gospels do you like best?" His answer: "Brother Monson, I love each of the Gospels."

Years later as I perused the pages of *Our Lord of the Gospels* and paused at the section entitled "The Miracles of Jesus," I remembered as though it were yesterday President Clark asking me to read to him several of these accounts while he sat back in his large leather chair and listened. He asked me to read aloud the account found in Luke concerning the man filled with leprosy. Then he asked that I continue reading from Luke concerning the man afflicted with palsy and the enterprising manner in which he was presented to the attention of the Lord, who healed him. President Clark removed from his pocket a handkerchief and wiped the tears from his eyes. He commented, "As we grow older, tears come more frequently." After a few words of good-bye, I departed from his office, leaving him alone with his thoughts and his tears.

Late one evening I delivered some press proofs to his office in his home in Salt Lake City. President Clark was reading from Ecclesiastes, and he was in a quiet and reflective mood. He sat back from his large desk, which was stacked with books and papers. He held the scriptures in his hand, lifted his eyes from the printed page, and read aloud to me: "Let us hear the conclusion of the whole matter: Fear God, and keep his commandments: for this is the whole duty of man." (Ecclesiastes 12:13.) He exclaimed, "A treasured truth! A profound philosophy!"

What a blessing was mine to learn daily at the feet of such a master teacher and a principal architect of the welfare program. Knowing that I was a newly appointed bishop presiding over a challenging ward, he emphasized the need for me to know my people, to understand their circumstances, and to minister to their needs.

One day he recounted the Savior's raising from the dead the son of the widow of Nain, as recorded in the Gospel of Luke. When President Clark closed the Bible, I noticed that he was weeping. In a quiet voice, he said, "Tom, be kind to the widow and look after the poor."

On another occasion he said: "You do not find truth groveling through error. You find truth by seeking truth."

Through the years these conversations have remained bright in my memory. (Thomas S. Monson, *Inspiring Experiences That Build Faith: From the Life and Ministry of Thomas S. Monson* [Salt Lake City: Deseret Book, 1994], 234)

SUMMARY

There are not enough words to expound upon the word of God—its sanctity, its monumental importance in the eternal scheme of things, its profound value as a gift of our Father in Heaven to His children. The simple truth is that we as the children of God must yield our hearts to His word, learn His will, and do it. We can then enjoy the blessings of the Lord in all facets of our lives. Let us humbly and diligently feast upon the word and thus receive the power of God unto salvation.

SELFISHNESS

Of all the destructive forces in a person's character, nothing is as devastating as selfishness. Selfishness cankers the soul, wreaks havoc in relationships, and makes communication almost nonexistent. In addition, selfishness can lead to lust, greed, seeking for unrighteous power, among other sins. Of all the negative traits of society and individuals, selfishness is one of the most grievous; therefore, we must all work to overcome it. Selfishness is diametrically opposed to charity, a fundamentally important element of the Christian lifestyle. In the presence of charity, selfishness vanishes. The Apostle Paul explained most eloquently: "Charity suffereth long, and is kind; charity envieth not; charity vaunteth not itself, is not puffed up" (1 Cor. 13:4). Let us strive to purge every ounce of selfishness from our lives, that charity may take its rightful place and provide the foundation for our spiritual salvation.

THE SCRIPTURES TEACH US

3 Nephi 6:15–16. *Now the cause of this iniquity of the people was this—Satan had great power, unto the stirring up of the people to do all manner of iniquity, and to the puffing them up with pride, tempting them to seek for power, and authority, and riches, and the vain things of the world. And thus Satan did lead away the hearts of the people to do all manner of iniquity; therefore they had enjoyed peace but a few years.*

Selfishness is part of the serious sin of pride, the downfall of the unrighteous. Satan tries to use pride to snare us and lead us away captive. Therefore, we must counteract selfishness with humility and love. Only by thinking of others and their welfare first can we ever destroy our selfish tendencies.

Doctrine and Covenants 121:35–36. *Because their hearts are set so much upon the things of this world, and aspire to the honors of men, that they do not learn this one lesson—That the rights of the priesthood are inseparably connected with the powers of heaven, and that the powers of heaven cannot be controlled nor handled only upon the principles of righteousness.*

Whenever we focus on "things" and attention for ourselves rather than on the well-being of others, we suffer from selfishness. In this state, we cannot be of use to God, but will remain in the downward spiral of self-aggrandizement. Selfishness is the sin of destruction: it destroys lives, it destroys the soul, leading us away from God.

MODERN PROPHETS SPEAK

Gordon B. Hinckley:
> Selfishness is the basis of our troubles . . . in this community and in this nation and in the world—a vicious preoccupation with our own comforts, with the satisfaction of our own appetites, . . . Selfishness is the cause of most of the domestic problems that afflict so many homes of our nation. . . . So many in the game of life get to first base, or second, or even third, but then fail to score. They are inclined to live unto themselves, denying their generous instincts, grasping for possessions and in their self-centered, uninspired living, sharing neither talent nor faith with others. . . . The antidote for selfishness is service, a reaching out to those about us—those in the home and those beyond the walls of the home. A child who grows in a home where there is a selfish, grasping father is likely to develop those tendencies in his own life. On the other hand, a child who sees his father and mother forgo comforts for themselves as they reach out to those in distress, will likely follow the same pattern when he or she grows to maturity. (*Teachings of Gordon B. Hinckley* [Salt Lake City: Deseret Book, 1997], 583)

Harold B. Lee:
> The selfishly ambitious man is never the happy man, for always beyond his covetous grasp there lies the receding horizons that mock his ill-gotten gains. Shun evil itself, and all things with a bad reputation, and remember again the warning words with which I introduced my theme: "Destined as such a soul as yours is for immortality, it must find all that is not eternal too short,

all that is not infinite too small." Never stoop to any material action that will bring you down from the highest position on the high throne of your eternal nature. (*The Teachings of Harold B. Lee,* ed. Clyde J. Williams [Salt Lake City: Bookcraft, 1996], 620)

IDEAS FOR DAILY LIVING

Here are four strategies for overcoming selfishness:

1. Ask yourself what kind of foundation you want for your life.

- *Build on enduring principles*—Examine the underlying principles of your life. If you have allegiance to our Savior Jesus Christ, you will possess honor, integrity, service, and love as a foundation for your life. These principles are incompatible with selfishness.
- *Cultivate self-respect*—Don't confuse selfishness with self-respect. One must be committed to self-respect, which leads one to optimize one's health, vitality, self-confidence, and self-development. These factors are essential to one's capacity to serve others, whereas selfishness degrades service and charity.
- *Seek to be humble*—In humility we erect the ultimate defense against selfishness. "Proud people are intolerably selfish," stated Ralph Waldo Emerson. Let us therefore avoid pride as the cancer of the soul.

2. Be clear about the consequences.

- *Consider the benefits*—Peace, joy, and spiritual calm will not result from selfishness. Instead, selfishness breeds alienation, rancor, greed, envy, jealousy, and anger. Any reasonable person would not commit to a life of selfishness if he or she understood the inevitable outcomes.
- *Know the source of joy*—Try to think of other's needs, desires, and happiness before your own. Such concern will surely turn your thoughts away from self, bringing joy to your life.
- *Understand what produces contentment*—Be happy for others when they succeed. Do not compete for everything. Having more than others or being better than others will not ensure your happiness, but helping others succeed will.

3. Use leadership to thwart selfishness.

- *Start with your thoughts and language*—In what ratio do the words "we" and "I" occur in your patterns of thinking and speaking? You can choose to emphasize the "we" over the "I" in how you conduct your life, thus controlling selfishness at a very fundamental level.
- *Leadership is essentially a selfless endeavor*—The decision to serve others on a regular basis and work toward their progress and productivity is the heart of leadership. There are those, of course, who attempt for selfish reasons to galvanize people into action serving false causes, but this is not genuine leadership. Genuine leadership is structured to optimize the well-being and happiness of the greatest possible number of people.
- *Think family*—Family commitment is the greatest bastion against selfishness. Are you doing all in your power to bring happiness to your spouse and your children? If not, then the canker of selfishness needs to be cured. Be service minded and teach your family members to be service minded as well.
- *Recognize the good in others*—Seek to praise and give credit to others. By illuminating the accomplishments of others, you also cast yourself in a good light. Remember that you are successful on the basis of your own sterling qualities and talents. You don't have to put others down in order for you to be good or successful.

4. Rely on the Lord.

- *Remember to be grateful*—Heavenly Father is the ultimate source of all that you have, including your very being. Hording the gifts He has blessed you with goes against the basic teachings of from the gospel. Selfishness is the ultimate expression of ingratitude for your blessings.
- *Give back generously*—Remember to give your tithes and offerings as well as your Christlike service. Give freely of your substance to help others. Such a pattern of action is an effective inoculation against the malaise of selfishness.
- *Ask for spiritual strength*—Pray and fast to be selfless instead of selfish. Ask for help from the Lord to rise above selfishness.

ILLUSTRATIONS FOR OUR TIMES

President James E. Faust explains what selfishness is, giving examples of people who exhibit this trait and suffer its consequences.

What's in It for Me?

Many years ago I was in a professional association with two older, more experienced men. We had been friends for many years and found it mutually beneficial to help one another. One day, one associate sought our help on a complex matter. As soon as the issue had been explained, the first thing the other associate said was, "What's in it for me?" When his old friend responded so selfishly, I saw the look of pain and disappointment on the face of the one who had invited our help. The relationship between the two was never quite the same after that. Our self-serving friend did not prosper, as his selfishness soon eclipsed his considerable gifts, talents, and qualities. Unfortunately, one of the curses of the world today is encapsulated in this selfish response, "What's in it for me?" . . .

In the Grand Council in Heaven, when the great plan of salvation for God's children was presented, Jesus responded, "Here am I, send me," and "Father, thy will be done, and the glory be thine forever." And thus He became our Savior. In contrast, Satan, who had been highly regarded as "a son of the morning," countered that he would come and "redeem all mankind, that one soul shall not be lost." Satan had two conditions: the first was the denial of agency, and the second, that he would have the honor. In other words, something had to be in it for him. And thus he became the father of lies and selfishness.

Taking up one's cross and following the Savior means overcoming selfishness; it is a commitment to serve others. Selfishness is one of the baser human traits, which must be subdued and overcome. We torture our souls when we focus on getting rather than giving. . . .

I have learned that selfishness has more to do with how we feel about our possessions than how much we have. The poet Wordsworth said, "The world is too much with us; late and soon, / Getting and spending, we lay waste our powers." A poor man can be selfish and a rich man generous, but a person obsessed only with getting will have a hard time finding peace in this life. . . .

Some years ago, Elder ElRay L. Christiansen told about one of his distant Scandinavian relatives who joined the Church. He was quite well-to-do and sold his lands and stock in Denmark to come to Utah with his family. For a while he did well as far as the Church and its activities were concerned, and he prospered financially. However, he became so caught up in his possessions that he forgot about his purpose in coming to America. The bishop visited him and implored him to become active as he used to be. The years passed and some of his brethren visited him and said: "Now, Lars, the Lord was good to you when you were in Denmark. He has been good to you since you have come here. . . . We think now, since you are growing a little older, that it would be well for you to spend some of your time in the interests of the Church. After all, you can't take these things with you when you go."

Jolted by this remark, the man replied, "Vell, den, I vill not go." But he did! And so will all of us! (James E. Faust, "What's in It for Me?" *Ensign,* Nov. 2002, 19)

SUMMARY

As we learn to overcome our selfish tendencies, we truly find ourselves. Putting others and their well-being first will drown out selfishness. This does not mean we must tolerate things that need to be changed, ignore improper behavior, or become permissive. Instead, it means we love and seek the well-being of our fellowmen. The ultimate antidote to selfishness, therefore, is charity, the pure love of Christ. Moroni records precious counsel given by his father, Mormon, regarding charity. He states that to combat selfishness we must develop the qualities of charity; we must be one who "suffereth long, and is kind, and envieth not, and is not puffed up, seeketh not her own, is not easily provoked, thinketh no evil, and rejoiceth not in iniquity but rejoiceth in the truth, beareth all things, believeth all things, hopeth all things, endureth all things" (Moro. 7:45). Selfishness is fleeting and temporally focused, but charity "endureth forever" (v. 47).

SIN

A sin is an unrighteous thought or action committed by an accountable person. Similarly, not doing good works that might be called for in keeping with righteous principles is often referred to as a sin of omission. Sinning entails transgressing the law of God (see 1 Jn. 3:4). It is following after ideas and actions that lead us away from the Lord. This is why the adversary "inviteth" and "enticeth" us to sin (see Moro. 7:12). He knows that when we sin, we withdraw ourselves from the Spirit of God (see Mosiah 2:36). If Satan can get us away from the Spirit, we are likely to sin more. Sin perpetuates sin; when we sin we become more easily influenced by the further temptations of Satan (see D&C 29:40), and are less aware of our sins. All have sinned (see 1 Jn. 1:8–10), and we need to repent daily of whatever has drawn us away from the Spirit. Fortunately, we are free to choose righteousness rather than sin (see 2 Ne. 2:27), and the test of life is to make good choices and to repent of our sins. The Lord cannot make allowance for sin in His presence, but He is compassionate and merciful to the repentant sinner (see D&C 1:31–32). When we confess and forsake our sins, the Lord remembers them no more (see D&C 58:42–43). If we do not repent, we can never return to the Lord.

THE SCRIPTURES TEACH US

John 8:34. *Jesus answered them, Verily, verily, I say unto you, Whosoever committeth sin is the servant of sin.*

When we succumb to sin, we subject ourselves to the consequences of the sin according to the natural law that applies. We lose the Spirit (see Mosiah 2:36), and we lose all the blessings associated with keeping the commandment we have broken.

James 4:17. *Therefore to him that knoweth to do good, and doeth it not, to him it is sin.*

Sins of omission are still sins. We can transgress the law of God by failing to act.

Alma 5:40. *For I say unto you that whatsoever is good cometh from God, and whatsoever is evil cometh from the devil.*

In deciding how to act, remember that all good comes from God and that all evil and sin are of the devil; he is the author of all sin (see Hel. 6:30).

Doctrine and Covenants 50:28. *But no man is possessor of all things except he be purified and cleansed from all sin.*

The Lord invites all to seek justification and sanctification through the Atonement and the Holy Ghost; otherwise, we cannot be empowered from on high to do all things. Certainly, repentance is the single greatest thing we can do in regard to our individual salvation, and helping others repent is the greatest good we can do for our fellowmen (see D&C 15:6; 31:5).

MODERN PROPHETS SPEAK

Spencer W. Kimball:

> Sin has great attraction. Whoever said that sin was not fun? Whoever claimed that Lucifer was not handsome, persuasive, easy, friendly? Whoever said that sin was unattractive, undesirable, or nauseating in its acceptance?

> Transgression wears elegant gowns and sparkling apparel. It is highly perfumed, has attractive features, a soft voice. It is found in educated circles and sophisticated groups. It provides sweet and comfortable luxuries. Sin is easy and has a big company of bedfellows. It promises immunity from restrictions, temporary freedoms. It can momentarily satisfy hunger, thirst, desire, urges, passions, wants, without immediately paying the price. But, it begins tiny and grows to monumental proportions. It grows drop by drop, inch by inch.

> The attractiveness of sin is a lie. Have you seen a real mirage in the distance with lakes and trees and dwellings and castles and water, but as the thirsty traveler moves on and on and on through it, he finds it but an illusion, and when he has gone too far to return he stumbles choking in the desert deception. That is like life—wealth and pride, wit and physical charm, popularity and flattery are the shadows of the nothingness that can bring us only disappointment and frustration.

> Sin is slavery. Carnal pleasures are fleeting and frothy and they always bring their retribution sooner or later. In the breaking of every law of God there is the breaking down of the divine elements of the man. Each command we obey sends us another rung up the ladder to perfected manhood and toward godhood; and every law disobeyed is a sliding toward the bottom where man merges into the brute world. Only he who obeys law is free. Serfdom comes to him who defies law. "The truth shall make

you free" (John 8:32) was another of the incontrovertible truths authored by the Master. He truly is free who is master of situations, habits, passions, urges, and desires. If one must yield to appetite or passion and follow its demands, he is truly the servant of a dictator.

Sin limits progress. Since the beginning there has been in the world a wide range of sins. Many of them involve harm to others, but every sin is against ourselves and God, for sins limit our progress, curtail our development, and estrange us from good people, good influences, and from our Lord.

The scriptures say that "God is not the God of the dead, but of the living." (Matthew 22:32.)

There are no dead except those who have chosen to be dead as to the law, dead as to the benefits, dead as to the blessings, dead as to the eternal nature of the gift. (*The Teachings of Spencer W. Kimball*, ed. Edward L. Kimball [Salt Lake City: Bookcraft, 1982], 153)

Joseph Fielding Smith:
>Here is something which those who contend that the Lord has granted immunity from their sins to some, if they have received certain sealings by the Holy Spirit of promise, have overlooked in this passage. I call attention to these two things. If covenants are broken and enormous sins are committed, but not unto death, there are certain punishments to be inflicted. The mere confession is not enough; the sinners are: 1—to "be destroyed in the flesh"; and 2—to "be delivered unto the buffetings of Satan unto the day of redemption."
>
>Who in the world is so foolish as to wish to sin with the hope of forgiveness, if such a penalty is to be inflicted? No one but a fool! To be "destroyed in the flesh" means exactly that. . . .
>
>Then to be turned over to the buffetings of Satan unto the day of redemption, which is the resurrection, must be something horrible in its nature. Who wishes to endure such torment? No one but a fool! I have seen their anguish. I have heard their pleadings for relief and their pitiful cries that they cannot endure the torment. This was in this life. Add to that, the torment in the spirit world before the redemption comes—all of this, mark you, coming after severe and humble repentance! (*Doctrines of Salvation*, 3 vols., ed. Bruce R. McConkie [Salt Lake City: Bookcraft, 1954–1956], 2:96)

Joseph Smith:
>Our Savior says, that all manner of sin and blasphemy shall be forgiven men wherewith they shall blaspheme; but the blasphemy against the Holy Ghost shall not be forgiven, neither in this world, nor in the world to come, evidently showing that there are sins which may be forgiven in the world to come, although the sin of blasphemy against the Holy Ghost cannot be forgiven. (*History of the Church*, 4:596)

IDEAS FOR DAILY LIVING

Here are several ideas to help us repent and avoid sin:

1. Build a world where sin is not welcome.
- *Control your thoughts*—Don't allow anything in your mind that is degrading or tempting.
- *Be selective*—Expose your mind only to the best and most noble material from books, magazines, the Internet, videos, movies, television, and radio.

- *Activate righteous defenses*—If an evil thought comes, have a method or system to dismiss it: sing a hymn, recite a scripture, view an image of the Savior, view yourself seen by your Heavenly Father or someone you respect deeply.
- *Control your environment*—Be in the right place at the right time, and if you find yourself in the wrong place, leave immediately. (Remember the sterling example of Joseph and Potiphar's wife.) President Harold B. Lee taught: "Not only must we avoid sin but we must avoid the very appearance of evil" (*Decisions for Successful Living* [Salt Lake City: Deseret Book, 1973], 37).
- *Remember the consequences*—Sin brings pain and suffering; obedience brings peace and joy.

2. Plan to succeed. Make a plan to stay on the straight and narrow path.
- *Remember the basics*—Pray, search the scriptures, faithfully attend church, and keep the commandments.
- *Start where you stand*—Confess and forsake your sins. Feelings of guilt leading to repentance are of the Lord. Guilt that makes you feel you are beyond repentance is of the devil. President James E. Faust counseled: "After our full repentance, the formula is wonderfully simple. Indeed, the Lord has given it to us in these words: 'Will ye not now return unto me, and repent of your sins, and be converted, that I may heal you?' (3 Nephi 9:13). In so doing, we have his promise that 'he healeth the broken in heart, and bindeth up their wounds' (Psalms 147:3)" (*Finding Light in a Dark World* [Salt Lake City: Deseret Book, 1995], 31).
- *Stay close to your family and righteous associates*—Counsel with your parents, family members, and Church leaders.
- *Avoid idleness*—As the saying goes, "an idle mind is the devil's workshop." Don't just avoid the bad in life; actively pursue good things (see D&C 58:27).
- *Cultivate love of the gospel*—Look outside yourself for opportunities to serve. President Harold B. Lee taught: "*We must love and obey the truth to avoid sin.* Satan knows truth, but he has no intelligence, or he would yield obedience to that truth. Knowing the truth isn't the thing that saves us. I think that perhaps loving the truth is the only thing that can give one the capacity to avoid sin. The scripture doesn't say: 'If ye know me, you will keep my commandments,' but it says, 'If ye love me, ye will keep my commandments' (see John 14:15)" (*The Teachings of Harold B. Lee,* ed. Clyde J. Williams [Salt Lake City: Bookcraft, 1996], 105).
- *Cultivate charity*—Sin is self-centered. As you strive to serve others, reaching outside yourself, you will no longer desire to sin.
- *Have hope*—Hope is your anchor of faith to do good. Regardless of your past, things can be better with hope in Christ our Savior. Without hope, sin is at the door.

ILLUSTRATIONS FOR OUR TIMES

The story of near-tragedy on a busy highway has parallels to the wisdom of avoiding sin by following our living prophets.

Wrong Way—Do Not Enter

Many years ago, our next-door neighbor performed an act of inordinate courage to save the lives of some strangers. He and his wife were driving along a stretch of interstate highway one day when he glanced across the median strip to behold a terrifying phenomenon. Incredibly, there was a car across the way driving parallel to his own car but moving directly into the line of traffic in the opposite lanes. My friend watched with utter horror as trucks and cars swerved to avoid collision with the intruding vehicle driving in the wrong direction along the innermost lane. What to do?

In a split second, my friend had made his decision. He accelerated to a high rate of speed and looked for the next opportunity to cross over the median. Soon he came to a connecting road and maneuvered quickly toward the opposite lanes of traffic, coming to a screeching halt on the inner shoulder of the opposite lanes. Despite significant dangers to himself, he then ran towards the errant vehicle and flagged it down amid the swerving and dodging vehicles.

Incredibly, the elderly couple whom he forced to stop off to the side of traffic were at first indignant at such treatment. What business did this stranger have interrupting their trip? Soon they realized, however, that he had surely saved their lives, and were grateful for the Christian act of charity and deliverance.

This true story is like a modern-day parable of the reactions of the world in nearly all ages to the ministry of the prophets of God. They see us heading the wrong way into sin, and do all they can to warn us and help us turn around and go the right way. The eternal message is one of warning: the call to repentance, the admonition to heed the word of God and be saved. In modern terms, it is the alarm sounded when one foolishly travels down a one-way street in the wrong direction. So often this warning is met with hardness of heart and with stubborn and prideful rebellion. "What business do you have to tell me I cannot propel myself into the jaws of destruction?" However, the alarm of the prophets is powered by the spirit of charity. As Samuel the Lamanite proclaimed to his obstinate Nephite audience from the walls of Zarahemla: "For behold, they have been a chosen people of the Lord; yea, the people of Nephi hath he loved, and also hath he chastened them; yea, in the days of their iniquities hath he chastened them because he loveth them" (Hel. 15:3).

Would we not all do well to choose our bearings in life based on eternal principles, and to observe with care the directions of our journey day-by-day? Should we not accept in the spirit of gratitude and humility the loving, though firm entreaties of the prophets of God as they teach us to move faithfully away from sin and securely toward a destination of peace and redemption?

—Richard J. Allen

SUMMARY

Our salvation, immortality, and eternal life depend on our overcoming and forsaking our sins. We must repent—there is no other way back into the presence of our Heavenly Father. The process of repentance through the Atonement of our Savior is a wonderful gift, yet how much less painful it is to make righteous choices than to learn by committing sin and repenting. Alma correctly stated, " O, remember, my son, and learn wisdom in thy youth; yea, learn in thy youth to keep the commandments of God" (Alma 37:35). Learning early in our lives to do right and avoid sin will save us much pain and difficulty, and will prove our loyalty and love to our Heavenly Father and our Savior Jesus Christ.

SPIRITUALITY

Spirituality can be defined in many ways. Herein, we refer to it as living an inspired life, or enjoying the companionship and blessings of the Holy Spirit. It involves using self-mastery to become Spirit directed rather than carnally minded. As we increase our spirituality, our spirit, by the power of the Holy Ghost, directs our life—our flesh is governed by our spirit. In this state, we can be shown all things to do by the Holy Ghost (see 2 Ne. 32:5). We have begun the process of sanctification to become clean and pure. We seek the will of Heavenly Father, yielding our hearts to Him. The blessings of spirituality received from the Holy Spirit are many and varied, enumerated as the gifts of the Spirit (see Moro. 10:7–19; D&C 46:8–31); the fruits of the Spirit (see Gal. 5:22–23); trust in the Spirit, which leads one to do good (see D&C 11:12–13); and many other blessings of the Spirit (see *Holy Ghost*).

A spiritual foundation in life is an essential ingredient in being well-adjusted and happy. Jacob explained, "Remember, to be carnally-minded is death, and to be spiritually-minded is life eternal" (2 Ne. 9:39). We can see the difficulty our society faces as it abandons its spiritual roots. A carnally-minded people tries to take God out of the world, rather than remove themselves from worldliness to find God. As we develop our spirituality, we find God, and we exercise faith and hope in Him.

THE SCRIPTURES TEACH US

Romans 8:5–14. *For they that are after the flesh do mind the things of the flesh; but they that are after the Spirit the things of the Spirit. For to be carnally minded is death; but to be spiritually minded is life and peace. Because the carnal mind is enmity against God: for it is not subject to the law of God, neither indeed can be. So then they that are in the flesh cannot please God. But ye are not in the flesh, but in the Spirit, if so be that the Spirit of God dwell in you. Now if any man have not the Spirit of Christ, he is none of his. And if Christ be in you, the body is dead because of sin; but the Spirit is life because of righteousness. . . . For if ye live after the flesh, ye shall die: but if ye through the Spirit do mortify the deeds of the body, ye shall live. For as many as are led by the Spirit of God, they are the sons of God.*

These glorious verses, written by the Apostle Paul to the Saints at Rome, remind us of the incomparable blessings of living by the Spirit. As we increase our spirituality, we transcend the earthly sphere and live in a higher plane; though we are still in the world, we are no longer "of the world."

Galatians 5:22–23. *But the fruit of the Spirit is love, joy, peace, longsuffering, gentleness, goodness, faith, Meekness, temperance: against such there is no law.*

When we receive the Spirit and partake of its fruits, we will see these qualities of spirituality expressed in our own lives. We can then use these qualities to serve our fellowmen and build the kingdom of God.

Alma 5:14. *And now behold, I ask of you, my brethren of the church, have ye spiritually been born of God? Have ye received his image in your countenances? Have ye experienced this mighty change in your hearts?*

In this scripture, Alma exhorts Church members to be spiritually minded—to be born of the Spirit, to radiate the light of Christ (see 3 Ne. 18:24), and to ensure that we have given our hearts to the will of God (see Mosiah 3:19; Hel. 3:35).

Doctrine and Covenants 11:12–13. *And now, verily, verily, I say unto thee, put your trust in that Spirit which leadeth to do good—yea, to do justly, to walk humbly, to judge righteously; and this is my Spirit. Verily, verily, I say unto you, I will impart unto you of my Spirit, which shall enlighten your mind, which shall fill your soul with joy.*

When we live by and trust in the Spirit, we increase our spirituality—our minds are enlightened with knowledge of who we are and how we should act, and we rejoice in this state.

Moroni 4:3. *O God, the Eternal Father, we ask thee in the name of thy Son, Jesus Christ, to bless and sanctify this bread to the souls of all those who partake of it; that they may eat in remembrance of the body of thy Son, and witness unto thee, O God, the Eternal Father, that they are willing to take upon them the name of thy Son, and always remember him, and keep his commandments which he hath given them, that they may always have his Spirit to be with them. Amen.* (See also Moro. 5:2; D&C 20:77, 79.)

The companionship of the Spirit and increased spirituality come as we keep the Lord's commandments and renew our covenants by worthily partaking of the sacrament each week.

MODERN PROPHETS SPEAK

Gordon B. Hinckley:

> If I were a bishop or stake president today, what would I do? I think that I would try to put my major efforts on building the spirituality of the people. I would work as hard as I knew how to work in building their faith in the Lord Jesus Christ, in God our Eternal Father, in the Prophet Joseph Smith and the restoration of this work and what it means and what it is all about. I would encourage my people to read the scriptures, to read the Book of Mormon, to read the New Testament. I would urge them with all the capacity I have to read quietly and thoughtfully and introspectively, if you please. I would urge them to read the teachings of the Prophet Joseph Smith.

> We need to build ourselves spiritually. We live in a world of rush and go, of running here and there and in every direction. We are very busy people. We have so much to do. We need to get off by ourselves once in awhile and think of the spiritual things and build ourselves spiritually. If you have a study at home, lock yourselves in it. If you have a place in the basement where you can be by yourself, go there. Get by yourself and think of things of the Lord, of things of the Spirit. Let gratitude swell up in your hearts. Think of all the Lord has done for you. How blessed you are, how very blessed you are. Think of your duty and your responsibility. Think of your testimony. Think of the things of God. Just meditate and reflect for an hour about yourself and your relationship to your Heavenly Father and your Redeemer. It will do something for you. (*Teachings of Gordon B. Hinckley* [Salt Lake City: Deseret Book, 1997], 608–609)

David O. McKay:

> Man's earthly existence is but a test as to whether he will concentrate his efforts, his mind, his soul upon things which contribute to the comfort and gratification of his physical instincts and passions, or whether he will make as his life's end and purpose the acquisition of spiritual qualities. (*Gospel Ideals: Selections from the Discourses of David O. McKay* [Salt Lake City: Improvement Era, 1953], 387)

Howard W. Hunter:

> Developing spirituality and attuning ourselves to the highest influences of godliness is not an easy matter. It takes time and frequently involves a struggle. It will not happen by chance, but

is accomplished only through deliberate effort and by calling upon God and keeping his commandments. . . .

We must take time to prepare our minds for spiritual things. The development of spiritual capacity does not come with the conferral of authority. There must be desire, effort, and personal preparation. This requires, of course, as you already know, fasting, prayer, searching the scriptures, experience, meditation, and a hungering and thirsting after the righteous life.

I find it helpful to review these admonitions from Almighty God:

"If thou shalt ask, thou shalt receive revelation upon revelation, knowledge upon knowledge, that thou mayest know the mysteries and peaceable things—that which bringeth joy, that which bringeth life eternal" (D&C 42:61).

"Ask the Father in my name, in faith believing that you shall receive, and you shall have the Holy Ghost, which manifesteth all things which are expedient unto the children of men" (D&C 18:18).

"Let the solemnities of eternity rest upon your minds" (D&C 43:34). . . .

"God shall give unto you knowledge by his Holy Spirit, yea, by the unspeakable gift of the Holy Ghost" (D&C 121:26).

These are promises that the Lord will surely fulfill if we prepare ourselves.

Take time to meditate, ponder, and pray on spiritual matters. (*The Teachings of Howard W. Hunter,* ed. Clyde J. Williams [Salt Lake City: Bookcraft, 1997], 36)

Harold B. Lee:
Within every one of you there dwells a spirit which is the exact counterpart of your full-grown physical body. To keep your physical body in vigor and health, food and drink must be provided at frequent intervals. Every germ cell of your bodies must have a nerve connection in order to maintain the vital life processes. Failure to maintain these nerve connections or to supply the required sustenance brings decay, stagnation, sickness, and finally death to the physical body.

Your spiritual body needs nourishment at frequent intervals in order to assure its health and vigor. Earthly food does not satisfy this need. Food to satisfy your spiritual needs must come from spiritual sources. Principles of eternal truth, as contained in the gospel, and the proper exercise by engaging in spiritual activities are essential to the satisfying of your spiritual selves. Vital processes of the spirit are likewise maintained only by intelligent connection with spiritual fountains of truth. Spiritual sickness and death, which mean separation from the fountain of spiritual light, are sure to follow the severance of your connection with the spiritual nerve center, the Church of Jesus Christ. . . .

To be spiritually minded is to live the gospel. The spiritually minded person seeks respect of the high-minded who obey the law, who revere womanhood and virtue and encourage purity of thought and action rather than cater to the applause of those who secretly despise the man who thinks and acts below the standards he professes.

When prospering in a material way, a person with great spirituality shows appreciation to God, to whom he is indebted for all that he has, by a thrifty, frugal husbanding of his substance and by extending generosity to the unfortunate according to the laws of the Church, rather than indulging in a reckless, riotous living as a prodigal in defiance of the laws of both God and man. (*The Teachings of Harold B. Lee,* ed. Clyde J. Williams [Salt Lake City: Bookcraft, 1996], 123)

IDEAS FOR DAILY LIVING

Here are three ideas to help us grow spiritually:

1. Savor the literature on spirituality.
- *Listen to the prophets*—Review carefully the prophets' counsel regarding spirituality.
- *Study the scriptures regularly*—Create a study plan for feasting daily on the word of God. Pray to understand the commandments and will of Heavenly Father.
- *Study the support literature*—Read and study the support literature provided by the Church. Manuals for Sunday School, priesthood/Relief Society lessons, or for institute and other Church Educational System programs are a great place to start.

2. Follow a step-by-step process for cultivating a spiritual mindset and lifestyle. Spirituality perpetuates spirituality. As we seek spirituality, our desire for spiritual things increases, and we come to enjoy the blessings of obedience and leading a Spirit-guided life. This process is eloquently summarized in the following passage:

> We seek spirituality through faith, repentance, and baptism; through forgiveness of one another; through fasting and prayer; through righteous desires and pure thoughts and actions. We seek spirituality through service to our fellowmen; through worship; through feasting on the word of God, in the scriptures and in the teachings of the living prophets. We attain spirituality through making and keeping covenants with the Lord, through conscientiously trying to keep all the commandments of God. Spirituality is not acquired suddenly. It is the consequence of a succession of right choices. It is the harvest of a righteous life. (Monte S. Nyman and Charles D. Tate Jr., eds., *Mosiah: Salvation Only through Christ* [Provo: BYU Religious Studies Center, 1991], 240)

3. Seek balance. Let us avoid compartmentalizing our life to such an extent that we separate gospel principles from our daily life. Living the principles of the gospel should be central in everything we do—not just on Sunday as part of our church attendance and worship.

ILLUSTRATIONS FOR OUR TIMES

In an excerpt from an *Ensign* article by Mary Ellen Edmunds, we learn the characteristics of people who have developed a deep spirituality in their lives.

Spirituality Is Integrity

> The story goes that someone once asked Michelangelo how he could transform ordinary rock into his marvelous statues. Reportedly, the artist replied that he just chiseled until everything that wasn't the statue wasn't there. To be spiritual means to have a sense of who we truly are and then to be that person.

Eventually, spirituality becomes such an integral part of our being that we can follow our heart's true desires without doing anything wrong. Nephi, the son of Helaman, reached that point where there was no conflict between what he wanted and what was right. The Lord promised him, "I will bless thee forever; and I will make thee mighty in word and in deed, in faith and in works; yea, even that all things shall be done unto thee according to thy word, *for thou shalt not ask that which is contrary to my will.*" (Hel. 10:5; italics added.)

This kind of spirituality requires that we consciously move away from all that is unkind, unholy, impure, or unchristian. It requires that we let go of anger and revenge. And it yields a peace of heart and soul. It makes us able to find good things to do without constantly being asked, pushed, or reminded. . . .

As I observe people who seem to have developed a deep spirituality, I notice several qualities they have in common. One is the ability to communicate in a meaningful, personal way with God, to enjoy meditating and pondering. Another is a cheerfulness, an optimism, a buoyancy of spirit. Those who are spiritual also seem to be grateful—not just for obvious blessings, but for the often unnoticed joys of life. They seem genuinely happy when others succeed or receive praise. They obey with a feeling of enlightenment and sense of progression, rather than out of duty or fear or in hopes of some honor. And they seem as much concerned with *being*—with the state of their souls—as they are with *doing*.

Perhaps the trait I enjoy most in those who seem to have reached higher levels of spirituality is that they show kind, tender, active concern for others. They don't seem to need much credit for genuine Christian service. And they seem to be able to help others without creating dependency or a feeling of indebtedness. They have a way of exalting those they help. (See D&C 104:15–16.)

They say, "Here we are, Lord. Send us!" Send us to Africa or South America. Send us next door with some warm bread. Send us to listen to a weary, struggling neighbor. Send us to visit a lonely friend. Send us into the next room to lift a heavy heart. Help us be in tune so that we can respond to all the big and little promptings that come. Help us go beyond "Just call if you need me" to anticipating and helping before there is desperation and helplessness.

The price God asks of each of us is the same: everything. The reward is also the same: a growing feeling of confidence and peace. I will always remember a tall Nigerian who stood in a testimony meeting and said with emotion, "I am convinced that I am a son of God!" I also like to think how Enos must have felt when he knew he was forgiven of his sins and his faith in Christ was rewarded: "Wherefore my soul did rest." (Enos 1:17.)

May we lift and love and nourish and smile. May we visit and share and sing and serve until joy fills our souls to overflowing. Then we, with Enos, may look forward to meeting God, for we will "see his face with pleasure." (Enos 1:27.) (Mary Ellen Edmunds, "Spirituality—More Than a Feeling," *Ensign,* October 1985, 14)

SUMMARY

Achieving spirituality is necessary in order to live a life in harmony with the gospel of Jesus Christ. Such a state of being is not a pious "holier than thou" attitude, but rather a God-fearing, humble state where we submit our will to the will of the Father. The fruits of spirituality include the Christlike qualities of goodness and compassion, and a disposition to serve others without trying to improve our own position or station. Spirituality is the gateway to understanding God, for whom all things have a spiritual foundation: "Wherefore, verily I say unto you that all things unto me are spiritual, and not at any time have I given unto you a law which was temporal; neither any man, nor the children of men; neither Adam, your father, whom I created" (D&C 29:34). So should our view be in life; nothing is of only temporal consequence. Let us therefore commit ourselves to cultivating a more spiritual lifestyle by keeping the commandments of God.

SUSTAINING CHURCH LEADERS

As members of the Church, we show our devotion to God by sustaining the prophets and leaders He has called and put in place for us. We do this by supporting them in their actions and requests and by hearkening to their words. The words they speak as our leaders are the words of God (see D&C 1:38; 21:4–6) and we should heed them lest we bring ourselves under great condemnation (see 3 Ne. 28:34–35). In addition, we are greatly blessed by believing on their words (see 3 Ne. 19:28). We give our Church leaders our sustaining vote by participating in the law of common consent, binding ourselves through that action to support them.

THE SCRIPTURES TEACH US

Matthew 10:40. *He that receiveth you receiveth me, and he that receiveth me receiveth him that sent me.*

When we accept the prophets and their direction, we accept our Savior and our Heavenly Father. If we are true and faithful, we can receive all that the Father has (see D&C 84:36–38).

2 Chronicles 20:20. *And they rose early in the morning, and went forth into the wilderness of Tekoa: and as they went forth, Jehoshaphat stood and said, Hear me, O Judah, and ye inhabitants of Jerusalem; Believe in the Lord your God, so shall ye be established; believe his prophets, so shall ye prosper.*

When we choose to follow the prophets, we prosper in our lives. Furthermore, we are favored of the Lord when we follow without murmuring (see 1 Ne. 3:6).

Doctrine and Covenants 107:22. *Of the Melchizedek Priesthood, three Presiding High Priests, chosen by the body, appointed and ordained to that office, and upheld by the confidence, faith, and prayer of the church, form a quorum of the Presidency of the Church.*

By the law of common consent, we sustain the First Presidency with our prayers and our faith (see D&C 26:2). We should pray daily for the welfare of the Brethren so that they may bless the Church and all the world.

MODERN PROPHETS SPEAK

James E. Faust:
> She [my mother] always taught us to sustain our bishop and our stake president and the General Authorities. She said that if we did not sustain our leaders, we were not sustaining our God, because

they are the representatives of the Lord. She also taught us that when we criticize the leaders of the Church, we are on the road to apostasy. I have tried to follow my mother's teachings in this regard. (*To Reach Even unto You* [Salt Lake City: Deseret Book, 1980], 65)

I do not believe members of the Church can be in full harmony with the Savior without sustaining his living prophet on the earth, the president of the Church. If we do not sustain the living prophet, whoever he may be, we die spiritually. Ironically, some have died spiritually by exclusively following prophets who have long been dead. Others equivocate in their support of living prophets, trying to lift themselves up by putting down the living prophets, however subtly. (*Reach Up for the Light* [Salt Lake City: Deseret Book, 1990], 111)

Howard W. Hunter:

As I have pondered the messages of the conference, I have asked myself this question: How can I help others partake of the goodness and blessings of our Heavenly Father? The answer lies in following the direction received from those we sustain as prophets, seers, and revelators, and others of the General Authorities. Let us study their words, spoken under the spirit of inspiration, and refer to them often. The Lord has revealed his will to the Saints in this conference. (*The Teachings of Howard W. Hunter,* edited by Clyde J. Williams [Salt Lake City: Bookcraft, 1997], 213)

Neal A. Maxwell:

It is exceedingly important for members of the Church to get experience following the prophets in little things, so that they can follow in large matters. By following the prophets in fair weather we become familiar with their cadence, so that we can follow them in stormy times too, for then both our reflexes and our experience will need to combine to help us; the stresses will be so very real. (*All These Things Shall Give Thee Experience* [Salt Lake City: Deseret Book, 1979], 102)

Joseph B. Wirthlin:

The Savior has declared that whether we receive the word of God "by [his] own voice or by the voice of [his] servants, it is the same." (D&C 1:38.) If we are to follow Christ, we must follow the prophet, the Lord's mouthpiece on earth. (*Finding Peace in Our Lives* [Salt Lake City: Deseret Book, 1995], 234)

IDEAS FOR DAILY LIVING

Here are some suggestions for sustaining the General Authorities and local leaders:

1. Pray for them. Pray for the well-being of our Church leaders, and for them to be inspired of the Lord. Our prophets and other General Authorities often express their gratitude for the prayers of the Saints.

2. Hearken to their counsel. Heed and conform your life to the counsel of Church leaders. Doing what they ask you to do is a symbol of your love for them and for the Lord.

3. Worthiness—Be worthy of blessings of the priesthood and to be directed by the Holy Ghost.

4. Be easily entreated and quick to obey. Receive the word of God from leaders with an eager heart and willingly follow their direction.

5. Never judge, criticize, find fault, or murmur. Do not speak evil of the Lord's chosen leaders, as this is a sure way to inactivity and apostasy. Rather, seek to understand and follow their words.

6. Give honest feedback when asked. When asked for information or your opinion, be honest and forthright so that needs can be accurately assessed and revelation received in regard to the situation.

7. Give freely of your time. Organize your life so you can take the time to serve well. When you magnify your callings, you are sustaining and following your leaders.

8. Increase your faith. Work to build your faith in the Lord Jesus Christ. When your faith is strong, you will be eager to receive and follow the Lord's servants.

ILLUSTRATIONS FOR OUR TIMES

Apostle L. Tom Perry tells of his father's interaction with the prophet Joseph F. Smith while living in his home, then uses one of his father's experiences to emphasize the importance of following and sustaining the prophet.

Heed the Prophet's Voice

> While my father attended L.D.S. High School, he worked and lived in the home of President Joseph F. Smith. He wrote in his life history about President Smith:

> "Most great men that I have known have been deflated by intimate contact. Not so with the prophet Joseph F. Smith. Each common everyday act added inches to his greatness. To me he was a prophet even while washing his hands or untying his shoes."

> My father tells of one experience in which the prophet taught him a practical lesson late one night as he entered the Beehive House. Again quoting from my father's life history:

> "I walked with guarded steps through the office, then into the private study to the door at the foot of the steps that led to my bedroom. But the door would not open. I pushed and I pushed to no avail. Finally I gave up and went back to a rug that I had noticed in the hall with the intention of sleeping there until morning.

> "In the darkness I bumped against another partially opened door and the collision awakened the prophet. He turned on the light and, seeing who it was, came down the stairway and inquired concerning my difficulty.

> "'The door is locked that leads to my room,' I explained. He went to the door and pulled instead of pushed, and the door opened. Had he been disturbed by my foolish blunder I would not have been surprised, for I had robbed him of a precious night's sleep by a thoughtless act. He only smiled and stopped to inquire of a strange stable boy what I had stumbled into. I pointed to the half open door at the other end of the hall.

> "'Let me show you something.' He took time at midnight to explain, 'When in the dark, never go groping with hands parted and outstretched; that permits doors to get by your guard and hit

you. Keep your arms in front, but hands together; then you will feel with your hands and not your head.' I thanked him and moved to my quarters. He waited until I reached the rear stairway and then he retired."

Isn't a prophet someone who teaches us to open doors we could not open ourselves—doors to greater light and truth? Isn't a prophet like a pair of hands clasped together in front of the body of the Church, helping members navigate through the dark corridors of the world? Isn't a prophet someone who watches and waits for us patiently while we get to where we need to be?

Never has there been a time when the written and spoken word can descend upon us from so many different sources. Through the media we find analysts analyzing the analysts, almost overwhelming us with opinions and different views.

What a comfort it is to know that the Lord keeps a channel of communication open to His children through the prophet. What a blessing it is to know we have a voice we can trust to declare the will of the Lord. As the prophet Amos taught, "Surely the Lord God will do nothing, but he revealeth his secret unto his servants the prophets" (Amos 3:7). (L. Tom Perry, "Heed the Prophet's Voice," *Ensign,* November 1994, 17)

SUMMARY

As we sustain and follow our Church leaders, we will be blessed and receive strength. The Lord Himself explains that we receive not only Him and the Father by receiving His servants, but entrance into the kingdom of God (see D&C 84:36–38). Let us remember that as we raise our hands to the square in common consent, we covenant to put forth effort and faith necessary to sustain our leaders. We do this by praying for them, by following their counsel, by not speaking evil of them, and by magnifying our callings.

TEACHING

The act of teaching has great potential for influencing the growth of others. Henry Adams said, "A teacher affects eternity. He can never tell where his influence stops." Whether by precept or example, a skillful teacher creates an atmosphere of learning and inspires change and improvement. For good or ill, all of us are teachers because invariably someone is watching or listening. Great teachers have the power, the skills, and the opportunity to make a difference in others' lives and society.

THE SCRIPTURES TEACH US

Mosiah 23:14. *And also trust no one to be your teacher nor your minister, except he be a man of God, walking in his ways and keeping his commandments.*

As teachers, we have the responsibility to seek to be worthy to teach by keeping the commandments. As learners, we should pray for those who teach to be worthy and prepared to teach by the Spirit. Whether or not we can teach or learn things of an eternal nature depends on our worthiness to receive the promptings of the Spirit.

Doctrine and Covenants 42:14. *And the Spirit shall be given unto you by the prayer of faith; and if ye receive not the Spirit ye shall not teach.*

We simply cannot teach properly or effectively without the assistance of the Holy Ghost. We must seek the Spirit in our teaching, for the Spirit will tell us the very things we need to say (see D&C 100:5–6). With the Spirit, we will teach by the power and authority of God (see Alma 17:3), and we will teach others to walk in His ways and to love and serve one another (see Mosiah 4:15). When we teach by the Spirit of Truth, those present will hear by that same Spirit (see D&C 50:17–22).

Doctrine and Covenants 68:25, 28. *And again, inasmuch as parents have children in Zion, or in any of her stakes which are organized, that teach them not to understand the doctrine of repentance, faith in Christ the Son of the living God, and of baptism and the gift of the Holy Ghost by the laying on of the hands, when eight years old, the sin be upon the heads of the parents. . . . And they shall also teach their children to pray, and to walk uprightly before the Lord.*

According to these verses, we have duties as parents that cannot be delegated to any other person or organization. We stand condemned if we fail to teach our children to understand gospel principles and to follow the ways of the Lord.

MODERN PROPHETS SPEAK

N. Eldon Tanner:

> In my opinion no greater call can come to anyone than to be a teacher in The Church of Jesus Christ of Latter-day Saints. We are all teachers in one way or another, whether we have been called and set apart as such or not. The Savior himself was known as the greatest of all teachers. Let us try in every way to emulate him and his example. ("Teaching Children of God," *Ensign,* October 1980, 2)

M. Russell Ballard:

> I believe there is no greater call in the Church than to be an effective teacher. Effective teaching by the Spirit can stir the souls of men with a desire to live the principles of the gospel of Jesus Christ more completely. ("Teaching—No Greater Call," *Ensign,* May 1983, 68)

Joseph Smith:

> Be careful that you teach not for the word of God the commandments of men, nor the doctrines of men, nor the ordinances of men, inasmuch as you are God's messengers. Study the word of God, and preach it and not your opinions, for no man's opinion is worth a straw. Advance no principle but what you can prove, for one scriptural proof is worth ten thousand opinions. We would moreover say, abide by that revelation which says "Preach nothing but repentance to this generation," and leave the further mysteries of the kingdom till God shall tell you to preach them, which is not now. (*History of the Church,* 3:395–96)

Ezra Taft Benson:

> We are to use the Book of Mormon as the basis for our teaching. The Lord states: "And again, the elders, priests and teachers of this church shall teach the principles of my gospel, which are . . . in the Book of Mormon, in the which is the fulness of the gospel." (D&C 42:12.) As we read and teach, we are to liken the Book of Mormon scriptures unto us "that it might be for our profit and learning" (1 Nephi 19:23). (*The Teachings of Ezra Taft Benson* [Salt Lake City: Bookcraft, 1988], 306)

IDEAS FOR DAILY LIVING

Here are six qualities of an effective teacher:

1. An effective teacher teaches by the Spirit. An effective teacher prepares to teach with the Spirit by being obedient to the commandments (see D&C 20:77, 79), being full of love (see D&C 76:116), and by exercising faith.

2. An effective teacher is motivated by love and respect.
- *The key ingredient is love*—Above all other qualities, an effective teacher has a generous measure of love for the student.
- *Show respect*—A part of showing love is showing respect. An effective teacher treats his or her students with dignity and encouragement.

3. An effective teacher is visionary.
- *Focus on the potential*—An effective teacher sees less of what is, and more of what might be. Above all, a good teacher has confidence in the outcome of the teaching process, because only where the teacher sees clearly the potential of the student can that student be taught to catch the vision of his or her own future.
- *Open the eyes of your students*—An effective teacher illuminates new pathways, better opportunities to seek growth, and better knowledge for living and learning.
- *Illuminate the understanding*—One key to effective teaching is to ensure that students understand the information and see its value. This improves their attitudes and increases their studious behavior.

4. An effective teacher is exemplary of the learning process.
- *Be diligent*—An effective teacher demonstrates the qualities of hard work, persistence, and the determination to excel so that he or she can model the very process by which the student, too, can master the subject.
- *Know your students*—An effective teacher knows the needs, concerns, strengths, and desires of his or her students. Effective teaching involves teamwork. No teaching can occur in a vacuum.
- *Earn their trust*—An effective teacher establishes relationships of trust and credibility with students.
- *Be humble*—An effective teacher is humble, ever willing to confess that he or she likewise is a student who must continue to learn each day, to increase in the mastery of the subject.
- *Be balanced*—The effective teacher demonstrates an interest in all areas of learning, both secular and spiritual, rather than confining intellectual curiosity to isolated concerns.

5. An effective teacher builds an environment for optimal growth.
- *Cultivate a genuine locus of learning*—Create an appealing atmosphere for learning and change. This does not refer to the classroom or to the physical space as much as to the framework for learning—the vision, the relationships, the opportunities, the excitement, and the encouragement.
- *Focus on desire*—When you create the desire to learn, the hardest step in the learning process has been taken. Desire is the fuel for learning. "Experience teaches only the teachable," counseled Aldous Huxley.
- *Listen*—A master teacher listens. This skill allows the teacher to discern the needs, strengths, and potential of the individual. Said one anonymous writer: "Until you know how they feel, think, and believe, you cannot teach with power."

- *Master the techniques that foster learning*—Teach efficiently and effectively. When the heart is touched, there is greater change.
- *Use action*—Involve students in the teaching process. Discovery learning is very powerful.
- *Use high energy*—Make learning fun and exciting. Learning can be one of the great adventures of life.
- *Encourage reach*—Help students stretch beyond their level. This inspires creativity and discovery.
- *Be honest and candid*—Be forthright with your students. Where a student is heading into unproductive pathways, the effective teacher will set forth with clarity the consequences so that the student can choose more wisely.
- *Be gracious*—Never embarrass a student in front of his or her peers.
- *Use praise*—Praise your students for work well done.
- *Be creative*—Be resourceful and innovative. No legitimate option for learning should be left unattended and unapplied where it might assist the individual student to have the "aha's" needed for true discovery.

6. An effective teacher is patient.

- *Never give up*—Be patient. Some students grasp concepts immediately; others take more time. You cannot force a young tree to grow up any faster than nature has provided for its growth. But you can continually nourish it, nurture it, prune it in wisdom, and provide an environment where it can rise to fulfill its destiny.
- *Watch for the straggler*—Encourage those who struggle and fall behind. Look for the signs of discouragement. Shore up the weak and instill hope in the fearful.
- *Have relentlessly high expectations*—Always expect the best out of students.
- *Start in the family*—The family setting is the seedbed for effective teaching. Sir Francis Drake reminded us: "see that ye hold fast the heritage we leave you, yea, and teach your children value."

ILLUSTRATIONS FOR OUR TIMES

In a general conference address, Vaughn J. Featherstone explains how great teachers teach souls, not just lessons.

Impact Teachers

> What miracles an impact teacher can achieve by giving honest appreciation and a sense of self-worth! The parent or teacher who honestly satisfies this heart hunger will hold a child or a class in the palm of his hand.
>
> Some years ago when Aldin Porter was president of the Boise North Stake, he dropped by the home of Glen Clayton, who was the Scoutmaster in his ward. Glen and his son were working together repairing a bicycle. President Porter stood and talked to them for a few minutes and then left. Several hours later he returned and the father and son were still working on the bike together. President Porter said, "Glen, with the wages you make per hour you could have bought a new bike, considering the time you have spent repairing this old one."
>
> Glen stood up and said, "I'm not repairing a bike, I'm training a boy!"
>
> That year twenty-one boys achieved the rank of Eagle Scout in Glen's troop. Impact teachers do not teach lessons, they teach souls. (Vaughn J. Featherstone, "The Impact Teacher," *Ensign,* November 1976, 103)

SUMMARY

There is an ancient Greek saying: "If a teacher influences but one, his influence never stops." To be effective teachers, we must ask ourselves, "How can I help my students?" "How can I strengthen their faith in Jesus Christ?" Let each of us seek to emulate the greatest teacher who ever lived, our Master Jesus Christ, who said, "Learn of me, and listen to my words; walk in the meekness of my Spirit, and you shall have peace in me" (D&C 19:23).

TEMPLE WORK AND FAMILY HISTORY

Temples are "The House of the Lord," erected and dedicated as sacred precincts where we can worship God and receive the ordinances of exaltation. Going hand in hand with temple work is family history work, wherein we search out our ancestors and perform their temple work. Family history and temple work are essential to eternal families—without this work, families could not be bound together through eternal ordinances. The restoration of the priesthood and the sealing power through Elijah has, as prophesied, caused the children and their fathers to turn towards each other (see D&C 2). As we complete our ancestors' temple work, we can be made perfect with them (see D&C 128:15). Preparing a written record of our family history also brings gratitude for the past and for the sacrifices made by our predecessors. Family histories can serve as inspiration and motivation for descendants to live righteous lives, and the process of preparing the histories can bring families closer together. Following family history research with performing the sacred temple ordinances gives our ancestors the keys to exaltation, while giving us increased knowledge and spirituality.

THE SCRIPTURES TEACH US

Doctrine and Covenants 2:1–3. *Behold, I will reveal unto you the Priesthood, by the hand of Elijah the prophet, before the coming of the great and dreadful day of the Lord. And he shall plant in the hearts of the children the promises made to the fathers, and the hearts of the children shall turn to their fathers. If it were not so, the whole earth would be utterly wasted at his coming.* (See also Mal. 4:5–6; 3 Ne. 25:5–6; JS–H 1:37–39.)

The sealing power restored by Elijah truly has changed the hearts of mankind. The Spirit of Elijah inspires us to turn back to those who have gone before and seek after them. In another important way, it has made family members turn to their immediate family in compassion and love. Part of the purpose of this existence is for us to experience family relationships and be bound through the ordinances of the temple. The question remains: Do we have the Spirit of Elijah in our hearts?

Doctrine and Covenants 128:15. *And now, my dearly beloved brethren and sisters, let me assure you that these are principles in relation to the dead and the living that cannot be lightly passed over, as pertaining to our salvation. For their salvation is necessary and essential to our salvation, as Paul says concerning the fathers—that they without us cannot be made perfect—neither can we without our dead be made perfect.*

Our exaltation is dependent upon our searching after our dead and performing the ordinances they cannot perform for themselves. The proxy work we do for them in the temple provides them with the saving ordinances, and it provides us with time in the temple to worship, learn, and grow spiritually. This work is our responsibility and it will bring us great joy.

Doctrine and Covenants 128:24. *Behold, the great day of the Lord is at hand; and who can abide the day of his coming, and who can stand when he appeareth? For he is like a refiner's fire, and like fuller's soap; and he shall sit as a refiner and purifier of silver, and he shall purify the sons of Levi, and purge them as gold and silver, that they may offer unto the Lord an offering in righteousness. Let us, therefore, as a church and a people, and as Latter-day Saints, offer unto the Lord an offering in righteousness; and let us present in his holy temple, when it is finished, a book containing the records of our dead, which shall be worthy of all acceptation.*

The vicarious work we do for our deceased ancestors is recorded in our temples. This "book" is our offering in righteousness unto the Lord, and as He accepts it, the temple work is recorded in heaven.

Doctrine and Covenants 138:53–58. *The Prophet Joseph Smith, and my father, Hyrum Smith, Brigham Young, John Taylor, Wilford Woodruff, and other choice spirits who were reserved to come forth in the fulness of times to take part in laying the foundations of the great latter-day work, Including the building of the temples and the performance of ordinances therein for the redemption of the dead, were also in the spirit world. I observed that they were also among the noble and great ones who were chosen in the beginning to be rulers in the Church of God. Even before they were born, they, with many others, received their first lessons in the world of spirits and were prepared to come forth in the due time of the Lord to labor in his vineyard for the salvation of the souls of men. I beheld that the faithful elders of this dispensation, when they depart from mortal life, continue their labors in the preaching of the gospel of repentance and redemption, through the sacrifice of the Only Begotten Son of God, among those who are in darkness and under the bondage of sin in the great world of the spirits of the dead. The dead who repent will be redeemed, through obedience to the ordinances of the house of God.*

As the children of God in this last dispensation, we have been called to lay the foundation of this great latter-day work: proclaiming the gospel, perfecting the Saints, and redeeming the dead. We build temples; we do vicarious work for the dead; we preach the gospel. We do vicarious temple work so that the spirits on the other side of the veil can enjoy the blessings of the ordinances of the temple.

MODERN PROPHETS SPEAK

Ezra Taft Benson:
> We have an obligation to do temple work for our kindred dead. This means that we must do the necessary research in order for their names to be sent to the temples. We cannot be exalted without being eternally linked to our ancestors. (*Come unto Christ* [Salt Lake City: Deseret Book, 1983], 105)

> I promise you that, with increased attendance in the temples of our God, you shall receive increased personal revelation to bless your life as you bless those who have died. ("The Book of Mormon and the Doctrine and Covenants," *Ensign*, May 1987, 85)

Gordon B. Hinckley:
> This vicarious work constitutes an unprecedented labor of love on the part of the living in behalf of the dead. It makes necessary a vast undertaking of genealogical research to find and identify those who have gone before. (*Be Thou an Example* [Salt Lake City: Deseret Book, 1981], 131)

The Lord has made it possible for us in these holy houses to receive our own [ordinances]. Then we have the opportunity and responsibility of extending these same blessings to those who have passed on without the privilege. But in the very process there comes into our own lives a refinement of character, together with increased spirituality. It is interesting to reflect on the fact that although many on the other side may not receive the ordinances done for them here, those who perform these ordinances will be blessed in the very process of doing so. (*Teachings of Gordon B. Hinckley* [Salt Lake City: Deseret Book, 1997], 622–23)

Boyd K. Packer:

Those who fail to partake of the privileges and blessings of temple work deprive themselves of some of the choicest gifts within the keeping of the Church. (*The Holy Temple* [Salt Lake City: Bookcraft, 1980], 3)

IDEAS FOR DAILY LIVING

Some things to remember and do as we strive to be worthy of temple ordinances:

1. Be clean and pure to enter the temple.

- *Repent of sins*—We should spare no effort to cleanse ourselves of the influence and burdens of sin. No unclean thing should enter the temple.
- *Keep our covenants and obey the commandments*—We must keep the covenants we have already made in preparation to going to the temple and making more covenants. We must pay our tithes and offerings, honor our baptismal and priesthood covenants, keep the Word of Wisdom, attend our meetings, and magnify our callings.

2. Strengthen our testimony.

- *Seek learning*—As we prepare to enter the temple, we should learn all we can about it beforehand. Attending temple preparation classes and studying the scriptures and Church materials about the temple will increase our enthusiasm to attend the temple and solidify our testimony of the importance of the work.
- *Be worthy of the Spirit*—Let us be worthy of the confirmation of the Spirit regarding these sacred truths: That God lives; that His Son accomplished the Atonement on behalf of all of God's children; that the Restoration brought back to Earth the kingdom of God, with living prophets and the power of the priesthood; and that the scriptures are true.

Some things to remember and do in regard to our temple ordinances and covenants:

1. Understand the temple ordinances.

- *Sanctification*—The sanctifying power of the Lord Jesus Christ is signified through the washings and anointings (initiatory work).
- *Endowment*—We learn about the plan of salvation and are empowered from on high as we receive our temple endowment.
- *Sealings*—Couples can be together forever and have an eternal family as they honor their covenants entered into as part of their temple marriage or sealing.

2. Attend the temple often.

- *Continue to learn*—Regular temple attendance refreshes our minds and deepens our understanding. Make a schedule to attend the temple as often as possible.

- *Inspiration*—We can gain great knowledge in the Lord's house, including answers to prayers and insights into our Church callings (see D&C 97:13–16).
- *Peace*—We will feel the peace of the Lord in His holy house. It is a refuge from the world and our temporal cares.

3. Remember to keep the covenants in daily life.
- *Safety and worthiness*—The covenants we make with Heavenly Father and our Savior apply to our daily lives. If we live these covenants, we will be protected both spiritually and temporally according to the Lord's will. Most importantly, keeping our covenants will help us be worthy to return to our Father's presence.
- *Blessings*—Remember the blessings of keeping our temple covenants. Elder Russell M. Nelson has stated, "The supreme benefits of membership in the Church can be realized only through the exalting ordinances of the temple. These blessings qualify us for 'thrones, kingdoms, principalities, and powers' in the celestial kingdom" (*Perfection Pending, and Other Favorite Discourses* [Salt Lake City: Deseret Book, 1998], 130).

Some things to remember and do in regard to redeeming the dead through vicarious service:

1. We become "saviors on Mount Zion" as we perform proxy service for those who have gone on before (see Obad. 1:21).
- *All righteous acts are motivated by love*—Our love for mankind is truly exhibited by our Christlike service in the temples.
- *The miracle of vicarious service*—We become perfected as we help perfect others through vicarious service in the temple (see D&C 128:15). We are "saviors" in performing a work for others that they cannot perform for themselves.

2. Family history is a legacy of love.
- *Blessings in writing*—Family histories, journals, letters, and other writings bless generations yet unborn.
- *Temple information*—Often we obtain information from family histories that allows us to prepare names for temple work.
- *Inspiration*—Family histories provide wonderful stories and examples of sacrifice that strengthen descendants. They provide teaching opportunities from those who have gone on before. Take the time and read your ancestors' histories and, better still, leave your own writings to your children.

3. Family history research (genealogical research) is our duty and our joy. Your ward family history consultant is a great resource to help you through each of the following steps.
- *Identify your ancestors by gathering information from all sources*—The Church's FamilySearch is the greatest asset in the world to aid in family history research. In addition, it is helpful to consult available family histories and visit your local Family History Center.
- *Record your information*—Become familiar with Personal Ancestral File (PAF) computer program from the Church to facilitate cataloging and using your family history information. PAF can be downloaded free of charge from the Church's website, www.lds.org.
- *Comply with temple guidelines*—Be aware of the information needed to submit your ancestors' information for temple work.
- *Analyze and search*—Determine which ancestors need temple ordinances.
- *Prepare names for submission*—Use PAF and TempleReady to prepare names for submission.

- *Submit the information*—Properly submit your ancestors' information to the temple of your choice.
- *Perform the ordinances*—Be sure all the temple work is done and recorded. Enlist your family and friends to complete the work if necessary.

Some things to remember and do in teaching your children about temple work and family history:

1. Set an example of regular attendance at the temple. When you go to the temple, let your children know where you are going, what you are doing, and why you are doing it.

2. Speak of the temple often to your children.
- *Testimony*—Bear your testimony of the temple and its importance.
- *Be thankful*—Express gratitude for the blessings of the temple and your eternal family.
- *Lay the foundation for celestial marriage*—Teach your children concerning temple marriage and its vital blessings.
- *Family gatherings*—Talk of the temple in family home evening and family council.
- *Vicarious work*—Arrange for children of age to do baptisms for the dead.

ILLUSTRATIONS FOR OUR TIMES

Elder Melvin J. Ballard recounts a story from his father's life that illustrates the importance of doing vicarious temple work for our kindred dead.

Take This to Your Father

> I recall an incident in my own father's experience. How we looked forward to the completion of the Logan Temple. It was about to be dedicated. My father had labored on that house from its very beginning, and my earliest recollection was carrying his dinner each day as he brought the rock down from the quarry. How we looked forward to that great event! I remember how in the meantime father made every effort to obtain all the data and information he could concerning his relatives. It was the theme of his prayer night and morning that the Lord would open up the way whereby he could get information concerning his dead.

> The day before the dedication while writing recommends to the members of his ward who were to be present at the first service, two elderly gentlemen walked down the streets of Logan, approached my two young sisters, and, coming to the older one of the two placed in her hands a newspaper and said:

> "Take this to your father. Give it to no one else. Go quickly with it. Don't lose it."

> The child responded and when she met her mother, her mother wanted the paper. The child said, "No. I must give it to father and to no one else."

> She was admitted into the room and told her story. We looked in vain for these travelers. They were not to be seen. No one else saw them. Then we turned to the paper.

> The newspaper, *The Newbury Weekly News,* was printed in my father's old English home, Thursday, May 15th, 1884, and reached our hands May 18, 1884, three days after its publication.

We were astonished, for by no earthly means could it have reached us, so that our curiosity increased as we examined it. Then we discovered one page devoted to the writings of a reporter of the paper, who had gone on his vacation, and among other places had visited an old cemetery. The curious inscriptions led him to write what he found on the tombstones, including the verses. He also added the names, date of birth, death, etc., filling nearly an entire page.

It was the old cemetery where the Ballard family had been buried for generations, and very many of my father's immediate relatives and other intimate friends were mentioned.

When the matter was presented to President Merrill of the Logan Temple he said, "You are authorized to do the work for those, because you received it through messengers of the Lord."

There is no doubt but that the dead who had received the gospel in the spirit world had put it into the heart of that reporter to write these things, and thus the way was prepared for my father to obtain the information he sought. (Melvin J. Ballard, *Three Degrees of Glory* [Salt Lake City: Magazine Printing Co., 1922].) (Jack M. Lyon, Linda Ririe Gundry, and Jay A. Parry, eds., *Best-Loved Stories of the LDS People* [Salt Lake City: Deseret Book, 1997], 254)

SUMMARY

There is no greater work than helping people come unto Christ. As Heavenly Father's work and glory is to bring to pass the immortality and eternal life of His children (see Moses 1:39), so our work and glory can be to assist in this labor. Family history and temple work is the culmination of Heavenly Father's plan in that it perfects the family and prepares us for our future roles in the worlds to come. We should take the time to make family history and temple work a key part of our lives, for as the Lord has said: "This is eternal lives—to know the only wise and true God, and Jesus Christ, whom he hath sent. I am he. Receive ye, therefore, my law" (D&C 132:24).

TEMPTATION

Temptation exists because there is opposition in all things (see 2 Ne. 2:11). Without opposition, which includes temptation, there can be no growth and progression. Even our Savior Jesus Christ was tempted in all things, though He never succumbed (see Heb. 4:15; Mosiah 3:7). Without temptation, we could not be "agents unto ourselves," learning and choosing good or evil (see D&C 29:39). Satan tempts us in a variety of ways: making us think that our decisions really don't matter, creating doubt and unbelief, enticing us with the lusts of the flesh (see James 1:12–15), and in many other devious and insidious ways. When we love the world and its allurements more than God, we are more susceptible to temptation— we become carnal, sensual, and devilish (see Moses 5:13). Recognizing the temptations that surround us helps us to prepare ourselves to resist these forces.

THE SCRIPTURES TEACH US

JST, Matthew 6:14. *And suffer us not to be led into temptation, but deliver us from evil.*

In the Lord's prayer, the King James version uses the phrase "lead us not into temptation." The Prophet Joseph made this correction in his translation, which shows us that the Lord would never "lead" us to be tempted (see James 1:13), but rather "allows" us to be tempted as we travel the pathways of mortality and exercise our agency.

2 Peter 2:9. *The Lord knoweth how to deliver the godly out of temptations, and to reserve the unjust unto the day of judgment to be punished.*

Heavenly Father knows how to help us, and He will always provide a way for us to succeed. We will be succored by the Lord according to our needs as we are tempted (see D&C 62:1).

James 1:12. *Blessed is the man that endureth temptation: for when he is tried, he shall receive the crown of life, which the Lord hath promised to them that love him.*

The crowning blessings for enduring all things here upon the earth will be exaltation. Overcoming temptation is part of the test in proving ourselves worthy during our second estate (see Abr. 3:25).

1 Nephi 15:24. *And I said unto them that it was the word of God; and whoso would hearken unto the word of God, and would hold fast unto it, they would never perish; neither could the temptations and the fiery darts of the adversary overpower them unto blindness, to lead them away to destruction.*

In this verse, Nephi refers to the iron rod, or the word of God. Searching the scriptures and feasting upon the word of God will help us stay on the straight and narrow path. As we hold to the iron rod, we will be able to avoid and overcome temptation.

2 Nephi 4:27. *And why should I yield to sin, because of my flesh? Yea, why should I give way to temptations, that the evil one have place in my heart to destroy my peace and afflict my soul? Why am I angry because of mine enemy?*

This section of the psalm of Nephi asks questions that each of us need to consider in regard to temptation. He answers his own questions in verses 28–35. To paraphrase Nephi's words, we need to: (1) Awaken our soul—do something; (2) Don't quit trying because of our problems or afflictions; (3) Pray for strength and realize the Savior is our rock; (4) Ask for redemption and succoring from the Lord and the capacity to abhor the very thought of sin; (5) Ask for His strength to provide the way through temptation and to be encircled with His righteousness; (6) Put our trust in the Lord (see Prov. 3:5–6) and not in the arm of flesh; and (7) Know that the Lord will help us if we ask Him to in faith (see Alma 13:28; 3 Ne. 18:18).

.

Mormon 9:28. *Be wise in the days of your probation; strip yourselves of all uncleanness; ask not, that ye may consume it on your lusts, but ask with a firmness unshaken, that ye will yield to no temptation, but that ye will serve the true and living God.*

In our prayers, we should ask for specific help in resisting temptation—not just sound out platitudes of generality. Our prayers to avoid temptation should be continual (see Alma 34:39), and we must remember to never ask that we might remain in and enjoy temptation.

Doctrine and Covenants 23:1. *But beware of pride, lest thou shouldst enter into temptation.*

Pride, a sin itself, is one of the primary precursors to others sins. It opens many doors by which Satan can enter in and tempt us. This is why the Lord continually admonishes us to beware of pride.

MODERN PROPHETS SPEAK

Harold B. Lee:

> To have strength to overcome temptation is God-like. The strong, the virtuous and the true of every generation have lived pure, clean lives, not because their emotions were less impelling nor because their temptations were fewer but because their will to do was greater and their faith in divine guidance won them strength through prayer that proved their kinship with the great Exemplar who gave us the pattern for the perfect life. (*Decisions for Successful Living* [Salt Lake City: Deseret Book, 1973], 43)

Howard W. Hunter:

> *A personal testimony of the Savior and his atonement can help us avoid temptation.* Strive to build a personal testimony of Jesus Christ and the atonement. A study of the life of Christ and a testimony of his reality is something each of us should seek. As we come to understand his mission, and the atonement which he wrought, we will desire to live more like him. We especially encourage the young men and young women to come to know the reason for the atoning sacrifice of our Lord. When temptations come, as they surely will, an understanding of the Savior's agony in Gethsemane and his eventual death on the cross will be a reminder to you to avoid any activity that would cause the Savior more pain. Listen to his words, "For behold, I, God, have suffered these things for all, that they might not suffer if they would repent; But if they would not repent, they must suffer even as I" (D&C 19:16–17). (*The Teachings of Howard W. Hunter,* ed. Clyde J. Williams [Salt Lake City: Bookcraft, 1997], 31)

Gordon B. Hinckley:

> You constantly are faced with difficult choices. Your problems are not new, but they are intensified. You are subjected to temptations that are attractive and appealing. You represent the future of this Church, and the adversary of truth would like to injure you, would like to destroy your faith, would like to lead you down paths that are beguiling and interesting, but deadly. (*Teachings of Gordon B. Hinckley* [Salt Lake City: Deseret Book, 1997], 642–43)

IDEAS FOR DAILY LIVING

Here is a list of some major temptations and ideas for overcoming them:

1. Pride. Pride totally degrades our relationship with Heavenly Father and short-circuits our dependence on Him. Pride pits our will against God's will, and it separates us from Him. It is a damning attribute that we should avoid at all costs. Not only does pride make us vulnerable to temptation, it is a sin itself.

Antidote: Humility. Humility is the antithesis of pride. It is the beginning virtue of exaltation.

2. Selfishness. The predominant concern for oneself, with little or no concern for others, is known as selfishness. It can destroy marriages and families.

Antidote: Love. Love is the ultimate concern for others that brings about righteous service. Love is the most pure motive for all good deeds.

3. Greed. Greed or avarice is an insatiable desire for gain. When we are greedy, we always want more, especially more than others. This often leads to dishonest practices to gain more.

Antidote: Charity. When we truly love our fellowmen, we desire for all to succeed. The love of Christ—or charity—is the answer to greed. The united order, practiced early in the Restoration, was a way in which people would have all things in common—no one would have "more" than his neighbor. This initiative failed because people were greedy and selfish, not centered upon the virtue of charity.

4. Lust. Lust is an insatiable desire commonly associated with sexual relations. This temptation carries many destructive consequences when contemplated or—much worse—acted out. Many souls and families are destroyed because of sexual transgression.

Antidote: Spiritual conversion. Understanding key gospel doctrines will help us in overcoming lust. These doctrines include the worth of souls, our divine nature, the fact that our bodies are temples, charity, and self-mastery, to mention a few. When these doctrines are internalized, we will want to protect and bless others and never destroy another person's virtue—or our own.

5. Jealousy, envy, gossip. These sins, which tend to lead to greater sin, are a result of resentment toward others for their achievements, qualities, and possessions. We often tear others down to aggrandize ourselves or raise ourselves higher in the eyes of others. This usually happens when we have low self-confidence or don't understand our self-worth.

Antidote: Love for others. Love for our fellowmen and understanding their divine nature can overcome jealousy, envy, and gossiping.

6. Apathy. When we fail to care about life or to feel anything toward others, we are apathetic. Apathy can lead us into many temptations and sins, because we think that important things just don't matter. Apathy often follows discouragement, both major tools of Satan and his followers.

Antidote: Love. If apathy is failing to care, then ultimate caring will overcome apathy. The opposite of apathy, love is caring.

7. Precepts of men. The moral conduct and values of mankind have deteriorated to such a point that we should beware of the standards and behaviors of society. We should not put our trust in the arm of flesh (see 2 Ne. 4:34).

Antidote: Word of God. Gospel knowledge from the scriptures and the living prophets will give us a standard and value system based on the foundation of the Lord Jesus Christ (see Hel. 5:12). Understanding the doctrines, principles, and covenants in the gospel of Jesus Christ will not only give us a standard for righteous behavior but will help us live the teachings of our Savior.

8. Fear of man. Peer pressure and the fear of condemnation by another person often tempt us and lead us to sin. Such was the case with Martin Harris and the lost 116 pages of the Book of Mormon manuscript (see D&C 3:7). Likewise, we often are not at our best when seeking to "fit in" with the crowd.

Antidote: Fear of God. Let us learn to fear the consequences of an offended God more than man. When we reverence our Heavenly Father, we will be exactly, immediately, and courageously obedient. We will seek to please God rather than man. When we love God, we will keep His commandments (see John 14:15).

9. Anger. When we become angry, we can be provoked and tempted into irrational behavior. If aroused to wrath and even rage, we behave in a completely unchristlike manner. From abuse to road rage, anger can leave a trail of victims to which the sinner must make recompense.

Antidote: Prayer. The presence of anger in a person is a character flaw. We can improve our character through prayer (see Hel. 3:35; Moro. 7:48), and we can pray for strength to overcome temptation (see 3 Ne. 18:18). In addition, we can search the scriptures and receive strength and courage to move forward. When we truly love another person, we will never strike out in anger, wreaking havoc or causing physical harm.

10. Hypocrisy. When we attempt to act by false pretense, pretending to be someone we are not, we are a hypocrite. The Lord condemned hypocrisy as a very grievous sin (see Matt. 6:2–5,16; 7:5; 23).

Antidote: Belief in our divine nature—Like anger, hypocrisy is a character flaw. When we are hypocritical, we seek to raise ourselves in the eyes of others. We were born with self-worth—we are the divine children of God the Father, and our value never changes in His eyes. When we believe this, we value the worth of others as well as ourselves. We should never seek to put others down in an attempt to elevate ourselves, and we should not seek to judge (see 3 Ne. 14:1). Let us seek to become like Christ and not just be a member of the Church in name only.

11. Vanity. When we are preoccupied with our appearance and achievements, we suffer from vanity. Vanity reeks of pride, because when we are vain we care more about ourselves than our fellowmen. We seek to appear better than others.

Antidote: Love. Love of fellowmen, recognizing your true worth, and humility—all these will help overcome vanity. There is also a great joy and a suppression of vanity in honestly praising others.

12. Unbelief. When we fail to accept gospel truths or suffer from a lack of conviction, we are in a state of unbelief. This creates a major problem in our value system by which we live—hence we are easily tempted and swayed by the sophistry of man. The Book of Mormon clearly teaches how unbelief can lead people astray (see 1 Ne. 12:22–23).

Antidote: A softened heart. Let us cultivate an easily entreated soul, a willingness to ask, and a genuine desire to be a seeker of truth. Yielding our heart and spirit to the Lord will surely help us begin to believe in the things of God.

13. Additional temptations. The list of temptations could go on, just as could a listing of the many ways we can sin (see Mosiah 4:29). General antidotes for other temptations include the following:
- *Charity*—As we exercise the pure love of Christ, we will gain the power to overcome temptation.
- *Humility*—Humility will give us strength in the Lord (see Ether 12:27).
- *The word of God*—Search the scriptures and hold to the iron rod on a daily basis (see 1 Ne. 15:24; Hel. 3:29).
- *Nurture*—Nurture the word with faith, diligence, and patience (see Alma 32:40–43).
- *Prayer*—Pray with all your heart (see Alma 13:28; 31:10; 34:39; 3 Ne. 18:15, 18; D&C 61:39).
- *Follow the Spirit*—Seek the Spirit in all things and you will not be led away into sin. The Spirit will lead you (see 1 Ne. 4:6), comfort you (Moro. 8:26), give you gifts for doing all things (Moro. 10 and D&C 46), show you all things to do (2 Ne. 32:5), and give you truths to live by (Moro. 10:5). When we yield to the enticings of the Holy Spirit, we put off the natural man, which is carnal, sensual, devilish, and unrepentant, and become a saint with more power to resist temptation (see Mosiah 3:19).
- *Obedience*—Righteousness begets righteousness and yields not to temptation (see Alma 11:23). Keeping the commandments through obedience will allow us to have the Spirit—and we will not sin when we are acting under the influence of the Holy Ghost.

ILLUSTRATIONS FOR OUR TIMES

Hugh B. Brown relates the training of Arabian horses to our ability to avoid temptation and hearken to the voice of the Lord.

When the Bell Rings

May I tell a story to illustrate the point that a man must respond to his better self if he is going to be a worthy holder of the priesthood.

The story is told that the Arabians, when they are training their horses, put them to a final test of character and stamina. It is said that the finest of the Arabian horses which are kept for breeding stock are trained from the time they are colts to respond to a bell which rings intermittently at the tent of the master. Wherever they are and whatever they are doing, they must run to the tent of the master when the bell rings. Their mothers were taught it before them, and they respond, and the colts, running beside the mother, habitually as time goes on respond to the bell and know that it is the call of duty.

When the colts are three years old, they are placed in a pole corral that they can see through. They are left there three days and nights without food or water. At the end of the third day hay and grain and water are placed just outside the corral.

You can imagine the eagerness of the young colts as they look through the bars at the food and water. When the gate is opened the young colts rush out, and just as they are about to reach the food and water, the bell rings. Only those of them that have stamina enough to respond to the bell and resist the urge of appetite are kept for the breeding stock of the future.

Brethren, as we go forward, we become increasingly aware of the fact that there is a bell which rings very frequently throughout life. Sometimes men become unresponsive or hard of hearing and disregard the bell to their own sorrow. You young men are going to hear it many times between now and the time you are our age. We plead with you to resist the call of appetite and passion and hearken to the bell which is your conscience. If you are tempted to do wrong, there will always be something within you saying, "Don't do it."

Hearken and respond to that bell, and you will be worthy of the confidence that the President of the Church has in you, worthy to take over the responsibilities now held by your fathers, your brothers, your leaders. (Hugh B. Brown, Conference Report, April 1963, 91)

SUMMARY

As we rely on the Lord, our spirit is strengthened and we can overcome and avoid temptations, thus becoming free from sin. Self-mastery comes as we become spiritually strong in the Lord. The Lord will always provide us a way to avoid temptation and to do His will. Let us build a value system based upon the gospel of Jesus Christ, make a commitment to keep our covenants, and not yield to temptation.

TESTIMONY

A testimony is the priceless knowledge of eternal truths received by the power of the Holy Ghost. As members of Jesus Christ's Church, we can have a witness of many eternal verities. These include the fact that God is our Father, that Jesus is the Christ, that revelation is the pattern for God's dealing with man, that Joseph Smith was the Prophet of the Restoration, that gospel truths were indeed restored through the Book of Mormon, and many other related matters. By the power of the Holy Ghost, we can know that The Church of Jesus Christ of Latter-day Saints is the Lord's Church once again established here upon the earth and that a living prophet leads us. The Lord Himself told us that we can know the truth of all things by the power of the Holy Ghost. When we sincerely bear our testimonies, the Spirit testifies of the truthfulness of our words, for the Spirit bears witness of all truths. Each of us should seek to have our own testimony of eternal truth.

THE SCRIPTURES TEACH US

2 Timothy 1:8. *Be not thou therefore ashamed of the testimony of our Lord, nor of me his prisoner: but be thou partaker of the afflictions of the gospel according to the power of God.*

If we are not ashamed of the gospel of Jesus Christ (see Rom. 1:16), we will never waver in bearing or living our testimony. Honoring our spiritual witness that the gospel is true makes us worthy of the blessings of the Lord and covenant candidates for the blessings of exaltation, based on our obedience, righteousness, and enduring to the end.

Mosiah 18:9. *Yea, and are willing to mourn with those that mourn; yea, and comfort those that stand in need of comfort, and to stand as witnesses of God at all times and in all things, and in all places that ye may be in, even until death, that ye may be redeemed of God, and be numbered with those of the first resurrection, that ye may have eternal life.*

At baptism, we covenant to stand as witnesses of Jesus Christ—to bear testimony of Him and testify of gospel truths—at all times. We are disciples of Jesus Christ and have taken upon us His name. All sincere testimonies are powerful, for they are born of the Spirit. When we bear witness of eternal truths, others will believe us because of the witness of the Spirit.

Alma 4:19. *And this he did that he himself might go forth among his people, or among the people of Nephi, that he might preach the word of God unto them, to stir them up in remembrance of their duty, and that he might pull down, by the word of God, all the pride and craftiness and all the contentions which were among his people, seeing no way that he might reclaim them save it were in bearing down in pure testimony against them.*

Alma knew the power of the word of God taught by the Spirit. Humble listeners believe the preaching of the truth because the Holy Ghost carries it unto their hearts (see 2 Nephi 33:1).

Alma 5:45–47. *And this is not all. Do ye not suppose that I know of these things myself? Behold, I testify unto you that I do know that these things whereof I have spoken are true. And how do ye suppose that I know of their surety? Behold, I say unto you they are made known unto me by the Holy Spirit of God. Behold, I have fasted* *and prayed many days that I might know these things of myself. And now I do know of myself that they are true; for the Lord God hath made them manifest unto me by his Holy Spirit; and this is the spirit of revelation which is in me. And moreover, I say unto you that it has thus been revealed unto me, that the words which have been spoken by our fathers are true, even so according to the spirit of prophecy which is in me, which is also by the manifestation of the Spirit of God.*

Alma, a prophet of God who had seen angels and experienced miracles, received his testimony the same way we receive ours. There is no substitute for the power of the Spirit. To gain a testimony like Alma's, we must fast and pray to know the things of God. The Holy Spirit will reveal to us that Jesus is the Christ (see Alma 7:13); this is the spirit of revelation (see Alma 6:8).

Doctrine and Covenants 62:3. *Nevertheless, ye are blessed, for the testimony which ye have borne is recorded in heaven for the angels to look upon; and they rejoice over you, and your sins are forgiven you.*

Standing up for truth and righteousness as we bear our testimonies blesses every facet of our lives. In addition, this scripture informs us that the testimonies we bear are recorded and read in heaven, and that through bearing our testimonies we receive forgiveness of our sins.

Joseph Smith—History 1:26. *I had now got my mind satisfied so far as the sectarian world was concerned—that it was not my duty to join with any of them, but to continue as I was until further directed. I had found the testimony of James to be true—that a man who lacked wisdom might ask of God, and obtain, and not be upbraided.*

We can learn of gospel truths as we follow the word of God and our prophets. We can receive a witness after the trial our faith, and we can know all things by the power of the Spirit (see Ether 12:6).

MODERN PROPHETS SPEAK

Gordon B. Hinckley:
> If there are any lacking that testimony, you can get it; and you must get it. How? The Lord has said that he that doeth the will of the Father shall know of the doctrine, "whether it be of God, or whether I speak of myself." (John 7:17.) That's the way you gain a testimony. You do the will of the Father, and as certainly as you do the will of the Father you will know of the truth of the gospel, including the knowledge that Jesus is the Christ, the Son of God. (*Teachings of Gordon B. Hinckley* [Salt Lake City: Deseret Book, 1997], 648)

Richard G. Scott:
> A strong testimony is the unshakable foundation of a secure, meaningful life where peace, confidence, happiness, and love can flourish. It is anchored in a conviction that an all-knowing God is in command of His work. He will not fail. He will keep His promises.
>
> A strong testimony is the sustaining power of a successful life. It is centered in an understanding of the divine attributes of God our Father, Jesus Christ, and the Holy Ghost. . . . A testimony is fortified by spiritual impressions that confirm the validity of a teaching, of a righteous act, or of a warning of pending danger. Often such guidance is accompanied by powerful emotions that make it difficult to speak and bring tears to the eyes. But a testimony is not emotion. It is the very essence of character woven from threads born of countless correct decisions. . . . A strong

testimony gives peace, comfort, and assurance. It generates the conviction that as the teachings of the Savior are consistently obeyed, life will be beautiful, the future secure, and there will be capacity to overcome the challenges that cross our path. A testimony grows from understanding truth, distilled from prayer and the pondering of scriptural doctrine. It is nurtured by living those truths in faith and the secure confidence that the promised results will be obtained. . . . Your personal security and happiness depend upon the strength of your testimony, for it will guide your actions in times of trial or uncertainty.

Honestly evaluate your personal life. How strong is your own testimony? Is it truly a sustaining power in your life, or is it more a hope that what you have learned is true? Is it more than a vague belief that worthwhile concepts and patterns of life seem to be reasonable and logical? Such mental assent will not help when you face the serious challenges that will inevitably come to you. Does your testimony guide you to correct decisions? To do so, fundamental truths must become part of the very fiber of your character. They must be an essential part of your being, more treasured than life itself. If an honest assessment of your own testimony confirms that it is not as strong as it should be, how can it be strengthened?

Your testimony will be fortified as you exercise faith in Jesus Christ, in His teachings, and in His limitless power to accomplish what He has promised. . . . A powerful testimony distills from quiet moments of prayer and pondering as you recognize the impressions that will accompany such effort. Humble, trusting prayer brings consolation, solace, comfort, direction, and peace the unworthy can never know. ("The Power of a Strong Testimony," *Ensign*, November 2001, 87–89)

IDEAS FOR DAILY LIVING

Here are several ideas to help us gain and strengthen our testimonies:

1. **Desire to know the truth.** Alma taught that desire is the beginning of the process of exercising faith to know the truth (see Alma 32:27). You must *want* to have a testimony.

2. **Study the word of God from the scriptures and living prophets.** The word of God has power to change you (see Alma 13:5), and it will tell you all things to do (see 2 Ne. 32:3). From the scriptures, you can learn of God and the Savior Jesus Christ (see John 5:39). Truth is found in the word of God (see John 17:17).

3. **Fast and pray to know the truth.** Heavenly Father will give you answers to your prayers (see James 1:5–6). He answered the Prophet Joseph. He answered Alma (see Alma 5:45–47), and He answered countless others. He will answer you, too, for He is no respecter of persons (see D&C 38:16). The Holy Ghost will make the truth of all things known unto you (see Moro. 10:5).

4. **Live your testimony**—When you live the things you believe, this practice becomes part of your nature. Your character is the result of living what you value. You will become what you believe.

5. **Bear your testimony.** The more you bear your testimony by the Spirit, the stronger it will become. Speaking of helping others gain a testimony, Elder Boyd K. Packer has taught us, "There are two dimensions to testimony. The one, a *testimony we bear to them,* has power to lift and bless them. The other, infinitely more important, *the testimony they bear themselves,* has the power to redeem and exalt them. You might say they can

get a testimony from what we say. *The* testimony comes when they themselves bear a witness of the truth and the Holy Ghost confirms it to them" (*Let Not Your Heart Be Troubled* [Salt Lake City: Bookcraft, 1991], 15).

ILLUSTRATIONS FOR OUR TIMES

Apostle Joseph B. Wirthlin, in an excerpt from a general conference address, witnesses to the truthfulness of the gospel as he explains how he gained his testimony.

Pure Testimony

May I tell you how I gained a testimony of the truth and divine nature of this great latter-day work? I'm afraid my experience isn't very dramatic. It is not a story of heavenly hosannas or thundering shouts. It is not a story of lightning, fire, or flood.

But I have always known the reality and goodness of God.

From my earliest memories it was there—a sure and abiding testimony of this great work. Sometimes that assurance comes when we feel the love of the Savior when we meet His servants. I remember when I was just five years old and my family moved into a new ward. That first Sunday, Bishop Charles E. Forsberg, who was born in Sweden, came up to me and called me by name. I knew then.

During the cold and gray days of the Great Depression I remember a wonderful servant of the Savior by the name of C. Perry Erickson. Brother Erickson, a contractor, had a difficult time finding work. He could have shut himself up. He could have become bitter and angry. He could have given up. Instead, when I was 12 he was my Scoutmaster. He spent countless hours helping me and others my age to learn, to grow, and to approach every difficulty with confidence and optimism. Without exception, every one of C. Perry Erickson's Scouts received an Eagle award. I knew then.

Yes, the testimonies of priesthood leaders and faithful ward members helped me to know.

I remember the words of my mother and father. I remember their expressions of faith and love for their Heavenly Father. I knew then.

I knew the reality of the Savior's compassion when, at the request of my father, the bishop of the ward, I delivered food and clothing to the widows and poor of the ward.

I knew, when as a young father, my wife and I gathered our children around us and expressed our gratitude to our Heavenly Father for our many blessings.

I knew last April, when I heard from this pulpit the words of our prophet, President Gordon B. Hinckley, who called Jesus his friend, exemplar, leader, Savior, and King. . . .

Now, I would like to bear my testimony—I know that Joseph Smith saw what he said he saw, that the heavens opened and God the Father and His Son, Jesus Christ, appeared to an unlearned youth reared in the backwoods of New York.

As a special witness of the name of Jesus Christ in all the world, I promise you that if you seek the Lord, you will find Him. Ask, and you shall receive.

I pray that you may do so and testify to the ends of the earth that the gospel of our Lord and Savior is restored to man! (Joseph B. Wirthlin, "Pure Testimony," *Ensign,* November 2000, 22)

SUMMARY

The pure knowledge given us by the Spirit is our testimony. In order to claim the blessings of our loving Heavenly Father, We must be valiant in our testimony. We must strengthen our testimony by studying, praying, living the gospel, and bearing witness of the truthfulness of the gospel and Church of Jesus Christ. As we seek to do these things, the grace of God will enable us to be instruments in His hands as we witness to the world of eternal truths. The Apostle Paul made it clear that "no man can say that Jesus is the Lord, but by the Holy Ghost" (1 Cor. 12:3). Therefore, let us live in a manner that will invite the sacred influence of the Holy Ghost to touch our lives and give us an abiding testimony of the Savior, His Atonement, and the saving truths of the gospel.

TITHES AND OFFERINGS

Offerings to the Lord are given in many forms. We pay ten percent of our increase to the Lord and we make other financial offerings. In addition, we offer unto Him the sacrifice of a broken heart and a contrite spirit (see 3 Ne. 9:20), and we offer our devotions to Him by serving others. Tithes and other monetary offerings will be covered herein, while other types of offerings will be discussed under such topics as *Charity, Consecration, Covenants, Magnifying Your Calling, Sacrifice, Good Works.* By way of commandment, we give temporal offerings to the Lord, in particular our tithes and our fast offerings (see D&C 119). We must pay an honest tithe in order to obtain a temple recommend. Payment of tithes brings a multitude of blessings from our Heavenly Father, both temporal and spiritual. However, such blessings are not always manifest in the way we expect, and should not be the prime motivation for our offerings. We must remember that we owe our Heavenly Father everything; therefore, we should not withhold our oblations from Him. "And it pleaseth God that he hath given all these things unto man; for unto this end were they made to be used, with judgment, not to excess, neither by extortion. And in nothing doth man offend God, or against none is his wrath kindled, save those who confess not his hand in all things, and obey not his commandments" (D&C 59:20–21). We pay our tithes and offerings not simply to receive God's blessings, but because we love Him and want to show Him our gratitude and obedience.

THE SCRIPTURES TEACH US

Malachi 3:8. *Will a man rob God? Yet ye have robbed me. But ye say, Wherein have we robbed thee? In tithes and offerings.*

Heavenly Father has given us everything, including our life (see Mosiah 2:20–21). We are indebted to Him for all things, yet He asks for so little in return. When we do not pay our tithes and offerings, we not only rob Him, but we rob ourselves of the opportunity to obey.

Doctrine and Covenants 64:23. *Behold, now it is called today until the coming of the Son of Man, and verily it is a day of sacrifice, and a day for the tithing of my people; for he that is tithed shall not be burned at his coming.*

There are specific consequences for keeping or not keeping every commandment, including the law of tithing. The Lord has promised us that we will be spared at His Second Coming if we have faithfully paid our tithing.

Doctrine and Covenants 119:3–4. *And this shall be the beginning of the tithing of my people. And after that, those who have thus been tithed shall pay one-tenth of all their interest annually; and this shall be a standing law unto them forever, for my holy priesthood, saith the Lord.*

The law of tithing is simple: we should give one-tenth of our "interest" or increase annually. We should avoid making this a complicated process and simply give one-tenth of our increase.

MODERN PROPHETS SPEAK

Joseph F. Smith:

> By this principle (tithing) the loyalty of the people of this Church shall be put to the test. By this principle it shall be known who is for the kingdom of God and who is against it. By this principle it shall be seen whose hearts are set on doing the will of God and keeping his commandments, thereby sanctifying the land of Zion unto God, and who are opposed to this principle and have cut themselves off from the blessings of Zion. There is a great deal of importance connected with this principle, for by it it shall be known whether we are faithful or unfaithful. In this respect it is as essential as faith in God, as repentance of sin, as baptism for the remission of sin, or as the laying on of hands for the gift of the Holy Ghost. For if a man keep all the law save one point, and he offend in that, he is a transgressor of the law, and he is not entitled to the fulness of the blessings of the gospel of Jesus Christ. But when a man keeps all the law that is revealed, according to his strength, his substance, and his ability, though what he does may be little, it is just as acceptable in the sight of God as if he were able to do a thousand times more. (*Gospel Doctrine: Selections from the Sermons and Writings of Joseph F. Smith,* comp. John A. Widtsoe [Salt Lake City: Deseret Book, 1939], 225)

Gordon B. Hinckley:

> The law of tithing is a law designed to bless us. It does not take from us, it adds to us. It is not so much a matter of money as it is a matter of faith, and great are the promises of the Lord to those who live honestly with Him in the payment of their tithes and their offerings. (*Teachings of Gordon B. Hinckley* [Salt Lake City: Deseret Book, 1997], 405)

Spencer W. Kimball:

> My dear brothers and sisters, my message today is not a new one. Prophets of all dispensations have clearly taught the law of tithing and the principles of the gospel with regard thereto. From the beginning we have been taught that "the earth is the Lord's, and the fulness thereof" (1 Cor. 10:26). From this fulness, the Lord requires that we dedicate one-tenth to him. Tithing is a law of God and is required of his followers. To fail to meet this obligation is to fail in a very weighty matter.
>
> In these times of troublous economic concern and worry, we must forcefully remind ourselves, both individually and as a church, that the Lord has given us a spiritual and economic law which,

when fully obeyed will bring promised blessings so great that "there will not be room enough to receive" them (Mal. 3:10).

I speak of the law of tithing, which can be our great blessing and safety, our great assurance of divine assistance. It has always been impressive to me that of all the teachings from Old Testament prophets that the Lord could have given anew to the Nephites when he visited them, he gave Malachi's stirring promise regarding tithing. ("He Did It with All His Heart, and Prospered," *Ensign,* March 1981, 3)

Marion G. Romney:

One of the important things the Lord has told us to do is to be liberal in our payment of fast offerings. I would like you to know that there are great rewards for so doing—both spiritual and temporal rewards. The Lord has said that the efficacy of our prayers depends upon our liberality to the poor. (See Alma 34:28.) ("The Blessings of the Fast," *Ensign,* July 1982, 2)

IDEAS FOR DAILY LIVING

Here are some suggestions for understanding and living the law of tithes and offerings:

1. Tithing is a commandment of God.
- *Clear expectations*—It is clear that the Lord expects us to return one-tenth of our "interest" or increase (see D&C 119:3–4). This is a very clear-cut command and needs no debate.
- *Clear implications*—If we do not pay our tithes and offerings, we are denied a myriad of blessings in this life—including temple attendance—as well as in the life to come.

2. There are blessings and consequences regarding tithing.
- *Spiritual and temporal blessings*—The Lord prospers us as we keep the commandments (see Mosiah 2:22). Elder Russell M. Nelson reminds us, "The law of tithing is a valuable key to the blessings of honesty and prosperity" (*The Power within Us* [Salt Lake City: Deseret Book, 1988], 133).
- *Protection*—We will not be burned at the Lord's Second Coming if we pay our tithing (see D&C 64:23). President Spencer W. Kimball taught, "The prophets of all dispensations have clearly taught the law of tithing for the blessing and protection of the Lord's people" (*President Kimball Speaks Out* [Salt Lake City: Deseret Book, 1981], 63).
- *Growth through obedience*—The main reason we pay tithes is because we love the Lord and want to be obedient to Him.

3. We are to teach the law of tithing.
- *Family learning environment*—Take the time to explain to your children that Heavenly Father has given us everything, including our lives, our homes, our money, and all our other material possessions. Help them realize they are simply giving back one-tenth of what is already Heavenly Father's.
- *Tracking*—Create a method for helping children keep track of tithes and offerings. For instance, they could make a box or container for tithing, one for other offerings, one for savings, and one for their personal spending. This will teach them many principles in regard to financial well-being.
- *Accounting*—Plan a special time each week or month for your children to make an accounting of their tithes.
- *Payment*—On a regular basis, have your children personally hand their donations to the bishop.

- *Tithing settlement*—Always take your children to tithing settlement so that they realize how important this sacred law is.
- *Understanding*—Teach your children how the Church uses the tithes and offerings to bless everyone, including members and people all over the world.

ILLUSTRATIONS FOR OUR TIMES

The prophet George Albert Smith relates how he helped a friend in the Church understand that he was not properly paying his tithing.

The Story of a Generous Man

One day on the street I met a friend whom I had known since boyhood. I had not visited with him for some time, and I was interested in being brought up to date concerning his life, his problems, and his faith, therefore I invited him to go to a conference in Utah County with me. He drove his fine car (the make of car I was driving had not been received into society at that time). He took his wife, and I took mine.

At the conference, I called on him to speak. I did not know what it might do to him, but I thought I would take a chance. He made a fine talk. He told of his trips to the East, how he explained the gospel to the people he met, and how grateful he was for his heritage. He stated that his opportunities in the world had been magnified and multiplied because his father and mother had joined the Church in the Old World.

As we drove home, he turned to me and said: "My this has been a wonderful conference. I have enjoyed it."

I thought to myself, he was like one of our sisters who came home from fast meeting and said to her family: "That is the best meeting I ever attended."

One of the daughters asked: "Well, Mother who spoke?" And then her mother replied, "I did."

I thought he had enjoyed it because he himself had participated. I was glad he had. Then he said: "You know I have heard many things in this conference, but there is only one thing that I do not understand the way you do."

I said: "What is it?"

"Well," he said, "it is about paying tithing."

He thought I would ask him how he paid his tithing, but I did not. I thought if he wanted to tell me, he would. He said: "Would you like me to tell you how I pay my tithing?"

I said, "If you want to, you may."

"Well," he said, "if I make ten thousand dollars in a year, I put a thousand dollars in the bank for tithing. I know why it's there. Then when the bishop comes and wants me to make a contribution for the chapel or give him a check for a missionary who is going away, if I think he needs the money, I give him a check. If a family in the ward is in distress and needs coal or food or clothing or anything else, I write out a check. If I find a boy or a girl who is having difficulty getting through school in the East, I send a check. Little by little I exhaust the thousand dollars, and every dollar of it has gone where I know it has done good. Now, what do you think of that?"

"Well," I said, "do you want me to tell you what I think of it?"

He said, "Yes."

I said: "I think you are a very generous man with someone else's property." And he nearly tipped the car over.

He said, "What do you mean?"

I said, "You have an idea that you have paid your tithing?"

"Yes," he said.

I said: "You have not paid any tithing. You have told me what you have done with the Lord's money but you have not told me that you have given anyone a penny of your own. He is the best partner you have in the world. He gives you everything you have, even the air you breathe. He has said you should take one-tenth of what comes to you and give it to the Church as directed by the Lord. You haven't done that; you have taken your best partner's money, and have given it away."

Well, I will tell you there was quiet in the car for some time. We rode on to Salt Lake City and talked about other things.

About a month after that I met him on the street. He came up, put his arm in mine, and said: "Brother Smith, I am paying my tithing the same way you do." I was very happy to hear that. (George Albert Smith, *Sharing the Gospel with Others,* [Salt Lake City: Deseret Book, 1948], 44)

SUMMARY

When we understand the law of tithing, we realize that tithes and offerings are used to build up the kingdom of God here upon the earth. These monies are necessary for building chapels and temples, and for caring for the poor and the needy. We should find great joy in living the law of tithing, knowing that we become part of building up the Lord's Church and blessing all of Heavenly Father's children. Let us commit to paying a full tithe and making generous donations to the Church, that we may be living proof of the verity of the Lord's promise: "Bring ye all the tithes into the storehouse, that there may be meat in mine house, and prove me now herewith, saith the Lord of hosts, if I will not open you the windows of heaven, and pour you out a blessing, that there shall not be room enough to receive it" (Mal. 3:10).

TOLERANCE

Tolerance is a form of love; it implies being considerate of others, including their feelings and behavior, even if we do not necessarily approve of them. When we exhibit tolerance, we recognize the rights of others, and we allow them their beliefs without taking action against them. As we strive to be tolerant, we become free of bigotry. We come to understand the goodness in others, and that they have a great deal to contribute to our world. Righteous behavior includes tolerance. However, we must be cautious in what we will tolerate. Much in the world is unworthy and immoral, and condoning lewdness and irreverence can perpetuate it in our own lives. We must beware this tendency when it comes to our values and principles, or the world and its morals will seduce us. Tolerance for others should not involve accepting violation of the law or accepting behavior that negatively affects the well-being of society, especially the family. To tolerate crime, drugs, illicit sex, and all manner of pernicious behavior that afflicts society would make one party to the problem. We must stand for truth and virtue. Tolerance is not permissiveness and apathy; rather, tolerance is understanding.

THE SCRIPTURES TEACH US

Ephesians 4:2. *With all lowliness and meekness, with longsuffering, forbearing one another in love.*

As disciples of Jesus Christ, we are commanded to show love to our fellowman. We should allow everyone the right and privilege of his or her own beliefs (see Alma 30:7; A of F 1:11).

Alma 7:23. *And now I would that ye should be humble, and be submissive and gentle; easy to be entreated; full of patience and long-suffering; being temperate in all things; being diligent in keeping the commandments of God at all times; asking for whatsoever things ye stand in need, both spiritual and temporal; always returning thanks unto God for whatsoever things ye do receive.*

In all things we should exercise patience and long-suffering, as well as humility in our own beliefs. This shows tolerance, charity, and love for our fellowmen.

MODERN PROPHETS SPEAK

Stephen L Richards:
> When people reach the point where they can say, "I do not understand that man's views; they do not appeal to me, but I have no reason to doubt his sincerity and he may be right," then, and then only, may we hope for the dissipation of dogmatic bigotry which so often precludes open-minded investigation. (*The Church in War and Peace* [Independence, MO: Zion's Printing and Publishing, 1943], 210)

Gordon B. Hinckley:
> Let us as Latter-day Saints cultivate a spirit of brotherhood in all of our associations. Let us be more charitable in our judgments, more sympathetic and understanding of those who err, more willing to forgive those who trespass against us. Let us not add to the measure of hatred that periodically sweeps across the world. Let us reach out in kindness to all men, even toward those who speak evil of us and who would, if they could, harm us. . . .

Teach [your children] tolerance. They need not surrender their own beliefs while extending tolerance to those with other beliefs.

Teach them civility toward others. Conflict between the races will fade when all of us recognize that we are all part of one great family.

Teach them respect—respect for others, respect for the property of others, respect for the opinions of others, respect on the part of men for women and women for men. (*Teachings of Gordon B. Hinckley* [Salt Lake City: Deseret Book, 1997], 661, 663)

IDEAS FOR DAILY LIVING

Here are five insights that can help us show tolerance toward our fellowmen:

1. Tolerance is a vision that sees the unseen.
- *Potential*—See the potential in others. See them as dynamic beings, not statically locked in their condition, but capable of learning, growing, and maturing in wisdom and productivity.
- *New perspectives*—Try to view life through the eyes of other people. How do they see the world? What are their dreams and aspirations? What are their fears and anxieties?
- *Whole person*—Avoid seeing a person as the embodiment of just one attribute, as that is mistaking the part for the whole. No one is totally bad or totally good—you can find good in nearly everyone.

2. Tolerance is understanding.
- *Knowledge*—Learn more about people—study, read, ask questions, explore history. Seek to understand others from the point of view of their culture and traditions. Knowledge often dispels intolerance.
- *Rights*—Recognize that all are not of the same persuasion and have a right to their own opinions.
- *Abilities*—Understand that all people do not possess the same abilities or skills. Be tolerant of others' shortcomings as they learn and make progress in different ways and at different rates than you do.
- *Age*—Remember that children and youth need more understanding and tolerance than most adults. They are in a dynamic stage of life with feelings and behavior that are often hard to deal with.

3. Tolerance has natural limits.
- *Inappropriate humor*—Never criticize others on the basis of race, creed, gender, or physical handicap. Never utter jokes that make fun of another race or class of people—and do not tolerate it when others do so.
- *Harm and injury*—Do not tolerate injury or threat to your person or your family.
- *Principles*—As you practice tolerance, remember that it does not require sacrifice of your principles. "Tolerance is the positive and cordial effort to understand another's beliefs, practices and habits without necessarily sharing or accepting them," counseled Joshua Loth Liebman.
- *Bigotry*—Make a valiant effort to dispel any incipient prejudice and take steps to foster understanding.

4. Tolerance is leadership.
- *Unity*—Proactively look for things that you have in common with others, rather than things that divide.
- *Common goals*—Find common goals and a common vision to work toward. Usually, when people of differing backgrounds "buy into" a long-range goal, they can find ways to work together and forget the things that separate them. Find a common cause, such as hunger, lack of education, lack of opportunity, the need to improve health and well-being, etc.

5. Tolerance is love.

- *Kindness*—Simple courtesy, benevolence, thoughtfulness, humanity, consideration—all these overpower intolerance. When you see these traits at work, you see intolerance slink away in shame.
- *Charity*—Intolerance neutralizes charity; it short-circuits the innate desire to serve and do good. On the other hand, tolerance is the gateway to unconditional love. Helen Keller taught: "No loss of flood and lightning, no destruction of cities and temples by hostile forces of nature, has deprived man of so many noble lives and impulses as those which his intolerance has destroyed."

ILLUSTRATIONS FOR OUR TIMES

The following story illustrates the fact that a little tolerance can make all the difference in our lives.

A Hard Lesson to Learn

A friend of mine related a story about a man who seemed like he had it all, but simply couldn't be happy and enjoy life. He had a wonderful family, a thriving business, a loving wife, and all the amenities that go along with financial success. Yet Tom (we will call him Tom) was always upset or disturbed about something. He was never satisfied with his children's grades or their friends. If someone disagreed with him, he took it personally and usually ended up calling the person an "idiot" or some other unfavorable title. He always compared others with himself and criticized those who didn't agree with him.

Everyone seemed to bother Tom—whether it was a coworker who approached problems differently, the bag-boy at the grocery store putting bread in with the canned goods, or the way the next-door neighbors always seemed so happy, like life was simply the greatest. Other drivers on the road were jerks, and his children were constantly needing help—from getting dressed to not getting their duties and homework done fast enough. No one was fast enough, smart enough, or good enough for Tom. Tom was dissatisfied with life, and yet he seemed to have it all. He thought, *Why is everybody so irritating?*

As my friend told me this story, he mentioned how one day a friend of Tom's pulled him aside and complimented him on his success and his wonderful family. Tom was taken aback and thought, *I really am blessed. Why am I so disgruntled? Why am I always upset? Why am I angry with others when they haven't really done anything to me?* Tom took a step back and started to think:

My children are great—not perfect, but great. I love them. They are just learning to become adults. Their friends are nice—just because one's hair is a little long, the funny girlfriend with that horrible foreign accent is hard to understand, or one boy is always blowing his nose—why should these things bother me? My friend at work really wants the company to succeed. Just because his ideas are different than mine doesn't mean he's wrong. When I changed lanes the other day without signaling and someone honked at me, maybe I was the jerk. When my neighbor came out smiling and mentioned how great everything was, I could have thought, "What a great attitude."

As Tom changed his way of looking at things, life started to be better. Tom became satisfied with his children—even praising them and their friends. He even mentioned to his coworker how he had been thinking about his idea and what a unique way of looking at the problem it was. Tom was no longer dissatisfied, upset, or unhappy—he had learned tolerance.

—Ed J. Pinegar

SUMMARY

As we show tolerance, we rise above the pettiness of intolerance and bigotry. Our world today needs the rekindling of virtue. We must be tolerant of others, but at the same time we must be champions of peace and purity. Charity does not require tolerance for abuse, war, or any manner of wickedness. In reality, tolerance is seeking to understand others and allow them to believe and act according to their desires, as long as it does not affect the freedom of others. Tolerance is to be practiced in righteousness. The heart and soul of tolerance can be found in the words of the Savior: "Thou shalt love thy neighbor as thyself" (D&C 59:6; see also Lev. 19:18; Matt. 19:19).

TRUST

A primary ingredient in strong and enduring relationships is trust. Trust is the confidence people place in each other, the reliability of a relationship. The oft-quoted statement, "It is better to be trusted than to be loved" is probably true in building relationships—especially as it relates to personal matters. Of course, it is best to be both trusted and loved, and trust and love go hand-in-hand. Trust enriches and ennobles love. The corollary holds true: "Without love, trust is nothing." Trust also derives from honesty and integrity, which must be absolute. In the world today, there is a critical need for people and nations to trust one another, and to be trustworthy. Our greatest lesson in trust and trustworthiness, though, comes from the Lord. Even more than trusting each other, we need to trust in Him, for He is ever constant and will not fail.

THE SCRIPTURES TEACH US

Proverbs 3:5–6. *Trust in the Lord with all thine heart; and lean not unto thine own understanding. In all thy ways acknowledge him, and he shall direct thy paths.*

Trust in the Lord empowers us to live righteously. We gain strength knowing that the Lord is there and that He knows all things, has all power, and will help us at all times (see D&C 84:88). When we rely on Him, He will lead us to do good, to do His will, and our trust in Him will dispel fear (see Isa. 12:2). Let us not assume that our understanding is adequate; rather, let us always be willing to receive counsel from the Lord (see 2 Ne. 9:28–29).

2 Nephi 4:34. *O Lord, I have trusted in thee, and I will trust in thee forever. I will not put my trust in the arm of flesh; for I know that cursed is he that putteth his trust in the arm of flesh. Yea, cursed is he that putteth his trust in man or maketh flesh his arm.*

Nephi wisely counsels us to always rely on the Lord and to never trust in the strength of humanity when it comes to eternal and exalting power. Only the Lord has power to save us spiritually. However, we can have confidence in our teachers and entrust to them the task of teaching us eternal truths—if they walk in the ways of the Lord (see Mosiah 23:14).

Alma 36:3. *And now, O my son Helaman, behold, thou art in thy youth, and therefore, I beseech of thee that thou wilt hear my words and learn of me; for I do know that whosoever shall put their trust in God shall be supported in their trials, and their troubles, and their afflictions, and shall be lifted up at the last day.*

We can always rely on the Lord, for He will bless us in our trials and our afflictions, and He will lift us up at the last day (see Mosiah 23:22). When we trust in the Lord, we will listen to His words, follow His prophets, and keep His commandments.

MODERN PROPHETS SPEAK

David O. McKay:

> Absolute trust in the Lord will awaken a desire, at least, to try to live in accordance with Christ's teachings, chief of which is to love, not hate one another. (*Gospel Ideals: Selections from the Discourses of David O. McKay* [Salt Lake City: Improvement Era, 1953], 35–36)

> These young men are instructed that they go out as representatives of the Church, and that a representative of any organization—economic or religious—must possess at least one outstanding quality, and that is Trustworthiness. He was right who said, "To be trusted is a greater compliment than to be loved." And whom do these missionaries represent? First, they represent their parents, carrying the responsibility of keeping their good name unsullied. Second, they represent the Church, specifically the ward in which they live. And third, they represent the Lord Jesus Christ, whose servants they are. These ambassadors, for such they are, represent these three groups and carry in that representation one of the greatest responsibilities of their lives. (*Pathways to Happiness* [Salt Lake City: Bookcraft, 1957], 179–180)

George Q. Cannon:

> We must be a tried people. We must walk by faith, putting our trust in the Lord and not, at present, by sight. In this way the leaders of the people of God, as well as the people themselves, have their faith tested. (*Gospel Truth: Discourses and Writings of President George Q. Cannon*, ed. Jerreld L. Newquist [Salt Lake City: Deseret Book, 1987], 300)

Gordon B. Hinckley:

> Accept responsibility in the Church, and trust in the Lord to make you equal to any call you may receive. Your example will set a pattern for your children. Reach out in love to those in distress and need. (*Teachings of Gordon B. Hinckley* [Salt Lake City: Deseret Book, 1997], 391)

IDEAS FOR DAILY LIVING

Here are four suggestions that can help in building trust:

1. Trust in God. The beginning of trust is trust in God. That is the standard of excellence you should strive for—to emulate the example of Deity, in whom you can have perfect trust. If you can be honest with our God, then you can learn to be honest with your fellow human beings.

2. To be trusted is a badge of honor that pays great dividends.
- *Trust generates peace*—The fruits of deceit and broken promises are discord, suspicion, anger, and even hatred. On the other hand, where trust governs human behavior, you will find balance, harmony, and peace.
- *Trust opens the door to opportunity*—Your word is a solemn bond that commits you to action and trust. Too often today, one's word is considered a casual thing, subject to all manner of silent contingencies, but it should never be so. If you give your word and make it your policy to keep it, people will trust you, and you will get the reputation as one in whom confidence can be vested.

- *Trust builds friendships*—Trust acts like a magnet, attracting allegiance and loyalty. It forges lasting bonds between you and others. Having a reputation of trust is a priceless asset for life.

3. Trust is a quality that can be cultivated.

- *Start with your word*—Make your word your bond: If you make a promise to anyone, keep it. To be trusted, you must be trustworthy.
- *Evaluate carefully before committing to an outcome*—Carefully weigh the projects you commit to. Make sure you have the skills, resources, and time to perform as required before you give your commitment. Don't create unrealized expectations—it destroys confidence and trust.
- *Become a master at follow-through*—Once you commit to others to do something, do it. Never become undependable. Do your duties well and on time. Be one of whom people say, "There's a person who keeps his (her) word."
- *Communicate clearly*—Make sure communication is understood in order to avoid unnecessary problems and questions regarding your commitments.
- *Avoid gossiping and backbiting*—Nothing will sully your reputation more quickly than gossiping or backbiting. Always treat others with dignity and respect, whether they are present or not.

4. Trust is an important dimension of leadership.

- *Start with the family*—Trust is inaugurated in the family, where it should be cultivated, taught, and made a high priority among to indispensable values.
- *Teach trust one step at a time*—Trust can be taught among children and subordinates little by little. Begin with small tasks and small commitments. Combine accountability with appropriate follow-up and rewards (or consequences). Gradually increase the responsibility until each individual is granted the seal of honor and trust, meaning that his or her word is a bond of value.
- *Stand up for trust and integrity*—Whatever the situation—in the community, in athletic competition, in business matters, in politics—make your voice known as one who stands for trust and honor.

ILLUSTRATIONS FOR OUR TIMES

The following personal story shows how one son learned to trust through a simple gardening lesson.

Pumpkins Really Come from Seeds—Trust Me

As a young parent I was trying to help my sons, Brett and Cory, learn about the power within a seed—how God had created this little seed that could grow and grow and grow. I said, "Trust me; these little seeds are going to become pumpkins. We are going to have jack-o-lanterns for Halloween." They looked at me with doubt, for they had never seen a pumpkin seed before, and not having been raised on a farm, they couldn't imagine that something as big as a pumpkin could come from these little seeds. I told them that there would be many pumpkins from each plant. I even showed them the package of seeds with the picture. They thought about it, then verified once more, "You mean, Dad, that these little seeds will actually become pumpkins?" I replied, "Yep, they sure will. Trust me."

I then explained how we had to plant the seeds, then water, fertilize, and weed the area so that the plants would grow. It would take work, and the hard thing was that it would take a long time. It would take patience. The boys would check to see how the seeds were doing every day. Nothing was happening. I reminded them it would take two to three months for the pumpkins to grow, but that pretty soon a little green sprout would come out of the ground. I reminded them, "Trust me."

The day finally came when the little green sprout started to come from all the "mounds" where we had planted the seeds. The boys were excited, and so was I. The summer passed, and the pumpkins grew. The boys said, "I can't believe it. Those little seeds made these great big pumpkins. We trust you, Dad." Sweet words to a daddy. It was a valuable lesson in my own trustworthiness. Perhaps, in a small way, it is how our Heavenly Father feels about us. We cannot always see the outcome of what He commands; we can't even imagine how what He tells us will work. But if we heed these simple words, "Trust in me," we too will see miracles occur.

—Ed J. Pinegar

* * *

In a story about Alexander the Great, we learn of the great value in choosing trustworthy friends.

The Cup of Vitality or the Cup of Death?

During his invasion of Persia, Alexander the Great was at one point taken seriously ill, thus causing a delay in the advance of his armies. Because of the political intrigue and atmosphere of suspicion that attended the grand movements of Alexander's entourage, the physicians on the scene did not dare to administer any medicine for fear of losing their reputation—or even their lives—should the outcome prove unseemly. Yet one physician, Philip the Acarnanian, a close friend of Alexander, stepped forward with medication he claimed was indispensable for the cure. As it turned out, at the very same time, Alexander had received a letter from one of his Macedonian staff warning him against Philip, claiming that the latter was involved in a conspiracy with the enemy, Darius III of Persia, to bring about Alexander's death. Alexander read the letter and then placed it beneath his pillow without showing it to anyone.

What happened next is worth revisiting in the words of the historian Plutarch: "when Philip came in with the potion, he [Alexander] took it with great cheerfulness and assurance, giving him meantime the letter to read. This was a spectacle well worth being present at, to see Alexander take the draught and Philip read the letter at the same time, and then turn and look upon one another, but with different sentiments; for Alexander's looks were cheerful and open, to show his kindness to and confidence in his physician, while the other was full of surprise and alarm at the accusation, appealing to the gods to witness his innocence, sometimes lifting up his hands to heaven, and then throwing himself down by the bedside, and beseeching Alexander to lay aside all fear, and follow his directions without apprehension."

In a short time, as a consequence of Philip's skillful treatment, Alexander recovered fully from his sickness and showed himself once again to his armies, much to their relief. Thus was memorialized one of the great illustrations in history of the implicit trust that a great personality had for one of his loyal friends. Philip must have in times past proven his great level of trustworthiness. How great to be known for such integrity. That level of trust which places one's life in the hands of another—even one accused of disloyalty and treachery—is indeed the highest possible level of trust.

—Richard J. Allen

SUMMARY

Within the family and society the element of trust is essential for harmony and peace. When trust is lost, one lives with anxiety and in extreme cases, even justifiable paranoia. Marriages are put in jeopardy and families are destroyed in the wake of the loss of trust. We can choose this outcome, or we can be people of integrity.

Let us make it our solemn goal to be trustworthy. Let us use the pattern given us by heaven: "And they that know thy name will put their trust in thee: for thou, Lord, hast not forsaken them that seek thee" (Ps. 9:10). And again: "Trust ye in the Lord for ever: for in the Lord Jehovah is everlasting strength" (Isa. 26:4).

TRUTH

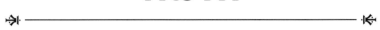

Truth is found in the Lord Jesus Christ. He is "the light, and the life, and the truth of the world" (Ether 4:12). One of the main purposes of our Savior is to "bear witness unto the truth" (John 18:37). Truth is found in all the things of God: His word (see John 17:17), His law (see Ps. 119:142), and His works (see Dan. 4:37). Truth is further described as "knowledge of things as they are, and as they were, and as they are to come" (D&C 93:24). Truth is enduring and eternal (see D&C 88:66). While a wealth of half-truths and non-truths exists, we have fortunately been given the means to discern truth. The Holy Ghost can testify to us of the truth of all things (see Moro. 10:5), but such revelation of truth is contingent on our worthiness. The process of enlightenment is clear: "He that keepeth his commandments receiveth truth and light, until he is glorified in truth and knoweth all things" (D&C 93:28). We are to seek diligently after truth, and the truth will make us free (see John 8:32).

THE SCRIPTURES TEACH US

John 14:6. *Jesus saith unto him, I am the way, the truth, and the life: no man cometh unto the Father, but by me.*

As we come unto Christ, we will be filled with truth and light. Our lives will have the standard of truth, and the life of Christ will not only save us through the infinite Atonement but will show us the way to live.

Doctrine and Covenants 93:36–37. *The glory of God is intelligence, or, in other words, light and truth. Light and truth forsake that evil one.*

Light and truth have power to overcome the evil one, and will not dwell in the presence of evil. Because we possess light and truth, we can more easily identify sin and therefore avoid it. When we seek the glory of God, our whole bodies are filled with light and we comprehend all things (see D&C 88:67).

Doctrine and Covenants 93:39. *And that wicked one cometh and taketh away light and truth, through disobedience, from the children of men, and because of the tradition of their fathers.*

Satan does not want us to know the truth, so he tempts us away from it. Whenever we choose to disobey the Lord, we lose the Spirit and diminish our light and truth.

Doctrine and Covenants 93:40. *But I have commanded you to bring up your children in light and truth.*

We have a duty to teach our children the truth of all things as pertaining to the gospel of Jesus Christ. Many have been chastened by the Lord for not teaching their children, and so shall we if we fail to teach them (see D&C 68:25–28; 93:42–48).

Doctrine and Covenants 123:12. *For there are many yet on the earth among all sects, parties, and denominations, who are blinded by the subtle craftiness of men, whereby they lie in wait to deceive, and who are only kept from the truth because they know not where to find it—*

We are blessed with the truth of the gospel, and we have an obligation to share it with everyone with whom we come in contact. Our fellow beings need to be invited to hear the word of God, because they need an alternative to the deceit the world offers. Let us stand up boldly as witnesses for the truth. Let us pray for all those who do not know God (see Alma 6:6).

MODERN PROPHETS SPEAK

Gordon B. Hinckley:

> The marvelous and wonderful thing is that any individual who desires to know the truth may receive that conviction. The Lord himself gave the formula when he said, "If any man will do [God's] will, he shall know of the doctrine, whether it be of God, or whether I speak of myself." (John 7:17.) (*Faith: The Essence of True Religion* [Salt Lake City: Deseret Book, 1989], 5)

Hugh B. Brown:

> Any open-minded search for truth requires courage, constancy, and humility. To quote an ancient prayer:
>
> From the cowardice that shrinks from new truth,
> From the laziness that is content with half truth,
> From the arrogance that thinks it knows all the truth,
> O God of truth, deliver us.
>
> Any thoughtful, prayerful search for truth reveals that God is our Father, and that He is a person, that His glory is intelligence, and that He had a will, a purpose, and a plan in creating the universe and providing for man's earth life. (*The Abundant Life* [Salt Lake City: Bookcraft, 1965], 276)

Thomas S. Monson:

> Fill your mind with truth. I'd like to suggest that when we search for truth, we search among those books and in those places where truth is most likely to be found. I've often referred to a simple couplet: "You do not find truth groveling through error. You find truth by searching the holy word of God." There are those who for direction and inspiration turn to the philosophies of man. There a smattering of truth may be found, but not the entire spectrum. (*Be Your Best Self* [Salt Lake City: Deseret Book, 1979], 169)

IDEAS FOR DAILY LIVING

Here are several ideas for finding and living the truth in Christ:

1. Seek His word, His law, and His commandments.
- *Listen to the Spirit* (see 2 Ne. 32:5).
- *Search and feast upon the scriptures* (see 2 Ne. 32:3).
- *Listen to the words of the living prophets* (see D&C 1:38; 21:4–6; 3 Ne. 28:34–35).
- *Fast and pray to understand the word of God* (see Alma 5:46).
- *Attend the temple regularly* (see D&C 97:13–14).

2. Discern truth from error.

- *Seek the truth*—Study and learn by faith that you might know the truth (see D&C 88:118). When we have a value system based on the truth, we will have a standard to judge all things and we will not be deceived. Declared Plato: "The true lover of knowledge must, from childhood up, be most of all a striver after truth in every form."
- *Love the truth*—That which we truly love will become our standard for knowledge as well as behavior. The truth will make us free from sin and error (see John 8:32).
- *Keep an eye single to the glory of God*—We can be filled with light, and we can attain a state where we can comprehend all things (see D&C 88:67) and discern between truth and error.
- *Use discernment*—Beware of the sophistries and false traditions of men, inspired by the devil. We must follow the prophets and the counsel of God and not depend upon the learning of man (see 2 Ne. 9:28–29).
- *Listen to the Spirit*—Always listen to the Spirit, for it will tell us the truth of all things (see Moro. 10:5) and we will judge righteously (see D&C 11:12). "It is by that Spirit that one is able to discern truth from untruth," confirmed Roy W. Doxey (*The Doctrine and Covenants Speaks* [Salt Lake City: Deseret Book, 1964], 1: 393).

3. Live the truth.

- *Avoid and overcome temptation*—Search the scriptures (see 1 Ne. 15:24) and pray (see 3 Ne. 18:18). As we come to further know the truth, we will be more likely to live it, avoiding even the temptation and deceit of sin.
- *Remember to keep the covenants*—As we renew our covenants by partaking of the sacrament, we will have renewed power to keep the commandments while always remembering our Savior, the source of truth.
- *Have faith in God*—The Lord will provide a way (see Ne. 3:7) and give us strength as we humble ourselves before Him (see Ether 12:27).
- *Surrender your will to the Lord*—Just as the Savior gave His will to Heavenly Father (see John 6:38), we must do likewise as servants of God (see Eph. 6:6). We must yield our hearts to God that we might be sanctified (see Hel. 3:35). "People cannot change truth—but truth can change people," declared one anonymous writer.
- *Set an example for your children*—When we realize that our children will follow our example, it will give us the strength to live the truth for their sakes, if for no other reason.
- *Recognize the blessings of living the truth*—We will receive all that the Father has (see D&C 84:38)—even a fulness of truth and light and knowledge of all things (see D&C 93:26–28).
- *Love God with all your heart, might, mind, and strength*—If we love God completely, our desires will be to Him and keeping His commandments (see John 14:15).

ILLUSTRATIONS FOR OUR TIMES

In the famous story of a man searching for diamonds, we learn that sometimes we search far and wide for truth when it exists in very close proximity.

The Truth Shall Make You Free

Pilate asked, "What is truth?" (John 18:38). People have been struggling with this question for centuries. Each man or woman has the responsibility to find the truth.

Another appropriate question is, "Where can truth be found?" Perhaps a clue to the answer can be found in the following story:

Ali Hafed, an ancient Persian, owned much land and many productive fields, with orchards and gardens, and had money out at interest. He had a lovely family and was "contented because he was wealthy, and wealthy because he was contented."

An old priest came to Ali Hafed and told him that if he had a diamond the size of his thumb, he could purchase a dozen farms like his. Ali Hafed said, "Will you tell me where I can find diamonds?"

The priest told him, "If you will find a river that runs through white sands, between high mountains, in those white sands you will always find diamonds."

Said Ali Hafed, "I will go."

So he sold his farm, collected his money that was at interest, and left his family in the charge of a neighbor, and away he went in search of diamonds, traveling through many lands.

The man who purchased Ali Hafed's farm led his camel out into the garden to drink, and as the animal put his nose into the shallow waters, the farmer noticed a curious flash of light in the white sands of the stream. Reaching in, he pulled out a black stone containing a strange eye of light. Not long after, the same old priest came to visit Ali Hafed's successor and found that in the black stone was a diamond. As they rushed out into the garden and stirred up the white sands with their fingers, they came up with many more beautiful, valuable gems. Thus were discovered the diamond mines of Golconda, the most valuable diamond mines in the ancient world. Had Ali Hafed remained at home and dug in his own cellar or anywhere in his own fields rather than traveling in strange lands, he would have had acres of diamonds (adapted from Russell H. Conwell, *Acres of Diamonds* [1915], 4–9).

The search for truth is often not unlike Ali Hafed's search for diamonds. The truth is not in distant lands but under our feet. Sir Winston Churchill once said of someone, "Occasionally he stumbled over the truth, but hastily picked himself up and hurried on as if nothing had happened" (in *The Irrepressible Churchill Stories,* ed. Kay Halle [1966], 113). (James E. Faust, "The Truth Shall Make You Free," *Ensign,* September 1998, 2)

SUMMARY

As the Lord said, the truth will make us free (see John 8:32). However, knowing the truth is not enough. We are commanded not only to know the truth and discern truth from error, but to *live* the truth. Our salvation depends upon making our life a pursuit of living the truth. Apostle Joseph B. Wirthlin confirmed this doctrine when he taught: "We must learn the truth, love the truth, and live the truth" (*Finding Peace in Our Lives* [Salt Lake City: Deseret Book, 1995], 139). When we live what we learn as it pertains to eternal truth, we become free from sin and the power of Satan, who seeks to destroy us and bring us down to hell. We become free to enjoy life and to pursue happiness. This should be our goal—to know the truth and live the truth, and thus enjoy the blessings of eternal life.

UNDERSTANDING

To understand and be understood is the essence of effective communication. When we come to understand something, we gain an appreciation for the underlying causes, logic, and operations pertaining to it. As we begin to understand the things of God, our attitude and behavior change, and we cultivate a sense of gratitude to our Heavenly Father. Understanding is the companion to faith, the mentor of hope, and the protector of covenant values. To understand something or someone requires effort, ability, perception, and a host of other intellectual and empathetic capacities. The ability to understand is of major importance in our lives. Our aim should be to understand universal concerns such as life, relationships, family values and roles, life after death, and many more important and meaningful things.

THE SCRIPTURES TEACH US

Psalms 119:34. *Give me understanding, and I shall keep thy law; yea, I shall observe it with my whole heart.*

Understanding the things of God will give us the power to keep the commandments with all of our hearts. Understanding provides a sense of purpose for our obedience. Our Savior and our prophets have counseled us to search the scriptures, fast and pray, and live by the Spirit in order to understand the things of God.

Proverbs 3:13. *Happy is the man that findeth wisdom, and the man that getteth understanding.*

Happiness is dependent upon our understanding. When we understand and receive the love of God, we avoid the effects of misunderstanding—contention, envy, and strife—and we are happy (see 4 Ne. 1:15–16).

Alma 32:28. *Now, we will compare the word unto a seed. Now, if ye give place, that a seed may be planted in your heart, behold, if it be a true seed, or a good seed, if ye do not cast it out by your unbelief, that ye will resist the Spirit of the Lord, behold, it will begin to swell within your breasts; and when you feel these swelling motions, ye will begin to say within yourselves—It must needs be that this is a good seed, or that the word is good, for it beginneth to enlarge my soul; yea, it beginneth to enlighten my understanding, yea, it beginneth to be delicious to me.*

When we plant the word of God in our hearts, we feel good. The word enlarges our soul, the Spirit enlightens our understanding, and the word is delicious to us. We then desire to feast upon the word, which will tell us all things to do (see 2 Ne. 32:3). This is because the word of God enlightens our understanding and kindles within us a sense of commitment and devotion to the truth and to the Savior.

Doctrine and Covenants 50:10–12. *And now come, saith the Lord, by the Spirit, unto the elders of his church, and let us reason together, that ye may understand; Let us reason even as a man reasoneth one with another face to face. Now, when a man reasoneth he is understood of man, because he reasoneth as a man; even so will I, the Lord, reason with you that you may understand.*

The Lord wants to help us understand, and He asks us to reason with Him (see Isa. 1:18). He told Nephi through the Spirit to take Laban's life—a very hard thing for Nephi to understand. Once Nephi understood, he said, "I did obey the voice of the Spirit," and he took Laban's life in order that a whole nation would not sink into ignorance and be lost (see 1 Ne. 4:10–18).

Doctrine and Covenants 50:22. *Wherefore, he that preacheth and he that receiveth, understand one another, and both are edified and rejoice together.*

With understanding comes edification by the Spirit. We should seek to understand the scriptures and the prophets through prayer, rather than finding fault or using the reasoning of man to accommodate our behavior or present situation.

Doctrine and Covenants 76:12. *By the power of the Spirit our eyes were opened and our understandings were enlightened, so as to see and understand the things of God.*

When we worthily seek the Spirit, we, like the Prophet Joseph and Sidney Rigdon, can have our eyes opened and understand the things of the Lord. Listening to the Spirit is the key to understanding. We should live worthy of the Spirit at all times, that we may receive inspiration, especially when we do not know what to do (see 1 Ne. 4:6).

MODERN PROPHETS SPEAK

Joseph F. Smith:
> But let every man seek earnestly to understand the truth and teach his children to become familiar with those truths of heaven that have been restored to the earth in the latter-days. (*Gospel Doctrine: Selections from the Sermons and Writings of Joseph F. Smith,* comp. John A. Widtsoe [Salt Lake City: Deseret Book, 1939], 5)

George Q. Cannon:
> If we do anything, let us do it understandingly. If we hear any principle taught from the stand that we do not understand, let us seek to comprehend it by the Spirit of God. . . . "I do not know whether this is true or not; I will not fight it, neither will I endorse it, but I will seek knowledge from God, for that is my privilege, and I will never rest satisfied until I have obtained the light I require."

> If you hear a doctrine that does not agree with your feelings or that you do not believe, take this course; do not reject nor endorse hastily without knowing or understanding. By taking this course you will develop the principle that God designs we should possess, and we will thus become a wise and understanding people, for we will be based on the rock of revelation. (*Gospel Truth: Discourses and Writings of President George Q. Cannon,* ed. Jerreld L. Newquist [Salt Lake City: Deseret Book, 1987], 270)

Marion G. Romney:
> When the witness comes, however, it is very real and powerful. He whose desire to know the living God is strong enough to induce him to follow the prescribed course can and will get the witness for himself. Then he will understand what the Lord was saying in these scriptures. However, he who does not so seek will never understand these scriptures, nor the revelations which God has given of himself. (*Look to God and Live* [Salt Lake City: Deseret Book, 1971], 21)

Bruce R. McConkie:
> Those who have faith and understanding always seek to harmonize into one perfect whole all the statements of the scriptures and all the pronouncements of the Brethren. (*Sermons and Writings of Bruce R. McConkie* [Salt Lake City: Bookcraft, 1998], 231)

Ezra Taft Benson:

> To study by faith is to seek understanding and the Spirit of the Lord through the prayer of faith. (*The Teachings of Ezra Taft Benson* [Salt Lake City: Bookcraft, 1988], 309)

IDEAS FOR DAILY LIVING

Here are four ideas and principles to help us learn how to understand:

1. Knowledge precedes understanding.

- *Get the facts*—Before taking action, first seek out information to appreciate the subject or the person. *This is absolutely essential.* "A man of understanding hath wisdom" (Prov. 10:23).
- *Go to informed sources*—Assemble the best information from the best sources—the scriptures, statements from the Brethren, books, experts, and other proven sources of wisdom.
- *Be prepared to invest effort*—Understanding takes initiative and effort; it is not a passive skill. Prepare to exert effort, whether in your studies or your relationships.
- *Be prepared to invest time*—Understanding sometimes comes over time. Therefore, time is your ally in coming to understand anything. Resist the urge to step in with judgment or recommendations until you have a knowledgeable grasp of the situation.

2. Using all your faculties gives you a greater ability to understand.

- *Use multiple points of view*—The key to a better understanding of people is to combine your sources of information: include their words, their body language, and their actions—both what they do and what they choose not to do.
- *Use the heart*—Listen not only with your ears, but with your heart. Don't judge solely on the words you hear, but also rely on what you feel.
- *Practice empathy*—You can never fully understand another person until you try to feel his or her emotions.
- *Adjust your perspective*—Remember that you see things by your perception—recognize this and account for it.
- *Remember the Spirit*—The highest form of listening is to discern and understand spiritual promptings. Responding to inspiration is a quality that demonstrates humility, and a desire to learn. Pray for more understanding and wisdom.

3. Leadership cultivates understanding and clarity.

- *Project the vision*—A principal role of leadership is to articulate vision and objectives with such clarity that the team understands and then takes action with purpose.
- *Cultivate clarity of expression*—Learn to express yourself with clarity and precision, so that you cannot be misunderstood.
- *Avoid misunderstanding*—Where helpful, use disclaimers such as: "In saying this, I do not mean to imply . . ." or "Please don't misunderstand. I am *not* saying . . ."
- *Close the loop*—Understanding is an interactive process. Test your own understanding by expressing what you believe you have heard, and then ask the simple question, "Is this what you mean?" Then listen closely to what the other person says.

4. Understanding is a gift to others.

- *Build self-confidence*—Realize that listening holds important consequences and benefits for the person you listen to. There are few human experiences that cause a person to increase in self-confidence more rapidly than when someone truly listens to him or her.

- *Provide the best resources*—Understanding a person means that you can better channel to him or her the correct resources at the right time in the right manner.
- *Foster freedom of choice*—It is an act of kindness to say to a person, after you have listened to all that has been said, "What are your options? What do you think you should do?" In doing this, you honor a person's right to choose.
- *Create harmony*—Would you rather preside over a home of strict control and structured order, or one of understanding and harmony? Understanding creates harmony and love.

ILLUSTRATIONS FOR OUR TIMES

A story by Thomas S. Monson demonstrates that the understanding of even a small child can lead to great understanding in others.

A Five-year-old Missionary

Our daughter, Ann, turned five shortly after we arrived in Canada, where I served as mission president. She saw the missionaries going about their work and she too wanted to be a missionary. My wife demonstrated understanding by permitting Ann to take to class a few copies of the *Children's Friend*. That wasn't sufficient for Ann. She wanted to take a copy of the Book of Mormon, and she talked to her teacher, Miss Pepper, about the Church.

I thought it rather thrilling that long years after our return from Toronto, we came home from a vacation and found in our mailbox a note from Miss Pepper that read:

Dear Ann,

Think back many years ago. I was your school teacher in Toronto, Canada. I was impressed by the copies of the Children's Friend *which you brought to school. I was impressed by your dedication to a book called the Book of Mormon.*

I made a commitment that one day I would come to Salt Lake City and see why you talked as you did and why you believed in the manner you believed. Today I had the privilege of going through your visitors' center on Temple Square. Thanks to a five-year-old girl who had an understanding of that which she believed, I now have a better understanding of The Church of Jesus Christ of Latter-day Saints.

Miss Pepper died not too long after that visit. How happy our daughter Ann was when she attended the Jordan River Temple and performed the temple work for her beloved teacher whom she had friendshipped long ago. (Thomas S. Monson, *Inspiring Experiences That Build Faith: From the Life and Ministry of Thomas S. Monson* [Salt Lake City: Deseret Book, 1994], 151)

SUMMARY

When you come to an understanding of something or someone, you learn to appreciate the value of that thing or that person. Our relationships in life are based upon understanding and trust. Without these qualities it would be difficult to maintain lasting relationships. Our power to comprehend and understand reflects on our ability to learn and to apply that knowledge for our betterment and for the betterment of others. As the scriptures confirm: "Understanding is a wellspring of life unto him that hath it" (Prov. 16:22).

UNITY

Unity among the Saints, being one even as the Father and the Son are one, is what Christ prayed for in Gethsemane (see John 17:11). We are to be one in thought, in purpose, and in all the desires of our heart. The Lord spoke plainly in our day concerning unity among His followers when He said, "I say unto you, be one; and if ye are not one ye are not mine" (D&C 38:27). This oneness was experienced in the primitive Church in the days of the early Apostles (see Acts 4:32), and among the Nephite nation following the personal ministry of the resurrected Christ (see 4 Ne. 1:15–16). Unity provides for increased service and blessings through concerted effort and cooperation. Unity overcomes contention (see 3 Ne. 11:27–28) and, in turn, the devil, the father of contention. Unity allows the Spirit to bless all those of one heart and one mind.

THE SCRIPTURES TEACH US

Romans 12:5. *So we, being many, are one body in Christ, and every one members one of another.*

"The unity of the Saints is unique and powerful. . . . We enjoy that unity through love. We can neither purchase nor force it. Our method is to 'persuade, . . . and bless with wisdom, love, and light, . . . but never force the human mind.' ['Know This, That Every Soul Is Free,' *Hymns,* no. 240.] To the extent we operate in other ways, we diminish our right to be recognized as disciples of Christ" (John K. Carmack, "United in Love and Testimony," *Ensign,* May 2001, 76).

Philippians 2:2. *Fulfil ye my joy, that ye be likeminded, having the same love, being of one accord, of one mind.*

We bring great joy to the Lord and to those who love us when we exhibit unity and togetherness, which reflects love, harmony, and peace. When we are unified we truly have compassion for one another (see 1 Pet. 3:8).

Doctrine and Covenants 38:27. *Behold, this I have given unto you as a parable, and it is even as I am. I say unto you, be one; and if ye are not one ye are not mine.*

It is vital that we seek unity of testimony and purpose in the Church and in our families. When all agree on a common value system, steps toward unity of action can commence.

Moses 7:18. *And the Lord called his people Zion, because they were of one heart and one mind, and dwelt in righteousness; and there was no poor among them.*

We cannot be a Zion people if we do not all align ourselves with the Lord. With the Nephites, this oneness brought peace and righteousness for a time. Unity should be our goal for our family and as members of the Church.

MODERN PROPHETS SPEAK

Brigham Young:

> The Savior sought continually to impress upon the minds of His disciples that a perfect oneness reigned among all celestial beings—that the Father and the Son and their Minister, the Holy

Ghost, were one in their administration in heaven and among the people pertaining to this earth. Between them and all the heavenly hosts there can be no disunion, no discord, no wavering on a suggestion, on a thought or reflection, on a feeling or manifestation; for such a principle would differ widely from the character of him who dictates them, who makes his throne the habitation of justice, mercy, equity, and truth. If the heavenly hosts were not one, they would be entirely unfit to dwell in the eternal burnings with the Father and Ruler of the universe. . . .

We must become of one heart and mind, in order to fully enjoy the blessings we anticipate.

If we are united, we are independent of the powers of hell and of the world. . . .

A perfect oneness will save a people, because intelligent beings cannot become perfectly one, only by acting upon principles that pertain to eternal life. (*Discourses of Brigham Young,* sel. John A. Widtsoe [Salt Lake City: Deseret Book, 1954], 282)

Henry B. Eyring:
> Where people have that Spirit with them, we may expect harmony. The Spirit puts the testimony of truth in our hearts, which unifies those who share that testimony. The Spirit of God never generates contention (see 3 Ne. 11:29). It never generates the feelings of distinctions between people which lead to strife (see Joseph F. Smith, *Gospel Doctrine,* 13th ed. [1963], 131). It leads to personal peace and a feeling of union with others. It unifies souls. A unified family, a unified Church, and a world at peace depend on unified souls. ("That We May Be One," *Ensign,* May 1998, 66)

Howard W. Hunter:
> Of course, the key to a unified church is a unified soul—one that is at peace with itself and not given to inner conflicts and tensions. So much in our world is calculated to destroy that personal peace through sins and temptations of a thousand kinds. We pray that the lives of the Saints will be lived in harmony with the ideal set before us by Jesus of Nazareth. ("That We May Be One," *Ensign,* May 1976, 105)

IDEAS FOR DAILY LIVING

Here are several ideas to help us increase unity in our personal lives, our families, and in our Church service:

1. Understand the benefits. Recognize the power of unity within one's personal life. If we go contrary to our values and standards, we violate ourselves. If we are not one with our values, we will suffer from self-deception, which turns into diminished self-worth and compromised self-respect. Unity of purpose and fidelity to our values brings self-confidence and enhances self-esteem.

2. Agreed-upon values bring unity. Seek to create a value system within the group that can be understood, appreciated, and applied by all involved. This brings unity to the family or group.

3. Synergy produces results. The power of cooperation is brought to bear when unity is strong.

4. Seek to understand. Understanding one another and the values each person stands for is the key to unity. We cannot stand together if we don't know where each other stands.

5. Seek eternal blessings. The blessings of unity include peace, purity of motive, being of one mind and of one purpose, dispelling contention, having the Spirit present, and being one in the Lord (see Gal. 3:28).

ILLUSTRATIONS FOR OUR TIMES

In the following personal story, the lack of harmony and unity in a ward was resolved by a resourceful brother who took action instead of joining in the contention.

Harmony: The Business of Saving Souls

When we first moved into the ward, we soon became aware of a controversy that was fomenting a good deal of discussion in hallway and classroom alike. It seemed that an evergreen tree near the front entrance had originally been planted somewhat too close to the building during the construction phase in 1937. Now the mature tree was growing at a considerable angle to the wall, which was of concern to many. The ward seemed to be divided into factions—one of them wanting to remove the tree, another insisting on doing nothing, and a third voting to trim the tree aesthetically. I noted that priesthood meetings were not infrequently given over to debating the issue. Finally, we came to church one Sunday and found that the tree had completely disappeared. It seems one resourceful brother, having had his fill of the bickering and murmuring, had come on Saturday and taken the tree out all by himself, removing all the debris clean as a whistle. He showed up at the meetings that day with a peaceful and satisfied look on his face, and many if not most of us said a silent prayer of thanks in our hearts that someone had had the wisdom to exorcise the spirit of contention and arguing over inconsequential matters. After that, it seemed much easier to get back to the business of saving souls.

It is so easy to find distraction in our course of righteousness. The devil would have us fret with one another over trivial matters to avoid becoming unified on the more weighty matters of life. The Savior said: "And there shall be no disputations among you, as there have hitherto been; neither shall there be disputations among you concerning the points of my doctrine, as there have hitherto been. For verily, verily I say unto you, he that hath the spirit of contention is not of me, but is of the devil, who is the father of contention, and he stirreth up the hearts of men to contend with anger, one with another. Behold, this is not my doctrine, to stir up the hearts of men with anger, one against another; but this is my doctrine, that such things should be done away" (3 Ne. 11:28–30). Our course is clear, and we ought to seek only to be unified in following the Savior's words: "Learn of me, and listen to my words; walk in the meekness of my Spirit, and you shall have peace in me" (D&C 19:23).

—Richard J. Allen

SUMMARY

Unity with our Heavenly Father and our Savior is essential to the work of the kingdom. Without unity, the Spirit cannot influence our lives or the people we serve. For this reason, the Lord prayed for this most important aspect in the lives of His disciples (see John 17:11). Let us seek unity by aligning our values and standards with the principles and ordinances of the gospel and having the courage and dedication to live them. The will of God will become our only desire when we will willingly submit to all things He commands us to do. Then we will be one with Him and our Savior.

VISITING TEACHING

Visiting teaching is similar to home teaching. Relief society sisters strengthen each other as they give messages pertaining to the gospel of Jesus Christ. Visiting teachers support and comfort their sisters in the Relief Society. As visiting teachers and disciples of the Lord Jesus Christ, they show charity and love (see John 13:34–35), strengthen and help others (see D&C 81:5; 108:7), and nurture them in love (see Moro. 6:4). So much pressure is put on today's women to abandon the values of previous generations. The women of the Church are able to support and lift one another unlike any other group of women. Visiting teachers should pray for strength and wisdom as they represent the Lord and Church leaders in this most important assignment.

THE SCRIPTURES TEACH US

James 1:27. *Pure religion and undefiled before God and the Father is this, To visit the fatherless and widows in their affliction, and to keep [her]self unspotted from the world.*

Visiting teachers display their devotion to God as they serve their fellow sisters. This is what the gospel is all about—living the principles of charitable service in our daily lives.

Doctrine and Covenants 108:7. *Therefore, strengthen your brethren [and sisters] in all your conversation, in all your prayers, in all your exhortations, and in all your doings.*

When we build caring relationships, we are better able to strengthen one another both temporally and spiritually. We can strengthen each other not only in visiting (conversation), but in sincere prayer, in our teaching, and in all our service.

MODERN PROPHETS SPEAK

Spencer W. Kimball:

> Visiting teaching is a great opportunity for service. To be successful, it seems to me that a visiting teacher would wish to have high purpose and remember it all the time, would want to have great vision, a terrific enthusiasm that cannot be worn down, a positive attitude, of course, and a great love. . . .

> There are many sisters who are living in rags—spiritual rags. They are entitled to gorgeous robes, spiritual robes, as in the parable. It is your privilege more than your duty. We talk so much about duty, but it is your privilege to go into homes and exchange robes for rags. . . .You cannot miss a home with impunity; you must not pass a sister by, even if she is a little uncomplimentary, or not too happy for your visit. . . .

> For a [home] teacher or a visiting teacher to accept a responsibility of four, five, six, or seven homes, and leave them in their spiritual rags and tatters is without excuse; and when you go into the homes, there should be no vain babblings or swelling words. You are going to save souls and who can tell but that many of the fine active people in the Church today are active because you

were in their homes and gave them a new outlook, a new vision. You pulled back the curtain. You extended their horizons. You gave them something new. Maybe they will never tell you about it in all their lives, but you did the work just the same.

You see, you are not only saving these sisters, but perhaps also their husbands and their homes. (*The Teachings of Spencer W. Kimball,* ed. Edward L. Kimball [Salt Lake City: Bookcraft, 1982], 527)

Howard W. Hunter:

Sisters, continue to seek opportunities for service. Don't be overly concerned with status. Do you recall the counsel of the Savior regarding those who seek the "chief seats" or the "uppermost rooms"? "He that is greatest among you shall be your servant." (Matt. 23:6, 11.) It is important to be appreciated. But our focus should be on righteousness, not recognition; on service, not status. The faithful visiting teacher, who quietly goes about her work month after month, is just as important to the work of the Lord as those who occupy what some see as more prominent positions in the Church. Visibility does not equate to value. ("To the Women of the Church," *Ensign,* November 1992, 95)

Joseph B. Wirthlin:

We urge home teachers and visiting teachers to look after their families in a spirit of charity. Home teaching and visiting teaching are vehicles for saving souls when they are done the right way with the right intent. (*Finding Peace in Our Lives* [Salt Lake City: Deseret Book, 1995], 216)

IDEAS FOR DAILY LIVING

Here are a few ideas to consider in your calling as a visiting teacher:

1. Recognize visiting teaching as a divine calling.

- *Realize the power of love and service*—You have more influence than you can know in befriending and serving. Even those strong in the gospel need to be lifted at times.
- *Acknowledge the power of true conversion*—The visiting teaching calling is designed to help sisters become more deeply converted. The program is inspired; miracles can happen through visiting teaching.
- *Understand the worth of souls*—Because the Lord cares so much for each of His children, He has asked us to look after one another. This is why He designed the visiting teaching program.
- *Increase your faith in the Savior*—This is His work. You represent Him.
- *Improve your prayer habits*—Sometimes the greatest service you can provide to your sisters is prayer. Often, in praying for a sister, you can be inspired with how you can help her.

2. Evaluate your efforts.

- *Do you truly show that you care for your sisters?*—Or are they merely an assigned "project"?
- *Do you recognize that you are on the errand of the Lord?*—Do you convey His love and His message?
- *Do you seek to understand your sisters' needs and attempt to fulfill them?*—Or do you assume everything is fine when it seems that way on the surface?
- *Do you really pray for your sisters and their well-being?*—Or do you just mention them in passing once in a while in your prayers?
- *Do you look for opportunities to serve your sisters and then do it?*—Or do you use the old cliché, "Let me know if I can help in any way."
- *Do you report our stewardship to our leaders regularly?*—Visiting teaching isn't done until it is reported.

3. Remember the important things.

- *Appointments*—Call and make appointments early in the month. This shows you care.
- *Special occasions*—Remember birthdays and special days in the lives of the sisters.
- *Honors*—Find out about any success or honors that each sister has received and seek to praise and encourage her. If it has been published, bring the newspaper article.
- *Surprises*—Learn each sister's favorite foods, hobbies, and activities and then surprise her with a simple gift.
- *Above all, teach the gospel*—Invite the Spirit to direct you and in turn bless the sister according to her needs.

ILLUSTRATIONS FOR OUR TIMES

In an *Ensign* article, a sister shares her experiences with visiting teaching and explains how she learned the true spirit of the program.

Learning to Cherish Visiting Teaching

For many years I envisioned visiting teachers as older women who delivered casseroles to each other. Not eager to enter that world, I reluctantly accepted my first visiting teaching assignment to visit four sisters in my BYU ward. The sisters I visited seemed as uncomfortable as I was, and I was relieved when visits ended early.

Shortly after I was married, I again was called to be a visiting teacher. I wondered what I could teach these sisters, who seemed so secure in their families and homes. When my visiting teaching partner, a 65-year-old widow, asked me to give the message, I stumbled through it—my gaze never leaving the manual.

My attitude gradually softened as I watched my visiting teaching partner prepare for each visit by praying that we would be able to discern the needs of the sisters we taught. The idea that these sisters, so outwardly radiant and successful, might have problems intrigued me. Although I began to look at them differently, my ideas about visiting teaching remained relatively unchanged.

During my next encounter with visiting teaching, I was assigned to visit four sisters, and I was determined to be the "perfect" visiting teacher. I gave the prepared message, visited early in the month, and brought cookies and cakes, birthday treats, and Christmas gifts.

But the feelings of sisterhood I had expected didn't materialize, and I blamed the visiting teaching program. If only I were assigned to visit women whose circumstances matched my own, if only the sisters appreciated the time and effort I spent in visiting them, if only . . .

These new feelings went unchanged for several years. I still tried to visit with promptness and enthusiasm. However, I paid scant attention to the *needs* of the sisters. All of my energy was devoted to meeting what I perceived as the requirements of a visiting teacher. I doubled my efforts—I remembered not only the sisters' birthdays but also those of their children. I tended their children and arranged meals at the arrival of a new baby.

Again I questioned why I didn't feel the promised rewards. Frightened by sisters with whom I had little in common, I avoided close relationships with them. Besides, I rationalized, visiting teaching took time away from my family. It required patience to juggle schedules and involved finding baby-sitters for my children.

When I was assigned to visit Ann, a widow in her sixties, I grumbled once more. After all, I thought, how could I expect to feel a commitment to someone who was so different from me? How could I possibly develop a lasting friendship with a woman who was twice my age and no longer had small children at home?

But I soon discovered that she and I shared an offbeat sense of humor, one that often baffled others. As we learned more about each other, our friendship grew. Both computer illiterate, we struggled to learn word processing together. We cried together when she was diagnosed with cancer.

I no longer tried to be the "perfect" visiting teacher—I was too busy being Ann's friend. It was a friendship that endured until several years later when she died.

Through visiting Ann I learned what I had lacked in my other visiting teaching assignments— love. I now try to share love and sisterhood with those I visit. I no longer fear differences—I appreciate them.

I've learned that the composition of visiting teaching is much like that of a symphony. The common melody of the gospel allows us to harmonize. However, the differences among us create an exquisite counterpoint, one all the more beautiful for its occasional unexpectedness. As each strain of the symphony is heard, a common theme emerges—one of love and compassion among sisters, strengthening each other and bringing us closer to our Heavenly Father. (Jane McBride Choate, "Learning to Cherish Visiting Teaching," *Ensign,* March 1995, 28)

SUMMARY

Visiting teaching can be a fulfilling and enjoyable experience as visiting teachers catch the vision and importance of this sacred work—blessing the lives of the sisters they visit. Once visiting teachers catch the true vision of visiting teaching, their desire will increase. They will prepare every needful thing in order to be good visiting teachers. They will be full of enthusiasm and will make and keep commitments. Effective visiting teachers are committed and devoted servants of the Lord and true undershepherds to their sisters. They honor their baptismal covenants (see Mosiah 18:8–9). As sisters serve as loving visiting teachers, acting with a humble and obedient spirit, the work will prosper and lives will be blessed.

WIFE

It is difficult to distinguish all the roles of womanhood; they form a seamless whole. The role of wife and mother is without equal in the world today. The wife is a companion, comfort, and partner to her husband. In his vision of the spirit world, President Joseph F. Smith beheld "our glorious Mother Eve, with many of her faithful daughters who had lived through the ages and worshiped the true and living God"

(D&C 138:39). What a transcendent view of wifehood and motherhood was vouchsafed the prophet as he confirmed the nobility of these sacred roles. It is a reminder to us all that the faithful and honorable woman holds an exalted place among all of God's children. As the poet Goethe exclaimed (in *Faust*): "Das ewig weibliche zieht us hinan"—*The eternal womanly draws us on.*

THE SCRIPTURES TEACH US

Genesis 2:18. *And the Lord God said, It is not good that the man should be alone; I will make him an help meet for him.*

We see here God's ordination of the first marriage. He points our the great and important role women play in the scheme of humanity. Wives and husbands are associates. They work together in council. They are partners in the greatest cause on earth—the immortality and eternal life of Heavenly Father's children.

1 Corinthians 11:11. *Nevertheless neither is the man without the woman, neither the woman without the man, in the Lord.*

Exaltation and eternal lives are reserved for those couples who are not only married for time and all eternity (see D&C 131:2–4), but also who live in love and harmony, being equally yoked in their eternal roles. They are one.

Ephesians 5:33. *Nevertheless let every one of you in particular so love his wife even as himself; and the wife see that she reverence her husband.*

Husbands are to love their wives even as Christ has loved the Church (see Eph. 5:25). Love translates into caring concern that serves others. Husbands should serve their wives and family even as Christ has served us. In reverencing their husbands, wives are involved in a reciprocating act—as each honors, respects, and treats the other with deference and kindness.

Moses 4:22. *Thy desire shall be to thy husband, and he shall rule over thee.*

A wife gives herself to her husband in righteousness. This act is one of turning one's heart with affection to the mate. Both husband and wife participate in this selfless act of love.

MODERN PROPHETS SPEAK

Gordon B. Hinckley:
> The most important decision of life is the decision concerning your companion. Choose prayerfully. And when you are married, be fiercely loyal one to another. Selfishness is the great destroyer of happy family life. I have this one suggestion to offer. If you will make your first concern the comfort, the well-being, and the happiness of your companion, sublimating any personal concern to that loftier goal, you will be happy, and your marriage will go on through eternity. (*Teachings of Gordon B. Hinckley* [Salt Lake City: Deseret Book, 1997], 328–29)

Harold B. Lee:
> Remember that great love is built on great sacrifice and that a daily determination in each other to please in things that are right will build a sure foundation for a happy home. That determination

for the welfare of each other must be mutual and not one-sided or selfish. Husband and wife must feel equal responsibilities and obligations to teach each other. Two of the things that today strike at the security of modern homes is that young husbands have never sensed their full obligation in supporting a family, and young wives have sidestepped the responsibility of settling down to the serious business of raising a family and of making a home. (*The Teachings of Harold B. Lee,* ed. Clyde J. Williams [Salt Lake City: Bookcraft, 1996], 252)

James E. Faust:

In marriage, neither is superior; each has a different primary and divine responsibility. Chief among these responsibilities for wives is the calling of motherhood. I firmly believe that our dear, faithful sisters enjoy a special spiritual enrichment that is inherent in their natures. (*Finding Light in a Dark World* [Salt Lake City: Deseret Book, 1995], 122)

IDEAS FOR DAILY LIVING

Here are four ideas for women to consider in their role as wives:

1. Improve the inner reality.
- *Elevate your vision*—You are a partner with God in the creation. You, in concert with your husband, are the pinnacle of the vital process of bringing new life into the world. There is nothing to equal it, nothing to surpass it in its significance.
- *Choose correct principles*—Anchor to rock-solid principles of integrity, honor, selflessness, loyalty, service, trustworthiness, and love. Set aside any excessive allegiance to things that fade: fads, fashions, or momentary pleasures.
- *Establish priorities*—Remember that you are a wife. This must be your most important priority.

2. Foster positive actions that bring benefits to yourself, your spouse, and your children.
- *Work toward long-term results*—You can do more to bring harmony, peace, contentment, and joy into the world in your function as wife and mother than in any other role. Vision is required.
- *Learn always*—Learn continuously from the best books, through meaningful conversations with chosen role models, via positive media and Internet sources, and by taking workshops and courses, etc. Life is always changing, and wives must be ready for such dynamic lifestyles.
- *Cultivate unity of purpose and action*—The poet Homer put it this way: "The best thing in the world [is] a strong house held in serenity where man and wife agree."

3. Strengthen your relationship.
- *Foster dialogue*—Communicate your needs and feelings frankly to your husband. Remember that sometimes the male ego prefers to remain aloof and self-contained. Help your husband to communicate freely.
- *Be supportive of your husband in his occupation*—Help him enhance his career as much as possible. If you must also help earn the living, then work toward a fair sharing of domestic responsibilities. This counsel applies to both husband and wife: Repress the tendency to nag or complain, for only hard feelings come from that type of behavior.
- *Know the differences*—Recognize that men have different needs—just as you do. Understanding will go a long way toward fostering unity and cooperation.
- *Praise and honor your husband*—As you encourage him, you will grow together, and share in each other's successes.

4. Find common ground and common purpose. Have many goals in common with your spouse: health, companionship, spiritual growth, and leaving a legacy of honor and harmony for the children. Here are some of the mutually important things for husband and wife to keep in mind:

- *Fidelity in all things*—Even "harmless" flirtation with others can lead to adultery, which destroys families.
- *Loyalty*—Be loyal to and supportive of your husband.
- *Selflessness*—Think of him first, before yourself.
- *Overcoming selfishness*—Selfishness is the cause of virtually all marital discord. It is evidenced in the inability to communicate and reason together, leading to misunderstandings, unrealized expectations, and demanding behavior, among other things.
- *Communication*—Be willing to counsel together. Discuss *all* things relating to your marriage, your family, and your lives.
- *Happiness*—Channel and sublimate your efforts for the well-being and happiness of your husband.
- *Togetherness*—Do things together: dining, vacationing, fun activities, domestic chores—simply everything where possible. Take time to plan a fun vacation together.
- *Empathy*—If you practice empathy and understanding, then you will appreciate your husband. Gratitude will abound. Your attitudes toward each other will change, as will your behavior. If it's important to your husband, it should be important to you.
- *Service*—Look for ways to serve each other and your children.
- *Uniqueness*—Recognize that each of you has unique roles in your marriage. Be understanding and supportive.
- *Praise*—Genuinely praise your sweetheart. Write him love notes. Give him sweet surprises.
- *Privacy*—Give him space, for friends, hobbies, etc.
- *Affection*—Be affectionate. Children need to know that you like to show affection to your husband and accept the same from him.
- *Worship together*—Search the scriptures together. Pray together. Genuinely seek spiritual growth with your husband. Nothing will add a more lasting glow to the relationship.

ILLUSTRATIONS FOR OUR TIMES

The following illustration, related by former general Relief Society president Sister Barbara B. Smith, shows how wives can uniquely support their husbands.

A Call to Action

Something of this relationship might be seen if I relate a conversation with a friend of mine. He said, "My wife and I decided to face the front of our home with rocks. So I called around and located a place where I could get them.

"I started to get into my truck when my wife called to me and said, 'Let me go with you. I want to help you.'

"When we got to the place where the rocks were located, we found them on the top of a hill. I complained, 'That's going to be a terrible job to get those rocks down.'

"My wife said, 'I'll go up to the top of the hill and roll the rocks down to you and then you'll just have to carry them over to the truck. How does that sound?'

"I thought that was a good idea," he said. "I watched her climb to the top of the hill and disappear for a few minutes. Soon she called out, 'Here comes the first rock. Here comes another one.' Then she said, 'Oh, this rock is a beauty. I hope this one won't be too heavy for you to carry.'

"I said, 'I'll carry anything you roll down.'

"Then she said, 'Look at this rock. It has real character. Here comes my favorite.'"

He said, "She actually had me waiting anxiously for each rock." And then he said, "In this endeavor, as in many other of our projects together, she had given me not only the help I needed but a perspective that often eludes men."

I would like to see all sisters . . . acting as [such] helpmeets. (Barbara B. Smith, "A Call to Action," *Ensign,* May 1977, 90)

SUMMARY

Unfortunately, many individuals do not find fulfillment in their roles. Today's society has shifted away from proven patterns in the definition of the roles of male and female—and much goodness and satisfaction has been lost in the transition. If each spouse could realize the importance of his or her unique position, then each could find fulfillment within the role of wife or husband. If things are not right, seek counsel from the Lord. If both husband and wife exercise faith in the strength of the Lord in righteousness, things will be better. Find happiness in your companionship. The wife should find joy in the success and achievement of her husband. Likewise, the husband should find joy in the success and achievement of his wife and say, with Shakespeare (in the play *Julius Caesar*): "Render me worthy of this noble wife." Let us seek to find joy in being one in purpose, cause, and action. Let us fulfill our wedding vows with honor and covenant fidelity by being the best partner for our spouse.

WISDOM

Wisdom is the ability to make good choices based on truth. Truth based on the principles of the gospel of Jesus Christ is the truth on which we can build a foundation for making wise decisions and good choices. Those who continually make good choices are enlightened by the light of Christ and inspired by the Holy Ghost. As we live worthy of the inspiration of the Holy Ghost, we can learn wisdom, for the Holy Ghost will testify of all truth (see Moro. 10:5) and show us all things to do (see 2 Ne. 32:5).

THE SCRIPTURES TEACH US

Proverbs 2:6. *For the Lord giveth wisdom: out of his mouth cometh knowledge and understanding.*

Wisdom is a gift of the Lord through His Spirit (see 1 Cor. 12:8). The Lord has commanded us to seek the best gifts, for they allow us to bless the lives of others. When we seek for wisdom, we gain understanding of gospel principles, and we also find happiness (see Prov. 3:13). Wisdom is greater than riches because it brings so many blessings (see Prov. 8:11).

Matthew 7:24. *Therefore whosoever heareth these sayings of mine, and doeth them, I will liken him unto a wise man, which built his house upon a rock.*

Hearing and knowing is one thing, but wisdom requires action—doing things according to correct principles. We must not be just hearers of the word but should be wise doers of the word (see James 1:22). In so doing we build upon a sure foundation—our Savior Jesus Christ—and we will not fall (see Hel. 5:12).

1 Corinthians 3:19. *For the wisdom of this world is foolishness with God. For it is written, He taketh the wise in their own craftiness.*

Secular learning and things of the world are not eternal verities. They change constantly, while the truth and wisdom of God is absolute and unchanging. Let us build our lives on gospel truths, take counsel from Heavenly Father, and not lean upon our own understanding (see 2 Ne. 9:28–29).

James 1:5. *If any of you lack wisdom, let him ask of God, that giveth to all men liberally, and upbraideth not; and it shall be given him.*

In order to learn the things of God, we must seek them out. Asking is a principle with a promise. God will give answers to our prayers just like He has done with Adam, Enoch, Noah, Abraham, Moses, Joseph Smith, and all of His other prophets. As we seek wisdom, we become rich as to the things of God, qualifying for His greatest gift, eternal life (see D&C 6:7). We are His children, and He has asked us to call upon His name in humility. If we do so, we will hear and see the things of God (see D&C 136:32) and receive blessings according to our faith.

Doctrine and Covenants 88:118. *And as all have not faith, seek ye diligently and teach one another words of wisdom; yea, seek ye out of the best books words of wisdom; seek learning, even by study and also by faith.*

We should seek learning from all sources. Obviously, the scriptures are the best books, but there are other good books as well. As we lean upon the Spirit, we can discern between truth and error. The Lord counsels us that wisdom will help us overcome wickedness (see D&C 38:30). Even in our weakness, the Lord will make us wise if we follow Him (see D&C 124:1).

MODERN PROPHETS SPEAK

Bruce R. McConkie:
> That wisdom which leads to salvation comes from God by revelation. Every person on earth, in or out of the Church, can gain wisdom from the Lord, who is the source and font of all truth and righteousness. Those outside the Church who diligently seek will be led to the gospel of salvation where perfect wisdom resides; those in the Church, when they seek righteousness with all their hearts, will be led along the path of truth and revelation until they know all things and have all wisdom. (*Doctrinal New Testament Commentary,* [Salt Lake City: Bookcraft, 1965–1973], 3:246)

Marvin J. Ashton:
> As with most simple formulas, all of us must analyze our own lives and use wisdom and free agency as we apply the basic principles. Jesus said, "This is my gospel; and ye know the things that ye must do in my church; for the works which ye have seen me do that shall ye also do; for that which ye have seen me do even that shall ye do." (3 Nephi 27:21.) The doing is always more difficult than the knowing. (*Be of Good Cheer* [Salt Lake City: Deseret Book, 1987], 11)

Joseph Fielding Smith:

> Intelligence, then, is more potent than knowledge. While there is no intelligence without knowledge, there is much knowledge without intelligent application. Pure intelligence is an attribute of God which will create in the heart of man a desire to come to the perfect knowledge of truth. He will therefore seek wisdom and knowledge, that he may have power; but all his efforts to know will be put forth to obtain glory, honor, and eternal life. (*The Way to Perfection* [Salt Lake City: Genealogical Society of Utah, 1949], 230)

Gordon B. Hinckley:

> We need not look far in the world to know that "the wisdom of the wise has perished and that the understanding of the prudent has come to naught." That wisdom for which the world should seek is the wisdom which comes from God. The only understanding that will save the world is divine understanding. (*Teachings of Gordon B. Hinckley* [Salt Lake City: Deseret Book, 1997], 500)

IDEAS FOR DAILY LIVING

Here are some ideas to help us gain wisdom:

1. Seek truth and knowledge.
- *Scriptures*—Search the word of God to gain the knowledge upon which to base correct decisions.
- *Discernment*—Do not be swayed by the learning of man when it conflicts with gospel truths. Learn to distinguish between temporal and eternal truths.
- *Faith*—We learn not only by study, but by also faith (see D&C 88:118).
- *Continual learning*—Be easily entreated when it comes to following the Brethren.
- *Standards*—Once you have a set of standards on which to base your decisions, you are prepared to make good and wise choices.

2. Use your God-given reason to apply wisdom in decision making.
- *Get the facts*—A wise person collects all pertinent information and makes sure of its accuracy before making a decision. A wise person makes decisions calmly, not in haste or under duress, but in a reasoned, judicious manner.
- *Look at all the options*—Study the pros and cons of a certain decision. Make the best choice you can, and then seek confirmation.

3. Keep your mind open and your heart close to the Spirit.
- *Seek wisdom out of the best books* (see D&C 88:118)—Latter-day Saints do not have the monopoly on wisdom. Throughout the ages, the Lord has inspired good men and women, and many of these recorded their wisdom. Be discerning, but don't be afraid to immerse yourself in the wisdom of good literature.
- *The Spirit*—Listen for the witness of the Spirit as to things being true or not.
- *Be aware of your environment*—Wisdom is knowing what's going on around you, and how your choices will play into that. Recognizing the effects of your words and actions on others is a sign of wisdom.

ILLUSTRATIONS FOR OUR TIMES

Perspective is an important part of wisdom, as we see in this humorous poem by John Godfrey Saxe.

The Blind Men and the Elephant

It was six men of Indostan
To learning much inclined,
Who went to see the elephant
(Though all of them were blind),
That each by observation
Might satisfy his mind.
The First approached the elephant,
And, happening to fall
Against his broad and sturdy side,
At once began to bawl:
"God bless me! but the elephant
Is nothing but a wall!"
The Second, feeling of the tusk,
Cried: "Ho! what have we here
So very round and smooth and sharp?
To me 'tis mighty clear
This wonder of an elephant
Is very like a spear!"
The Third approached the animal,
And, happening to take
The squirming trunk within his hands,
Thus boldly up and spake:
"I see," quoth he, "the elephant
Is very like a snake!"
The Fourth reached out his eager hand,
And felt about the knee:
"What most this wondrous beast is like
Is mighty plain," quoth he;
"'Tis clear enough the elephant
Is very like a tree."
The Fifth, who chanced to touch the ear,
Said: "E'en the blindest man
Can tell what this resembles most;
Deny the fact who can,
This marvel of an elephant
Is very like a fan!"
The Sixth no sooner had begun
About the beast to grope,
Than, seizing on the swinging tail
That fell within his scope,
"I see," quoth he, "the elephant
Is very like a rope!"
And so these men of Indostan
Disputed loud and long,
Each in his own opinion

Exceeding stiff and strong,
Though each was partly in the right,
And all were in the wrong!
So, oft in theologic wars
The disputants, I ween,
Rail on in utter ignorance
Of what each other mean,
And prate about an elephant
Not one of them has seen!
(John Godfrey Saxe in *Best Loved Poems of the LDS People,* Jay A. Parry, Jack M. Lyon, and Linda
Ririe Gundry eds. [Salt Lake City: Deseret Book, 1997], 196–98)

SUMMARY

Each of us can develop wisdom by gaining knowledge based on truth and exercising our judgment based on sound principles. When we follow the light of Christ and the Holy Spirit, we will have the power to make wise decisions. Many great people in the past, regardless of the situations facing them, made wise choices that made a difference in their lives and in the lives of many of others. The consequences of wise decisions enrich our lives every day.

WORD OF WISDOM

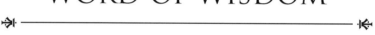

The Word of Wisdom, Doctrine and Covenants Section 89, is a principle with a promise—a law with blessings predicated on our obedience. It is primarily concerned with dietary matters—what we should or should not eat or drink—as well as the use of tobacco. The law also extends logically to the use of harmful and addictive drugs (see Howard W. Hunter, "Let Lives Reflect the Gospel," *Church News,* December 17, 1994). There are other important precepts to follow in regard to good health that are not included in the Word of Wisdom. For example, in the Word of Wisdom, the Lord does not specifically mention dietary extremes, but He does counsel that we are to do things "with prudence and thanksgiving" (v. 11). With all the extremes in diet and "health-promoting" trends, it is reassuring that the Lord has given us a tried and proven health plan.

THE SCRIPTURES TEACH US

Romans 14:17. *For the kingdom of God is not meat and drink; but righteousness, and peace, and joy in the Holy Ghost.*

The Mosaic law, as recorded in Leviticus, lists many dietary restrictions. In this admonition to the Roman Saints, however, Paul teaches that there is more to religion and spirituality than simply what you eat and drink. The Lord suggested the same thing in the New Testament (see Mark 7:18–19). We must be careful that we don't become extremists in regard to the Word of Wisdom.

1 Corinthians 3:17. *If any man defile the temple of God, him shall God destroy; for the temple of God is holy, which temple ye are.*

We are temples of God where His Spirit may dwell. Therefore, we should seek to make our bodies as pure and clean as possible. The Lord has told us how to do this in His Word of Wisdom.

Doctrine and Covenants 89:4. *Behold, verily, thus saith the Lord unto you: In consequence of evils and designs which do and will exist in the hearts of conspiring men in the last days, I have warned you, and forewarn you, by giving unto you this word of wisdom by revelation.*

In our day, conspiring individuals have deceived the public in regard to tobacco. Such purveyors are now paying billions of dollars in damages. However, they can never replace the lives ruined or cut short by their heinous acts of greed. Likewise, many harmful substances are offered to us as pleasurable pastimes. The Lord knew the consequences of partaking of these harmful things, and He forewarned us in the Word of Wisdom.

Doctrine and Covenants 89:7–9. *And, again, strong drinks are not for the belly, but for the washing of your bodies. And again, tobacco is not for the body, neither for the belly, and is not good for man, but is an herb for bruises and all sick cattle, to be used with judgment and skill. And again, hot drinks are not for the body or belly.*

Alcohol and hot drinks (tea and coffee) are addictive and cause nothing but harm to our bodies. Vaughn J. Featherstone has reminded us: "The leaders of the Church have advised, and we do now specifically advise, against use of any drink containing harmful habit-forming drugs" (in Conference Report, April 1975, 102). We should seek to be free from dependence on anything that is harmful to the body.

Doctrine and Covenants 89:12–13. *Yea, flesh also of beasts and of the fowls of the air, I, the Lord, have ordained for the use of man with thanksgiving; nevertheless they are to be used sparingly; And it is pleasing unto me that they should not be used, only in times of winter, or of cold, or famine.*

Meat is ordained of God for the use of man and is beneficial to us if used in moderation. However, as recent medical research attests, too much meat is detrimental to our health. Let us use prudence and wisdom, not extreme measures, in regard to dietary habits.

Doctrine and Covenants 89:18–21. *And all saints who remember to keep and do these sayings, walking in obedience to the commandments, shall receive health in their navel and marrow to their bones; And shall find wisdom and great treasures of knowledge, even hidden treasures; And shall run and not be weary, and shall walk and not faint. And I, the Lord, give unto them a promise, that the destroying angel shall pass by them, as the children of Israel, and not slay them. Amen.*

The blessings of keeping the Word of Wisdom are clear: health, long life, wisdom and hidden knowledge, strength and stamina, and protection from many life-threatening illnesses. We can claim these blessings through simple obedience.

MODERN PROPHETS SPEAK

Joseph Smith:
> No official member in this Church is worthy to hold an office, after having the Word of Wisdom properly taught him, and he, the official member, neglecting to comply with or obey it. (*History of the Church,* 2:35)

Gordon B. Hinckley:

> One appreciates the incomparable wisdom of the Lord who in 1833 in a rural town on the frontier of America spoke these simple and encompassing words: " . . . tobacco . . . is not good for man, . . ." (D&C 89:8.)
>
> He did not say that one would get lung cancer, develop heart or respiratory problems if he smoked. He did not produce mountainous statistics or recite case histories. He simply declared that " . . . tobacco . . . is not good for man, . . ."
>
> That declaration was given as "a principle with promise," (V. 3.)
>
> It was given as a warning and a forewarning, "in consequence of evils and designs which do and will exist in the hearts of conspiring men in the last days, . . ." (V. 4.) How aptly descriptive these words are in light of what we today observe. . . .
>
> Can there be any doubt that it is a Word of Wisdom when great forces, with millions of dollars at their command and some of the cleverest minds in the art of advertising, promote that which sober men of science also now say "is not good for man"?
>
> One cannot read the testimony without recognizing that true freedom lies in obedience to the counsels of God. (*Teachings of Gordon B. Hinckley* [Salt Lake City: Deseret Book, 1997], 699–700)

Joseph F. Smith:

> Now, I do wish with all my heart—not because I say it, but because it is written in the word of the Lord—that you would give heed to this Word of Wisdom. It was given unto us "not by commandment"; but by the word of President Brigham Young, it was made a commandment unto the Saints. It is written here for our guidance, for our happiness and advancement in every principle that pertains to the kingdom of God, in time and throughout eternity, and I pray you to observe it. It will do you good; it will ennoble your souls; it will free your thoughts and your hearts from the spirit of destruction; it will make you feel like God, who sustains even the sparrow, that it does not fall to the ground without his notice; it will bring you nearer to the similitude of the Son of God, the Savior of the world, who healed the sick, who made the lame to leap for joy, who restored hearing to the deaf and sight to the blind, who distributed peace, joy, and comfort to all with whom he came in contact, and who cured and destroyed nothing, save it was the barren fig tree, and that was to show forth his power more than anything else. (*Gospel Doctrine: Selections from the Sermons and Writings of Joseph F. Smith*, comp. John A. Widtsoe [Salt Lake City: Deseret Book, 1939], 365)

The First Presidency:

> That in these dire days, we may, each in his own place, enjoy the abundant physical blessings of the righteous life, we call upon all true Latter-day Saints, in or out of office, to keep this law of health,—completely to give up drink, to quit using tobacco, which all too often leads to drink, to abandon hot drinks and the use of harmful drugs, and otherwise to observe the Word of Wisdom. We urge the Saints to quit trifling with this law and so to live it that we may claim its promises. (*Messages of the First Presidency of The Church of Jesus Christ of Latter-day Saints*, 6 vols., comp. James R. Clark (Salt Lake City: Bookcraft, 1965–75), 6:173)

IDEAS FOR DAILY LIVING

Here are some ideas to help us more faithfully keep the Word of Wisdom:

1. Set goals and make plans.

- *Menu planning*—Organize your meals to include the foods recommended and specified in the Word of Wisdom. Remember that extreme measures are not part of the Lord's law of health.
- *Commitment*—Make a commitment to abstain from alcohol, tobacco, hot drinks (tea and coffee), other harmful drinks, and illegal drugs.
- *Counsel*—If you struggle with the Word of Wisdom, seek counsel from your Church leaders, ask for a blessing, seek medical help, and do everything within your power to overcome the habit.

2. Consider all the blessings.

- *Health*—As you follow the Word of Wisdom, you will be healthier in every respect: physically, mentally (a clear mind), emotionally (self-control), and spiritually (blessings of obedience).
- *Clean temples (you are a temple)*—Physical purity enables one to receive the inspiration of the Lord.
- *Treasures*—"And shall find wisdom and great treasures of knowledge, even hidden treasures" (D&C 89:19–20).
- *Savings*—By avoiding alcohol, tobacco, and similar harmful substances, you can have significant monetary savings over a lifetime.
- *Clarity of thought and judgment*—You are in control of yourself when not under the influence of alcohol and other harmful drugs. In addition, when your body is healthy, you are less stressed and better able to function in your thinking.
- *Being a self-starter*—You are not dependent on *any* harmful thing for your strength or motivation.
- *Temple*—Keeping the Word of Wisdom is a requirement for a temple recommend.

ILLUSTRATIONS FOR OUR TIMES

The following personal story illustrates an additional blessing that came from following the Word of Wisdom—respect for adhering to one's beliefs.

I Brewed It Myself

As a graduate student at the Johns Hopkins University many years ago, I learned that keeping the honor of God and the honor of the world separate is much less challenging if you have wise allies looking out for you. My senior faculty advisor, Dr. Harold Jantz, world-renowned in his discipline, was also a careful student of human affairs and human values. He regularly convened seminars in his home, where he served the graduate students coffee and tea. At my first such event, he served all of my colleagues their coffee or tea, and then turned to me and handed me a cup of herbal tea. "It's rose-hips," he said with a friendly twinkle in his eyes. "I brewed it myself from my rose plants. I know you don't drink coffee or regular tea, so this is for you." His generosity was matched only by his magnanimous respect for my values and standards. Thereafter, at each such occasion, he hospitably prepared and served me a portion of delicious and nutritious rose-hips tea. With such a hospitable host and mentor, I couldn't have compromised my values—even if I had wanted to! It was a small thing, but it had great implications. Not only was my obedience at stake, but others' judgments of the Church. Members of the Church never know how many eyes are watching, nor how many hearts can be influenced for good when they strive in all diligence to keep the commandments.

—Richard J. Allen

SUMMARY

All counsel from the Lord is a commandment to the righteous (see Jacob 4:10). Keeping the Word of Wisdom is a requirement if we desire to serve in the temple. Furthermore, the prophets have made it clear that it is a commandment for us to obey the Word of Wisdom. With the help of the Lord, we can keep the Word of Wisdom. He will provide a way for us if we have the desire, exercise our faith, and work diligently to follow His law of health (see 1 Ne. 3:7; 17:2–3; Alma 26:11–12; Ether 12:27; Moro. 7:33).

WORK

Work is the price of success, and it is essential in the building of character. Work protects us from the consequences of idleness, and it is the standard of excellence in every field. From the farmers of yesterday to the superstar athletes of today, the work ethic is the difference between the success and failure. Great people and super performers understand the value of working hard and working smart.

In the early years of this country, most people lived in rural farming communities. Work was simply a part of life—a large part. With our modern cities and affluence, it seems as though many youth today do not enjoy the blessing of work in their lives. What can be done to address this problem? It is up to parents and to leaders of the Church, community, and nation to show a better example.

THE SCRIPTURES TEACH US

Genesis 3:18–19. *Thorns also and thistles shall it bring forth to thee; and thou shalt eat the herb of the field; In the sweat of thy face shalt thou eat bread, till thou return unto the ground; for out of it wast thou taken: for dust thou art, and unto dust shalt thou return.*

From the very beginning, work was set forth by the Lord as a remedy for sin. The Lord commanded Adam to work (see Moses 5:1) for his own benefit and growth.

2 Nephi 5:17. *And it came to pass that I, Nephi, did cause my people to be industrious, and to labor with their hands.*

Physical labor is good for us. When we are industrious, we are busy, diligent, steady, and tireless. These attributes serve us well in all facets of life. Idleness, a tool of the devil, will not be a curse to anyone that is industrious.

Doctrine and Covenants 58:27. *Verily I say, men should be anxiously engaged in a good cause, and do many things of their own free will, and bring to pass much righteousness.*

The Lord is pleased with the willing worker—one who does not require continual prodding. A work ethic learned early can carry us throughout our lives. In raising children, it is paramount to teach them the value of work.

Doctrine and Covenants 75:29. *Let every man be diligent in all things. And the idler shall not have place in the church, except he repent and mend his ways.*

The Lord has counseled us clearly about our work ethic: We must be diligent (work hard) in all things. There will never be a substitute for work. Many of our blessings are predicated on the principle of work.

MODERN PROPHETS SPEAK

David B. Haight:
> They (the early saints) had a majestic dream of great things and lofty ideals: of homes and gardens, temples and meetinghouses, schools and universities. It would take work—hard work—and everyone's best efforts to make it happen. They became experienced colonizers and benefactors to our nation and to humanity. Many of us are a product of that early, inspired colonization—its teachings and blessings of the value of hard work coupled with desire and faith for a better way of life. (*A Light unto the World* [Salt Lake City: Deseret Book, 1997], 138)

Ezra Taft Benson:
> Work hard educationally and in your vocation. Put your trust in the Lord, have faith, and it will work out. The Lord never gives a commandment without providing the means to accomplish it. (See 1 Ne. 3:7.) (*Come, Listen to a Prophet's Voice* [Salt Lake City: Deseret Book, 1990], 53)

> One of the greatest secrets of missionary work is *work*. If a missionary works, he will get the Spirit; if he gets the Spirit, he will teach by the Spirit; if he teaches by the Spirit, he will touch the hearts of the people, and he will be happy. Then there will be no homesickness nor worrying about families, for all time and talents and interests are centered on the work of the ministry. Work, work, work—there is no satisfactory substitute, especially in missionary work. (*Come unto Christ* [Salt Lake City: Deseret Book, 1983], 95)

Joseph B. Wirthlin:
> The foundation of self-reliance is hard work. Parents should teach their children that work is the prerequisite to achievement and success in every worthwhile endeavor. Children of legal age should secure productive employment and begin to move away from dependence on parents. None of us should expect others to provide for us anything that we can provide for ourselves. (*Finding Peace in Our Lives* [Salt Lake City: Deseret Book, 1995], 44)

IDEAS FOR DAILY LIVING

Here are five things to consider to improve your work ethic and to help others learn to work:

1. How you view your work is just as important for the outcome as your performance.
- *See work as a natural law*—Look at work as a key part of the natural law of consequences. If you desire certain outcomes, rewards, and benefits, then you must work to obtain them. In this way, work is not enslaving, but liberating, for it is the doorway to the freedoms you desire.
- *See work as something you do one day at a time*—Don't work hard all your life—just *today*, and *each* day. Keep your eye on the goal, but face your tasks one day at a time.
- *See work as the fulcrum of self-confidence*—The inner spirit always feels good after a good, hard day of work.

- *See yourself as the "boss"*—Mentally fire your boss and hire another one—*you*. Reframe your work situation so that you are working for yourself. No matter who is above you in the chain of command, work for yourself. Build quality into your work, because it is *your* work.

2. Work smart, as well as hard.

- *Work toward meaningful goals*—Work smart at those things that will bring you closer to your goals each day. Henry David Thoreau acknowledged the need for meaningfulness when he said, "It is not enough to be busy . . . the question is: what are we busy about?"
- *Know your place of importance*—Understand how you fit in with the overall vision. People work better when they understand their role in a project.
- *Focus on effectiveness and productivity*—Understand the parameters of your work so you will be not only efficient, but effective. As part of your work ethic, always make your best effort at everything you do.
- *Concentrate*—When working diligently, your mind is focused productively on the task, which is crucial for optimum performance.

3. Choose to do what you love, and love what you do.

- *Make wise career decisions*—Seek a career that you find stimulating and rewarding—or make it so by bringing the right attitude to the workplace. "Blessed is he who has found his work; let him ask no other blessedness. He has a work, a life purpose; he has found it and will follow it," observed Thomas Carlyle.
- *Put joy to work*—Transform any unpleasant but necessary task by investing joy in it. No matter what the job—washing dishes, mopping floors, changing diapers, doing routine tasks for long hours—you can radiate joy to others in spite of the challenging circumstances.

4. Govern your life with balance.

- *Have fun*—Set a good example for your family by working hard, but put balance in your life so that you also have fun with them and enjoy life. The Lord Himself commands us to rest from our work at times (see Ex. 20:8–9).
- *Have a diversified "work portfolio"*—Spread your work ethic evenly over all the important facets of your life: personal development, career, family, community service, and spiritual development.
- *Avoid extremes*—Be careful not to be obsessed with work. Some people actually become so attached to their work that all other things in life are put on hold, and this is not wise.

5. Teach others the principles of work.

- *Bless lives by teaching correct principles*—Teach your family that desirable rewards require considerable effort. Don't give them the world; rather, show them how to earn it.
- *Create meaningful opportunities*—Give children opportunities to work. It is your responsibility to help them learn to work.
- *Praise often*—People always work better with praise and appreciation.

ILLUSTRATIONS FOR OUR TIMES

The following illustration describes how a work ethic instilled at a young age can be a blessing throughout life.

A Treasure in the Weeds

The bus ride home was about eight miles. I was a young fifth-grader in Central Elementary School. I was always excited to tell my mother about the day at school. I would jump off the bus and run the 100 yards-plus up the farm road to the house. My mother would be waiting. She gave me homemade bread, butter, jam, and a big glass of milk for my after-school treat. I would tell her about my school day and then do my chores. Then I would hope to play a while before dark. But invariably my father would say—or at least it seemed invariably so—"Ed, go pull burdock." Burdock was a large leafy plant with "burs" that would stick to your clothes. There were thousands of these plants growing wild on our farm. I could never pull all the weeds. I didn't like to weed. I hate to weed to this day—and I'm a senior citizen. So I would try to run and play before my Dad could find me. It was to no avail. He always found me, and he said, "Go pull burdock, Ed." So I did. Farm life was great except it always seemed like we had to work.

We eventually moved from the farm. My father passed away almost two years later. Living in the city was different, but there was still work—though fortunately not so many weeds. My angel mother raised our family all alone. And she was the perfect mother in every way. Life went on. I got married. One day when I was thinking about life and the growth that I had experienced, I came to a great realization: I owed to my father much of my success in life—whether on the athletic field, in schoolwork, or in life's experiences. It was the ability to work hard, never to give up, and to finish the job—now—that had made the difference in my life. I learned to work as a young boy. It was as simple as the order to pull burdock, but it truly made all the difference. In today's world, the ethic of work has almost become a forgotten virtue for the youth. Idleness will eventually destroy the individual, while work will bring out the virtue of character and will result in success in life.

—Ed J. Pinegar

SUMMARY

Thomas Jefferson observed: "I'm a great believer in luck, and I find that the harder I work the more I have of it." The ethic of work truly needs to be re-established in our society, where the problem of idleness is manifest all around us. The blessings of work must become better understood by all, especially our youth. Those who learn the work ethic early tend to be outstanding students and good employees. The great welfare program of the Church is centered on re-enthroning the principle of work and self-sufficiency among the Saints. Work is key to success and accomplishment in all human endeavor, and "the laborer is worthy of his hire" (D&C 31:5; 84:79; 106:3; Luke 10:7). Our Savior counsels: "Verily I say, men should be anxiously engaged in a good cause, and do many things of their own free will, and bring to pass much righteousness; . . . And inasmuch as men do good they shall in nowise lose their reward" (D&C 58:27–28).

WORSHIP

To worship God is to show Him reverence, honor, devotion, and love. True worship is more than just a feeling or attitude—it is accompanied by an offering of self and service. Unfortunately, we are often inclined to worship things of the world rather than our Heavenly Father and our Savior. In caring more about things than we do about God, we eventually forget God, the source of life and all our blessings. The commandments are clear: "Ye cannot serve God and mammon" (Matt. 6:24); "Thou shalt have no other gods before me" (Ex. 20:3); "Worship God, in whatsoever place ye may be in, in spirit and in truth" (Alma 34:38). In another clear example, we read: "Master, which is the great commandment in the law? Jesus said unto him, Thou shalt love the Lord thy God with all thy heart, and with all thy soul, and with all thy mind. This is the first and great commandment" (Matt. 22:36–38). In short, we are to worship God with our attention single to His glory (see D&C 82:19; 88:67).

THE SCRIPTURES TEACH US

Exodus 20:3–5, 7–8. *Thou shalt have no other gods before me. Thou shalt not make unto thee any graven image, or any likeness of any thing that is in heaven above, or that is in the earth beneath, or that is in the water under the earth: Thou shalt not bow down thyself to them, nor serve them. . . . Thou shalt not take the name of the Lord thy God in vain; for the Lord will not hold him guiltless that taketh his name in vain. Remember the sabbath day, to keep it holy.*

The Ten Commandments have never been revoked or changed, and they are still in effect. So important is it to our Heavenly Father that we honor Him and acknowledge our relationship to Him that the first four of His commands have to do with worshipping Him. The first commandment, "Thou shalt have no other gods before me," means that no other thing or entity should be put ahead of, or in place of, our Heavenly Father. We are to live a life focused upon our Heavenly Father and His Son Jesus Christ, keeping the commandments they have given us.

John 4:23–24. *But the hour cometh, and now is, when the true worshippers shall worship the Father in spirit and in truth: for the Father seeketh such to worship him. God is a Spirit: and they that worship him must worship him in spirit and in truth.*

We should worship God the Father at all times, not just when we are in church or in the temple. When we truly worship Him, we acknowledge and keep His laws and commandments, and we acknowledge His Son and the glorious Atonement.

2 Nephi 9:37. *Yea, wo unto those that worship idols, for the devil of all devils delighteth in them.*

Anything other than God, His Church, and His law is of the world, whether it be an image or a material thing such as position, title, station, power, or money. All worldly things are false gods. It is so easy to become obsessed with material things that we must always be on guard and not forget our God due to the ease of the way (see Hel. 12:2–3).

2 Nephi 25:29. *And now behold, I say unto you that the right way is to believe in Christ, and deny him not; and Christ is the Holy One of Israel; wherefore ye must bow down before him, and worship him with all your might, mind, and strength, and your whole soul; and if ye do this ye shall in nowise be cast out.*

We worship our Savior as well as God the Father. This does not take away from our complete adoration for, and worship of, our Heavenly Father, for they are one in purpose. This scriptural passage helps us realize the important role of Jesus Christ—Jehovah—the God of the Old Testament and the Savior of the world.

Alma 32:9–11. *Behold thy brother hath said, What shall we do?—for we are cast out of our synagogues, that we cannot worship our God. Behold I say unto you, do ye suppose that ye cannot worship God save it be in your synagogues only? And moreover, I would ask, do ye suppose that ye must not worship God only once in a week?*

Alma teaches a profound truth by explaining that we should worship God at all times and not just in church or on the Sabbath day. Daily worship of Heavenly Father consists of prayer, scripture study, pondering and meditating, and, above all, living the gospel of Jesus Christ by seeking to bless our fellowmen.

Alma 33:3. *Do ye remember to have read what Zenos, the prophet of old, has said concerning prayer or worship?*

Prayer is the most personal form of worship. In prayer, we acknowledge our relationship with Heavenly Father—that we are His children. The phrase, "We ask Thee" implies that we recognize our total dependence upon Him. When we submit ourselves in humble prayer to our God, we worship Him, seeking to do His will and keep His commandments.

Alma 34:38. *That ye contend no more against the Holy Ghost, but that ye receive it, and take upon you the name of Christ; that ye humble yourselves even to the dust, and worship God, in whatsoever place ye may be in, in spirit and in truth; and that ye live in thanksgiving daily, for the many mercies and blessings which he doth bestow upon you.*

We should follow Amulek's advice to the Zoramites to live daily in thanksgiving to our God. Gratitude is a transcendent principle in worshipping God, for He truly gives us everything.

MODERN PROPHETS SPEAK

Gordon B. Hinckley:
> Strange as it seems, we alone, among all the great organizations that worship God, have a true description and a true definition of him. The experience of Joseph Smith in a few moments in the grove on a spring day in 1820, brought more light and knowledge and understanding of the personality and reality and substance of God and his Beloved Son than men had arrived at during centuries of speculation. (*Teachings of Gordon B. Hinckley* [Salt Lake City: Deseret Book, 1997], 236)

Neal A. Maxwell:
> Not only are we urged to worship God but, astoundingly, we are instructed to become like Him! (Matthew 5:48; 3 Nephi 12:48; 27:27.) (*Meek and Lowly* [Salt Lake City: Deseret Book, 1987], ix)

> As we worship God with all of our mind, soul, and strength we move from appreciation to adoration and on to emulation. Our minds are involved in studying and pondering. Our souls are extended in service. Finally we reach a consecration of all things. (*Men and Women of Christ* [Salt Lake City: Bookcraft, 1991], 102)

IDEAS FOR DAILY LIVING

Here are eight suggestions for making our worship more meaningful:

1. Seek to understand Deity. We should make knowing and worshiping God one of our highest goals. The word "worship" comes from two Old English words, *weorth* (worth) and *-scipe* (-ship). The obvious implication is that we respond with a worshipful attitude when considering something of immense worth. Who could be of more worth to us than the Being who created the universe, gave us life, sustains us from moment to moment, and laid the foundation for our unlimited progress based on our choices?

2. Cultivate a spirit of reverence. Once we gain a knowledge of the nature and character of God, we will have a desire to worship Him and hold Him in great reverence. We should recognize our utter dependence upon Deity—our nothingness when compared with Him, and yet our divine destiny as children of God, created in His image, to be like Him. Humility and reverence are not groveling; they are a quiet, worshipful attitude of thanksgiving for blessings received, and a sincere commitment to be more like the Creator.

3. Worship more devoutly within the family. With gratitude and reverence for God taking root in our souls, our attitude toward Him and His children will change. We will want to obey Him and we will want to bless His children. Find common purpose with loved ones. There is no more fulfilling context for family life than a mutual appreciation for moral good, togetherness, health and vitality, gratitude for blessings, and sincere worship. "Worshipping together generates worth, leverages goodness, and magnifies the light of love" (Anonymous).

4. Expand worship into everyday behavior. With an attitude of love towards God, we will change our everyday behavior. We will want to keep His commandments, and we will want to live a righteous and moral life. An important preparation for authentic worship is to cleanse oneself of the cankerous malaise of hate, envy, jealousy, holding grudges, and designing ill against one's fellow beings.

5. Learn to pray. As we proceed along this worshipful path, we will have a desire to communicate with God, to pray more frequently. Prayer is the purest form of worship. Listen to the Spirit's promptings to pray always.

6. Seek after spiritual things. In our prayers, we should seek to know God's will and pray for strength to do it. We can also seek for wisdom, comfort, assistance, the easing of our burdens, and a myriad of other blessings.

7. Make enduring gratitude a founding principle in your life. When we truly worship God, we will thank Him for *all* things. In the wonderful book entitled *The Hiding Place*, Corrie Ten Boom expresses gratitude even for fleas, for fleas became a protector for her and others against Nazi guards.

8. Sense your own divine nature. As we communicate with God through prayer, we will realize more fully that He is our Father and we are His children. If we truly worship God, we will follow His direction and enjoy life here and hereafter. Thomas Carlyle said that "Worship is transcendent wonder."

ILLUSTRATIONS FOR OUR TIMES

Using a personal story, S. Michael Wilcox explains how true worship is imitation and how we can be lifted by the Lord as we worship Him.

True Worship

> We must learn what it means to truly worship God. My six-year-old son taught me the meaning of worship one day while I was preparing a lesson. He was playing when he noticed that I was

underlining my scriptures. He dropped his toys, ran into his room, and returned with his own copies of the scriptures. He lay beside me on the bed, duplicating my exact position, and opened his scriptures.

During the next half hour I was aware that he was underlining with my colored pencils. When I looked up, he showed me his work. Somehow he had found the page I was working on. There in his own book was an exact replica of my own work. He had highlighted the same words in the same colors. My arrows, lines, and numbers were there. He had even duplicated my marginal notes until his large handwriting forced him to stop. Apologetically and almost in tears, he said: "My lines aren't straight like yours."

This small incident helped me see a greater principle: true worship is imitation. It happens when we drop our worldly toys, study deeply the Savior's life, and try to imitate the tiniest details of his character. In doing so, we also imitate the Father. Our lives are not sin-free as his, but the Atonement's power is sufficient if our love and effort are sincere and deep. The eventual result of our worship will be godhood, not to mention a happier, more stable society here and now.

Becoming like God demands effort and sacrifice, but the Lord promises his constant help. To ancient Israel he said: "Hearken unto me, O house of Jacob, and all the remnant of the house of Israel, which are borne by me from the belly, which are carried from the womb:

"And even to your old age I am he; and even to hoar hairs will I carry you: I have made, and I will bear; even I will carry, and will deliver you.

"To whom will ye liken me, and make me equal, and compare me, that we may be like?" (Isa. 46:3–5.)

We can worship the gods of the world and bear them like a burden, or we can be lifted and carried by the Lord from birth to the grave. (S. Michael Wilcox, "No Other Gods before Me," *Ensign,* January 1994, 22)

SUMMARY

God-fearing people—those who show reverence, those who worship their God—live with hope. Life has more meaning for those who trust in God and who make Christlike behavior their standard. Because earth life is a proving ground prior to immortality, and because there is opposition in all things, we must use our moral agency to make choices. These choices can affect all mankind for good or ill, and we will be accountable to God for our actions. Our time on earth is the time to prepare to meet our God and to learn to worship and obey Him.

ZION

The Lord calls His people Zion. Specifically, He called Enoch's city Zion because the Saints were righteous, were of one heart and mind, and had no poor among them (see Moses 7:18). To be a Zion people we must be pure in heart (see D&C 97:21). Our affections, our decisions, and the very center of our being are said to be in our heart, for as a man "thinketh in his heart, so is he" (Prov. 23:7). A broken heart and a contrite spirit is our offering to the Lord that makes the Atonement efficacious in our lives and enables us to become pure in heart. As we treat the subject of Zion, we will deal primarily with Zion as a people rather than a place. Our goal as a Church and as a community of Saints should be to become a Zion people—pure in heart. We should seek to bring forth and build up the cause of Zion all the days of our lives.

THE SCRIPTURES TEACH US

1 Nephi 13:37. *And blessed are they who shall seek to bring forth my Zion at that day, for they shall have the gift and the power of the Holy Ghost; and if they endure unto the end they shall be lifted up at the last day, and shall be saved in the everlasting kingdom of the Lamb.*

When we help others come unto Christ and receive the blessings of exaltation, we are working for the cause of Zion. As we do this, we are blessed with the Holy Ghost, who will show us all things we need to do (see 2 Ne. 32:5). We should commit to endure to the end so that we and our brothers and sisters can enjoy all the blessings our Heavenly Father has in store for us.

2 Nephi 26:31. *But the laborer in Zion shall labor for Zion; for if they labor for money they shall perish.*

Church service is a labor of love that we do because we love God, our Savior, and our fellowmen. We seek the glory of God rather than riches and glory of man. When we seek to bring forth the cause of Zion, we will be made rich, for we shall have eternal life (see D&C 6:6–7).

3 Nephi 12:8. *And blessed are all the pure in heart, for they shall see God.*

Zion is composed of the pure in heart. Purity of heart indicates that our intentions and behavior, as well as our affections towards God, reflect an obedient and righteous spirit. When we have a change of heart, we become pure and receive the blessings of the Spirit, with the promise of someday being in the presence of God.

Doctrine and Covenants 97:21. *Therefore, verily, thus saith the Lord, let Zion rejoice, for this is Zion—the pure in heart; therefore, let Zion rejoice, while all the wicked shall mourn.*

We create a Zion for ourselves when we are pure in heart. When we, as a group of Saints, are pure in heart, we create a Zion community. This is what the Lord wants—to bring forth a Zion people, His people, reflecting purity and righteousness.

Doctrine and Covenants 105:5. *And Zion cannot be built up unless it is by the principles of the law of the celestial kingdom; otherwise I cannot receive her unto myself.*

The Saints of Zion, the pure in heart, understand and practice the law of the celestial kingdom. The Sermon on the Mount (in Jerusalem) and the Sermon at the Temple (in Bountiful during the visit of the resurrected Savior) contain the celestial law. These are the principles and commandments that will help us, through the Atonement, to become perfected and to become like our Savior Jesus Christ and our Heavenly Father (see 3 Ne. 12:48). It is imperative to spiritual perfection that we understand and live the principles and commandments of our Savior.

MODERN PROPHETS SPEAK

Ezra Taft Benson:

Only a Zion people can bring in a Zion society. And as the Zion people increase, so we will be able to incorporate more of the principles of Zion until we have a people prepared to receive the Lord. (*The Teachings of Ezra Taft Benson* [Salt Lake City: Bookcraft, 1988], 123–24)

Gordon B. Hinckley:

If we are to build that Zion of which the prophets have spoken and of which the Lord has given mighty promise, we must set aside our consuming selfishness. We must rise above our love for comfort and ease, and in the very process of effort and struggle, even in our extremity, we shall become better acquainted with our God. . . .

Our forebears dreamed of Zion. "Come to Zion," they said. "Even if you have to walk all the way. Come to Zion. Leave Babylon and gather to the mountains of Ephraim." No one can read the words of Brigham Young, John Taylor, or Wilford Woodruff without knowing that they thought of these mountain valleys as a great gathering place for people of one heart and one mind and one faith, a place where the mountain of the Lord's house should be established in the tops of the mountains and where all nations would flow unto it. (*Teachings of Gordon B. Hinckley* [Salt Lake City: Deseret Book, 1997], 725–26)

John Taylor:

When Zion descends from above, Zion will also ascend from beneath, and be prepared to associate with those from above. The people will be so perfected and purified, ennobled, exalted, and dignified in their feelings and so truly humble and most worthy, virtuous and intelligent that they will be fit, when caught up, to associate with that Zion that shall come down from God out of heaven. (As quoted in *Doctrines of the Book of Mormon: 1991 Sperry Symposium on the Book of Mormon* [Salt Lake City: Deseret Book, 1992], 76)

Joseph F. Smith:

This should be the condition of the people of Zion. Every individual should be in a position to add something to the wealth of the whole. Everyone should be increasing, improving, and advancing in some way, and accomplishing something for his or her good and for the good of the whole. (Conference Report, October 1898, 23)

IDEAS FOR DAILY LIVING

Here are some doctrines and principles to help us understand how to become a Zion people:

1. Acquire the attributes of a pure heart.
- *Love*—Motives should be founded on love for others rather than selfish concerns.
- *Desires*—Desires should be to serve and build up our fellowmen.
- *Thoughts*—Thoughts should be upon wholesome and righteous ideas. Remember that thoughts dwelled upon become desires, which, if encouraged, result in action.
- *Attitudes*—Attitudes should be positive and full of hope.
- *Repentance*—Repentance is crucial to becoming pure in heart. Repentance requires a broken heart and a contrite spirit so that our hearts can be made pure through the Savior's Atonement. As we repent, the Holy Ghost sanctifies us and we become clean and pure.

- *Humility*—When we are humble, we recognize our dependence upon our Savior and our Heavenly Father. Humility—being submissive and easily entreated—allows our hearts to become soft and pure.

2. Learn that Zion people seek to bring forth the cause of Zion.

- *The cause of Zion*—Zion's cause is to build up the kingdom of God and preach the gospel to every nation, kindred, tongue, and people.
- *A personal quest*—Each individual working toward Zion should have a personal quest to become pure in heart.
- *The example of the Redeemer*—All true Saints of Zion attempt to live a Christlike life by serving their fellowmen and helping them come unto Christ.
- *Blessing others*—Everyone should seek personal improvement and by so doing bless those around them.

3. Create a Zion family as the basic unit for a Zion society.

- *Teach your family the concept of Zion*—Teach your children to become pure in heart and to help others to do likewise.
- *The celestial law*—Help your children understand the celestial law as set forth in the teachings of our Savior.
- *Example*—Set an example for your family of one possessed with a pure heart, both in motives and actions.
- *Missionary spirit*—As individuals and as families, be missionary-minded for the living and the dead.
- *Unity*—Seek to be "one" as a family. Unity brings peace and the Spirit to the family.

4. Receive the blessings of a Zion people.

- *Eternal life*—If we become a Zion people, we shall receive the blessings of eternal life (see D&C 6:7).
- *Zion fellowship*—When Zion comes down from above, we—if we are a Zion people—will be righteous and worthy of their association (see John Taylor, in *Journal of Discourses* [London: Latter-day Saints' Book Depot, 1854–86], 10:147).
- *Happiness*—As a Zion people, we will be happy, for we will have the love of God in our hearts. There will be no envyings, strifes, tumults, whoredoms, lyings, murders, or any manner of lasciviousness (see 4 Ne. 1:15–16). "Prophets of God have been concerned continuously with the establishment of a righteous people of Zion, a social condition among men where justice, mercy, peace, and good will may prevail" (Lowell L. Bennion, *The Best of Lowell L. Bennion: Selected Writings 1928–1988,* ed. Eugene England [Salt Lake City: Deseret Book, 1988], 187).

ILLUSTRATIONS FOR OUR TIMES

Heidi S. Swinton uses the examples of various pioneers to demonstrate the faith of those seeking to establish Zion.

Come to Zion

"Come to Zion" was the gathering call to the Saints in the early days of the Church. And come they did, from England and neighboring European nations, from Nauvoo and Winter Quarters. Some crossed oceans, most journeyed across the plains, and they settled in the Salt Lake Valley and a host of other communities throughout the sprawling territory of Deseret. That pioneer spirit—their belief in the restoration of the gospel of Jesus Christ and their desire to live it in its fulness—is what brought them together. This gathering shaped a spiritual heritage that is being extended by pioneers around the world today.

Modern-day pioneers do not travel to Zion by wagon trains and ox teams, or endure starvation and bitter weather on the plains of Wyoming. But they face journeys of a lifetime just the same. They are the first members of the Church in their homelands or families; they learn and then teach the gospel in many languages and nations; they are the congregations that stand as one to sing "The Spirit of God" in the dedication of a new temple; they are the faithful who sometimes feel they trudge through daily living, their experiences their own pioneer footprints in the sandy soil of secular society. All are guided by the Lord, who said, "I will take you one of a city, and two of a family, and I will bring you to Zion." (Jeremiah 3:14.)

Pioneers are those who walk a difficult trail to distant frontiers. Gospel pioneers are those who break new ground, who press forward into a wilderness believing fervently that they are building the kingdom of God and that God is directing the way. . . .

Pioneers do not set out to be heroes. Yet, they become examples to those who follow because they carry on by applying righteous principles. For the most part, they are good people quietly doing their part. Said President Young to those preparing to cross the plains in one of the early companies, "I just do the thing that I know to be right and the Lord blesses me." (Thomas Bullock Journal, 8 Mar. 1847, LDS Church Historical Department.)

Our pioneer heritage is yoked to distinguishing traits that characterize a latter-day Zion people. Those strengths were described by the Lord to Joseph Smith in 1829:

"O ye that embark in the service of God, see that ye serve him with all your heart, might, mind and strength. . . . And faith, hope, charity and love, with an eye single to the glory of God, qualify him for the work. Remember faith, virtue, knowledge, temperance, patience, brotherly kindness, godliness, charity, humility, diligence." (D&C 4:2, 5–6.)

It was with faith that William Atkin and his wife approached the Green River with their handcart only to find that the wagon train they were with had already crossed and gone on. Turning to his wife, William said, "We cannot cross this river alone." She responded, "No, but the Lord will help us over." . . .

It was with faith that the first Latter-day Saint meetings in Estipac, Mexico, were held. At first the missionaries and their investigators met in an electrical shop. Water was sprinkled on the dirt floor to keep the dust down, and a fifty-gallon oil drum was rolled to the front to serve as a pulpit. A borrowed white tablecloth was draped over the cardboard box sacrament table. Makeshift, yes, but the first pioneers into the Salt Lake Valley met for Sunday services in the field and leaned against wagon wheels for support. Twenty people came that first week in Estipac, but the next Sunday the electrical shop was closed. Brother Nicolas Gonzalez offered, "You may use my house. I have been building two extra rooms. I don't need the rooms. I don't know why I was building them. But now I know. There is space there for the people." The missionaries knew God had prepared a place for them.

It was with charity that Relief Society sisters, led by their president Iby Subowo, cared for each other in Indonesia in 1976, even though they had little to share. Every morning before they began their cooking, each sister would hold back a spoonful of rice. By Sunday each sister had a small bag of rice to take to the meeting. The sisters would pray to know who needed the rice, and then all would go for the visit. The frontier ethic is one of sharing, not hoarding, however scant the supplies.

It was with courage that Russian Andrei Seminov joined the Church. For years he had been an agnostic. "I had looked for truth," he said, "but when I first heard the Latter-day Saint doctrines I was afraid. The standards seemed too high, too impossible to live. Since then I've learned that there is a source of strength to help me live this way."

It was with patience that members in East Germany and other countries behind the Iron Curtain waited for decades to reestablish Church association. For decades their governments limited and often forbade their meeting and their teaching the gospel to others. In the meantime, the members did what they could. They fasted the third Sunday of every month for the return of the missionaries. When the doors were finally opened, a young missionary, one of the first sent into East Germany, exclaimed, "It was a great honor to be the answer to someone's forty-year-old prayers."

Pioneers. Today they are building Zion in Sweden and South Africa, South Carolina and Peru. Diligent gospel pioneers have always led the way, not just in this dispensation but in earlier ones, too. Moses led his people out of Egypt, and they wandered in the wilderness for forty years before finally reaching the promised land. Lehi and his family faced countless unknowns in their journey to their promised land. And the apostle Peter leaped over the side of the Galilean fishing boat to begin his pioneering in the Church by walking on water. Their experiences and those of the pioneers who crossed the plains of North America in the mid-1800s remind us that the most critical journey of all is to come unto Christ. Pioneers—may we be in their company. "I will take you one of a city, and two of a family, and I will bring you to Zion." (Jeremiah 3:14.) (Heidi S. Swinton, *Pioneer Spirit: Modern-Day Stories of Courage and Conviction* [Salt Lake City: Deseret Book, 1996], 5)

SUMMARY

Returning to the presence of our Heavenly Father requires that we become pure in heart, that we become like our Savior Jesus Christ. This is the purpose of earth life, to become even as He is (see 3 Ne. 27:27) and to prepare to return to God. When we do return to Him, we will be judged according to our works and the desires of our hearts (see Alma 41:3), to see if we belong in Zion. Therefore, our hearts must be pure. A Zion person can make a great difference in the lives of all the people he or she associates with. We can become a Zion people, one person at a time and one family at a time. This is the cause of Zion—to bless the children of our Heavenly Father, that they too can be partakers of eternal life.

ABOUT THE AUTHORS

ED J. PINEGAR is a retired dentist and long-time teacher of early-morning seminary and religion classes at Brigham Young University. He teaches at the Joseph Smith Academy and has served as a mission president in England and at the Missionary Training Center in Provo, Utah. He has been a bishop and a stake president and is a temple sealer. Ed and his wife, Patricia, have eight children, thirty-five grandchildren, and five great-grandchildren and reside in Orem, Utah.

RICHARD J. ALLEN is a husband, father, teacher, and writer. He has served on several high councils, in several stake presidencies, and as a bishop. Richard's teaching assignments in the Church have included service as a full-time missionary, instructor in various priesthood quorums, gospel doctrine teacher, and stake institute director. He has served as a faculty member at both Brigham Young University and Johns Hopkins University. Richard has coauthored many articles, manuals, and books and has served on a number of national educational boards. He and his wife, Carol Lynn Hansen Allen, have four children and five grandchildren.